Recent Advances in Digital Media Impacts on Identity, Sexuality, and Relationships

Michelle F. Wright
Penn State University, USA

IGI Global
DISSEMINATOR OF KNOWLEDGE

A volume in the Advances in Human and Social Aspects of Technology (AHSAT) Book Series

Published in the United States of America by
IGI Global
Information Science Reference (an imprint of IGI Global)
701 E. Chocolate Avenue
Hershey PA, USA 17033
Tel: 717-533-8845
Fax: 717-533-8661
E-mail: cust@igi-global.com
Web site: http://www.igi-global.com

Library of Congress Cataloging-in-Publication Data

Names: Wright, Michelle F., editor.
Title: Recent advances in digital media impacts on identity, sexuality, and relationships / Michelle F. Wright, editor.
Description: Hershey, PA : Information Science Reference, [2020] | Includes bibliographical references and index. | Summary: "This book examines the role of digital media and its impact on identity development, behavioral formations, and the inter-personal relationships of young adults"-- Provided by publisher.
Identifiers: LCCN 2019024170 (print) | LCCN 2019024171 (ebook) | ISBN 9781799810636 (hardcover) | ISBN 9781799810643 (paperback) | ISBN 9781799810650 (ebook)
Subjects: LCSH: Young adults--Social conditions. | Young adults--Psychology | Young adults--Sexual behavior. | Digital media--Social aspects.
Classification: LCC HQ799.5 .R43 2020 (print) | LCC HQ799.5 (ebook) | DDC 305.242--dc23
LC record available at https://lccn.loc.gov/2019024170
LC ebook record available at https://lccn.loc.gov/2019024171

This book is published in the IGI Global book series Advances in Human and Social Aspects of Technology (AHSAT) (ISSN: 2328-1316; eISSN: 2328-1324)

British Cataloguing in Publication Data
A Cataloguing in Publication record for this book is available from the British Library.

For electronic access to this publication, please contact: eresources@igi-global.com.

Advances in Human and Social Aspects of Technology (AHSAT) Book Series

Ashish Dwivedi
The University of Hull, UK

ISSN:2328-1316
EISSN:2328-1324

Mission

In recent years, the societal impact of technology has been noted as we become increasingly more connected and are presented with more digital tools and devices. With the popularity of digital devices such as cell phones and tablets, it is crucial to consider the implications of our digital dependence and the presence of technology in our everyday lives.

The **Advances in Human and Social Aspects of Technology (AHSAT) Book Series** seeks to explore the ways in which society and human beings have been affected by technology and how the technological revolution has changed the way we conduct our lives as well as our behavior. The AHSAT book series aims to publish the most cutting-edge research on human behavior and interaction with technology and the ways in which the digital age is changing society.

Coverage

- Philosophy of technology
- Digital Identity
- Public Access to ICTs
- Human-Computer Interaction
- End-User Computing
- Technology Dependence
- Human Rights and Digitization
- Human Development and Technology
- Technology and Social Change
- Computer-Mediated Communication

IGI Global is currently accepting manuscripts for publication within this series. To submit a proposal for a volume in this series, please contact our Acquisition Editors at Acquisitions@igi-global.com or visit: http://www.igi-global.com/publish/.

The Advances in Human and Social Aspects of Technology (AHSAT) Book Series (ISSN 2328-1316) is published by IGI Global, 701 E. Chocolate Avenue, Hershey, PA 17033-1240, USA, www.igi-global.com. This series is composed of titles available for purchase individually; each title is edited to be contextually exclusive from any other title within the series. For pricing and ordering information please visit http://www.igi-global.com/book-series/advances-human-social-aspects-technology/37145. Postmaster: Send all address changes to above address.

Titles in this Series

For a list of additional titles in this series, please visit:
https://www.igi-global.com/book-series/advances-human-social-aspects-technology/37145

Handbook of Research on Politics in the Computer Age
Ashu M. G. Solo (Maverick Technologies America Inc., USA)
Information Science Reference • copyright 2020 • 436pp • H/C (ISBN: 9781799803775) • US $245.00 (our price)

Human Behavior and Another Kind in Consciousness Emerging Research and Opportunities
Shigeki Sugiyama (Independent Researcher, Japan)
Information Science Reference • copyright 2019 • 102pp • H/C (ISBN: 9781522582175) • US $135.00 (our price)

Impacts of Mobile Use and Experience on Contemporary Society
Xiaoge Xu (Mobile Studies International, Singapore)
Information Science Reference • copyright 2019 • 354pp • H/C (ISBN: 9781522578857) • US $185.00 (our price)

Managing Screen Time in an Online Society
Lídia Oliveira (University of Aveiro, Portugal)
Information Science Reference • copyright 2019 • 393pp • H/C (ISBN: 9781522581635) • US $185.00 (our price)

Critical Issues Impacting Science, Technology, Society (STS), and Our Future
Heather Christina Lum (Pennsylvania State University, USA)
Information Science Reference • copyright 2019 • 345pp • H/C (ISBN: 9781522579496) • US $185.00 (our price)

Digital Humanities and Scholarly Research Trends in the Asia-Pacific
Shun-han Rebekah Wong (Hong Kong Baptist University, Hong Kong) Haipeng Li (University of California – Merced, USA) and Min Chou (New Jersey City University, USA)
Information Science Reference • copyright 2019 • 310pp • H/C (ISBN: 9781522571957) • US $195.00 (our price)

Handbook of Research on Industrial Advancement in Scientific Knowledge
Vicente González-Prida Diaz (Universidad de Sevilla, Spain & Universidad Nacional de Educación a Distancia (UNED), Spain) and Jesus Pedro Zamora Bonilla (Universidad Nacional de Educación a Distancia (UNED), Spain)
Information Science Reference • copyright 2019 • 442pp • H/C (ISBN: 9781522571520) • US $235.00 (our price)

Gender Gaps and the Social Inclusion Movement in ICT
Idongesit Williams (Aalborg University, Denmark) Olga Millward (Aalborg University, Denmark) and Roslyn Layton (Aalborg University, Denmark)
Information Science Reference • copyright 2019 • 325pp • H/C (ISBN: 9781522570684) • US $195.00 (our price)

IGI Global
DISSEMINATOR OF KNOWLEDGE

701 East Chocolate Avenue, Hershey, PA 17033, USA
Tel: 717-533-8845 x100 • Fax: 717-533-8661
E-Mail: cust@igi-global.com • www.igi-global.com

Table of Contents

Detailed Table of Contents

The music video for Eminem and Rihanna's hit single "Love the Way You Lie" (2010) reproduces commonly held myths about intimate partner violence (IPV), primarily that many women instigate their abuse or even enjoy it. Music video culture has been of concern to parents, researchers, and policymakers because youth are considered developmentally susceptible to gendered sexual scripts. However, some scholars suggest that audience members, rather than being passive consumers, are practical actors who filter information according to first- and secondhand experiences. This study examined how young adults' respond to the depiction of IPV in the music video for "Love the Way You Lie." Findings indicated strong emotional response, a tendency to filter media through personal experiences, and a continuation of gendered blame. However, participants also demonstrated critical analysis. Thus, even when depictions are sensational or reinforce myth-based beliefs and gendered biases, young adults are capable of being critical consumers of popular culture.

Chapter 6

The Trouble With Tinder: Emerging Adults With Disabilities Dating Online 99

Elizabeth Mazur, Penn State Greater Allegheny, USA

Although research indicates that almost all emerging adults in the U.S. use the internet, little is known about the online dating experiences of persons with disabilities. Particularly in developed countries, online dating currently accounts for a substantial proportion of the initiation of romantic relationships and promises numerous advantages for persons with disabilities. Online dating includes a way to escape disability stigma, at least initially, access to a wide network of potential partners, and a convenient, private, and efficient method of meeting them. Online daters can be strategic in how they present both themselves and their disabilities, the manner in which they communicate with potential partners, and whether they join a large, popular dating site or a specialized disability-oriented one. The chapter discusses how the nine-step process of online dating might differ for or challenge emerging adults with various types of disabilities, sharing relevant research and media examples when available. The implications of popular mobile dating apps are also considered.

Chapter 7

Send Nudes? : Sexting Experiences and Victimization Relating to Attachment and Rejection Sensitivity – Incorporating Sexual Minority Perspectives 119

Alaina Brenick, University of Connecticut, USA
Kaitlin M. Flannery, State University of New York College at Cortland, USA
Emily Karr, University of Connecticut, USA
Daniell Carvalheiro, University of Connecticut, USA

As texting continues to serve as an increasingly common method of communication among emerging adults, increases in rates of sexting, or sending sexually explicit messages, pictures, or videos, have also been observed. While consensual sexting can facilitate intimacy in relationships, when used as a tool to victimize others, it has been shown to yield a range of negative outcomes: from embarrassment to severe depression and suicide. This chapter aims to review the existing literature on emerging adults' engagement in and evaluations of sexting, while also considering the risks associated with sexting victimization. The role that individual characteristics, such as attachment style and rejection sensitivity as well as demographic characteristics such as gender, sexual orientation, and relationship status, play in the relation between experiences with and evaluations of using sexting as a tool for victimization will also be explored.

Previous studies have found that individuals with various health issues use social media for various purposes. Social media help them obtain support from other users and manage identity. However, past research also pointed out risks and challenges associated with the use of social media by those with health issues. One of the risks is stigmatization they could experience when using social media. Even though previous studies revealed serious issues related to stigma in face-to-face settings, the negative effects of stigmatization on social media are left unexplored. To facilitate research on the issues, first, this chapter reviews past works focusing on the use of social media by those with various health issues. Next, previous studies on stigma associated with these illnesses and disabilities are reviewed. Finally, this chapter proposes future directions of research on the issues.

In this chapter, the author is interested in studying self-comparison in social media and its effect to the self-esteem in emerging adults. In Indonesia, social media are widely used by various groups. Jakarta is even referred as the capital of a text-based social media. Data in 2016 indicated that social media users in Indonesia have reached high ranking. Indonesia ranked fourth in the world for social media users and ranked first with Facebook with 111 million users, followed by Twitter. Indonesian Internet Service Provider Association explained that the biggest users were dominated by adolescents, amounting to 75.50% of the total users. The use of social media can be influenced by collective culture. This culture can influence how individuals evaluate themselves, including their self-esteem. The topic of the psychological effects of social media has been much discussed. A lot of research conducted on the effect of social on development of self-esteem. Social media becoming a place for comparing oneself to others and it turn out it has a great effect.

Preface

The purpose of this book is to present a framework for how emerging adults navigate developmental tasks, opportunities, and issues utilizing digital media and technologies. Emerging adults are growing up in a technologically connected world and it is important to understand how such technology might harm or aid in their development. Ultimately, many individuals in emerging adulthood do not know a time in which digital media and technology were not instrumental parts of their life – they have grown up fully connected! Emerging adulthood is a unique developmental period in the human lifespan. It is sometimes described as a transitional period between adolescence and adulthood. Characteristics of this age group include individuals who might not live on their own and who do not have sufficient income to be fully independent in their early to late 20s. Even if living independently, working, and making their own decisions, emerging adults might still rely on their parents for monetary help. Some emerging adults leave the family home, only to come back home a few years later due to issues with making livable wages. The period is also characteristic of identity exploration, instability, self-focus, and feeling that one is not yet completely an adult but not a child either. Emerging adults explore their identity through various ways. One such way is through digital media and technology which can be used to help explore, develop, and maintain emerging adults' identity, behaviors, sexuality, and interpersonal relationships.

The aim of this book is to synthesize research on emerging adults' digital media and technology use, and to describe how such use could hinder or facilitate their identity development and formation, contribute to aggression and prosocial behaviors, understand and explore their sexuality, and influence their relationships with their parents, friends, and romantic partners. There are some gaps in the literature on the navigation of developmental tasks using digital media and technology among emerging adults. When such gaps occur, research from the face-to-face context will be used as a starting point for understanding the same topics in relation to digital media and technologies. Throughout the book, gaps in the literature will be addressed and future research will be proposed to fill these gaps. The book is grouped based on broader topics, including identity development and formation, sexuality, interpersonal relationships, and behaviors. Specific topics include aggression, stalking, relationship intimacy, "hooking up", relationship violence, dating, sexting, pornography, addiction, self-disclosure, social media use, social comparison, and identity exploration. The majority of chapters in the book focus on interpersonal relationships, specifically romantic relationships, suggesting that digital media and technologies have permeated emerging adults' relationships and serve the function of forming, establishing, and/or maintaining these relationships.

THE ORGANIZATION OF THE BOOK

The book is organized according to various broader contexts of how emerging adults connect with digital technologies. These contexts were described above and include behaviors, interpersonal relationships, social media and smartphone use, addiction, and identity exploration and development. Some of the chapters include overlapping information, especially when describing the nature and characteristics of emerging adulthood. It was difficult to conceptualize of one context separate from the others or how such contexts might overlap. Authors of chapters employ different terminology to refer to the emerging adulthood period, including adults, youths, young people, college students, students, and young adults. Regardless of the terminology used, authors focus on individuals from the ages of 18 through 29, with the majority of focus on individuals from ages of 18 through 25. Some of the chapters involve emerging adults from the United States but also from China and other countries (e.g., Greece, Turkey, Indonesia), as well as emerging adults with disabilities. Such inclusion was purposeful for providing details on the diverse voices of emerging adults as culture and disability status could have a role in the navigation of their developmental tasks.

Chapters 1 and 2 focus on cyber behaviors, specifically emerging adults' involvement in cyber aggression and cyberstalking. Chapter 1 describes the author's research on the longitudinal relationships between adjustment difficulties (e.g., depression, loneliness, anxiety, grade point average, non-suicidal self-harm, suicidal ideation) and cyber aggression involvement among emerging adults. The author discusses future research directions for understanding the adjustment difficulties associated with emerging adults' cyber aggression perpetration and victimization and explains possible intervention programs aimed at reducing these behaviors. There is also some additional attention given to recommendations for colleges and universities as they also have a role in helping to reduce their students' involvement in negative online behaviors, especially considering that aggression and victimization negatively impact psychological and academic adjustment.

Chapter 2 explores the author's research on the prevalence, behaviors, and tactics of cyberstalking perpetration among Greek emerging adults. She also explains the correlates associated with cyberstalking perpetration and victimization, including personality characteristics, attachment styles, and relating to others. The findings of the research suggest the importance of considering psychological, interpersonal, and social consequences of cyberstalking perpetration and victimization. A number of recommendations are provided for intervention programs to prevent cyberstalking or mitigate the negative effects of cyberstalking. A call is also made for law enforcement and criminal justice officials to be trained to recognize the tactics used by cyberstalkers and to respond effectively to victims of cyberstalking. Service providers are also urged to develop websites for victims to exchange information and design formal and informal support networks to address the needs of victims and enhance their safety.

Chapters 3 through 8 focus on interpersonal relationships. As noted, more chapters are included in the context of interpersonal relationships, highlighting how far research has come on this topic. Chapter 3 focuses on the role of digital technology, especially the internet, in facilitating various opportunities for social interactions among emerging adults. The authors argued that the increasing global connectivity afforded by the internet affects developmental paths and allows for exposure to various cultures and ideas during a "fluid time in development". The next portion of the chapter focuses on the developmental task of intimacy during emerging adulthood and explains how this developmental period encompasses greater depth in the formation of romantic relationships than formed in adolescence, with particular focus on emerging adult women. The evolution of romantic relationships in emerging adulthood is also described within the context of digital media and technologies. The chapter also incorporates the role identity plays in the formation and evolution of romantic relationships. The authors conclude the chapter by discussing a qualitative, interview-based study on women's experiences with dating relationships in the context of digital media and technologies.

The authors of Chapter 4 focus on hookup culture among emerging adults. They explain that the identity-seeking desires of emerging adulthood draws emerging adults to hookup culture where they are able to experiment with the presentation of self and sample intimate relations without having to commit themselves to a restrictive relationship. Furthermore, the authors highlight the role of technology and online resources for streamlining the process of seeking out potential romantic and sexual partners by developing applications that can be downloaded on user's mobile devices. The next part of the chapter focuses on the risks of using mobile dating/hookup applications, which are argued to be some of the same features that draw emerging adults to hookup culture. Ultimately, the authors suggest that dating/hookup applications could result in degradation of authenticity and a systematic undermining of the capacity to trust. Deceptive practices might become a normalized part of the mobile dating experience, undermining the ability to trust one another. The chapter concludes with the authors' concern that mobile hookup and dating practices could result in a reduction in commitment to stable social relations and to the degradation in the quality of relationships.

Switching technologies slightly, Chapter 5 describes emerging adults' responses to the depictions of intimate partner violence in the music video, "Love the Way You Lie". The authors begin the chapter by explaining how the music video reproduces commonly held myths about intimate partner violence through the depiction of women instigating their abuse or even enjoying such abuse. Focus groups were conducted with emerging adults to provide an in-depth and contextualized discussion of how they received the music video content and their perceptions and knowledge of intimate partner violence. Emerging adults perceived the video as making the song more powerful and intensifying the meaning of the lyrics. They also identified intimate partner violence as a common experience within their generation, with some disclosing firsthand or secondhand experiences. Even if an emerging adult had not experienced intimate partner violence, they indicated that they could relate to the video's storyline. Many of the emerging adults were concerned with the video's harmful effect on younger adolescents, believing that young people might have a difficult time understanding the difference between reality and media sensationalizing. Ultimately, the authors argued that while popular media may sensationalize, reduce, or romanticize common social problems, such media provides a starting point for engaging critical dialogue on such contemporary issues.

Chapter 6 focuses on the online dating experiences of people with disabilities by describing how these people communicate with potential partners and escape disability stigma. The author draws on scientific literature on emerging adults with disabilities (referred to as "people with disabilities") and their personal relationships, internet interactions, and online dating. It is argued that online dating has the potential to improve what is an often frustrating activity for people with disabilities. Online dating has the potential to help people with disabilities communicate with multiple potential partners conveniently and efficiently, which is an appealing alternative to relying on traditional ways to seek romantic relationships. Furthermore, online communication allows users to "meet" without an initial focus on disability. Despite the promise of online dating, there are challenges to online dating for people with disabilities, including creating attractive profiles and accessibility. The chapter concludes by indicating that online dating is a good opportunity for people with disabilities to interact with multiple interested daters and is a positive venue for relationship development.

Chapter 7 reviews the literature on emerging adults' engagement in and evaluations of sexting by describing the prevalence of this experience. The authors also describe risk factors associated with sexting victimization, including attachment style and rejection sensitivity. Furthermore, the chapter focuses on the experiences of emerging adults who identify as lesbian, gay, or bisexual. Such a focus is important because the authors argues that these individuals are sometimes absent from the literature on sexting, even though they are at increased risk of victimization due to their marginalized status. Attention is also needed to this topic because individuals who identify as lesbian, gay, or bisexual participate in sexting more regularly than their heterosexual peers. Later in the chapter, the authors describe their research on the role of insecure attachment and rejection sensitivity in sexting among emerging adults who are lesbian, gay, or bisexual. The chapter concludes with a discussion of the results of the authors' research.

The purpose of Chapter 8 is to review the existing literature on the nature of pornography use among emerging adults and how pornography impacts their romantic relationships. Ultimately the authors are interested in exploring the connection between emerging adult pornography use and the processes in their romantic relationships. They address the following questions: What is the nature of pornography use among emerging adults? and What is the relationship between pornography use and pornography-related anxiety in emerging adult romantic relationships? The chapter begins by discussing emerging adults and their romantic relationships, approaches to pornography research, and theoretical foundations (i.e., social learning theory, sexual script theory). The rest of the chapter presents the authors' research on the influence of pornography use on emerging adults' attitudes about and behaviors in forming romantic relationships.

The authors of Chapter 9 conducted an online survey with emerging adults in Hong Kong, China to examine potential associations among loneliness, Facebook use, and self-disclosure on Facebook. Their findings revealed that loneliness was not associated with Facebook use, but it was associated with disclosure. Thus, the lonelier the Facebook user, the less he or she disclosed negative information. The pattern of association between Facebook use and self-disclosure indicated that the more time users spent on Facebook, the more they revealed positive disclosures and the less likely they were to reveal negative disclosures. The authors argue that the findings indicate evidence of a "remain positive" norm among emerging adult Facebook users in Hong Kong. Culture might play a role in Facebook users' communication patterns. They also suggest that Facebook norms might be culture specific and measuring self-disclosure valence may provide a more nuanced understanding for such norms.

While Chapter 9 focused on some of the positive aspects of social media use, Chapter 10 describes mobile phone addiction. Research on mobile phone addiction suggests that smartphone addiction is becoming a prevalent problem among emerging adults. The main purpose of the chapter is to present the authors' research on smartphone use and addiction among emerging adults in Turkey. The authors found that smartphone use and addiction were positively associated among Turkish emerging adults. Particularly surprising was that 22.5% of the emerging adults in the authors' sample looked at their devices over 100 times a day! They found that the strongest predictor of smartphone addiction was accompany/fellowship and withdrawal. Thus, emerging adults tended to use their smartphones more when they felt isolated or lonely and they experienced withdrawal symptoms when the battery was low and became agitated when their smartphone was not in sight.

Chapter 11 discusses the potential of social networking websites to provide social support and help the psychological well-being of individuals with health issues, including mental illness, depression, schizophrenia, HIV/AIDS, cancer, intellectual disabilities, and diabetes. The author argues that social networking websites are helpful for emerging adults with health issues who often have a hard time developing close relationships with others and obtaining interpersonal support. Despite the positives associated with social networking use among emerging adults with disabilities, there are potential risks, such as experiencing stigma, which can have a negative impact of identity management. The author proposed research questions to help facilitate future studies to explore the potential positives and negatives associated with social networking website use to develop close relationships and explore identity formation and development among emerging adults with health issues.

Chapter 12 focuses on Indonesian emerging adults' self-comparisons through social media. The author also explains how social media influences how emerging adults view themselves. Furthermore, the author also describes how the collectivistic nature of Indonesia might influence emerging adults' social media environments as they might evaluate themselves differently, which impacts their self-esteem and psychological outcomes. The author argues that the danger of social media is that emerging adults can compare themselves to others without realizing it, and this can influence how they feel about themselves and lead to poorer well-being. The chapter concludes with making the argument that more awareness is needed about the role of social media in human welfare and for individuals to not blame social media for their problems. Ultimately, the author indicates that we can still use social media and stay human.

Like other authors in this book, the authors of Chapter 13 make the argument that emerging adults are at a critical stage in their life where they explore and experiment with changing relationships, world views, and work arrangements. The authors of Chapter 13 indicate that social media is designed to foster and maintain relationships and provide an understanding for the intersection between personal characteristics and motivations. Chapter 13 presents the authors' research on emerging adults' use of social media and the internet, how self-esteem, social support, and self-control influence internet use, and how these relationships might vary for younger (18-24 years old) and older (25-29 years old) emerging adults. The findings revealed that older emerging adults and younger emerging adults differed in their use of different social media platforms, with older emerging adults preferring email and LinkedIn compared to younger emerging adults. Online social support, offline social support, self-control, and self-esteem predicted internet use, particularly problematic internet use. Higher self-esteem related to higher functional internet use and less problematic internet use.

Chapter 1
Negative Psychological Outcomes Associated With Emerging Adults' Cyber Aggression Involvement

Michelle F. Wright
Penn State University, USA

ABSTRACT

The first objective of the present study was to describe the nature of cyber aggression and victimization among emerging adults by focusing on what digital technologies are used and the relationship between the perpetrator and the victim. The second objective of the present study was to investigate the longitudinal, reciprocal relationships between cyber victimization, cyber aggression, suicidal ideation, non-suicidal self-harm, depression, loneliness, anxiety, and grade point average among emerging adults over four years, using cross-lagged modeling. The findings of the study were consistent with cross-sectional studies, with the present study revealing longitudinal and reciprocal relationships between cyber aggression, cyber victimizations, suicidal ideation, non-suicidal self-harm, depression, anxiety, and GPA over four years. Additional research attention should be given to understanding more about these associations.

INTRODUCTION

Emerging adults are enmeshed in a digitally connected world. Being digitally connected to just about anyone in a matter of seconds and having access to an assortment of information at the "click of a button" are just a few of the benefits associated with emerging adults' internet and digital technology use. Many emerging adults go online or utilize digital technologies at least once a day (Smith, Rainie, & Zickuhr, 2011). Although the internet and digital technologies provide various opportunities and conveniences in emerging adults' lives, they might be at risk for internet addiction, identity theft, sexual predation and exploitation, and cyber aggression (Copes, Kerby, Huff, & Kane, 2010; Finn, 2004; Weigman & van Schie, 1998; Wright & Li, 2012). Utilizing digital technologies increases the likelihood of experi-

DOI: 10.4018/978-1-7998-1063-6.ch001

encing or perpetrating cyber aggression (Alvarez-Garcia, Nunez Perez, Gonzalez, & Perez, 2015; Holt, Fitzgerald, Bossler, Chee, & Nq, 2016; Mishna, Khoury-Kassabri, Gadalla, & Daciuk, 2012; Perrin & Duggan, 2015). Emerging adults' high levels of internet and digital technology consumption increase their online risks, particularly their risk of cyber aggression.

Despite emerging adults using the internet and digital technologies at similar or higher levels than children and adolescents, little attention has been devoted to their exposure and perpetration of cyber aggression. Such a gap in the literature is unfortunate as many high profile cases of cyber aggression sometimes involve emerging adults, although the general public typically believes that these behaviors are a concern for children and adolescents. Failure to acknowledge emerging adults' vulnerability to cyber aggression might neglect the development of intervention programs aimed at reducing risks among this population. Furthermore, not recognizing that cyber aggression is a concerned for emerging adults might exacerbate their psychological, social, academic, and behavioral difficulties, and reduce the likelihood that someone might intervene and reduce the impact of negative outcomes. Research on cyber aggression and emerging adults is increasing, although much of this research involves studies utilizing cross-sectional research designs, which limits our understanding of the long-term predictors and consequences of these behaviors. The first objective of the present study was to describe the nature of cyber aggression and victimization among emerging adults by focusing on what digital technologies are used and the relationship between the perpetrator and the victim. The second objective of the present study was to investigate the longitudinal, reciprocal relationships between cyber victimization, cyber aggression, suicidal ideation, non-suicidal self-harm, depression, loneliness, anxiety, and grade point average among emerging adults over four years, using cross-lagged modeling.

BACKGROUND

Definition of Emerging Adulthood

More and more high school students plan to attend college nowadays, delaying their plans for marriage and families (Badger, Nelson, & Barry, 2006). Consequently, many people in college do not consider themselves to be adults. Coalescing together, these factors have created a unique developmental period, often referred to as "emerging adulthood" (Arnett, 2000). Emerging adulthood is characterized by an increased level of exploration and instability until one reaches their mid to late twenties, before taking on adult roles and responsibilities. Other characteristics of emerging adulthood include pursuing personal goals (e.g., traveling, school), creating an identity that is influenced by work, school, or interpersonal relationships, becoming involved in intimate relationships, and engaging in risky behaviors, such as using illegal drugs or driving while drunk (Arnett & Jensen, 2002; Nelson & Barry, 2005). Given these characteristics, many researchers consider emerging adulthood a unique developmental period, separate from adolescence and adulthood. The aim of this study is focus on cyber aggression and victimization exclusively among emerging adults. This developmental period represents a unique developmental stage for understanding the impact of negative interactions on emerging adults' mental health.

Definition of Cyber Aggression and Victimization

Typically conceptualized as an extension of face-to-face traditional aggression, cyber aggression involves purposefully and hostilely embarrassing or intimidating others (Ferdon & Hertz, 2007; Kowalski & Limber, 2007; Topcu, Erdur-Baker, & Aydin, 2008; Wolak, Mitchell, & Finkelhor, 2007; Ybarra, Diener-West, & Leaf, 2007). Unlike the traditional definition of face-to-face aggression and victimization, cyber aggressive behaviors do not necessarily have to include repetition or an imbalance of power between the perpetrator and the victim (Grigg, 2010). Cyber aggressive behaviors are usually malicious, and might include sending abusive emails, impersonating others, and sending harassing messages via text messages, instant messenger, and social networking sites (Walker, Sockman, & Koehn, 2011; Wolak et al., 2007; Wright & Li, 2012; Ybarra & Mitchell, 2004). Other cyber aggressive behaviors include harassment, insults, physical threats, verbal taunts, malicious teasing, social exclusion, and humiliation. There are also more severe forms of cyber aggressive behaviors, such as distributing explicit videos or images of others, happy slapping, hacking, and flaming (Rideout, Roberts, & Foehr, 2005; Smith et al., 2008). Happy slapping is defined as a group of people insulting another person, while filming the incidence on a mobile phone, and then later posting the images or videos online. Hacking is defined as gaining access to someone's computer system or other online accounts in an effort to get information. Flaming is defined as posting provocative and/or offensive messages in a public forum with the intention to provoke angry responses or agreement from members of the public forum. Cyber aggression can be perpetuated or experienced through a variety of digital technologies and tools, including cell phones, social networking sites, emails, gaming consoles, chatrooms, blogs, Youtube, and chat programs.

Cyber Aggression and Victimization Among Emerging Adults

Research on cyber aggression is advancing, with many of the earliest studies focused on the prevalence rates of these behaviors among children and adolescents. One of the first studies conducted on cyber aggression among emerging adults was published by Finn in 2004. In her study, she found that 10-15% of her sample experienced email and/or instant messenger victimization, equating to 1 in 10 emerging adults being targeted by cyber victimization. Changes in emerging adults' access to an assortment of digital technologies have transformed the avenues to perpetrate cyber aggression. Therefore, more current research has focused on cyber aggression through various digital technologies. In particular, Walker, Sockman, and Koehn (2011) focused on cyber victimization among emerging adults via Facebook and text messages. They found that 56% of their sample reported that they were harassed through Facebook. Furthermore, 45% of their participants experienced victimization through text messages. In another study, Wright and Li (2012) investigated how often emerging adults experience cyber aggression, with the majority of their participants reporting cyber victimization every 2 to 4 months. Less attention has been given to the frequency of cyber aggression perpetration among emerging adults. Dilmac (2009) examined Turkish emerging adults' engagement in cyber aggression. His findings revealed that 22.5% of emerging adults in his study perpetrated cyber aggression at least once in their lifetime. Ultimately, emerging adults' involvement in cyber aggression ranges from 8.6% to 43.3% (Crosslin & Crosslin, 2014; Finn, 2014; Hinduja & Patchin, 2010; Schenk & Fremouw, 2012). It is worth noting that the differences between the frequency rates of these studies is not important as variations in these rates reflect differences in the samples used, the measurement of cyber aggression involvement, and the definitions of cyber aggression and cyber victimization. Other research has focused on the consequences associated with cyber aggression and victimization among emerging adults.

Consequences of Cyber Aggression Involvement

Few studies have focused on the consequences associated with cyber aggression involvement among emerging adults. In this literature, emerging adults' cyber victimization was related to eating disorders, suicidal ideation, and depression (Cowie, 2013). Furthermore, emerging adults who were victims of cyber aggression experienced depression, anxiety, phobias, and paranoia (Cowie, 2013; Schenk & Fremouw, 2012). Their feelings of isolation and loneliness increased, resulting in diminished opportunities for forming new friendships (Crosslin & Crosslin, 2014). Problematic alcohol use is also increased among female emerging adults who were involved in cyber aggression (Selkie, Kota, Chan, & Moreno, 2015). Like cybervictims, emerging adults who were cyberaggressors also experienced depression. Less attention has been given to how cyber aggression involvement might impact the academic performance of emerging adults. The literature on this topic among adolescents indicates that cyberaggressors and cybervictims experienced more academic difficulties and engaged in more non-suicidal self-harm than uninvolved adolescents (Tang et al., 2013; Wright, 2015).

Present Study

The first goal of the study was to understand the nature of cyber aggression involvement among emerging adults through examining the digital technologies used to harm others and the relationship between the perpetrator and the victim. Another goal of the study was to investigate the longitudinal, reciprocal relationships between cyber victimization, cyber aggression, suicidal ideation, non-suicidal self-harm, depression, loneliness, anxiety, and grade point average over four years, while accounting for prior levels of these variables and face-to-face aggression and victimization. Bidirectional or reciprocal relationships were hypothesized because research indicates that cyber victimization and cyber aggression are predictors of suicidal ideation, non-suicidal self-harm, depression, loneliness, anxiety and grade point average, and that these variables also predict cyber victimization and cyber aggression (Cappadocia, Craig, & Pepler, 2013; Cowie, 2013; Crosslin & Crosslin, 2014; Schenk & Fremouw, 2012; Wright, 2015; Ybarra & Mitchell, 2004; Ybarra et al., 2007). Magnitudes or ordering of the variables were not hypothesized due to a lack of research on this topic. An important consideration of the present study was to include time parameters for emerging adults' self-reported cyber aggression involvement. Many studies focusing on emerging adults do not specify time parameters, with many of these studies examining lifetime prevalence versus estimates of cyber aggression involvement within the past 60 days or the past year. By specifying time parameters, it is possible to determine whether cyber aggression and victimization are important developmental concerns for emerging adults. The present study had the following aims:

1. Describe the frequency of cyber aggression involvement among emerging adults through various technologies over four years.
2. Describe the frequency of who perpetrates cyber aggression among emerging adults over four years.
3. Examine the reciprocal and longitudinal associations between cyber victimization, cyber aggression, suicidal ideation, non-suicidal self-harm, depression, loneliness, anxiety, and grade point

average among emerging adults over four years, while controlling for face-to-face aggression and victimization.

METHOD

Participants

There were 1,483 emerging adults (ages 21-29; M_{age} = 24.67 years; 60% female) who participated in this study. The sample was from one of three 4-year universities located in the Southeastern United States. These universities enrolled between 29,636 to 59,770 students in 2014. The participants self-identified as White (65%), Black/African American (15%), Latino/a (10%), Asian (6%), and biracial (4%). The majority of participants were classified as college seniors, with 10% classified as juniors. Family incomes ranged from $23,000 to $461,000. Most of the participants were from middle-class families and 85% received financial assistance, typically student loans, scholarships, or work-study programs. The demographic background of the participants reflects the overall general student population at each of the universities.

Procedures

Recruitment began during participants' first year of college. The information about the study was posted on the universities' psychology subject pool websites, which included a short description of the study, how long students would be expected to participate, and what they would do (i.e., answer questionnaires). The recruitment ad explained that the study would take place over four years and that students would be expected to complete a set of questionnaires per year.

The first wave of data was collected during the fall of participants' first year in college. Participants came to a research laboratory for the first wave of data collection. During this data collection session, participants had to be first-year college students to be eligible for the study. Thirty-five students were not eligible for the study. These students still received credit for attending the session. After determining eligibility, participants read and completed an informed consent document, which included information about the nature of the study, length of the study, what they would do over the four years, and how much they would be compensated ($10 per wave for a total of $40 over the course of the study). Research assistants explained to participants that they could still participate in the study even if they were unsure whether they wanted to commit to the four-year duration of the study. Participants were informed that their participation was voluntary and that they could stop participating in the study at any time, while still receiving credit through the psychology subject pool. There were thirty-five students who declined to participate for various reasons, and they were thanked for their time and given subject pool credit. Two thousand and twenty-seven first-year college students provided their consent to participate in the study. Before completing questionnaires, participants were interviewed regarding demographic information. They were asked again to confirm that they were first-year college students as well as provide their gender, ethnicity, family income (348 participants were unsure), and information about their financial assistance. Research assistants also asked participants for their permanent home address, a school-affiliated email address, a personal email address, and their phone number. This information was used to contact participants over the four years of the study and research assistants routinely contacted participants via a school-affiliated email address to confirm contact information. All participants were assigned an ID that was used throughout the duration of the study. The study was approved by the universities' institutional review boards, and APA standards were followed throughout the completion of this study. At all waves of data collection, participants completed measures on self-reported cyber aggression and victimization, self-reported face-to-face aggression and victimization, suicidal ideation, non-suicidal self-harm, depression, loneliness, anxiety, and grade point average (GPA).

The psychology subject pool was used at Wave 1 only. Other waves of data collection occurred after 2 years (Wave 2), 3 years (Wave 3), and 4 years (Wave 4). Before sending participants an email with a website address directing them to the online questionnaires for waves two through four, research assistants contacted them via the phone. During the phone conversation, research assistants verified their home address, school-affiliated email address, and personal email address. The information was updated as needed over the next three years. In the second year, 52 participants did not have a working phone number. Research assistants were able to reconnect with 10 of these participants, and a phone meeting was scheduled to verify their personal information. Once contact information was verified, emails were sent to participants. When participants clicked on the website address in the email, they were then taken to the informed consent document. If they agree to participate, they were taken to the questionnaires. If participants did not agree to participate, they were not taken to the questionnaires and thanked for their time. On the last page of the website, participants were asked to provide an email address that they checked frequently, if they wanted to receive the gift card. A $10 Amazon gift card was emailed to participants who wished to receive one after each wave of data collection. The same procedure was used for data collection in the third and fourth years. Depending on the year of data collection, around 60-73% of participants requested the gift card. Attrition during the second year was 154, with 112 declining to participate and 42 who were unreachable. The third year attrition rate was 138, with 78 declining to participate and 60 who were unreachable. For the fourth year, the attrition rate was 230, with 167 declining to participate and 63 who were unreachable. Thus, the attrition rate for the full study was between 9% and 15%, such that 522 of the 2,227 participants from the first wave did not participate by the end of the fourth wave. Attrition for the first school was 521, 514 for the second school, and 501 for the third school. Typical attrition for longitudinal studies is between 30-70%, indicating that attrition from the present study was much less than previous longitudinal studies (Fischer, Dornelas, & Goethe, 200).

Measures

Self-reported Cyber Aggression and Victimization

Participants were asked to report how often they experienced or perpetrated aggression online or through text messages. Ten items were included for cyber victimization and ten items were included for cyber aggression. Some of the cyber aggression behaviors included having rumors spread about oneself / spreading rumors about someone, being teased / teasing someone, having mean or hurtful comments posted about oneself / posting mean or hurtful comments about someone, and having someone threaten to hurt them / threatening to hurt someone (Wright & Li, 2012). All items were rated on a scale of 1 (*never*) to 9 (*daily*). Before answering the items, participants were asked to respond to the questionnaires according to what has happened to them in the last 60 days. Behaviors for cyber victimization and cyber aggression were combined separately, with acceptable Cronbach's alphas at Wave 1 (.88 for cyber victimization and .86 for cyber aggression), Wave 2 (.87 for cyber victimization and .86 for cyber aggression), Wave 3 (.91 for cyber victimization and .87 for cyber aggression), and Wave 4 (.90 for cyber victimization and .88 for cyber aggression).

Cyber Aggression and Victimization Across Various Technologies

Participants were asked how often they experienced cyber aggression for ten items across seven technologies and tools (i.e., social networking sites, chat programs, email, chatrooms, blogs, online gaming, and text messages), which resulted in seventy items for cyber victimization. The same items were included for cyber aggression perpetration, across the seven technologies. A sample item included: Having rumors spread about oneself through social networking sites / spreading rumors about someone through social networking sites (e.g., Twitter, Facebook, Myspace). The behavior stem was replaced with a different behavior for each of the items and the technology stem was replaced with each of the digital technologies or tools. Items were answered using yes or no. All items were combined separately for each of the technologies for cyber aggression (seven total scores for each of the four waves) and cyber victimization (seven total scores for each of the four waves).

Cyber Aggression and Victimization Within the Relationship Between the Aggressor and the Perpetrator

Like the previous questionnaire, participants answered ten items according to how often six different individuals (i.e., ex-significant other, ex-friend, current significant other, current friend, acquaintance, and someone whom they did not know) victimized the participants online or through text messages, resulting in 60 items. The same items were used for cyber aggression, except these items were reworded to indicate who the participants targeted. The behavior stem was replaced with a different behavior for each of the items and the relationship stem was replaced with each of the individuals. Items were answered using yes or no. All items were combined separately for each of the relationships for cyber aggression (seven total scores for each of the four waves) and cyber victimization (seven total scores for each of the waves).

Self-Reported Face-To-Face Aggression and Victimization

Like the self-reported cyber aggression and victimization questionnaire, participants also reported how often they were victimized or perpetrated aggression in the offline world (Wright, Li, & Shi, 2014). These items were the same as those used for the previous questionnaire, except the "online or through text messages" portion of the item was removed. Twenty items were included for this questionnaire (10 items for face-to-face aggression and 10 items for face-to-face victimization), which were rated on a scale of 1 (*never*) to 9 (*daily*). Before answering the items, participants were asked to respond to the questions according to what they have experienced or perpetrated within the last 60 days. The items for face-to-face aggression and face-to-face victimization were averaged separately to form separate scores. Cronbach's alphas were acceptable for Wave 1 (.90 for face-to-face victimization and .89 for face-to-face aggression), Wave 2 (.86 for face-to-face victimization and .86 for face-to-face aggression), Wave 3 (.86 for face-to-face victimization and .85 for face-to-face aggression), and Wave 4 (.88 for face-to-face victimization and .87 for face-to-face aggression).

Suicidal Ideation

To assess suicidal ideation, participants were asked to respond to two questions (i.e., during the past 12 months, how often have you seriously considered attempting suicide, and during the past 12 months, did you make a plan about how you would attempt suicide; Center for Disease Control, 2011). The original items included yes or no responses, and these responses were updated to a 5-point Likert-type scale for this study, with ratings on a scale of 1 (*never*) to 5 (*very often*). The two items were combined to form scores on suicidal ideation. Cronbach's alphas were acceptable for Wave 1 (.73), Wave 2 (.73), Wave 3 (.71), and Wave 4 (.70).

Non-Suicidal Injury

Participants completed the Self-Harm Inventory. This questionnaire consists of 22 items asking participants if they have ever intentionally engaged in a described behavior (Sansome, Wiederman, & Sansone, 1998). All 22 items were answered with yes or no responses. These responses were updated to a 5-point Likert-type scale for this study, with ratings on a scale of 1 (*never*) to 5 (*very often*). Sample items included: Hit yourself, Cut yourself on purpose, and Prevented wounds from healing. All items were combined to form a final score on non-suicidal self-harm. Cronbach's alpha was acceptable for Wave 1 (.81), Wave 2 (.78), Wave 3 (.78), and Wave 4 (.80).

Depression

The Beck Depression Inventory was used to assess depression among emerging adults (Beck, Steer, & Brown, 1996). The questionnaire included 21 items with four statements per item. Participants rated each statement on a scale of 0 (*I do not feel sad*) to 3 (*I am sad and unhappy that I can't stand it*) on how they felt in the past 2 weeks. Items were combined to form a final score on depression, with Cronbach's alphas of .86 for Wave 1, .88 for Wave 2, .88 for Wave 3, and .86 for Wave 4.

Loneliness

The Revised UCLA Loneliness Scale was used to measure participants' feelings and experience of loneliness (Russell, 1996). There were 20 items included for this questionnaire, which were rated on a scale of 1 (*never*) to 4 (*often*). A sample item included: I feel isolated from others. The items were combined to form a final score on loneliness, with acceptable Cronbach's alphas of .83 for Wave 1, .84 for Wave 2, .80 for Wave 3, and .81 for Wave 4.

Anxiety

The Beck Anxiety Inventory was used to measure participants' symptoms of anxiety over the past month, including the day they completed the questionnaire (Beck & Steer, 1993). Participants responded to 21 items representing symptoms of anxiety (e.g., numbness or tingling and feeling hot). The items were rated on a scale of 0 (*not at all*) to 3 (*severely - it bothered me a lot*). All 21 items were combined to form a final score for anxiety, with acceptable Cronbach's alphas of .83 for Wave 1, .81 for Wave 2, .81 for Wave 3, and .84 for Wave 4.

Grade Point Average

Participants responded to an open-ended question that asked them their cumulative GPA using a 4.0 grading system. During the first wave, participants were asked for their final high school cumulative GPA. For the second through the fourth waves, they were asked for their current cumulative GPA in the previous semester. They wrote in their cumulative GPA.

Analytic Plan

To investigate cyber aggression and cyber victimization for various technologies and the relationship between the aggressor and the victim, frequencies were calculated (Aims 1 through 2). To examine the longitudinal, reciprocal relationships among cyber aggression, cyber victimization, suicidal ideation, non-suicidal self-harm, depression, loneliness, anxiety, and GPA over four years, various autoregressive cross-lagged path models were constructed using *Mplus* 7.31 (Aim 3; Bollen & Curran, 2006). All variables were regressed on proceeding variables, which allows for the ability to examine bivariate effects between variables, while accounting for previous levels of these variables over time. Face-to-face aggression and victimization were controlled for in the analyses by allowing these two variables to predict all variables in the models. Accounting for face-to-face aggression and victimization is important because these variables are highly correlated with cyber aggression and victimization (Wright & Li, 2012). Paths were added from cyber aggression and cyber victimization to suicidal ideation, non-suicidal self-harm, depression, loneliness, anxiety, and GPA for each of the waves. A missing at random test was performed to determine whether the data were missing completely at random (Little & Rubin, 1989; Rubin & Coplan, 2010). The findings revealed that all data were missing completely at random, $\chi^2 = 91.03$, $df = 116$, $p = .96$. Therefore, only complete cases were included in the analyses. There was missing data for 53 participants and therefore these cases were dropped from the analyses, resulting in a final sample size of 1,483.

RESULTS

Descriptive Statistics

Before conducting the autoregressive cross-lagged models, descriptive statistics were computed for each of the study's variables. Next, correlational analyses were conducted among all variables examined in the study (see Table 1). The findings revealed that cyber aggression and cyber victimization at all waves were associated positively with suicidal ideation, non-suicidal self-harm, depression, loneliness, anxiety, and GPA. On the other hand, cyber aggression and cyber victimization were related negatively to GPA for all waves. Furthermore, all adjustment variables were related positively to each other, except for GPA. GPA was associated negatively with suicidal ideation, depression, loneliness, and anxiety, but it was unrelated to non-suicidal self-harm.

The frequencies of cyber aggression and victimization occurring through various technologies and tools, such as social networking sites, chat programs, email, chatrooms, blogs, online gaming, and text messages, were conducted (see Table 2). The most used technology for cyber aggression was text messages, followed by social networking sites, chat programs and email, chatrooms, blogs, and online gaming across all four waves. Similar patterns were found for cyber victimization across all four waves as well. Frequencies were conducted for the relationship between the perpetrator and the victim (see Table 3). For cyber aggression, the most frequently targeted individual was an ex-friend, followed by ex-significant other, someone they did not know offline, current friend, and current significant other. The same patterns were found for cyber victimization. Overall, the frequency of cyber aggression and cyber victimization diminished from wave one through wave four for all technologies and across each of the relationships between the perpetrator and the victim.

Cyber Aggression

The model fit for suicidal ideation ($\chi^2 = 98.54$, $df = 12$, $CFI = .98$, $RMSEA = .06$, $SRMR = .04$), non-suicidal self-harm ($\chi^2 = 106.13$, $df = 12$, $CFI = .97$, $RMSEA = .05$, $SRMR = .05$), depression ($\chi^2 = 114.01$, $df = 12$, $CFI = .97$, $RMSEA = .06$, $SRMR = .05$), loneliness ($\chi^2 = 118.69$, $df = 12$, $CFI = .97$, $RMSEA = .06$, $SRMR = .05$), anxiety ($\chi^2 = 125.71$, $df = 12$, $CFI = .99$, $RMSEA = .05$, $SRMR = .05$), and GPA ($\chi^2 = 89.89$, $df = 12$, $CFI = .99$, $RMSEA = .05$, $SRMR = .05$) demonstrated excellent fit indices (see Table 1 for all path models). The coefficients for the paths revealed stability for cyber aggression, suicidal ideation, non-suicidal self-harm, depression, loneliness, anxiety, and GPA over time. Wave 1, Wave 2, Wave 3, and Wave 4 of cyber aggression predicted all adjustment outcomes, after accounting for previous levels of these variables and face-to-face aggression, while all adjustment outcomes predicted cyber aggression for each wave as well. The strengths of the magnitudes were weaker when all adjustment outcomes predicted cyber aggression than when cyber aggression predicted all adjustment outcomes.

Cyber Victimization

The model fit for suicidal ideation ($\chi^2 = 96.13$, $df = 12$, $CFI = .99$, $RMSEA = .05$, $SRMR = .04$), non-suicidal self-harm ($\chi^2 = 106.78$, $df = 12$, $CFI = .95$, $RMSEA = .05$, $SRMR = .05$), depression ($\chi^2 = 119.23$, $df = 12$, $CFI = .97$, $RMSEA = .06$, $SRMR = .05$), loneliness ($\chi^2 = 113.69$, $df = 12$, $CFI = .98$, $RMSEA = .05$, $SRMR = .05$), anxiety ($\chi^2 = 123.03$, $df = 12$, $CFI = .96$, $RMSEA = .06$, $SRMR = .05$), and GPA ($\chi^2 = 88.67$, $df = 12$, $CFI = .98$, $RMSEA = .05$, $SRMR = .05$) demonstrated excellent fit indices (see Table 2 for all path models). The coefficients for the paths revealed stability for cyber victimization, suicidal ideation, non-suicidal self-harm, depression, loneliness, anxiety, and GPA over time. Wave 1, Wave 2, Wave 3, and Wave 4 of cyber victimization predicted all adjustment outcomes, after accounting for previous levels of these variables and face-to-face victimization, while all adjustment outcomes predicted cyber victimization for all waves as well. The strengths of the magnitudes were weaker when all adjustment outcomes predicted cyber victimization than when cyber victimization predicted all adjustment outcomes.

DISCUSSION

Findings from a handful of studies have linked cyber aggression and cyber victimization to suicidal ideation, depression, and anxiety among emerging adults, utilizing cross-sectional research designs (Kokkinos, Antoniadou, & Markos, 2014; Schenk & Fremouw, 2012; Tennant, Demaray, Coyle, & Malecki, 2015; Wright & Li, 2012, 2013). Most of the available research on the longitudinal relationships between cyber

Table 1. Correlations among all waves of the variables in the study

	Cyber Aggression				Cyber Victimization			
	Wave 1	Wave 2	Wave 3	Wave 4	Wave 1	Wave 2	Wave 3	Wave 4
W1 CA	---	---	---	---	---	---	---	---
W2 CA	.51***	---	---	---	---	---	---	---
W3 CA	.43***	.43***	---	---	---	---	---	---
W4 CA	.37***	.37***	.41***	---	---	---	---	---
W1 CV	.35***	.35***	.36***	.35***	---	---	---	---
W2 CV	.34***	.34***	.33***	.30***	.54***	---	---	---
W3 CV	.34***	.33***	.34***	.30***	.46***	.50***	---	---
W4 CV	.30***	.33***	30***	.31***	.42***	.47***	.44***	---
W1 SI	.29***	.29**	.28**	.24*	.39***	.37***	.42***	.48***
W2 SI	.27**	.26**	.26**	.22*	.36***	.36***	.43***	.48***
W3 SI	.25*	.25*	.24*	.19*	.34***	.33***	.45***	.46***
W4 SI	.20*	.22*	.23*	.18*	.35***	.41***	.42***	.41***
W1 SH	.31***	.33***	.30***	.29**	.32***	.30***	.29***	.31***
W2 SH	.29**	.28**	.29**	.26**	.29**	.31***	.31***	.30***
W3 SH	.26*	.26*	.25*	.23*	.30***	.31***	.28**	.27**
W4 SH	.23*	.21*	.19*	.20*	.27**	.26**	.27**	.23*
W1 DEP	.41***	.37***	.33***	.29**	.51***	.53***	.49***	.50***
W2 DEP	.33***	.42***	.33***	.30***	.48***	.49***	.46***	.50***
W3 DEP	.36***	.37***	.39***	.36***	.46***	.51***	.50***	.51***
W4 DEP	.35***	.33***	.31***	.36***	.46***	.56***	.46***	.46***
W1 LONE	.33***	.31***	.27**	.27**	.30***	.27**	.25*	.22*
W2 LONE	.30***	.30***	.27**	.25*	.29**	.28**	.25*	.22*
WE LONE	.28**	.27**	.25*	.19*	.27**	.29**	.26**	.21*
W4 LONE	.25*	.20*	.19*	.19*	.23*	.23*	.26**	.19*
W1 ANX	.27**	.30***	.28**	.25*	.26***	.29***	.30***	.29***
W2 ANX	.25*	.29**	.27**	.21*	.21**	.31***	.32***	.29***
W3 ANX	.19*	.21*	.20*	.23*	.25***	.22**	.28***	.27***
W4 ANX	.19*	.19*	.20*	.19*	.18*	.17*	.24**	.25**
W1 GPA	-.36***	-.31***	-.27**	-.25*	-.31***	-.26**	-.23*	-.19*
W2 GPA	-.31***	-.30***	-.28**	-.26*	-.30***	-.29**	-.27**	-.25*
W3 GPA	-.31***	-.29**	-.23*	-.23*	-.30***	-.27**	-.29**	-.27**
W4 GPA	-.27**	-.27**	-.26*	-.21*	-.26**	-.26**	-.21*	-.25*

Note. W1 = Wave 1; W2 = Wave 2; W3 = Wave 3; W4 = Wave 4; CA = cyber aggression; CV = cyber victimization; SI = suicidal ideation; SH = non-suicidal self-harm; DEP = depression; LONE = loneliness; ANX = anxiety; GPA = grade point average.

*p < .05. **p < .01. ***p < .001.

Table 2. Frequency of cyber aggression and cyber victimization across digital technologies and tools

	Cyber Aggression				Cyber Victimization			
	Wave 1	**Wave 2**	**Wave 3**	**Wave 4**	**Wave 1**	**Wave 2**	**Wave 3**	**Wave 4**
SNS	24.6%	22.3%	21.6%	20.2%	30.7%	30.1%	28.9%	28.1%
Chat	12.7%	10.9%	10.0%	8.9%	9.1%	8.7%	7.3%	6.9%
Email	12.7%	11.1%	9.6%	8.8%	4.5%	4.0%	4.0%	3.8%
Chatrooms	3.1%	2.9%	2.2%	1.9%	1.6%	1.3%	1.1%	0.8%
Blogs	1.3%	1.1%	0.9%	0.9%	1.6%	0.9%	0.6%	0.6%
Online Gaming	3.0%	3.0%	2.7%	2.0%	10.3%	10.1%	9.5%	9.0%
Text Messages	39.1%	37.8%	35.8%	33.4%	28.2%	28.2%	27.8%	26.3%

aggression involvement and adjustment difficulties (i.e., suicidal ideation, depression, anxiety) have been conducted among children and adolescents (Bannink, Broeren, van de Looij-Jasen, de Waart, & Raat, 2014; Hay & Meldrum, 2010; Shpiegel, Klomek, & Apter, 2015). These studies revealed that suicidal ideation, depression, and anxiety increased after children and adolescents experienced or perpetrated cyber aggression. Finding that suicidal ideation, non-suicidal self-harm, depression, loneliness, anxiety, and GPA are antecedents and consequences of cyber aggression and victimization among emerging adults demonstrates the importance of understanding more about this topic. Cyber aggression and victimization are typically considered problems for primary and secondary school students. Acknowledging that these behaviors occur among emerging adults is an important step in the prevention of cyber aggression involvement and helping to alleviate the negative consequences associated with such behaviors. The first purpose of the present study was to describe the digital technologies and tools that emerging adults utilize more often to harm others and to understand the nature of the relationship between the perpetrator and the victim. The second purpose of the study was to investigate the longitudinal and reciprocal relationship of cyber aggression and cyber victimization to suicidal ideation, non-suicidal self-harm, depression, loneliness, anxiety, and GPA across fours year among emerging adults, while accounting for previous levels of these variables and face-to-face aggression and victimization.

The findings from the present study were similar to those found in cross-sectional studies on the associations of cyber victimization to various psychological, social, academic, and behavioral difficulties

Table 3. Frequency of cyber aggression and cyber victimization across different relationships between the perpetrator and the victim

	Cyber Aggression				Cyber Victimization			
	Wave 1	**Wave 2**	**Wave 3**	**Wave 4**	**Wave 1**	**Wave 2**	**Wave 3**	**Wave 4**
Ex-significant other	15.2%	15.0%	14.5%	13.3%	21.4%	19.8%	19.0%	18.4%
Ex-friend	16.8%	16.1%	15.6%	15.0%	35.3%	33.8%	32.8%	30.9%
Current significant other	1.0%	0.8%	0.8%	0.7%	1.3%	1.0%	0.8%	0.6%
Current friend	7.7%	7.1%	6.4%	6.1%	8.4%	8.1%	7.6%	7.1%
Acquaintance	11.3%	10.8%	10.1%	8.8%	11.3%	10.8%	9.2%	8.3%
Someone do not know offline	10.3%	9.8%	8.6%	8.0%	15.9%	15.0%	14.1%	13.5%

among emerging adults (Feinstein, Bhatia, & Davila, 2014; Kokkinos et al., 2014; Landoll, La Greca, & Lai, 2013; Schenk & Fremouw, 2012; Tennant et al., 2015). Furthermore, the results of the present study expand on the existing literature by demonstrating longitudinal and bidirectional associations between cyber victimization, suicidal ideation, non-suicidal self-harm, depression, loneliness, anxiety, and GPA. Such relationships were highly stable over the four years of the study, revealing that prior levels of cyber aggression and cyber victimization predicted later cyber aggression involvement and psychosocial and academic difficulties. Prolonged exposure to cyber aggression might potentially weaken emerging adults' ability to effectively cope with victimization. Utilizing maladaptive coping strategies might lead emerging adults to suicidal ideation, non-suicidal self-harm, depression, loneliness, anxiety, and GPA. Stable patterns of cyber victimization were experienced by some emerging adults in this study, combined with poor coping strategies, which might increase their risk for additional victimization and further adjustment difficulties (Ybarra, Alexander, & Mitchell, 2005).

Less attention has been given in the literature to cyber aggression perpetration among children, adolescents, and emerging adults, with even fewer studies conducted on the association between cyber aggression perpetration and adjustment difficulties among emerging adults. Cyber aggression perpetration is linked to depression, anxiety, and loneliness, findings that are consistent with the current study's results (Brighi et al., 2012; Gradinger, Strohmeier, & Spiel, 2009; Sontag, Clemans, Graber, & Lyndon, 2011). Research also indicates that adolescent cyberaggressors experience academic difficulties, such as failing grades, classroom disruptions, and poor achievement scores (Wright, 2015). This finding can also be applied to the current study's results, revealing connections between cyber aggression perpetration and lower GPA. Thus far, no research has focused on the association between cyber aggression perpetration, suicidal ideation, and non-suicidal self-harm. In the face-to-face aggression literature, the perpetration of aggression is correlated with suicidal ideation and self-harm among adolescents (Barker, Arsenault, Brendgen, Fontaine, Maughan, 2008; Kim, Leventhal, Koh, & Boyce, 2009). It is proposed that individuals with externalizing problems, like aggression, are more impulsive and indulge in anger-related behaviors, which increases their suicide and self-harm risk (Apter et al., 1991). Therefore, cyber aggression perpetrators might be more impulsive and anger-prone, leading them more vulnerable to suicidal ideation and self-harm.

The magnitudes of the associations of cyber aggression and cyber victimization to suicidal ideation, non-suicidal self-harm, depression, loneliness, anxiety, and GPA were stronger than the reciprocal associations. Tennant and colleagues (2015) consider cyber aggression to be "a more persistent and pervasive form of aggression." Due to the pervasiveness of cyber aggression, emerging adults' psychological and academic difficulties might increase over time. Cyber victimization might lead some emerging adults to continuously experience a cycle of victimization, leading to repeated exposure to negative messages. The repeated exposure to negative messages and interactions might make it difficult for victims to perceive positive social interactions. The inability to perceive positive social interactions might reduce cyber-victims' self-concept, leading to greater levels of suicidal ideation, non-suicidal self-harm, depression, loneliness, anxiety, and lower GPAs (Lipton, 2011). Victims of cyber aggression might find it more difficult to escape from victimization as they are not able to receive sanctuary in their homes (Kowalski & Limber, 2012). Furthermore, emerging adults are typically away from home and experience changes in their social relationships and identity. These changes in emerging adults' lives might make them more vulnerable to the adjustment difficulties associated with cyber victimization.

SOLUTIONS AND RECOMMENDATIONS

Raising awareness of cyber aggression and cyber victimization on college and university campuses is needed. Colleges and universities need to develop clear policies concerning cyber aggression involvement and provide details about the sanctions against perpetrators at the school level. The sanctions for perpetrations of cyber aggression should be clearly conveyed with college students to reduce their desire to engage in such behavior. It might be helpful to distribute materials on cyber aggression involvement and the associated adjustment difficulties during freshmen orientations. The resource can explain the dangers related to cyber victimization, what constitutes cyber aggression, and include contact information for the counseling center that students. The counseling center should also employ trained and knowledge staff regarding recognizing the signs of cyber aggression and the psychological, academic, and behavioral consequences. Faculty and staff, particularly those individuals who serve as advisors, might also benefit from understanding more about cyber aggression and victimization, with specific knowledge on the risk factors associated with involvement and the negative outcomes. Universities/colleges implement various training program for faculty and staff, such as training on internet safety or working with student workers. In tandem with these programs, faculty and staff might benefit from a training module on recognizing the risks factors and outcomes of cyber aggression among college students. These programs might be interactive and allow for faculty and staff to implement their skills in an immersive environment. It might also be important to have a faculty and staff run committee at the university/college level which focuses on providing training and updates to knowledge regarding cyber aggression and victimization.

There is a need to establish theoretically based and empirically proven prevention and intervention programs in cyber aggression for college students. Most of the available programs focus on stopping or reducing cyber aggression among children and adolescents between the ages of 11 and 14 (e.g., Lee, Zi-Pei, Sanstrom, & Dalal, 2013; Williford et al., 2014). Some of these programs are aimed at older adolescents who are the age of 17 (e.g., Wolfer, Schultze, Zagorscak, Gobel, & Scheithauer, 2014) or among students 14 to 20 years (e.g., Menesini, Nocentini, & Palladino, 2012). Specific programs are needed at the college level, and these programs should focus on cyber aggression perpetration, cyber bystander behavior, and cyber victimization. To date, one theoretically based and empirically tested prevention programs has been developed for reducing cyber aggression among college students (Doane, Kelley, & Pearson, 2016). It might also help to encourage college students to be activists for more positive internet and technology experiences. This could involve having college students serve as college-level peer mentors for encouraging safe internet practices across the school campus. These students could campaign at school fairs and other events, as well as have booths during specific campus events. Having outreach made by college students to their peers might be especially useful for promoting positive internet and technology use. Activities carried out by college students might be much more effective than having a standalone prevention or intervention program. Therefore, such social activism on the school campus could be coupled with a university/college-wide program for reducing negative online behaviors and promoting positive interactions in cyberspace.

Programs devoted to cyber aggression among college/university students might benefit from recognizing that the most common perpetrators of these behaviors are ex-friends and ex-partners. Although it might be difficult for people to recognize that their friendships or romantic relationship might end, college/university students might benefit from realizing that it could happen and what the implications might be of such dissolutions of the relationship. They might benefit from learning strategies to mitigate the negative impacts of relationship dissolution by developing positive coping strategies or finding ways to block or ignore technology-based contact with the ex-partner or ex-friend. Many programs designed to reduce cyber aggression ignore the relationship-based or former relationship between the individuals involved in these behaviors. Such programs might be further beneficial for college/university students who undergo various transitions, including changing relationships. These programs might also assume that there are social support systems, but such systems might be absent or diminished in college/university students' lives, given the amount of transitions they experience. There might be a need for these programs to focus on building new support systems or engaging in other activities to reduce the negative impacts of cyber aggression and victimization. If existing support systems are accessible, it might be encouraged for college/university students to continue to foster these systems to gain additional support for what they might experience. Harnessing existing support systems might reduce the likelihood of experiencing negative adjustment and academic difficulties associated with cyber aggression involvement.

FUTURE RESEARCH DIRECTIONS

The four-wave longitudinal design of the present study is a strength of this research. More attention should be given to investigating cyber aggression and cyber victimization among emerging adults, as findings from the present study indicate that these experiences and behaviors are harmful to emerging adults' psychological health. This study employed self-reports of both face-to-face and cyber aggression and victimization. Follow-up research should be conducted using multi-informants, such as friends and parents. This research might also consider investigating clinical forms of suicidality, non-suicidal self-harm, depression, anxiety, and loneliness to better understand their linkages to cyber aggression and cyber victimization over time. This study relied on a convenience sample of emerging adults. More attention should be given to conducting follow-up studies on cyber aggression and cyber victimization among other adults as well.

Based on the prevalence rates of cyber aggression across different technologies, it appears that social networking websites and text messages through mobile devices are the most frequent tools used. It is important to recognize the role of different technologies and behaviors when trying to fully understand college students' involvement in cyber aggression. Follow-up research should be conducted to understand why or the motivations for college students to utilize different technologies and behaviors to perpetrate cyber aggression. Such a focus might allow for the development of individually tailored programs to help increase coping skills and technical skills of victims. The advice in these programs could be tailored to the specific technology used to harm someone. Furthermore, college/university students reported that they were most often victimized by ex-friends and ex-partners. More research should be conducted to better understand why relationship dissolution might trigger negative interactions, as well as understand the ways to mitigate the negative impacts.

Another aim of future research might be to understand how different variables could mitigate or exacerbate the relationship between cyber aggression and cyber victimization and psychological and academic adjustment difficulties among college students. Some variables, such as coping strategies and technical skills, might reduce or elevate the negative adjustment following cyber aggression and cyber victimization. It might also be important to investigate the variables that might predict cyber aggression and cyber victimization, and whether different forms of cyber aggression have differential impacts on adjustment problems for college students. For example, non-anonymous forms of cyber aggression might not hinder psychological processes more so than anonymous forms of cyber aggression involving a friend or a significant other.

CONCLUSION

This study adds to the growing body of literature on cyber aggression and cyber victimization among emerging adults, and how such experiences relate to psychological and academic difficulties. The findings of the study were consistent with cross-sectional studies, with the present study revealing longitudinal and reciprocal relationships between cyber aggression, cyber victimizations, suicidal ideation, non-suicidal self-harm, depression, anxiety, and GPA over four years. Additional research attention should be given to understanding more about these associations by focusing on mitigating or moderating variables. More awareness should be given to cyber aggression and cyber victimization among emerging adults as oftentimes these behaviors are considered concerns associated with children and adolescence. This mentality prevents additional research conducted on cyber aggression and cyber victimization among emerging adults, which diminishes our ability to deal with these behaviors and the associated psychological and academic difficulties. Awareness of cyber aggression and cyber victimization among emerging adults is necessary to prevent these behaviors and to alleviate the negative outcomes of such behaviors. Universities/colleges must incorporate the mental health and focus on positive behaviors of college students within their mission. Academic excellence is important but so is educating college students in a setting that promotes positive interactions and diminishes negative interactions in cyberspace.

REFERENCES

Alvarez-Garcia, D., Nunez Perez, J. C., Gonzalez, A. D., & Perez, C. R. (2015). Risk factors associated with cyber victimization in adolescence. *International Journal of Clinical and Health Psychology*, *15*(3), 226–235. doi:10.1016/j.ijchp.2015.03.002 PMID:30487840

Apter, A., Kotler, M., Sevy, S., Plutchik, R., Brown, S. L., Foster, H., ... van Praag, H. M. (1991). Correlates of risk of suicide in violent and nonviolent psychiatric patients. *The American Journal of Psychiatry*, *148*(7), 883–837. doi:10.1176/ajp.148.7.883 PMID:2053628

Arnett, J. (2000). Emerging adulthood: A theory of development from late teens through the twenties. *The American Psychologist*, *55*(5), 469–480. doi:10.1037/0003-066X.55.5.469 PMID:10842426

Arnett, J., & Jensen, L. (2002). A congregation of one: Individualized religious beliefs among emerging adults. *Journal of Adolescent Research*, *17*(5), 451–467. doi:10.1177/0743558402175002

Badger, S., Nelson, L., & Barry, C. M. N. (2006). Perceptions of the transition to adulthood among Chinese and American emerging adults. *International Journal of Behavioral Development*, *30*(1), 84–93. doi:10.1177/0165025406062128

Bannink, R., Broeren, S., van de Looij-Jansen, P. M., de Waart, F. G., & Raat, H. (2014). Cyber and traditional bullying victimization as a risk factor for mental health problems in adolescents. *PLoS One*, *9*, e94026. doi:10.1371/journal.pone.0094026 PMID:24718563

Barker, E. D., Arseneault, L., Brendgen, M., Fontaine, N., & Maughan, B. (2008). Joint development of bullying and victimization in adolescence: Relations to delinquency and self-harm. *Journal of the American Academy of Child and Adolescent Psychiatry*, *47*(9), 1030–1038. PMID:18665001

Beck, A. T., & Steer, R. A. (1993). *Beck anxiety inventory manual*. San Antonio, TX: Harcourt Brace.

Beck, A. T., Steer, R. A., & Brown, G. K. (1996). *Manual for the beck inventory-II*. San Antonio, TX: Psychological Corporation.

Bollen, K. A., & Curran, P. J. (2006). *Latent curve models: A structural equation perspective*. New York, NY: Wiley.

Brighi, A., Melotti, G., Guarini, A., Genta, M. L., Ortega, R., Mora-Merchan, J., … Thompson, F. (2012). Self-esteem and loneliness in relation to cyberbullying in three European countries. In Q. Ling, D. Cross, & P. K. Smith (Eds.), Cyberbullying in the global playground (pp. 52-56). West Sussex, UK: Blackwell Publishing.

Cappadocia, M. C., Craig, W. M., & Pepler, D. (2013). Cyberbullying: Prevalence, stability and risk factors during adolescence. *Canadian Journal of School Psychology*, *28*(2), 171–192. doi:10.1177/0829573513491212

Center for Disease Control and Prevention (CDC). (2011). *Self-directed violence surveillance: Uniform definitions and recommended data elements*. Retrieved from: http://www.cdc.gov/violenceprevention/pdf/SelfDirected-Violence-a.pdf

Copes, H., Kerley, K., Huff, R., & Kane, J. (2010). Differentiating identity theft: An exploratory study of victims using a national victimization survey. *Journal of Criminal Justice*, *38*(5), 1045–1052. doi:10.1016/j.jcrimjus.2010.07.007

Cowie, H. (2013). Cyberbullying and its impact on young people's emotional health and well-being. *The Psychiatrist*, *37*(5), 167–170. doi:10.1192/pb.bp.112.040840

Crosslin, K. L., & Crosslin, M. B. (2014). Cyberbullying at a Texas university—A mixed-methods approach to examining online aggression. *Texas Public Health Journal*, *66*, 26–31.

Dilmac, N. (2009). Psychological needs as a predict of cyber bullying: A preliminary report on college students. *Educational Sciences: Theory and Practice*, *9*(3), 1307–1325.

Feinstein, B. A., Bhatia, V., & Davila, J. (2014). Rumination mediates the association between cybervictimization and depressive symptoms. *Journal of Interpersonal Violence*, *29*(9), 1732–1746. doi:10.1177/0886260513511534 PMID:24346650

Ferdon, C. D., & Hertz, M. F. (2007). Electronic media, violence, and adolescents. An emerging public health problem. *The Journal of Adolescent Health*, *41*(6), 1–5. doi:10.1016/j.jadohealth.2007.08.020 PMID:17577527

Finn, J. (2004). A survey of online harassment at a university campus. *Journal of Interpersonal Violence*, *19*(4), 468–483. doi:10.1177/0886260503262083 PMID:15038885

Fischer, E. H., Dornelas, E. A., & Goethe, J. W. (2001). Characteristics of people lost to attrition in psychiatric follow-up studies. *The Journal of Nervous and Mental Disease*, *189*(1), 49–55. doi:10.1097/00005053-200101000-00009 PMID:11206665

Gradinger, P., Strohmeier, D., & Spiel, C. (2015). Traditional bullying and cyberbullying: Identification of risk groups for adjustment problems. *The Journal of Psychology*, *217*, 205–213.

Grigg, D. W. (2010). Cyber-aggression: Definition and concept of cyberbullying. *Australian Journal of Guidance & Counselling*, *20*(2), 143–156. doi:10.1375/ajgc.20.2.143

Hay, C., & Meldrum, R. (2010). Bullying victimization and adolescent self-harm: Testing hypotheses from General Strain Theory. *Journal of Youth and Adolescence*, *39*(5), 446–459. doi:10.100710964-009-9502-0 PMID:20072852

Hinduja, S., & Patchin, J. W. (2010). Bullying, cyberbullying, and suicide. *Archives of Suicide Research*, *14*(3), 206–221. doi:10.1080/13811118.2010.494133 PMID:20658375

Holt, T. J., Fitzgerald, S., Bossler, A. M., Chee, G., & Nq, E. (2016). Assessing the risk factors of cyber and mobile phone bullying victimization in a nationally representative sample of Singapore youth. *International Journal of Offender Therapy and Comparative Criminology*, *60*(5), 598–615. doi:10.1177/0306624X14554852 PMID:25326463

Kim, Y. S., Leventhal, B. L., Koh, Y. J., & Boyce, W. T. (2009). Bullying increased suicide risk: Prospective study of Korean adolescents. *Archives of Suicide Research*, *13*(1), 15–30. doi:10.1080/13811110802572098 PMID:19123106

Kokkinos, C. M., Antoniadou, N., & Markos, A. (2014). Cyber-bullying: An investigation of the psychological profile of university student participants. *Journal of Applied Developmental Psychology*, *35*(3), 204–214. doi:10.1016/j.appdev.2014.04.001

Kowalski, R. M., & Limber, S. P. (2007). Electronic bullying among middle school students. *The Journal of Adolescent Health*, *41*(6), 22–30. doi:10.1016/j.jadohealth.2007.08.017 PMID:18047942

Kowalski, R. M., & Limber, S. P. (2012). Psychological, physical, and academic correlates of cyberbullying and traditional bullying. *The Journal of Adolescent Health*, *53*, 513–520. PMID:23790195

Landoll, R. R., La Greca, A. M., & Lai, B. S. (2013). Aversive peer experiences on social networking sites: Development of the Social Networking-Peer Experiences Questionnaires (SN-PEQ). *Journal of Research on Adolescence*, *23*(4), 695–705. doi:10.1111/jora.12022 PMID:24288449

Lipton, J. D. (2011). Combating cyber-victimization. *Berkeley Technology Law Journal*, *26*, 1104–1126.

Little, R. J. A., & Rubin, D. B. (1989). The analysis of social science data with missing values. *Sociological Methods & Research*, *18*(2-3), 292–326. doi:10.1177/0049124189018002004

Mishna, F., Khoury-Kassabri, M., Gadalla, T., & Daciuk, J. (2012). Risk factors for involvement in cyber bullying: Victims, bullies and bully-victims. *Children and Youth Services Review*, *34*(1), 63–70. doi:10.1016/j.childyouth.2011.08.032

Nelson, L., & Barry, C. (2005). Distinguishing features of emerging adulthood: The role of self-classification as an adult. *Journal of Adolescent Research*, *20*(2), 242–262. doi:10.1177/0743558404273074

Perrin, A., & Duggan, M. (2015). *Americans' internet access: 2000-2015*. Retrieved from: http://www.pewin ternet.org/2015/06/26/americans-internet-access-2000-2015/

Rideout, V. J., Roberts, D. F., & Foehr, U. G. (2005). *Generation M: Media in the lives of 8-18-year-olds: Executive summary*. Menlo Park, CA: Henry J. Kaiser Family Foundation.

Rubin, K. H., & Coplan, R. (2010). *The development of shyness and social withdrawal*. New York, NY: Guilford Press.

Russell, D. (1996). UCLA Loneliness Scale (Version 3): Reliability, validity, and factor structure. *Journal of Personality Assessment*, *66*(1), 20–40. doi:10.120715327752jpa6601_2 PMID:8576833

Sansone, R. A., Wiederman, M. W., & Sansone, L. A. (1998). The Self-Harm Inventory (SHI): Development of a scale of identifying self-destructive behaviors and borderline personality disorder. *Journal of Clinical Psychology*, *54*(7), 973–983. doi:10.1002/(SICI)1097-4679(199811)54:7<973::AID-JCLP11>3.0.CO;2-H PMID:9811134

Schenk, A. M., & Fremouw, W. J. (2012). Prevalence, psychological impact, and coping of cyberbully victims among college students. *Journal of School Violence*, *11*(1), 21–37. doi:10.1080/15388220.2011.630310

Selkie, E. M., Kota, R., Chan, Y., & Moreno, M. (2015). Cyberbullying, depression, and problem alcohol use in female college students: A multisite study. *Cyberpsychology, Behavior, and Social Networking*, *18*(2), 79–86. doi:10.1089/cyber.2014.0371 PMID:25684608

Shpiegel, Y., Klomek, A. B., & Apter, A. (2015). Bullying, cyberbullying, depression and suicide ideation among youth. Comparing online to paper-and-pencil questionnaires. *International Journal of Child and Adolescent Health*, *8*, 161–167.

Smith, A., Rainie, L., & Zickuhr, K. (2011). *College students and technology*. Retrieved from http://www.pe winternet.org/2011/07/19/college-students-and-technology/

Smith, P. K., Mahdavi, J., Carvalho, M., Fisher, S., Russell, S., & Tippett, N. (2008). Cyberbullying: Its nature and impact in secondary school pupils. *Journal of Child Psychology and Psychiatry, and Allied Disciplines*, *49*(4), 376–385. doi:10.1111/j.1469-7610.2007.01846.x PMID:18363945

Sontag, L. M., Clemans, K. H., Graber, J. A., & Lyndon, S. T. (2011). Traditional and cyber aggressors and victims: A comparison of psychosocial characteristics. *Journal of Youth and Adolescence*, *40*(4), 392–404. doi:10.100710964-010-9575-9 PMID:20680425

Tang, J., Ma, Y., Guo, T., Ahmed, N. I., Yu, Y., & Wang, J. (2013). Association of aggression and non-suicidal self-injury: A school-based sample of adolescents. *PLoS One*, *8*(1), e78149. doi:10.1371/journal.pone.0078149 PMID:24205132

Tennant, J. E., Demaray, M. K., Coyle, S., & Malecki, C. K. (2015). The dangers of the webs: Cybervictimization, depression, and social support in college students. *Computers in Human Behavior*, *50*, 348–357. doi:10.1016/j.chb.2015.04.014

Topcu, C., Erdur-Baker, O., & Capa, A. Y. (2008). Examination of cyber-bullying experiences among Turkish students from different school types. *Cyberpsychology & Behavior*, *11*(6), 644–648. doi:10.1089/cpb.2007.0161 PMID:18783345

Walker, C., Sockman, B., & Koehn, S. (2011). An exploratory study of cyberbullying with undergraduate university students. *TechTrends*, *55*(2), 31–38. doi:10.100711528-011-0481-0

Weigman, O., & Schie, E. (1998). Video game playing and its relations with aggressive and prosocial behaviors. *British Journal of Social Psychology*, *37*(3), 367–378. doi:10.1111/j.2044-8309.1998.tb01177.x PMID:9738313

Wolak, J., Mitchell, K., & Finkelhor, D. (2007). Does online harassment constitute bullying? An exploration of online harassment by known peers and online-only contacts. *The Journal of Adolescent Health*, *41*(6), 51–58. doi:10.1016/j.jadohealth.2007.08.019 PMID:18047945

Wright, M. F. (2015). Cyber victimization and perceived stress: Linkages to late adolescents' cyber aggression and psychological functioning. *Youth & Society*, *47*(6), 789–810. doi:10.1177/0044118X14537088

Wright, M. F., & Li, Y. (2012). Kicking the digital dog: A longitudinal investigation of young adults' victimization and cyber-displaced aggression. *Cyberpsychology, Behavior, and Social Networking*, *15*(9), 44–454. doi:10.1089/cyber.2012.0061 PMID:22974350

Wright, M. F., & Li, Y. (2013). Normative beliefs about aggression and cyber aggression among young adults: A longitudinal investigation. *Aggressive Behavior*, *39*(3), 161–170. doi:10.1002/ab.21470 PMID:23440595

Wright, M. F., Li, Y., & Shi, J. (2014). Chinese adolescents' social status goals: Associations with behaviors and attributions for relational aggression. *Youth & Society*, *46*(4), 566–588. doi:10.1177/0044118X12448800

Ybarra, M. L., Alexander, C., & Mitchell, K. J. (2005). Depressive symptomology, youth internet use, and online interactions: A national survey. *The Journal of Adolescent Health*, *36*(1), 9–18. doi:10.1016/j.jadohealth.2003.10.012 PMID:15661591

Ybarra, M. L., Diener-West, M., & Leaf, P. J. (2007). Examining the overlap in internet harassment and school bullying: Implications for school intervention. *The Journal of Adolescent Health*, *41*(6), S42–S50. doi:10.1016/j.jadohealth.2007.09.004 PMID:18047944

Ybarra, M. L., & Mitchell, K. J. (2004). Online aggressor/targets, aggressors, and targets: A comparison of associated youth characteristics. *Journal of Child Psychology and Psychiatry, and Allied Disciplines*, *45*(7), 1308–1316. doi:10.1111/j.1469-7610.2004.00328.x PMID:15335350

ADDITIONAL READING

Bauman, S. (2011). *Cyberbullying: What counselors need to know*. Alexandria, VA: American Counseling Association.

Bauman, S., Cross, D., & Walker, J. (2013). *Principles of cyberbullying research: Definitions, measures, and methodology*. New York, NY: Routledge.

Feinberg, T., & Robey, N. (2010). Cyberbullying: Intervention and prevention strategies. Retrieved from: http://www.nasponline.org/resources/bullying/cyberbullying.pdf

Hinduja, S., & Patchin, J. W. (2015). *Bullying beyond the schoolyard: Preventing and responding to cyberbullying*. Thousand Oaks, CA: Sage Publications.

Li, Q., Cross, D., & Smith, P. K. (2012). *Cyberbullying in the global playground*. Malden, MA: Blackwell Publishing. doi:10.1002/9781119954484

Menesini, E., & Spiel, C. (2012). *Cyberbullying: Development, consequences, risk and protective factors*. New York, NY: Psychology Press.

Shariff, S., & Churchill, A. H. (2010). *Truths and myths of cyber-bullying: International perspectives on stakeholder responsibility and children's safety*. New York, NY: Peter Lang Publishing, Inc.

Tokunaga, R. S. (2010). Following you home from school: A critical review and synthesis of research on cyberbullying victimization. *Computers in Human Behavior*, *26*(3), 277–287. doi:10.1016/j.chb.2009.11.014

Chapter 2
Cyberstalking Victimization and Perpetration Among Young Adults:
Prevalence and Correlates

Argyroula Kalaitzaki
https://orcid.org/0000-0002-6416-9740
Laboratory of Interdisciplinary Approaches for the Enhancement of Quality of Life, Hellenic Mediterranean University, Greece

ABSTRACT

Cyberstalking is becoming more common among young adults. The aim of this study was to investigate (1) the prevalence, behaviours, and tactics of both victims and perpetrators of cyberstalking among a sample of Greek undergraduate students; (2) the correlates of victimization and perpetration of cyberstalking to personality, attachment style, and relating to others; and (3) the impact of cyberstalking on victims' mental health. Results showed that 23.9% of the students were victims and 9% were perpetrators, with females, disproportionately experiencing and inflicting cyberstalking. Negatively close relating (i.e., intrusive and possessive relating) increased the risk of perpetration, whereas relating to others distantly (suspicious and avoidant relating) decreased the risk of victimization. Agreeableness decreased the risk of perpetration. Mother's affectionless control increased the risk of both perpetration and victimization, and mother's neglectful parenting increased the risk of perpetrating cyberstalking. Fear, anxiety, and depression were reported by the victims.

INTRODUCTION

Although stalking is not a new behaviour, its emergence into the cyber-world is. Stalking is defined as the behaviors by an individual who engages in a pattern of harassing or threatening acts (Ashcroft, 2001), such as following a person, appearing at a person's home or place of business, making harassing phone calls, leaving written messages or objects, or vandalizing a person's property (Tjaden & Thoennes,

DOI: 10.4018/978-1-7998-1063-6.ch002

1998). The advancement of information and communication technologies, such as the Internet, has offered stalkers an additional and perhaps more effective, though dubious and insidious, way to target their victims and commit their malevolent act; thus, some stalkers have become Cyberstalkers.

Despite experts' and legislators' attempts to define cyberstalking, there is no commonly accepted definition of *cyberstalking* or *technology-aided stalking*. In general, the term is used to refer to the repeated pursuit or monitoring of an individual using electronic (e.g., e-mails, blogs, instant messaging, video, chat rooms, on-line social networks, or other websites) or tracking technologies/ Internet-capable devices that induces the victim to feel distress, fear, alarm, or concerned for his/her safety (Dreßing, Bailer, Anders, Wagner, & Gallas, 2014; Reyns, 2010; Reyns, Henson, & Fisher, 2012). This may involve threatening, coercive, harassing, or intimidating messages or sexual overtones or other unwanted, persistent, and intrusive contact. Cyberstalking is one form of cyberviolence or interpersonal cybercrimes, such as cyberbullying, sexting, cyber dating abuse, and revenge porn (e.g., Backe, Lilleston, & McCleary-Sills, 2018; Clevenger, Navarro, & Gilliam, 2018).

To the author's knowledge, there is no other study on cyberstalking in Greece. The prevalence of both cyberstalking perpetration and victimization worldwide is also unknown because of considerable disparities in estimates, which are likely due to different definitions, study samples, methodological, and measurement differences across studies. While there is abundant research on cyberstalking victimization, few studies are available on cyberstalking perpetration, particularly due to the difficulty in obtaining offending data (Roberts, 2008).

There are studies that estimate that roughly 5% of college students admit to cyberstalking (Marcum, Higgins, & Ricketts, 2014; Reyns, 2018; Reyns et al., 2012; Reyns, Fisher, & Randa, 2018), whereas there are other studies that indicate significantly higher rates (e.g., 26.5% by Strawhun, Adams, & Huss, 2013). The profile of a cyberstalker is also not well-known, as few studies have examined this topic. Among the demographics that have been identified as risk factors are being women (Reyns, 2018; Smoker & March, 2017; van Baak & Hayes, 2018), over 21 years old and nonsingle (Reyns, et al., 2012), and being known by the victim, such as ex-partners, friends, or acquaintances (Dreßing et al., 2014). However, other studies have reported that the harasser is predominately male (Dreßing et al. 2014; Reyns et al., 2012; WHOA, 2013) and single (WHOA, 2013).

Studies have also found that cyberstalking often occurs simultaneously with offline stalking (Dreßing et al. 2014; Groban, 2016; Reyns & Fisher, 2018), and with other forms of violence, such as sexual (Buzawa, Buzawa, & Stark, 2017) or physical assault (Dreßing et al. 2014; Strawhun et al., 2013), and sexting (Reyns, 2018). Studies have found that there is an overlap between different forms of online offending (Holt & Bossler, 2014; Reyns, 2018).

Demographic data on perpetrators are relatively limited. Cyberstalking behaviors are likely to be more prevalent in the population of emerging adults (aged between 18–25 years old; Arnett, 2000; Backe et al., 2018), than in other age groups as they are the highest users of social media and are more likely to use technology to connect with partners in their intimate relationships (Boyle & O'Sullivan, 2014; Dewing, 2010). Moreover, the relationships in this age group are characterized by greater emotional intensity, importance, and commitment compared to earlier ages (Collins, 2003), which might increase potential distress over loss and "difficulty letting go" during the process of adjusting to a breakup (Lee & O'Sullivan, 2014).

Scarce research exists on the personality of cyberstalkers and cyberstalking victims. Cyberstalkers are low on agreeableness, conscientiousness, and emotional stability, and high on extraversion (O'Riordan & O'Connell, 2014), while other studies have described cyberstalkers as introverted (Wall, 2007). Other risk factors of perpetrating cyberstalking are having low self-control (Reyns, 2018; Reynes, Henson, et al., 2018; van Baak & Hayes, 2018) or having the Dark Tetrad personality traits (i.e., Machiavellianism, narcissism, psychopathy, and sadism; Smoker & March, 2017). Not much is known about the personality of cyberstalking victims. However, victims of cyberbullying have been described as low on agreeableness and high on extraversion and openness (Festl & Quandt, 2013; Peluchette, Karl, Wood, & Williams, 2015).

Several studies among university students have reported relatively high, though diverse prevalence rates of cyberstalking victimization, ranging from 20% (e.g., 18.9% reported by Holt & Bossler, 2009) to 40% (Tokunaga & Aune, 2017) or higher (46.3%; Reyns et al., 2012). Being female (e.g., Reyns et al, 2012; Dreßing et al. 2014) and in young adulthood (between 18 and 30 years of age; e.g., Brownstein, 2000; Lenhart et al. 2016) are risk factors for cyberstalking victimization. Studies have consistently found that women disproportionally experience cyberstalking compared to men (e.g., Reyns et al., 2012; Working to Halt Online Abuse, 2013). For instance, Duggan (2014) found that 26% of women compared to 7% of men aged 18 to 24 were reportedly cyberstalked. In general, Spitzberg & Cupach (2007) have reported that prevalence rates range between 2% to 13% for males and 8% to 32% for females. Approximately 1 in 4 stalking victims reported some form of cyberstalking, such as e-mail (83%) or instant messaging (35%; Baum, Catalano, Kristina, Michael, 2009).

There is inconsistent evidence regarding the responses that victims use to deal with cyberstalking. Alexy, Burgess, Baker, and Smoyak (2005) found that most victims do not report cyberstalking, whereas other studies have found that victims do report cyberstalking (e.g., Finn, 2004; WHOA, 2011, 2013). Cyberstalking can have major psychosocial impacts on individuals (Worsley, Wheatcroft, Short, & Corcoran, 2017). Victims have reported increased suicidal ideation, fear, anger, depression, and post-traumatic stress disorder (PTSD) symptomology (Short, Linford, Wheatcroft, & Maple, 2014). In addition, poorer well-being (Nobles, Reyns, Fox, & Fisher, 2014), behavioral problems (i.e., increased sleeplessness and social withdrawal; Dreßing et al., 2014) have also been reported. The main coping strategies that victims employ are avoidance, ignoring the perpetrator, confrontation, support seeking, and cognitive reframing (Worsley et al., 2017).

To the author's knowledge, effects on cyberstalking perpetrators have not been reported. However, cyberbullies have poorer quality of life and psychological difficulties such as more hyperactivity and conduct problems (Fletcher et al., 2014). Due to its serious negative implications, cyberstalking should be an issue of great concern by both legal authorities and victim assistance professionals.

Studies have revealed that cyberstalkers have an insecure-anxious adult attachment style (MacKenzie, Mullen, Ogloff, McEwan, & James, 2008; Patton, Nobles, & Fox, 2010; Tonin, 2004). Fox and Warber (2014) found that people with "preoccupied" and "fearful" attachment styles reported higher levels of "relationship uncertainty" within a romantic relationship and higher levels of interpersonal electronic surveillance (IES) of romantic partners (i.e., checking up more often on their romantic partners). Interpersonal electronic surveillance of a partner after breaking up could lead to cyberstalking provided that it is not just checking up or seeking information about the partner but also instilling fear in the victim. Furthermore, research has shown that attachment styles influence reactions to breakups, with anxious attachment styles having a longer recovery period and continuing to seek information about their partner after the breakup (e.g., Fagundes, 2012).

The current study will add to this limited, yet growing body of research on cyberstalking, by investigating: (a) the prevalence, behaviors, and tactics/responses, (b) personality, attachment style, and type of relating to others as risk factors associated with cyberstalking perpetration and victimization, and (c) the impact of cyberstalking on victims' mental health. Identifying consistent risk factors related to cyberstalking is challenging. The findings will address the gaps in the empirical literature, provide new insights into the field, and make recommendations for further research on cyberstalking and the prevention of these behaviors.

METHOD

Participants

Data were collected via a Web-based survey administered to a random sample of undergraduate college students at the Hellenic Mediterranean University in southern Greece. The sample consists of 442 undergraduate students (78.7% woman) aged 17-21 (42.2%), 22-27 (44.12%), or 28 and over (13.7%).

Procedure

The questionnaire was prepared using Google Forms and the link to the online questionnaire was posted on personal and group webpages and social networks available to the students (e.g., Facebook). Once volunteers read the informed consent, which assured them that all information was confidential and anonymous, they were invited to complete the questionnaire which asked about their experience with cyberstalking, both as victims and offenders.

Measures

The questionnaire asked participants their demographic characteristics (e.g., gender, age, and department) as well as questions regarding traditional (offline) stalking. Next, the definition of cyberstalking was introduced along with examples of cyberstalking acts (e.g., compiling online information, stealing a person's online identity, threatening, false accusations, defamation). The following questionnaires were administered to participants:

The Big Five Inventory (BFI; John & Srivastava, 1999) was administered to measure the Big Five factors (i.e., dimensions) of personality (i.e., extraversion, agreeableness, conscientiousness, neuroticism, openness). It is a self-report inventory of 44 items initiated with the phrase "I see myself as someone who..." Participants responded to each item using a five-point Likert type scale ranging from 1 (*Strongly Disagree*) to 5 (*Strongly Agree*). Certain items were reverse scored, and scores were summed to produce five subscale scores, which corresponded to the five dimensions of personality. Extraversion encompasses traits like talkative, energetic, and assertive. Agreeableness includes traits like sympathetic, kind, and affectionate. Conscientiousness includes traits like organized, thorough, and planful. Neuroticism encompasses traits like tense, moody, and anxious. Openness to Experience includes traits like having wide interests, being imaginative, and insightful. This questionnaire has been shown to have good convergent and discriminant validity, acceptable reliability, and factorial structure across 56 nations, including Greece (John, Donahue, & Kentle, 1999; Schmitt, Allik, McCrae, & Benet-Martinez, 2007). The Greek reliabilities were satisfactory (extraversion: 0.92, agreeableness: 0.91, conscientiousness: 0.89, neuroticism: 0.90, openness: 0.89).

The Person's Relating to Others Questionnaire – Shortened version (PROQ3; Birtchnell, Hammond, Horn, De Jong, & Kalaitzaki, 2013; Kalaitzaki & Birtchnell, 2016) measures a persons' negative (i.e. maladaptive) tendencies to relate to others. It is a 48-item, self-administered questionnaire, with six items contributing to each of the eight scales: upper neutral (e.g., domination), upper close (e.g., intrusiveness), neutral close (e.g., dependence), lower close (e.g., fear of rejection), lower neutral (e.g., helplessness), lower distant (e.g., subservience), neutral distant (e.g., withdrawal), and upper distant (e.g., tyranny). These scales correspond to the negative relating styles within the eight octants of a theoretical structure called the interpersonal octagon, proposed by Relating Theory (Birtchnell, 1996). The six items for each subscale comprise five negative items that contribute to the score and one unscored positive item. The response options include "Nearly always true," "Quite often true," "Sometimes true" and "Rarely true," which carry a score of 3, 2, 1 or 0, respectively. The PROQ3 is scored by computer and the scores are represented both numerically and graphically as shaded areas across the eight octants of an octagon. Higher scores represent more relating deficits. Example items for each scale are: Upper Neutral (UN): *I try to arrange things so that people do what I want*, Upper Close (UC): *I keep a firm hold on someone who is close to me*, Neutral Close (NC): *I have a tendency to cling to people*, Lower Close (LC): *I have a dread of being rejected*, Lower Neutral (LN): *I prefer it when someone else is in control*, Lower Distant (LD): *I easily give in to people*, Neutral Distant (ND): *I do not let people get too close to me*, and Upper Distant (UD): *I tend to get back at people who offend me*. The PROQ3 has been found to possess good psychometric properties (Birtchnell et al., 2013; Newberry & Birtchnell, 2011). In this study the reliabilities were satisfactory (UN: 0.88, UC: 0.89, NC: 0.90, LC: 0.87, LN: 0.86, LD: 0.84, ND: 0.93, UD: 0.84).

The Parental Bonding Instrument (mother-father version) (PBI; Parker, Tupling, & Brown, 1979) was used to assess participants' retrospective accounts of care and protection during their first 16 years of life. It consists of two identical forms (one for each parent) of 25 items each rated on a 4-point Likert scale. A care score, measured by 12 items, and a control score, measured by 13 items, is obtained for each parent. Low scores on the care scale reflect parental indifference, neglect, and rejection whereas high scores reflect parental warmth and affection, and high scores on the protection scale reflect excessive control and intrusive parenting whereas low scores reflect encouragement of autonomy and independence. Four types of bonding were extracted: Optimal bonding / parenting (high care and low protection), weak or absent bonding / neglectful parenting (low care and low protection), affectionate constraint (high care and high protection), affectionless control (low care and high protection). In the present study, the Greek-validated PBI was used, which possesses satisfactory test–retest reliability and internal consistency (Avagianou & Zafiropoulou, 2008). In this study the reliabilities were satisfactory for both mother's and father's version, respectively (optimal parenting: 0.87 and 0.85, neglectful parenting: 0.86 and 0.84, affectionate constraint: 0.89 and 0.90, affectionless control: 0.86 and 0.87).

The Brief Symptom Inventory (BSI-18; Derogatis, 2001) is a short 18-item self-report questionnaire adapted from the 53-item Brief Symptom Inventory (BSI; Derogatis, 1993) to measure psychological distress and psychiatric disorders using three symptom scales of six items each, including Somatization (i.e., distress caused by the perception of bodily dysfunction, focusing on symptoms arising from cardiovascular, gastrointestinal, and other physiological systems that have powerful autonomic mediation), Depression (i.e., symptoms of disaffection and dysphoric mood, such as those reflecting self-deprecation, anhedonia, loss of hope, and suicidal ideation), and Anxiety (i.e., symptoms of nervousness, tension, motor restlessness, apprehension, and panic states). It also includes an overall summary score, the Global Severity Index (GSI). The scale possesses satisfactory reliability indexes (Derogatis, 2001) and psychometric structure (Meijer, de Vries, & van Bruggen, 2011). In this study, the reliabilities were very good (somatization: 0.95, depression: 0.97, anxiety: 0.97, overall scale: 0.95).

The victims of cyberstalking also completed the Impact of Event Scale-Revised (IES-R; Weiss & Marmar, 1996). This is a 22-item self-report questionnaire to measure subjective distress caused by traumatic events (i.e., post-traumatic stress). Respondents rated their degree of distress during the past seven days and items were rated on a 5-point scale ranging from 0 (*not at all*) to 4 (*extremely*). A sample item is "Any reminders brought back feelings about it". The IES-R yields a total score (ranging from 0 to 88) and subscale scores can also be calculated for the Intrusion (intrusive thoughts, nightmares, intrusive feelings and imagery, dissociative-like re-experiencing), Avoidance (numbing of responsiveness, avoidance of feelings, situations, and ideas), and Hyperarousal (anger, irritability, hypervigilance, difficulty concentrating, heightened startle) scales. Scores over 24 are indicative of at least some Post Traumatic Stress Disorder (PTSD) symptoms, whereas scores over 33 are indicative of a probable diagnosis of PTSD. In this study, the reliabilities were very good (intrusion: 0.94, avoidance: 0.92, hyperarousal: 0.91, overall scale: 0.93).

RESULTS

Victimization

Results showed that 43.3% were victims of stalking ($N = 190$) and 21.8% were victims of cyberstalking (N=95), with 2.1% being victims currently ($N = 9$). Females (80.7%) and younger participants (17-21; 58.1%) were disproportionately cyberstalked. Cyberstalking was most likely to be experienced less than 4 times in one's lifetime (84.3%), mainly by one person (60.0%), who had a close proximity to the victim (38.6%; e.g., friend, (ex)-partner, classmate) as opposed to an unknown person (31.6%). Cyberstalking lasted 1 to 2 weeks (64.7%), one month (13.7%), or up to one year (19.6%). The incidence was not reported in 82.5% of the cases. Those who did report the incidence typically told a friend (45.6%). The victims were likely to have experienced the following behaviors (once to three times a year): harassment (42.7%), web exclusion (34.7%), theft of personal code (29.2%), defamation/denigration (22.7%), publishing personal data (18.1%), and fraudulence and video recording through cell-phone (14.3% each). Cyberstalking occurred predominantly (42.1%) through social networking websites (i.e., Facebook, MySpace, Twitter) or text messages (28.1%).

Victims were predominantly intrusive, restrictive, and possessive to others, which are features of relating from an upper close position ($M = 13.9$, $SD = 3.4$). They were open ($M = 34.3$, $SD = 5.3$), conscientious ($M = 29.6$, $SD = 4.8$) and agreeable ($M = 28.8$, $SD = 5$) in terms of their personality characteristics. Victims recalled both their mothers and fathers as being low in care and high in protection (i.e., affectionless control; $M = 0.3$, $SD = 0.5$ and $M = 0.4$, $SD = 0.5$, respectively).

Cyberstalking reportedly instilled fear among victims in 58.6% of the cases, and symptoms of anxiety ($M = 6.8$, SD = 5.7) and depression ($M = 6.6$, SD = 6.5). Hyperarousal was the predominant response by those who had experienced cyberstalking ($M = 1.2$, $SD = 0.8$), as opposed to avoidance ($M = 1.1$, $SD = 0.8$) and intrusion ($M = 1.0$, $SD = 0.8$); the difference between the three coping strategies was not significant ($F_{(2)} = 1.248$, p=.289). Victims reported the use of the following coping strategies: 'behaved more carefully than before' (66.6%), 'limited the disclosure of personal data /information online' (62.8%), and 'reduced the importance of the problem or refused it' (49%). The following responses were 'not at all likely' to be used: 'retaliated using electronic methods' (82.0%), 'met with the police to estimate the cyberstalking' (76.0%), 'substantiated a legal case' (72.0%), and 'negotiated the relationship with the cyberstalker' (64.7%).

Perpetration

A percentage of 19.1% admitted to being stalkers in the offline environment (*N* = 84) and 8.2% were cyberstalkers (N = 34), with 1.0% being presently involved as cyberstalkers (*N* = 4). Female students were statistically more likely (60.7%) than male students to perpetrate cyberstalking. They were typically between the ages of 22 and 27 years old (46.7%) or younger (17 – 21: 40%). Offending occurred less than 4 times (69.2%) or more than 10 times (19.2%) in one's lifetime, predominantly at the age of 17-21 (69.2%), against one victim (53.8%) and cyberstalking lasted for 1 to 2 weeks (53.8%) or approximately one month (34.6%). Cyberstalkers were engaged in the following behaviors a few times a year (up to 7 times): interception of personal code (36.9%), web exclusion (34.6%), harassment (30.8%), defamation/denigration (30.7%), publishing personal data (26.9%), fraudulence (26.9%), and video recording through cell-phone (19.2%). Cyberstalking occurred predominantly through social networking websites (i.e., Facebook, MySpace, Twitter) and text messages (32.1% each) or emails (21.4%).

Like victims, offenders' predominant type of relating to others (*M* = 13.9, *SD* = 3.4) was negative relating from a position of upper closeness (i.e., being intrusive, restrictive, and possessive). In addition, they were open (*M* = 36.4, *SD* = 4.8), conscientious (*M* = 29.9, *SD* = 4.5) and agreeable (*M* = 29.6, *SD* = 3.4). They recalled affectionless control by their mother that was low in care and high in protection (*M* = 0.4, *SD* = 0.5) and affectionate constraint by father that was high in care and high in protection (*M* = 0.3, *SD* = 0.5).

Differences Between Victims and Perpetrators

One-way ANOVA was conducted to compare types of relating, personality, and parenting types between victims and perpetrators. Perpetrators demonstrated significantly higher negative lower distant (LD) relating scores than victims; they were also less agreeable, but the difference failed to reach statistical significance (see Table 1). No differences were found regarding the parenting types among perpetrators and victims (optimal, neglectful, affectionate constraint, and affectionless control).

Risk Factors

A binary logistic regression was performed to examine the effects of the eight types of negative relating to others (i.e., upper neutral, upper close, neutral close, lower close, lower neutral, lower distant, neutral distant, and upper distant) and the five personality factors (i.e., extraversion, agreeableness, conscientiousness, neuroticism, and openness) on the likelihood that students were perpetrators of cyberstalking. Personality and relating variables were entered in the same model as they are both intrapersonal features. The logistic regression model (Table 2) was statistically significant ($\chi^2_{(2)} = 16.685, p < .001$). The model explained 21.5% (Nagelkerke R^2) of the variance in cyberstalking perpetration and corrected classified 91.0% of cases. Higher scores in negative neutral close (NC) relating were associated with a higher likelihood of cyberstalking perpetration, but higher scores on agreeableness were associated with reduced likelihood of perpetration. A separate binary logistic regression examined the effects of

Table 1. Differences between victims (N=95) and perpetrators (N=34)

	Victims	Perpetrators	F (p)
Relating to Others (PROQ3)			
Upper Neutral (UN)	12.3 (3.5)	12.4 (2.1)	.001 (.977)
Upper Close (UC)	13.9 (3.4)	15.0 (1.9)	1.105 (.297)
Neutral Close (NC)	12.4 (3.1)	14.1 (2.0)	2.802 (.099)
Lower Close (LC)	12.8 (3.2)	13.5 (1.6)	.485 (.489)
Lower Neutral (LN)	13.4 (3.1)	13.9 (2.5)	.321 (.573)
Lower Distant (LD)	**13.0 (2.4)**	**14.5(1.4)**	**4.437 (.039)**
Neutral Distant (ND)	12.3 (3.8)	12.5(3.6)	.051 (.821)
Upper Distant (UD)	12.7 (2.9)	12.7(3.0)	.004 (.951)
Total score (TOT)	102.6 (17.7)	108.6 (7.6)	1.201 (.277)
Personality Factors (BFI)			
Extraversion	24.7 (4.4)	24.5 (5.2)	.065 (.799)
Agreeableness	28.8 (5.0)	27.0 (3.9)	3.318 (.071)
Conscientiousness	29.6 (4.8)	28.4 (5.9)	1.189(.278)
Neuroticism	25.0 (5.4)	24.7 (5.2)	.064 (.801)
Openness	34.4 (5.2)	33.6 (7.6)	.324(.571)
Parenting Styles (PBI)			
Affectionate constraint (Mother)	0.3 (0.4)	0.1 (0.3)	2.550(.113)
Affectionate constraint (Father)	0.2 (0.4)	0.3 (0.4)	.104(.748)
Affectionless control (Mother)	0.4 (0.5)	0.5 (0.5)	2.040 (.156)
Affectionless control (Father)	0.4 (0.5)	0.4 (0.5)	.081 (.777)
Optimal parenting (Mother)	0.3 (0.4)	0.2 (0.4)	.369(.545)
Optimal parenting (Father)	0.2 (0.4)	0.1 (0.4)	.036(.849)
Neglectful parenting (Mother)	0.1 (0.3)	0.2 (0.4)	1.214(.273)
Neglectful parenting (Father)	0.2 (0.4)	0.2 (0.4)	.032(.859)

the four attachments styles (i.e., affectionate constraint, affectionless control, optimal parenting, and neglectful parenting) on perpetration. The model was statistically significant ($\chi^2_{(2)} = 9.25, p < .01$). It explained 8.3% (Nagelkerke R^2) of the variance and corrected classified 91.1% of cases. Higher scores in mother's affectionless control and neglectful parenting were associated with a higher likelihood of cyberstalking perpetration.

Two binary logistic regressions were also performed to examine the effects of the same independent variables on cyberstalking victimization (Table 3). The first logistic regression model was statistically significant ($\chi^2_{(2)} = 4.125, p = .042$), and it explained 3.8% of the variance and corrected classified 76.1% of cases. Higher scores on negative distant relating (ND) were associated with reduced likelihood of cyberstalking victimization. Personality factors failed to be associated with cyberstalking victimization. The second logistic regression model was also statistically significant ($\chi^2_{(2)} = 4.177, p = .041$), it ex-

Table 2. Negative relating styles, personality factors (first regression model) and parenting styles (second regression model) as independent variables (sorted by effect size) in the logistic regressions where the dependent variable is cyberstalking perpetration

Variables	B	S.E.	Wald	p	Exp(B)	95% C.I. for EXP(B)	
						Lower	Upper
Model A							
Agreeableness	-.184	.058	10.159	.001	.832	.742	.931
PROQ3 (NC)	.192	.077	6.164	.013	1.211	1.041	1.409
Model B							
Mother's AC	1.138	.405	7.886	.005	3.121	1.410	6.906
Mother's NP	1.068	.537	3.959	.047	2.909	1.016	8.329

Note: Mother's AC=Mother's affectionless control; Mother's NP= Mother's neglectful parenting

plained 2.5% of the variance and corrected classified 78.0% of cases. Affectionless control by mothers increased cyberstalking victimization.

DISCUSSION

Consistent with the results of other studies (e.g., Finn, 2004), cyberstalking occurred commonly among participants (23.9%) and females were more likely to be cyberstalked than males (e.g., Duggan, 2014; Reyns et al., 2012). Although the literature has revealed high rates of cyberstalking (e.g., Holt & Bossler, 2009), in this study a lower than expected rate was revealed (9%). It is believed that the true prevalence of offending might have been under-estimated. Respondents might have been willing to conceal unpleasant information such as cyberstalking. Higher rates of women engaged in cyberstalking perpetration. There is sufficient research evidence indicating that the majority of cyberstalkers are males (e.g., WHOA, 2013), although a few other studies have suggested that females admit higher rates of cyberstalking (e.g., Strawhun et al., 2013).

Table 3. Negative relating styles, personality factors (first regression model) and parenting styles (second regression model) as independent variables (sorted by effect size) in the logistic regressions where the dependent variable is cyberstalking victimization

Variables	B	S.E.	Wald	p	Exp(B)	95% C.I. for EXP(B)	
						Lower	Upper
Model A							
PROQ3 (ND)	- 0.85	.042	4.040	.044	.919	.846	.998
Model B							
Mother's AC	5.19	.252	4.264	.039	1.681	1.027	2.752

Note: Mother's AC=Mother's affectionless control

Another finding that was consistent with other studies was that cyberstalking most frequently occurred via social networking websites and that perpetrators were usually known to the victim (Dreßing et al., 2014). In this study, most of the victims did not report the incidence (e.g., Alexy et al., 2005). However, cyberstalking had significant negative impacts on victims' mental health; fear, anxiety, and depression were the predominant mental health outcomes inflicted by cyberstalking, which are in line with other study findings (Short et al., 2014). The coping strategies used by victims were intrusion, avoidance, and hyperarousal. Avoidance is one of the most used strategies (e.g., Worsley et al., 2017).

Negatively neutral close (NC) relating was the predominant type of relating to others by both victims and offenders, which reflects an intrusive, restrictive, and possessive type of relating and a need for attention and admiration. This may suggest the need by victims and offenders to cling to others and fear of separation and of being alone. This makes absolute sense only in cases where offenders and victims were known, such as ex-partners. NC relating was also found to increase the odds of cyberstalking perpetration. Newberry (2016) found that NC was significantly correlated with psychopathy (i.e., which reflects one's callousness of caring about the pain that inflicts to others). The findings of the present study suggest that cyberstalkers need to maintain a close, though negative, relationship with the victim in order to inflict their malicious acts. It can also be assumed that young adults might resort to cyberstalking as a reaction to being fearful of separation and/or rejection. These findings coincide with Ganck and Vanheule's (2015) assertion that people react with violence in their interpersonal relationships as a result of the threat they experience from untrustworthy people.

On the other hand, negative distant (ND) relating was associated with reduced likelihood of cyberstalking victimization. ND relating reflects suspiciousness, avoidance, fear of invasion and intrusion, need of personal space, and privacy. It seems that this type of relating is a protective factor against victimization. It might be that people with this type of predominant relating style might limit the extent of inappropriate disclosure of personal information. Avoiding being a target of cyberstalking requires revealing nothing personal about oneself and maintaining a certain distance from the offender.

Of the personality factors, agreeableness (i.e., sympathy, kindness, and affection) was associated with a lower likelihood of one being a cyberstalker, which is consistent with other findings (e.g., O'Riordan & O'Connell, 2014). No statistically significant results were found for victims. It might be that another instrument for measuring personality might be more appropriate and could provide statistically significant results for victims. Besides, other variables not included in this study might affect victimization. For instance, Fox, Gover, and Kaukinen (2009) found that the lack of self-control was associated with stalking victimization for college women.

In this study, cyberstalking perpetration was associated with mother's affectionless control and neglectful parenting, and cyberstalking victimization was associated only with mother's affectionless control. Affectionless control predicted both perpetration and victimization. Parental monitoring has protective effects against offending, whereas negative parental control reflects rejection and hostility and increases delinquency (Hoeve et al., 2009). Moreover, authoritative parenting (i.e., high control and responsiveness) has been found to predict lower levels of cyberbullying, while permissive parenting (i.e., low control and high responsiveness) has been found to predict higher levels of risk-taking behavior, such as disclosing personal information and meeting people only known by text (Carson, 2014). Similar patterns might be found for cyberstalking.

Parenting styles are associated with attachment (Karavasilis, Doyle, & Markiewicz, 2003) and attachment is associated with cyberstalking-related behaviors (Fox & Warber, 2014; Strawhun, et al., 2013). For instance, studies have linked anxious attachment to cyberstalking (e.g., Ménard & Pincus,

2012; Strawhun, et al., 2013). Fox and Tokunaga (2015) found that avoidantly attached people employ distance in their relationships, evade relational commitment, and are more likely to look for alternatives to the relationship, in comparison to anxiously attached people who demand intimacy and approval from partners, and who become overly dependent or excessively attached to partners and are more likely to try to establish a reconnection and resort to Facebook stalking following a break-up. Moreover, Zeinali, Sharifi, Enayati, Asgari, and Pasha (2011) found that authoritative and permissive parenting styles were associated with secure partner attachment, which in turn was associated with high levels of self-regulation and decreased addiction susceptibility, whereas authoritarian and neglectful parenting styles were associated with insecure attachment, which in turn was associated with a low level of self-regulation and increased addiction susceptibility. Self-regulation might be an important factor in cyberstalking as well.

The primary limitations of this study are the use of a convenience sample rather than a representative one and its limited size, which may have affected sampling error. Perpetrators were particularly underrepresented. It is possible that with a larger sample a notable percentage of offenders and victims could be located and consequently, more of the results would have been significant. Prevalence rates may have been underestimated due to a tendency for socially desirable responding. However, because the findings are in accordance with those of other studies, they may be considered to provide an accurate account of the situation in Greece. This sample was also heavily skewed toward females and heterosexual participants. Future research should address homosexual participants and samples equally spread across genders. Because of the cross-sectional type of this study, causal inferences are not warranted without longitudinal verification. It would have been interesting to have compared scores between perpetrators, victims and those that were both perpetrators and victims or those that were neither perpetrators nor victims, but the smallness of the size of the sampling groups did not permit the comparison. The potential moderating relationship of resilient coping on the association between cyberstalking victimization and the outcome variables needs to be explored, since there is a vast literature indicating the significance of this variable (e.g., Spitzberg & Cupach, 2001; Spitzberg & Hoobler, 2002). Future studies need to address other mediating variables too.

Despite these limitations, the implications drawn from the results of this study extend the knowledge of this phenomenon in Greece. Given the increased prevalence of cyberstalking worldwide, future studies should be conducted to determine its psychological, interpersonal, and social consequences. Continued research will maximize the likelihood of an accurate and comprehensive understanding of cyberstalking, the implications of which would be to establish effective prevention and appropriate intervention programs to prevent cyberstalking or mitigate its effects. Recommendations for law enforcement and criminal justice officials include training service providers to recognize the tactics used by cyberstalkers and to respond to the needs of victims. Service providers should develop websites for victims to exchange information and design or expand formal and informal support networks to meet the needs of victims and enhance their safety.

Efforts should also target the perpetrators of cyberstalking. Enhancing their interpersonal skills and modifying cyberstalkers' negative relating styles to positive styles would be useful. Counsellors can also assist people from disadvantaged backgrounds to acquire positive perceptions of their stressful developmental trajectories and help them develop a strong identity, fulfilling intimate relationships and skills to adapt to the constantly changing environments. Moreover, buffering or strengthening resiliency against negative parenting rearing could have positive impacts in overcoming adversity. Counselling centres can adopt therapeutic interventions and approaches to address parenting issues and provide advices on positive parenting practices. Raising public awareness about the tactics used by cyberstalkers, the detrimental impact of cyberstalking on victims, and the steps that can be taken to prevent this phenomenon are important for preventing and/or combating cyberstalking.

REFERENCES

Alexy, E. M., Burgess, A. W., Baker, T., & Smoyak, S. A. (2005). Perceptions of cyberstalking among college students. *Brief Treatment and Crisis Intervention*, *5*(3), 279–289. doi:10.1093/brief-treatment/mhi020

Arnett, J. J. (2000). Emerging adulthood. A theory of development from the late teens through the twenties. *The American Psychologist*, *55*(5), 469–480. doi:10.1037/0003-066X.55.5.469 PMID:10842426

Ashcroft, J. (2001). *Stalking and domestic violence: A report to Congress (No. NCJ 186157)*. Washington, DC: U.S. Department of Justice.

Avagianou, P. A., & Zafiropoulou, M. (2008). Parental bonding and depression: Personality as a mediating factor. *International Journal of Adolescent Medicine and Health*, *20*(3), 261–270. doi:10.1515/IJAMH.2008.20.3.261 PMID:19097563

Backe, E. L., Lilleston, P., & McCleary-Sills, J. (2018). Networked individuals, gendered violence: A literature review of cyberviolence. *Violence and Gender*, *5*(3), 135–146. doi:10.1089/vio.2017.0056

Baum, K., Catalano, S., Rand, M., & Rose, K. (2009). *Stalking victimization in the United States*. Washington, DC: Department of Justice Bureau of Justice Statistics. Available from https://www.justice.gov/sites/default/files/ovw/legacy/2012/08/15/bjs-stalking-rpt.pdf

Birtchnell, J. (1996). *How Humans Relate: A New Interpersonal Theory*. Hove, UK: Psychology Press.

Birtchnell, J., Hammond, S., Horn, E., De Jong, C., & Kalaitzaki, A. (2013). A cross-national comparison of a shorter version of the Person's Relating to Others Questionnaire. *Clinical Psychology & Psychotherapy*, *20*(1), 36–48. doi:10.1002/cpp.789 PMID:21960317

Boyle, A. M., & O'Sullivan, L. F. (2016). Staying connected: Computer-mediated and face-to-face communication in college students' dating relationships. *Cyberpsychology, Behavior, and Social Networking*, *19*(5), 299–307. doi:10.1089/cyber.2015.0293 PMID:27148761

Brownstein, A. (2000). In the campus shadows, women are stalkers as well as the stalked. *The Chronicle of Higher Education*, *47*(15), 40–42.

Buzawa, E. S., Buzawa, C. G., & Stark, E. D. (2017). *Responding to domestic violence: The integration of criminal justice and human services* (5th ed.). New York, NY: Sage. doi:10.1007/978-3-319-56721-1

Carson, R. (2014). *Adolescent cyberbullying in New Zealnd and the implications of parenting styles* (Unpublished doctoral thesis). University of Canterbury.

Clevenger, S. L., Navarro, J. N., & Gilliam, M. (2018). Technology and the endless "cat and mouse" game: A review of the interpersonal cybervictimization literature. *Sociology Compass*, *12*(12), e12639. doi:10.1111oc4.12639

Collins, W. A. (2003). More than myth: The developmental significance of romantic relationships during adolescence. *Journal of Research on Adolescence*, *13*(1), 1–24. doi:10.1111/1532-7795.1301001

Derogatis, L. R. (1993). *BSI, Brief Symptom Inventory: Administration, scoring & procedures manual*. Minneapolis, MN: National Computer Systems.

Derogatis, L. R. (2001). *Brief Symptom Inventory (BSI)-18. Administration, scoring and procedures manual*. Minneapolis, MN: NCS Pearson, Inc.

Dewing, M. (2010). *Social media: Who uses them?* Library of Parliament Background Paper. Retrieved from publications.gc.ca/site/eng/370191/publication.html

Dreßing, H., Bailer, J., Anders, A., Wagner, H., & Gallas, C. (2014). Cyberstalking in a large sample of social network users: Prevalence, characteristics, and impact upon victims. *Cyberpsychology, Behavior, and Social Networking*, *17*(2), 61–67. doi:10.1089/cyber.2012.0231 PMID:24106979

Duggan, M. (2014). *Online harassment*. Washington, DC: Pew Research Center. Retrieved from http://www.pewinternet.org/2014/10/22/onlineharassment/#

Fagundes, C. P. (2012). Getting over you: Contributions of attachment theory for postbreakup emotional adjustment. *Personal Relationships*, *19*(1), 37–50. doi:10.1111/j.1475-6811.2010.01336.x

Festl, R., & Quandt, T. (2013). Social relations and cyberbullying: The influence of individual and structural attributes on victimization and perpetration via the internet. *Human Communication Research*, *39*(1), 101–126. doi:10.1111/j.1468-2958.2012.01442.x

Finn, J. (2004). A survey of online harassment at a university campus. *Journal of Interpersonal Violence*, *19*(4), 468–483. doi:10.1177/0886260503262083 PMID:15038885

Fletcher, A., Fitzgerald-Yau, N., Jones, R., Allen, E., Viner, R. M., & Bonell, C. (2014). Brief report: Cyberbullying perpetration and its associations with socio-demographics, aggressive behaviour at school, and mental health outcomes. *Journal of Adolescence*, *37*(8), 1393–1398. doi:10.1016/j.adolescence.2014.10.005 PMID:25448835

Fox, J., & Tokunaga, R. S. (2015). Romantic Partner Monitoring After Breakups: Attachment, Dependence, Distress, and Post-Dissolution Online Surveillance via Social Networking Sites. *Cyberpsychology, Behavior, and Social Networking*, *18*(9), 491–498. doi:10.1089/cyber.2015.0123 PMID:26348808

Fox, J., & Warber, K. M. (2014). Social networking sites in romantic relationships: Attachment, uncertainty, and partner surveillance on facebook. *Cyberpsychology, Behavior, and Social Networking*, *17*(1), 3–7. doi:10.1089/cyber.2012.0667 PMID:23952623

Fox, K. A., Gover, A. R., & Kaukinen, C. (2009). The rffects of low self control and childhood maltreatment on stalking victimization among men and women. *American Journal of Criminal Justice*, *34*(3-4), 181–197. doi:10.100712103-009-9064-4

Groban, M. S. (2016). Intimate partner cyberstalking - Terrorizing intimate partners with 21st Century technology. United States Attorneys'. *Bulletin*, *64*(3), 12–16.

Hoeve, M., Dubas, J. S., Eichelsheim, V. I., van der Laan, P. H., Smeenk, W., & Gerris, J. R. M. (2009). The relationship between parenting and delinquency: A meta-analysis. *Journal of Abnormal Child Psychology*, *37*(6), 749–775. doi:10.100710802-009-9310-8 PMID:19263213

Holt, T. J., & Bossler, A. M. (2009). Examining the applicability of lifestyle-routine activities theory for cybercrime victimization. *Deviant Behavior*, *30*(1), 1–25. doi:10.1080/01639620701876577

Holt, T. J., & Bossler, A. M. (2014). An assessment of the current state of cybercrime scholarship. *Deviant Behavior*, *35*(1), 20–40. doi:10.1080/01639625.2013.822209

John, O. P., Donahue, E. M., & Kentle, R. L. (1991). *The Big Five Inventory--Versions 4a and 54*. Berkeley, CA: Institute of Personality and Social Research.

John, O. P., & Srivastava, S. (1999). The Big Five trait taxonomy: History, measurement, and theoretical perspectives. In L. A. Pervin & O. P. John (Eds.), *Handbook of personality: Theory and research* (pp. 102–138). New York: Guilford Press.

Kalaitzaki, A. E. (2017). Cyberstalking victimization and perpetration among Greek college students. In M. F. Wright (Ed.), *Identity, Sexuality, and Relationships among Emerging Adults in the Digital Age*. IGI Global. doi:10.4018/978-1-5225-1856-3.ch015

Kalaitzaki, A. E., & Birtchnell, J. (2016). The Person's Relating to Others Questionnaire (PROQ). In J. Birtchnell, M. Newberry, & A. E. Kalaitzaki (Eds.), *Relating Theory: Clinical, Forensic and other Applications*. London: Palgrave Macmillan. doi:10.1057/978-1-137-50459-3_3

Karavasilis, L., Doyle, A. B., & Markiewicz, D. (2003). Associations between parenting style and attachment to mother in middle childhood and adolescence. *International Journal of Behavioral Development*, *27*(2), 153–164. doi:10.1080/0165025024400015

Lee, B. H., & O'Sullivan, L. F. (2014). The ex-factor: Characteristics of online and offline post-relationship contact and tracking among canadian emerging adults. *The Canadian Journal of Human Sexuality*, *23*(2), 96–105. doi:10.3138/cjhs.2415

Lenhart, A., Ybarra, M., Zickuhr, K., & Price-Feeney, M. (2016). *Online Harassment, Digital Abuse, and Cyberstalking in America*. Data & Society Research Institute. Retrieved from https://www.datasociety.net/pubs/oh/Online_Harassment_2016.pdf

MacKenzie, R. D., Mullen, P. E., Ogloff, J. R. P., McEwan, T. E., & James, D. V. (2008). Parental bonding and adult attachment styles in different types of stalker. *Journal of Forensic Sciences*, *53*(6), 1443–1449. doi:10.1111/j.1556-4029.2008.00869.x PMID:18798773

Marcum, C. D., Higgins, G. E., & Ricketts, M. L. (2014). Juveniles and cyber stalking in the United States: An analysis of theoretical predictors of patterns of online perpetration. *International Journal of Cyber Criminology*, *8*, 47–56.

Meijer, R. R., de Vries, R. M., & van Bruggen, V. (2011). An evaluation of the Brief Symptom Inventory-18 using item response theory: Which items are most strongly related to psychological distress? *Psychological Assessment*, *23*(1), 193–202. doi:10.1037/a0021292 PMID:21280957

Ménard, K. S., & Pincus, A. L. (2012). Predicting overt and cyber stalking perpetration by male and female college students. *Journal of Interpersonal Violence, 27*(11), 2183–2207. doi:10.1177/0886260511432144 PMID:22203630

Newberry, M. (2016). Negative Relating and Psychopathy. In J. Birtchnell, M. Newberry, & A. E. Kalaitzaki (Eds.), *Relating Theory: Clinical, Forensic and other Applications*. London: Palgrave Macmillan. doi:10.1057/978-1-137-50459-3_20

Newberry, M., & Birtchnell, J. (2011). Negative relating and offense type. *Journal of Criminal Psychology, 1*(1), 24–35. doi:10.1108/20093829201100003

Nobles, M. R., Reyns, B. W., Fox, K. A., & Fisher, B. S. (2014). Protection against pursuit: A conceptual and empirical comparison of cyberstalking and stalking victimization among a national sample. *Justice Quarterly, 31*(6), 986–1014. doi:10.1080/07418825.2012.723030

O'Riordan, C., & O'Connell, M. (2014). Predicting adult involvement in crime: Personality measures are significant, socio-economic measures are not. *Personality and Individual Differences, 68*, 98–101. doi:10.1016/j.paid.2014.04.010

Parker, G., Tupling, H., & Brown, L. B. (1979). A Parental Bonding Instrument. *The British Journal of Medical Psychology, 52*(1), 1–10. doi:10.1111/j.2044-8341.1979.tb02487.x

Patton, C. L., Nobles, M. R., & Fox, K. A. (2010). Look who's stalking: Obsessive pursuit and attachment theory. *Journal of Criminal Justice, 38*(3), 282–290. doi:10.1016/j.jcrimjus.2010.02.013

Peluchette, J. V., Karl, K., Wood, C., & Williams, J. (2015). Cyberbullying victimization: Do victims' personality and risky social network behaviors contribute to the problem? *Computers in Human Behavior, 52*, 424–435. doi:10.1016/j.chb.2015.06.028

Reyns, B. W. (2010). A situational crime prevention approach to cyberstalking victimization: Preventive tactics for Internet users and online place managers. *Crime Prevention and Community Safety, 12*(2), 99–118. doi:10.1057/cpcs.2009.22

Reyns, B. W. (2018). Online pursuit in the twilight zone: Cyberstalking perpetration by college students. *Victims & Offenders*. doi:10.1080/15564886.2018.1557092

Reyns, B. W., & Fisher, B. S. (2018). The relationship between offline and online stalking victimization: A gender-specific analysis. *Violence and Victims, 33*(4), 769–786. doi:10.1891/0886-6708.VV-D-17-00121 PMID:30567773

Reyns, B. W., Fisher, B. S., & Randa, R. (2018). Explaining cyberstalking victimization against college women using a multitheoretical approach: Self-control, opportunity, and control balance. *Crime and Delinquency, 64*(13), 1742–1764. doi:10.1177/0011128717753116

Reyns, B. W., Henson, B., & Fisher, B. S. (2012). Stalking in the twilight zone: Extent of cyberstalking victimization and offending among college students. *Deviant Behavior, 33*(1), 1–25. doi:10.1080/01639625.2010.538364

Roberts, L. (2008). Jurisdictional and definitional concerns with computer related interpersonal crimes: An analysis on cyber stalking. *International Journal of Cyber Criminology*, *2*, 271–285.

Schmitt, D. P., Allik, J., McCrae, R. R., & Benet-Martinez, V. (2007). The geographic distribution of Big Five personality traits: Patterns and profiles of human self-description across 56 nations. *Journal of Cross-Cultural Psychology*, *38*(2), 173–212. doi:10.1177/0022022106297299

Short, E., Linford, S., Wheatcroft, J. M., & Maple, C. (2014). The impact of cyberstalking: The lived experience-a thematic analysis. *Studies in Health Technology and Informatics*, *199*, 133–137. doi:10.3233/978-1-61499-401-5-133 PMID:24875706

Smoker, M., & March, E. (2017). Predicting perpetration of intimate partner cyberstalking: Gender and the dark tetrad. *Computers in Human Behavior*, *72*, 390–396. doi:10.1016/j.chb.2017.03.012

Spitzberg, B. H., & Cupach, W. R. (2001). Paradoxes of pursuit: Toward a relational model of stalking-related phenomena. In J. A. Davis (Ed.), *Stalking crimes and victim protection: Prevention, intervention, threat assessment, and case management* (pp. 97–136). Boca Raton, FL: CRC Press. doi:10.1201/9781420041743.ch6

Spitzberg, B. H., & Cupach, W. R. (2007). The state of the art of stalking: Taking stock of the emerging literature. *Aggression and Violent Behavior*, *12*(1), 64–86. doi:10.1016/j.avb.2006.05.001

Spitzberg, B. H., & Hoobler, G. (2002). Cyberstalking and the technologies of interpersonal terrorism. *New Media & Society*, *4*(1), 71–92. doi:10.1177/14614440222226271

Strawhun, J., Adams, N., & Huss, M. T. (2013). The assessment of cyberstalking: An expanded examination including social networking, attachment, jealousy, and anger in relation to violence and abuse. *Violence and Victims*, *28*(4), 715–730. doi:10.1891/0886-6708.11-00145 PMID:24047049

Tjaden, P., & Thoennes, N. (1998). *Stalking in America: Findings from the National Violence Against Women Survey (Research in Brief NCJ 169592)*. Washington, DC: National Institute of Justice and Centers for Disease Control and Prevention.

Tokunaga, R. S., & Aune, K. S. (2017). Cyber-defense: A taxonomy of tactics for managing cyberstalking. *Journal of Interpersonal Violence*, *32*(10), 1451–1475. doi:10.1177/0886260515589564 PMID:26082443

Tonin, E. (2004). The attachment styles of stalkers. *Journal of Forensic Psychiatry & Psychology*, *15*(4), 584–590. doi:10.1080/14789940410001729644

van Baak, C., & Hayes, B. E. (2018). Correlates of cyberstalking victimization and perpetration among college students. *Violence and Victims*, *33*(6), 1036–1054. doi:10.1891/0886-6708.33.6.1036 PMID:30573549

Wall, D. (2007). *Cybercrime: The Transformation of Crime in the Information Age*. Polity.

Weiss, D. S., & Marmar, C. R. (1996). The Impact of Event Scale - Revised. In J. Wilson & T. M. Keane (Eds.), *Assessing psychological trauma and PTSD* (pp. 399–411). New York: Guilford.

Working to Halt Online Abuse (WHOA). (2011). *Cyberstalking statistics*. Retrieved on 8th January 2015, from http://www.haltabuse.org/resources/stats/2011Statistics.pdf

Working to Halt Online Abuse. (2013). *Online Harassment / Cyberstalking statistics*. Retrieved on 25th March, 2019, from http://www.haltabuse.org/resources/stats/2013Statistics.pdf

Zeinali, A., Sharifi, H., Enayati, M., Asgari, P., & Pasha, G. (2011). The mediational pathway among parenting styles, attachment styles and self-regulation with addiction susceptibility of adolescents. *Journal of Research in Medical Sciences*, *16*(9), 1105–1121. PMID:22973379

Chapter 3
Relationship Fluidity:
The Changing Nature of Intimacy for Emerging Adult Women

Megan Lindsay Brown
Arizona State University, USA

Judy Krysik
Arizona State University, USA

Walter LaMendola
University of Denver, USA

Drishti Sinha
Arizona State University, USA

Lauren Reed
Arizona State University, USA

ABSTRACT

Emerging adults are persistent users of information and communication technology (ICT), with young women between 18-29 being the highest users of ICT in the United States. Relatively little research has investigated how young women internalize experiences of emerging adulthood in the context of their development, and especially intimate relationships. Using qualitative interviews with young adult women, this chapter will explore how high ICT use mediates the developmental tasks of forming an adult identity and intimate relationships. Emerging adult women (18-29) who were high users of ICT (N=22) described their user habits and discussed their developmental trajectories and experiences. Findings demonstrated that identity and intimacy are still pertinent developmental tasks for emerging adults but have changed in nature allowing a fluidity that challenges the bounds of traditionally developmental theories.

DOI: 10.4018/978-1-7998-1063-6.ch003

INTRODUCTION

Traditional roles for women dictate that they should prioritize developing intimate relationships over other concerns; but as culture and gender roles change, women may now negotiate the tensions between identity and intimacy to suit the roles most important to their envisioned life-course. According to the developmental theory of emerging adulthood young people aged 18-29 are focused on two primary tasks: expressing their personal identity and exploring intimate relationships. Current day conceptions of this developmental period are marked by fluidity and increased experimentation, as young adults aim to explore and try out various adult social roles (Arnett, 2000). Arnett & Schwabb (2012) argued that the in-depth personal exploration and the postponing of certain social roles among today's young adults created the need for a more clearly distinguished and entirely different psychosocial developmental stage that separates adolescence from adulthood. This chapter will explore how young adult women are impacted by the complications of these fluid relationships, shifting gender roles, and the proliferation of technology.

These tasks are not easily navigated. On their face, expressing individuality and nurturing intimate relationships may appear to be conflicting goals, and young adults are further influenced by an increasingly dynamic social landscape. Arnett's emerging adulthood theory (2000) emphasizes the advantages and social benefits of in-depth identity exploration, but less attention is given to the impact this new phase will have for practicing intimacy. Emerging adulthood also abandoned assumptions about women found in Erikson's original theories, specifically that women experienced intimacy before identity. Modern relationships are complicated by the changing social roles and opportunities for women and technology is another contributing factor. Drawing from Arnett's theory, this chapter will analyze the experiences of emerging adult women and how the developmental tasks of identity exploration and intimacy have been shaped by digital technologies.

Given the onset of digital technology, particularly the internet, emerging adults are experiencing expanded and vast opportunities for social interactions that ultimately inform the adult social roles they acquire. Jensen and Arnett (2012) recognized that this increasing global connectivity affects developmental paths, allowing for exposure to more cultures and ideas. Instead of forming an identity in the context of the local environment, which is an assumption of earlier developmental theories, individuals now create a *hybrid identity* that is derived from both local and global cultures (Jensen & Arnett, 2012). A *hybrid identity* is born out of the ability to observe multiple, global societies in order to understand what fits with one's personal identity.

The internalization of hybrid identities affects young women's development because they have the agency to reject local social norms based on traditional values of womanhood and instead adopt global ideas of what it means to be a woman (Arnett, 2002). Additionally, because a *hybrid identity* expands the potential identities an individual can partake in, it can be assumed that the expansion applies to how individuals develop intimacy with a wider set of individuals. Emerging adults are actively discussing and developing their own personal narratives about the types of relationships they seek in relation to who they want to be, as emerging adulthood encompasses the formation of romantic relationships with greater depth than those formed in adolescence.

A study of emerging adults found that narratives of true love and true friendship were predictive of maturing and advancing to the middle adulthood stage, and these narratives are developed in conjunction with peers (Mackinnon et al., 2011). Emerging adults continue to make meaning with one another, but prioritize intimate relationships over peers. Another indicator that intimacy is fundamental to this developmental stage comes from exhibiting an increase in romantic behaviors, the desire to influence within relationships, engagement with sexual experiences, and exchange of support (Giordano, Manning, Longmore, & Flanigan, 2009). Generally, the behavior differences among emerging adults indicate their romantic relationships have advanced beyond their adolescent years.

Yet, experimentation continues to be a key aspect of emerging adults' exploration of intimacy, and the levels of experimentation and time spent engaged in fluid relationships may be influenced and increasing due to new technologies. The fluid movement between relationships manifests as an intense focus on dating during this developmental period (Dailey, Rossetto, Pfiester & Surra, 2009; Dailey, Jin, Pfiester, & Beck, 2011; Halpern-Meekin, Manning, Giordano & Longmore, 2013b). For example, in a longitudinal study of how young people form dating and romantic relationships, emerging adult young women 18-29 years old were found to be more likely than adolescents to experiment with different types of relationships, such as hook-ups, same sex, and long-distance (Giordano et al., 2009; Halpern-Meekin, Manning, Giordano & Longmore, 2013a). Additionally, emerging adults are likely to experience relationship instability as they are exploring identity and relationship possibilities simultaneously. An example of this instability is seen in relationship *churning*, which is defined as breaking up and getting back together and/or having sexual relations with an ex-partner (Halpern-Meekin et al., 2013). Essentially, young people now experience a period of time where the commitment to the relationship, while important, is still secondary to establishing an individual identity outside of the context of marriage and other traditional romantic relationships.

Tensions of Intimacy and Identity

The developmental tasks of identity and intimacy as described above are not likely to be mastered simultaneously. For example, the goal of a sustainable romantic relationship is often at odds with balancing the start of a career, revealing potential conflicts between identity and intimacy (Archer, 2007). Instead, emerging adults must resolve this tension by reflexively deciding which combination of these tasks fit with their priorities. Some emerging adults may choose to prioritize identity development by choosing not to date, emphasizing their career, seeking economic stability, or engaging in low-commitment romantic relationships and platonic relationships instead of traditional routes such as marriage (Lanz & Tagliabue, 2007). Consequently, these tasks are not independent of each other. Emerging adults often seek to relationally confirm and develop these tasks – they seek out intimate partners who reaffirm their identity as well as further develop their sense of identity through the process of dating (Manning, Giordano, Longmore, & Hocevar, 2009). In contemporary society, emerging adult women explore these tasks in parallel, while simultaneously existing in a dynamic social structure with changing social roles for women (Archer, 2012; Castells, 1997).

Evolution of the Intimate Relationship

The aforementioned effect of globalization on the creation of new developmental pathways to identity provides a unique perspective on how relationships manifest since the advent of everyday internet (Jensen & Arnett, 2012). Specifically, in Western cultures, individualism has been valued over the collective, and this has led to an intense emphasis on personal autonomy over predetermined social roles (Arnett, 2000; Archer, 2000; Archer, 2007; Archer, 2012; Schwartz, Côté & Arnett, 2005). The emphasis on individualism may be connected to the decline in social alignment with the traditional family structure, as evidenced by the increased age of first marriage, a higher percentage of children born outside of marriage, an increased divorce rate, and an overall decrease in marriage rates (Castells, 1997; Geiger & Livingston, 2019). In the United States, the increased importance placed on individualism and personal identity is demonstrated through the decline and rarity of marriages across political party lines (Geiger & Livingston, 2019).

In the past two decades, the incidence of cohabitation has been rising. However, unlike marriage, the age of first cohabitation has not been increasing in the past 20 years – those with the highest levels of education were found to wait longer to both cohabitate and marry (Manning et al., 2014). Population changes in relationship characteristics and marriages illustrate shifting developmental norms, particularly for women. For example, an increased cultural focus on personal autonomy is reflected in present-day marriage rates, in which age at first marriage is highest among college-educated women when compared to all adult women in the U.S. This likely reflects a shift in what society values – women who are educated are valued more for their financial contributions (Manning, Brown, & Payne, 2014). Alternately, this could be a result of economic pressure to have a two-income household, as demonstrated by the increase in dual-income families since 1970 (Parker & Livingston, 2018). Delaying marriage is likely tied to socioeconomic status, with economically-disadvantaged young women postponing marriage for pragmatic reasons (Manning et al., 2014). The age of first cohabitation remaining stable, and the marriage rate declining while women continually pursue personal goals like higher education, provides evidence that romantic relationships are established after a sense of personal identity and economic accomplishment.

Dating and sexual behavior are also shaped by developmental and cultural norms. Given the decision to postpone a serious long-term monogamous relationship, many individuals choose to treat dating as an exploratory activity. Current emerging adults are often considered to be a part of the "hook-up generation," characterized as a generational cohort which engages in higher rates of casual sex. However, a recent study of a nationally representative sample of Americans found that a higher percentage of millennials have not had a sexual partner before the age of 18 compared to previous generations, and millennials, especially young women, were more likely to be sexually inactive (Twenge, Sherman, & Wells, 2017). This delay in sexual activity may be due to specific factors that affect the millennial generation; for example, a higher percentage of millennials live with their parents' post-recession, which may limit opportunities to engage in sexual activities (Twenge et al., 2017). Regardless of the reasons, the expanded period of dating and intimate relationship exploration further indicates that experiences of present-day dating are marked by significant cultural changes.

Emerging Technologies, Intimate Relationships, and Identity

The prevalence and accessibility of Information and Communication Technologies (ICT), devices that create, manage, and support information transmission and communication, have enabled global connectivity and a highly networked society that is shifting toward niche networks and new forms of sociality (LaMendola, 2010). The advent of social media, a salient form of ICT, in the late 20th century diverged from traditional media because of its ability to connect individuals through interaction across the internet. This interaction forms through individuals creating an online presence that reflects themselves, and users have the opportunity to observe and interact with others' online presentations (Donnath & Boyd, 2004; Marwick, 2015). The advent of social media has expanded the ability to have a platform from an elite group of traditional celebrities to every individual (Duggan, 2014; Senft, 2008). The term "lifestreaming" was coined by Marwick (2011) to describe daily activities in the online space, which requires a careful, selective process in which an individual sifts through his/her daily life and chooses to emphasize certain parts. This selection process is highly emotional and deliberate, wherein a user aims to presents information that would be relevant to those in their network and interesting enough to attract others to his/her page. How individuals present themselves online likely ranges from shared information that is intended to garner attention from a wider audience to that which is meant for a smaller network (Baym, 2010; Turkle, 2011; Marwick, 2015).

Emerging adult women are the highest and most active users of social media compared to all other groups (Smith & Duggan, 2013). Their high rates of social media activity are demonstrated through their greater likelihood of curating online content, particularly photos and videos (Duggan, 2014). A more recent study by Smith and Anderson (2018) demonstrates similar trends, with a higher percentage of women users on most social media platforms included in the study, along with a higher percentage of 18-29 year old's using most of the platforms included in the study. Even if young men and women are spending comparable time on social media sites, the young women on the sites are more active and expressive posters (Smith & Duggan, 2013). Given the salient nature of social media in the lives of young women, it is likely that social media will mediate social interactions that are important in shaping adult identity and exploring intimacy, thereby affecting developmental trajectories.

Just as ICT has changed the environment in which emerging adults develop identity, a more networked society has implications for the exploration of intimacy as well. A growing body of literature has assessed the impact of ICT on dating relationships among emerging adults (Coyne, Stockdale, Busby, Iverson, & Grant; 2011; Draucker & Marstolf, 2010; Fox, Warber, & Makstaller, 2013; Mansson & Myers, 2011; Muise, Christofedes, Demaris, 2009; Odaci & Kalkan, 2010; Stevens & Morris, 2007; Tokunga, 2011). Social media has presented the opportunity to engage in new social interactions that have modified how intimate relationships are formed.

The use of dating apps, online dating websites, and social media for flirting and communicating with romantic partners is often evolving along with the technology trends themselves. A sample of adolescents and young adults reported that ICTs have changed the way that dating partners interact with each other and may lead to less in-person communication (Vaterlaus, Tulane, Porter, & Beckert, 2018). An increasingly common way for emerging adults to meet is through dating/hookup apps like Tinder (Greenfield, 2013). This platform, which allows users to reject or accept people based on their visual appearance, allows users a generous interpretation about dating fit and requires them to rely on images to understand an individual's identity. The app thereby perpetuates white heteronormativity and may not be the easiest way for those whose identity is grounded beyond this norm to find potential partners (Duguay, 2017; Peterson, 2014). However, ICT can facilitate the initiation of relationships in other ways. Stevens and Morris (2007) hypothesized that individuals experiencing social anxiety may find it easier to maintain social relationships through social media.

Furthermore, Stienfield, Ellison, and Lampe (2008) and Yang et al. (2013) found that emerging adults believed that gathering social information online about a potential partner could relieve the pressure that the individual felt when initiating a relationship. In fact, over a third of emerging adults have reported researching their potential partners online before meeting them in person (Smith & Duggan, 2013). Social media interactions have also become an expected norm at the initiation of a relationship, in which flirting occurs in both offline and online spaces, with almost half of 18-24 year olds reporting online flirting with a potential partner (Smith & Duggan, 2013; Hardey 2004; Yang et al., 2013). Relationship activity has also translated to the online space, and Papp et al. (2012) found that Facebook status played an important role in defining a significant commitment to the relationship. Beyond changing relationship status on the site, changing an individual's profile picture to include his/her partner predicted greater relationship satisfaction.

Some believe new avenues for communicating with a partner complicate the situation. For example, individuals may want to send a signal of apathy as opposed to desperation by not answering calls or responding to texts immediately (Bergdall et al., 2012). Pacing the integration of the couple, and maintaining a strict individual presence online, can be a part of the implicit communication that occurs within relationships to set boundaries, and self-reflection on social media representation of a relationship can determine these boundaries. For example, a participant from a study conducted by Zhao et al. (2012) mentioned that noticing she and her partner stopped posting pictures of each other was a negative indicator of the status of their relationship. Additionally, social media presentation of a relationship may reflect gender-based and heteronormative social roles. In a study conducted by Mansson & Meyers (2011), female undergraduates were more likely to post public displays of affection compared to their male counterparts. As such, social media presentation of a relationship may be used to genuinely enhance intimacy between individuals in a romantic relationship, to reflect the status of intimacy in the romantic relationship, to represent social expectations and roles in a relationship, or to present an ideal image of a relationship for an online audience.

New modes of communication have been documented as beneficial as well. Within a formed intimate relationship, ICT has been demonstrated to help strengthen the relationship by facilitating extra communication and allowing for open sharing of information and interests, providing a space to express sexuality, and increasing the accessibility and number of communication channels (Murray & Campbell, 2015). Long distance relationships, now easily facilitated by new technologies, may be a way for those who have anxiety or fear of dating to experiment with relationships and feel less pressure (Stevens & Morris, 2007).

Technology-Based Abuse

The new opportunities made available through ICT have potentially deleterious effects on the quality of relationships and may even encourage abusive behaviors. Similar to off-line forms of abuse and harassment, these behaviors range from unhealthy isolated behaviors to a systematic pattern of behaviors to exert power and control over a dating partner, which characterizes abuse. Abuse through ICT can occur when daily and normalized activities, such as surveillance, escalate or cross into harassment. Unfortunately, given the ambiguity of communication on the internet, it can be difficult to understand where this line lies. To demonstrate this subjectivity, the contextual nature of each mediated communication can lead to multiple interpretations.

Paasonen, Light, and Jarrett (2019) illustrate how social media platforms and gender dynamics affect the perception of a "dick pic" (explicit photograph of a penis) as harassment. For example, an unsolicited dick pic through private message is primarily seen as disturbing and humiliating, a way for men to show dominance and leave the receiver feeling robbed of his/her sexual agency. However, in an online space like Tumblr, when publicly shared with an audience and curated, an explicit picture may be seen as an art form and an expression of sexuality because of the online community (Paasonen et al., 2019). Therefore, it is imperative that online harassment be read within the multiple digital cultures and communities that exist.

ICTs give partners exposure to an unprecedented amount of information about their dating partners' whereabouts and activities, create an expectation of constant and immediate contact, and instantly broadcast digital interactions and humiliations to entire social networks. Burke, Wallen, Vail-Smith, and Knox (2011) found that 50% of surveyed college students reported either being a perpetrator or a victim of controlling or monitoring behaviors online. Several studies have documented that ICT use exasperates unhealthy relationship characteristics like jealousy (Elphinston & Noller, 2011; Muise et al., 2009; Marshall, Benjanyan, Di Castro, & Lee, 2013). Specifically, Elphinston & Noller (2011) found that easy accessibility of a partner's personal information on Facebook encouraged surveillance and jealousy while negatively impacting the building of intimate relationships. Reed, Tolman, Ward, & Safyer (2015) proposed that for anxious emerging adults, accessibility of information about partners via ICTs may trigger anxiety and lead to digital monitoring and control in an attempt to alleviate anxiety. At its most severe, ICT abuse can involve public digital exposure (such as the distribution of sexual or embarrassing photos without permission), threats of physical violence, or hurtful and demeaning posts or messages. The highest risk of unwanted network exposure is young women, with one in ten women under the age of 30 reporting threats of nonconsensual image sharing (Lenhart, Ybaraa, Price-Feeney, 2016).

Intimate partner violence scholars have found that rather than a new form of abuse, ICT abuse is a new context for abusive behaviors that occur off-line. Previous research with adolescents and young adults found a strong positive correlation between on-line and off-line victimization experiences (Borrajo, Gámez-Guadix, & Calvete, 2015; Choi, Ouytsel, & Temple, 2015; Doucette, Collibee, Hood, Stone, DeJesus, & Rizzo, 2018; Reed, Tolman, & Ward, 2016; Stonard, 2018; Zweig, Dank, Yahner, & Lachman, 2013). Similar to off-line forms of abuse and harassment, these behaviors range from unhealthy isolated behaviors to a systematic pattern of behaviors to exert power and control over a dating partner, which characterizes abuse. Most research on ICT abuse identifies several types of potentially problematic digital behaviors: *direct aggression* and *control/monitoring* (Taylor & Xia, 2018), whereas other authors argue that *sexual abuse* using ICTs is an additional salient category of potentially abusive digital behaviors in dating relationships (Reed, Tolman, & Ward, 2017; Zweig et al, 2013).

Although most forms of ICTs are conceptually similar to off-line psychological abuse, researchers argue that these subcategories of ICT abuse are useful because their frequency and impact differ by gender (Bennett et al., 2011; Reed, Tolman, & Ward, 2017). Although both young men and women report frequency of ICT abuse victimization at about equal rates, like in off-line abuse, preliminary evidence from studies of adolescents indicates that girls may experience more emotional distress and consequences from ICT victimization than boys (Reed, Tolman, & Ward, 2017). Young women are more likely to experience coercion to send sexually explicit photos (Kernsmith, Victor, & Smith-Darden, 2018; Lippman & Campbell, 2014), and may be influenced by gender socialization to engage in certain types of ICT monitoring/control to ensure partner fidelity and affection (Lucero, Weisz, Smith-Darden, & Lucero, 2014; Reed, Tolman, Ward, Lippman, & Seabrook, 2018).

The availability of the information can lead to arguments between individuals in a relationship and a questioning of the deeper meaning and intent of the individual's engagement and actions online (Fox et al., 2014). Finally, Clayton, Nagurny, and Smith (2013) found that newer relationships were more likely to experience negative outcomes in their relationship when the partner spent more time on social media. These correlations cannot point to social media as a direct cause of mistrust, but an increasing number of studies suggest that if you are predisposed to mistrust the abundance of information and interactions, it can serve as a trigger for anxiety (Reed et al., 2016). How emerging adults navigate multiple interactions of relationship communications, unprecedented levels of information about a new partner, while establishing trust will need to be researched further to help individuals adapt.

Methods

Driving the study were two primary research questions, the first being "What are the concerns of emerging adult women and how do they fit with the traditional developmental tasks of identity and intimacy?" Our second research question, "How does ICT use influence emerging adult women and their reflexivity during the developmental process?" yielded discussions related to the process of dating in the context of the ICT landscape, communication mediated by ICT within a romantic relationship, and lastly, experiences of abuse through ICT.

Interviews were conducted with young women (18-29) who self-identified as high ICT users (N = 22). To qualify as a high-ICT user the participants checked social media accounts every day, owned a smartphone, and had profiles on multiple platforms. Participants were interviewed twice; the initial interview used a structured schedule comprised of 20 open ended questions. The second interview was an informal conversation personalized to the participants' interests, experiences, and opinions about the topic as expressed during interview one. The study recruitment and interview process were informed using Markham's (2013) Remix Method, encouraging qualitative researchers to engage the online environment and digital cultures researchers strive to describe. Participants were recruited from across the country using Craigslist, Facebook, Tumblr, Twitter, and personal referrals. The diversity in the sample mirrors the heterogeneous nature of the emerging adult population. During the ongoing analysis process, a third party transcribed all interviews. Qualitative interviews produced 1,351 pages, with the average of 61 pages of transcript per participant. Data from the study was organized into 6 major themes, and approximately 15 subthemes. The express purpose of this chapter is to give an in depth review of six of the subthemes that all fell under the primary theme of Dating Relationships and ICT.

Two forms of qualitative analysis were used, open thematic coding and narrative analysis. This chapter will focus on the open thematic coding, but first discuss briefly the narrative analysis used. These techniques allowed the lead researcher to review each participant's interview(s) and draw out a story that described a sequence of events and consequences based on her/their experiences during emerging adulthood (Riessman & Quinney, 2005). Each participant was given an individual and unique narrative summary before the open thematic coding began. The interviews were intended to draw stories about individuals' lives as they came to understand intimacy and identity. Through a careful reading of the data, the researcher constructed a story based on information presented, keeping a critical eye to notice what parts of the story are left out and how the narrative influenced perceptions (Riessman & Quinney, 2005). This first round of analysis began immediately after the data collection ended. Revisions, editing, and refining of the narrative summaries became an ongoing practice during the second round of analysis, and provided organization and structure.

After the transcripts had been reviewed using the narrative methods, a second reading was conducted to look for patterns among the individual participants by using open thematic coding. Open coding was used to first interpret data with no (or minimal) expectations or interpretations of possible variables. A second step of axial coding was used for an intensive analysis to sort individual codes by relevant categories, such as relationship type or online behaviors, and then the codes were organized by themes and subthemes through the writing process. I started with approximately 112 codes; through the initial read of the data major themes were identified and selected for review.

The writing process allowed the first author to collapse codes when the content was similar enough to be combined for the purpose of discussion. As an example, an excerpt from the codes for "dating relationship" and "physical intimacy" are written coinciding a discussion about a long-distance relationship. In other instances, the lead author collapsed and combined codes for the sake of organization. Rather than review "sexual assault," "child abuse," and "intimate partner violence," codes were under the umbrella of "abuse experiences." Because of the nature of certain codes, often an excerpt would be given multiple codes. Original review of the data required interpreting transcripts and narrative while simultaneously writing and examining the codebook. Authors discussed and reviewed the themes and codes in conjunction with writing and finalizing this chapter, offering additional validity checks.

Findings

The following quotes were demonstrative of how developmental trajectories take form and how intimacy is experienced by emerging adults in the present day. Specific attention was given to the new social opportunities and interactions that were facilitated, mediated, or afforded because of the individuals time spent online. Regrading research question one, four primary themes will be discussed; individualism, which ultimately influences when and to what extent emerging adults engage in intimate relationships, intimacy and self-defined womanhood, the theme of healthy relationships and what this means in the present day as an emerging adult, and last the abuse experiences that revealed the ongoing conflict and burden women bear when practicing intimate relationships. The second research question specifically addressed the role of ICT; three themes will be discussed, dating relationships and ICT, romantic relationship communication, and abuse experiences. Each theme is supported by quotes from the interviews and discussion of the context.

Individualism

Currently, emerging adult women have a period of heightened identity exploration and this instability in social roles lived in their early twenties is reflected in the fluid nature of intimate relationships as well. Individualism and a rejection of predefined social roles and social institutions are now an integral part of emerging adulthood. The developmental trajectory of participants has shifted toward two individuals committing out of desire rather entering marriage to meet the expectations of the historical social order. Thus, we can conceptualize the exploration of intimacy as an extension of identity, or *identimacy.* In contrast to prior conceptualizations of developmental milestones by Erikson (1964), which emphasized that women must prioritize marriage over exploring other social roles, the present participants seek to confirm their identity through their intimate relationships. Instead of a reliance on traditional social, intimate roles of the mother and the wife as defining a young woman's identity, these social roles are negotiated with the romantic partner in accordance with an individual's personal concerns and values.

The participants were focused on gaining independence and living individualistically. Defining one's self and having at least a sense of what one's own sexuality and career aspirations were seemed to be two primary goals before entering committed relationships. The women interviewed envisioned living a life that was shaped by passions, interests, and commitment to self-defined-values (Archer, 2007). This reflects prior literature that has noted the increased effects of individualism on developmental trajectories (Arnett, 2000; Archer, 2000; Archer, 2007; Archer, 2012; Schwartz, Côté & Arnett, 2005). When asked about success, Kami (28) responded, *"Independence. It's the first word I think of..."* Kai (23) described individualism as *"knowing what you like and what makes you happy and like going after it."* Thus, the definition of success was largely individualized to participants. For them, an integral part of success was financial stability, but ultimately, they defined success as maintaining a life balance, for example between career and relationships. Life balance was important especially in the face of job insecurity and financial instability, such as being able to derive happiness outside of financial independence. Specifically, one young woman described that attaining a romantic relationship was a sign of maturity, through balancing financial independence with support through relationships. However, Holly (19) highlights the difficulty of seeking a romantic relationship in the current tumultuous economic climate conducive to job insecurity:

So, you know, I think there is like this pressure back then to like, you know get married at like 20 and have a child at like 24 and then have a career by 25. And, I think not all of those were possible because, you know... to get like a stable job at 25 and sustain that until they were 70. But, you know, I think also with like job market, like people need to like focus on finding their career first before they can like cultivate this like relationship, like, this stable romantic relationship. (Holly, 19)

The individualism embraced by young women in the study can be found in their self-concept – they identify as separate and whole outside of the context of others, but still incorporate intimate relationships as a part of who they are. The proliferation of information about different sexualities and sexual expressions was often represented in individuals' *hybrid identity* born out of globalization and an easier exchange of ideas (Jensen & Arnett, 2012). Participants dismissed more conventional labels and social roles, instead choosing to exist outside of the limits of traditional definitions of identity. When Tina (23) was asked to identify her sexual orientation, she responded *"I don't."* For Olivia (26), discovering her sexuality was an important part of understanding herself. Coming out to friends and family on Facebook was less about the label, and even seeking intimate relationships, sharing this part of herself online was a chance for her own sense of integration and an important step towards dating other women.

And, part of the struggle was like me not understanding myself enough. So, I went on to talk about like labels and boxes and then just saying like I no longer wanted to, you know, be put in a box and, so I wasn't going to..... I also just really don't like labels. So, I get... I'm like just like throw your study out of the window. But, yeah, I think... I don't know. (Olivia, 26)

As a result of the highly individualized values and concerns of these emerging adults, participants believed that while relationships were important for emotional growth and could be a source of happiness, the ability to flexibly self-identify took precedence. However, individualistic tendencies of these emerging adults were not the sole impact on their sense of self and decision-making. Participants mentioned that their love and respect for others was a consistent driving force in their decision making, despite their individualism.

Like will this hurt other people or something or will it offend someone? So basically I think about myself and the other guy. I try to employ that into my decision making.(Ryan, 18)

Yes. Me and my husband have kind of like a motto and mainly because we come from two very different cultures and often times those, our values are very different so we try to say like "Whatever choice you're gonna make, do it like by coming from a place of love." We have a very diverse family and like my husband's brother is gay and he, well basically he lives in Missouri so recently they passed the law that gay people can get married in Missouri and people often wanna give us a lot of opinions about that and we always just kind of like is your opinion or your idea coming from a place of love or judgment? And so, whenever we, I don't know, I'd say like our main family value is just be respectful and whatever you're doing come from that place of love, don't come from hate or judgment, you know? (Casey, 29)

For Casey (29), her interracial romantic relationship has affected her decision-making; she thoughtfully considers the impacts of her view and strives to make choices from a place of love and compassion. She attributes this openness to her marriage. Thus, in addition to a strong sense of individualism that these young women feel, their relationships with others have instilled values of compassion and kindness that influence their actions. Other studies have confirmed that social conventions, like marrying within your cultural group, is low on the priorities for millennials and Gen Z (Geiger & Livingston (2019). Women in the study not only in the context of interracial marriages, but diverging gender and sexual expressions, stressed the importance of incorporating love into their actions and that creating social bonds between cultural groups was an ongoing part of identity work and intimate relationship.

Intimacy and Self-Defined Womanhood

Many of the participants' views regarding marriage mirror the shifting trends; these changes indicate an increasing delay of first marriage and an overall decrease in marriage rate (Geiger & Livingston, 2019). Instead of marriage being considered a social requirement when experiencing intimacy in emerging adulthood, marriage is becoming a choice that reflects personal values. Additionally, attitudes around marriage are affected by the increasing importance placed on developing identity. For example, Ryan (18) discusses the conflict between identity and intimacy, in which attaining success in education and career can take precedence over finding and marrying an intimate partner.

I think marriage and kids have become less important now compared to a generation or 2 ago. That much I've noticed for to being adult women. I feel like a lot more independence is put more into women like you should be more independent and you should get your education and you should get a job which is a lot better than like a generation or two ago was. (Ryan, 18)

Participants believed that there was value in marriage, but they also believed that it was not a necessary milestone for development, heavily contrasting the work of Erikson (1964). No participant expressed a belief that an individual would be incomplete if they were not married. Additionally, the expression of emotional closeness did not have to take the form of marriage. Participants in the study demonstrated varying beliefs about marriage, each of which fit their individualized world views. For example, with regard to roles and shared responsibility within a marriage, Vanessa expressed a desire to separate herself from her mother's traditional role in her marriage, whereas Margret believed that emulating traditional roles in marriage allowed her to retain part of her Sudanese heritage.

I'm like basing off of my Mom just because with my Mom's generation, I feel like a lot of men are more of like, 'You're the woman of the house. You have to cook for me. You have to iron my clothes for me. You have to do...' Like, the woman has to do everything? (Vanessa, 26)

I still keep my culture. Like, you know, keeping your house clean is a must and always cooking like for your man. You have to do that every day. And, like you have to like respect every adult. It doesn't matter who it is. (Margret, 20)

Healthy Relationships

When discussing with participants what being in a healthy, authentic relationship means to them, threads of individualism were present throughout their responses. Participants discussed how their experiences and values shaped what they wanted out of romantic relationships. As a result, no participants discussed universal "rules" of a relationship and instead emphasized that identity must be compatible with the nature of the relationship, and decision-making in the relationship must be balanced amongst the partners. This emphasis on compatibility with assumed identity is supported by a Pew study that found 88% of Americans stated that they married for love, as opposed to seeking recognition by a religion, financial stability or legal benefits (Geiger & Livingston, 2019). This is congruent to the work of Archer (2012), who argues that young people reflexively resolve the conflict between the development of identity and intimacy simultaneously, through understanding how these developmental goals fit with their own personal concerns.

The theme of shared-decision making and individual agency to shape intimacy was carried throughout a discussion on sexual attitudes. No participants believed that sex was only acceptable within a marriage. Even participants who held more conservative beliefs on premarital sex believed that their own sexual attitudes were specific to their own values and lives. Across all participants, the only standard for sex that was mentioned was consent. For example, Jordan (24) resisted labelling a specific, appropriate time to have sex in a relationship. Instead, she emphasized that this is a decision that is mutually based on each partner's personal standards.

Ahm. Honestly I think it's when both people, I don't think there's a certain time for say like 3 months or 90 days or whatever, I think it's a when we're both of one accord, when we both consent, when we both feel like this is the next step and we both want to. It's not necessarily like what's you know, what society deems right or you know this all these double standards for women and all this stuff. I think it's when both- or if you both want to that's when the time is right. (Jordan, 24)

With regard to shared decision-making in relationships, including decisions around sexual intercourse, communication is necessary to share values with each other. For example, Olivia recounts the end of her first serious relationship and recognizes the integral role of communication to maintain emotional closeness.

No. I just think that we like view the world differently. I tend to look more optimistically. She's more pessimistic. And, so I just think that there... And, like, I would say communication was huge. We have very different communication styles. And, I know... You know, it was hard for me to be that vulnerable and, so I think that there were times... and, like I don't wanna speak for her. But, I know like myself aware [pause] I would like shut down and then I wouldn't communicate at all—(Olivia, 26)

Churning, as described by Halpern-Meekin et al. (2013), is a process that exemplifies the relationship instability often experienced by emerging adults. The instability of on-again off-again relationships allows for time between the re-initiations of the relationship to develop identity and reevaluate personal concerns in a context away from the partner. In some cases, like that of Casey (29), time for personal growth can make a relationship stronger if both partners mature similarly. This is a perfect example of the conflict between identity and intimacy. Intimacy is re-evaluated after a break-up, and focus is shifted to identity as the individual considers their concerns. This pattern of relationship instability reinforces the idea that individualism is a strong value among emerging adults, and intimacy is formed in accordance with individual concerns.

I think I first knew I was in love with my husband when so, we like dated for a while and then we like took a break and I decided to take a month and go to Spain. I decided like I just gotta get out of here so saved up my money and I went to Spain and when I came back we kind of reevaluated our relationship and those few months afterwards. We really connected on a different level, I really was, I don't know, I think in a better, more open mindset, I had like cleared my mind and I think I'm really allowing myself to like fall for him so, I feel like the time, I can remember like the place we were, I remember we were like eating at this restaurant called Flat Ranch in Missouri and we're just staying there, eating something and just like looked at each other kind of like started laughing about something and I just realized like 'I love him' I love that guy and yeah, just I think once I was like in a better more open mindset...(Casey, 29)

A milestone of maturity for participants was self-reflection of one's emotions and evaluating the fit of personal relationships in accordance to these feelings. Additionally, broken trust, whether in platonic or romantic relationships, was seen as a learning experience. For example, Tina (23) has learned to recognize what bothers her in her relationships, what she values in relationships, and ultimately, how she chooses to form relationships, through reflecting upon her experiences with relationships in the past.

No. So, I said that I trust no one before, right? So, I guess my like definition of intimacy would be like, you know, anybody that I'm in a friendship or like in a relationship with, that I like trust to be like consistently not saying shitty things all the time. Like, a lot of people just say horrible things all the time. That really bothers me. So, I definitely like value my relationships with people who are also critical thinkers. So, yeah, I mean all of my close friends are very similar to me in that way. (Tina, 23)

Through the exploration of young women's developmental concerns in the current day, there was a clear, sustained struggle between balancing the development of identity and intimacy. The participants' sense of generational identity, which is rooted in a strong sense of individualism, led to a prioritization of identity, with intimacy as an extension of an individual's sense of self. Participants avoided using formalized labels to define their relationships. Ultimately, it was participants' experiences with balancing identity and intimacy through self-reflection that led to developmental growth, rather than age.

Dating Relationships and ICT

Social media platforms have become an integral part of romantic relationship initiation. Specifically, Casey (29) shares how she and her current partner of more than five years began their relationship and how social media mediated this interaction. Although Casey (29) did not first meet her significant other online, Facebook allowed for easier access to her partner, from which she was able to grow their mutual intimacy. Even at a time when social media interactions were not as salient as they are currently, Casey (29) recognized the important role of social media in the initiation of her relationship.

...when I first met my husband he owns a restaurant and I went into that restaurant with people and it's funny because like 2 years before that I ran a summer program at a Hispanic resource center and my current husband's sister was enrolled in that program, I taught her but I never met my husband even though his sister was there and then 2 years later I show up at his restaurant that I've never been to and I, in his restaurant he was like "Hey! You should comeback without your friends sometime." And I was like "What?" that's weird but obviously he wanted to see me again and I wanted to see him too because you know, I thought he was cute so when we got in the car I asked one of my friends like 'Do you remember that girl who was in that program? Do you remember her last name?' and then like, 'Oh yeah, it's Oldivia' and so I went on Facebook and I found him on Facebook and I friend requested him and then he sent me a message like, I can't remember what I posted but he was something like 'Oh, we should get to know each other more.' And so through that we like ran into each other at a bar and he got my phone number and we started dating and now that's that... (Casey, 29)

Flirting through ICT has also become a part of the relationship initiation process, in support of findings by Smith and Duggan (2013) that report flirting online supplemented face-to-face interactions. Experiences with flirting online were varied; Kai (23) found their experiences with flirting online to be uncomfortable due to prior experiences they described as "stalkerish." However, Kara (26) found these interactions endearing and emulates flirting in person but in a more public space. This discrepancy in experiences with flirtatious interactions online mirrors previous work by Spitzberg and Cupach (2007), in which they state it is often difficult to distinguish between acceptable courtship behaviors and harassment behaviors in an online space that obscures meaning conveyed during in-person interaction. Kai (23) describes how they are able to differentiate between platonic and flirtatious interactions.

I can tell they're hitting on me based on the comments they make or them suddenly deciding to message or text me after. I also feel like the primary people who like my statuses/pics are ones who have previously said they like me. (Kai, 23)

Some participants felt that ICT-mediated flirting actually made it more difficult to cultivate authentic relationships because of the false barriers in the online space. For example, Alex (22) believed that these false barriers could increase confusion regarding communication, and this ambiguity could be exploited purposefully to "play games" with a potential partner.

It [technology] enhances [dating games] because I mean I think it puts a level of distance between two people. I mean at least the game within like the past has been like face-to-face to a certain extent and there's still like conversation happening, but you know, now it's a text message. You know, you get to know someone through a text message, opposed to like a voice call or you get to know them through like Facebook or they're like through Instagram opposed to like talking about it or whatever and you know, there's positives and negatives to it you know? (Alex, 22)

However, participants' responses did support data from Stevens and Morris (2007), which showed that additional information about a potential partner online can ease uncertainty and tension, especially amongst those with social anxiety. One participant, Jennifer (25), who has self-reported social anxiety, recounts her experience with cultivating her romantic relationship online after meeting her partner through an online game, in which the online space became a safe space to share intimacy with her partner.

...we just started talking about our issues and getting to know each other. And, he sent me a picture of him like three weeks later and I'm like, 'Oh, you're pretty cute,' and, then I sent him a picture of me. And, that's when I had my weight problem and I sent him a picture of just my face 'cause I was so self-conscious. And he's like, you're really pretty. And, so then we saw each other picture-wise and then we email each other back and forth and then we got on Skype. (Jennifer, 25)

In contrast to Jennifer's experience, when Lea (22) found out more information about a potential partner online, she felt betrayed. Prior to finding additional information she felt uncertain as she was unable to foster clear communication between herself and her partner, and additional information confirmed the relationship was not stable. While ICT can be useful to maintain the connection and excitement surrounding a new relationship, the decoding required in the online space can be confusing and overwhelming when the bounds of a relationship are not clear.

So I was about to follow him [on Twitter] and then I saw like all these porn stars he was talking to... And I was like 'What?!' like I know we weren't in a relationship but at the same time, I don't know, I kinda felt betrayed and I was like "ah!"... In that moment I was like, I felt betrayed, I was like, why is he talking to like these women who he doesn't know, like what? Why? Like why are you telling women you wanna have sex with them like we just hooked up like why, I know we weren't in a relationship like I said but at the same time it was like I don't know. (Lea, 22)

Communicating online is most often just an extension of relationships and communications offline. However, information transmitted through ICT is in fact mediated, and the degree to which ICT can mediate this information is dependent on both the individuals involved in the interaction and the intimacy of the relationship between these individuals. To some, the superficiality of online interactions can be off putting and confusing, while to others, online interactions can enhance closeness to a partner, and this may be determined by stage in the dating process.

Romantic Relationship Communication and ICT

After the initiation of a new romantic relationship, ICT can be extremely useful in maintaining closeness and intimacy for those who are already in relationships (Murray & Campbell, 2015). For example,

Kendall recounts when a small gesture on social media by her boyfriend, who was not particularly interested in utilizing social media, redefined her relationship and made her feel closer to her partner. The small act of changing a profile picture to one that included Kendall was mediated by the context of her relationship, which in turn revalidated her relationship.

...he's like not really a big Facebook person but, we're at a wedding for one of his friends a couple of weeks ago and we like took a picture and he's like, 'I'm making that my profile picture. You can't steal it.' and, I was like, 'Okay. You can have it.' So, that was like funny. That's the most like Facebook-y thing he's probably ever done in his life.(Kendall, 24)

While the use of ICT to communicate within an established relationship can be beneficial to its health, ICT can amplify issues within a relationship. One of the younger participants in the study, Margret (20), who would be more likely to experience relationship jealousy at her age (Elphinston et al., 2011), reported that her boyfriend wanted to exchange phones after witnessing a social media interaction of Margret's that he did not like. This experience is consistent with those reported in the literature, in which women are more likely to report jealousy in their relationships arising from social media interactions with others (Muise et al., 2009). Surveillance of partner's online interactions deserves attention--these behaviors could be a form of relationship control that is spilling into the online space. Social media can magnify specific patterns of behavior seen offline in a relationship, while also providing new avenues to further develop a relationship through online communications.

Abuse Experiences

As ICT creates a more networked society, access to individuals increases. Regrettably, this increased ease of access also provides new avenues for the manifestation of abuse in romantic relationships. Modes of violence heavily researched in intimate partner violence and sexual violence literature have leaked into the online space. Unfortunately, the young women in the study experienced abuse online in varied ways. For example, Carly (25) discussed her abuse experience when using ICT and how this not only changed her perception of intimacy but also her perception of her own sexuality.

I actually, I kind of have, in some ways I have a negative view of it because when I was a teenager, I got abused online. I understand people, so I kind of have, like, a negative view on sexuality because of that. (Carly, 25)

Carly's abuse experience occurred in chat rooms, in which she was unknowingly lured into sexual roleplaying as a minor. Despite Carly's and other young women's experiences, none reported that they were permanently staying away from online interactions, likely due to the salience of the online space in identity and self-concept. Similar to the response to broken trust that we previously discussed, participants conceptualized these abuse experiences as a learning experience. Unfortunately, trust is fragile and difficult to decipher, and trust is further obscured in the anonymity of the online space.

CONCLUSION/DISCUSSION

When investigating the concerns of emerging adult women in the study, it became clear that while the developmental tasks of exploring identity and intimacy are salient in the lives of the women, these tasks were not viewed as separate. Rather, intimacy was viewed as an extension of identity, which we describe as *identimacy*. The theme of individualism emerged while discussing identity, individualism is priority but not above and beyond the desire for meaningful relationships. Hybrid identities, or integrated worldviews strayed away from traditional social expectations and previous practices of marriage for the primary pathway to adulthood. Instead, these women's sense of individualism affected their relationality – they refused to limit their identity to bounds of traditional social roles, and they believed the same agency should be available for others. While individualism played an important role in the participant's prioritization of tasks, intimacy was not disregarded but was instead molded to be compatible with identity tasks and postponed until the individual felt some level of security within their own social identity.

Related to the theme of individualism is self-directed womanhood in the context of intimacy. Participants' aversion to labelling themselves and others carried into discussions regarding their own development, in which they refused to set a requirement of intimate experiences to define adulthood. Instead, beliefs about marriage and other romantic relationships were personalized to each woman's world views, and these identities were maintained as individual needs. Therefore, marriage has transformed into a personal choice, as opposed to a social expectation. Those who did choose to get married did not necessarily do so for institutional approval but rather to align with personal concerns.

The shift toward individualism influenced the lives of those who chose to engage in a romantic relationship. The young women in the study refused to define a singular view of an authentic relationship, and instead emphasized relationships are defined equally by the partners themselves based on their shared worldviews. It is clear that identity is driving the choices these women made about their relationships, rather than their romantic decisions defining their identity. Practices like *churning* emphasize how intimacy is constantly reevaluated in the context of identity development.

Social media habits shift and change as well, Facebook use has stagnated from 2016 to 2018, with other social media sites, like Instagram, Pinterest, and Twitter gaining users in this timeframe (Smith & Anderson, 2018). One possibility is that a migration back to Facebook will happen as individual users maturate and their relationship status changes. Put more simply, do users avoid Facebook until they are in committed and serious adult relationships? It is important to consider how newer social media platforms are modifying the initiation and definition of relationships. When looking specifically at the role of ICT in the developmental trajectory of emerging adult women, it becomes clear that ICT not only provides a new outlet of expression and communication, but it ultimately mediates how this information is perceived. Due to ICT's salience as a communication channel, its effects on relationship formation and longevity are expansive. At the start of a relationship, ICT is used both to initiate contact and to supplement in-person contact. Ease and comfort of relationship initiation depended both on the identity of the individual and the context of the interaction. For some, the ambiguity and false barriers of communication in the online space can be off putting, while for others, it can provide a sense of security.

While ICT use at the start of a potential relationship can be difficult to navigate, ICT use within a relationship had a clear role. ICT amplified the characteristics present in the existing relationship. ICT allowed for the further fostering of closeness between individuals and helped maintain excitement and connection, amplifying the positive aspects of a relationship. However, unhealthy characteristics of a relationship, like jealousy are also augmented. Easy access to information facilitates negative behaviors like increased surveillance of partners' actions, tempting those who feel insecure within relationships to act on their distrust (Reed et al., 2016). ICTs are complex in nature, and the subjective interactions require analysis within the individuals' goals and the broader relationship context. This chapter provides further evidence that emerging technologies support and further a fluid relationship experience as emerging adults establish an individual identity.

REFERENCES

Archer, M. S. (2000). *Being human: The problem of agency*. Cambridge University Press. doi:10.1017/CBO9780511488733

Archer, M. S. (2007). *Making our way through the world: Human reflexivity and social mobility*. Cambridge University Press. doi:10.1017/CBO9780511618932

Archer, M. S. (2012). *The reflexive imperative in late modernity*. Cambridge University Press. doi:10.1017/CBO9781139108058

Arnett, J. J. (2000). Emerging adulthood: A theory of development from the late teens through the twenties. *The American Psychologist, 55*(5), 469–480. doi:10.1037/0003-066X.55.5.469 PMID:10842426

Arnett, J. J. (2002). The psychology of globalization. *The American Psychologist, 57*(10), 774–783. doi:10.1037/0003-066X.57.10.774 PMID:12369500

Arnett, J. J., & Schwab, J. (2012). *The Clark University Poll of Emerging Adults: Thriving, Sturgglin, & Hopeful*. Retrieved from: https://www.clarku.edu/clarkpoll-emerging-adults/pdfs/clark-university-poll-emerging-adults-findings.pdf

Baym, N. (2010). *Personal connections in the digital age*. Cambridge, UK: Polity Press.

Bennett, D. C., Guran, E. L., Ramos, M. C., & Margolin, G. (2011). College students' electronic victimization in friendships and dating relationships: Anticipated distress and associations with risky behaviors. *Violence and Victims, 26*(4), 410–429. doi:10.1891/0886-6708.26.4.410 PMID:21882666

Bergdall, A. R., Kraft, J. M., Andes, K., Carter, M., Hatfield-Timajchy, K., & Hock-Long, L. (2012). Love and hooking up in the new millennium: Communication technology and relationships among urban African American and Puerto Rican young adults. *Journal of Sex Research, 49*(6), 570–582. doi:10.1080/00224499.2011.604748 PMID:21854226

Borrajo, E., Gámez-Guadix, M., & Calvete, E. (2015). Cyber dating abuse: Prevalence, context, and relationship with offline dating aggression. *Psychological Reports, 116*(2), 565–585. doi:10.2466/21.16.PR0.116k22w4 PMID:25799120

Burke, S. C., Wallen, M., Vail-Smith, K., & Knox, D. (2011). Using technology to control intimate partners: An exploratory study of college undergraduates. *Computers in Human Behavior, 27*(3), 1162–1167. doi:10.1016/j.chb.2010.12.010

Castells, M. (1997). *The power of identity: The information age. Economy, Society and Culture* (Vol. 2). West Sussex, UK: John Wiley & Sons.

Choi, H., Ouytsel, J. V., & Temple, J. R. (2016). Association between sexting and sexual coercion among female adolescents. *Journal of Adolescence, 53*, 164–168. doi:10.1016/j.adolescence.2016.10.005 PMID:27814493

Clayton, R. B., Nagurney, A., & Smith, J. R. (2013). Cheating, breakup, and divorce: Is Facebook use to blame? *Cyberpsychology, Behavior, and Social Networking, 16*(10), 717–720. doi:10.1089/cyber.2012.0424 PMID:23745615

Coyne, S. M., Stockdale, L., Busby, D., Iverson, B., & Grant, D. M. (2011). "I luv u:)!": A descriptive study of the media use of individuals in romantic relationships. *Family Relations, 60*(2), 150–162. doi:10.1111/j.1741-3729.2010.00639.x

Dailey, R. M., Jin, B., Pfiester, A., & Beck, G. (2011). On-again/Off-again dating relationships: What keeps partners coming back? *The Journal of Social Psychology, 151*(4), 417–440. doi:10.1080/00224545.2010.503249 PMID:21755653

Dailey, R. M., Rossetto, K. R., Pfiester, A., & Surra, C. A. (2009). A qualitative analysis of on-again/off-again romantic relationships: "It's up and down, all around". *Journal of Social and Personal Relationships, 26*(4), 443-466. doi:10.1177/0265407509351035

Donath, J., & Boyd, D. (2004). Public displays of connection. *BT Technology Journal, 22*(4), 71–82. doi:10.1023/B:BTTJ.0000047585.06264.cc

Doucette, H., Collibee, C., Hood, E., Gittins Stone, D. I., DeJesus, B., & Rizzo, C. J. (2018). Perpetration of electronic intrusiveness among adolescent females: Associations with in-person dating violence. *Journal of Interpersonal Violence*. PMID:30516429

Draucker, C. B., & Marstolf, D. S. (2010). The role of electronic communication technology in adolescent dating violence. *Journal of Child and Adolescent Psychiatric Nursing, 23*(3), 133–142. doi:10.1111/j.1744-6171.2010.00235.x PMID:20796096

Duggan, M. (2014). *Pew Research Center. Photo and Video Sharing Grow Online*. Available at: http://pewInternet.org/Reports/2013/Photos-and-videos.aspx

Duguay, S. (2017). Dressing up Tinderella: Interrogating authenticity claims on the mobile dating app Tinder. *Information Communication and Society, 20*(3), 351–367. doi:10.1080/1369118X.2016.1168471

Elphinston, R. A., & Noller, P. (2011). Time to face it! Facebook intrusion and the implications for romantic jealousy and relationship satisfaction. *Cyberpsychology, Behavior, and Social Networking, 14*(11), 631–635. doi:10.1089/cyber.2010.0318 PMID:21548798

Erikson, E. H. (1964). Inner and outer space: Reflections on womanhood. *Daedalus, 93*(2), 582–606. Retrieved from http://www.jstor.org/stable/20026847

Fox, J., Osborn, J. L., & Warber, K. M. (2014). Relational dialectics and social networking sites: The role of Facebook in romantic relationship escalation, maintenance, conflict, and dissolution. *Computers in Human Behavior, 35*, 527–534. doi:10.1016/j.chb.2014.02.031

Fox, J., Warber, K. M., & Makstaller, D. C. (2013). The role of Facebook in romantic relationship development: An exploration of Knapp's relational stage 216 model. *Journal of Social and Personal Relationships*, *30*(6), 771–794. doi:10.1177/0265407512468370

Geiger, A., & Livingston, G. (2019, February 13). *8 facts about love and marriage in America*. Retrieved April 29, 2019, from https://www.pewresearch.org/fact-tank/2019/02/13/8-facts-about-love-and-marriage/

Giordano, P. C., Flannigan, C. M., Manning, W. D., & Longmore, M. A. (2009). *Developmental shifts in the character of romantic relationships from adolescence to early adulthood*. National Center for Family & Marriage Research Working Paper Series.

Greenfield, R. (2013). Tinder: A hook-up app women actually use. *Atlantic (Boston, Mass.)*.

Halpern-Meekin, S., Manning, W. D., Giordano, P. C., & Longmore, M. A. (2013). Relationship churning in emerging adulthood on/off relationships and sex with an ex. *Journal of Adolescent Research*, *28*(2), 166–188. doi:10.1177/0743558412464524 PMID:24535913

Halpern-Meekin, S., Manning, W. D., Giordano, P. C., & Longmore, M. A. (2013). Relationship churning, physical violence, and verbal abuse in young adult relationships. *Journal of Marriage and the Family*, *75*(1), 2–12. doi:10.1111/j.1741-3737.2012.01029.x PMID:24000263

Hardey, M. (2004). Mediated relationships. *Information Communication and Society*, *7*(2), 207–222. doi:10.1080/1369118042000232657

Jensen, L. A., & Arnett, J. J. (2012). Going global: New pathways for adolescents and emerging adults in a changing world. *The Journal of Social Issues*, *68*(3), 473–492. doi:10.1111/j.1540-4560.2012.01759.x

Kernsmith, P. D., Victor, B. G., & Smith-Darden, J. P. (2018). Online, offline, and over the line: Coercive sexting among adolescent dating partners. *Youth & Society*, *50*(7), 891–904. doi:10.1177/0044118X18764040

LaMendola, W. (2010). Social work and social presence in an online world. *Journal of Technology in Human Services*, *28*(1-2), 108–119. doi:10.1080/15228831003759562

Lanz, M., & Tagliabue, S. (2007). Do I really need someone in order to become an adult? Romantic relationships during emerging adulthood in Italy. *Journal of Adolescent Research*, *22*(5), 531–549. doi:10.1177/0743558407306713

Lee, E., Choi, T. R., Lee, T. D., & Sung, Y. (2019). Using Instagram While "In a Relationship". *Journal of Individual Differences*, *40*(2), 111–117. doi:10.1027/1614-0001/a000282

Lenhart, A. Ybaraa, M., & Price-Feeney, M. (2016). *Nonconsensual Image Sharing: One in 25 Americans has been a Victim of "Revenge Porn."* Academic Press.

Lippman, J. R., & Campbell, S. W. (2014). Damned if you do, damned if you don't... if you're a girl: Relational and normative contexts of adolescent sexting in the United States. *Journal of Children and Media*, *8*(4), 371–386. doi:10.1080/17482798.2014.923009

Lucero, J. L., Weisz, A. N., Smith-Darden, J., & Lucero, S. M. (2014). Exploring gender differences: Socially interactive technology use/abuse among dating teens. *Affilia*, *29*(4), 478–491. doi:10.1177/0886109914522627

Mackinnon, S. P., Nosko, A., Pratt, M. W., & Norris, J. E. (2011). Intimacy in young adults' narratives of romance and friendship predICT's Eriksonian generativity: A mixed method analysis. *Journal of Personality*, *79*(3), 587–617. doi:10.1111/j.1467-6494.2011.00692.x PMID:21534965

Manning, W. D., Brown, S. L., & Payne, K. K. (2014). Two decades of stability and change in age at first union formation. *Journal of Marriage and the Family*, *76*(2), 247–260. doi:10.1111/jomf.12090 PMID:25147410

Manning, W. D., Giordano, P. C., Longmore, M. A., & Hocevar, A. (2009). *Romantic relationships and academic/career trajectories in early adulthood*. Retrieved from The Center for Family and Demographic Research website: http://www.bgsu.edu/organizations/cfdr

Mansson, D. H., & Myers, S. A. (2011). An initial examination of college students' expressions of affection through Facebook. *The Southern Communication Journal*, *76*(2), 155–168. doi:10.1080/1041794090331 7710

Markham, A. (2013). Remix Cultures, Remix Methods. Global Dimensions of Qualitative Inquiry, 63-81.

Marshall, T. C., Bejanyan, K., Di Castro, G., & Lee, R. A. (2013). Attachment styles as predictors of Facebook-related jealousy and surveillance in romantic relationships. *Personal Relationships*, *20*(1), 1–22. doi:10.1111/j.1475-6811.2011.01393.x

Marwick, A. E. (2015). Instafame: Luxury Selfies in the Attention Economy. *Public Culture, 27*(175), 137-160.

Marwick, A. E., & boyd. (2011). I tweet honestly, I tweet passionately: Twitter users, context collapse, and the imagined audience. *New Media & Society*, *13*(1), 114–133. doi:10.1177/1461444810365313

Muise, A., Christofides, E., & Desmarais, S. (2009). More information than you ever wanted: Does Facebook bring out the green-eyed monster of jealousy? *Cyberpsychology & Behavior*, *12*(4), 441–444. Retrieved from http://sexresearchandthecity.com/content/uploads/2011/04/Facebook-Jealousy.pdf doi:10.1089/cpb.2008.0263 PMID:19366318

Murray, C. E., & Campbell, E. C. (2015). The pleasures and perils of technology in intimate relationships. *Journal of Couple & Relationship Therapy*, *14*(2), 116–140. doi:10.1080/15332691.2014.953651

Odaci, H., & Kalkan, M. (2010). Problematic Internet use, loneliness and dating anxiety among young adult college students. *Computers & Education*, *55*(3), 1091–1097. doi:10.1016/j.compedu.2010.05.006

Paasonen, S., Light, B., & Jarrett, K. (2019). The dick pic: harassment, curation, and desire. *Social Media+ Society, 5*(2).

Papp, L., Danielewicz, J., & Cayemberg, C. (2012). "Are we Facebook official?" Implications of dating partners' Facebook use and profiles for intimate relationship. *Cyberpsychology & Behavior*, *15*(2), 85–99. doi:10.1089/cyber.2011.0291 PMID:21988733

Parker, K., & Livingston, G. (2018, June 13). *7 facts about American fathers*. Retrieved April 29, 2019, from https://www.pewresearch.org/fact-tank/2018/06/13/fathers-day-facts/

Peterson, A. (2014). *How I rebuilt Tinder and discovered the shameful secret of attraction*. Academic Press.

Reed, L. A., Tolman, R. M., & Ward, L. M. (2016). Snooping and sexting: Digital media as a context for dating aggression and abuse among college students. *Violence Against Women*, *22*(13), 1556–1576. doi:10.1177/1077801216630143 PMID:26912297

Reed, L. A., Tolman, R. M., & Ward, L. M. (2017). Gender matters: Experiences and consequences of digital dating abuse victimization in adolescent dating relationships. *Journal of Adolescence*, *59*, 79–89. doi:10.1016/j.adolescence.2017.05.015 PMID:28582653

Reed, L. A., Tolman, R. M., Ward, L. M., & Safyer, P. (2016). Keeping tabs: Attachment anxiety and electronic intrusion in high school dating relationships. *Computers in Human Behavior*, *58*, 259–268. doi:10.1016/j.chb.2015.12.019

Reed, L. A., Ward, L. M., Tolman, R. M., Lippman, J. R., & Seabrook, R. C. (2018). The association between stereotypical gender and dating beliefs and digital dating abuse perpetration in adolescent dating relationships. *Journal of Interpersonal Violence*. PMID:30261802

Riessman, C. K., & Quinney, L. (2005). Narrative in social work: A critical review. *Qualitative Social Work: Research and Practice*, *4*(4), 391–412. doi:10.1177/1473325005058643

Schwartz, S. J., Côté, J. E., & Arnett, J. J. (2005). Identity and Agency in Emerging Adulthood Two Developmental Routes in the Individualization Process. *Youth & Society*, *37*(2), 201–229. doi:10.1177/0044118X05275965

Senft, T. (2008). *CamGirls: Celebrity and Community in the Age of Social Networks*. New York: Peter Lang Publishing.

Smith, A., & Anderson, M. (2019, April 17). *Social Media Use 2018: Demographics and Statistics*. Retrieved April 29, 2019, from https://www.pewinternet.org/2018/03/01/social-media-use-in-2018/

Smith, A., & Duggan, M. (2013). *Online Dating & Relationships*. Pew Internet & American Life Project. Retrieved from http://www.pewInternet.org/Reports/2013/Online-Dating.aspx

Spitzberg, B. H., & Cupach, W. R. (2007). The state of the art of stalking: Taking stock of the emerging literature. *Aggression and Violent Behavior*, *12*(1), 64–86. doi:10.1016/j.avb.2006.05.001

Steinfield, C., Ellison, N. B., & Lampe, C. (2008). Social capital, self-esteem, and use of online social network sites: A longitudinal analysis. *Journal of Applied Developmental Psychology*, *29*(6), 434–445. doi:10.1016/j.appdev.2008.07.002

Stevens, S. B., & Morris, T. L. (2007). College dating and social anxiety: Using the Internet as a means of connecting to others. *Cyberpsychology & Behavior*, *10*(5), 680–688. doi:10.1089/cpb.2007.9970 PMID:17927536

Stonard, K. E. (2018). The prevalence and overlap of technology-assisted and offline adolescent dating violence. *Current Psychology (New Brunswick, N.J.)*, 1–15.

Taylor, S., & Xia, Y. (2018). Cyber partner abuse: A systematic review. *Violence and Victims*, *33*(6), 983–1011. doi:10.1891/0886-6708.33.6.983 PMID:30573547

Tokunaga, R. S. (2011). Social networking site or social surveillance site? Understanding the use of interpersonal electronic surveillance in romantic relationships. *Computers in Human Behavior, 27*(2), 705–713. doi:10.1016/j.chb.2010.08.014

Turkle, S. (2011). *Alone together: Why we expect more from technology and less from each other*. New York: Basic Books.

Twenge, J. M., Sherman, R. A., & Wells, B. E. (2017). Sexual inactivity during young adulthood is more common among us millennials and igen: Age, period, and cohort effects on having no sexual partners after age 18. *Archives of Sexual Behavior, 46*(2), 433–440. doi:10.100710508-016-0798-z PMID:27480753

Vaterlaus, J. M., Tulane, S., Porter, B. D., & Beckert, T. E. (2018). The Perceived Influence of Media and Technology on Adolescent Romantic Relationships. *Journal of Adolescent Research, 33*(6), 651–671. doi:10.1177/0743558417712611

Yang, C., Brown, B. B., & Braun, M. F. (2013). From Facebook to cell calls: Layers of electronic intimacy in college students' interpersonal relationships. *New Media & Society, 0*(0), 1–19. doi:10.1177/1461444812472486

Zhao, X., Schwanda Sosik, V., & Cosley, D. (2012). It's complicated: how romantic partners use Facebook. In *Proceedings of the SIGCHI Conference on Human Factors in Computing Systems* (pp. 771-780). ACM. 10.1145/2207676.2207788

Zweig, J. M., Dank, M., Yahner, J., & Lachman, P. (2013). The rate of cyber dating abuse among teens and how it relates to other forms of teen dating violence. *Journal of Youth and Adolescence, 42*(7), 1063–1077. doi:10.100710964-013-9922-8 PMID:23412689

Chapter 4
The Electric Hookup:
Individual and Social Risks Related to Hookup App Use Among Emerging Adults

Brenna Helm
Michigan State University, USA

Thomas Vander Ven
Ohio University, USA

Howard T. Welser
https://orcid.org/0000-0002-6715-1335
Ohio University, USA

ABSTRACT

Social critics claim that emerging adults are subjecting themselves and one another to a variety of risks through the use of mobile dating and hookup applications, or "apps." These narratives emphasize concerns about authenticity, the threat of sexual predators, and changing expectations about the nature and emotional intimacy of relationships. The use of apps among emerging adults presents risks for individual users and for social relational patterns, both in the digital world and "on the ground." In this chapter, the authors analyze the theoretical and empirical risks of mediating hookup culture through the use of mobile dating apps and discuss the potential risks to app users, such as harassment, cyberstalking, and sexual violence. Next, the authors explore the social risks pertaining to authenticity, trust, the quality of relationships, and conflicting understandings of social norms and acceptable behaviors. Finally, the chapter concludes with suggestions for future directions in research related to the use of hookup apps and its related risks.

DOI: 10.4018/978-1-7998-1063-6.ch004

INTRODUCTION

Emerging adults are especially vulnerable to a variety of risks, both "on the ground" and in the digital world. According to Arnett (2000), emerging adulthood is a period of development located between late adolescence and the early twenties, most specifically between the ages of 18 and 25. Emerging adults operate between adolescence and adulthood in a way that Erikson (1968) described as a sort of psychological dizziness where young people struggle with the transition from childhood to adulthood. Thus, much of their focus is trained on identity development and exploration. According to Klinger (2016), this unique identity-seeking feature of emerging adulthood draws them to hookup culture where they can experiment with the presentation of self and sample intimate relations without having to commit themselves to a restrictive relationship.

Hookup culture can be understood as a social climate in which engaging in casual, romantic, or sexual interactions outside of a committed relationship is deemed acceptable and, in fact, encouraged by changing sociosexual scripts (Bogle, 2008; Garcia, Reiber, Massey & Merriwether, 2012; Monto & Carey, 2014; Wade, 2017). In Lisa Wade's book, *American Hookup: The New Culture of Sex on Campus* (2017), she describes hookup culture as an overwhelming presence that we are entrenched in, regardless of whether or not we are actively participating. As a result, many college students in particular feel as though hookup culture is, as Wade puts it, a "dominating force" in their lives and those of their peers (Armstrong, Hamilton, & England 2010; Wade, 2017).

"Hooking up" has become a common topic in popular discourse, but it is one that is difficult to explicitly define as it is based on the subjective sexual experiences one has within the larger culture. In an effort to better define hooking up, we summarize it as *brief, but sometimes repeated, uncommitted sexual or romantic encounters between individuals who are not romantic partners or dating one another* (Garcia, Reiber, Massey, & Merriwether, 2012). In this way, hooking up is an ambiguous term, as it can refer to anything ranging from simply kissing to sexual intercourse (Wade, 2017). An Online College Social Life Survey found that sexual intercourse occurs during approximately 40% of hookups; while foreplay- a sexual experience referring to nudity and genital touching- and open-mouth kissing occur in 12% and 35% of hookups respectively (England, 2011; Wade, 2017).

Technology and online resources have streamlined the process of seeking out potential romantic and sexual partners by developing applications, or "apps," that can be downloaded on user's mobile devices. These mobile dating apps, also commonly referred to as dating or "hookup apps," have grown in popularity over the years. In fact, the percentage of those aged 18-24 who used dating apps went from a meager 10% in 2013 to 27% in 2015 (Smith, 2016). Research on the motivations of Tinder (a popular app) users identified a variety of objectives, including love, casual sex, ease of communication, thrill of excitement, self-worth validation, and trendiness (Sumter, Vandenbosch, & Ligtenberg, 2017). These motivations differ based on gender identity, as men are more highly motivated by casual sex, ease of communication, and thrill of excitement. These differences are partly attributable to deeply ingrained gender socialization that make engaging in casual sex and hookups more anxiety-producing for women (Klinger, 2016; Petersen & Hyde, 2011; Ranzini & Lutz, 2017; Sumter, Vandenbosch, & Ligtenberg, 2017; Widman et al., 2006).

According to recent scholarship, one of the dominant characteristics of hookup culture is a reliance on assumptions and a lack of direct communication (Klinger, 2016; Wade, 2017). Often, participants are operating on assumptions, in some measure due to the ambiguity of the term "hookup," but also due to the comorbidity between hookup culture and alcohol use (Fielder & Carey, 2010; Klinger, 2016; Vander

Ven, 2011; Wade, 2017). In this capacity, alcohol serves as a social lubricant as well as an excuse for a failed or regrettable hookup experience (Klinger 2016; Vander Ven, 2011; Wade, 2017). Fielder and Carey (2010) found that 64% of first semester college students gave an account of alcohol presence in their hookup experiences. Other scholars found that 80% of their participants used alcohol in the initiation of their hookup experience (Downing-Matibag & Geisinger 2009; Klinger 2016).

Hookup participants often participate in "reality management," in which students overemphasize the positive aspects and good sexual experiences they have had when relaying the events to their friends (Klinger 2016). While these positive aspects are aggrandized, the negative experiences- such as dissatisfaction- are simultaneously understated. The implications of reality management are twofold: On one hand, reality management serves as a way of presenting themselves and their sexual experiences in an ideal way; on the other, reality management contributes to the overestimation that is distinctive of hookup culture (Klinger 2016:4). In 2016, a study found that male and female college students were engaging in twice the number of hookups compared to first dates (Klinger 2016). However, studies have also shown that the number of estimated hookups reportedly experienced by graduating college students throughout their college experience is, on average, one per semester (Wade, 2017). Based on existing literature, we know that engaging in hookups is not as common as implied, and that those who do participate are not hooking up frequently (Wade, 2017).

The arrangement of a hookup is built upon the mutual lack of commitment to a relationship and the desire for "no strings attached" sexual interaction. This causes a distinct barrier to communication between app users and the larger population of those engaged in casual hookups. As a result, participants- especially women- often find themselves hesitant to voice concerns or seek out deeper connections, as that would violate the unspoken understanding about nature of the relationship (Klinger, 2016). Concerns pertaining to uncertainty about the status of the relationship and future directions go unexpressed, and personal feelings are not articulated (Klinger 2016; Bisson & Levine, 2009). These anxieties are amplified among female participants due to fear of adhering to stereotypes portraying women as emotional and unable to participate in "no strings attached" sex (Klinger, 2016).

Danger, High Voltage: Cultural Narratives About Harms Related to Electric Hookups

As the popularity of mobile dating apps has grown, so too has social anxiety about their consequences. Articles aimed at making the potential risks clear have become increasingly common on high-traffic sites and social media. These concerns can be organized thematically, with three primary categories: 1) Concerns about authenticity and trust; 2) The presence of sexual predators, harassers, and antisocial users on dating/hookup apps; and 3) the commodification of love and dating, which could result in the widespread decline in relationships and connectedness.

Given the nature of these applications, a common warning involves confirming the identity of the person you matched with and are talking to. As with any online forum, the anonymity of a screen allows space for users to present themselves in ideal ways, guided by the expectations of a desired audience. However, with hookup apps there is an underlying expectation of eventually meeting your match, and, theoretically, one can only realistically manipulate their self-presentation during the initial stages of app interaction (Hobbs, Owen, & Gerber, 2017). There is a delicate balance between accuracy and strategic self-improvement in user representation. Cultural narratives about hookup apps are heavily focused on the risk of user deception. In one campus news source, a police sergeant is quoted: "Confirming anyone's identity is a difficult task. How do you confirm someone is who they say they are?" (Park, 2018). The common narrative is primarily focused on the deception used by sexual predators rather than general user duplicity to improve self-presentation.

The fear of sexual predators and harassment is not isolated to claims about authenticity, it is also evidenced in general warnings of using the apps themselves. Jason Lawrence, a 50-year-old man from Hampshire was given a life sentence after raping and assaulting seven women he met on Match.com. His case is a typifying example of "mobile dating gone wrong" (Rayner, 2016). After meeting and marrying someone he met on the site, he continued contacting "thousands of women online" and was reported online by four of his victims (Rayner, 2016). Another media report focused on the abuse and harassment that women face on the well-known hookup app, Tinder (Sprankles, 2015). In it, the author argues that the anonymity serves as a "tool for emboldenment" in which male users in particular use the app to threaten, harass, and send unwarranted nude images to female users. Furthermore, statistics taken from the book *Instant Checkmate's Playbook for Winning Love Online* are used to paint an image for readers and makes the claim that 42% of women have been harassed or made to feel uncomfortable at some point while using online dating (Sprankles, 2015). The questions that arise revolve around proper supervision and action on these sites and apps, and whether or not the lack of proper guardianship creates a digital hunting ground that, along with other characteristics of the apps and larger hookup culture, create a "perfect storm" for predatory behavior and victimization.

It has also been theorized that these apps pose a threat to relationships and intimacy, that they turn relationships, intimacy, and sex into a sort of commodified game (Bauman, 2003; Hobbs et al., 2017). Bauman (2003) suggests that with rising individualism and technological change, dating is becoming a recreational activity used to derive enjoyment or pleasure, and as a result we pose the risk of people becoming seen as expendable or as conquests (Klinger 2016). This relates to the process of rebranding that hookup apps have undergone. Companies are seemingly pushing narratives that Tinder and other apps are as fundamental to your social experience as your first time drinking or engaging in sexual intercourse, and that bad dates are humorous and can be seen as "exciting misadventures" (Bromwich, 2018; Singh-Kurtz, 2018). Thus, dating/hookup apps are portrayed as essential tools in the adolescent journey.

Mobile Dating/Hookup Apps: Risks to Users

The same features that draw young adults to hookup culture present a variety of risks. A large body of criminological research findings demonstrate that emerging adults are disproportionately represented as both criminal offenders and victims. Known as "the age-crime curve" (Loeber & Farrington, 2014), the relationship between young adulthood and criminality is well established. Scholars suggest that this relationship owes to many factors including the social turbulence, uncertainty, and stress that accompany developmental transitions, the relatively weak bonds to social institutions (e.g., work and family) experienced by youth, and to increasing attachment to peers in adolescence (Rocque, Posick, & Hoyle, 2016).

Theorizing Risk for Mobile Dating/Hookup App Users

The disproportionate risks faced by emerging adults may be amplified by the use of mobile dating/hookup apps. While hookup app use may indeed provide an efficient forum for communicating with potential partners and may facilitate consensual romantic or sexual encounters between users, scholars suggest that some users may use them as a vehicle for executing antisocial goals (Duncan & March, 2019).

Furthermore, according to Mishna, McLuckie, and Saini (2009), predatory online dating can produce a variety of negative effects including depressive symptoms, feelings of guilt and shame, self-harm, and a retreat from social interaction.

The risks presented by these applications can be vividly seen through the lens of a criminological perspective known as the routine activities approach. First articulated by Cohen and Felson (1979; Felson & Cohen, 1980) and later elaborated by Felson and Eckert (2016), the routine activities approach suggests that predatory crime requires the convergence in space and time of *motivated offenders*, *suitable targets*, and the *absence of capable guardianship*. According to Felson and Cohen (1980, 392), the completion of a predatory crime "requires at a minimum an offender with both criminal inclinations and the ability to carry out those inclinations, a person or object providing a suitable target for the offender, and the absence of capable guardians capable of preventing the violation." Any social force or set of contextual circumstances that facilitates the convergence of these elements, then, should increase the risk of victimization.

Mobile dating/hookup app use, it seems, may systematically provide each of the ingredients described by the routine activities approach. First, motivated offenders may be drawn to dating/hooking app use because of the deep pool of victims (i.e., suitable targets) that it provides. Choi (2008) argues, in fact, that motivated offenders and suitable targets are truly ubiquitous in the online community. Furthermore, scholars suggest that certain predatory personality attributes may be more commonly found among users of hookup apps, like Tinder. For example, Duncan and March (2019) assert that individuals with Machiavellian traits (i.e., the use of social manipulation and disdain for traditional morality) and those with psychopathic tendencies may see dating/hookup apps as effective vehicles for employing deceptive dating strategies. And while scholars have observed a variety of motivations for dating/hookup app use (e.g., romantic goals, passing time, relaxing, thrills and excitement) the quest to satisfy sexual desires is a common goal (Sumter, Vandenbosch, & Ligtenberg, 2017). Thus, it is likely that some opportunistic users see the world of virtual dating as a fertile context for sexual coercion.

Second, dating/hookup app users may be especially suitable as targets because they are higher-than-average risk takers and, thus, may find themselves in vulnerable social spaces. In an analysis of mobile dating app user behavior, Sevi (2018) found that Tinder users take more health and safety risks than non-users (e.g., engaging in unprotected sex) and have lower levels of sexual disgust sensitivity (e.g., low level of repulsion to various sexual scenarios) than non-users do. Like Sevi, other scholars found that mobile dating/hookup app subscribers may take more sexual risks than non-users which manifests itself in an increased risk for sexually transmitted infections (Beymer et al., 2014; Bhattacharya, 2015). However, the research findings linking mobile dating/hookup app use to sexual risk behavior are complex and inconsistent. Some scholars suggest that app users report greater sexual risk behavior (Landovitz et al., 2013; Sevi, 2018) and others report that app subscribers exhibit lower risk behavior (Green, Turner & Logan, 2018; Hahn et al, 2018; Rice et al., 2012).

Third, according to the logic of routine activities approach, the world of app dating and mobile hookups may be especially rife with risk because of the low level of guardianship in the virtual world. The anonymity and isolation of app dating reduces the probability that potential victims of harassment or app-initiated violence will be protected from harm by friends and bystanders. This is clearly the case when app users are harassed, insulted, or sexually objectified by other users within the confines of the app. And when dating/hookup apps lead to face-to-face meetings in the real world, motivated offenders may strategically arrange to isolate victims in social spaces where guardianship is low. Thus, mobile app communication may involve luring victims to dangerous locations. Furthermore, dating app users inadvertently allow predators to track their location through the geolocation data provided in many dating apps. According to Murphy (2018, 113), "Mobile dating apps have also been known to share the geolocation of its users for up to one hundred and sixty-five days after the initial location share, even if the user has not been using the app," which could facilitate stalking, unwanted interaction, and violence.

The routine activities approach provides a practical framework for hypothesizing the victimization risks embedded in mobile dating app behavior. The empirical literature on virtual dating apps and risk, however, draws from a variety of disciplines, theoretical perspectives, and research methods to investigate this issue. In this context, we summarize the research focused on the victimization experiences of mobile dating and hookup app users.

Dating/Hookup Apps, Harassment, and Stalking Behavior

Dating/Hookup app users may experience cyberbullying or online harassment which is defined here as repeated unwanted, hurtful, harassing, and/or threatening interaction through electronic communication media (Rafferty & Vander Ven, 2014).

To be fair, it must be noted that many dating/hookup app users are generally satisfied with their virtual dating experience. Lefebvre (2018), for instance, found that 46% of Tinder users felt that mobile dating improved their pool of potential partners. Furthermore, it appears that many dating/hookup app users do not see harassment as a significant problem. Of the Tinder users that reported deleting their account in Lefebvre's study, barely 1% reported harassment as the reason for abandoning mobile dating.

It is difficult to estimate the prevalence and frequency of dating/hookup app harassment and antisocial behavior as the empirical research findings in this area are scattered across small, non-representative samples. Much of the research aimed at online dating app harassment has focused on the mobile app, Tinder. According to Duncan and March (2019), Tinder users are likely to experience predatory behavior such as invasion of privacy, harassment and objectification. Moreover, researchers report that women are especially vulnerable to harassment on Tinder (Guadagno et al., 2012; Lopes & Vogel, 2017). Some estimates imply that antisocial behavior is commonplace on dating apps and that gendered harassment is fairly widespread in the world of mobile app dating—Burgess (2016) reported that 57% of female Tinder users experienced harassment on the app while just 21% of male users reported the same. And qualitative research highlights the gendered content of dating app harassment as well. Thompson (2018), for example, analyzed inflammatory, sexually demeaning, and threatening messages that women received from men on dating apps. On the other hand, Duncan and March (2019) did not identify gender as a significant predictor of antisocial Tinder use and March et al. (2017) found no gender patterns in trolling behaviors on Tinder.

Much of the scholarship directed at the complexities of dating/hookup app use analyzes samples of gay men and male sexual minorities. One of the first mobile dating/hookup apps, Grindr, was primarily used by gay, bisexual, genderqueer, and sexually curious men who used the geolocation instrumentation on Grindr to find other users in time and space (LeFebvre, 2018). Thus, much of the early work in this area features gay men and their mobile dating/hookup experiences. Although it appears that gay and lesbian mobile app users are ambivalent about their app experiences (Chan, 2018; Tang, 2017), some studies show that gay men report instances of deception, catfishing, and sexual coercion (Lauckner et al., 2019) as well as sexual harassment (Albury & Byron, 2016), and unflattering comparisons to idealized social types (Uteda, 2017).

A related concern about the unintended consequences of mobile dating/hookup app use relates to the risk of cyberstalking—the use of electronic media to perpetrate "the persistent unwanted following of a person, causing the victim to feel unsafe" (Purcell et al., 2004). It appears that some mobile app users have some concern over whether their use will result in cyberstalking. Over 48 percent of the Tinder users surveyed by Lutz and Ranzini (2017) reported that they had at least moderate concern that other users would use their personal data stalk them. While social critics and journalists claim that cyberstalking (and face-to-face) stalking is a common consequence of mobile dating app activity (see Murphy, 2018), there are currently no systematic, empirical data to support or challenge this claim.

Dating/Hookup Apps and Sexual Violence

Journalists and police agencies have made dramatic claims about the alarming increase in dating app-facilitated sexual violence. Drawing from British news reports, for example, Murphy (2018) asserts that police reports of rape attributed to the use of mobile dating apps increased by 450% in just five years. Furthermore, media accounts of predators using mobile dating apps to lure and then sexually assault victims frequent the news. An internet search of sexual assaults attributed to dating/hookup app use will produce hundreds of media reports. In 2015, for example, a California man was arrested for using Tinder to arrange for meetings with four unsuspecting women who he subsequently sedated and raped. And in 2018, an Indiana man was arrested and charged with raping an 11-year old girl that he met on Tinder. Empirical research on the pathway between mobile dating/hookup app use and sexual assault, however, is scarce.

The most comprehensive attempts to study the risk of sexual assaults among mobile dating/hookup app users were conducted by Shapiro et al. (2017) and Choi, Wong, and Fong (2018). In their survey of 166 Tinder users and 249 nonusers, Shapiro et al. (2017) found that Tinder use was significantly associated with non-consensual sexual encounters (i.e., ''has someone who you met tried to have oral and/or genital intercourse with you without your consent?'). While the investigators did not specifically link assault to meetings arranged through mobile app use, they found that greater odds of reporting non-consensual sex were associated with Tinder use. And in their examination of mobile dating and sexual abuse outcomes in Hong Kong university students, Choi, Wong, and Fong (2018) found that users of dating apps were more likely to be sexually abused in the last year than nonusers and that dating app use was a risk factor of lifetime sexual abuse. While these studies did not establish a concrete link between mobile dating activity and sexual assault, the findings are suggestive that risks exist. Strategic attempts to trace dating/hookup apps to meetings that result in sexual assault are needed.

Mobile Dating/Hookup Apps: Risks to Social Relations

This section explores some of the negative social implications of mobile dating apps in the context of hookup culture. As new technology is adopted it alters how people interact, how they behave towards others, and how those behaviors are interpreted (Smith, 2000, Shirky, 2008). It is often the case that the unintentional consequences of social technology are more profound than the intended effects. For instance, the international rise of mobile phone technology has spurred small businesses in rural parts of the African continent. These developments are partly attributable to the use of cell minutes for payment and exchange rather than simply making communication easier (Asongu, 2013).

While mobile dating applications have been available since 2012, they have only recently become ubiquitous within the young adult cohorts (Smith, 2016; "U.S. Dating Websites," 2019). Clay Shirky (2008) remarked that when technology becomes commonplace it can become socially interesting-- and by this standard, the increase in mobile dating app use has developed from unusual, to commonplace, to socially interesting. What social risks are made more likely by the widespread use of mobile dating apps? We see three general classes of social risks: (1) degradation of authenticity and the capacity to trust, (2) reduction in commitment and quality of relationships, (3) distorted perceptions of behavior and social norms.

Degradation of Authenticity and Undermining the Capacity to Trust

The key to success is sincerity. If you can fake that you've got it made. George Burns[1]

The normalization of deception and manipulation in mobile dating culture increases both individual and social risks. Deception involves deliberate communications designed to produce false beliefs in the eyes of others (Levine, 2014). Participation in hookup culture embeds dating adults in social settings where overly honest modes of self-presentation are discouraged and may be naive. Participants and researchers are aware that self-presentations are, at least partly, exercises in strategic impression management where men become taller and more wealthy, women are slimmer and more attractive, and everyone becomes clever and more desirable (Toma, 2015; Toma, Hancock, & Ellison 2008; Kashy & DePaulo, 1996). Profile construction and interactions during the discovery phase are shaped by the awareness of the need to self-promote in a market of close alternatives. People who are placed in situations where they are expected to promote the most favorable view of themselves tend to engage in more deception and to strategically self-enhance (Feldman, Forrest, & Happ, 2002). To the extent that the prime motive is to seem more desirable, interactions during the matching and discovery phases are likely to lead to an increase in deception and a degradation of authenticity. Sharing evidence of deceptions is popular on blogs and twitter, and these prominent examples can lead to exaggerated perceptions of how common deceptive practices are. A social risk is a normalization of strategic distortion that leads to a degradation in authenticity, where participants expect others to be inauthentic and they also feel a pressure to present in ways that they may not feel are authentic.

The awareness of inauthenticity in the mobile dating context is in sharp contrast to what researchers term the truth bias, or the well documented tendency for people to interact with a baseline level of honesty and expectation that others will themselves act truthfully (Levine, 2014; Levine, Kima, & Hamela, 2010). Expectation for truthful and honest dealings are cornerstones of social order, without which everyday coordination of actions becomes costly and contentious. To the extent that our default truth bias is at odds with the game of how people interact in mobile dating contexts, it can lead to collective costs. First, the need to second guess the presentations of others increases the difficulty and costs in finding a fitting match. All other things being equal, perceived prevalence of deceptive practices make search and selection a more difficult and costly process for all participants.[2] Two commonly recognized barriers to achieving coordination in online social systems are the problem of too much information and the signal to noise problem (Rheingold, 2012), both of which are exacerbated by proliferation of deception in mobile dating profiles and communications. Participants in such systems need to cultivate platform specific digital literacy skills (Rheingold, 2012) such as how to recognize matches that are more likely to be trustworthy, the ability to read and respond appropriately to the normative expectations of a potential partner (Yeo & Fun, 2016), and the competency to use communication to develop a shared expectation for the encounter.

High levels of involvement in mobile dating apps may undermine our capacity to trust through the deception consensus effect. In a pair of studies Markowitz and Hancock (2018) investigate mobile dating app users' perceptions of deception during the discovery phase, or the time period of electronic exchanges that occur after a match is made, but before face to face contact is initiated. Markowitz and Hancock found a strong correlation between the number of lies a mobile dater perceives in their partners and the number of lies they recognize in their own communications. In other words, participants who actively deceive their partners perceive higher levels of deception in the communications of those partners. As app users are socialized, they become more skilled and successful at navigating mobile dating app interactions and they will also become more aware of uses of deception. In the social learning process, they may also become more willing to use deception themselves. To the degree that use of mobile dating apps leads to greater exposure to, and use of deceptive practices, then, the widespread use of dating apps can shift social settings towards a greater sense of distrust, cynical perceptions of deception, and anxiety about the risk of being victimized by manipulation and deception. A social risk of the mobile dating culture where deception is prevalent will be a degradation in the capacity to trust. This has extra risk when we consider that attitudes that embrace deception are consistent with exploitative ideologies.

Tis impossible to separate the chance of good from the risk of ill. -David Hume

Mobile dating apps create opportunities for people to engage in interactions that both parties hope to benefit from, and thus they must find a ground on which to trust each other. Without enough trust to act on the match, the potential benefit of the interaction is lost. But to engage in a trust interaction with an unworthy partner can lead to a wide range of negative experiences (described above in the individual risk section). This general trust problem has been extensively studied from a rational action perspective which highlights how interests, sanctioning capacity, reputation, and timing can allow or impede the development of trust (Hardin, 2002; Berg, Dickhaut, & McCabe 1995).

Trust situations are shaped by how the interests of the parties align or compete as well as how this interaction may alter opportunities for future interactions. The decision to engage in trust will often require past experience (with that person) as well as an accurate understanding of the sanctions the trusted can expect to receive for fulfilling or for violating that trust. The trusted will be more likely to behave as trusted when there is an opportunity for future interactions, when there are strong reputational costs for violations of trust, and when their reputation is durable and easily reviewed by future interaction partners. Based on this logic users of mobile dating apps can expect violations to be more common when they engage in one time interactions with partners that are otherwise unknown to them, and when using systems where it is easy for participants to create a new online identity. This suggests that the user interface that lacks effective internal sanctioning systems, and the tendency to use an app for one time encounters ought to increase the likelihood of failures of trust.

Systems like eBay maintain extensive reputation systems to facilitate trust fulfilling behavior and make it temporally costly to build up a good reputation (Friedman & Resnick, 2001), while mobile dating apps do not integrate effective and fair sanctioning systems to help prevent abuses of trust. The rise of 3rd party contexts for public sanctioning (like "Tinder Nightmares") underscores the unmet demand for effective sanctioning systems that can help reduce the chance of trust violations.

This lack of effective systems for fostering trust worthiness carries several social implications, the most notable involves violations of consent. Greater use of mobile dating apps for hookups may lead to an increased perception of the legitimacy, inevitability, and acceptability to violations of consent. Consent violations may become seen by both victims and perpetrators as just another "occupational hazard" that inevitably accompanies sexual life in a digitally facilitated hook up culture.

Reduction in Commitment and Degradation in Quality of Relationships

Central features of mobile dating apps include the low cost of searching for matches, high availability of potential partners, rapid communication, and the capacity for communicating with many possible matches concurrently. Similarly, even when one is currently involved with one partner, the app makes users well aware of the availability of many potential new matches. Mobile dating apps facilitate quicker initiation of relationships and shorter time horizons compared to online dating and especially with traditional methods of findings romantic partners (like those that arise organically from social interaction in work, organizations, and avocations).

Attributes of relationships such as commitment, dedication, and solidarity depend upon the parties involved as well as the social context in which such relationships are formed. From the perspective of social exchange (Emerson 1976) the more dependent a person is on a partner the stronger their commitment will be. Conversely, when alternative sources are readily available exchange partners are likely to feel weak commitment, and relationship partners will feel less solidarity with each other (Hechter 1988). This implies that the availability of new partners and rapid development of intimacy will undermine the quality of the relationships that are likely to develop in the mobile dating app context.

Some users of mobile dating apps recognize that rapid temporality of relationship formation and the availability of close alternatives seems to degrade the quality of relationships formed. Yeo and Fun (2016) focused on young gay men using a dating app in Hong Kong, collecting in-depth interviews and focus group discussions from 74 participants. They found that the platform and the message alert system decreased the time between communications, raising the tempo of interactions and prompting users to transition rapidly from matching, to chatting, to having sex (2016, 2). Users contrasted their experience with the mobile dating apps to more traditional format online dating and remarked that the speed of the mobile dating system reduced their capacity to get to know their partners, and which turn made their relationships feel less special. Users also recognized that the focus on photos and rapid response altered the structure of courtship in ways that skip the process of forming a friendship, and therefore, the instantaneity of the relationship made it less stable. This is consistent with expectations from identity theory where commitment generally (to organizations, activities and relationships) depends on the range of identity relevant roles that are enacted in that relation. With only one relevant dimension (sex / hotness), commitment levels in hookup relationships are not likely to become strong. Yeo and Fun (2016, 4) suggested that rapid relationships formed on the basis of physical attraction are not expected to last.

Distortions of Behavior and Conflict about Social Norms

What is acceptable? What types of actions are normative in a given context? Which are deplorable and which are worthy of esteem? These questions are answered through fundamental processes of socialization, social learning, and contestations of norms. Increasingly these processes are embedded in the broader social context of the electrified interaction order (Smith, 2009). The electrified interaction order includes mobile dating apps and extends far beyond to everything from text messages to blog posts and can combine in ways that create unexpected risks as well as opportunities.

Social norms are learned through social interaction in the context of roles (Korte, 2009). Mobile dating apps create a virtual social space where users can witness self-presentations of others and develop a sense of norms and expectations through interaction. Screenshots and other records of interactions provide evidence of attempted interactions, and these can be viewed as evidence of what is acceptable, and by others as a target of approval or for public shaming and informal social control. These instances, to the extent that they draw attention and are shared with others. can contribute disproportionately to perceptions of what is common or normal (Tversky & Kahneman, 1973). We know that memes, urban myths, and false beliefs are spread and amplified through social media networks (Spitzberg, 2014; Bessi et al, 2015). We also know that there are many possible sources of cognitive and social biases that confuse us (Gilovich, Griffin, & Kahneman, 2002). So, the first risk of the integration of mobile dating apps with the electrified interaction order is that our perceptions are distorted, but we are not sure exactly how.

The second risk (and also opportunity) connects the risk of skewed perceptions with personal social networks. Use of the mobile dating apps and screen captures from app interactions can be interpreted as indicative of normative expectations and can weigh strongly on our decisions of how to behave even when those interpretations do not reflect what is actually common, approved or consistent with norms of our social network. In other words, depending on how our social networks are structured we can easily conclude that behaviors that are rare are actually common, and behaviors that are deeply problematic are accepted and even respected. The principle of homophily in social networks (people seeking self-similarity on beliefs and values) can lead to an echo chamber and distorted perceptions about the general distribution of beliefs (Del Vicario et al., 2016; Boutyline & Willer, 2017). The combination of social learning and embedded learning in social networks implies that the way we learn about dating and hookup norms is likely to result in contingently varied patterns and possible conflicts between users with contrasting social networks. On the positive side, this implies that people with social networks that emphasize compassion and respect are likely to have those behaviors reinforced through their networks. The negative side is that those with exploitative, manipulative and dishonest exemplars in their networks are susceptible to having those behaviors promoted and adopted.

The third risk/opportunity arises from the formation of communities and social movements related to issues of sex and dating. A social risk that arises from the socially mediated context of hooking up is the development of communities that use evidence of interactions from mobile dating apps to reinforce misogynistic, exploitive, and predatory ideologies. These sub-cultural groups increase the risk of assault and non-consensual acts in the context of mobile dating app use. Almog and Kaplan (2017) describe the situation of young masculinity existing in Guyland (Kimmel 2008), where white, single, middle class men exist in a hedonistic obligation free lifestyle of recreation and consumption (2017: 28). In this context, socially awkward nerds are attracted to online communities with "seduction workshops" that cater to nerds and encourage them to see courtship as solved by a dehumanizing and exploitative gaming logic.

On the side of opportunities, users have created 3rd party resources for presenting and sanctioning negative behaviors for the purpose of awareness raising and public demonstration of negative sanctions. Vitis and Gilmour (2017) describe how an Instagram art project, Instagranniepants, and similar systems for public shaming of harassment, contradict the image of women as passive victims of technologically facilitated violence.

The final type of risk/opportunity of mobile dating apps relating to community and norms arises from the opportunity to experience a sense of community through the app itself. For some same sex app users, the mobile dating app social space can become the only social context where they are able to witness others and interact in a manner consistent with their identity (Blackwell et al, 2018). This is especially true for location based mobile dating apps where the population of users is limited, such as gay men participating in Grindr while living in relatively small and isolated towns. Because awareness of community held norms and expectations are developed informally through social interaction, the mobile dating app context might be the only "gay space" for app users to interact.

This opportunity to manage normative expectations extends to the use of the mobile dating apps. Mobile dating apps allow users to see the types of relationships they prefer, and conflict can arise when users differ in terms of what types of relationships they seek and how they should present themselves while seeking those relationships. While some mobile dating app users are not interested in developing longer term commitments, users are motivated by a range of relationship goals, and even some of those intending to hook up may develop into a more committed relationship (Timmermans & Courtois, 2018; LeFebvre, 2018). This can lead to conflicts between users who see mobile dating apps simply as a way to find quick partners for sex, and those that are trying to find a friend or date. This tension is well-articulated by one user who reported, "I get a little frustrated . . . when there are these guys who sort of pretend like this is something like you're supposed to meet like friends or like find dates and that sort of thing. I'm sure there are guys who use it for that, but the fact of the matter is that the majority of people on there are to fuck" (Blackwell et al 2014: 12). Users of apps have developed signals and shorthand to help others quickly identify if this user is primarily interested in long term relationships, or in short term sex (Teo & Fun 2016; Blackwell et al 2014). As apps evolve and develop to serve different populations with different motivations for mobile dating, these motivational tensions may be relieved either through community or design innovations.

CONCLUSION

Emerging adults are active seekers of opportunities to build identity and to explore relationships and sexual experiences in hookup culture. Mobile dating and hookup apps provide efficient and user-friendly channels to deepen their potential partner pools and to experiment with coupling rituals. The efficiency and excitement of mobile dating, however, is not without potential risks. Routine activities approach is a useful theoretical lens for imagining the sources of vulnerability for app users. First, researchers have demonstrated that some users, especially young women, face harassment and deceptive presentation tactics through app interaction. And some studies suggest that antisocial app users (i.e., motivated offenders) may be drawn to mobile dating and hookup mechanisms because of the deep pool of suitable human targets and the anonymous nature of digital hookup settings.

Furthermore, while studies have produced inconsistent findings, some researchers have found that mobile dating app users are higher-than-average risk takers, providing offenders with a steady stream of suitable targets. Moreover, mobile dating/hookup rituals generally take place outside of the purview of capable guardianship. Thus, antisocial behaviors may go unchecked when predators harass and objectify app users and guardianship may be strategically minimized by motivated offenders when they track other users through geolocation tools or arrange to meet matches in isolated social spaces. That being said, while media reports frequently publish high profile stories of victimization, few studies have attempted to document the prevalence of stalking victimization or sexual assault that results from mobile dating practices. The true risks of app-facilitated sexual violence, then, are currently unknown. Thus, more systematic research attempts to estimate the risk of sexual assault to mobile dating/hookup app users are needed.

Furthermore, this chapter attempted to theorize more broadly about the general social risks of mobile dating. First, we suggest that increasing patterns of dating/hookup app use could result in the degradation of authenticity and a systematic undermining of the capacity to trust. If deceptive practices become increasingly normalized as part of the mobile dating experience, users may come to expect that the social actors they meet in the digital world are prone to exaggeration and manufactured self- presentation and may feel obliged to distort their own identities in inauthentic ways. These practices may undermine our fundamental abilities to trust one another. These risks and conflicts originate in the unhealthy social dynamic that is inherent in the design of these apps. The lack of efficiency and perceived deception of users make finding a match more difficult and increases engagement with the application. And it is not in the best business interests of mobile dating app companies to make matching more effective. Other online systems designed to facilitate in-person interactions, such as eBay or Lyft, employ reputation systems that may help mend some of the structural shortcomings of hookup apps. Mobile dating app designers may respond to the deception existing in mobile dating by adding reputation systems or user grading features to amplify trust.

We also speculated that the growth of mobile hookup and dating practices could result in a reduction in commitment to stable social relations and to the degradation in the quality of relationships. The easy access and availability of new potential partners and the rapid development of intimacy could undermine the quality of the relationships that are likely to develop in the mobile dating app context. Mobile dating and hookup practices may also lead to distortions of behavior and social conflict about what counts as acceptable behavior. When users principally interact with those that promote the degradation of women and advocate sexual aggressiveness, for example, these attitudes may appear to be normative and socially acceptable and, thus, get produced and reproduced in these settings. Future investigators interested in the consequences of mobile dating and hookup practices might extend their research agendas to illuminate some of these broader social consequences of mobile dating and hookup trends.

REFERENCES

Albury, K., & Byron, P. (2016). Safe on my phone? Same-sex attracted young people's negotiations of intimacy, visibility, and risk on digital hook-up apps. *Social Media+Society, 2*(4).

Almog, R., & Kaplan, D. (2017). The nerd and his discontent: The seduction community and the logic of the game as a geeky solution to the challenges of young masculinity. *Men and Masculinities*, *20*(1), 27–48. doi:10.1177/1097184X15613831

Armstrong, E. A., Hamilton, L., & England, P. (2010). Is Hooking Up Bad for Young Women? *Contexts*, *9*(3), 22–27. doi:10.1525/ctx.2010.9.3.22

Arnett, J. J. (2000). Emerging adulthood: A theory of development from the late teens through the twenties. *The American Psychologist*, *55*(5), 469–480. doi:10.1037/0003-066X.55.5.469 PMID:10842426

Asongu, S. A. (2013). How has mobile phone penetration stimulated financial development in Africa? *Journal of African Business*, *14*(1), 7–18. doi:10.1080/15228916.2013.765309

Bauman, Z. (2003). *Liquid Love: On the frailty of human bonds*. John Wiley & Sons.

Berg, J., Dickhaut, J., & McCabe, K. (1995). Trust, reciprocity, and social history. *Games and Economic Behavior*, *10*(1), 122–142. doi:10.1006/game.1995.1027

Bessi, A., Coletto, M., Davidescu, G. A., Scala, A., Caldarelli, G., & Quattrociocchi, W. (2015). Science vs conspiracy: Collective narratives in the age of misinformation. *PLoS One*, *10*(2), e0118093. doi:10.1371/journal.pone.0118093 PMID:25706981

Beymer, M. R., Weiss, R. E., Bolan, R. K., Rudy, E. T., Bourque, L. B., Rodriguez, J. P., & Morisky, D. E. (2014). Sex on demand: Geosocial networking phone apps and risk of sexually transmitted infections among a cross-sectional sample of men who have sex with men in Los Angeles county. *Sexually Transmitted Infections*, *90*(7), 567–572. doi:10.1136extrans-2013-051494 PMID:24926041

Bhattacharya, S. (2015). Swipe and burn. *New Scientist*, *225*(3002), 30–33. doi:10.1016/S0262-4079(15)60032-X

Bisson, M. A., & Levine, T. R. (2009). Negotiating a friends with benefits relationship. *Archives of Sexual Behavior*, *38*(1), 66–73. doi:10.100710508-007-9211-2 PMID:17851750

Blackwell, C., Birnholtz, J., & Abbott, C. (2015). Seeing and being seen: Co-situation and impression formation using Grindr, a location-aware gay dating app. *New Media & Society*, *17*(7), 1117–1136. doi:10.1177/1461444814521595

Bogle, K. A. (2008). *Hooking up: sex, dating, and relationships on campus*. New York: New York University Press.

Boutyline, A., & Willer, R. (2017). The social structure of political echo chambers: Variation in ideological homophily in online networks. *Political Psychology*, *38*(3), 551–569. doi:10.1111/pops.12337

Bromwich, J. E. (2018, December 20). Tinder and Bumble Are Hungry for Your Love. *The New York Times*. Retrieved from https://www.nytimes.com/2018/12/18/style/dating-apps-tinder-bumble-content.html

Burgess, K. (2016). *Consumer survey: The best way to "swipe" a mate*. Retrieved from http://consumersresearch.org/consumer-survey-the-best-way-to-swipe-amate/

Chan, L. S. (2018). Ambivalence in networked intimacy: Observations from gay men using mobile dating apps. *New Media & Society*, *20*(7), 2566–2581. doi:10.1177/1461444817727156

Choi, E. P. H., Wong, J. Y. H., & Fong, D. Y. T. (2018). An emerging risk factor of sexual abuse: The use of smartphone dating applications. *Sexual Abuse*, *30*(4), 343–366. PMID:27698090

Choi, K. (2008). Computer crime victimization and integrated theory: An empirical assessment. *International Journal of Cyber Criminology*, *2*, 308–333.

Cohen, L. E., & Felson, M. (1979). Social change and crime rate trends: A routine activity approach. *American Sociological Review*, *44*(4), 588–608. doi:10.2307/2094589

Del Vicario, M., Vivaldo, G., Bessi, A., Zollo, F., Scala, A., Caldarelli, G., & Quattrociocchi, W. (2016). Echo chambers: Emotional contagion and group polarization on facebook. *Scientific Reports*, *6*(1), 37825. doi:10.1038rep37825 PMID:27905402

Downing-Matibag, T. M., & Geisinger, B. (2009). Hooking up and sexual risk taking among college students: A health belief model perspective. *Qualitative Health Research*, *19*(9), 1196–1209. doi:10.1177/1049732309344206 PMID:19690202

Duncan, Z., & March, E. (2019). Using Tinder® to start a fire: Predicting antisocial use of Tinder® with gender and the Dark Tetrad. *Personality and Individual Differences*, *145*, 9–14. doi:10.1016/j.paid.2019.03.014

Emerson, R. M. (1976). Social exchange theory. *Annual Review of Sociology*, *2*(1), 335–362. doi:10.1146/annurev.so.02.080176.002003

England, P. (n.d.). *Online College Social Life Survey, 2005-2011*. New York University [data file and codebook]. Retrieved from: http://www.nyu.edu/projects/england/ocsls/

Erikson, E. H. (1968). *Identity: Youth and crisis*. New York, NY: Norton.

Feldman, R. S., Forrest, J. A., & Happ, B. R. (2002). Self-presentation and verbal deception: Do self-presenters lie more? *Basic and Applied Social Psychology*, *24*(2), 163–170. doi:10.1207/S15324834BASP2402_8

Felson, M., & Cohen, L. E. (1980). Human ecology and crime: A routine activity approach. *Human Ecology*, *8*(4), 389–406. doi:10.1007/BF01561001

Felson, M., & Eckert, M. (2016). *Crime and everyday life*. Sage publications.

Fielder, R. L., & Carey, M. P. (2010). Predictors and consequences of sexual "hookups" among college students: A short-term prospective study. *Archives of Sexual Behavior, 39*(5), 1105–1119. doi:10.100710508-008-9448-4 PMID:19130207

Friedman, E. J., & Resnick, P. (2001). The social cost of cheap pseudonyms. *Journal of Economics & Management Strategy, 10*(2), 173-199.

Garcia, J. R., Reiber, C., Massey, S. G., & Merriwether, A. M. (2012). Sexual Hookup Culture: A Review. *Review of General Psychology, 16*(2), 161–176. doi:10.1037/a0027911 PMID:23559846

Gilovich, T., Griffin, D., & Kahneman, D. (Eds.). (2002). *Heuristics and biases: The psychology of intuitive judgment*. Cambridge university press. doi:10.1017/CBO9780511808098

Green, S. M., Turner, D., & Logan, R. G. (2018). *Exploring the effect of sharing common Facebook friends on the sexual risk behaviors of tinder users*. Academic Press.

Green, S. M., Turner, D. A., & Logan, R. G. (2018, July). Exploring the Effect of Sharing Common Facebook Friends on the Sexual Risk Behaviors of Tinder Users. *Cyberpsychology, Behavior, and Social Networking, 21*(7), 457–462. doi:10.1089/cyber.2017.0581

Guadagno, R. E., Okdie, B. M., & Kruse, S. A. (2012). Dating deception: Gender, online dating, and exaggerated self-presentation. *Computers in Human Behavior, 28*(2), 642–647. doi:10.1016/j.chb.2011.11.010

Hahn, H. A., You, D. S., Sferra, M., Hubbard, M., Thamotharan, S., & Fields, S. A. (2018). Is it too soon to meet? Examining differences in geosocial networking app use and sexual risk behavior of emerging adults. *Sexuality & Culture, 22*(1), 1–21. doi:10.100712119-017-9449-3

Hardin, R. (2002). *Trust and trustworthiness*. Russell Sage Foundation.

Hechter, M. (1988). *Principles of group solidarity*. Univ of California Press.

Hobbs, M., Owen, S., & Gerber, L. (2017). Liquid love? Dating apps, sex, relationships and the digital transformation of intimacy. *Journal of Sociology (Melbourne, Vic.), 53*(2), 271–284. doi:10.1177/1440783316662718

Hume, D. (2003). *A treatise of human nature*. Courier Corporation.

Kashy, D. A., & DePaulo, B. M. (1996). Who lies? *Journal of Personality and Social Psychology, 70*(5), 1037–1051. doi:10.1037/0022-3514.70.5.1037 PMID:8656334

Kimmel, M. (2008). *Guyland: The perilous world where boys become men*. New York: Harper Perennial.

Klinger, L. (2016). Hookup Culture on College Campuses: Centering College Women, Communication Barriers, and Negative Outcomes. *College Student Affairs Leadership, 3*(2), 5.

Korte, R. F. (2009). How newcomers learn the social norms of an organization: A case study of the socialization of newly hired engineers. *Human Resource Development Quarterly, 20*(3), 285–306. doi:10.1002/hrdq.20016

Landovitz, R. J., Tseng, C. H., Weissman, M., Haymer, M., Mendenhall, B., Rogers, K., ... Shoptaw, S. (2013). Epidemiology, sexual risk behavior, and HIV prevention practices of men who have sex with men using GRINDR in Los Angeles, California. *Journal of Urban Health, 90*(4), 729–739. doi:10.100711524-012-9766-7 PMID:22983721

Lauckner, C., Truszczynski, N., Lambert, D., Kottamasu, V., Meherally, S., Schipani-McLaughlin, A. M., ... Hansen, N. (2019). "Catfishing," cyberbullying, and coercion: An exploration of the risks associated with dating app use among rural sexual minority males. *Journal of Gay & Lesbian Mental Health*, 1–18.

LeFebvre, L. E. (2018). Swiping me off my feet: Explicating relationship initiation on Tinder. *Journal of Social and Personal Relationships, 35*(9), 1205–1229. doi:10.1177/0265407517706419

Levine, T. R. (2014). Truth-Default Theory (TDT): A theory of human deception and deception detection. *Journal of Language and Social Psychology, 33*(4), 378–392. doi:10.1177/0261927X14535916

Levine, T. R., Kima, R. K., & Hamela, L. M. (2010). People Lie for a Reason: Three Experiments Documenting the Principle of Veracity. *Communication Research Reports, 4*(4), 271–285. doi:10.1080/08824096.2010.496334

Loeber, R., & Farrington, D. P. (2014). Age-Crime Curve. In G. Bruinsma & D. Weisburd (Eds.), *Encyclopedia of Criminology and Criminal Justice*. New York, NY: Springer. doi:10.1007/978-1-4614-5690-2_474

Lopes, M. R., & Vogel, C. (2017, August). Women's perspective on using Tinder: a user study of gender dynamics in a mobile device application. In *Proceedings of the 35th ACM International Conference on the Design of Communication* (p. 12). ACM. 10.1145/3121113.3121220

Lutz, C., & Ranzini, G. (2017). Where dating meets data: Investigating social and institutional privacy concerns on tinder. *Social Media+ Society, 3*(1).

March, E., Grieve, R., Marrington, J., & Jonason, P. K. (2017). Trolling on Tinder® (and other dating apps): Examining the role of the Dark Tetrad and impulsivity. *Personality and Individual Differences, 110*, 139–143. doi:10.1016/j.paid.2017.01.025

Markowitz, D. M., & Hancock, J. T. (2018). Deception in mobile dating conversations. *Journal of Communication, 68*(3), 547–569. doi:10.1093/joc/jqy019

Mishna, F., McLuckie, A., & Saini, M. (2009). Real-world dangers in an online reality: A qualitative study examining online relationships and cyber abuse. *Social Work Research, 33*(2), 107–118. doi:10.1093wr/33.2.107

Monto, M. A., & Carey, A. G. (2014). A new standard of sexual behavior? Are claims associated with the "hookup culture" supported by general social survey data? *Journal of Sex Research, 51*(6), 605–615. doi:10.1080/00224499.2014.906031 PMID:24750070

Murphy, A. (2018). Dating Dangerously: Risks Lurking within Mobile Dating Apps. *Catholic University Journal of Law and Technology, 26*(1), 7.

Park, M. (2018, March 26). *Dating app dangers: is swiping safe?* Retrieved May 12, 2019, from The Daily Universe website: https://universe.byu.edu/2018/03/26/dating-apps-can-present-predatory-dangers-to-users1/

Petersen, J. L., & Hyde, J. S. (2011). Gender Differences in Sexual Attitudes and Behaviors: A Review of Meta-Analytic Results and Large Datasets. *Journal of Sex Research*, *48*(2–3), 149–165. doi:10.1080/00224499.2011.551851 PMID:21409712

Purcell, R., Pathé, M., & Mullen, P. E. (2004). Stalking: Defining and prosecuting a new category. *International Journal of Law and Psychiatry*, *27*(2), 157–169. doi:10.1016/j.ijlp.2004.01.006 PMID:15063640

Rafferty, R., & Vander Ven, T. (2014). "I hate everything about you": A qualitative examination of cyberbullying and on-line aggression in a college sample. *Deviant Behavior*, *35*(5), 364–377. doi:10.1080/01639625.2013.849171

Ranzini, G., & Lutz, C. (2017). Love at first swipe? Explaining Tinder self-presentation and motives. *Mobile Media & Communication*, *5*(1), 80–101. doi:10.1177/2050157916664559

Rayner, G. (2016, March 3). *Match.com rapist jailed for life as judge raises concerns about safety of dating websites.* Retrieved from https://www.telegraph.co.uk/news/uknews/crime/12181869/Match.com-rapist-Jason-Lawrance-jailed-for-attacking-women-met-on-dating-site.html

Reyns, B. W., Henson, B., & Fisher, B. S. (2016). Guardians of the cyber galaxy: An empirical and theoretical analysis of the guardianship concept from routine activity theory as it applies to online forms of victimization. *Journal of Contemporary Criminal Justice*, *32*(2), 148–168. doi:10.1177/1043986215621378

Rheingold, H. (2012). *Net smart: How to thrive online*. Mit Press.

Rice, E., Holloway, I., Winetrobe, H., Rhoades, H., Barman-Adhikari, A., Gibbs, J., ... & Dunlap, S. (2012). Sex risk among young men who have sex with men who use Grindr, a smartphone geosocial networking application. *Journal of AIDS and Clinical Research*, (Suppl. 4).

Rocque, M., Posick, C., & Hoyle, J. (2016). Age and crime. In W. G. Jennings, G. E. Higgins, D. N. Khey, & M. M. Maldonado-Molina (Eds.), *Encyclopedia of Crime and Punishment*. Hoboken, NJ: Wiley.

Sevi, B. (2019). Brief Report: Tinder Users Are Risk Takers and Have Low Sexual Disgust Sensitivity. *Evolutionary Psychological Science*, *5*(1), 104–108. doi:10.100740806-018-0170-8

Shapiro, G. K., Tatar, O., Sutton, A., Fisher, W., Naz, A., Perez, S., & Rosberger, Z. (2017). Correlates of Tinder use and risky sexual behaviors in young adults. *Cyberpsychology, Behavior, and Social Networking*, *20*(12), 727–734. doi:10.1089/cyber.2017.0279 PMID:29211500

Shirky, C. (2008). *Here comes everybody: The power of organizing without organizations*. Penguin.

Singh-Kurtz, S. (2018). *Dating apps are trying to spin your terrible dates as exciting misadventures.* Retrieved May 9, 2019, from Quartzy website: https://qz.com/quartzy/1500645/dating-apps-are-trying-to-spin-your-terrible-dates-as-exciting-misadventures/

Smith, A. (2016). *15% of American adults use online dating sites or mobile apps*. Retrieved from PEW Research Center website: http://www.pewinternet.org/2016/02/11/15-percent-of-american-adults-have-used-online-dating-sites-or-mobile-dating-apps/

Smith, M. A. (2000). Some social implications of ubiquitous wireless networks. *Mobile Computing and Communications Review*, *4*(2), 25–36. doi:10.1145/367045.367049

Smith, M. A. (2009, February 18). Electrification of the interaction order, or, eGoffman. *Connected Action*.

Spitzberg, B. H. (2014). Toward a model of meme diffusion (M3D). *Communication Theory*, *24*(3), 311–339. doi:10.1111/comt.12042

Sprankles, J. (2015, October 26). *The Most Common Abuse On Tinder Faced by Women Is Truly Revolting — INFOGRAPHIC*. Retrieved May 12, 2019, from https://www.bustle.com/articles/119408-the-most-common-abuse-on-tinder-faced-by-women-is-truly-revolting-infographic

Sumter, S. R., Vandenbosch, L., & Ligtenberg, L. (2017). Love me Tinder: Untangling emerging adults' motivations for using the dating application Tinder. *Telematics and Informatics*, *34*(1), 67–78. doi:10.1016/j.tele.2016.04.009

Tang, D. T. S. (2017). All I get is an emoji: Dating on lesbian mobile phone app Butterfly. *Media Culture & Society*, *39*(6), 816–832. doi:10.1177/0163443717693680

Thompson, L. (2018). "I can be your Tinder nightmare": Harassment and misogyny in the online sexual marketplace. *Feminism & Psychology*, *28*(1), 69–89. doi:10.1177/0959353517720226

Timmermans, E., & Courtois, C. (2018). From swiping to casual sex and/or committed relationships: Exploring the experiences of Tinder users. *The Information Society*, *34*(2), 59–70. doi:10.1080/01972243.2017.1414093

Toma, C. L. (2015). Online dating. In C. Berger & M. Roloff (Eds.), *The international encyclopedia of interpersonal communication* (pp. 1–5). Hoboken, NJ: John Wiley & Sons, Inc. doi:10.1002/9781118540190.wbeic118

Toma, C. L., Hancock, J. T., & Ellison, N. B. (2008). Separating fact from fiction: An examination of deceptive self-presentation in online dating profiles. *Personality and Social Psychology Bulletin*, *34*(8), 1023–1036. doi:10.1177/0146167208318067 PMID:18593866

Tversky, A., & Kahneman, D. (1973). Availability: A heuristic for judging frequency and probability. *Cognitive Psychology*, *5*(2), 207–232. doi:10.1016/0010-0285(73)90033-9

U.S. Dating Website or App Usage by Age Group. (2019). Retrieved from Statista: www.statista.com/statistics/310344/us-online-dating-app-site-usage-age/

Uteda, A. (2017). *Young Gay Adults' Personal Engagement with Contemporary Hookup Culture Through the Use of Mobile Apps*. Unpublished M.A. thesis.

Vander Ven, T. (2011). *Getting wasted: why college students drink too much and party so hard*. New York: New York University Press.

Vitis, L., & Gilmour, F. (2017). Dick pics on blast: A woman's resistance to online sexual harassment using humour, art and Instagram. *Crime, Media, Culture*, *13*(3), 335–355. doi:10.1177/1741659016652445

Wade, L. (2017). *American Hookup: The New Culture of Sex on Campus*. W.W. Norton & Company, Inc.

Widman, L., Welsh, D. P., McNulty, J. K., & Little, K. C. (2006). Sexual Communication and Contraceptive Use in Adolescent Dating Couples. *The Journal of Adolescent Health*, *39*(6), 893–899. doi:10.1016/j.jadohealth.2006.06.003 PMID:17116521

Yeo, T. E. D., & Fung, T. H. (2016, July). Relationships form so quickly that you won't cherish them: mobile dating apps and the culture of instantaneous relationships. In *Proceedings of the 7th 2016 International Conference on Social Media & Society* (p. 2). ACM. 10.1145/2930971.2930973

ENDNOTES

1. This quote, sometimes attributed to George Burns, was probably coined by someone else. https://quoteinvestigator.com/2011/12/05/fake-honesty/
2. It is worth noting that 'free' social services like mobile dating apps have no incentive for reducing this cost for users. In fact, to the extent that deception and inefficient matching increases engagement in the app the use generates more contextual data which creates more monetary benefits for the app makers.

Chapter 5
Depictions of Intimate Partner Violence:
Responses of College-Aged Youth to the Music Video "Love the Way You Lie"

Jonel Thaller
Ball State University, USA

Megan Lindsay Brown
Arizona State University, USA

Jill Theresa Messing
Arizona State University, USA

ABSTRACT

The music video for Eminem and Rihanna's hit single "Love the Way You Lie" (2010) reproduces commonly held myths about intimate partner violence (IPV), primarily that many women instigate their abuse or even enjoy it. Music video culture has been of concern to parents, researchers, and policymakers because youth are considered developmentally susceptible to gendered sexual scripts. However, some scholars suggest that audience members, rather than being passive consumers, are practical actors who filter information according to first- and secondhand experiences. This study examined how young adults' respond to the depiction of IPV in the music video for "Love the Way You Lie." Findings indicated strong emotional response, a tendency to filter media through personal experiences, and a continuation of gendered blame. However, participants also demonstrated critical analysis. Thus, even when depictions are sensational or reinforce myth-based beliefs and gendered biases, young adults are capable of being critical consumers of popular culture.

DOI: 10.4018/978-1-7998-1063-6.ch005

INTRODUCTION

Intimate partner violence (IPV) has been described as a significant public health issue with serious health and mental health outcomes (Black et al., 2011). In the United States, 1 in 3 women and 1 in 4 men have reported ever experiencing rape, physical violence, or stalking by an intimate partner, and women are more likely than men to report multiple forms of abuse and to experience serious mental health consequences, injury, or death as a result (Black et al., 2011; Campbell et al., 2003). Women experience the greatest risk of IPV during the stage of young adulthood (18-29 years; Tjaden & Thoennes, 2000; Black et al., 2011), with as many as 78% of female college students reporting at least one violent incident in their current or most recent relationship (Helweg-Larsen, Harding, & Kleinmen, 2008). However, despite high rates of victimization, many young women do not engage in help seeking behaviors, partially due to feelings of shame and stigmatization (Helweg-Larsen et al., 2008; Henning & Klesges, 2002; Murray & Kardatzke, 2007). Worden and Carlson (2005) found that 1/4 of respondents in a public opinion survey in the United States believed that some women secretly desire to be abused. Likewise, both female and male university students in the US reported a common belief that victims are at least somewhat responsible for their abuse (Nabors et al., 2006; Peters, 2008). Notably, young women under the age of 30 were more likely than men of the same age to blame the victims (Waltermaurer, 2012). These beliefs can be detrimental because they lead to support for policy decisions that criminalize and/or withhold support for victims, placing them in increased danger (Policastro & Payne, 2013).

Berns (2001) has identified the perpetuation of *gendered shame* in relation to IPV, theorizing that an inordinate amount of blame and responsibility is typically placed upon female victims as a gendered form of social control. Women are held responsible for their own victimization because, for example, they "elect to stay" with their abusers. Some studies have found that education about IPV is associated with one's ability to distinguish myth-based beliefs from empirically based research evidence (e.g., Fox & Cook 2011; McMahon et al., 2013; Nabors, Dietz & Jasinksi 2006; Worden & Carlson 2005). An individual's first- or second-hand experience with IPV may also play a part. In her study of perceptions of IPV, Berns (2004) observed that individuals with first- and secondhand experience with IPV are more likely to understand the complexity of IPV situations and the needs of victims. In contrast, individuals with no first- or secondhand experience will likely acquire knowledge of IPV from various institutional ideologies or the media, both of which tend to reduce the experience of abuse to stereotypes rather than acknowledge individual experiences.

Activists have advocated for victims of IPV by working to bring visibility to the problem, but they have had little control over how the media or various visual or performing artists have represented this issue or how consumers have received the depictions. The hit single "Love the Way You Lie," released by Eminem (aka. Marshall Mathers) and R&B singer Rihanna in June of 2010, is one such depiction of IPV. The lyrics, sung by Eminem, describe a physically and emotionally abusive relationship and culminate with a chilling threat:

If she ever tries to fucking leave again

I'mma tie her to the bed

And set the house on fire

Rihanna responds with the chorus:

Just gonna stand there and watch me burn

But that's alright because I like the way it hurts

Just gonna stand there and hear me cry

But that's alright because I love the way you lie

I love the way you lie

This single was well-received, remaining #1 on the Billboard Top 100 list for seven consecutive weeks, and the music video, starring popular movie actress Megan Fox and actor Dominic Monoghan, amassed 6.6 million views on YouTube within the first 24 hours of release (Copsey, 2010). For anyone who follows popular culture, it is typically well known that Rihanna was violently victimized in 2009 by her boyfriend, Chris Brown, but the song's lyrics are also thought to depict Eminem's notoriously turbulent relationship with his ex-wife, Kim. Earlier in Eminem's career, he sang about wanting to murder his ex-wife and her new family, though he more recently re-emerged on the hip-hop scene with a more humanized and relaxed image following a biopic film and a series of memoirs. Public reactions to the music video for "Love the Way You Lie" varied widely, ranging from hope that it might raise awareness of IPV to concern that it might further normalize or even glamorize relationship violence (McCartney, 2010). While it could be argued, as Rihanna did, that the lyrics for "Love the Way You Lie" accurately portray the cycle of violence in a physically and emotionally abusive relationship (Access Hollywood, 2010), one could also argue that young people may not be sophisticated enough to understand that this behavior is something to be avoided, not emulated.

The ubiquity of the music video medium has led to inquiry about its potential effect on attitudes, behavior, and self-image of young consumers (APA, 2011). Some scholars suggest audiences are "practical actors" who filter information according to first- and second-hand experiences (Loseke, 2001; Berns, 2004), yet the extent to which individuals employ these experiences to trump popular culture and myth-based beliefs about IPV is debatable (Postmus et al., 2011; Black, Weisz, & Bennett, 2010; Fox & Cook, 2011; Peters, 2008; Nabors, Dietz, & Jasinksi, 2006; Worden & Carlson, 2005). Research has found an association between music video imagery that is sexually degrading to women and greater tolerance, by both males and females, of rape myths, stereotypical sex-role behavior, and IPV (e.g., Coyne & Padilla-Walker, 2015; Franiuk, Coleman, & Apa, 2017; Hyatt et al., 2017; Kalof, 1999; Peter & Valkenburg, 2007; Rhodes, Potocki, & Masterson, 2018). Moreover, because they offer concrete imagery, music videos can "play a major role in the transfer of ideas from the video world to one's own real-world situations" (Anderson, Carnagey & Eubanks, 2003, p.961). Youth are considered particularly susceptible to absorbing harmful sexual scripts because they are in the process of developing their values and identities, often through popular culture (Martino et al., 2007). Many youth are also developing intimate sexual or romantic relationships for the first time, and the health of these early relationships may influence emotional development, school performance, and the health of intimate relationships in adulthood (Arnett, 2007; Barry et al., 2009).

The depiction of IPV in the music video for "Love the Way You Lie" can be seen as problematic in several ways. In a content analysis of the video, Thaller and Messing (2014) observed a significant disjunction between the song lyrics and music video narrative. Most notably, Eminem threatens to burn his girlfriend alive within the song lyrics, but within the video narrative, the young woman is the primary physical aggressor and ignites the fire that engulfs their home. Thaller and Messing theorized that gender roles were reversed in the music video in order to render it more palatable to a large audience and to alleviate psychological distress that can result from acknowledging gendered inequalities, specifically the vulnerability of women to violence from men (Peters, 2008). In contrast, the young woman in the video is depicted as both the physical and sexual aggressor. She not only professes to love the way her partner abuses her, but she is also sexually aroused by their physical altercations—far from the typical "worthy victim" (Meyers, 1994) of IPV. This gendered reversal of roles, the sexualization of relationship violence, and the aesthetic depiction of fire within the music video all minimize the dire emergency of the ultimatum delivered in the song lyrics. However, content analyses of lyrics and music video imagery do little to elucidate how audiences actually receive and process this content. Thus, the next step in this research was to study audience reactions to the music video.

Method

The purpose of this study was to examine young adults' reactions to the depiction of IPV in the music video for "Love the Way You Lie." Qualitative research methods were employed to initiate an in-depth and contextualized understanding of the meaningful ways in which the young people received this content. Focus groups were used to allow the researchers to observe the participants communicating with peers in their own linguistic registers and to allow them to challenge each other's interpretations of the video content and perceptions and knowledge of IPV. Feminist research has relied on focus groups to provide a more authentic social experience wherein groups construct meaning and knowledge through peer interaction (Wilkinson, 1998), and young adults, in particular, rely heavily on peer interaction to make sense of their intimate relationships (Morgan & Korobov, 2012).

Sample and Procedure

A purposive sample of young adults (N=22, M=20.7 years, Range=18-23 years), evenly split between male and female, was recruited from a large public university in the Southwest US to participate in focus groups. The self-reported racial/ethnic identity of participants roughly mirrored that of the university, with the majority being Caucasian (54.5%, n=12) or Hispanic/Latino (22.7%, n=5). The remaining participants identified as Biracial, African-American or East-Indian. All participants were enrolled in college courses at the time of data collection and reported a variety of declared major areas of study. The sample was recruited via campus listservs, classroom announcements, public flyers, and word of mouth. The resulting sample was diverse in age, experience, area of study, and prior knowledge of IPV. Researchers stopped recruiting for the study when they felt that the sample had reached a point of saturation with phenomenal and demographic variation (Sandelowski, 1995).

Six focus groups, in duration of approximately 1.5 hours each, were conducted and audiotaped with IRB approval from the researchers' higher education institution. At the time of recruitment, students were told they would be participating in a study about media consumption and asked to view a music video with mild adult content. Each focus group interview, led by co-facilitators, began with a broad inquiry into participants' music consumption habits—their music genre preferences, how often and when they were most likely to listen to music, how often and why they might decide to view a music video, to what extent peers influenced their music consumption, and to what extent this consumption was likely to occur alone or among friends. Next, the researchers transitioned to more specific questions by asking participants to view the music video for "Love the Way You Lie." They then asked participants to discuss the content of the song and music video. More specifically, participants were asked whether they thought the music video presented an accurate depiction of certain types of relationships. When necessary, probing questions were used throughout the focus group interviews to encourage participants to clarify or expand on their statements and to dialogue with each other.

The majority of participants stated that they listen to music as a regular habit and often share recommendations with friends and siblings. More than one participant asserted that they listen to music "all the time." Most stated that they had heard the song "Love the Way You Lie" prior to the focus group session. Participants reported listening to a variety of music genres (including pop, hip hop, R&B, country, and heavy metal), but explained that the type of music they listened to on a particular day was usually related to an "emotion," "mood," or "something I'm going through." When elaborating on their music preferences, many participants noted that they did not always share the same taste in music as friends and family members—they insisted that they ultimately made their own listening choices despite social influence and current trends. Still, many participants reported that word-of-mouth was an important factor in determining whether they would take the time to look up and view a music video. They stated they might look up a music video if they really liked the song or had heard that the video was "interesting" or "funny." Several young men stated that they had already searched for and viewed the music video prior to the focus group session because it featured Megan Fox, an attractive young actress (GRP 2). In another group, a young man stated he had "clicked on" the music video because "there was fire and that kind of interests me" (GRP 6).

Plan of Analysis

Prior to analysis, researchers collectively reflected on their own biases regarding music genre preferences and performing artists, popular depictions of IPV, and the particular song and music video. After each researcher had written personal reflections about the preceding topics, all members of the research team exchanged reflections. During in-person and telephonic meetings, biases and reactions were discussed. A shared document recording the researchers' reflections was referenced throughout the data analysis process to minimize researcher influence and personal projections (Lietz, Langer, & Furman, 2006). Researchers then developed a codebook for analysis based upon participants' 1) reactions to the music video, 2) first- and secondhand experiences with IPV, and 3) perceptions of whether the music video depiction of IPV was helpful or harmful. Two members of the research team used the "Tracked Changes" function in Word to independently mark areas in the transcripts where themes from the codebook were present. The final codebook was compiled into a Word document and shared with the third researcher who independently reviewed these analyses for consistency (Lietz, Langer, & Furman, 2006).

Results

Most participants had heard the song "Love the Way You Lie" at least once prior to the focus group session. One young woman commented on the ubiquity of the song, stating, "This is typically the kind of song I would listen to on the radio while I'm driving. It's basically because I don't have a choice. They play it on the radio all the time, and I listen to it" (GRP 2). Several participants reported that they had previously sung or danced along to the song, enjoying its "catchy beat" (GRP 2). Regardless, many had not seen the music video prior to the focus group session. While viewing the video within the group, participants reacted with expressions such as "damn," "wow," and "that sucks." Further, they described the video storyline and imagery as "intense," "sad," "violent," and "graphic." One participant argued that the storyline was "Way too much for a music video…I didn't even know they were allowed to show stuff like that" (GRP 5), whereas another insisted that the video was not particularly "offensive or edgy or controversial," except maybe for "smaller kids" (GRP 6). Another participant described the video as "typical" and noted the tendency for music videos to be "shocking," especially those that are "kind of like a porno" (GRP 3).

Many noted that the depiction of relationship violence in the video made the song "even more powerful" (GRP4) and "intensified the meaning of the words" (GRP 6). One participant explained, "You'll sing it, but you really won't think about it…[seeing the music video] leaves a totally different impression on you" (GRP 4). Yet, regardless of its graphic content, a majority of participants reported that they held a mostly favorable view of the song: "I like this song because it's very catchy. The tune—I guess even the lyrics—they make sense. They tell a story" (GRP 2) and "As much as I'm totally *not* for domestic violence, I think this song is, actually, one of my favorite songs" (GRP 4).

Focus group participants identified IPV as a common experience within their generation, which may at least partially explain the song's swift popularity among youth. Many disclosed that they had experienced IPV either firsthand (as a victim/survivor) or secondhand (as a witness to IPV), and these experiences appeared to influence their responses to the music video. One female participant who had experienced IPV firsthand related to the volatile nature of the relationship depicted based upon her own relationship experience. She was able to identify and articulate the problematic consequences of emotional abuse, including its tendency not only to persist but also to escalate. She explained,

[It makes me think of] my past relationship—not that it was anything hard-beating and stuff like that—but me and my ex, we were like that. We would argue and then it was like "Oh, that was yesterday." It was like a bipolar mood swing…Now that I'm out of the relationship I just see it like this [type of violence] could have happened, but it stopped. (GRP 3)

Other participants similarly recalled firsthand experiences with IPV as a result of viewing the video, for example: "It hits close to home because I was in an abusive relationship" (GRP 4) and "Like, your little [relationship] bubble just bursts. It's not the whole fairy tale story. It's not this whole perfect world. Once you start going through all these difficult things in your life, that's when you start waking up" (GRP 4). For these participants, the pattern of abuse depicted within the video storyline held enough similarity to their own experiences to evoke strong feelings.

Study participants who had not experienced IPV firsthand also reported being able to relate to the video storyline through their secondary experience with IPV, and they reported feeling similarly strong emotion as a result of viewing the video:

It's such a relatable song...It's like even if you haven't directly been in that type of situation, it's like everyone either knows someone or has been. Even though I never was hit or anything, there's an emotional tie. Even if you haven't directly been in that, you can relate back to that song in some way. (GRP 4)

Participants reported knowing couples who had behaved like the couple in the video. One related, "Honestly, I feel that it's a lifestyle now, a couple being like that" (GRP 3). Another participant recalled helping a friend ("It got really bad and to the point where there was an intervention") and mourning a family member ("I also had a relative that went through the same experience, and it led to suicide") as a result of IPV. She reported, "Just seeing the video is emotional. It's just like all these past images coming up" (GRP 1).

Many participants also acknowledged that they may have known victims of IPV without realizing it. They stated, "I think people hide [an abusive relationship] because they feel like it may be their fault or that they brought it upon themselves. So looking at someone I wouldn't realize it just by first glance" (GRP 2) and "I don't think I've ever known anybody that has been beat like that, or I probably did but I'm not aware of it" (GRP 3). One young woman who reported that she had been a victim of IPV confirmed, "You can never really know the number [of victims] because many of the people will not report it because it's shameful. It's embarrassing. It's like, how can this happen to me?" (GRP 4). Additionally, many participants, even if they had no experience with IPV, expressed empathy for the couple depicted in the video: "I can see how you know that something is not healthy for you but you can't get out of it" (GRP 2). However, opinions were ultimately mixed regarding whether the music video depiction of IPV was harmful or helpful in creating awareness of IPV.

Positive Perceptions of the Music Video as Educational

Participants who perceived the music video depiction of IPV as realistic also tended to see educational value in it: "It's teaching people there is abusive relationships out there" (GRP 6) and "I think it's bringing awareness what these types of situations are, what it looks like" (GRP 4). Some suggested that the music video was educational for them specifically because they had no first- or secondhand experience with IPV. One participant explained, "Personally I don't know anyone who's had an experience with domestic violence [but] I know that it happens and stuff. This opens your mind to see that there's other kind of situations out there" (GRP 1). Likewise, another participant stated, "I've never personally experienced it—I've heard about it happening, but I've never experienced it happening with people that I know, [but] the way it's portrayed, it seems fairly realistic" (GRP 6).

Several participants compared the couple in the video to couples they had known. One stated, "Obviously [the relationship in the music video] was unhealthy, but I feel like a lot of people have relationships like that." She explained knowing couples who would make "a public display of violence, and then they get back together again within like half an hour...He yells at her and then she yells back, and it gets very heated and one of them hits the other. And then they're fine perfectly after that" (GRP 2). Other participants suggested, "It's just a very explosive relationship. That's relatable. That does happen a lot" (GRP 4) and "Obviously, they get their ideas to put on a television show or make this video happen from somewhere" (GRP 3).

Some participants perceived the video as educational for women in particular. Two male participants stated, "I think it's sending the message out that, if you're a female, don't go for the wrong guy. Females nowadays tend to go for the cruelest guys ever" (GRP 6) and "I think we should teach the ladies out there don't go for that guy because he drinks, he smokes, he hangs out with the cool kids…It actually teaches the young ladies out there" (GRP 1). Similarly, a female participant suggested that Rihanna's presence in the music video was to remind viewers that any woman, no matter how famous or successful, can become victim to IPV. She asserted, "Rihanna wasn't really part of the story [in the video]. She was just put in there for the warning part of it" (GRP 3). Another young woman noted the significance of Rihanna's presence in the video, given her history with IPV. She described Rihanna's involvement in the project as inspirational because "her face was messed up [but] that didn't let her down; she still came back. She started making more music. She became probably even more popular with the music video" (GRP 1).

One of the myths potentially perpetuated by the song and music video is that women enjoy being victimized by partners or that IPV is a normal part of relationships. However, for many participants, the depiction of IPV in the video seemed realistic: "I think it's just like a behind-the-scenes to like what really happens behind a relationship. The way they showed it was accurate, though a little over exaggerated. It's what kind of world we're living in right now" (GRP 1). One young man felt that the video was an accurate portrayal of a "revenge relationship" where "if this person did something, I'm just gonna do this just to make them feel mad or to make them do this. Then it just goes back and forth until someone just wants to stop and then let go of it. That's how I saw it" (GRP 6). In response, another young man in the group equated violence with passion: "They have passion towards one another and the fact that they're actually arguing and fighting means that there's something there. There is some sort of foundation, and so they just kinda see that raw passion—you know, displaying with their anger and punching holes" (GRP 6). In regard to the scene where the couple begins a sexual encounter during a heated and violent argument, several young women agreed amongst themselves that it seemed realistic "to be together and have sex like that after you guys just got through arguing" (GRP 3).

Negative Perceptions of the Music Video as Glamorizing/Normalizing IPV

Other participants expressed anger or disappointment in the music video because they felt it contributed to the normalization of relationship violence. One young woman, who identified as having been in an emotionally abusive relationship, argued that the normalization of IPV through popular culture could be disempowering for victims attempting to leave an abusive situation. She explained,

[The video] got me really upset because it's advertising domestic violence, and it's making it OK...He's bringing her a teddy bear, making her happy, and then hitting her. Then they're back to doing OK, they're making out—it's the whole cycle of it. It's making it OK, but it's not OK. I feel like I understand what she would be going through, but there's a point where it's like, "Enough." You don't need that kind of media making you feel even more powerless. (GRP 4)

Similarly, another young woman stated, "I feel like [the video] creates a culture where people think that [relationship violence] is an OK thing to do and an OK way to live your life." She explained,

I work at a domestic violence shelter, and it's very clear that women don't leave situations for a variety of reasons, [such as] lack of support. I think music and videos like that—it's just taking one more tool away from a woman who's in that situation because she feels like it's culturally accepted for men to do that and that maybe she's the anomaly. (GRP 5)

Other participants were unsure how the music video might impact individual behavior, but expressed concern about cultural effects, for example: "We grew up with some really soft stuff, and you get to the current situation where it's stuff like this. I mean, maybe it's not necessarily good or bad, but it is what it is, and we'll see if that adds to domestic abuse" (GRP 6) and "I don't think people see [the video] and they're gonna go do something like that, but you put something out there, and it becomes a part of the collective unconscious, and that's like it's making it OK to do that" (GRP 5). One participant suggested that media culture might even directly impact IPV prevalence. She said, "Maybe why there's a big teen dating violence problem is because they're seeing things like this, and they're like, this is normal" (GRP 4).

Participants who were worried about the individual and cultural impact of the music video depiction primarily voiced concern for its effect on children and adolescents. One participant stated, "It's fine that it's out there, but on the levels that they're showing it, it's kind of a bit too much for younger kids" (GRP 6). Many agreed that adolescents lack the experience and/or education to make good relationship decisions: "We're in college, we're trying to get an education. But who are [the media] really targeting? They're not really targeting us, they're targeting teenagers…[and] they act based on what they're seeing" (GRP 4). A young woman remarked,

I knew when I saw [the video], I didn't want [my little sister] watching it. They make it seem like it's OK to have a relationship like that. Like, "Oh it's all about love, and all of that goes with it." They make it seem like, it's violent, but then at the end of the day she takes him back, and they love each other, and what counts is the love. (GRP 5)

Likewise, another participant argued, "The worst thing is they're targeting kids that are like 12 and 13. My little sister is 12, so it's irritating to hear her sing those kinds of songs. It's disturbing" (GRP 3).

Several participants noted that having a boyfriend or girlfriend is often a status symbol in adolescence, but young people lack the experience to navigate relationship difficulties. One young woman explained, "High school's a total mess—junior high as well. Once you're able to get out of that, you actually see the world for how it is. That's when you're able to pick out what's real and what's not." She continued, "Every girl wants a fairy tale. The thing is, these girls haven't been through experience enough to be like, this isn't what's going to happen. [But] I feel like I've had my fair share of relationships. I know what's up" (GRP 4). The young adults in this group also expressed concern that adolescents learn primarily from popular culture because they typically reject relationship advice from adults and even older siblings: "You can give all the advice to them, but if they're not ready to take that stuff, then they won't. If they have not experienced what you're telling them, then it's not going to click in. Because it's unreal to them because they've never gone through anything like that" (GRP 4). Another young woman agreed, "I had a younger brother. It was like talking to a wall. He'd roll his eyes every time I tried to lecture him. I'm like, I'm trying to help you here, to save you some time and pain" (GRP 4).

Some participants also asserted that the music video "glorified" and even sexualized IPV, pointing out that Megan Fox "looked hot" even when her boyfriend was assaulting her (GRP 5). One participant observed that Rihanna was wearing "a little bra and shorts" while performing in the video and asked, "Why?" (GRP 3). Another argued that the song was "just another [music video] where Rihanna glamorizes dysfunction" (GRP 5). Only one participant noticed the significant discrepancy between how the song and music video portray the final act of violence, that Eminem delivers the line about setting his girlfriend on fire, but, in the video, Megan Fox actually ignites the fire (GRP 4). Participants who engaged in this level of deep analysis of the song and video typically mentioned college courses they had taken. For example, one stated,

I took a sociology class. We talked about feminism and the media. To me it's just kind of sad how when you look at those videos and you hear the music, they think we're tricks...I mean it's good music to dance to, but they make us feel like we're sex slaves, and we're just hos, and we need to do whatever they say. (GRP 3)

Another participant, who had taken a course in domestic violence, argued that the video's normalization/glamorization of IPV was problematic because then "a lot of people don't see certain things as abuse" (GRP 4).

Gendered Blame

The music video aroused strong emotion for most of the focus group participants. Perhaps the strongest and most common sentiment to emerge from both men and women was disappointment, disgust, and even aggression toward Rihanna. Many participants filtered their judgment of the video through their knowledge of the IPV incident between Rihanna and Chris Brown in 2009 as well as their impression of Rihanna as a performing artist. While at least one participant saw Rihanna as inspirational, most reported disapproval of her participation in the video: "[Rihanna] is an attention whore and—I'm very against guys ever laying their hands on girls or anything like that, *but* when I heard it was Rihanna..." (GRP 3) and "I didn't really give [Rihanna] much sympathy. I'm like 'You must've done something to provoke him.' It's just like 'Whatever. Rihanna can just get slapped'" (GRP 3). One young woman expressed an expectation that Rihanna would provide an accurate depiction of IPV, not only because she is a woman, but also because she herself had been a victim of IPV:

I feel like [because] she's a woman, she should be advocating for domestic violence [victims]. If the male is [misrepresenting abuse], it's more normal. But when you see a woman [misrepresenting abuse], it's just like, "What are you doing?"—especially because she had the whole thing with Chris Brown. (GRP 4)

Yet another participant argued: "I think she also has to be aware of the people, her fans, and the age. Because I think girls who would see her say, 'Hey, it's okay. I'm dating him again. Or I'm thinking about dating him again.'" She explained, "It's sending totally the wrong message. I think there should have been a consideration for all the people that do look up to her" (GRP 5).

Whereas Rihanna was assigned responsibility for preventing IPV, this task was not assigned to Eminem or men generally. In contrast to the high expectations and harsh judgment for Rihanna, both female and male participants were likely to express *admiration* for Eminem despite his known history of perpetrating severe psychological abuse, including public death threats, toward his ex-wife. It is possible that participants focused more on Rihanna's past than Eminem's because the incident with Chris Brown was more current than any publicized incident between Eminem and his ex-wife Kim. Still, participants seemed to be aware of Eminem's past behavior, stating "I think he's overcome a lot. People are always out to get him, but somehow he always makes a comeback" (GRP 2) and "He stepped off the stage for a while and then came back years later and had this big transformation. He's a different person" (GRP 5).

Another participant stated, "I think I really mostly like him because of how he talks about his daughter. Like how she's like his world and he'd do anything for her. I think that's really sweet" (GRP 2).

Eminem was also perceived as more authentic than Rihanna. For example, one participant argued, "[Eminem] actually writes about stuff that's going on in life. He's real. Rihanna, to me she's just like—a joke. But with Eminem I feel like it's coming from his heart, everything he says, cuz he's either experienced that or it's going on" (GRP 3). However, several participants argued that Rihanna had sexualized her image (becoming "fake") in order to achieve fame, for example: "I remember Rihanna when she first came out. She had dance songs, then she started getting crazy. She started getting weird. She's dirty now. I remember the old, innocent Rihanna" (GRP 2) and "She started very pop, very towards teenagers, compared to now where I think she's done a total 180…not really keeping in mind of the people that she's also brought in" (GRP 5). One participant lamented,

She does all these weird sexual things…like aggressively sexual. It makes me uncomfortable. I'll be in the grocery store, and S&M will be playing and there are like old people and children. I just—I want to be ten miles away from that situation. There's children around!" (GRP 6).

Another complained that Rihanna was always "touching herself" in music videos, stating "[Rihanna] is in her rights as a woman to do [her own music and performance], but I don't think she's being a very responsible artist by doing it. She will be so empowering and then she does stuff like that" (GRP 5). Eminem, however, seemed to be allowed to opt out of being a role model, for example: "I think he's always made it clear that he wasn't always a role model. He's always made it clear that, 'If you like my music, great. But don't look up to me or don't expect anything out of me cuz I am who I am'" (GRP 3).

The tendency to blame Rihanna for her victimization, and to so easily forgive Eminem for his perpetration, points to the existence of gendered blame, a phenomenon that is both a result and cause of male entitlement in a patriarchal society (Berns, 2001). However, at least one astute participant observed this discrepancy within her group and argued, "I don't think people give [Eminem] enough responsibility in the messages that he sends. I think Rihanna gets a lot more heat for the things that she says and does… I think generally men are held less accountable for their actions" (GRP 6). In another group, a young woman noted, "I think women always will have that stereotype—to be the good one" (GRP 5). Many noted that the expectations of women set by popular culture had become overwhelming. They maintained that "a lot of the media influences girls to want to fit a certain mold" (GRP 3). Several participants noted that women on television were required to be sexy: "It's almost like we're pieces of meat. It's all about looks. It's frustrating" (GRP 4) and "I'm trying to think of when I've seen a woman not be portrayed so sexual…I can't think of anything, but I feel that they've always portrayed us as pretty" (GRP 5). Another young woman remarked,

A couple years ago I was able to walk out of my house without makeup and feel pretty about myself, but now you have all these celebrities like Kim Kardashian, like these beautiful girls and guys are uploading pictures of her saying "I want my girl to look like that," and girls don't feel as pretty anymore. (GRP 3)

She added, "They feel like they have to look like this special someone to get everybody's attention" (GRP 3).

It is difficult to determine to what extent the participants' animosity toward Rihanna resulted from internalized sexism and gendered blame or an expression of disappointment that they do not have an adequate female role model to look up to. One participant noted that the over-sexualization of female performing artists was a popular culture trend in no way unique to Rihanna: "I think a lot of artists like her, they're taking it to a whole different level. They're just being too ridiculous with how seductive and how they dress up and how they portray themselves…being overly seductive, really sexual…in a gross way" (GRP 3). No doubt, the expectations placed upon female performing artists from both media producers and consumers are different than for male artists. In the case of Rihanna and Eminem, Rihanna bore the brunt of responsibility for educating the public about IPV, though focus group participants argued that her frequent displays of sexuality eroded at her personal credibility as a survivor.

Discussion and Implications

Rather than being immune to the sensational content of the music video for "Love the Way You Lie," the young adults in the focus groups generally expressed a strong emotional reaction to it. Many stated that they had known adults—their own parents or friends' parents—who had been in abusive relationships. Moreover, several reported that they knew other young people who had experienced relationship abuse or that they had experienced it themselves. Several participants noted that they had previously danced to or sung along to the song without actually considering the gravity of the topic or how it was depicted. Thus, they reported a more casual consumption of the song lyrics until the music video imagery depicting IPV was attached. The participants communicated a wide range of reactions to the music video in regard to whether it was an accurate depiction of IPV and could be educational in nature. This variation in opinion about the video among participants suggests that we should not assume young people are mere passive consumers of popular culture; rather, several factors in relation to a given topic influence how they interpret depictions. Further, during the focus group sessions, young people appeared to be comfortable expressing their dissenting opinions and constructively agreeing or disagreeing with peers. It is also important to note how willing these participants appeared to share their experiences as a whole, despite the sensitive nature of the topic. Young adults have a tendency to discuss their romantic relationships and the dynamics within them with their peers in order to make sense of their experiences; media, specifically its depiction of intimate relationships, is another common contributor to this ongoing discussion (Mackinnon et al., 2011). Those who saw the video as harmful were mostly concerned about its effect on younger adolescents. They stated that they did not feel that young people had enough experience to know the difference between reality and media sensationalizing. They concluded that life experience and education had led them to a better understanding of relationship norms and realistic expectations. Though some students were not quite able to articulate the cause of the discomfort they felt at the music video's portrayal of IPV, they demonstrated a capacity for beginning to explore these ideas through dialogue amongst themselves, even without heavy prodding from the focus group facilitators.

Findings from this focus group study demonstrate that young people actively filter their media consumption. In the absence of first- and secondhand experience, most will learn of IPV from the media or popular culture, where depictions are likely to be incomplete, inaccurate, and/or sensationalized. Likewise, health and mental health practitioners-in-training, may make sense of important issues, such as IPV, based upon common cultural assumptions or media images if they lack first- and secondhand experience with them (Dill, 2009; Berns, 2001). Although critical education is not the goal of entertainment media, educators can engage students and generate meaningful discussion by working within popular culture, rather than ignoring it., Excerpts from popular film can be used to examine attitudes, beliefs, and emotional reactions to difficult topics, such as IPV. This instructional strategy, referred to as *cinemeducation,* uses popular film to generate discussion and allow students to work through emotional responses (theirs and others) that arise from exposure to heavy topics, (Darbyshire & Baker, 2012; Lenahan & Shapiro, 2005; Membrives, Isern, & Mathau, 2016). Film and video have a unique pedagogical value in that it is typically consumed in groups and its imagery is intended to stir emotion and elicit thoughtfulness and conversation (Byrne, 2009; Collins & Carmody, 2011; Liles, 2007). Thus, by utilizing a format in which emotion is commonly accessed, students can receive an "emotional education" around these social issues, "enabling them to recognize and resolve complex personal reactions…to examine stereotypes and assumptions, and develop a more knowledgeable and humane attitude toward pervasive problems" (Lenahan & Shapiro, 2005, p.544).

Lastly, it is important to note the fervor at which participants, even young women, held Rihanna (but not Eminem) responsible for empowering young people to participate in healthy relationships. In a patriarchal society, it is not uncommon for women to shoulder the blame for IPV as well as the responsibility for eradicating it. Indeed, participants who perceived the music video as educational were likely to specify that this education should be directed toward women. These beliefs emerged within all focus groups, even without prompting from facilitators. Additionally, many young women expressed frustration about how women are portrayed in music culture and the consequences these depictions have on their treatment from men as well as their self-esteem. Participants lamented the sexualization of women in music videos in general, and expressed disappointment that Rihanna had turned toward the trend of over-sexualization for the sake of "attention." All in all, it appeared that the young people disproportionately blamed Rihanna and held her responsible; however, they also conveyed a desire for a strong female role model who did not buy into sexist demands from popular culture and who could advocate for equal portrayal and treatment of women. This finding supports the need for feminist constructions of relationships and sexuality where women are not held to impossible and contradictory expectations. Moreover, women's seeming inclination to act as avid agents of gendered blame requires closer examination (Waltermaurer, 2012). Though this finding may point to internalized sexism and group thinking, it is also important to note, again, that some participants did challenge myth-based beliefs about IPV and who is responsible for its perpetration. These results, taken as a whole, support the notion that young people are capable of critically analyzing potentially harmful depictions of IPV in dialogue with one another and in response to a video prompt. While popular media may sensationalize, reduce, or romanticize common social problems, this potentially harmful messaging around IPV can be used as a starting point for engaging in critical dialogue.

REFERENCES

Access Hollywood. (2010). *Access extended: Rihanna: 'I couldn't say no to Eminem' for 'Love the Way You Lie'.* Accessed January 22, 2018: http://www.accesshollywood.com/rihanna-icouldnt-say-no-to-eminem-to-record-love-the-way-you-lie_video_1240713

Anderson, C. A., Carnagey, N. L., & Eubanks, J. (2003). Exposure to violent media: The effects of songs with violent lyrics on aggressive thoughts and feelings. *Journal of Personality and Social Psychology, 84*(5), 960–971. doi:10.1037/0022-3514.84.5.960 PMID:12757141

Arnett, J. J. (2007). Socialization in emerging adulthood: From the family to the wider world, from socialization to self-socialization. In J. E. Grusec & P. D. Hastings (Eds.), *Handbook of Socialization: Theory and Research* (pp. 208–231). New York: Guilford Press.

Barry, C. M., Madsen, S. D., Nelson, L. J., Carroll, J. S., & Badger, S. (2009). Friendship and romantic relationship qualities in emerging adulthood: Differential associations with identity development and achieved adulthood criteria. *Journal of Adult Development, 16*(4), 209–222. doi:10.100710804-009-9067-x

Berns, N. (2001). Degendering the problem and degendering the blame: Political discourse on violence and women. *Gender & Society, 15*(2), 262–281. doi:10.1177/089124301015002006

Berns, N. (2004). *Framing the victim: Domestic violence, media, and social problems*. New York: Taylor & Francis.

Black, B. M., Weisz, A. N., & Bennett, L. W. (2010). Graduating social work students' perspectives on domestic violence. *Affilia, 25*(2), 173–184. doi:10.1177/0886109910364824

Black, M. C., Basile, K. C., Breiding, M. J., Smith, S. G., Walters, M. L., Merrick, M. T., & Stevens, M. R. (2011). National intimate partner and sexual violence survey. Atlanta, GA: Centers for Disease Control and Prevention.

Byrne, P. (2009). Why psychiatrists should watch films (or What has cinema ever done for psychiatry?). *Advances in Psychiatric Treatment, 15*(4), 286–296. doi:10.1192/apt.bp.107.005306

Campbell, J. C., Webster, D., Koziol-McLain, J., Block, C., Campbell, D., Curry, M. A., ... Sharps, P. (2003). Risk factors for femicide in abusive relationships: Results from a multisite case control study. *American Journal of Public Health, 93*(7), 1089–1097. doi:10.2105/AJPH.93.7.1089 PMID:12835191

Collins, V. E., & Carmody, D. C. (2011). Deadly love images of dating violence in the "Twilight Saga.". *Affilia, 26*(4), 382–394. doi:10.1177/0886109911428425

Copsey, R. (2010). Eminem and Rihanna break YouTube record. *Digital Spy*. Accessed January 22, 2018. http://www.digitalspy.com/music/news/a258634/eminem-andrihanna-break-youtube-record.html

Coyne, S. M., & Padilla-Walker, L. M. (2015). Sex, violence, & rock n'roll: Longitudinal effects of music on aggression, sex, and prosocial behavior during adolescence. *Journal of Adolescence, 41*, 96–104. doi:10.1016/j.adolescence.2015.03.002 PMID:25828552

Darbyshire, D., & Baker, P. (2012). A systematic review and thematic analysis of cinema in medical education. *Medical Humanities*, *38*(1), 28–33. doi:10.1136/medhum-2011-010026 PMID:22282424

Dill, K. E. (2009). *How fantasy becomes reality: Seeing through media influence*. Oxford University Press.

Fox, K. A., & Cook, C. L. (2011). Is knowledge power? The effects of a victimology course on victim blaming. *Journal of Interpersonal Violence*, *26*(17), 3407–3427. doi:10.1177/0886260511403752 PMID:21602202

Franiuk, R., Coleman, J., & Apa, B. (2017). The influence of non-misogynous and mixed portrayals of intimate partner violence in music on beliefs about intimate partner violence. *Violence Against Women*, *23*(2), 243–257. doi:10.1177/1077801216637473 PMID:26985047

Helweg-Larsen, M., Harding, H. G., & Kleinman, K. E. (2008). Risk perceptions of dating violence among college women: The role of experience and depressive symptoms. *Journal of Social and Clinical Psychology*, *27*(6), 600–617. doi:10.1521/jscp.2008.27.6.600

Henning, K. R., & Klesges, L. M. (2002). Utilization of counseling and supportive services by female victims of domestic abuse. *Violence and Victims*, *17*(5), 623–636. doi:10.1891/vivi.17.5.623.33714 PMID:12477102

Hyatt, C. S., Berke, D. S., Miller, J. D., & Zeichner, A. (2017). Do beliefs about gender roles moderate the relationship between exposure to misogynistic song lyrics and men's female-directed aggression? *Aggressive Behavior*, *43*(2), 123–132. doi:10.1002/ab.21668 PMID:27527124

Kalof, L. (1999). The effects of gender and music video imagery on sexual attitudes. *The Journal of Social Psychology*, *139*(3), 378–385. doi:10.1080/00224549909598393 PMID:10410622

Lenahan, P., & Shapiro, J. (2005). Facilitating the emotional education of medical students: Using literature and film in training about intimate partner violence. *Family Medicine*, *37*(8). PMID:16145628

Lietz, C., Langer, C., & Furman, R. (2006). Establishing trustworthiness in social work research: Implications from a study regarding spirituality. *Qualitative Social Work: Research and Practice*, *5*(4), 441–458. doi:10.1177/1473325006070288

Liles, R. E. (2007). The use of feature films as teaching tools in social work education. *Journal of Teaching in Social Work*, *27*(3-4), 45–60. doi:10.1300/J067v27n03_04

Loseke, D. R. (2001). Lived realities and formula stories of "battered women." In J. F. Gubrium & J. A. Holstein (Eds.), *Institutional selves: Troubled identities in a postmodern world* (pp. 107–126). New York: Oxford University Press.

Mackinnon, S. P., Nosko, A., Pratt, M. W., & Norris, J. E. (2011). Intimacy in young adults' narratives of romance and friendship predicts Eriksonian generativity: A mixed method analysis. *Journal of Personality*, *79*(3), 587–617. doi:10.1111/j.1467-6494.2011.00692.x PMID:21534965

Martino, S. C., Collins, R. L., Elliott, M. N., Strachman, A., Kanouse, D. E., & Berry, S. H. (2007). Exposure to degrading versus nondegrading music lyrics and sexual behavior among youth. *Pediatrics*, *118*(2), e430–e441. doi:10.1542/peds.2006-0131 PMID:16882784

McCartney, J. (2010). Eminem and Rihanna's brutality chic is a bit beyond me. *The Telegraph*. Retrieved from http://www.telegraph.co.uk/comment/columnists/jennymccartney/7957505/Emimen-and-Rihannas-brutality-chic-is-a-bit-beyond-me.html

McMahon, S., Postmus, J. L., Warrener, C., Plummer, S., & Schwartz, R. (2013). Evaluating the effect of a specialized MSW course on violence against women. *Journal of Social Work Education*, *49*(2), 307–320. doi:10.1080/10437797.2013.768484

Membrives, M. D., Isern, M. T. I., & Matheu, M. C. L. (2016). Literature review: Use of commercial films as a teaching resource for health sciences students. *Nurse Education Today*, *36*, 264–267. doi:10.1016/j.nedt.2015.10.002 PMID:26490325

Meyers, M. (1994). News of battering. *Journal of Communication*, *44*(2), 47–63. doi:10.1111/j.1460-2466.1994.tb00676.x

Morgan, E. M., & Korobov, N. (2012). Interpersonal identity formation in conversations with close friends about dating relationships. *Journal of Adolescence*, *35*(6), 1471–1483. doi:10.1016/j.adolescence.2011.09.005 PMID:21986354

Murray, C., & Kardatzke, K. (2007). Dating violence among college students: Key issues for college counselors. *Journal of College Counseling*, *10*(1), 79–89. doi:10.1002/j.2161-1882.2007.tb00008.x

Nabors, E. L., Dietz, T. L., & Jasinski, J. L. (2006). Domestic violence beliefs and perceptions among college students. *Violence and Victims*, *21*(6), 779–795. doi:10.1891/0886-6708.21.6.779 PMID:17220019

Peter, J., & Valkenburg, P. M. (2007). Adolescents' exposure to a sexualized media environment and their notions of women as sex objects. *Sex Roles*, *56*(5-6), 381–395. doi:10.100711199-006-9176-y

Peters, J. (2008). Measuring myths about domestic violence: Development and initial validation of the domestic violence myth acceptance scale. *Journal of Aggression, Maltreatment & Trauma*, *16*(1), 1–21. doi:10.1080/10926770801917780

Policastro, C., & Payne, B. K. (2013). The blameworthy victim: Domestic violence myths and the criminalization of victimhood. *Journal of Aggression, Maltreatment & Trauma*, *22*(4), 329–347. doi:10.1080/10926771.2013.775985

Postmus, J. L., McMahon, S., Warrener, C., & Macri, L. (2011). Factors that influence attitudes, beliefs, and behaviors of students toward survivors of violence. *Journal of Social Work Education*, *47*(2), 303–319. doi:10.5175/JSWE.2011.200900122

Rhodes, N., Potocki, B., & Masterson, D. S. (2018). Portrayals of intimate partner violence in music videos: Effects on perceptions of IPV warning signs. *Media Psychology*, *21*(1), 137–156. doi:10.1080/15213269.2016.1267648

Sandelowski, M. (1995). Sample size in qualitative research. *Research in Nursing & Health*, *18*(2), 179–183. doi:10.1002/nur.4770180211 PMID:7899572

Thaller, J., & Messing, J. T. (2014). (Mis) Perceptions around intimate partner violence in the music video and lyrics for "Love the Way You Lie.". *Feminist Media Studies, 14*(4), 623–639. doi:10.1080/14680777.2013.826267

Tjaden, P., & Thoennes, N. (2000). *Full report of the prevalence, incidence, and consequences of violence against women series: Research report.* Atlanta, GA: Centers for Disease Control and Prevention.

Waltermaurer, E. (2012). Public justification of intimate partner violence: A review of the literature. *Trauma, Violence & Abuse, 13*(3), 167–175. doi:10.1177/1524838012447699 PMID:22643069

Wilkinson, S. (1998). Focus groups in feminist research: Power, Interaction, and the Co-construction of meaning. *Women's Studies International Forum, 21*(1), 111–125. doi:10.1016/S0277-5395(97)00080-0

Worden, A. P., & Carlson, B. E. (2005). Attitudes and beliefs about domestic violence: Results of a public opinion survey II. Beliefs about causes. *Journal of Interpersonal Violence, 20*(10), 1219–1243. doi:10.1177/0886260505278531 PMID:16162487

Chapter 6
The Trouble With Tinder:
Emerging Adults With Disabilities Dating Online

Elizabeth Mazur
Penn State Greater Allegheny, USA

ABSTRACT

Although research indicates that almost all emerging adults in the U.S. use the internet, little is known about the online dating experiences of persons with disabilities. Particularly in developed countries, online dating currently accounts for a substantial proportion of the initiation of romantic relationships and promises numerous advantages for persons with disabilities. Online dating includes a way to escape disability stigma, at least initially, access to a wide network of potential partners, and a convenient, private, and efficient method of meeting them. Online daters can be strategic in how they present both themselves and their disabilities, the manner in which they communicate with potential partners, and whether they join a large, popular dating site or a specialized disability-oriented one. The chapter discusses how the nine-step process of online dating might differ for or challenge emerging adults with various types of disabilities, sharing relevant research and media examples when available. The implications of popular mobile dating apps are also considered.

INTRODUCTION

Being upfront about my disability on Tinder and other dating sites has liberated me (Ladau, 2017).

According to the Census Bureau, in 2014 approximately 14.4% of Americans ages 18 to 24 had some type of disability and about 7.7% had a severe disability (Taylor, 2018). Although dating during emerging adulthood is an important part of building long-term relationships (Holmes, Brown, Shafer, & Stoddard, 2017), research suggests that emerging adults with disabilities may have more difficulty dating and finding romantic and sexual partners than do their peers without disabilities (Miller, Chen, Glover-Graf, & Kranz, 2009; Wiegerink, Roebroeck, Donkervoort, Stam, & Cohen-Kettenis, 2006).

DOI: 10.4018/978-1-7998-1063-6.ch006

This is distressing and unfortunately ironic because the quality of close relationships strongly contributes to physical health and longevity (Holt-Lunstad, Robles, & Sbarra, 2017; Pietromonaco & Collins, 2017). College students in committed romantic relationships also experience fewer mental health problems (Braithwaite, Delevi, & Fincham, 2010). Similarly, for a community sample of racially diverse sexual minority youth, initially ages 16 to 20, being in a romantic relationship promoted mental health for many participants over a five year period, especially those who were Black and/or gay (Whitton, Dyar, Newcomb, & Mustanski, 2018). Furthermore, emerging adults report spending more time with romantic partners than with friends, and they are significantly more likely than adolescents to consider their partner a source of influence and reference (Giordano, Longmore, Schroeder, & Seffrin, 2008).

The challenges forming longterm romantic relationship are demonstrated by low marriage rates among people with disabilities (PWDs). Overall, just 41% of U.S. adults with disabilities are married as compared to 52% of adults without disabilities. For persons between ages 18 and 34, the percent never married among those with disabilities is 74% as compared to 65% for their peers without disabilities (Schur, Kruse, & Blanck, 2013). The marriage rate for PWDs over the life span is lower as well. According to the 2010 U.S. Census, just 41% of U.S. adults ages 18 and older with disabilities are married as compared to 52% of U.S. adults without disabilities (Schur et al., 2013). Data over the last two decades indicate that this disparity in U.S. marriage rates by disability status has been increasing (Tumin, 2016).

Not all types of disabilities have a similar influence on people's chances of getting married. Using data from the National Longitudinal Study of Adolescent Health, MacInnes (2011) found that among individuals between the ages of 24 and 32 in the U.S., 43% of individuals with learning disabilities, 37% of those with mental disabilities, and 21% of those with multiple disabilities reported having experienced a first marriage as compared to 53% of their peers with physical disabilities and 50% of those without disabilities. In the National Longitudinal Transition Study-2, marriage rates eight years after high school graduation ranged from 1% for U.S. emerging adults with Autism Spectrum Disorder (ASD) or multiple disabilities to 11% for those with mental retardation, emotional disturbances, hearing impairment, or traumatic brain injury, 13% for those with speech/language impairment, and 15% for those with other health impairments and with learning disabilities (Newman et al., 2011).

PWDs in Western nations also are less likely than those without disabilities to socialize with friends, relatives, or neighbors (McDonald, 2010; Pfeiffer & Pinquart, 2011;Wiegerink et al., 2006). Disabled children and adolescents are less likely than their peers without disabilities to engage in developmentally appropriate social endeavors outside of school, such as dating and organized and informal peer group activities (Feragen, Stock, Sharratt, & Kvalem, 2016; Nosek, Howland, Rintala, Young, & Chanpong, 2001; Pinquart & Pfeiffer, 2012). These activities create opportunities for adolescents and emerging adults to feel socially accepted, to develop romantic relationships, and to learn helpful social skills, such as flirting (Feragen et al., 2016; Shuttleworth, 2000; Wiegerink, Roebroeck, Van Der Slot, Stam, & Cohen-Kettenis, 2010). In addition, people without disabilities are often reluctant or unwilling to engage in a meaningful or intimate manner with PWDs and appear to hold negative attitudes and stereotypes, especially when the disability is severe or includes cognitive or psychiatric impairments (Miller, Chen, Glover-Graf, & Kranz, 2009).

Disabled women are much more likely to have problems finding and keeping partners than disabled men and women without disabilities (Gill, 1996; Howland & Rintala, 2001; Nosek et al., 2001). Gender and disability stereotypes interact in unique ways, especially when forming social judgments of women. According to traditional societal stereotypes, women with physical disabilities do not, and should not, engage in dating behavior, and they are typically considered asexual and ineligible for the attentions of those who desire a romantic relationship (Gill,1996; Howland & Rintala, 2001; Liddiard & Slater, 2018; Olkin, 1999; Pausch et al., 2016). However, the type of disability matters in terms of this desire. For example, research with American undergraduates found that they viewed women with intellectual disabilities as more physically attractive than those with physical disabilities, although students felt more comfortable with the idea of interacting with the latter (Coleman, Brunell, & Haugen, 2015). However, students' attitudes did not differ when judging men with the same two types of disabilities. In addition, culture and gender matter in terms of the perceiver; there is evidence that emerging adult American women have fewer stereotypes of PWDS than do American men and Asian men and women. In a study of male and female undergraduates in the U.S., Taiwan, and Singapore, American women showed the most favorable attitudes toward people with disabilities in the context of dating and marriage (Chen, Brodwin, Cardoso, & Chan, 2002). Similarly, a study of German professional students found that women were more likely than men to accept the idea of a spouse with a cleft lip, and acceptance also differed by professional background (Pausch et al., 2016).

One way that both men and women with disabilities may escape such stigma is to use the internet. Online dating, particularly in developed countries, currently accounts for a substantial proportion of the initiation of romantic relationships. Recent data by Pew Internet indicates that 27% of 18-24-year-olds in the U.S. have used online dating (Smith, 2016). Over half (57%) of Pew's respondents ages 18-24 knew someone who had used online dating sites or mobile dating apps, and 34% of them knew someone who had entered into a long-term relationship or marriage in which they had met their partner online. Furthermore, a majority of adult online daters considered the online dating experience to be positive; specifically, they agreed that online dating is a good way to meet people, helps people find a better match for themselves, and is easier and more efficient than other ways of dating.

There are many examples of how individuals with disabilities use the internet for social interaction and support. For example, online support groups offer social interaction for groups of PWDs, typically consisting of discussion forums specifically for the individual with the disability and/or their families and friends (Gozza-Cohen & May, 2012). For PWDs who are unable to leave home, have limited access to others with the same or similar disability, are challenged by learning disabilities, or who live in more rural areas, these online sites can provide emotional support and assist with building relationships with people with similar concerns and interests (Gozza-Cohen & May, 2012; Holmes & O'Loughlin, 2014).

Yet little is known specifically about internet use for romance by emerging adults with a disability. Research indicates that almost all (98%) of 18 to 29-year-olds in the U.S. report using the internet (Anderson, Perrin, & Jiang, 2018), and PWDs in this age group are likely to use sites that are popular with their peers and include persons with disabilities, such as Snapchat, Instagram, and Twitter (Smith & Anderson, 2018). For example, a study of adolescents in the Netherlands found that access to and use of the internet is similar between physically disabled and nondisabled adolescents (Lathouwers, de Moor, & Didden, 2009). A qualitative study in Sweden also indicated that young adults with intellectual disabilities use the internet in similar ways as their peers, mainly for social and romantic reasons (Lofgren-Martenson, 2008).

The objective of this chapter is to draw on the accumulated scientific literature on emerging adults' personal relationships, internet interactions, and online dating to consider how online dating might be similar or different for PWDs during emerging adulthood as compared to their peers without disabilities. Because there are only a handful of studies that directly address the topic of online dating for PWDs, and even fewer that include emerging adults, the author will often extrapolate from related topics to examine how Internet dating is likely to affect the process and outcomes relevant to the romantic relationships of PWDs. This literature spans multiple research domains such as clinical psychology, developmental psychology, social psychology, personality psychology, rehabilitation, sociology, communications, medicine, and computer and information studies. The chapter will culminate with an analysis of daters' progression through the nine steps of online dating.

BACKGROUND

A unique component of Internet interactions for emerging adults is that it allows them to play with their public persona, an important aspect of identity exploration while engaging with others (Mazur & Kozarian, 2010). More specifically, research suggests that such social interactions can be considered to a large extent as conscious public performance (Bargh, McKenna, & Fitzsimons, 2002, Mazur & Kozarian, 2010). And herein lie the opportunity and the challenges for PWDs; online, they need not reveal their disability unless or until desired (Gozza-Cohen & May, 2012), if they acknowledge it at all. Across all age groups, disability self-identification appears to be rare relative to the prevalence of health conditions (Bogart, Rottenstein, Lund, & Bouchard, 2017). The few empirical studies suggest that on the internet, young people with disabilities find themselves caught in a bind between concealment and disclosure, even when they consider their disability to be a natural part of their everyday lives (Soderstrom, 2013).

These issues of identity and representation come to the fore with online dating, which has been growing in popularity and acceptance among Americans over the past decade. Current data indicate that 27% of 18-24-year-olds have tried online dating, 22% report using mobile dating apps, and more than half of the users of Tinder, the most popular dating app in the U.S. and the world, are ages 18 to 25 (Bromwich, 2018; Smith & Anderson, 2016); however, one-third of adult online daters (of all ages) have never progressed to the date stage (Smith & Anderson, 2016).

PWDs have decribed how they can be strategic in the way they present themselves and interact on internet dating sites (Goodman, 2012; Heideman, 2014; Sykes, 2014). Results from research on this topic are similar; for example, most of the Swedish adults ages 18 to 31 years that Lofgren-Martenson (2008) interviewed reported that they presented themselves in cyberspace, typically on a popular virtual meeting-place called LunarStorm, without mentioning their intellectual disability. Many participants explained that they wanted to meet friends and partners without intellectual disabilities. Thus, they informed others only about their age, interests, and purpose for using the Internet.

Online dating offers other benefits in terms of finding romantic relationships for PWDs. One advantage is that online dating provides access to a wider network of potential partners who would have been previously unknown or inaccessible to PWDs; individuals do not need to leave home to find a potential date (Finkel, Eastwick, Karney, Reis, & Sprecher, 2012; Roth & Gillis, 2015). Furthermore, dating sites provide convenient computer-mediated communication as a way to learn about potential partners. However, these considerable advantages are mitigated somewhat by the strategy of introducing users to potential partners through profiles, which according to Levitin (2014) and Finkel and his colleagues (2012), typically fail to capture the essence of a person.

THE NINE STEPS OF ONLINE DATING: CHALLENGES AND DIFFERENCES FOR PWDS

For people with disabilities, dating is Mount Everest. (Olkin, 1999, p. 223)

In their seminal analysis of online dating, Finkel and his colleagues (2012) delineated a nine-step process of online dating. The remainder of the chapter will discuss in turn how these nine steps might differ for or challenge PWDs during emerging adulthood, including relevant research and media examples as available.

Seeking Information About One or More Dating Sites

The two strongest predictors of American adults engaging in online dating, being an Internet user and being single (Finkel et al., 2012), are likely to be as true of PWDs as people without disabilities; online daters typically have difficulty locating potential romantic partners (Finkel et al., 2012). According to personality research, adults who are more sensitive to rejection, and more specifically, emerging adults who fear being judged, are more likely to use online dating sites and mobile dating apps like Tinder, respectively, than those who are less sensitive and more extraverted (Blackhart, Fitzpatrick, & Williamson, 2014; Timmermans & De Caluwé, 2017). As the research about disability suggests, this vulnerability is likely to be grounded in reality for PWDs, especially for women (Coleman et al., 2015; Gill, 1996; Rintala et al., 1997)

In terms of garnering information, a British survey of internet daters ages 16 and older found that the most frequently mentioned sources of information about online dating were advertising seen on the internet and visiting an online dating website (Gunter, 2007). Users of online dating websites, especially women, were most likely to have considered using such services following a personal recommendation. For example, one 26-year-old British man explained in a news article, "I had felt a bit snobby about internet dating but some friends had tried it, so it felt less intimidating" (Urquhart & Fraser-Thoms, 2012, p. 11). Because research is lacking, one can only surmise that disability-only dating sites are promoted primarily by word of mouth rather than by mass advertising.

Registering for Dating Sites

There is little research available that has studied the decisions of emerging adults to choose one specific dating site over another. The general site, Plenty of Fish (POF), which claims "more dates, more relationships, more visits than any other dating site," suggests that adults will choose dating sites that their friends have used successfully when it asserts that the site visitor will "know of at least 1 person that has found someone on POF" (Plentyoffishmedia, 2015, para. 1). In Gunter's (2007) study of British dating site users of all ages, choice of dating service was influenced by cost, quality of contacts, and the potential number and variety of contacts a site may be able to supply. For women, the site's reputation and the preservation of anonymity were also particularly important.

The consideration for PWDs is whether to register for large, popular dating sites, such as OkCupid, Match.com, eHarmony, and Plenty Of Fish that include mostly people without disabilities, or to register with smaller free or low-cost websites that are aimed specifically at heterosexual and homosexual PWDs with a variety of disabilities. For example, the sites Whispers4u and Dating4Disabled target people with physical and mobility-related disabilities. In addition to targeting people with physical and mobility-related disabilities, Disabled Passions includes daters with chronic health conditions and depression. Other specialty sites include DeafSinglesMeet, NoLongerLonely for adults with mental illness, and POZ Personals for people who are H.I.V. positive.

The major advantage of such specialized sites is the commonality of disability. Research on disability friendship networks of adults of all ages has found that PWDs derive unique informational and emotional benefits from friends who also have a disability, and it need not be the same diagnosis (Silverman, Molton, Smith, Jensen, & Cohen, 2017). Also, as one man with H.I.V. explained, "Getting to know someone in an online community of people with H.I.V. allows relationships to form without the burden of the big reveal hovering overhead. Here everyone knows you have H.I.V., so it gets the barrier out of the way" (Barrow, 2010, paras. 12-13). However, other online users with disabilities believe that dating sites targeting different disabilities are limiting. Writing for *The Daily Beast*, Heideman (2014) noted that the women she interviewed believed that their disability should not restrict them to a smaller dating pool of only people with disabilities.

Finkel and his colleagues (2012) proposed that users' choose a particular dating site after conducting a cost/benefit analysis. For example, a user might ask himself or herself, "Do the benefits, such as efficiency, access to attractive potential partners, and the possibility of forming strong relationships outweigh the costs, money, time, and the potential awkwardness of having one's dating profile available to strangers?" (p. 15). It is unclear whether this type of cost/benefit analysis occurs among emerging adults with disabilities. Furthermore, this cost/benefit analysis might be impacted by other variables, such as gender, type of disability, and time since acquiring the disability. Gill (1996) suggests that heterosexual women with disabilities are often open to the idea of partnering with a PWD but that men with disabilities are often more interested in finding a partner without a disability. Olkin (1999) suggested that daters with early-acquired disabilities may have a fear of rejection based on real experiences with rejection in childhood, particularly during adolescence. Thus, while most emerging adults with disabilities will seek out dating opportunities, the choice of dating site appears much more fraught than it is for their peers without disabilities.

Strategically Creating a Profile and, Possibly, Completing a Matching Questionnaire

Strategic presentation is a challenging issue for many online daters, of whom 22% have asked someone else to help them create or review their profile (Smith & Anderson, 2016). Women are especially likely to enlist a friend in helping them craft the perfect profile. In particular, 30% of female online daters have asked a friend for help when creating a profile as compared to 16% of men (Smith & Anderson, 2016). Whitty (2008) found that crafting an attractive profile is considered important by nearly all online daters and that the physical image was more important than any other characteristic.

Research with people without obvious disabilities suggests that the information that online users present tends not to be entirely truthful, partly because people of all ages, consciously or not, typically engage in strategic self-presentation when constructing their profiles (Finkel et al., 2012). On an online Australian dating site, adults without obvious physical disabilities most commonly misrepresented themselves in terms of their physical appearance; this is the characteristic that daters most highly value in their potential partners (Whitty, 2008). Online dating sites that offer matching, such as eHarmony and Match.com, require users to complete extensive questionnaires that potential partners cannot view. One's answers can be crucial because such sites only allow users to view profiles of potential partners whom the algorithm declares, based on the responses, to be a match (Finkel et al., 2012). Online users' motivation for strategic presentation while completing these questionnaires is likely to be as strong as their desire to represent themselves well in their profiles.

The stakes for creating a "perfect" profile or questionnaire are likely to be high for PWDs, who are aware that people without disabilities tend to be socially uncomfortable around them. Americans often associate disability with charity campaigns, poster children, and telethons that depict people with disabilities as objects of pity. As Jaeger (2012) explains, "It is a rare person with an obvious disability whose personal interactions with new acquaintances aren't dictated by the expectations of being viewed as a pathetic wretch burdened by the disability, or an amazing overachiever who can serve as an inspiring story" (p. 150).

One's disability identity can be complex and varied. Extrapolating from research studying disability in the workplace, a dater's decision to disclose disability is unlikely to be straightforward. Even PWDs with visible disabilities might not disclose their disability if they do not identify as a PWD or they anticipate negative reactions from potential matches (Milbrodt, 2019; Santuzzi & Waltz, 2016; Sharratt, Jenkinson, Moss, Clarke, & Rumsey, 2018). Interviews with British adults with a variety of visible differences indicate that the moment of disclosure of their difference assumes central importance in their romantic life. Despite the conviction that telling a partner is very important, disclosures were characterized by uncertainty and anxiety regarding how, where, and when to do so and how that other person would react (Sharratt et al., 2018). Yet some daters strategically use disclosure as a way to avoid matches who would be unaccepting of their disability (Bennett, 2017).

An online dater's profile construction need not be a static process. Whitty (2008) found that online daters experiment with self-descriptions and photos to increase their success at attracting others to their profile as did Sykes (2014), who described his own online dating experience. He noted that after adding disability status to his Match.com profile, he received as much online attention as before the update yet felt more secure in the knowledge that people were interested in him despite his disability. It appears that constructing an online dating profile is, at least in part, an exercise in self-identity through the perception of potential partners' opinions. Milbrodt (2019), who compared profiles of men and women ages 20 to 45 on the sites Match.com and Dating4Disabled, noted that some PWDs highlighted their "normality", while other profiles could be "interpreted as disability awareness efforts (p. 93)". In contrast, Dating-4Disabled daters appeared to assume that potential partners would have a positive or neutral attitude toward disability, sometimes including in their profiles specific details about their impairment or clearly connecting their identity to disability pride.

Browsing Other User Profiles

Research on mate preferences in online dating has found that dating site users prefer partners who are similar to them on numerous attributes (Hitsch, Hortacsu, & Ariely, 2010). These variables include education level, ethnicity, race, religion, marital status, political views, smoking habits, the presence or absence of children, and the desire for a long term relationship. Women show a stronger preference than men for income relative to physical attributes, such as facial attractiveness, height, and body mass index, and they are less willing to date someone of a different race (Hitsch et al., 2010; Hwang, 2013; Whitty, 2008). There is little research about whether such preferences would differ for emerging adults with disabilities. In one study that addressed this topic, Pinquart and Pfeiffer (2012) found that German adolescents with visual impairments were less likely than their sighted peers to consider physical attractiveness and material resources when seeking a partner on an online dating site. Rather, they were more likely to consider emotional maturity as important for partner selection.

The concern for PWDs who use dating sites is likely to relate to being accepting of those with different disabilities than their own as well as evaluating others' profiles for likely acceptance of their disabilities. The anonymity of the Internet allows online users to be honest about what traits they are truly seeking in a partner. According to Barrow (2010), many of the almost 12,000 members of Dating4Disabled specify the types of disabilities they would accept when seeking a long-term relationship. Barrow (2010) quotes the head of member services, "Like anyone else, people with disabilities have different preferences. Someone with good mobility may prefer someone also mobile, others don't limit at all" (para. 19.).

People tend to be comfortable with the disability that they know (Wright, 1983); thus, emerging adults with mobility limitations might fear reactions from potential partners with cognitive or sensory disabilities, or might stereotype people with those disabilities in a way similar to daters without disabilities. Dunn (2015) summarized the research on this topic, revealing that attitudes of individuals without disabilities become increasingly negative as one moves on the continuum from physical to cognitive and mental health-related disabilities as well as the presence of other factors, such as the disability's perceived severity, visibility, contagiousness, and unpredictability. U.S. college students who were uncertain whether they would date a person who stutters reported that they would base their decision partly on the prospective partner's level of stuttering severity, in addition to personality, appearance, and intelligence (Mayo & Mayo, 2013). Unfortunately, there is no research that specifically studies the variables that attracts PWDs to view certain online profiles and not others.

Initiating Contact Through the Dating Site

As in traditional dating, online users' decisions regarding whether to contact potential partners are not random; users are especially likely to initiate contact with people who appear physically attractive or even more physically attractive than they, have similar interests and values as them, and are similar in age and educational attainment (Finkel et al., 2012; Kreager, Cavanaugh, Yen, & Yu, 2014; Whitty, 2008). However, this last variable of educational attainment may be complicated for PWDs. For example, the high school graduation rate, while increasing, still lags for students with disabilities (Heasley, 2019). PWDs in the U.S. also are half as likely to have a college degree or higher (20.4%) as people without a disability (42.8%, Taylor, 2018). Graduation rates also vary among those emerging adults with different disabilities. Eight years after high school, emerging adults with visual and hearing impairments were more likely to have attended college or university than those with emotional disturbances, ASD, other health impairments, multiple disabilities, or mental retardation (Newman et al., 2011).

Some online daters with disabilities may decline to initiate any contact with people with disabilities, viewing their decision as refusing to "settle" (Nemeth, 2000). Olkin (1999) argues that a PWD's decision to date a person with or without a disability can represent either self-acceptance or self-loathing. Similar to the decision to register for a large, popular dating site or a smaller disability-focused one, "neither choice is inherently right or wrong or better or worse" (p. 225), although Olkin believes that the decision is likely to be grounded in the dater's self-esteem.

Receiving Contact Through the Dating Site

According to the large online dating site OkCupid, female users are more likely to get responses to their first contacts (40% chance) than are males (25% chance), and half of those responses are sent to women within 7 hours after the initial message (May, 2013). Neither women or men appear to have difficulty ignoring requests from less desirable suitors (Yeager et al., 2014). Unlike people without disabilities, PWDs experience a challenge to their self-concept if "disability trolls" reply to their profiles. Daters with obvious disabilities often sift through "the literally hundreds of messages … from people who… simply want to know how exactly you're 'broken' and whether or not you can still have sex" (Heideman, 2014). After continually fielding such questions, users with visible disabilities begin to feel like the people online are dating your wheelchair, rather than dating you ((Heideman, 2014). In an online essay, Ladau (2017) described how after divulging her disability and the "wheelchair bomb", she would "have to brace myself for their reactions, which were always a mixed bag, often ranging from indifference to ghosting", occasionally receiving an accepting response.

In Saltes' (2013) study, female PWDs discussed the challenge of "devotees," people who are specifically interested in and sexually aroused by PWDs. Men with disabilities did not report such experiences. According to Solvang (2007), some women with amputations dismiss devotees, whereas others welcome the sexual way in which their bodies are desired. The internet provides a relatively easy opportunity for devotees to connect with PWDs, especially those who use disability dating web sites. For emerging adults who may just be learning how to get people to see them as people rather than as their disabilities, comments from disability trolls might have a profound effect on their online and offline dating experiences (Heideman, 2014). It may be enlightening, however, for some PWDs, to see the myth that able-bodied daters will never find PWDs desirable as romantic and sexual partners demolished. Yet, some emerging adults with disabilities may feel suspicious of people without disabilities who desire to initiate a romantic relationship with them (Nemeth, 2000). Some of that prejudice may be based on experience or may occur because of the internalized stigma that something must be wrong with a person without disability who voluntarily desires to be with a person with a disability (Dunn, 2015; Sharratt et al., 2018; Nemeth, 2000).

Engaging in Mutual Mediated Communication

There is only about a 30% chance that a reply to a first message will turn into an actual conversation (May, 2013), defined as a correspondence that lasts for at least three exchanges. Once a conversation begins, the internet facilitates disclosure and may be especially helpful for those people who are socially anxious, shy, or lack social skills (McKenna, Green, & Gleason, 2002). Users are more likely to feel that they can better express their real selves. Research has found that people are likely to disclose more information about themselves online than when face-to-face (Bargh et al., 2002; Joinson, 2001). Because of the reciprocity norm surrounding self-disclosure, online daters who consciously disclose more about themselves may enable "deal breakers" for themselves and for their potential dating partners to surface before the first face-to-face meeting (Gibbs, Ellison, & Heino, 2006). Saltes (2013) argues that online dating may enable a level of interaction with others that is more difficult offline for some PWDs. In particular, the privacy and asynchronous online interactions enable PWDs to communicate more effectively and feel more at ease and comfortable disclosing their impairment. However, online interactions are not always as efficient and effective as offline interactions, which can be a fertile source of misunderstandings and insults, intentional or not (Seymour & Lupton, 2004).

The process of mutual mediated communication may differ depending on the type of disability. For example, people with intellectual disabilities, those who display speech difficulties, and those with visual impairment may have an easier time writing texts and emails with voice-recognition software, spelling with software spelling and grammar assistance, and communicating orally with text-to-speech software (Lofgren-Martenson, 2008), although the latter might disconcert people without similar disabilities. Screen readers may assist people with reading disabilities, intellectual disabilities, or visually impairments to listen aurally to content on the dating website and in their received emails and messages.

Yet, these new technologies, however advantageous, may limit the online dating opportunities of PWDs if they are too expensive or are inaccessible (Schur et al., 2013). For multiple practical reasons, such as unreliable technology and lack of technical support and training, individuals with disabilities often do not use or discontinue using assistive technology (Alper & Raharinirina, 2006; Bowker, 2010; Reimer-Reiss & Wacher, 2000). For example, Bennet (2017), who describes herself as blind, describes significant challenges engaging with text profiles and messaging features of online dating apps, even while using a screen reader.

Online daters may resist using assistive technology for psychological reasons, viewing devices such as hearing aids and speech synthesizers as markers of dependency and stigmatization (Blood, 1997; Parant, Schiano-Lomoriello, & Marchan, 2017; Ravneberg, 2012). The mere presence of a hearing aid and other assistive technology devices trigger negative social reactions in oneself and in others (Blood, 1997; Parant et al., 2017). Thus, while utilizing assistive technology may allow a person with speech and language disabilities to communicate online with other daters, accessing and acknowledging the use of an assistive device can be large psychological steps for many PWDs.

Due to likely experience with stigma, PWDS are typically aware that assistive technology may produce prejudicial reactions from potential daters as well as curiosity and embarrassment. According to Milbrodt (2019), wheelchair users on the dating site Match.com often articulate anxiety about how their assistive devices will be perceived, whether the chair will disqualify them as prospective partners, and insinuating that the wheelchair has repelled potential daters in the past.

Meeting Face-To-Face

One-third of adult online daters in the U.S. have never progressed to the date stage (Smith & Anderson, 2016). Most of the Australian online daters that Whitty (2008) interviewed claimed that the first face-to-face meeting was the true beginning of the screening out process. However, the first offline meeting may be especially complicated for those with mobility challenges, disfigurement issues, and stigmatized illnesses, such as bowel disease, who do not disclose their disability in their profiles or online communications. For example, Mathias and Harcourt (2014) described how women ages 18 to 29 with below-knee amputation preferred potential partners to be aware of their prosthesis from the outset, helping to reduce anxiety about how and when to "reveal" it. Adults with visible differences such as alopecia, cleft lip, and psoriasis, indicated that they used their new romantic partner's reaction to their appearance as a way to measure that person's character (Sharratt et al., 2018). On the other hand, other online daters may conceal disability as long as possible; as one media informant explained about his nondisclosing brother who suffered from Crohn's disease: "He was a good-looking boy. But when do you tell a girl that you have a colostomy bag? The first date? The third? There's no good time" (Barrow, 2010, para. 15).

Emerging adults with disabilities who have communication problems, such as hearing or oral speech limitations, are likely to find it more difficult to meet a potential dating partner in person than those without communication problems, and they are less satisfied with dating overall (Nosek et al., 2001). Rintala and her colleagues (1997) found that communication problems often interact with low self-esteem. A person with low self-esteem may be unable to effectively communicate interest in a potential dating partner or to maintain a relationship through clearly understood communication (Nosek et al., 2001).

The first date is likely to be awkward for most emerging adults, but having to figure out clear pathways for communication and physical accessibility can be additional stressors. There is little research on deaf-hearing adult relationships. In one study, McIntosh (1999) found that hearing people welcome a hearing-impaired person who speaks, but experience discomfort in most deaf-hearing interactions. Allard and Williams (2008) revealed college students' negative stereotypes about the self-esteem, intelligence, and employability of individuals with speech and language disorders, such as stuttering and poor articulation. Another study of American undergraduates specified that male undergraduates have significantly more negative attitudes toward profoundly hearing impaired and deaf individuals than do their female peers (LaBelle, Booth-Butterfield, & Rittenour, 2013).

In terms of oral communication, people who view their stuttering as an obstacle to forming relationships find it difficult to talk to potential romantic partners (Mayo & Mayo, 2013). Shuttleworth (2000) found that men with cerebral palsy and speech impairments often perceive communication as a barrier to developing intimacy but may employ nonverbal strategies such as making "puppy dog eyes" and giving back rubs, even with ones' feet. People who are visually impaired yet skilled oral communicators report that they frequently interact with fully sighted people who display unease or confusion. Smith and Kandath (1999) provide multiple examples of sighted people's inappropriate responses, such as speaking too loudly or not treating the visually impaired person as an adult peer.

For daters with mobility challenges, meeting in public can be complicated by accessibility issues, such as steps into a building or bathroom, or whether or how easily a wheelchair, power chair, or scooter will fit into a car or public transportation. Olkin (1999) explains that people with disabilities need a unique skill for social interactions, that of getting others to view them as people, not as disabilities and, thus, how to comfortably present their disability to others. Emerging adults' feelings of ease with their disability will set the tone for the potential dating relationship much more than the extent of their disability (Olkin, 1999).

Developing an Offline Relationship by Proceeding to a Second Date and/or Removing Their Online Dating Profile

Having a physical disability may present challenges at the start of a relationship. As Elizabeth, a 23-year-old female amputee explained, "I need someone who won't be weird about my scars, who will carry my purse if I'm on crutches, who doesn't mind when I ask him to get me stuff because I already took my leg off" (Mathias & Harcourt, 2014, p. 398). For some daters, positive encounters are defined as ones in which disability, as in this example, are treated neutrally or is not mentioned (Bennett, 2017). In addition, for some emerging adults with physical and intellectual disabilities there may be issues that they might need to discuss sooner than is typical for their peers without disabilities, such as independent living, pregnancy, childbirth, and raising children. For example, Elizabeth clarifies that the qualities she is looking for in her ideal partner include "considering the long-term, like the fact that I might be physically dependent earlier in life, childbirth, raising a child, things like that" (Mathias & Harcourt,

2014, p. 398). According to Nemeth (2000), couples with at least one partner with a disability must understand that they have disability-related "baggage" before they can negotiate relationships that work. Part of this negotiation can include a redefinition of or a complete rejection of traditional gender roles and attitudinal shifts in definitions of acceptable and fulfilling sex.

Gill (1996) describes how stigma contagion and the fear of gender and disability stereotypes are powerful variables when women with disabilities try to establish romantic relationships. Partners without disabilities commonly report that strangers treat them differently because of their relationship with a PWD. Olkin (1999) notes that a commonly held belief is that no able-bodied person will find a PWD desirable as a sex partner, and if they do, it is because there is either something wrong with the nondisabled partner or they are "settling," thus, the partner without disability is often seen as either a loser or a saint (Smart, 2011). It may be difficult for individuals without a disability to cope with such prejudice, especially if there are other online dating profiles waiting to be considered. As with traditional offline dating, a romantic relationship can proceed for a long time, only to founder when the issue of long-term commitments, such as marriage or starting a family, forces the partner of a PWD to reassess his or her desires for a particular life partner (Gill, 1996). At the same time, most PWDs state that people without disabilities typically ascribe far more importance and limitations to their disability than they do (Smart, 2011). Perhaps as a result, married adults with childhood-onset disabilities are significantly less likely than adults without disabilities to have a nondisabled spouse (Tumin, 2016).

Research with online daters has found that success in finding a partner may be partially a "numbers game" of multiple first dates, as reported by many of the interview participants in Gibbs' and her colleagues' (2006) survey of heterosexual Match.com members in the U.S. Romantic success, the researchers suggest, also requires the cognitive ability to reflect and learn from one's encounters, which people with intellectual disabilities might find difficult. Because they are less likely than their peers to be experienced daters, emerging adults with other disabilities whose relationships founder also may find it challenging to process the termination (Howland & Rintala, 2001). PWDs commonly feel angry and helpless in reaction to the real and perceived pervasive rejection and discrimination of dating situations (Olkin, 1999). They may not know whether their lack of success was due to their specific impairment, a more general disability stigma, or for the same reasons that relationships end for emerging adults without disabilities. Some PWDS, similar to daters without disabilities, will develop a committed relationship with someone they have met online. Other emerging adults with disabilities may become discouraged if they perceive fewer dating opportunities than their nondisabled peers, especially in an online environment with "plenty of fish."

FUTURE RESEARCH DIRECTIONS

Online dating is much more culturally acceptable than it was a decade ago (Smith & Anderson, 2016). Yet, despite the preponderance of online dating sites and, more recently, mobile dating apps, which are particularly popular among American emerging adults, most marriages and committed relationships still begin offline. Only 12% of Americans who have been with their spouse or partners for 5 years or less, the ones most likely to have used online services, report that they met their partner with the help of an internet dating site (Smith & Anderson, 2016). There is no frequency of use information for PWDs to guide them or comparisons of success for emerging adults between the large internet sites, like Match.com, and the smaller specialty disability dating sites, between men and women with disabilities, or between heterosexual and homosexual users of online sites. There is no research to support recommendations about the best time or manner to disclose one's disability during the process of online dating and the ramifications for long-term success. In fact, as is likely evident throughout the chapter, there has been little research published about online dating for PWDS and even less that includes more than a few emerging adults.

Emerging adults have been migrating to mobile phone apps for online dating, such as Tinder, as well as those launched by traditional dating sites such as Match.com, eHarmony, and OkCupid (Smith & Anderson, 2016). As the president of Match.com in North America bragged, Tinder "opened up this young demographic – 18- to -25-year-olds – that no product could open up before" (Wood, 2015, p. B8). Because Tinder profiles are more pictorial and less textual, with a maximum biography of 500 words and an average of 5.62 photos (LeFebvre, 2018), the implications for PWDs are likely to be complicated. Apps like Tinder facilitate more frequent meetings with nearby daters than traditional dating websites because they discourage communication via a laptop screen, and instead, encourage face-to-face interaction. For a PWD, there is likely much worrying over construction of the brief dating profiles, less time spent profile browsing, and quicker disclosure of disability, either through the profile photos or during the in-person meeting. Thus, dating apps, like Tinder, might challenge the dating prospects of emerging adults with disabilities by elevating the importance of their physical appearance and presence of visible disabilities over their personality attributes and common interests as early as the first meeting.

More philosophically, the availability of apps that help daters identify potential romantic partners living nearby may create the impression that it should be easy to meet romantic partners. If there are – supposedly - no more excuses for being single, and despite evidence of an intensification of social exclusion of disabled people in recent years (Tumin, 2016), being involuntarily unpartnered might be both experienced and perceived as particularly stigmatizing (Sumter, Vandenbosch, & Ligtenberg, 2017). This is an important area for new research.

CONCLUSION

Online dating has the potential to improve what is an often frustrating activity for PWDs: the pursuit of a committed, emotionally satisfying romantic relationship during one's emerging adulthood. Online dating provides the opportunity to communicate with multiple potential partners conveniently and efficiently, an appealing alternative to relying on more traditional ways of seeking romantic relationships. Online communication also allows users to "meet" without an initial focus on disability. However, there are many online dating challenges for PWDs. Some of these challenges are similar to those for people without disabilities, such as the creation of attractive profiles. Some are unique, such as the question of when and how to disclose one's disability. Some challenges, such as those related to accessibility as well as stigma, may differ depending on the type of disabilities one experiences. Despite these complexities, online dating, with its opportunity to interact with multiple interested daters, appears to offer emerging adults with disabilities a positive, though complex, venue for relationship development.

REFERENCES

Allard, E. R., & Williams, D. F. (2008). Listeners' perceptions of speech and language disorders. *Journal of Communication Disorders*, *41*(2), 108–123. doi:10.1016/j.jcomdis.2007.05.002 PMID:17586521

Alper, S., & Raharinirina, S. (2006). Assistive technology for individuals with disabilities: A review and synthesis of the literature. *Journal of Special Education Technology*, *21*(2), 47–64. doi:10.1177/016264340602100204

Anderson, M., Perrin, A., & Jiang, J. (2018). 11% of Americans don't use the internet. Who are they? *Pew Research Center.* Retrieved from http://www.pewresearch.org/fact-tank/2018/03/05/some-americans-dont-use-the-internet-who-are-they/

Bargh, J. A., McKenna, K. Y. A., & Fitzsimons, G. M. (2002). Can you see the real me? Activation and expression of the "true self" on the Internet. *The Journal of Social Issues*, *58*(1), 33–48. doi:10.1111/1540-4560.00247

Barrow, K. (2010, December 27). Difference is the norm on these dating sites. *The New York Times.* Retrieved from http://www.nytimes.com

Bennett, C. L. (2017). Disability-disclosure preferences and practices in online dating communities. *XRDS*, *24*(2), 30–33. doi:10.1145/3155120

Blackhart, G. C., Fitzpatrick, J., & Williamson, J. (2014). Dispositional factors predicting use of online dating sites and behaviors related to online dating. *Computers in Human Behavior*, *33*, 113–118. doi:10.1016/j.chb.2014.01.022

Blood, I. M. (1997). The hearing aid effect: Challenges for counseling. *Journal of Rehabilitation*, *63*, 59–62.

Bogart, K. R., Rottenstein, A., Lund, E. M., & Bouchard, L. (2017). Who self-identifies as disabled? An examination of impairment and contextual predictors. *Rehabilitation Psychology*, *62*(4), 553–562. doi:10.1037/rep0000132 PMID:28581320

Bowker, N. I. (2010). Understanding barriers to online experience for people with physical and sensory disabilities using discursive social psychology. *Universal Access in the Information Society*, *9*(2), 121–136. doi:10.100710209-009-0162-3

Braithwaite, S. R., Delevi, R., & Fincham, F. D. (2010). Romantic relationships and the physical and mental health of college students. *Personal Relationships*, *17*(1), 1–12. doi:10.1111/j.1475-6811.2010.01248.x

Bromwich, J. E. (2017, December 18). Tinder and Bumble are hungry for your love. *The New York Times.* Retrieved from https://www.nytimes.com/2018/12/18/style/dating-apps-tinder-bumble-content.html

Chen, R. K., Brodwin, M. G., Cardoso, E., & Chan, F. (2002). Attitudes toward people with disabilities in the social context of dating and marriage: A comparison of American, Taiwanese, and Singaporean college students. *Journal of Rehabilitation*, *68*, 5–11.

Coleman, J. M., Brunell, A. B., & Haugen, I. M. (2015). Multiple forms of prejudice: How gender and disability stereotypes influence judgments of disabled men and women. *Current Psychology (New Brunswick, N.J.)*, *34*(1), 177–189. doi:10.100712144-014-9250-5

Dunn, D. (2015). *The social psychology of disability*. New York: Oxford University Press.

Feragen, K. B., Stock, N. M., Sharratt, N. D., & Kvalem, I. L. (2016). Self-perceptions of romantic appeal in adolescents with a cleft lip and/or palate. *Body Image*, *18*, 143–152. doi:10.1016/j.bodyim.2016.06.009 PMID:27459395

Finkel, E. J., Eastwick, P. W., Karney, B. R., Reis, H. T., & Sprecher, S. (2012). Online dating: A critical analysis from the perspective of psychological science. *Psychological Science in the Public Interest*, *13*(1), 3–66. doi:10.1177/1529100612436522 PMID:26173279

Gibbs, J. L., Ellison, N. B., & Heino, R. D. (2006). Self-presentation in online personals: The role of anticipated future interaction, self-disclosure, and perceived success in internet dating. *Communication Research*, *33*(2), 152–177. doi:10.1177/0093650205285368

Gill, C. J. (1996). Dating and relationship issues. *Sexuality and Disability*, *14*(3), 183–190. doi:10.1007/BF02590076

Giordano, P. C., Longmore, M. A., Schroeder, R. D., & Seffrin, P. M. (2008). A life-course perspective on spirituality and desistance from crime. *Criminology*, *46*(1), 99–132. doi:10.1111/j.1745-9125.2008.00104.x

Goodman, S. (2012, March 22). Online dating with a disability. *The Guardian*. Retrieved from http://www.theguardian.com/lifeandstyle/2012/mar/22/online-dating-with-disability

Gozza-Cohen, M., & May, D. (2012). Individuals with disabilities and internet use. In Z. Yan (Ed.), *Encyclopedia of Cyber Behavior* (pp. 242–258). Hershey, PA: IGI Global. doi:10.4018/978-1-4666-0315-8.ch021

Gunter, B. (2007). Internet dating: A British survey. *Aslib Proceedings*, *60*(2), 88–98. doi:10.1108/00012530810862437

Heasley, S. (2019, January 30). Graduation rate for students with disabilities shows improvement. *Disability Scoop*. Retrieved from https://www.disabilityscoop.com/2019/01/30/graduation-rate-shows-improvement/25962/

Heideman, E. (2014, August 1). Disabled woman tackles the dating site trolls. *The Daily Beast*. Retrieved from http://www.thedailybeast.com/articles/2014/08/01/dropping-the-d-bomb- online-dating-with-a-disability.html

Hitsch, G. J., Hortacsu, A., & Ariely, D. (2010). What makes you click? – Mate preferences in online dating. *Quantitative Marketing and Economics*, *8*(4), 393–427. doi:10.100711129-010-9088-6

Holmes, E. K., Brown, G., Shafer, K., & Stoddard, N. (2017). Healthy transitions to family formation. In L. M. Padilla-Walker & L. J. Nelson (Eds.), *Flourishing in emerging adulthood: Positive development during the third decade of life* (pp. 70–97). New York, NY: Oxford University Press.

Holmes, K. M., & O'Loughlin, N. (2014). The experience of people with learning disabilities on social networking sites. *British Journal of Learning Disabilities*, *42*(1), 1–5. doi:10.1111/bld.12001

Holt-Lunstad, J., Robles, T. F., & Sbarra, D. A. (2017). Advancing social connection as a public health priority in the United States. *The American Psychologist*, *72*(6), 517–530. doi:10.1037/amp0000103 PMID:28880099

Howland, C. A., & Rintala, D. H. (2001). Dating behaviors of women with physical disabilities. *Sexuality and Disability*, *19*(1), 41–70. doi:10.1023/A:1010768804747

Hwang, W. (2013). Who are people willing to date? Ethnic and gender patterns in online dating. *Race and Social Problems*, *5*(1), 28–40. doi:10.100712552-012-9082-6

Jaeger, P. T. (2012). *Disability and the internet: Confronting a digital divide*. Boulder, CO: Lynne Rienner Publishers.

Joinson, A. N. (2001). Self-disclosure in computer-mediated communication: The role of self-awareness and visual anonymity. *European Journal of Social Psychology*, *31*(2), 170–192. doi:10.1002/ejsp.36

Kreager, D. A., Cavanagh, S. E., Yen, J., & Yu, M. (2014). "Where have all the good men gone?" Gendered interactions in online dating. *Journal of Marriage and the Family*, *76*(2), 387–410. doi:10.1111/jomf.12072 PMID:24910472

LaBelle, S., Booth-Butterfield, M., & Rittenour, C. E. (2013). Attitudes toward profoundly hearing impaired and deaf individuals: Links with intergroup anxiety, social dominance orientation, and contact. *Western Journal of Communication*, *77*(4), 489–506. doi:10.1080/10570314.2013.779017

Ladau, E. (2017, Sept. 27). Playing the online dating game, in a wheelchair. *The New York Times*. Retrieved from https://www.nytimes.com/2017/09/27/opinion/online-dating-disability.html

Lathouwers, K., de Moor, J., & Didden, R. (2009). Access to and use of Internet by adolescents who have a physical disability: A comparative study. *Research in Developmental Disabilities*, *30*(4), 702–711. doi:10.1016/j.ridd.2008.09.003 PMID:19022618

LeFebvre, L. (2018). Swiping me off my feet: Explicating relationship initiation on Tinder. *Journal of Social and Personal Relationships*, *35*(9), 1205–1229. doi:10.1177/0265407517706419

Levitin, D. J. (2014). *The Organized Mind*. New York: Penguin Random House.

Liddiard, K., & Slater, J. (2018). "Like, pissing yourself is not a particularly attractive quality, let's be honest": Learning to contain through youth, adulthood, disability and sexuality. *Sexualities*, *21*(3), 319–333. doi:10.1177/1363460716688674

Limoncin, E., Carta, R., Gravina, G. L., Carosa, E., Ciocca, G., Di Sante, S., ... Jannini, E. A. (2014). The sex.ual attraction toward disabilities: A preliminary internet- based study. *International Journal of Impotence Research*, *26*(2), 51–54. doi:10.1038/ijir.2013.34 PMID:24048013

Lofgren-Martenson, L. (2008). Love in cyberspace: Swedish young people with intellectual disabilities and the internet. *Scandinavian Journal of Disability Research*, *10*(2), 125–138. doi:10.1080/15017410701758005

MacInnes, M. (2011). Altar-bound? The effect of disability on the hazard of entry into a first marriage. *International Journal of Sociology*, *41*(1), 87–103. doi:10.2753/IJS0020-7659410105 PMID:23946548

Mathias, Z., & Harcourt, D. (2014). Dating and intimate relationships of women with below-knee amputation: An exploratory study. *Disability and Rehabilitation*, *36*(5), 395–402. doi:10.3109/09638288.2013.797509 PMID:23721496

May, K. T. (2013, February 14). 7 things we learned about online dating from the co-founder of OKCupid [blog post]. Retrieved from http://blog.ted.com/7- things-we-learned-about-online-dating-from-the-co-founder-of-okcupid/

Mayo, R., & Mayo, C. M. (2013). College students' perspectives on dating a person who stutters. *College Student Journal*, *47*, 169–177.

Mazur, E., & Kozarian, L. (2010). Self-presentation and interaction in blogs of adolescents and young emerging adults. *Journal of Adolescent Research*, *25*(1), 124–144. doi:10.1177/0743558409350498

McDonald, S. M. (2010, July 26). As ADA turns 20, Harris interactive survey finds lifestyle and economic gaps still remain between Americans with and without disabilities. *The Kessler Foundation.* Retrieved from http://www.2010disabilitysurveys.org/

McIntosh, A. (1999). When the deaf and the hearing interact: Communication features, relationship, and disability issues. In D. O. Braithwaite & T. L. Thompson (Eds.), *Handbook of Communication and People with Disabilities: Research and Application* (pp. 353–368). Mahwah, NJ: Routledge.

McKenna, K. Y., Green, A. S., & Gleason, M. E. J. (2002). Relationship formation on the Internet: What's the big attraction? *The Journal of Social Issues*, *58*(1), 9–31. doi:10.1111/1540-4560.00246

Milbrodt, T. (2019). Dating websites and disability identity: Presentations of the disabled self in online dating profiles. *Western Folklore*, *78*, 66–100.

Miller, E., Chen, R., Glover-Graf, N. M., & Kranz, P. (2009). Willingness to engage in personal relationships with persons with disabilities. *Rehabilitation Counseling Bulletin*, *52*(4), 211–224. doi:10.1177/0034355209332719

Nemeth, S. A. (2000). Society, sexuality, and disabled/ablebodied romantic relationships. In D. O. Braithwaite & T. L. Thompson (Eds.), *Handbook of communication and people with disabilities (* (pp. 37–48). Mahwah, NJ: Lawrence Erlbaum.

Newman, L., Wagner, M., Knokey, A. M., Marder, C., Nagle, K., Shaver, D., … Schwarting, M. (2011). *The post-high school outcomes of young adults with disabilities up to 8 years after high school. A report from the National Longitudinal Transition Study-2 (NLTS2)* (NCSER 2011-3005). Menlo Park, CA: SRI International.

Nosek, M. A., Howland, B. A., Rintala, D. H., Young, M. E., & Chanpong, G. (2001). National study of women with physical disabilities: Final report. *Sexuality and Disability, 19*, 5-39.

Olkin, R. (1999). *What psychotherapists should know about disability*. New York: Guilford Press.

Parant, A., Schiano-Lomoriello, S., & Marchan, F. (2017). How would I live with a disability? Expectations of bio-psychological consequences and assistive technology use. *Disability and Rehabilitation. Assistive Technology*, *12*(7), 681–685. doi:10.1080/17483107.2016.1218555 PMID:27677931

Pausch, N. C., Winter, K., Halama, D., Wirtz, C., Yildirim, V., & Nattapong, S. (2016). Psychosocial acceptance of cleft patients: Has something changed? *Oral and Maxillofacial Surgery*, *20*(1), 19–26. doi:10.100710006-015-0518-1 PMID:26212596

Pfeiffer, J. P., & Pinquart, M. (2011). Attainment of developmental tasks by adolescent with visual impairments and sighted adolescents. *Journal of Visual Impairment & Blindness*, *105*(1), 33–44. doi:10.1177/0145482X1110500104

Pietromonaco, P. R., & Collins, N. L. (2017). Interpersonal mechanisms linking close relationships to health. *The American Psychologist*, *72*(6), 531–542. doi:10.1037/amp0000129 PMID:28880100

Pinquart, M., & Pfeiffer, J. P. (2012). What is essential is invisible to the eye: Intimate relationships of adolescents with visual impairment. *Sexuality and Disability*, *30*(2), 139–147. doi:10.100711195-011-9248-y

Plentyoffishmedia. (2015, October 23). Retrieved from http://www.pof.com/

Ravneberg, B. (2012). Usability and abandonment of assistive technology. *Journal ofAssistive Technologies*, *6*(4), 259–269. doi:10.1108/17549451211285753

Reimer-Reiss, M. L., & Wacher, R. R. (2000). Factors associated with assistive technology discontinuance among individuals with disabilities. *Journal of Rehabilitation*, *66*, 44–50.

Rintala, D. H., Howland, C. A., Nosek, M. A., Bennett, J. L., Young, M. E., Foley, C. C., ... Chanpong, G. (1997). Dating issues for women with physical disabilities. *Sexuality and Disability*, *15*(4), 219–242. doi:10.1023/A:1024717313923

Roth, M. E., & Gillis, J. M. (2015). "Convenience with the click of a mouse": A survey of adults with autism spectrum disorder on online dating. *Sexuality and Disability*, *33*(1), 133–150. doi:10.100711195-014-9392-2

Saltes, N. (2013). Disability, identity, and disclosure in the online dating environment. *Disability & Society*, *28*(1), 96–109. doi:10.1080/09687599.2012.695577

Santuzzi, A. M., & Waltz, P. R. (2016). Disability in the workplace: A unique and variable identity. *Journal of Management*, *42*(5), 1111–1135. doi:10.1177/0149206315626269

Schur, L., Kruse, D., & Blanck, P. (2013). *People with Disabilities: Sidelined or Mainstreamed?* New York: Cambridge University Press. doi:10.1017/CBO9780511843693

Seymour, W., & Lupton, D. (2004). Holding the line online: Exploring wired relationships for people with disabilities. *Disability & Society*, *19*(4), 291–305. doi:10.1080/09687590410001689421

Sharratt, N. D., Jenkinson, E., Moss, T., Clarke, A., & Rumsey, N. (2018). Understanding and experiences of visible difference and romantic relationships: A qualitative exploration. *Body Image*, *27*, 32–42. doi:10.1016/j.bodyim.2018.08.002 PMID:30125758

Shuttleworth, R. P. (2000). The search for sexual intimacy for men with cerebral palsy. *Sexuality and Disability*, *18*(4), 263–282. doi:10.1023/A:1005646327321

Silverman, A. M., Molton, I. R., Smith, A. E., Jensen, M. P., & Cohen, G. L. (2017). Solace in solidarity: Disability friendship networks buffer well-being. *Rehabilitation Psychology*, *62*(4), 525–533. doi:10.1037/rep0000128 PMID:28394146

Smart, J. (2011). *Disability across the developmental lifespan*. New York: Springer.

Smith, A. (2016, February 11). 15% of American adults have used online dating sites or mobile dating apps. *Pew Research Center*. Retrieved from http://www.pewinternet.org/2016/02/11/15-percent-of-american-adults- have-used-online-dating-sites-or-mobile-dating-apps/

Smith, A., & Anderson, M. (2016, February 29). 5 facts about online dating. *Pew Research Center.* Retrieved from http://www.pewresearch.org/fact-tank/2016/02/29/5-facts-about-online- dating/

Smith, A., & Anderson, M. (2018, March 1). Social media use in 2018. *Pew Research Cente*r. Retrieved from http://www.pewinternet.org/2018/03/01/social-media-use-in-2018/

Smith, J. W., & Kandath, K. (1999). Communication and the blind or visually impaired. In D. O. Braithwaite & T. L. Thompson (Eds.), *Handbook of Communication and People with Disabilities: Research and Application* (pp. 389–404). Mahwah, NJ: Routledge.

Soderstrom, S. (2013). Digital differentiation in young people's internet use – eliminating or reproducing disability stereotypes. *Future Internet*, *5*(2), 190–204. doi:10.3390/fi5020190

Solvang, P. (2007). The amputee body desired: Beauty destabilized? Disability re-valued? *Sexuality and Disability*, *25*(2), 51–64. doi:10.100711195-007-9036-x

Sumter, S. R., Vandenbosch, L., & Ligtenberg, L. (2017). Love me Tinder: Untangling emerging adults' motivations for using the dating application Tinder. *Telematics and Informatics*, *34*(1), 67–78. doi:10.1016/j.tele.2016.04.009

Sykes, T. (2014, January 18). Online dating is hard enough. Try doing it with a disability. *The Guardian.* Retrieved from http://www.theguardian.com/commentisfree/2014/jan/18/online-dating-with-disability-match

Taylor, D. M. (2018, November). *Americans with Disabilities: 2014.* Current Population Reports, P70-152, U.S. Census Bureau, Washington, DC. Retrieved from https://www.census.gov/content/dam/Census/library/publications/2018/demo/p70-152.pdf

Timmermans, E., & De Caluwé, E. (2017). To Tinder or not to Tinder, that's the question: An individual differences perspective to Tinder use and motives. *Personality and Individual Differences*, *110*, 74–79. doi:10.1016/j.paid.2017.01.026

Tumin, D. (2016). Marriage trends among Americans with childhood-onset disabilities, 1997-2013. *Disability and Health Journal*, *9*(4), 713–718. doi:10.1016/j.dhjo.2016.05.004 PMID:27265773

Urquhart, C., & Fraser-Thoms, E. (2012, December 30). Online dating surges as lonely hearts look to kickstart some post-Christmas romance. *The Observer.* Retrieved from http://www.theguardian.com/lifeandstyle/2012/dec/29/online-dating-christmas-romance

Whitton, S. W., Dyar, D., Newcomb, M. E., & Mustanski, B. (2018). Romantic involvement: A protective factor for psychological health in racially-diverse young sexual minorities. *Journal of Abnormal Psychology*, *127*(3), 265–275. doi:10.1037/abn0000332 PMID:29389141

Whitty, M. T. (2008). Revealing the "real" me, searching for the "actual" you: Presentations of self on an internet dating site. *Computers in Human Behavior*, *24*(4), 1707–1723. doi:10.1016/j.chb.2007.07.002

Wiegerink, D., Roebroeck, M. E., Donkervoort, M., Stam, H. J., & Cohen-Kettenis, P. T. (2006). Social and sexual relationships of adolescents and young adults with cerebral palsy: A review. *Clinical Rehabilitation*, *20*(12), 1023–1031. doi:10.1177/0269215506071275 PMID:17148513

Wiegerink, D., Roebroeck, M. E., Van Der Slot, W. M., Stam, H. J., & Cohen-Kettenis, P. T. (2010). Importance of peers and dating in the development of romantic relationships and sexual activity of young adults with cerebral palsy. *Developmental Medicine and Child Neurology*, *52*(6), 576–582. doi:10.1111/j.1469-8749.2010.03620.x PMID:20187888

Wood, M. (2015, February 4). Led by Tinder, the mobile dating game surges. *The New York Times,* p. B8.

Wright, B. (1983). *Physical disability: A psychosocial approach*. New York: Harper & Row. doi:10.1037/10589-000

KEY TERMS AND DEFINITIONS

Disabilities: An umbrella term, covering impairments, activity limitations, and participation restrictions.

Mutual Mediated Communication: Ways of communicating through and around dating sites, such as by email-like messages and instant messaging on the dating site, personal email, text messaging, webcam conversations, or speaking on the phone.

Online Dating: The use of commercial or nonprofit internet sites that provide dating services to users seeking romantic relationships.

Profile: An online user's description and summary of themselves typically including basic demographic information, behaviors and interests, description of the traits sought in a potential partner, and one or more photos of oneself.

Self-Disclosure: Confiding intimate aspects of oneself to others.

Self-Esteem: Individuals' feelings of high or low self-worth.

Self-Presentation: Behaviors that are designed to convey an image about ones' self to other people.

Stigma: An attribute or identity that is perceived by others to have a broadly negative quality within a culture or situation.

Chapter 7
Send Nudes? :
Sexting Experiences and Victimization Relating to Attachment and Rejection Sensitivity - Incorporating Sexual Minority Perspectives

Alaina Brenick
https://orcid.org/0000-0002-9534-8231
University of Connecticut, USA

Kaitlin M. Flannery
https://orcid.org/0000-0003-0057-5982
State University of New York College at Cortland, USA

Emily Karr
University of Connecticut, USA

Daniell Carvalheiro
University of Connecticut, USA

ABSTRACT

As texting continues to serve as an increasingly common method of communication among emerging adults, increases in rates of sexting, or sending sexually explicit messages, pictures, or videos, have also been observed. While consensual sexting can facilitate intimacy in relationships, when used as a tool to victimize others, it has been shown to yield a range of negative outcomes: from embarrassment to severe depression and suicide. This chapter aims to review the existing literature on emerging adults' engagement in and evaluations of sexting, while also considering the risks associated with sexting victimization. The role that individual characteristics, such as attachment style and rejection sensitivity as well as demographic characteristics such as gender, sexual orientation, and relationship status, play in the relation between experiences with and evaluations of using sexting as a tool for victimization will also be explored.

DOI: 10.4018/978-1-7998-1063-6.ch007

INTRODUCTION

As technology use increasingly dominates the social lives of emerging adults (EAs), intimate communication—and potentially victimization—between romantic partners is transforming. This shift is especially apparent in rates of sexting, or the sending or receiving of sexually suggestive written messages, pictures, or videos. Sexting has become an increasingly common relationship ritual in young adults' romantic lives, with a conservative estimate of nearly 43% of youth between the ages of 18-24 years having sexted (Gordon-Messer, Bauermeister, Grodzinski, & Zimmerman, 2013). In another sample, 80.9% of 697 undergraduate participants reported having sent a sext at least once in their lifetime, and nearly half of the entire sample (48.5%) had sent a sext within the last 30 days (Hudson & Fetro, 2015). Given its ubiquity in emerging adulthood, it is essential to consider that although consensual sexting can facilitate intimacy in relationships (e.g., Burkett, 2015), when individuals are coerced into sexting or when sexting is used as a tool to victimize others, it can yield a range of negative outcomes from embarrassment to severe depression and suicide (Celizic, 2009; Judge, 2012). Nonetheless, little research has examined EAs' actual engagement in and evaluations of sexting as they relate to individual characteristics that might be associated with heightened vulnerability to the potential negative outcomes of sexting. Even more, individuals who identify as lesbian, gay, or bisexual (LGB), are largely absent from the literature on sexting, and are at an increased risk of victimization due to their marginalized status. Studies have found that individuals who identify as LGB participate in sexting more regularly than their heterosexual peers (Albury, 2014), yet they remain out of focus for most of the current studies. In an attempt to understand those individuals who might be most at risk, this chapter presents an original study that addresses this gap in the literature by assessing EAs' engagement in and evaluations of sexting and sexting victimization, together with individual characteristics—insecure attachment and rejection sensitivity—that are associated with other types of relational victimization (e.g., Downey & Feldman, 1996; Drouin & Tobin, 2014), and sexual orientation, which has thus far been largely left out of the literature on sexting victimization, all of which might be linked to heightened vulnerability to the negative aspects of sexting, such as sexting victimization.

BACKGROUND

General Trends in Sexting

Though sexting prevalence rates vary from study to study (see Klettke, Hallford, & Mellor, 2014), even conservative estimates (e.g., Gordon-Messer et al., 2013) indicate that sexting has become common practice among EAs. The variability in estimates of sexting behaviors is likely due to the complexity in operationalizing sexting altogether (Klettke et al., 2014). In a review of young adults' sexting, Klettke and colleagues (2014) found on average 53% of young adults send sexual texts and photos (49% reported sending sexts specifically with photo images), while 56% of young adults report having received sexts. Furthermore, studies have shown that individuals who identify as LGB demonstrate higher rates of participation in sexting than their heterosexual peers (Albury, 2014). These rates are specifically high in gay males, but are overall higher than heterosexual peers because of social pressures to keep homosexual relationships out of the public view. As a result, many LGB individuals turn to online sources to find partners and engage in sexting behaviors as a way of communicating sexual and romantic desires when finding a partner in real life may serve to be more challenging.

Klettke and colleagues (2014) emphasized the importance of breaking down sexting prevalence rates by type of sext (e.g., text or image) and the role of the individual (e.g., sender or recipient). In line with this recommendation, Brenick, Flannery, and Rankin (2017) assessed EAs' sexting in terms of sending and receiving text, image, and video messages, and found that 57% of EAs sent or received text based sexts, 43% sent and 49% received photo sexts, and 17% sent and 20% received video sexts. With new data from a larger and more representative sample, the authors of the present chapter, using the same methodology, found even higher rates of sexting; 68% of EAs sent and 77% received text-based sexts, 60% sent and 73% received photo sexts, and 33% sent and 47% received video sexts. Broken down further by demographics, 82% of LB females reported sending and 86% receiving text-based sexts, 68% sending and 75% receiving photo sexts, and 40% sending and 52% receiving video sexts, respectively. For GB males, 86% sent and 91% received text-based sexts, 85% sent and 88% received photo sexts, and 61% sent and 76% received video sexts. For heterosexual females, 62% sent and 75% received text-based sexts, 59% sent and 71% received photo sexts, and 28% sent and 38% received video sexts. Finally, for heterosexual males, 62% sent and 70% received text-based sexts, 50% sent and 69% received photo sexts, and 26% sent and 45% received video sexts.

As sexting in all forms has become a more normative manner of communication within relationships, a body of literature has emerged suggesting that sexting might not only be normative, but also a positive experience in emerging adulthood, fostering intimacy and pleasure within a close relationship (Burkett, 2015; Parker, Blackburn, Perry, & Hawks, 2013), as evidenced in studies assessing EAs' motivations for sexting. For instance, Hudson and Fetro (2015) found that in a sample of college students, attitudes toward sexting, perceptions of sexting norms, and behavioral intentions of sexting all significantly predicted activity with sexting; Kopecký (2011) found that individuals reported sexting to be viewed as arousing or to initiate sexual activity. Additionally, for those who were considered current sexters (i.e., had sent a sext within the last 30 days), the strongest predictor of their sexting activity was their attitude toward sexting, which the authors suggest indicated that current sexters were intentional in their sexting, and were motivated to sext because they wanted to and not because they felt social pressure to do so (Hudson & Fetro, 2015). These motivations to sext were mirrored in work by Lee and Crofts (2015), who argued that the gendered discourse surrounding females' motivations to engage in sexting does not accurately reflect the motivations most females actually express. Lee and Crofts (2015) acknowledge the existence of the widely discussed scenarios involving females experiencing pressure to send sexts to males; however, they suggest that most females decide to engage in sexting to pursue pleasure or because they desire to do so. Work by Dir and Cyders (2015) similarly implies that, although many people discuss sexting in terms of negative outcomes, these were rarely reported in that sample (the most common negative experience was having sexts shared with others, which happened to 12% of the sample). Renfrow and Rollo (2014) suggested that undergraduates were aware of the risk of having their sexts shared, but engaged in sexting anyway and attempted to minimize these risks by keeping sexts fun and less explicit, maintaining deniability in their sexts, and citing the normalcy of their actions. These participants also suggested that they saw benefits to sexting, such that it helped maintain their relationships, especially long-distance relationships (Burkett, 2015; Drouin et al., 2013). From these studies, it is clear that sexting can serve a unique purpose in romantic relationships, and despite an overwhelmingly negative narrative surrounding sexting, emerging adults do not all perceive it to be victimizing or risky.

Sexting Victimization

Despite the perceived benefits of sexting, research has established that there can be significant risks associated with sexting victimization. Contrary to Lee and Crofts (2015), work by Drouin, Ross, and Tobin (2015), for instance, demonstrated that approximately one fifth of a sample of EAs felt coerced into engaging in sexting. In fact, across a number of studies (e.g., Englander, 2012; Kopecký, 2011; Walker, Sanci, Temple-Smith, 2013), pressure or coercion from peers or partners was listed as a frequent motivation for sexting. Drouin and colleagues (2015) found that although the reported coercion was typically subtle, as opposed to containing threats, participants still reported trauma associated with this coercion, especially when looking back at the events. This study also revealed that sexting coercion was associated with intimate partner violence, as well as coercion into engaging in physical sex, indicating that sexting is another outlet through which intimate partner violence can be perpetrated (Drouin et al., 2015). Thus, even rare occurrences of sexting victimization should be diligently addressed.

Moreover, victimization can occur through the unauthorized sharing of sexts—an occurrence that is often viewed as a peer-encouraged means to obtain popularity amongst young men (Burkett, 2015; Ringrose, Harvey, Gill, & Livingstone, 2013). Media coverage offers additional evidence for such sexting victimization, although typically with extreme cases. For example, the widely broadcast story of an 18-year-old female who sent a sexual photo to her boyfriend. When the couple ended their relationship, the boyfriend distributed the sexual photo to their peers at school. Peers then began to humiliate the female, calling her degrading names, which left her feeling depressed, and afraid to attend school; soon after, she committed suicide (Celizic, 2009). Furthermore, homophobia and hate crimes keep LGB individuals "closeted", and as a result, many turn to online forums and profiles to safely express their sexual orientation. While simultaneously providing a safe-haven for communication, these forums can also create a dangerous space in terms of sexting. Individuals who choose to sext face the risk of being "outed", bullied, and if they are rejected for their sexual orientation, increased rates of homelessness or drug usage (Maziarz et al., 2012). Yet despite this unique and complex relation between sexting and identity, LGB voices remain largely absent from research on sexting victimization. Although suicide, homelessness, and drug use are extreme and rarer outcomes associated with sexting, the evidence for this possibility of victimization clearly necessitates an understanding of what individual characteristics might place a person at greater risk for the negative rather than positive outcomes of sexting. Two such risk factors might be the attachment security of an individual as well as their sensitivity to rejection. Both of these characteristics have been shown to increase vulnerability to and expectations of interpersonal victimization through personal experiences of loneliness, exclusion, abandonment, or worry about partner availability (Weisskirch & Delevi, 2011; Zimmer-Gembeck, Trevaskis, Nesdale, & Downey, 2013; Drouin & Tobin, 2014), and therefore necessitate further study into their relationship to sexting and sexting victimization.

ATTACHMENT, REJECTION SENSITIVITY, AND SEXTING

Individuals with insecure attachment or rejection sensitivity experience higher levels of victimization and vulnerability in their romantic relationships (Drouin & Tobin, 2014). However, to date, only two studies have assessed attachment in relation to sexting (see Klettke et al., 2014), and no research has examined the potentially moderating relation of attachment and rejection sensitivity with participants' engagement in and attitudes about sexting and sexting victimization. In addition, there has been a dearth of literature in the field of attachment and rejection sensitivity amongst the LGB community, and as such they remain absent to this field of study. In this chapter, the authors will review the extant literature on engagement in and evaluations of sexting and sexting victimization as well as present findings from a recent study that assessed EAs' engagement in sexting, their perceptions of sexting and sexting victimization, and their self-reports of attachment security and rejection sensitivity. Gaining a deeper understanding of the relationship between these individual characteristics and individuals' engagement in and evaluations of sexting will be important in order to identify those most at risk for sexting victimization and inform potential intervention or awareness strategies for those individuals, in particular.

Insecure Attachment

Attachment refers to how individuals process and reflect on their thoughts and feelings regarding their own intimate relationship experiences. A wealth of previous research has demonstrated the relation between attachment and experiences of victimization and vulnerability in romantic relationships (see Drouin & Tobin, 2014). Attachment can be defined as a deep and enduring emotional bond between two people developed through the interactions a child has with his/her caregivers; such interactions can result in that child developing either a secure or insecure (e.g., anxious or avoidant) attachment. Whereas attachment is often used to describe the relationship a child has with his/her caregivers, many theorists have examined adult and couple attachment as well, noting many similarities in the unique context of adult romantic attachment, including the need for close physical contact, deep interest in one another, and experiencing a sense of safety when the other is nearby (see George, 2009). Adults often integrate their childhood attachment experiences into their adult relationships by seeking out similar characteristics in their partners that they experienced with their caregivers (Cassidy, 2001). Attachment classification, or the pattern of relating to others, develops into an internal working model that is thought to be the foundation for an individual's intimate relationships in the present and in the future (see Weisskirch & Delevi, 2011). Some studies have shown that individuals who identify as LGB may experience higher rates of anxious attachment due to parental rejection of their sexual orientation. This rejection leaves children anxious that they will not be loved due to their orientation, and can often transfer over to their romantic partners and can manifest as a fear of being abandoned or being unlovable for their orientation (Brown, 2010).

Previous research has shown that individuals with insecure attachment experience higher levels of victimization and vulnerability in their romantic relationships (Drouin & Tobin, 2014). However, to date, only a few studies have assessed attachment in relation to sexting (see Klettke et al., 2014, for exception see Brenick et al., 2017) and none with LGB youth. From those studies, there is evidence to suggest that EAs who demonstrate insecure attachment (i.e., anxious; Weisskirch & Delevi, 2011, or avoidant; Drouin & Landgraff, 2012), are more likely to engage in sexting, and to view their sexting experiences as more victimizing (Delevi & Weisskirch, 2013). As such, it is a logical extension of attachment theory to further investigate how an individual's anxious or avoidant attachment style relates to his or her experiences of sexting within intimate relationships.

Sexting can be used for a variety of reasons in romantic relationships, and those with differing attachment styles may vary in their motivations for sexting, which may in turn relate to sexting victimization. For some, sexting may serve as a new way to explore romantic relationships by providing a means of connection and reassurance, whereas for others sexting may provide distance within a relationship while also sustaining intimacy. Regardless of these potential uses and benefits, sexting can also leave a sexter vulnerable to victimization. By utilizing sexting as a tool for intimacy, or lack thereof, a sexter may be exposing him or herself to the potential for victimization through the distribution of their sexual images and messages. Below, the authors discuss the relation between anxious and avoidant attachment with motivations for and experiences of sexting and sexting victimization.

Anxious attachment, on one hand, is characterized as having a strong desire for intimacy with others but also an intense fear of being abandoned. Individuals with anxious attachment are likely to seek approval from others and will attempt to build closeness with their partner out of fear that their partner will lose interest in the relationship. These individuals may be worried or preoccupied about the availability and responsiveness of their romantic partner (see Delevi & Weisskirch, 2013; Weisskirch & Delevi, 2011). Those with anxious attachment often experience more pressure to send sexual messages to keep a romantic partner's interest or to satisfy relational expectations (Drouin & Tobin, 2014). Anxious individuals may use sexting to gain reassurance from their romantic partner and to ensure that their partner is emotionally invested (Drouin & Landgraff, 2012).

Those with anxious attachment also are more likely to experience sexting victimization in the form of unwanted but consensual sexting. In this context, individuals sext, but do so because they feel obliged to participate. Heterosexual women who participate in unwanted but consensual sexting may display characteristics such as passivity, feeling responsible for maintaining relationship bonds, perceiving men's sexual urges as being uncontrollable and therefore unable to be resisted and, for men, experiencing social pressure to have sex (Delevi & Weisskirch, 2012; Drouin & Tobin, 2014).

Avoidant attachment, on the other hand, is characterized as having a fear of being intimate or dependent on others. Individuals with avoidant attachment attempt to distance themselves from their partners to avoid being dependent or relied upon for emotional closeness and support (Drouin & Landgraff, 2012). Those with avoidant attachment styles may be less likely to talk on the phone with their partner and often try to distance themselves, perhaps utilizing sexting as preferred means of communication (Weisskirch & Delevi, 2011; Drouin & Landgraff, 2012). Thus, sexting could be appealing to avoidant individuals because it serves as a reasonable substitute for physical intimacy (Drouin & Landgraff, 2012). It is an open question as to whether this would be the case with LGB individuals as well.

Attachment theory also states that individuals develop expectations about whether loved ones will fulfill their needs or reject them (Erozkan, 2009). Insecure attachment has been linked to rejection sensitivity, which is characterized by fear of being deserted, abused, betrayed or victimized with a high degree of sensitivity towards rejection (Natarajan, Somasundaram, & Sundaram, 2011). A person with an insecure attachment also may be influenced by feelings of rejection and be more likely to experience victimization when they encounter rejection. Therefore, it is important to consider the interaction between insecure attachment styles and levels of rejection sensitivity when considering one's positive and negative experiences of sexting and sexting victimization and one's evaluations of such experiences.

Rejection Sensitivity

Rejection sensitivity is defined as a disposition to cognitively and affectively process information in such a way that rejection is both expected and perceived in the actions of others (Downey & Feldman, 1996). People who are highly sensitive to rejection fear being deserted, abused, or betrayed by others, and tend to react very strongly to instances of actual and perceived rejection (Downey & Feldman, 1996). Rejection sensitivity is associated with a range of problematic behaviors in intimate relationships. For instance, these individuals are likely to believe that their partner is dissatisfied with their relationship and have been found to rate partners' behaviors as being more conflictual than do third-party observers (Norona, Salvatore, Welsh, & Darling, 2014). Consequently, those high in rejection sensitivity react accordingly and display behaviors such as jealousy, suspicion, and seeking control over a partner (Downey & Feldman, 1996). Alternatively, individuals high in rejection sensitivity may act submissively toward their partner and defer to their wishes in hopes of avoiding rejection (Hafen, Spilker, Chango, Marston, & Allen, 2014; Young & Furman, 2007). High levels of rejection sensitivity also have been linked to higher levels of depression, loneliness, exclusion, and, of particular importance for the present chapter, victimization from others (Zimmer-Gembeck et al., 2013). Given these characteristics associated with rejection sensitivity, it is unsurprising that rejection sensitivity is linked to both an increased risk for victimization and a greater negative response to the experience of victimization in the form of self-rated negative moods, and experimenter rated reactions of confusion, anger, or sadness (Downey & Feldman, 1996; Zimmer-Gembeck et al., 2014).

Because young people who are sensitive to rejection are highly motivated to avoid experiencing rejection, they may engage in behaviors that put them at risk for victimization (Young & Furman, 2007). In fact, rejection sensitivity has been linked to increased risk of victimization in multiple contexts including peer networks, friendships, and romantic relationships (Hafen et al., 2014; Zimmer-Gembeck & Duffy, 2014; Zimmer-Gembeck et al., 2014). Rejection sensitivity also has implications for the quality of these relationships, such that young adults who were high in rejection sensitivity in adolescence were less likely to be engaged in romantic relationships in emerging adulthood, and those who were in romantic relationships tended to report more negativity and anxiety within that relationship (Hafen et al., 2014); this study also revealed that females who increased in rejection sensitivity from adolescence to emerging adulthood were more likely to take on a role of submissiveness within their relationship, and defer power within the relationship to their partner.

Although these risks for victimization are clear, perhaps most related to patterns of sexting in emerging adulthood is the relation between rejection sensitivity and risk for sexual victimization as reported by Young and Furman (2007). Just as adolescent girls were more likely to feel pressured to act in ways that they believed were 'wrong' as a means to avoid losing their partner (Purdie & Downey, 2000), this study found that adolescents high in rejection sensitivity were more likely to experience sexual aggression into emerging adulthood (Young & Furman, 2007). However, as stressed by Edwards and Barber (2010), it is critically important to consider the context of sexual victimization; they astutely highlight that not just physically forced sexual interactions, but also compliant or consensual engagement in an activity in which someone does not really wish to partake, constitute sexual victimization, though contextually variant. While it is readily apparent that forced sexual interaction is victimization, coercion into consensual acts is also a form of victimization. Evaluations of victimization and responses to victimization differ based on the context in which victimization occurs (see Brenick & Romano, 2016; Rutland, Killen, & Abrams, 2010). Edwards and Barber (2010) examined sexual victimization in the context of condom use during intercourse, and the study found that rejection sensitive individuals who wanted to use condoms during intercourse were less likely to use condoms if they believed that their partner did not want to use them. Similarly, sexual victimization also can take place through sexting, a context that also does not include forced sexual interaction. Given Edwards and Barber's (2010) findings on condom use, it is likely that those EAs who are highly rejection sensitive would be much more likely to yield to their partner's wishes to engage in sexting if that is what they believed their partner would want. Furthermore, this allows for potential continued victimization through unauthorized sharing of those sexts with unintended recipients.

Although sexting is becoming an important part of relationships that inherently requires negotiations of roles within a relationship, no research thus far has considered sexting as a context for victimization that might be influenced by an individual's rejection sensitivity.

Beyond the direct influence of rejection sensitivity on the potential for victimization, rejection sensitivity is also highly related to insecure attachment styles (Natarajan et al., 2011). Given the literature linking attachment style to victimization both theoretically and empirically (Natarajan et al., 2011), and the clear association between rejection sensitivity and attachment (Erozkan, 2009; Natarajan et al., 2011), it is important to consider both individual characteristics in tandem. This was demonstrated in a study by Ozen, Sumer, and Demir (2010) in which relationship satisfaction (in this case, friendship) was predicted by both attachment and rejection sensitivity. Attachment had a direct effect on relationship satisfaction; however, rejection sensitivity moderated this effect such that rejection sensitivity influenced friendship satisfaction only for adolescents highly avoidant in their attachment style (Ozen et al., 2010). As suggested above, it is possible that rejection sensitivity might act as a moderator with insecure attachment to predict negative sexting experiences. If so, this situation sets the stage for individuals to be vulnerable to victimization, such as coercion into sexting, and then experience its negative outcomes as highly rejection sensitive individuals experience in their relationships. Altogether, it is clear that both attachment and rejection sensitivity are important individual characteristics to consider in relation to sexting patterns and victimization in emerging adulthood, but further research is needed to more clearly understand the relationship.

Current Research on Insecure Attachment, Rejection Sensitivity, and Sexting

The authors' present work set out to address these gaps in the literature by administering an online survey comprised of Collins' (1996) attachment scale, Downey and Feldman's (1996) rejection sensitivity questionnaire, and Alderson and Samimi's (2014) sexting experiences questionnaire. A sample of 770 EAs between 18-25 years of age (M_{age}=19.17, SD=1.44; 7.1% African-American, 15.7% Asian-American, 58.7% European-American, 10.4% Hispanic-Latino, 10% Other) was obtained through online recruitment using email listservs sent out to the entire student body of a large public university in New England. The majority of participants self-identified as female (54.9%), as heterosexual (69.9%), and as being single (57.3%).

Measures

The online survey assessed participant demographics, attachment style, level of rejection sensitivity, and beliefs about and experiences with sexting. First participants were asked to identify their gender, ethnicity, sexual orientation, age, and relationship status. Participants then completed the attachment, rejection sensitivity, and sexting experiences scales detailed below. Although the three measures have been widely used and are well established and validated, we pilot tested the combined instrument. Test fatigue was minimal, and comprehension was high, so no changes were made to the protocol.

Attachment

The *Revised Adult Attachment Scale* (Collins, 1996; alternative scoring) was used to assess participants' levels of insecure attachment. In the 18-item questionnaire, participants were asked to think about all of their relationships (past and present), and then respond to items in terms of how they experience their relationships. A scale of 1 (not at all characteristic of me) to 5 (very characteristic of me) was used to respond to items such as, *"I find that people are never there when you need them"* and *"I often wonder whether romantic partners really care about me."* The measure addressed two components of attachment: attachment anxiety (*M*=3.06, *SD*=1.04) and attachment avoidance (*M*=2.82, *SD*=0.74). Previous studies have demonstrated that this is a reliable and valid measure (Mikulincer & Shaver, 2016), and the Cronbach's alpha for the current sample was .89.

Rejection Sensitivity

Participants were administered the 18-item *Adult Rejection Sensitivity Questionnaire* (Downey & Feldman, 1996) to assess rejection sensitivity. The questionnaire asks participants to imagine themselves in hypothetical social situations and rate how concerned or anxious they would be about potential rejection in the scenarios. A scale of 1 (very unconcerned) to 6 (very concerned) was used to evaluate situations such as *"Your boyfriend/ girlfriend has plans to go out with friends tonight, but you really want to spend the evening with him/her, and you tell him/her so."* Participants were then asked to rate how concerned or anxious they would be over whether or not their boyfriend or girlfriend would decide to stay in. Scoring for this measure ranges from 2.00 to 26.00; the current participants' average score was 8.84 (*SD*=3.32). Previous studies have demonstrated that this is a reliable and valid measure (Downey & Feldman, 1996), and the Cronbach's alpha for the current sample was .90.

Sexting Experiences

A subsample of questions from Alderson and Samimi's (2014) questionnaire of potential sexting outcomes was used to assess participants' sexting experiences. This instrument provides a previously validated multifaceted conceptualization of sexting, assessing both the behaviors and beliefs of the participant in regards to the positive, negative, and neutral aspects of sexting. Specifically, the measure includes questions on five distinct sexting themes: *sexting entertainment*- participants' ratings of sexting as enjoyable and fun, Cronbach's alpha = .80; *sexting expectation*- participants' ratings of how typical and expected it is to engage in sexting, Cronbach's alpha = .84; *sexting sharing*- participants' reports of sharing sexts that they have received, Cronbach's alpha = .72; *sexting risk*- participants' beliefs that sexting is risky and could yield negative outcomes, Cronbach's alpha = .89; and *sexting regret*- participants' reports of having sent a sext that they later regretted sending (1 item). Responses were scaled from 1 (strongly disagree) to 7 (strongly agree). Sample questions include: *"Sexting is a regular part of romantic relationships nowadays"* (expectation; *M*=3.68, *SD*=1.15); *"Sexting is fun"* (entertainment; *M*=4.18, *SD*=1.35); *"Sending sexually suggestive photos or videos is risky"* (risk; *M*=5.98, *SD*=1.19); *"I share the sexts I receive with my friends"* (sharing; *M*=2.05; *SD*=1.34); *"I have sent a sext and then regretted sending it later on"* (regret; *M*=3.42, *SD*=1.95).

Results

For each of the dependent measures of sexting experiences, hierarchical multiple regressions were conducted with four steps: the first model included the control variables—gender, sexual orientation, and relationship status—as predictors. The second model added rejection sensitivity, anxious attachment, and avoidant attachment as predictors. The third and fourth models added all two- and three-way interaction terms, respectively, between the three predictor variables of interest. The data met all relevant statistical assumptions for this analysis. Given that interaction terms were examined in these regressions, all variables were mean centered (the variable mean was subtracted from each variable value) prior to analyses to increase interpretability of the results and reduce multicollinearity. This analysis revealed significant findings for all of the dependent variables: sexting entertainment, expectation, sharing, risk, and regret. Below we detail the significant results.

Sexting Entertainment

First, it is possible that insecure attachment and rejection sensitivity might not only leave an individual more likely to experience the negative and victimizing experiences of sexting, but also less likely to experience the positive experiences of sexting (e.g. seeing it as enjoyable and fun). To assess this possible influence, the authors analyzed the relation between insecure attachment, rejection sensitivity, and sexting entertainment. The results of the multiple regression analysis were significant in the first model ($F(1,673)=21.45$, $p<.001$) with the following significant predictors: gender, sexual orientation, and relationship status (see Table 1 for all coefficients). These results reveal that males, as compared to females, LGB individuals, as compared to heterosexual, and partnered individuals in a romantic relationship, as compared to those who are single, were more likely to find sexting entertaining. Additionally, there was a significant main effect of rejection sensitivity, such that those who were lower in rejection sensitivity were more likely to rate sexting as entertaining. However, the addition of the second step predictors did not explain significantly more variance than the first step ($\Delta R = .01$, $p = .11$), and therefore we do not explore this relationship further.

Sexting Expectations

Next, sexting expectations were assessed as participants' beliefs about the typicality in which sexting is engaged among EAs. The multiple regression analysis was significant in the second model ($F(3,670)=2.70$, $p<.05$) such that males, as compared to females, partnered individuals, as compared to those who are single, and individuals who were higher in anxious attachment rated sexting as a highly typical experience in which they are expected to engage in intimate relationships (see Table 1 for coefficients).

Sexting Sharing

Results from the multiple regression analysis on participants' experiences of sharing a sext that they received from someone else also showed significant effects. Only the first model was significant ($F(3,669)=17.54$, $p<.001$), with gender, sexual orientation, and relationship status as significant predictors (see Table 1 for coefficients). These results suggest that males are more likely than females to share the sexts they receive with others, and individuals who are single, as compared to those who are in a relationship, are more likely to share the sexts they receive with others. A 2-way interaction between rejection sensitivity and anxious attachment also was significant, but again the additional variance explained by the third step of the model was not statistically significant so it was not prudent to explore further with these data ($F(3,666)=2.01$, $p=.11$).

Table 1. Multiple regression analysis for sexting experiences by attachment and rejection sensitivity

Step	Predictors	Sexting Entertainment		Sexting Expectations		Sexting Sharing		Sexting Risk		Sexting Regret	
		ΔR^2	β	ΔR^2	β	ΔR^2	β	ΔR^2	β	ΔR^2	β
1	Gender	0.09***	-0.21***	0.04***	-0.20***	0.07***	-0.11**	0.02**	0.07	0.01*	0.05
	Sexual Orientation		0.13***		0.06***		-0.11**		0.11**		0.09*
	Relationship Status		-0.23***		-0.07		0.20***		0.09		-0.02
2	RS	0.01	-0.10*	0.01*	-0.03	0.00	-0.06	0.00	-0.04	0.05***	-0.01
	ANX		0.06		0.12*		0.01		0.06		0.26***
	AVOID		-0.02		0.02		0.05		0.01		-0.04
3	RS x ANX	0.00	-0.05	0.00	-0.01	0.01	-0.10*	0.02*	0.13**	0.00	0.02
	RS x AVOID		0.01		0.01		0.03		0.00		-0.03
	ANX x AVOID		0.06		0.05		-0.03		-0.09		0.01
4	RS x ANX x AVOID	0.00	0.01	0.00	0.08	.00	0.02	0.00	0.07	0.01*	0.13*
	Total R^2	0.10		0.06		0.09		0.04		0.07	

Note. n = 770. RS: Rejection Sensitivity; ANX = Anxious Attachment; AVOID = Avoidant Attachment.
Gender entered as a "dummy" variable: 0= male; 1= female. Sexual Orientation entered as a "dummy" variable: 0 = LGB, 1 = heterosexual. Relationship status entered as a "dummy" variable: 0= in a relationship, 1= single.
$^*p < .05$; $^{**}p < .01$; $^{***}p < .001$. Tables show βs for all predictors in highest significant step.

Sexting Risk

Another multiple regression analysis explored whether any of the aforementioned predictors were associated with how risky participants perceived sexting to be. Results indicated that the third step of the model, which included all mean level predictors and two-way interactions, was significant ($F(3,667) = 3.64$, $p <.05$). Of the demographic variables, only sexual orientation was a significant predictor, such that LGB participants are more likely to rate sexting as riskier (see Table 1 for coefficients). There also was a significant two-way interaction between rejection sensitivity and anxious attachment, such that for people with low rejection sensitivity, low anxious attachment is associated with higher ratings of sexting risk, whereas for people who are highly rejection sensitive, low anxious attachment is associated with lower ratings of sexting risk (see Figure 1).

Sexting Regret

Finally, significant predictors of sexting regret, or how much an individual regrets engaging in sexting, emerged. The results for the multiple regression analysis were significant in the final model ($F(1,660) = 6.35$, $p<.05$). Anxious attachment was as a significant predictor, such that participants with greater anxious attachment reported more regret after engaging in sexting (see Table 1 for coefficients). A 3-way interaction between rejection sensitivity, anxious attachment, and avoidant attachment also emerged. As shown in Figure 2, at low levels of avoidant attachment, low anxious attachment was associated with low levels of regret in individuals low in rejection sensitivity, but high levels of regret for individuals high in rejection sensitivity. For individuals high in avoidant attachment, however, those with low anxious attachment were more likely to show sexting regret if they were low in rejection sensitivity, and less likely to show sexting regret when they were high in rejection sensitivity.

Figure 1. Sexting risk: 2-way interaction between rejection sensitivity and anxious attachment

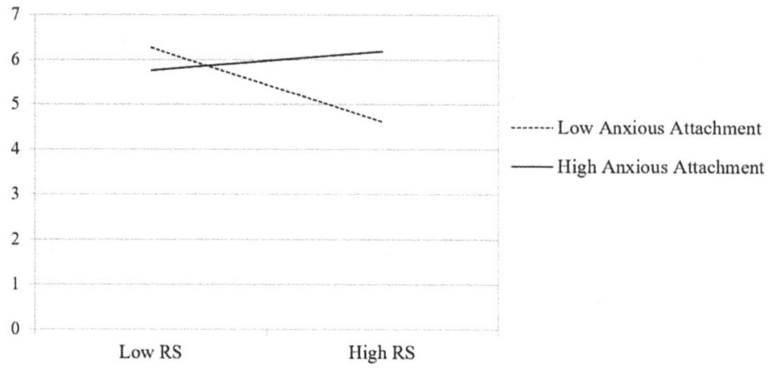

The Social Domain Theory and Evaluations of Sexting Victimization

These findings clearly demonstrate the benefit of examining both insecure attachment and rejection sensitivity in relation to EAs' engagement in and attitudes about sexting. It is equally important, though, to consider EAs' social and moral evaluations of sexting victimization. The Social Domain Theory (Smetana, Jambon, & Ball, 2014; Turiel, 1983) provides a theoretical and methodological framework through which this can be accomplished. The theory asserts that "morality is primarily about ways of approaching social relationships and how people ought to treat each other" (Turiel, 2014, p.19). This framework has been utilized extensively to assess children's, adolescents', and adults' social and moral evaluations of a myriad of social interactions—and potential transgressions—ranging from interpersonal rejection (Park & Killen, 2010) and exclusion (Brenick & Killen, 2014), to harassment (Horn & Nucci, 2006), retribution (Ardila-Rey, Killen, & Brenick, 2009), and deception (Perkins, & Turiel, 2007). However, to date, no research has focused on evaluations of victimization through sexting.

The Social Domain Theory conceptualizes social interactions as the quintessential context in which individuals coordinate three distinct domains of social thought: *the moral, the societal,* and *the psychological.* Research guided by the Social Domain Theory often employs the use of real or hypothetical scenarios of social interactions involving transgressions. Participants are asked to comprehensively evaluate the rightness or wrongness of the transgression; these evaluations are directly related to the coordination of the three domains of social knowledge.

Moral constructs manifest as universal, generalizable concerns regarding potential harm, welfare, and justice. Such moral concerns are used to determine and justify the level of acceptability or objection warranted by a social transgression (Smetana et al., 2014; Turiel, 1983); for instance, the unauthorized sharing of a sext beyond the intended recipient.

The *societal* domain involves conventions that define acceptable social interaction based on group norms, expectations, and authority within a given context. Transgressions within the societal domain are considered wrong only so long as the social norms and rules dictate, but would be evaluated as acceptable if those rules and norms were removed or changed (Smetana et al., 2014; Turiel, 1983). As an example, consider a high school with the following rule: cellphone use is banned in the classroom and any student caught using their cellphone in class must show school administrators their phone content. In this situation, a sext might be shared beyond the intended recipient, but it would be viewed as a more acceptable transgression due to the context defined rules governing cellphone usage.

Figure 2. Sexting regret: 3-way interaction between rejection sensitivity, anxious attachment, and avoidant attachment

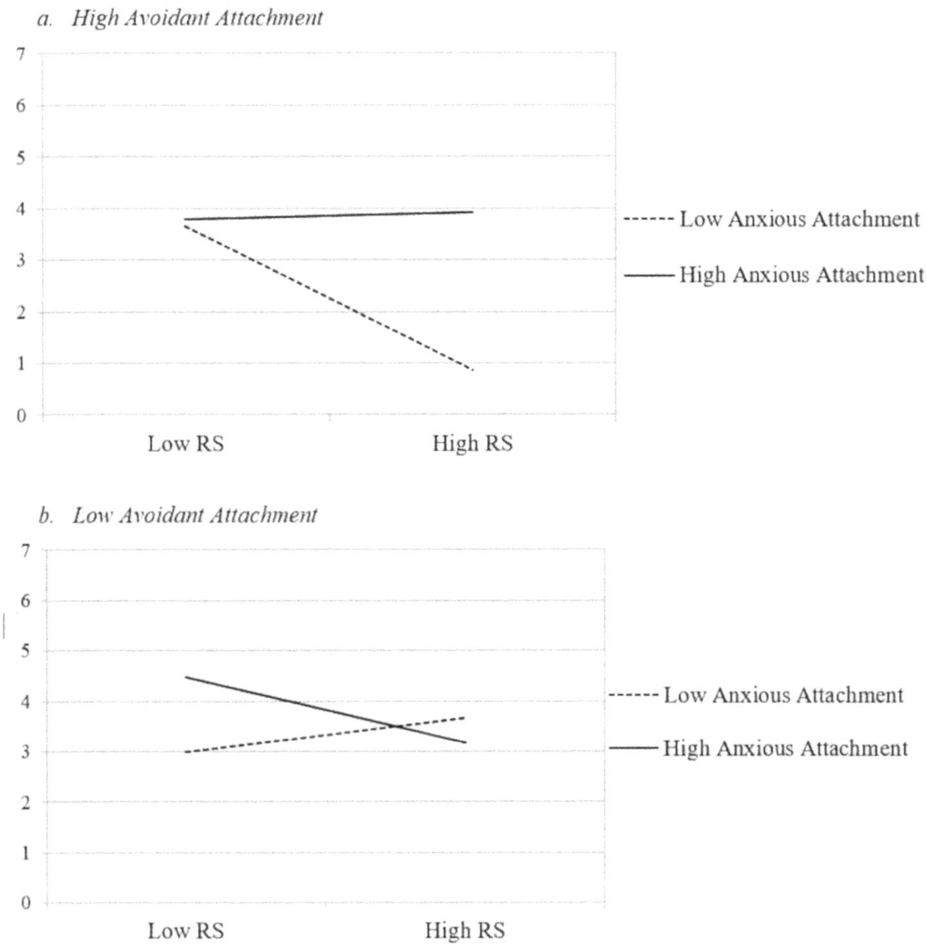

Finally, *psychological* constructs deal with person preferences. Issues within the psychological domain are considered "rights…grounded in notions of self and personal agency" (Smetana et al., 2014, p.25) rather than transgressions. An EA might believe that a sext that was sent to him is now his property to do with as he pleases- that it is his personal choice.

When a social interaction falls squarely within the moral domain, a transgression will be viewed as highly unacceptable, regardless of societal rules or personal preferences (see Brenick & Killen, 2014; Crystal, Killen, & Ruck, 2008; Heinze & Horn, 2014; Horn & Nucci, 2006). Transgressions in the societal domain are seen as less wrong than moral transgressions, as the context specificity of the acceptability of the transgression is considered in the former. Psychological transgressions are often not even considered to be wrong, but rather personal prerogatives (Smetana et al., 2014). However, social interactions are complex and typically appeal to multiple domains of social thought; multifaceted transgressions are often viewed as more acceptable given that moral concerns are coordinated with competing societal or psychological concerns (Brenick & Romano, 2016; Killen, Lee-Kim, McGlothlin, & Stangor, 2002;). The coordination of these competing concerns directly relates to whether an act is even viewed as victimizing, and, if so, what action, if any, should be taken in response (see Rutland et al., 2010). At its core, EAs may believe it is wrong to victimize the original sext creator by sharing a sext without permission (a transgression squarely in the moral domain), but what if peer conventions dictate that everyone shares sexts they receive (societal domain)?

Does it matter if a sext is simply shown to a friend in close physical proximity rather than forwarded to the cellphone of another individual in any location? In the former, the sext, though shared, does not transfer possession again and cannot be shared further, yet the opposite is true for the latter. Moreover, do EAs differentiate between the sharing of sexts in which the person depicted in the sext is known from those in which the person depicted is a stranger? Finally, how might these evaluations relate to an individual's attachment and rejection sensitivity, and what about the sexual orientation of those involved? The current study provides empirical assessment of participants' evaluations of hypothetical sexting victimization scenarios amongst heterosexual and LGB EAs.

Current Research on Evaluations of Sexting Victimization

In addition to assessing EAs' attachment styles, rejection sensitivity, and sexting experiences, the study presented here also assessed participants' evaluations of sexting victimization. In collaboration with two EA research assistants, multiple scenarios and the accompanying follow-up questions were developed specifically for use in this study. The measure was pilot tested with a sample of EAs to assess testing fatigue, comprehension, and ecological validity of the scenarios as presented. Only minor changes were made to the scenario wording.

Participants were presented with hypothetical situations depicting scenes in which one male individual, while out with male friends, received a picture sext of a woman (different-gender scenario). The situations differed in only one way; in the unknown condition the sext recipient and his friends did not know the woman depicted in the sext, but in the known condition, the sext recipient and his friend knew the female depicted in the sext. In line with Social Domain Theory established methodological protocol (see Brenick & Killen, 2014; Killen et al., 2002) the unknown condition was always presented first so that the scenario order reflected increasing levels of intimacy (from an unknown woman to a known woman). The text of the unknown scenario read as follows: *"Bob is hanging out with his best friends Sean and Mike. Bob's phone rings, he has just received a message from his friend AJ. AJ just forwarded Bob a sexual picture of a female that none of them know."* These hypothetical situations were then presented told depicting scenes in which one female/male, while out with female/male friends, received a picture sext of a woman/man from another female/male (same-gender scenario). For all conditions, participants rated the acceptability (i.e., how good or bad) of two potential responses by the scenario protagonist: 1. showing the sext to his/her friends nearby, or 2. electronically forwarding the sext to others. Participants also justified their answers in open-ended responses. Responses were coded into five justification categories: 1. Authority sanctioning - concerns about societal consequences imparted for participating in the victimization (*"it's illegal"*; *"they could get in trouble"*); 2. Direct victimization - moral concerns about the personal harm that would come upon the victim (*"The photo could have devastating effects on the woman's future"*); 3. Relational and group functioning - societal concern about how the friendship or friendship group will/not be affected by the actions (*"They don't know this female, so it seems less bad..."*); 4. Rights violations - moral appeals to broader concerns about undeniable rights that should be afforded to all (*"It's not acceptable [to] promote this type of sexual objectification"*; *"It's an invasion of privacy."*); and 5. Risk of the Sexter and status quo - appeals to accepted societal rules that govern sexting and the sharing of sexts ("*The sexter put themself in this predicament by taking the photo in the first place.*"; "*It's just typical to share something to those around you on your phone if you weren't expecting such a message. It probably would be done without even thinking twice about who saw it.*").

A mixed within- and between- subjects design was used to investigate participants' evaluations of sexting scenarios. A 2 (sexual orientation: heterosexual, LGB) x 2 (gender: female, male) x 2 (relationship status: single, in a relationship) x 2 (familiarity of target: known, unknown) x 2 (message type: show sext, forward sext) x 2 (scenario: different-gender, same-gender) repeated measures analysis of variance (ANOVA), with anxious attachment, avoidant attachment, and rejection sensitivity as covariates, was conducted for the following dependent measures: showing acceptability and forwarding acceptability. For analysis of participants' justifications, an additional 5 (justification: authority sanctioning, direct victimization, relational & group functioning, rights violation, risk of the sexter & status quo) within-subjects factor was included with the analysis model described above.

Comparable to rates found by Brenick et al., (2017), the vast majority of participants considered sharing sexts through methods of both showing the sext to friends close-by (72% when the sext depicts someone in a different-gender dyad unknown to the group, 73% when same-gender dyad unknown, 85% when different gender known, and 88% when same-gender known) and forwarding the sext to others electronically (91% different-gender unknown; 96% different-gender known; 91% same-gender unknown; 96% same-gender unknown) to be wrong and unacceptable. However, the actual ratings of acceptability differed significantly by familiarity ($F(1,471)=6.39, p<.05; \eta_p^2=.01$), indicating that participants rated it as more wrong for the protagonist to share a sext when the target was known to the group than when the target was unknown. The main effects for message type ($F(1,471)=30.44, p<.001; \eta_p^2=.06$), and gender ($F(1,471)=19.83; p<.001; \eta_p^2=.04$) were qualified by a more complex understanding of EAs' evaluations of sexting victimization. A significant 4-way interaction between scenario, message type, gender, and sexual orientation ($F(1,471)=5.60, p<.05, n_p^2=.00$) revealed that whereas all participants rated it equally un/acceptable to share a sext in the same-gender scenario, heterosexual male participants rated it significantly more acceptable to show a sext in the different-gender scenario than all other participants and to forward a sext in the same-gender scenario than the GB participants (see Table 2).

To justify their evaluations of the sexting victimization scenarios, the participants most often appealed to moral concerns about general rights violations, in particular gross invasions of privacy and consent. Next, participants voiced concerns about the direct victimization and potential harm that would be brought upon the victim, ranging from harassment, to bullying, to a completely ruined life. Participants similarly appealed to societal concerns about group and relational functioning that addressed how the victimization may or may not affect the group of friendship dynamic. Participants said that the victimization "*wasn't as bad if they didn't know the person in the sext,*" but it could harm their friend group if the sext got around to people they all knew. Alternatively, participants also talked about friends expecting others to share sexts with them and how not sharing could harm their own relationships. Less frequently, participants brought up social norms regarding sexting to justify potential victimization, claiming that the sexter knows they are at risk for their message being shared as soon as they send it, and that most peers have the mentality that once "*they have the photo on their phone [they] can do what they want with it,*" and "*It's typical to share without thinking twice.*" Moreover, with the addition of the same-gender scenario a new justification emerged reflecting the societal concern about being mistaken as gay; "*Possession of content may call into question perceived orientation, making it less likely to share.*" Participants used authority sanctioning significantly least frequently of all justification, indicating they did not prioritize

Table 2. Means and standard errors of participants' evaluations of sexting victimization across between- and within-subjects factors

Relationship Status	Gender	Sexual Orientation	Different Gender Scenario				Same Gender Scenario			
			Unknown Victim		Known Victim		Unknown Victim		Known Victim	
			Show	Forward	Show	Forward	Show	Forward	Show	Forward
Single	Male	Heterosexual	2.47 (.10)	1.64 (.08)	2.60 (.10)	1.57 (.06)	2.01 (.11)	1.54 (.08)	1.64 (.09)	1.36 (.06)
		GB	2.03 (.16)	1.35 (.13)	1.47 (.15)	1.18 (.10)	1.83 (.18)	1.37 (.13)	1.43 (.14)	1.21 (.10)
	Female	Heterosexual	1.75 (.09)	1.29 (.07)	1.39 (.09)	1.08 (.06)	2.00 (.10)	1.29 (.07)	1.53 (.08)	1.12 (.06)
		LB	1.74 (.12)	1.14 (.09)	1.27 (.11)	1.10 (.07)	1.69 (.13)	1.35 (.10)	1.48 (.10)	1.16 (.07)
Partnered	Male	Heterosexual	2.20 (.14)	1.67 (.11)	1.88 (.13)	1.49 (.09)	2.04 (.16)	1.71 (.12)	1.71 (.13)	1.49 (.09)
		GB	2.39 (.28)	1.76 (.22)	2.02 (.26)	1.46 (.18)	2.48 (.31)	1.74 (.23)	1.73 (.25)	1.46 (.17)
	Female	Heterosexual	1.81 (.10)	1.30 (.08)	1.36 (.09)	1.12 (.06)	1.95 (.11)	1.28 (.08)	1.50 (.09)	1.17 (.06)
		LB	1.82 (.13)	1.41 (.10)	1.48 (.12)	1.21 (.08)	2.00 (.14)	1.54 (.10)	1.53 (.11)	1.23 (.08)

potential consequences of the action as a major detriment for carrying out the victimization (main effect for justification: $F(4,1664)=15.65$, $p<.001$, $n_p^2=.04$).

Below we describe two higher order interactions that qualify this main effect for justification. First, there was a 3-way interaction between justification, message type, and gender ($F(4,1664)=2.89$, $p<.05$, $n_p^2=.01$). Females, as compared to males, used more rights violation and fewer risk of the sexter and status quo justifications for both show and forward message types and less relational and group functioning justifications for the forward message type. Second, there was a 4-way interaction between justifications, sexual orientation, relationship status, and scenario ($F(4,1664)=4.04$, $p<.05$, $n_p^2=.01$), such that all participants used authority sanctioning and relational and group functioning justifications more in the different-gender scenario than the same-gender scenario, whereas the reverse was true of the risk of the sexter and status quo justifications. However, the direct victimization justification was used less frequently across scenarios but only by partnered LGB participants in comparison to single heterosexual participants. At the same time, partnered and single LGB participants used rights violation justification significantly more often than single heterosexual participants.

Perhaps what is most striking though, is the discrepancy between individuals' perceptions of sexting victimization, their actual sexting activity, and their perceptions of others' sexting activity. Clearly, participants found unauthorized sharing of sexts as wrong—a harmful moral violation of privacy and decency. At the same time, 98% of our participants agreed to having shared or forwarded a sext they received. In relation to the scenarios, 27% of participants believed it was likely or very likely that the scenario protagonist would forward the sext of an unknown woman in the different-gender scenario; 30% in the same gender scenario. Incredibly, 75% of participants believed it was likely or very likely the scenario protagonist would show their friends the sext of an unknown person in the different-gender scenario and 42% in the same gender scenario—50% for a known person in the different gender scenario and 41% in the same-gender scenario. Participants see not just sexting, but this type of sexting *victimization* as a typical and expected occurrence.

SOLUTIONS AND RECOMMENDATIONS

The findings reviewed and newly presented in this chapter further establish the scientific knowledge that sexting, particularly with text and images, is an increasingly common behavior among young adults. In line with Klettke and colleagues' (2014) charge to the field, the newly presented findings extend Brenick et al.'s (2017) findings by assessing EAs' engagement in multiple, clearly defined acts of sexting- breaking sexting down by content (i.e. text, image, video) and by the act of sending or receiving a sext. Additionally, sexting experiences were broken down into multiple dimensions reflecting both positive (entertainment) and negative (risk and regret) qualities of sexting experiences, as well as expectations surrounding sexting behaviors, and explored the viewpoints of marginalized communities in regard to sexting and sexting victimization. Although the literature reports varying rates of the negative experiences of victimization through sexting, the present review emphasizes that even rare instances of sexting victimization have been shown to yield highly detrimental consequences (Drouin et al., 2015). As a result, it is imperative to explore all aspects of the multifaceted nature of sexting as well as potential indicators of vulnerability toward sexting victimization.

Accordingly, this chapter presented anxious and avoidant attachment and rejection sensitivity as three such significant predictors of sexting experiences and evaluations of sexting and sexting victimization. Previously, only a handful of studies had explored attachment and sexting, yet those findings indicate a significant relation between the two; specifically, individuals with insecure attachment may engage in sexting more frequently because of overestimated beliefs that sexting is expected of them. This result was replicated in the findings of Brenick et al. (2017), but also further expanded upon here by examining both insecure attachment and rejection sensitivity as they relate independently and interactively to young adults' experiences and evaluations of sexting. The novel results demonstrate that individuals with higher levels of rejection sensitivity found sexting to be less entertaining and those with anxious attachment styles were more likely to endorse the idea that sexting is typical and expected. This is in line with the few previous studies in the field that have described persons with anxious attachment as using sexual intimacy as a way to reduce tension, maintain a romantic partner's interest, and to build closeness with a romantic partner (Delevi & Weisskirch, 2011; Delevi & Weisskirch, 2013). However, people with anxious attachment styles also were more likely to report regret from engaging in sexting. Further interactions between insecure attachment and rejection sensitivity revealed more complex relations; rejection sensitivity related to ratings of sexting as more risky only when an individual also was high in anxious attachment. Similarly, a significant 3-way interaction suggests that individuals high in rejection sensitivity, anxious attachment, and avoidant attachment, report the least sexting regret. These results are important to frame and understand in the context of LGB adults, who have largely been absent from such studies, and cannot contribute to the overall impact of these results. Future research should explore these findings in relation to the previous research showing heightened levels of anxious attachment among the LGB population as well as increased rates of sexting participation. It is possible that a significant interaction did not emerge in our data because we did not have an adequate range of representation for anxious attachment among our limited LGB sample. As a result, the interplay between rejection sensitivity and insecure attachment offers more comprehensive and precise insights about the proclivities toward and experiences of sexting and sexting victimization and should be examined further with heterosexual and sexual minority samples.

Additionally, the current study made significant contributions to the literature by emphasizing demographic perspectives often missing from this literature. Larger samples of male and LGB participants allowed for gender and sexual orientation findings to be fully explored. Males were more likely to perceive sexting as entertaining and expected, and also were more likely to share sexts that they received than females. Heterosexual individuals, on the other hand, rated sexting as less entertaining and less risky than their non-heterosexual peers, but also reported a greater likelihood of sharing sexts. LGB individuals also rated sexting victimization as less acceptable than their heterosexual peers. In an interaction of gender and sexual orientation, heterosexual males were found to be the most accepting of sharing and forwarding sexts than all other participants. LGB participants viewed sexting victimization as a matter of rights violation that is applied equally to everyone, regardless of gender or sexual orientation. Heterosexual participants, however, viewed it as a matter of direct victimization that resulted in personal harm inflicted primarily on women by men—an act that is gendered. This mindset is, in and of itself, harmful to women and sexual minorities. This set of findings adds a multifaceted layer of complexity in the study of how people experience sexting and sexting victimization.

Beyond this, the authors have presented new insight into how EAs *evaluate* sexting and sexting victimization to complement our understanding of EAs' own *experiences* with sexting. To best address sexting victimization, it is essential to understand the ways in which EAs find sexting to be victimizing. For instance, when societal convention dictates the expectation to sext with an intimate partner, is it viewed as victimizing to be coerced into sexting? Similarly, when it is the real and perceived norm to share sexts with others without permission, is this form of victimization still viewed as a moral transgression? Does all this apply equally for heterosexual and LGB scenarios? EAs view sexting as something that is risky, but they also feel obliged to engage in it within their relationships—thus, demonstrating a tendency to knowingly engage in risky behaviors. They rate it as wrong, as a violation of privacy and decency, to share sexts without permission, yet the vast majority also admitted to having shared a sext and believing others would as well. This demonstrates a clear disconnect between their behaviors and beliefs. Providing a comprehensive account of how EAs make sense of their own and others' sexting experiences is critical to addressing any discrepancies in frequency of sexting victimization as well as preventing and effectively responding to sexting victimization.

These conceptual and methodological approaches had not previously been reported in the published literature, but can help identify individuals who are more likely to experience the negative consequences (and less likely to experience the positive outcomes) of sexting. Additionally, these approaches clarify the ways in which sexting is enacted and viewed as victimizing. This knowledge not only has the power to inform the ways in which EAs approach sexting, but also can reveal the most effective methods of preventing and responding to sexting victimization.

FUTURE RESEARCH DIRECTIONS

This chapter has clearly delineated the need for additional research examining EAs' engagement in and evaluations of sexting and sexting victimization—including how both of these factors relate to attachment dimensions and sensitivity to rejection. The presented study contributed valuable information about the influence of individual characteristics on evaluations of sexting; however, though comparable to other late-adolescent/EA samples (e.g., Norona, Roberson, & Welsh, 2016), rates of rejections sensitivity were relatively low in the current sample. Future research could target samples with a larger range of rejection sensitivity, including those who are extremely rejection sensitive, and, to a lesser extent, a sample with a wider array of attachment styles; results from such studies could expand the field's understanding of the effects of these individual characteristics across a larger spectrum. Furthermore, our sample targeted male and LGB youth but future research would benefit from including greater ethnic diversity, relationship diversity, as well as including a larger sample of males, and expanding the literature to include transgender, gender diverse, or asexual participants. This may necessitate widening the age range in future samples with more diverse participants as sexting may begin at different ages for youth and young adults who are on different gender and sexual identity developmental trajectories. Future research also should identify additional individual characteristics that influence sexting and sexting victimization; such identification may provide a deeper understanding of which individuals are at greatest risk following engagement in sexting. Such individual characteristics might include factors such as a history of victimization, social competence, and other instances of risk-taking behavior.

In addition to continuing to examine individual characteristics that predispose EAs for risk of victimization through sexting, the dyadic context within which sexting occurs also may be important to examine. Another limitation of the current study is the reliance on a single reporter design. This presents the potential of inflated correlations between measures when relying on self-report, but also misses valuable information that can be obtained from other sources, especially given that sexting often takes place in dyads. A dyadic design would reveal much needed information about the relationship contexts in which sexting takes place. For instance, victimization might occur more readily when partners have discrepant desires for sexting, and, despite their reservations, one partner agrees to sext the other because they believe it is what the other wants. In these instances, it would be important to examine how accurately partners guessed the desires of their partners. The pressure experienced by one partner may be imposed by other sources, such as general social convention, and, in fact, may not be coming from their partner. Moreover, certain types of dyads may engage in more or more varied sexting behaviors, and, in turn, those behaviors may be evaluated differently (e.g., whether people judge sexting within committed relationships less negatively or as less risky than sexting between casual sexual partners). Future research might aim to answer questions including whether the quality of the relationship, experienced intimacy, status, or trust between partners influences engagement in, evaluations of, and risk for experiencing victimization via sexting.

Additional avenues of research that could expand our understanding of sexting include a fuller examination of social and moral reasoning about sexting victimization. For instance, how do young adults coordinate societal, moral, and psychological concerns (Smetana et al., 2014; Turiel, 1983) when pertaining to contexts of sexting victimization? Does an EA's own engagement in sexting relate to reasoning about the likelihood and acceptability of sexting victimization? Do these evaluations change when victimization involves gender of sexual minorities? Studies addressing research questions of this type may provide a more detailed assessment of the perceived risks of sexting and a more explicit conceptualization of what sexting victimization entails.

Finally, though the study presented in this chapter provides valuable insight into how current university students evaluate sexting and sexting victimization, a much broader understanding of the changing societal landscape in terms of engagement in and acceptance of sexting and sexting victimization is warranted. This suggested research would require a more complex operationalization of sexting and sexting victimization, including risk and regret, than is typically used, and could not just lump the sending, receiving, sharing, or forwarding of texts together under the broad umbrella of sexting.

CONCLUSION

As the prevalence of sexting and presumed typicality of sexting victimization continue to increase, continued research and the treatment of sexting as a multifaceted phenomenon is warranted. The current chapter explored how often EAs reported engaging in different modes of sexting (e.g., text, image, or video) and their evaluations of various sexting scenarios. Our findings revealed that many EAs reported engaging in sexting. Furthermore, they viewed sexting as risky, but nonetheless obligatory in their intimate relationships—demonstrating a tendency to knowingly engage in risky behaviors. Importantly, these results were influenced by participants' attachment and rejection sensitivity. Individuals with insecure attachment and rejection sensitivity possess characteristics that might leave them more vulnerable to sexting victimization, pointing to the need for future research to examine these potential areas of risk. This chapter also took an exploratory look into the previously untouched lens of sexting victimization in relation to sexual orientation. Our findings revealed that those who identify as LGB are less accepting of instances of sexting victimization than their heterosexual peers, despite being more frequent participants in sexting behaviors in an effort to keep their sexual identities a secret. Individuals who identify as LGB may have more knowledge and sensitivity to the dangers that can come with sexting victimization due to their own risk of being victimized or harassed due to their sexual orientation. This same risk does not exist with heterosexual participants, specifically heterosexual males who are typically the perpetrators, and not the victims of sexting victimization. We believe our results are indicative of underlying sexual and gender dynamics that perpetuate the victimhood of women and sexual minorities.

This research could inform future education and intervention efforts aimed at providing training to EAs on how to address and avoid coercion into sexting and combat norms of victimization through unauthorized sharing of sexts. These training efforts could be tailored to individuals who experience attachment insecurity and sensitivity to rejection, avoiding a one-size-fits-all approach. For instance, on the one hand, individuals who are insecurely attached and sensitive to rejection might benefit the most from communication (e.g., about expectations) and boundary-setting skills training. On the other hand, efforts targeting all EAs more broadly might be most successful by working to change societal norms about sexting and sexting victimization (e.g., challenging the notion that women are expected by men to sext; taking action as a bystander to stop unauthorized sharing of sexts). Intervention efforts also might be effective with younger adolescent populations, and encompass more detailed preventative education about the multiple ways in which sexting can pose a risk to their social, emotional, and professional lives, while highlighting ways in which they may be more vulnerable to those negative consequences. Overall, sexting has become a common means of communication and expression within the intimate relationships of EAs, and given the significant developmental implications this has for EAs' cognition and behavior, as well as social and emotional well-being, the topic warrants further examination.

REFERENCES

Albury, K., & Byron, P. (2014). Queering sexting and sexualization. *Media International Australia, 153*(1), 138–147. doi:10.1177/1329878X1415300116

Alderson, K., & Samimi, P. (2014). Sexting among undergraduate students. *Computers in Human Behavior, 31*, 230–241. doi:10.1016/j.chb.2013.10.027

Ardila-Rey, A., Killen, M., & Brenick, A. (2009). Moral reasoning in violent contexts: Displaced and non-displaced Colombian children's evaluations of moral transgressions, retaliation, and reconciliation. *Social Development, 18*(1), 181–209. doi:10.1111/j.1467-9507.2008.00483.x PMID:25722543

Brenick, A., Flannery, K., & Rankin, E. (2017). Victimization or entertainment? How attachment and rejection sensitivity relate to sexting experiences, evaluations, and victimization. In M. F. Wright (Ed.), *Identity, Sexuality, and Relationships among Emerging Adults in the Digital Age* (pp. 201–223). Hershey, PA: IGI Global. doi:10.4018/978-1-5225-1856-3.ch013

Brenick, A., & Killen, M. (2014). Moral judgments about Jewish–Arab intergroup exclusion: The role of cultural identity and contact. *Developmental Psychology, 50*(1), 86–99. doi:10.1037/a0034702 PMID:24188040

Brenick, A., & Romano, K. (2016). Perceived peer and parent outgroup norms, cultural identity, and adolescents' reasoning about peer intergroup exclusion. *Child Development, 87*(5), 1392–1408. doi:10.1111/cdev.12594 PMID:27684394

Brown, J., & Trevethan, R. (2010). Shame, internalized homophobia, identity formation, attachment style, and the connection to relationship status in gay men. *American Journal of Men's Health, 4*(3), 267–276. doi:10.1177/1557988309342002 PMID:20413384

Burkett, M. (2015). Sex(t) talk: A qualitative analysis of young adults' negotiations of the pleasures and perils of sexting. *Sexuality & Culture: An Interdisciplinary Quarterly, 19*(4), 835–863. doi:10.100712119-015-9295-0

Cassidy, J. (2001). Truth, lies, and intimacy: An attachment perspective. *Attachment & Human Development, 3*(2), 121–155. doi:10.1080/14616730110058999 PMID:11708734

Celizic, M. (2009). *Her Teen Committed Suicide Over Sexting*. Retrieved from http://www.today.com/parents/her-teen-committed-suicide-over-sexting-2D80555048#.VRwMLvnF-So

Collins, N. (1996). *Revised Adult Attachment Scale* [Measurement Instrument]. Retrieved from https://labs.psych.ucsb.edu/collins/nancy/UCSB_Close_Relationships_Lab/Resources_files/Adult%20Attachment%20Scale.doc

Crystal, D. S., Killen, M., & Ruck, M. (2008). It is who you know that counts: Intergroup contact and judgments about race-based exclusion. *British Journal of Developmental Psychology, 26*(1), 51–70. doi:10.1348/026151007X198910 PMID:25505355

Dake, J., Price, J., Maziarz, L., & Ward, B. (2012). Prevalence and correlates of sexting behavior in adolescents. *American Journal of Sexuality Education, 7*(1), 1–15. doi:10.1080/15546128.2012.650959

Delevi, R., & Weisskirch, R. (2012). Its ovr b/n u n me: Technology use, attachment styles, and gender roles in relationship dissolution. *Cyberpsychology, Behavior, and Social Networking, 15*(9), 486–490. doi:10.1089/cyber.2012.0169 PMID:22823329

Delevi, R., & Weisskirch, R. (2013). Attachment style and conflict resolution skills predicting technology use in relationship dissolution. *Computers in Human Behavior, 29*(6), 2530–2534. doi:10.1016/j.chb.2013.06.027

Dir, A. L., & Cyders, M. A. (2015). Risks, risk factors, and outcomes associated with phone and Internet sexting among university students in the United States. *Archives of Sexual Behavior, 44*(6), 1675–1684. doi:10.100710508-014-0370-7 PMID:25358950

Downey, G., & Feldman, S. (1996). Implications of rejection sensitivity for intimate relationships. *Journal of Personality and Social Psychology, 70*(6), 1327–1343. doi:10.1037/0022-3514.70.6.1327 PMID:8667172

Downey, G., Freitas, A., Michaelis, B., & Khouri, H. (1998). The self-fulfilling prophecy in close relationships: Rejection sensitivity and rejection by romantic partners. *Journal of Personality and Social Psychology, 75*(2), 545–560. doi:10.1037/0022-3514.75.2.545 PMID:9731324

Downey, G., Nesdale, D., Trevaskis, S., & Zimmer-Gembeck, M. (2014). Relational victimization, loneliness and depressive symptoms: Indirect associations via self and peer reports of rejection sensitivity. *Journal of Youth and Adolescence, 43*(4), 568–582. doi:10.100710964-013-9993-6 PMID:23955324

Drouin, M., & Landgraff, C. (2012). Texting, sexting, and attachment in college students' romantic relationships. *Computers in Human Behavior, 28*(2), 444–449. doi:10.1016/j.chb.2011.10.015

Drouin, M., Ross, J., & Tobin, E. (2015). Sexting: A new, digital vehicle for intimate partner aggression? *Computers in Human Behavior, 50*, 197–204. doi:10.1016/j.chb.2015.04.001

Drouin, M., & Tobin, E. (2014). Unwanted but consensual sexting among young adults: Relations with attachment and sexual motivations. *Computers in Human Behavior, 31*, 412–418. doi:10.1016/j.chb.2013.11.001

Drouin, M., Vogel, K. N., Surbey, A., & Stills, J. R. (2013). Let's talk about sexting, baby: Computer-mediated sexual behaviors among young adults. *Computers in Human Behavior, 29*(5), A25–A30. doi:10.1016/j.chb.2012.12.030

Edwards, G., & Barber, B. (2010). The relationship between rejection sensitivity and compliant condom use. *Archives of Sexual Behavior, 39*(6), 1381–1388. doi:10.100710508-009-9520-8 PMID:19760145

Erozkan, A. (2009). Rejection sensitivity levels with respect to attachment styles, gender, and parenting styles: A study with Turkish students. *Social Behavior and Personality, 37*(1), 1–14. doi:10.2224bp.2009.37.1.1

Gordon-Messer, D., Bauermeister, J. A., Grodzinski, A., & Zimmerman, M. (2013). Sexting among young adults. *The Journal of Adolescent Health, 52*(3), 301–306. doi:10.1016/j.jadohealth.2012.05.013 PMID:23299018

Hafen, C., Spilker, A., Chango, J., Marston, E., & Allen, J. (2014). To accept or reject? The impact of adolescent rejection sensitivity on early adult romantic relationships. *Journal of Research on Adolescence*, *24*(1), 55–64. doi:10.1111/jora.12081 PMID:24729668

Heinze, J., & Horn, S. (2014). Do adolescents' evaluations of exclusion differ based on gender expression and sexual orientation? *The Journal of Social Issues*, *70*(1), 63–80. doi:10.1111/josi.12047

Horn, S. S., & Nucci, L. (2006). Harassment of gay and lesbian youth and school violence in America: An analysis and directions for intervention. In C. Daiute, Z. F. Beykont, C. Higson-Smith, & L. Nucci (Eds.), *International perspectives on youth conflict and development* (pp. 139–155). New York, NY: Oxford University Press. doi:10.1093/acprof:oso/9780195178425.003.0009

Hudson, H. K., & Fetro, J. V. (2015). Sextual activity: Predictors of sexting behaviors and intentions to sext among selected undergraduate students. *Computers in Human Behavior*, *49*, 615–622. doi:10.1016/j.chb.2015.03.048

Judge, A. (2012). Sexting among U.S. adolescents: Psychological and legal perspectives. *Harvard Review of Psychology*, *20*(2), 86–96. doi:10.3109/10673229.2012.677360 PMID:22512742

Killen, M., Lee-Kim, J., McGlothlin, H., Stangor, C., & Helwig, C. C. (2002). How children and adolescents evaluate gender and racial exclusion. *Monographs of the Society for Research in Child Development*, *67*, i-129. PMID:12557595

Killen, M., & Rutland, A. (2011). *Children and Social Exclusion: Morality, Prejudice, and Group Identity*. Hoboken, NJ: Wiley. doi:10.1002/9781444396317

Klettke, B., Hallford, D., & Mellor, D. (2014). Sexting prevalence and correlates: A systematic literature review. *Clinical Psychology Review*, *34*(1), 44–53. doi:10.1016/j.cpr.2013.10.007 PMID:24370714

Kopecký, K. (2014). Cyberbullying and sexting between children and adolescents –Comparative study. *Procedia: Social and Behavioral Sciences*, *149*, 467–471. doi:10.1016/j.sbspro.2014.08.292

Lee, M., & Crofts, T. (2015). Gender, pressure, coercion and pleasure: Untangling motivations for sexting between young people. *British Journal of Criminology*, *55*(3), 454–473. doi:10.1093/bjc/azu075

Mikulincer, M., & Shaver, P. R. (2016). *Attachment in adulthood: Structure, dynamics, and change* (2nd ed.). New York: Guilford Press.

Natarajan, G., Somasundaram, C. P., & Sundaram, K. R. (2011). Relationship between attachment security and rejection sensitivity in early adolescence. *Psychological Studies*, *56*(4), 378–386. doi:10.100712646-011-0108-8

Norona, J. C., Roberson, P. N. E., & Welsh, D. P. (2016). Rejection sensitivity and depressive symptoms: Longitudinal actor-partner effects in adolescent romantic relationships. *Journal of Adolescence*, *51*, 6–18. doi:10.1016/j.adolescence.2016.05.007 PMID:27254083

Norona, J. C., Salvatore, J. F., Welsh, D. P., & Darling, N. (2014). Rejection sensitivity and adolescents' perceptions of romantic interactions. *Journal of Adolescence*, *37*(8), 1257–1267. doi:10.1016/j.adolescence.2014.09.003 PMID:25282535

Ozen, A., Sumer, N., & Demir, M. (2010). Predicting friendship quality with rejection sensitivity and attachment security. *Journal of Social and Personal Relationships*, 163–181. doi:10.1177/0265407510380607

Park, Y., & Killen, M. (2010). When is peer rejection justifiable? Children's understanding across two cultures. *Cognitive Development, 25*(3), 290–301. doi:10.1016/j.cogdev.2009.10.004 PMID:21076660

Parker, T. S., Blackburn, K. M., Perry, M. S., & Hawks, J. M. (2013). Sexting as an intervention: Relationship satisfaction and motivation considerations. *The American Journal of Family Therapy, 41*(1), 1–12. doi:10.1080/01926187.2011.635134

Perkins, S. A., & Turiel, E. (2007). To lie or not to lie: To whom and under what circumstances. *Child Development, 78*(2), 609–621. doi:10.1111/j.1467-8624.2007.01017.x PMID:17381793

Purdie, V., & Downey, G. (2000). Rejection sensitivity and adolescent girls' vulnerability to relationship-centred difficulties. *Child Maltreatment, 5*(4), 338–349. doi:10.1177/1077559500005004005 PMID:11232261

Renfrow, D. G., & Rollo, E. A. (2014). Sexting on campus: Minimizing perceived risks and neutralizing behaviors. *Deviant Behavior, 35*(11), 903–920. doi:10.1080/01639625.2014.897122

Ringrose, J., Harvey, L., Gill, R., & Livingstone, S. (2013). Teen girls, sexual double standards and 'sexting': Gendered value in digital image exchange. *Feminist Theory, 14*(3), 305–323. doi:10.1177/1464700113499853

Rutland, A., Killen, M., & Abrams, D. (2010). A new social-cognitive developmental perspective on prejudice: The interplay between morality and group identity. *Perspectives on Psychological Science, 5*(3), 279–291. doi:10.1177/1745691610369468 PMID:26162160

Smetana, J. G., Jambon, M., & Ball, C. (2014). The social domain approach to children's moral and social judgments. In M. Killen & J. G. Smetana (Eds.), *Handbook of moral development* (2nd ed.; pp. 23–45). New York, NY: Psychology Press. doi:10.4324/9780203581957.ch2

Turiel, E. (1983). *The Development of Social Knowledge: Morality and Convention Cambridge*. Cambridge University Press.

Turiel, E. (2014). Morality: Epistemology, development, and social opposition. In M. Killen & J. G. Smetana (Eds.), *Handbook of moral development* (2nd ed.; pp. 3–22). New York, NY: Psychology Press. doi:10.4324/9780203581957.ch1

Vanden Abeele, V., Campbell, M., Eggermont, S., & Roe, K. (2014). Sexting, mobile porn use, and peer group dynamics: Boys' and girls' self-perceived popularity, need for popularity, and perceived peer pressure. *Media Psychology, 17*(1), 6–33. doi:10.1080/15213269.2013.801725

Walker, S., Sanci, L., & Temple-Smith, M. (2013). Sexting: Young women's and men's views on its nature and origins. *The Journal of Adolescent Health, 52*(6), 697–701. doi:10.1016/j.jadohealth.2013.01.026 PMID:23587784

Weisskirch, R., & Delevi, R. (2011). "Sexting" and adult romantic attachment. *Computers in Human Behavior, 27*(5), 1697–1701. doi:10.1016/j.chb.2011.02.008

Young, B. J., & Furman, W. (2007). Interpersonal factors in the risk for sexual victimization and its recurrence during adolescence. *Journal of Youth and Adolescence*, *37*(3), 297–309. doi:10.100710964-007-9240-0

Zimmer-Gembeck, M., & Duffy, A. (2014). Heightened emotional sensitivity intensifies associations between relational aggression and victimization among girls but not boys: A longitudinal study. *Development and Psychopathology*, *26*(3), 661–673. doi:10.1017/S0954579414000303 PMID:25047290

Zimmer-Gembeck, M., Trevaskis, S., Nesdale, D., & Downey, G. (2014). Relational victimization, loneliness and depressive symptoms: Indirect associations via self and peer reports of rejection sensitivity. *Journal of Youth and Adolescence*, *43*(4), 568–582. doi:10.100710964-013-9993-6 PMID:23955324

KEY TERMS AND DEFINITIONS

Anxious Attachment: An insecure attachment style that is characterized by having a deep desire for intimacy, while simultaneously fearing abandonment.

Attachment: The lasting emotional and affectionate bond (either secure or insecure in nature) that we develop in childhood with our caregiver and that manifests through the lifespan with the most important people in our lives (e.g., romantic partners).

Avoidant Attachment: An insecure attachment style that is characterized by having an aversion to being dependent on another individual or having another individual dependent on you.

Evaluations of Sexting: The ways in which people judge and reason about the positive, negative, and neutral aspects of sexting behaviors.

Rejection Sensitivity: The tendency to expect or perceive others to act in ways that reject the individual.

Sexting: Sending or receiving sexually suggestive text, picture, or video messages.

Sexting Victimization: Being harmed by sexting. Sexting victimization can occur in various ways, ranging from feelings of coercion and pressure to sext, to the threat or act of having a sext shared with others without the prior consent of the individual depicted.

Chapter 8
The Influence of Pornography on Romantic Relationships of Emerging Adults

Bonnie Young-Petersen
Brigham Young University, USA

Brian J. Willoughby
Brigham Young University, USA

ABSTRACT

Scholars have studied emerging adults and pornography extensively, but to date there is no research on how pornography influences how emerging adults approach and act in relationships. The purpose of this chapter is to explore the nature of pornography use among emerging adults, as well as to look at the relationship between pornography use and pornography-related relational anxiety among emerging adults. The authors describe existing research on pornography and emerging adults, introduce their own study, and explain the results and implications.

INTRODUCTION

Researchers have been drawn to the study of emerging adulthood since Dr. Jeffrey Arnett introduced the term almost twenty years ago (Arnett, 2000). Emerging adulthood, defined as the stage from the late teens through the twenties, has attracted scholars because of the distinct relational patterns of today's emerging adults. Scholars have noted how this cohort differs in attachment patterns (Umemura, Lacinova, & Macek, 2014), ideas about marriage (Willoughby & Hall, 2015), technology use (Swanson & Walker, 2015), and religiosity (Salas-Wright, Vaughn, & Maynard, 2014). While extensive research explores multiple aspects of emerging adult life, scholars have paid special attention to the changing romantic relationship and sexuality patterns of this group (Perry & Longest, 2018; Stanley, Rhoades, & Fincham, 2011; Willoughby, Hall, & Luczak, 2013; Lefkowitz & Gillen, 2006). This particular study examines pornography use patterns of emerging adults as well as how pornography influences attitudes

DOI: 10.4018/978-1-7998-1063-6.ch008

and feelings experienced in emerging adult romantic relationships.Similar to the recent prevalence of research on emerging adults, sexuality scholars have increasingly studied the effects of pornography on its consumers. The Internet boom in the western world increased the accessibility and use of pornography around the same time Arnett articulated his ideas about a new pre-adulthood phase (Young, 2008). Today's emerging adults are part of a unique cohort that has had essentially unlimited access to high-speed pornography and are some of the most frequent consumers of pornography (Traen, Nilsen, & Stigum, 2006; Stack, Wasserman, & Kern, 2004; Coyne, Padilla- Walker, & Howard, 2013; Carroll et al., 2008). Yet to date, scholarship on how emerging adult romantic relationships are influenced by pornography use is limited. In this chapter, the authors will look at connections between emerging adult pornography use and processes in romantic relationships. More specifically, our chapter will address the following questions: What is the nature of pornography use among emerging adults? What is the relationship between pornography use and pornography-related anxiety in emerging adult romantic relationships?

Emerging Adults and Romantic Relationships

The romantic relationships of today's emerging adults (mostly Gen Z-ers) are quite distinct from romantic relationships of previous generations. Traditionally, the period between age 18 and 30 was viewed as a time to make major decisions like marriage and occupation and also to assume one's position as an adult in society (Levinson, 1978). Scholars have noted that in contrast to generations past, today's young people are delaying those major decisions, and spend their twenties preparing for their futures individually. According to Schulman and Connolly (2013), the romantic relationships of today's emerging adults are characterized by postponement of marriage and are heavily influenced by individualistic ambitions. Many emerging adults believe it is important to travel extensively or to have an experience of self-discovery before settling down. Others postpone marriage until they have become financially secure. Most emerging adults today also believe that it is important to "test run" their relationships before marriage, and cohabit with their potential partner, adding another step into the path to marriage (Fincham & Cui, 2010).

Emerging adults aren't unique simply because of waiting to tie the knot or postponing the transition to adulthood. Popular culture portrays that while many young people in the United States are waiting to marry, they are replacing stable, committed relationships with "friends with benefits" or hookups, defined as brief, uncommitted sexual encounters (Garcia, Reiber, Massey, Merriweather, 2012). Books like "The Happy Hook Up: A Single Girl's Guide to Casual Sex" (Sherman & Tocantins, 2004) or "The Hookup Handbook: A Single Girl's Guide to Living it Up" (Rozler & Lavinthal, 2010) perpetuate this idea, and reflect emerging adults' ideas about how to approach and behave in relationships during this relatively new stage of life. While recent research has suggested that "hookup culture" might be not as prevalent as supposed (Monto & Carey, 2014), other studies suggest that up to 80% of college students have engaged in a hookup (Garcia, Reiber, Massey, Merriweather, 2012; Owen, Fincham, Moore, 2011). One study of undergraduate college students showed that both men and women had nearly double thenumber of hookups compared to first dates (Bradshaw, Kahn, & Saville, 2010). These sexual practices are often void of emotional ties or expectations of permanence. In fact, research suggests that emerging adults engaging in hookups do not disclose their feelings about sex with their partners and communicate their sexual likes more than their dislikes (Byers & Demmons, 1999). This falls in line well with sexual communication research that has found that sexual communication increases as the relationship matures and becomes exclusive (Fincham & Cui, 2010). Combined, these results suggest that emerging adults are seeking the sexual experiences traditionally shared in committed relationships in non-committal hookups. But how does pornography relate to these behaviors?

Today's emerging adults are the first cohort that has had unlimited access to endless high-speed internet pornography throughout their adolescence and early adult years. The current availability and use of pornography is unprecedented, and such changes have implications for emerging adult sexuality and relationship formation. In their 2018 study, Leonhardt and Willoughby found that emerging adult pornography use predicted lower perceptions that marriage will play a central role in one's life, perhaps pointing to pornography's effect on emerging adult relationship scripts. Similarly, Perry and Longest's longitudinal study showed that higher levels of pornography use among emerging adult men was associated with a lower likelihood of marriage (2018). Other scholars argue that the popularity of pornography use serves to drive down the "price of sex" with real women as pornography gives men attractive sexual options and experiences without relationship commitments (Regnerus, 2017; Regnerus & Uecker, 2010). In other words, emerging adult men may be delaying or placing less importance on marriage because they are able to get sex in a more convenient, immediate way. Further, emerging adult pornography users have been found to have more permissive sexual attitudes and place greater emphasis on having sexual experience before marriage (Leonhardt & Willoughby, 2018). Together, these findings point to pornography's influence on relationship patterns, thus it can be expected that pornography will also influence how emerging adults will approach and experience anxiety in romantic relationships.

Approaches to Pornography Research

While pornography outcome research in the last decade has been prolific (Tolman et al., 2014), not all results point to the same outcomes. Often, researchers' backgrounds inform the questions they ask about pornography's effects. As Hald, Seaman, and Linz (2014) suggest, the three most common approaches to pornography research have been the liberal, conservative, and feminist perspectives. All three perspectives hold unique views on pornography interacts with emerging adult development. The liberal perspective, which commonly supports positive outcomes of pornography use, is often supported by research focused on the neutrality or positive sexual outcomes of pornography use. For example, some such research has shown that female pornography use may be positively associated with female sexual quality (Willoughby & Leonhardt, 2018; Poulsen, Busby, & Galovan, 2013), and that pornography is a source of knowledge and a resource for intimate practices (Attwood, 2005). From this perspective, increased pornography use may help emerging adults become more sexually knowledgeable and promote more female-centric sexual scripts.

Pornography outcome research from the conservative perspective focuses heavily on negative sexual and relational outcomes. For example, a 2011 study conducted by E.M. Morgan showed that higher use of pornography among emerging adults was associated with more risky sexual behavior, such as more casual sex encounters and lower age at first intercourse. Another study found that less progressive gender role attitudes and sexual harassment perpetration were predicted by early exposure to pornography (Brown & L'Engle, 2009). Similarly, Stewart and Szymanski's 2012 study found that women's reports of their male partner's frequency of pornography use were negatively associated with their relationship quality, and that perceptions of problematic use of pornography were negatively correlated with self-esteem, relationship quality, and sexual satisfaction. From this perspective, pornography use during emerging adulthood may elevate harmful or risk-taking behaviors and be associated with negative individual and relational developmental outcomes (Wright, Tokunaga, & Kraus, 2015).

Research from the feminist perspective is generally centered around pornography's negative influence on attitudes and treatment of women. One 2007 study showed that for both males and females, exposure to online pornography was significantly related to beliefs that women are sex objects (Peter & Valkenburg, 2007). Similarly, Malamuth, Hald, and Koss examined pornography use and attitudes supporting violence against women, and found that among emerging adult males, an overall positive association between these factors existed (2011). Other studies, however, have found that exposure to pornography was a non-significant predictor of misogynist attitudes (McKee, 2007; Padgett, Brislin-Slutz, Neal, 1989; Barak, Fisher, Belfry, & Lashambe, 1999). This perspective would suggest the emerging adults (mostly men) who use pornography frequently may be more likely to harbor negative or inaccurate beliefs about women, and that these beliefs that may influence their ability to have healthy relationships with those of the opposite sex.

The liberal, conservative, and feminist approaches to pornography research provide unique understandings of pornography outcomes during emerging adulthood, but alone, these perspectives are limited in their ability to produce or support a comprehensive framework for organizing the effects of pornography. To this end, more inclusive approaches for pornography outcomes have been found when scholars have grounded their outcome research in social science theory.

Theoretical Foundations

Approaching research theoretically provides validity to research and enables scholars to extend and connect their results to other findings. Pornography outcome scholars use an array of theories to put their findings into context, as well as to organize the outcomes of pornography use. Below the authors summarize two of the major theories used when examining pornography use and emerging adulthood.

Social Learning Theory

Social learning theory states that individuals learn not only by their own experiences, but also through the observation of the actions and behaviors of others (Bandura, 1977; Check & Malamuth, 1986). When applied in a sexual context, social learning theory suggests that sexual behaviors, attitudes, and roles can be influenced and even created by pornography, and that this happens in a context where no punishment or social norms can prevent or negatively reinforce such attitudes, and behaviors (Malamuth & Check, 1985; Seto, Maric, & Barbaree, 2001). Multiple studies have shown support for social learning theory and pornography (Bridges, Sun, Ezzell, & Johnson, 2016; (Regnerus & Uecker, 2010; Fincham & Cui, 2010; Wright, Tokunaga, & Kraus, 2015; Hald, Malamuth, & Yuen, 2010).

Some scholars argue that behaviors portrayed in pornography are likely learned and acted out – even if at a small level—in sexual imaginations and relationships. These claims are partially supported by research. One study found that higher pornography use is associated with higher engagement in or interest in trying sexual behavior consistent with pornographic scripts (Bridges, Sun, Ezzell, & Johnson, 2016). Recent meta-analyses have found that pornography consumption is linked with more aggressive attitudes and behaviors toward women (Wright, Tokunaga, & Kraus, 2015; Hald, Malamuth, & Yuen, 2010). Other scholars, pointing to the frequency of anal sex in pornography (Bridges, Wosnitzer, Scharrer, Sun, & Liberman, 2010) report that the rate of heterosexual emerging adult couples who had engaged in anal sex has increased over the last few decades. According to their research, by the age of 23, around 30%

of emerging adults experienced anal sex. This increase in popularity of anal sex is viewed as evidence of porn-inspired practices (Regnerus & Uecker, 2010; Fincham & Cui, 2010).

A recent content analysis revealed that, in the internet's most popular pornographic videos, men were more likely to be portrayed as having sex for their own pleasure than women. Men were also more often manually and orally stimulated than women, were more likely to experience orgasms than women, and women were more frequently as being submissive during sex compared to men. Further, more than a quarter of the most popular pornographic videos depicted men spanking women and almost a fifth depicted men gagging women (e.g. inserting the penis very far in the woman's mouth), and the responses of these women being spanked or gagged was largely neutral (spanking: 57.4%; gagging: 61.3%) or positive (spanking: 38%; gagging: 12%). A fifth of the women being gagged gave mixed signals, such as at first appearing to be in displeasure, then changing to show pleasure. Across all pornographic videos, the average sex scenes lasted about 16 minutes (Klaassen & Peter, 2015). Previous content analyses have found similar patterns in best-selling pornography (Bridges, Wosnitzer, Scharrer, Sun, & Liberman, 2010). According to social learning theory, consuming such pornographic content can create beliefs about women's sexual preferences and behavior (i.e. women enjoy being spanked, sex acts should continue even when a partner expresses dislike, or men's pleasure is the priority), as well as how much time is being spent on sex. These implications may have weighty consequences, as time spent on sex, sexual communication, trust, focus on one's partner, and empathy are significantly related to sexual and relationship satisfaction (Leonhardt, Spencer, Butler, & Theobald, 2018; Blair & Pukall, 2014; Campbell et al., 2009).

Sexual Script Theory

Social learning theory shares multiple ideas with sexual script theory, and like social learning theory, sexual script theory is used by researchers to explain outcomes of pornography use (Štulhofer, Buško, & Landripet, 2010). Sexual script theory is rooted in the widely used script theory, which teaches that human behavior is dictated by patterns called "scripts" that individuals "act out" due to exposure and conditioning. According to sexual script theory, sexual scripts, or culturally available messages that define what 'counts' as sex, what is erotic, or how to act during a sexual encounter, may be altered by messages and images portrayed in pornography (Frith & Kitzinger, 2001). While it is acknowledged that pornography is not the only element influencing sexual scripts, this theory proposes that it may be used as a guide or educational tool for many users, young and old.

According to this theory, pornography leads users to adopt attitudes about where and how sex happens due to the "scripts" they have observed in pornography. One study conducted by Braithwaite, Couslon, Keddington, and Fincham examined how pornography influenced emerging adults' hooking up behavior via sexual scripts (2015). These researchers found that more frequent viewing of pornography was associated with more frequent hook ups and higher numbers of hook up partners, and plans to have higher numbers of sexual partners, and that more permissive sexual scripts mediated the association between more frequent pornography viewing and hooking up. Similarly, a 2010 study that utilized scripting theory found that viewing pornography influenced willingness to explore new sexual relationships. This study, however, found that viewing pornography extended sexual scripts rather than replacing them completely (Weinberg, Williams, Kleiner, & Irizarry). Depictions of committed relationships are rare and infidelity is a common theme in popular pornography, and such pornography may communicate a script that sex is casual, impersonal, and pleasure-focused (Rasmussen, Millar, & Trenchuk, 2018). Grubbs et al.'s study from 2019 echoes this and found that pornography consumption predicts more pleasure-oriented approaches to sex, as well as increases in casual attitudes about sexual involvement. According to this theory, pornography can also create scripts about what is sexually arousing or erotic. A 2019 study of sexually-active females found that masturbating to pornography was associated with increased recall of pornographic images and heightened reliance on pornography for achieving and maintaining arousal (Johnson, Ezzell, Bridges, & Sun, 2019).

In conclusion, scholars who include theory in their scope of pornography outcome research find more universal and applicable findings. In addition to the importance of theory, scholars also acknowledge the importance of individual and contextual factors in pornography outcomes related to emerging adults. These factors give a more comprehensive scope and understanding of pornography use, explaining and providing nuance for different outcomes.

Major Individual and Contextual Factors in Pornography Research

Scholars have suggested that individual and contextual factors are vital to understanding the correlates and outcomes of pornography use. Important factors that have been addressed include gender, age, religiosity, beliefs about pornography, and relationship status (individual factors), as well as if pornography is used alone vs. with partner and discrepancy in partner use (contextual factors) (Hald, 2006; Willoughby, Carroll, Nelson, & Padilla-Walker, 2014; Willoughby, Carroll, Busby, & Brown, 2015; Patterson & Price, 2012). Such results have demonstrated that pornography outcome research is multifaceted and complicated.

Among the most important individual factors is gender. Social scientists have repeatedly highlighted the differences between males and females in pornography use and outcomes (Carroll, Busby, Willoughby, & Brown, 2017; Malamuth, 1996; Romito, Beltramini, 2001) and very few studies exclude gender from analyses. Studies have found significant differences between genders in pornography consumption patterns, including age of exposure (men were younger), frequency of viewing pornography (men viewed more), patterns of viewing pornography with partners (women more likely to view with partners), as well as interest in hardcore pornography (men more interested) (Hald, 2006; Willoughby, Young-Petersen, & Leonhardt, 2018). Another study assessing sexual arousal and behavior as an outcome of watching X-rated videos found that emerging adult males reported more positive psychosexual responses than women (Mosher & Maclan, 1994). Females have also been found to perceive greater negative effects of viewing pornography than males and are more ready to support stricter guidelines for internet pornography (Lo & Wei, 2002). Clearly, the context of gender is one of the most – if not the most – important characteristic in approaching pornography outcomes (Carroll et al., 2008).

Another important individual factor that influences pornography outcomes is that of religion. This is for multiple reasons. For one, religious individuals often receive negative messages about pornography that non-religious individuals seldom hear. Religious organizations frequently have strict rules about sexuality both outside and within marriage, and using pornography is rarely a part of what is deemed an appropriate script of either context. It seems logical, then, that religious individuals would use less pornography – and the research supports that (Nelson, Padilla-Walker, & Carroll, 2010). Recent studies have shown that while nearly two thirds of young men and one half of young women in the United States agree that viewing pornography is acceptable, and nearly ninety percent of young men and one third of women report using it (Carroll et. al., 2008), studies on religious young adults have found a negative relationship between pornography use and religiosity, and that this group unanimously believes that pornography use is unacceptable (Nelson, Padilla-Walker, & Carroll, 2010).But what about religious individuals who do use pornography? Because of religious teachings, religiously devout individuals who compulsively – or even willfully – use pornography often experience unique feelings of guilt or shame (Fisher, Montgomery-Graham, & Kohut, 2019). This idea is supported by a 2012 study by Patterson and Price which showed that the mental health costs of using pornography was greater for religious individuals than non-religious individuals. Another study found that religious emerging adults experienced extreme distress as a result of their pornography use, and commonly perceived their use to be addictive, even without clinical evidence of addiction (Sessoms, 2011). Conversely, religious emerging adults who "stick to their morals" regarding pornography high levels of self-worth and low levels of depression (Nelson, Padilla-Walker, & Carroll, 2010). Further, religious emerging adults define pornography and interpret pornographic material differently than non-religious emerging adults, and often have a lower threshold for what types of sexual media constitute "pornography" (Grubbs & Perry, 2019; Willoughby & Busby, 2015).

Relationship context, including if one is in a relationship or if pornography use is utilized individually versus relationally, has also been seen to influence pornography acceptability and use. One study exploring pornography use of college students in committed romantic relationships found that three main groups emerged from the sample: The first group (70.8% of men, 45.5% of women) reported that solo and partner use was acceptable, the second group (22.3% of men, 26.2% of women) reported that pornography unacceptable because of being in a committed relationship and the final group(5.4% men, 12.9% women) reported that pornography use was unacceptable in any context or circumstance (Olmstead, Negash, Pasley, & Fincham, 2013). Other studies have shown that in a relationship context, discrepancies in pornography use at the couple level are related to negative outcomes (Carroll et al., 2017; Willoughby, Carroll, Busby, & Brown, 2016).

As can be seen, previous research on pornography use and emerging adults offers a wide array of findings and perspectives. Despite growing research this area, continued work is needed to address a multitude of scholarly gaps. For example, most research has focused exclusively on individual outcomes or relational outcomes. No research to date has explored how pornography use may alter an emerging adult's attitudes about forming romantic relationships or communicating about pornography in those relationships. In addition, since Carroll et al.'s landmark study on emerging adults and pornography in 2008, no scholarship has given a detailed account of the current pornography use patterns of emerging adults. Having reviewed previous literature on pornography use outcomes and emerging adults, the authors will now turn to a new analysis to provide us more information regarding pornography use patterns of emerging adults and the unique influence that pornography has on emerging adults' attitudes about and behaviors in forming romantic relationships.

METHODS

Participants

This study uses data collected in 2015 from an international sample of 929 emerging adults who took an online survey via Amazon's Mechanical Turk (MTurk) website. Scholars have noted that samples from MTurk are very similar to other diverse behavioral research samples, and several studies have been replicated using MTurk to provide evidence for the validity of the sample (Paolacci, Chandler, & Ipeirotis, 2010; Suri & Watts, 2011). The participants were predominantly from Southeast Asia and the United States. The sample included 437 male and 488 female respondents. For the purpose of this study (to compare pornography use among female and male emerging adults), the authors excluded transgender individuals from our analyses. The participants ranged in age from 18-30 and the mean age of the sample was 25.25 years (SD=3.22). Fifty percent of the sample was White, 34.1% were Asian, 6.3% were Black, and 5.4% were Latino. Participants reported a variety of religious affiliations: 34.3% reported Christian (15.8% Catholic, 15.1% Protestant, 3.4% Latter- day Saint), 25.7% reported Hindu, 3.5% reported Muslim, 1.2% reported Jewish, and 31.1% reported no religious affiliation. Four percent reported an "other" religious affiliation. Twenty-eight percent of the sample were dating and never married, 29.3% were married, and 33.6% were single.

Procedures

Participants were recruited to take an online survey via Amazon's Mturk website in the spring of 2015. Informed consent was obtained online, and only after participants indicated consent were they able to take the 20-30 minute survey and receive the compensation (.25$) through Mturk. Sections of the survey addressed areas such as religiosity, life satisfaction, depression, impulsivity, risky behavior, history of pornography use, compulsive pornography use, attitudes about pornography, and relationship history.

MEASURES

Pornography

In the survey participants took, pornography was defined as "any material intended for the sexual arousal of its viewer." Pornography use was measured by frequency of viewing and type of pornography viewed. Participants indicated if they had (1) or had not (0) ever viewed pornography. Of those who indicated that they had ever viewed pornography, participants indicated if they had viewed pornography daily (7), 2-6 times a week (6), about every other week (5), about every month (4), about once every few months (3), about twice a year (2), or about once a year or less (1). Specific types of pornography were explained in different items on the survey, with items asking participants to indicate whether they had (1) or had not (0) viewed photos of women in lingerie or swimsuits, photos of women exposing breasts, photos of women exposing breasts and genitals, photos of men exposing genitals, photos of sexual intercourse, videos depicting sexual intercourse, or videos depicting other sexual acts.

Compulsive pornography use was assessed with an adapted scale from the Sexual Compulsivity Scale, created by Kalichman and Rompa (1995). Five items were included on the survey: "My thoughts about pornography are causing problems in my life," "My desires to view pornography disrupt my daily life," "I sometimes fail to meet my commitments and responsibilities because of my pornography use," "Sometimes my desire to view pornography is so great I lose control," "I have to struggle to not view pornography." The scale was reliable (Chronbach's α = .89), and participants responded on a 6-point Likert Scale from "Very strongly disagree" (1) to "Very strongly agree" (6).

Control Variables

Previous research has suggested that there are several individual characteristics that are associated with pornography use and outcomes including gender, impulsivity, relationship status, culture, and religiosity (Perry & Schleifer, 2019; Carroll et al., 2008). Thus, the control variables used when running our regressions included gender, race, relationship status, impulsivity, age, and religiosity. Categorical variables were recoded into bivariate controls. Gender was measured by male (0) and female (1). Because approximately 50 percent of our sample was white, race was simplified into two categories: white (0) and non-white (1). Relationship status also divided into two categories. Those who were engaged, in a committed relationship, married, or cohabiting were "in a relationship" (1) and individuals who were divorced, separated, widowed, or single were "not in a relationship" (0).

To measure religiosity, individuals were asked, "How important is your religious faith to you?" and were able to choose from "very important," "important," "somewhat important," and "not important." They also were asked to indicate their religious affiliation, and were able to choose from "Catholic," "Protestant," "Hindu," "Muslim," "LDS," "Jewish," "None," or "Other." Using these items, we divided our sample into "religious" (1) and "non-religious" (0) categories. Those who reported high religious importance (religious faith was "very important" or "important") and a religious affiliation were labeled as "religious." Non-religious individuals where those who either did not report a religious affiliation or scored low on religious importance ("somewhat important" or "not important") were labeled as "non-religious." Thus, "religious" individuals were those who scored high on religious importance and also identified with an organized religion, while those who were "not religious" either did not identify with a religious affiliation or did belong to a religion but did not consider their religion personally important.

The authors measured impulsive behavior with the impulsivity scale validated by Novak and Clayton (2001). The scale was reliable (Chronbach's $\alpha = .879$) and items on this scale included "I have difficulty controlling my temper," "I get so frustrated I am ready to explode," "I get upset easily," "Often I am afraid I will lose control over my feelings," and "I slam doors when I am mad." Participants responded on a five-point Likert scale from "Never true" (1) to "Always true" (5).

Anxiety Related to Pornography Use

For the purposes of this study and to explore how pornography may associate with relational fears and anxieties, the research team created items measuring pornography-related relational anxiety. The items were created through a collaborative effort of the research team and drawing from previous research. After collecting our data, a principal axis factor analysis using a varimax rotation procedure was computed on the proposed items of the dataset analyzed. Two factors were extracted with eigenvalues greater than 1 that accounted for 70.66% of the total factor variance. All items loaded on their specified scales with no cross-loadings between factors. Additional analyses indicated that the two measures were reliable (see below).

The first measure, which the authors called "Relationship Anxiety Surrounding Pornography Use," measured an individual's belief that his/ her pornography use negatively impacts their ability to form and maintain romantic relationships. "Relationship Anxiety Surrounding Pornography Use," was reliable (Chronbach's $\alpha = .954$) and was composed of 9 items. Items on this scale included questions statements such as "My pornography use affects the way I see my dates," "I stop dating when I am using pornography," and "I feel that my relationship will end if I disclose my pornography use to my partner."

Responses were on a 6-point agreement scale from "very strongly disagree" (1) to "very strongly agree" (6). Individuals who scored higher on this scale had more beliefs that his/her pornography use impaired his/her relationship formation and maintenance.

The second factor that emerged the authors named "Communication Anxiety Surrounding Pornography Use." "Communication Anxiety Surrounding Pornography Use" refers to an individual's stress about or fear of talking about pornography with their partner. This measure was also reliable (Chronbach's $\alpha = .848$) and was composed of 4 items. Participants indicated their agreement with the following statements: "I feel anxious talking about pornography with my romantic partners," "I have withheld details about my pornography use because I am afraid my partner will react negatively," "I have withheld details about my pornography use because I do not know how to communicate about it," and "My partner would react negatively if I disclosed pornography use to him/her." Responses were on a 6-point agreement scale from "very strongly agree" (1) to "very strongly disagree" (6). Individuals who scored higher on this scale experienced or believed they would experience more anxiety when talking about pornography with their romantic partner.

Other Variables

Other measures the authors used included items reflecting individuals' past experiences and beliefs of pornography use. These items were not used in a scale but were used to gather preliminary data and to observe trends in our sample. These items included: "Have you ever had a relationship end solely because of pornography use?" "Have you ever had a relationship end partially because of pornography use?" "Have you discussed your pornography use with your spouse, fiancée, significant other, friend of the same gender, and friend of the opposite gender?" Participants responded "yes" (1) or "no" (0) to each of these items. The authors used these items in our T-tests analysis to compare male and female emerging adults' experience with pornography.

NATURE OF PORNOGRAPHY USE AMONG EMERGING ADULTS

Of our emerging adult sample including men and women from ages 18-30, 86% percent reported "ever viewing pornography." This statistic aligns well with other reports of emerging adult pornography-viewing behaviors: other studies have found that 60% to 87% of young people have consumed pornography (Carroll et al., 2008; Braun-Courville & Rojas, 2009). Of the 86% in our study that had ever viewed pornography, 88.4% had viewed pornography in the last 12 months, indicating that if an emerging adult has viewed pornography, he/ she is likely to view it at least yearly. Of those who viewed pornography in the last year, 8.9% reported daily use, 25.4% 2-5 times per week, 19% every other week, 16.3% once a month, 12.2% every few months, 5% twice a year, and 13.1% about once a year or less. Of the 86% of emerging adults that reported ever viewing pornography, 34.3% used pornography daily or weekly. Most emerging adults in our sample disagreed that their pornography viewing behavior is compulsive. Almost half of our sample (48.5%) "very strongly disagreed" that they were "addicted" to pornography. Only thirteen percent agreed, 6.5% "strongly agreed," and 2.8% "very strongly" agreed that they were addicted to pornography (see Figure 1). In other words, almost a quarter of emerging adults who view pornography self-reported as having some degree of compulsive pornography use. To systematically measure compulsive pornography use (vs. trusting self-reports), the authors combined scores from the

Figure 1. Percent of emerging adults' agreement to the item "I am addicted to pornography"

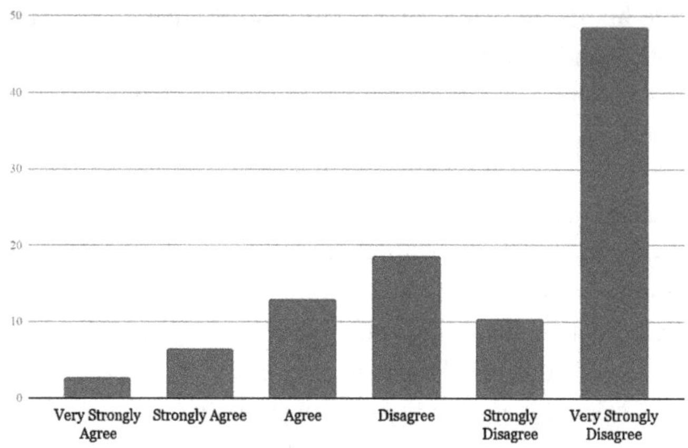

pornography compulsion scale, translated from the sexual compulsion scale (Kalichman & Rompa, 1995), with weekly or daily use. Those who scored above the median for compulsive pornography use and also reported using pornography daily or weekly were considered to be "compulsive" pornography users. According to this criterion, almost 9% of our sample reported behaviors necessary to be considered "compulsive" pornography users. These numbers give us an idea of the pornography viewing behavior of today's emerging adults, but the data is better understood when put in the context of gender.

Differences in Gender

Perhaps the most influential factor explaining sexual differences between groups of individuals is gender. To explore the differences between male and female emerging adults' pornography patterns, we performed an MANOVA analysis. Significant multivariate differences were found between men and women on our dependent variables (Wilks $\lambda = .670$, $F (1, 748) = 36.321$, $p < .001$). The authors therefore proceed to univariate results. Univariate F-tests were significant for viewing pornography in the last 12 months ($F (1, 748) = 24.66$, $p < .001$; partial $\eta 2 = .032$), overall frequency of viewing pornography ($F (1, 748) = 151.55$, $p <.001$; partial $\eta 2 = .17$), viewing photos of women in lingerie ($F (1, 748) = 53.33$, $p < .001$; partial $\eta 2 =.067$), viewing photos of women showing breasts and/or genitals ($F (1, 748) = 53.92$, $p < .001$; partial $\eta 2 = .067$), viewing photos of men showing their genitals ($F (1, 748) = 25.05$, $p < .001$; partial $\eta 2 = .033$), viewing photos of sexual intercourse ($F (1, 748) = 43.07$, $p < .001$; partial $\eta 2 = .054$), viewing videos of sexual intercourse ($F (1, 748) = 10.90$, $p < .001$; partial $\eta 2 = .014$), viewing videos of other explicit sexual acts ($F (1, 748) = 7.76$, $p < .01$; partial $\eta 2 = .010$), and viewing violent sex, child sex, and rape ($F (1, 748) = 22.73$, $p < .001$; partial $\eta 2 = .029$). Post-hoc tests were run using the Bonferonni method to control for multiple comparisons.

These analyses showed that generally, emerging adult males viewed pornography more frequently. Men were more likely than women to have viewed pornography in the last 12 months (men: $M = 1.058$; women: $M = 1.172$) and to view pornography more frequently in that time (men: $M = 5.106$; women: $M = 3.597$). There were also significant differences between men and women in the type of pornography viewed (see Table 1 depicting percentages of men and women viewing different types of pornography. The MANOVA analyses confirm the significant differences depicted all tables below). As is expected

Table 1. Type of pornography viewed in the last twelve months

	Female	Male
Women in Lingerie	47.4%**	74.4%
Photos of women exposing breasts and/or genitals	46.3%**	75.2%
Photos of men exposing genitals	45.8%**	35.5%
Photos of sexual intercourse	47.3%**	72.4%
Videos of sexual intercourse	63.5%**	79.8%
Videos of other explicit sexual acts	58.1%*	73.9%

**p<.001, *p<.01

with traditional heterosexuality, men were more likely than women to view pictures of women in lingerie (men: M = .775; women: M = .530) and photos of women exposing breasts and/ or genitals (men: M = .783; women: M = .538). Similarly, women were more likely than men to view photos of men exposing genitals (men: M = .354; women: M = .535). However, more men (75.2%) than women (48.5%) reported viewing pictures of the opposite sex exposing genitals. Men also reported higher levels of consuming media portraying sexual acts than women. Men were more likely than women to view photos of sexual intercourse (men: M = .767; women: M = .546), videos of sexual intercourse (men: M = .844; women: M = .747), and videos of other explicit sexual acts than women (men: M = .778; women: M = .688).

Differences in Religiosity

To explore differences in religious vs. non-religious emerging adults, the authors performed a MANOVA analysis. Significant multivariate differences were found between religious and non-religious emerging adults on our dependent variables (Wilks $\lambda = .890$, $F(1, 747) = 9.135$, $p < .001$). The authors therefore proceed to univariate results. Univariate F-tests were significant for viewing pornography in the last 12

Figure 2. Emerging adults and frequency of viewing pornography, by gender

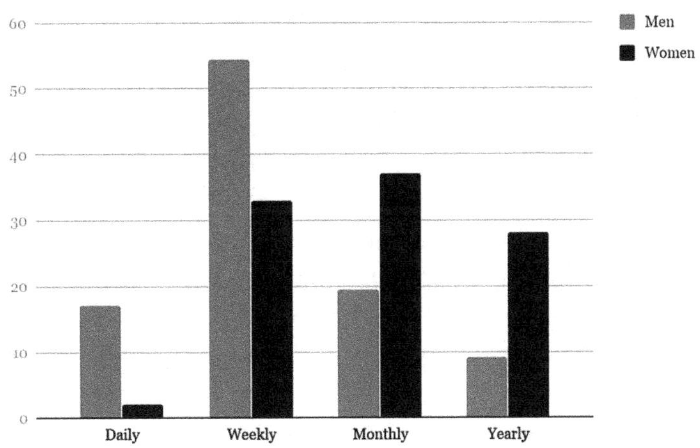

months ($F (1, 747) = 7.53$, $p < .01$; partial $\eta2 = .010$), overall frequency of viewing pornography ($F (1, 747) = 17.12$, $p <.001$; partial $\eta2 = .022$), viewing photos of women showing breasts and/or genitals ($F (1, 747) = 6.774$, $p < .01$; partial $\eta2 = .009$), viewing photos of men showing their genitals ($F (1, 747) = 6.056$, $p < .05$; partial $\eta2 = .008$), viewing photos of sexual intercourse ($F (1, 747) = 9.554$, $p < .01$; partial $\eta2 = .013$), viewing videos of sexual intercourse ($F (1, 747) = 12.852$, $p < .001$; partial $\eta2 = .017$), and viewing videos of other explicit sexual acts ($F (1, 747) = 10.567$, $p < .01$; partial $\eta2 = .014$). Post-hoc tests were run using the Bonferonni method to control for multiple comparisons.

These analyses showed that generally, non-religious emerging adults viewed pornography more frequently than religious emerging adults. Religious emerging adults (R) were more likely than non-religious (NR) emerging adults to have viewed pornography in the last 12 months (NR: M = 1.086 ; R: M = 1.149), but non-religious emerging adults viewed pornography more frequently than religious emerging adults (NR: M = 4.596 ; R: M = 4.043), perhaps revealing a pattern of religious emerging adults attempting (and failing) to abstain from pornography while non-religious emerging adults use pornography more frequently, except for those who choose not to (and don't). There were also significant differences between religious and non-religious emerging adults in the type of pornography consumed. Non-religious emerging adults were more likely than religious emerging adults to view pictures of women in lingerie (NR: M =6.82 ; R: M = 6.25), photos of women exposing breasts and/ or genitals (NR: M = .703; R: M = .613), photos of men exposing genitals (NR: M = .489 ; R: M = .399), photos of intercourse (NR: M = .708 ; R: M =.601), videos of intercourse (NR: M = .843 ; R: M = .738), and videos of other sexually explicit acts (NR: M = .779 ; R: M = .674).

PORNOGRAPHY USE AND RELATIONAL ANXIETY AMONG EMERGING ADULTS

The authors also explored feelings of pornography-related anxiety among emerging adults. From our findings, it is apparent that pornography is generally a significant factor in the levels of anxiety that emerging adults experience when forming or maintaining romantic relationships.

Relational Anxiety and Gender

To explore the differences between men and women who ended romantic relationships because of pornography use, the authors ran MANOVA analyses. Significant multivariate differences were found between men and women on our dependent variables (Wilks $\lambda = .992$, $F (1, 860) = 3.471$, $p < .05$). The authors therefore proceed to univariate results. Univariate F-tests were significant for "ending a relationship solely because of pornography use" ($F (1, 860) = 6.339$, $p < .05$; partial $\eta2 = .007$), but not for "ending a relationship partially because of pornography use" ($F (1, 860) = .994$, $p =.319$; partial $\eta2 = .001$). Post-hoc tests were run using the Bonferonni method to control for multiple comparisons. These analyses showed that while the differences were small, women were more likely than men to report that a relationship ended solely because of pornography use (men: M= 1.898, women: M= 1.841). From these results, it may be suggested that emerging adult females are more reactive to pornography use than emerging adult males and are reporting that more relationships have ended because of pornography use than men.

The authors also ran a MANOVA analysis to explore the differences between genders in disclosing/discussing pornography use with others. Participants indicated whether or not they had talked about their pornography use with spouses, fiancées, significant others, friends of the same gender, and friends of the opposite gender. Significant multivariate differences were found between men and women on our dependent variables (Wilks $\lambda = .900$, $F(1, 717) = 11.227$, $p < .001$). The authors therefore proceed to univariate results. Univariate F-tests were significant for discussing one's pornography use with a significant other ($F(1, 717) = 30.510$, $p < .001$; partial $\eta 2 = .041$) and with a spouse ($F(1, 717) = 7.765$, $p < .01$; partial $\eta 2 = .011$). Post-hoc tests using the Bonferonni method controlling for multiple comparisons indicated that men who had used pornography were more likely than women who had used pornography to discuss their pornography use with a significant other (men: M= 1.539 women: M= 1.339) and with a spouse (men: M= 1.728, women: M= 1.631). From these results, it appears that men are more likely than women to disclose their pornography use to individuals they are in a committed relationship with. Such findings may suggest that men are being expected to speak about pornography in relationships more than females, or that men simply use pornography more, and thus will report more conversation than women.

Predictors of Relational Anxiety Surrounding Pornography Use

Next, the authors conducted a multiple regression analysis with gender, race, impulsivity, relationship status, age, and religiosity as predictors of "relationship anxiety surrounding pornography use." All measures were entered simultaneously into the model. As outlined above, relationship anxiety surrounding pornography use refers to an individual's belief that he or she is capable of forming and maintaining a healthy relationship. The higher an individual's relationship anxiety surrounding pornography use, the less likely he or she believes his/herself capable of having a successful relationship. The linear combination of the six predictors was significantly related to relationship anxiety surrounding pornography use, $R^2 = .343$, adjusted $R^2 = .337$, $F(6,713) = 61.421$, $p< .001$. Of all of the measures, religiosity was the strongest predictor of relationship anxiety surrounding pornography use ($\beta= .594$, SE=.082, $p< .001$), followed by gender ($\beta= -.523$, SE=.079, $p< .001$). More religious emerging adults were more likely to believe that their pornography use would negatively influence their ability to initiate or carry on a committed relationship. Emerging adult males were also more likely than emerging adult women to believe that their consumption of pornography would have a negative impact on their relationships. This may illuminate the higher frequency of male pornography use or male's negative experiences surrounding pornography in past relationships. Impulsivity was the third strongest predictor of relationship anxiety surrounding pornography use ($\beta= .406$, SE=.041, $p< .001$). The more impulsive an emerging adult was, the more he believed that his pornography use could negatively influence his relationships. Race ($\beta= .345$, SE=.083, $p< .001$) and relationship status ($\beta=-.312$, SE=.085, $p< .001$) were also significant predictors of relationship anxiety surrounding pornography use. Non-white and single individuals were more likely to experience "relationship anxiety surrounding pornography use" than white individuals or emerging adults in a committed relationship. Age was not a significant predictor of relationship anxiety among emerging adults (see Table 3).

The authors also conducted a multiple regression analysis with gender, race, impulsivity, relationship status, age, and religiosity as predictors of anxiety of communication anxiety surrounding pornography use. As outlined above, communication anxiety surrounding pornography use refers to an individual's stress about or fear of talking about pornography with their partner. The linear combination of the six

Table 2. Percentages of emerging adults that have ended relationships solely and partially because of pornography use

	Female	Male
Solely because of pornography use	10.2%**	15.9%
Partially because of pornography use	12.7%*	15.1%

**p<.001, *p<.01

predictors was significantly related to pornography-related communication anxiety, R^2= .207, adjusted R^2 = .201, F (6,821) = 35.310, p< .001. Of all of the measures, gender was the strongest predictor of communication anxiety surrounding pornography use (β= -.577, SE=.084, p< .001), followed by religiosity (β= .435, SE=.087, p< .001). This indicates that, of all the predictors, gender is the factor that most explains the amount of communication anxiety surrounding pornography use among emerging adults. Emerging adult males are significantly more anxious about discussing pornography in romantic relationships than women. More religious emerging adults are more anxious about talking about pornography than less religious emerging adults. Impulsivity was the third strongest predictor of communication anxiety surrounding pornography use (β= .360, SE=.043, p<.001), indicating that more impulsive individuals feel higher amounts of anxiety around talking about pornography in relationships. Relationship status (β= -.255, SE=.090, p< .05) was also a significant (yet weak) predictor of communication anxiety surrounding pornography use. Emerging adults in romantic relationships were slightly less anxious talking about pornography with a significant other than those not in relationships. Neither age nor race were significant predictors of communication anxiety surrounding pornography use among emerging adults (see Table 4).

CONCLUSION

It is inaccurate to assume that all emerging adults are experiencing anxiety because of pornography use in their relationships. However, the authors see from the results that certain individual and contextual variables influence levels of anxiety for emerging adults. Similar to previous studies focused on

Table 3. Regression model predicting relationship anxiety surrounding pornography use

Variable	Model 1		
	b	SE	β
Gender	-.523**	.079	-.209
Race	.345**	.083	.138
Impulsivity	.406**	.041	.310
Relationship Status	-.312**	.085	-.117
Age	.014	.012	.037
Religiosity	.594**	.082	.236

R^2 = .343
**p<.001

Table 4. Regression model predicting communication anxiety surrounding pornography use

Variable	Model 1		
	b	SE	β
Gender	-.577**	.084	-.221
Race	.104	.089	.040
Impulsivity	.360**	.043	.268
Relationship Status	-.255*	.090	-.092
Age	.017	.013	.043
Religiosity	.435**	.087	.166

$R^2 = .024$
*p<.01, **p<.001

pornography use, being male and religious appeared to be key individual factors and predicted more pornography-related anxiety for emerging adults.

Gender

Generally, gender was the strongest predictor of pornography related anxiety differences in emerging adults. Notwithstanding the widely accepted cultural script that men are more sexual than women (Crawford & Popp, 2003), men may feel that they have to hide their pornography use more than women. Men were also more likely than women to believe that their pornography use will negatively influence their ability to form and maintain a relationship. For male emerging adults, it seems that pornography use is something that feels vulnerable, uncomfortable, or intimidating to share in a committed relationship (Willoughby & Leonhardt, 2018).

Perhaps this is because of male's perception that women find their partners' pornography use hurtful, inappropriate, or dishonest. From cultural or societal norms, emerging adult males may feel that pornography is an acceptable pastime for single, not committed, males. Thus, to fit into existing norms, males may decline from disclosing such information to their partner. Here, secrecy may explain the anxiety that many men may be experiencing. In addition, a male's perceptions of his female partner's eagerness to discuss pornography may add to the levels of anxiety that he feels, especially if that readiness is not matched or felt by the male. However, avoiding anxiety-producing topics (such as pornography) in romantic relationships often leads to lower relationship satisfaction (Velotti et al., 2015), thus it is imperative that today's young adults engage in such conversations. Despite its widespread use, pornography seems to be something that today's emerging adult males are not wanting to bring to (or bring up in) relationships. To explore these ideas further, future research should look at pornography acceptance by relationship status.

Religiosity

In this analysis, the authors found that religiosity was a more significant predictor than gender for emerging adults' beliefs that their pornography use made them inadequate partners in committed relationships. Religiosity was also a strong predictor for anxiety related to communicating about pornography. These findings can be explained by the social (and sexual) scripts that are often learned in religious settings. Religious emerging adults may hold strong beliefs about the importance of "worthiness" when forming a committed relationship. Pornography use that would make a religious individual "unworthy," is also bound to lead him or her to feeling more anxiety in forming and communicating their "unworthiness" in relationships (Wright & Perry, 2019). Communicating in healthy ways about pornography in romantic relationships will also be vital for religious emerging adults, especially because of the negative labels and reactions attached to pornography use in religious circles (Leonhardt, Willoughby, & Young-Petersen, 2018).

LIMITATIONS AND FUTURE DIRECTIONS

This study carries many limitations. Using Amazon's mechanical Turk online crowdsourcing system may have introduced sample bias into our study. There may be certain characteristics of individuals who utilized Amazon's mechanical Turk site that made them more or less likely to report their attitudes and behaviors relating to pornography use and relationships. Further, because the authors utilized individual data (vs. dyadic data), the study should not be interpreted to measure couple outcomes, but rather individual outcomes/ individuals' perceptions of couple outcomes. Future research should employ dyadic data from romantic partners to further examine relationship outcomes. Also, although our sample demographics reflect an impressive level of diversity on relationship and religious factors, our sample was predominantly white. Thus, our sample may not be as internationally representative as possible. For future studies, it may be important to analyze differences in behavior between emerging adults in different parts of the world, or to compare emerging adults in America with emerging adults from other countries.

In terms of religious representation, because our sample was comprised predominantly of Christian and Hindu individuals, the authors are unable to generalize these findings to all religious circles. There may be specific scripts and rules within Hinduism and Christianity that teach about pornography in a way that the effects of its use are magnified compared to other religious groups. In order to produce more generalizable results, the authors would employ random stratified sampling and include equal proportions of major religious groups. In the future, it would be valuable to study the differences between religious groups regarding pornography use. Further, no variables representing cultural attitudes toward pornography were included in this study. Taking cultural and societal norms surrounding pornography into consideration will be an important factor for researchers to consider when looking at pornography outcomes, as different cultural attitudes and beliefs about pornography and sexuality have been seen to alter its effects (Löfgren-Mårtenson & Månsson, 2010).Despite these limitations, the data presented here, combined with previous scholarship on emerging adults suggests that pornography has a significant influence on emerging adult's behaviors and relationships. While only 9% of our sample displayed compulsive pornography viewing behaviors, the majority of today's emerging adults use pornography, and most emerging adult males use pornography frequently. Emerging adult males also consume a wider spectrum of pornographic material with higher frequency than women. Pornography use seems to be associated with anxiety in relationship formation and a certain discomfort for emerging adults in established relationships. This anxiety is most apparent among male and religious emerging adults, but also exists among non-religious and female emerging adults. As pornography use becomes more widespread, emerging adults may experience more pornography-related anxieties and relational dynamics in romantic relationships.

In order to address the issues at hand, emerging adults will need to learn to talk about pornography in healthy ways as to lessen the anxiety they experience in the relationship, and thereby improve overall quality of their relationships. Further, relationship and sexual educators should consider including curriculum that can prepare young people and emerging adults to address the topic of pornography with romantic partners. Individual and couple therapists can also help their young clients to explore these topics in a safe and structured atmosphere, allowing them to practice and prepare to discuss them with future partners. Doing so will help lessen the anxiety or discomfort that these individuals experience and prepare them for healthier relationships.

REFERENCES

Arnett, J. J. (2000). Emerging adulthood: A theory of development from the late teens through the twenties. *The American Psychologist*, *55*(5), 469–480. doi:10.1037/0003-066X.55.5.469 PMID:10842426

Attwood, F. (2005). What do people do with porn? Qualitative research into the consumption, use, and experience of pornography and other sexually explicit media. *Sexuality & Culture*, *9*(2), 65–86. doi:10.100712119-005-1008-7

Bandura, A. (1977). *Social Learning Theory*. Englewood Cliffs, NJ: Prentice-Hall.

Barak, A., Fisher, W. A., Belfry, S., & Lashambe, D. R. (1999). Sex, guys, and cyberspace: Effects of internet pornography and individual differences on men's attitudes toward women. *Journal of Psychology & Human Sexuality*, *11*(1), 63–91. doi:10.1300/J056v11n01_04

Bartholomew, K., & Horowitz, L. M. (1991). Attachment styles among young adults: A test of a four-category model. *Journal of Personality and Social Psychology*, *61*(2), 226–244. doi:10.1037/0022-3514.61.2.226 PMID:1920064

Bersamin, M. M., Zamboanga, B. L., Schwartz, S. J., Donnellan, M. B., Hudson, M., Weisskirch, R. S., & Caraway, S. J. (2014). Risky business: Is there an association between casual sex and mental health among emerging adults? *Journal of Sex Research*, *51*(1), 43–51. doi:10.1080/00224499.2013.772088 PMID:23742031

Blair, K. L., & Pukall, C. F. (2014). Can less be more? Comparing duration vs. frequency of sexual encounters in same-sex and mixed-sex relationships. *The Canadian Journal of Human Sexuality*, *23*(2), 123–136. doi:10.3138/cjhs.2393

Bradshaw, C., Kahn, A. S., & Saville, B. K. (2010). To hook up or date: Which gender benefits? *Sex Roles*, *62*(9-10), 661–669. doi:10.100711199-010-9765-7

Braithwaite, S. R., Coulson, G., Keddington, K., & Fincham, F. D. (2015). The influence of pornography on sexual scripts and hooking up among emerging adults in college. *Archives of Sexual Behavior*, *44*(1), 111–123. doi:10.100710508-014-0351-x

Braun-Courville, D. K., & Rojas, M. (2009). Exposure to sexually explicit websites and adolescent sexual attitudes and behaviors. *The Journal of Adolescent Health*, *45*(2), 156–162. doi:10.1016/j.jadohealth.2008.12.004 PMID:19628142

Bridges, A. J., Sun, C. F., Ezzell, M. B., & Johnson, J. (2016). Sexual scripts and the sexual behavior of men and women who use pornography. *Sexualization, Media, & Society*, *2*(4).

Bridges, A. J., Wosnitzer, R., Scharrer, E., Sun, C., & Liberman, R. (2010). Aggression and sexual behavior in best-selling pornography videos: A content analysis update. *Violence Against Women*, *16*(10), 1065–1085. doi:10.1177/1077801210382866 PMID:20980228

Brown, J. D., & L'Engle, K. L. (2009). X-rated sexual attitudes and behaviors associated with US early adolescents exposure to sexually explicit media. *Communication Research*, *36*(1), 129–151. doi:10.1177/0093650208326465

Byers, E. S., & Demmons, S. (1999). Sexual satisfaction and sexual self-disclosure within dating relationships. *Journal of Sex Research*, *36*(2), 180–189. doi:10.1080/00224499909551983

Campbell, M., Kleinplatz, P. J., Mehak, L., Menard, A. D., Paquet, M. P., Paradis, N., & Zuccarino, D. (2009). The components of optimal sexuality: A portrait of" great sex. *The Canadian Journal of Human Sexuality*, *18*(1-2), 1–14.

Carroll, J. S., Busby, D. M., Willoughby, B. J., & Brown, C. C. (2017). The porn gap: Differences in men's and women's pornography patterns in couple relationships. *Journal of Couple & Relationship Therapy*, *16*(2), 146–163. doi:10.1080/15332691.2016.1238796

Carroll, J. S., Padilla-Walker, L. M., Nelson, L. J., Olson, C. D., Barry, C. M., & Madsen, S. D. (2008). Generation XXX: Pornography acceptance and use among emerging adults. *Journal of Adolescent Research*, *23*(1), 6–30. doi:10.1177/0743558407306348

Carroll, J. S., Willoughby, B., Badger, S., Nelson, L. J., Barry, C. M., & Madsen, S. D. (2007). So close, yet so far away: The impact of varying marital horizons on emerging adulthood. *Journal of Adolescent Research*, *22*(3), 219–247. doi:10.1177/0743558407299697

Check, J. V., & Malamuth, N. M. (1986). Pornography and sexual aggression: A social learning theory analysis. *Annals of the International Communication Association*, *9*(1), 181–213. doi:85.1986.11678607 doi:10.1080/238089

Coleman, E. (2011). Impulsive/compulsive sexual behavior: Assessment and treatment. The Oxford Handbook of Impulse Control Disorders, 375.

Coyne, S. M., Padilla-Walker, L. M., & Howard, E. (2013). Emerging in a digital world: A decade review of media use, effects, and gratifications in emerging adulthood. *Emerging Adulthood*, *1*(2), 125–137. doi:10.1177/2167696813479782

Crawford, M., & Popp, D. (2003). Sexual double standards: A review and methodological critique of two decades of research. *Journal of Sex Research*, *40*(1), 13–26. doi:10.1080/00224490309552163 PMID:12806528

Eyal, K., & Kunkel, D. (2008). The effects of sex in television drama shows on emerging adults sexual attitudes and moral judgments. *Journal of Broadcasting & Electronic Media*, *52*(2), 161–181. doi:10.1080/08838150801991757

Feeney, J. A., & Noller, P. (1990). Attachment style as a predictor of adult romantic relationships. *Journal of Personality and Social Psychology*, *58*(2), 281–291. doi:10.1037/0022-3514.58.2.281

Fincham, F. D., & Cui, M. (Eds.). (2010). *Romantic relationships in emerging adulthood*. Cambridge University Press; doi:10.1017/CBO9780511761935

Frith, H., & Kitzinger, C. (2001). Reformulating sexual script theory: Developing a discursive psychology of sexual negotiation. *Theory & Psychology*, *11*(2), 210. doi:10.1177/0959354301112004

Garcia, F. D., & Thibaut, F. (2010). Sexual addictions. *The American Journal of Drug and Alcohol Abuse*, *36*(5), 254–260. doi:10.3109/00952990.2010.503823 PMID:20666699

Giugliano, J. R. (2013). Sex addiction as a mental health diagnosis: Coming together or coming apart? *Sexologies*, *22*(3), e77–e80. doi:10.1016/j.sexol.2012.08.018

Grubbs, J. B., & Perry, S. L. (2019). Moral incongruence and pornography use: A critical review and integration. *Journal of Sex Research*, *56*(1), 29–37. doi:10.1080/00224499.2018.1427204 PMID:29412013

Grubbs, J. B., Wright, P. J., Braden, A. L., Wilt, J. A., & Kraus, S. W. (2019). Internet pornography use and sexual motivation: a systematic review and integration. *Annals of the International Communication Association*, 1-39.

Hald, G. M. (2006). Gender differences in pornography consumption among young heterosexual Danish adults. *Archives of Sexual Behavior*, *35*(5), 577–585. doi:10.100710508-006-9064-0 PMID:17039402

Hald, G. M., Kuyper, L., Adam, P. C., & Wit, J. B. (2013). Does viewing explain doing? Assessing the association between sexually explicit materials use and sexual behaviors in a large sample of Dutch adolescents and young adults. *Journal of Sexual Medicine*, *10*(12), 2986–2995. doi:10.1111/jsm.12157 PMID:23621804

Hald, G. M., & Malamuth, N. M. (2008). Self-perceived effects of pornography consumption. *Archives of Sexual Behavior*, *37*(4), 614–625. doi:10.100710508-007-9212-1 PMID:17851749

Hald, G. M., Malamuth, N. M., & Yuen, C. (2010). Pornography and attitudes supporting violence against women: Revisiting the relationship in non-experimental studies. *Aggressive Behavior*, *36*(1), 14–20. doi:10.1002/ab.20328 PMID:19862768

Hald, G. M., Seaman, C., & Linz, D. (2014). Sexuality and pornography. In D. Tolman, L. Diamond, J. Bauermeister, W. George, J. Pfaus, & L. Ward, (Eds.), APA Handbook of Sexuality and Psychology, Vol. 1: Person-based approaches. American Psychological Association. doi:10.1037/14194-001

Hall, P. (2014). Sex addiction–An extraordinarily contentious problem. *Sexual and Relationship Therapy*, *29*(1), 68–75. doi:10.1080/14681994.2013.861898

Johnson, J. A., Ezzell, M. B., Bridges, A. J., & Sun, C. F. (2019). Pornography and heterosexual women's intimate experiences with a partner. *Journal of Women's Health*, *28*(9), 1254–1265. doi:10.1089/jwh.2018.7006 PMID:30998084

Kalichman, S. C., & Rompa, D. (1995). Sexual sensation seeking and sexual compulsivity scales: Validity, and predicting HIV risk behavior. *Journal of Personality Assessment, 65*(3), 586–601. doi:10.120715327752jpa6503_16 PMID:8609589

Kelley, H. H., & Thibaut, J. W. (1978). *Interpersonal relations: A theory of interdependence*. New York: Wiley-Interscience.

Kingston, D. A., & Malamuth, N. M. (2011). Problems with aggregate data and the importance of individual differences in the study of pornography and sexual aggression: Comment on Diamond, Jozifkova, and Weiss (2010). *Archives of Sexual Behavior, 40*(5), 1045–1048. doi:10.100710508-011-9743-3

Klaassen, M. J., & Peter, J. (2015). Gender (in) equality in Internet pornography: A content analysis of popular pornographic Internet videos. *Journal of Sex Research, 52*(7), 721–735. doi:10.1080/00224499.2014.976781 PMID:25420868

Kuzma, J. M., & Black, D. W. (2008). Epidemiology, prevalence, and natural history of compulsive sexual behavior. *The Psychiatric Clinics of North America, 31*(4), 603–611. doi:10.1016/j.psc.2008.06.005 PMID:18996301

Lefkowitz, E. S., & Gillen, M. M. (2006). *"Sex is just a normal part of life": Sexuality in emerging adulthood*. Academic Press.

Leonhardt, N. D., Spencer, T. J., Butler, M. H., & Theobald, A. C. (2018). An organizational framework for sexual media's influence on short-term versus long-term sexual quality. *Archives of Sexual Behavior*, 1–17. PMID:30014336

Leonhardt, N. D., & Willoughby, B. J. (2018). Longitudinal links between pornography use, marital importance, and permissive sexuality during emerging adulthood. *Marriage & Family Review, 54*(1), 64–84. doi:10.1080/01494929.2017.1359811

Leonhardt, N. D., Willoughby, B. J., & Young-Petersen, B. (2018). Damaged goods: Perception of pornography addiction as a mediator between religiosity and relationship anxiety surrounding pornography use. *Journal of Sex Research, 55*(3), 357–368. doi:10.1080/00224499.2017.1295013 PMID:28287845

Levinson, D. J. (1978). *The seasons of a man's life*. Random House LLC.

Lo, V. H., & Wei, R. (2002). Third-person effect, gender, and pornography on the internet. *Journal of Broadcasting & Electronic Media, 46*(1), 13–33. doi:10.120715506878jobem4601_2

Löfgren-Mårtenson, L., & Månsson, S. A. (2010). Lust, love, and life: A qualitative study of Swedish adolescents perceptions and experiences with pornography. *Journal of Sex Research, 47*(6), 568–579. doi:10.1080/00224490903151374

Malamuth, N. M. (1996). Sexually explicit media, gender differences, and evolutionary theory. *Journal of Communication, 46*(3), 8–31. doi:10.1111/j.1460-2466.1996.tb01486.x

Malamuth, N. M., & Check, J. V. (1985). The effects of aggressive pornography on beliefs in rape myths: Individual differences. *Journal of Research in Personality, 19*(3), 299–320. doi:10.1016/0092-6566(85)90021-2

Malamuth, N. M., Hald, G. M., & Koss, M. (2012). Pornography, individual differences in risk and mens' acceptance of violence against women in a representative sample. *Sex Roles*, *66*(7-8), 427–439. doi:10.100711199-011-0082-6

McKee, A. (2007). The relationship between attitudes towards women, consumption of pornography, and other demographic variables in a survey of 1,023 consumers of pornography. *International Journal of Sexual Health*, *19*(1), 31–45. doi:10.1300/J514v19n01_05

Mikulincer, M. (2006). Attachment, caregiving, and sex within romantic relationships. *Dynamics of Romantic Love: Attachment, Caregiving, and Sex*, 23-42.

Miller, S. A., & Byers, E. S. (2004). Actual and desired duration of foreplay and intercourse: Discordance and misperceptions within heterosexual couples. *Journal of Sex Research*, *41*(3), 301–309. doi:10.1080/00224490409552237 PMID:15497058

Montgomery-Graham, S., & Kohut, T. (2019). Pornography problems due to moral incongruence. *Archives of Sexual Behavior*, *48*(2), 425–429.

Monto, M. A., & Carey, A. G. (2014). A new standard of sexual behavior? Are claims associated with the hookup culture supported by general social survey data? *Journal of Sex Research*, *51*(6), 605–615. doi:10.1080/00224499.2014.906031 PMID:24750070

Morgan, E. M. (2011). Associations between young adults use of sexually explicit materials and their sexual preferences, behaviors, and satisfaction. *Journal of Sex Research*, *48*(6), 520–530. doi:10.1080/00224499.2010.543960 PMID:21259151

Mosher, D. L., & MacIan, P. (1994). College men and women respond to X-rated videos intended for male or female audiences: Gender and sexual scripts. *Journal of Sex Research*, *31*(2), 99–113. doi:10.1080/00224499409551736

Nelson, L. J., Padilla-Walker, L. M., & Carroll, J. S. (2010). I believe it is wrong but I still do it: A comparison of religious young men who do versus do not use pornography. *Psychology of Religion and Spirituality*, *2*(3), 136–147. doi:10.1037/a0019127

Novak, S. P., & Clayton, R. R. (2001). The influence of school environment and self-regulation on transitions between stages of cigarette smoking: A multilevel analysis. *Health Psychology*, *20*(3), 196–207. doi:10.1037/0278-6133.20.3.196 PMID:11403217

Olmstead, S. B., Negash, S., Pasley, K., & Fincham, F. D. (2013). Emerging adults expectations for pornography use in the context of future committed romantic relationships: A qualitative study. *Archives of Sexual Behavior*, *42*(4), 625–635. doi:10.100710508-012-9986-7 PMID:22886349

Owen, J., Fincham, F. D., & Moore, J. (2011). Short-term prospective study of hooking up among college students. *Archives of Sexual Behavior*, *40*(2), 331–341. doi:10.100710508-010-9697-x

Padgett, V. R., Brislin-Slütz, J. A., & Neal, J. A. (1989). Pornography, erotica, and attitudes toward women: The effects of repeated exposure. *Journal of Sex Research*, *26*(4), 479–491. doi:10.1080/00224498909551529

Paolacci, G., Chandler, J., & Ipeirotis, P. G. (2010). Running experiments on amazon mechanical turk. *Judgment and Decision Making*, *5*(5), 411–419.

Patterson, R., & Price, J. (2012). Pornography, religion, and the happiness gap: Does pornography impact the actively religious differently? *Journal for the Scientific Study of Religion, 51*(1), 79–89. doi:10.1111/j.1468-5906.2011.01630.x PMID:22616090

Paul, E. L., McManus, B., & Hayes, A. (2000). Hookups: Characteristics and correlates of college students spontaneous and anonymous sexual experiences. *Journal of Sex Research, 37*(1), 76–88. doi:10.1080/00224490009552023

Perry, S. L., & Schleifer, C. (2019). Race and trends in pornography viewership, 1973–2016: Examining the moderating roles of gender and religion. *Journal of Sex Research, 56*(1), 62–73. doi:10.1080/00224499.2017.1404959 PMID:29244541

Peter, J., & Valkenburg, P. M. (2007). Adolescents exposure to a sexualized media environment and their notions of women as sex objects. *Sex Roles, 56*(5-6), 381–395. doi:10.100711199-006-9176-y

Phillips, B., Hajela, R., & Hilton, D. L. Jr. (2015). Sex addiction as a disease: Evidence for assessment, diagnosis, and response to critics. *Sexual Addiction & Compulsivity, 22*(2), 167–192. doi:20162.2015.1036184 doi:10.1080/107

Poulsen, F. O., Busby, D. M., & Galovan, A. M. (2013). Pornography use: Who uses it and how it is associated with couple outcomes. *Journal of Sex Research, 50*(1), 72–83. doi:10.1080/00224499.2011.648027 PMID:22449010

Regnerus, M., & Uecker, J. (2010). *Premarital sex in America: How young americans meet, mate, and think about marrying*. Oxford University Press. doi:10.1093/acprof:oso/9780199743285.001.0001

Reich, R. R., Cummings, J. R., Greenbaum, P. E., Moltisanti, A. J., & Goldman, M. S. (2015). *The temporal "pulse" of drinking: Tracking 5 years of binge drinking in emerging adults*. Academic Press.

Resch, M. N., & Alderson, K. G. (2014). Female partners of men who use pornography: Are honesty and mutual use associated with relationship satisfaction? *Journal of Sex & Marital Therapy, 40*(5), 410–424. doi:10.1080/0092623X.2012.751077 PMID:23898992

Romito, P., & Beltramini, L. (2011). Watching pornography: Gender differences, violence and victimization. An exploratory study in Italy. *Violence Against Women, 17*(10), 1313–1326. doi:10.1177/1077801211424555 PMID:21997464

Rozler, J., & Lavinthal, A. (2010). *The hookup handbook: A single girl's guide to living it up*. Simon and Schuster.

Salas-Wright, C. P., Vaughn, M. G., & Maynard, B. R. (2014). Profiles of religiosity and their association with risk behavior among emerging adults in the United States. *Emerging Adulthood.*

Sessoms, J. (2011). *The cyber pornography use inventory: Comparing a religious and secular sample*. Academic Press.

Seto, M. C., Maric, A., & Barbaree, H. E. (2001). The role of pornography in the etiology of sexual aggression. *Aggression and Violent Behavior, 6*(1), 35–53. doi:10.1016/S1359-1789(99)00007-5

Shaver, P., & Hazan, C. (1987). Being lonely, falling in love: Perspectives from attachment theory. *Journal of Social Behavior and Personality*.

Sherman, A. J., & Tocantins, N. (2004). *The happy hook up: A single girl's guide to casual sex*. Springer Science & Business.

Shulman, S., & Connolly, J. (2013). The challenge of romantic relationships in emerging adulthood: Reconceptualization of the field. *Emerging Adulthood*, *1*(1), 27–39. doi:10.1177/2167696812467330

Stack, S., Wasserman, I., & Kern, R. (2004). Adult social bonds and use of Internet pornography. *Social Science Quarterly*, *85*(1), 75–88. doi:10.1111/j.0038-4941.2004.08501006.x

Stanley, S. M., Rhoades, G. K., & Fincham, F. D. (2011). *Understanding romantic relationships among emerging adults: The significant roles of cohabitation and ambiguity*. Cambridge University Press.

Stewart, D. N., & Szymanski, D. M. (2012). Young adult women's reports of their male romantic partners pornography use as a correlate of their self-esteem, relationship quality, and sexual satisfaction. *Sex Roles*, *67*(5-6), 257–271. doi:10.100711199-012-0164-0

Štulhofer, A., Buško, V., & Landripet, I. (2010). Pornography, sexual socialization, and satisfaction among young men. *Archives of Sexual Behavior*, *39*(1), 168–178. doi:10.100710508-008-9387-0 PMID:18561012

Suri, S., & Watts, D. J. (2011). Cooperation and contagion in web-based, networked public goods experiments. *PLoS One*, *6*(3), e16836. doi:10.1371/journal.pone.0016836 PMID:21412431

Swanson, J. A., & Walker, E. (2015) Academic versus non-academic emerging adult college student technology use. *Technology, Knowledge and Learning*, 1-12.

Tolman, D. L., Diamond, L. M., Bauermeister, J. A., George, W. H., Pfaus, J. G., & Ward, L. (2014). APA Handbook of Sexuality and Psychology, Vol. 2: Contextual approaches. APA.

Traen, B., Nilsen, T. S., & Stigum, H. (2006). Use of pornography in traditional media and on the internet in Norway. *Journal of Sex Research*, *43*(3), 245–254. doi:10.1080/00224490609552323 PMID:17599247

Umemura, T., Lacinová, L., & Macek, P. (2014). Is emerging adults' attachment preference for the romantic partner transferred from their attachment preferences for their mother, father, and friends? *Emerging Adulthood*.

Velotti, P., Balzarotti, S., Tagliabue, S., English, T., Zavattini, G. C., & Gross, J. J. (2015). Emotional suppression in early marriage: Actor, partner, and similarity effects on marital quality. *Journal of Social and Personal Relationships*.

Weinberg, M. S., Williams, C. J., Kleiner, S., & Irizarry, Y. (2010). Pornography, normalization, and empowerment. *Archives of Sexual Behavior*, *39*(6), 1389–1401. doi:10.100710508-009-9592-5 PMID:20127507

Willoughby, B. J., & Busby, D. M. (2015). In the eye of the beholder: Exploring variations in the perceptions of pornography. *Journal of Sex Research*, 1–11. PMID:26643148

Willoughby, B. J., Carroll, J. S., Busby, D. M., & Brown, C. C. (2015). Differences in pornography use among couples: Associations with satisfaction, stability, and relationship processes. *Archives of Sexual Behavior*, ▪▪▪, 1–14.

Willoughby, B. J., Carroll, J. S., Busby, D. M., & Brown, C. C. (2016). Differences in pornography use among couples: Associations with satisfaction, stability, and relationship processes. [PubMed]. *Archives of Sexual Behavior*, *45*(1), 145–158. doi:10.100710508-015-0562-9

Willoughby, B. J., Carroll, J. S., Nelson, L. J., & Padilla-Walker, L. M. (2014). Associations between relational sexual behaviour, pornography use, and pornography acceptance among US college students. *Culture, Health & Sexuality*, *16*(9), 1052–1069. doi:10.1080/13691058.2014.927075 PMID:25023726

Willoughby, B. J., & Hall, S. S. (2015). Enthusiasts, delayers, and the ambiguous middle: Marital paradigms among emerging adults. *Emerging Adulthood*, *3*(2), 123–135. doi:10.1177/2167696814548478

Willoughby, B. J., Hall, S. S., & Luczak, H. P. (2013). Marital paradigms: A conceptual framework for marital attitudes, values, and beliefs. *Journal of Family Issues*.

Willoughby, B. J., Young-Petersen, B., & Leonhardt, N. D. (2018). Exploring trajectories of pornography use through adolescence and emerging adulthood. *Journal of Sex Research*, *55*(3), 297–309. doi:10.1080/00224499.2017.1368977 PMID:28972398

Wright, P. J., Tokunaga, R. S., & Kraus, A. (2015). A meta-analysis of pornography consumption and actual acts of sexual aggression in general population studies. *Journal of Communication*.

Young, K. S. (2008). Internet sex addiction risk factors, stages of development, and treatment. *The American Behavioral Scientist*, *52*(1), 21–37. doi:10.1177/0002764208321339

KEY TERMS AND DEFINITIONS

Compulsive Pornography Use: In this study, compulsive pornography use was measured by combining the pornography compulsion scale (translated from the sexual compulsion scale) with weekly or daily use. Those who scored above the median for compulsive pornography use and also reported using pornography daily or weekly were considered to be "compulsive" pornography users.

Emerging Adulthood: The stage from the late teens through the twenties, encompassing 18 to 30-year-olds.

Hookup: A brief, uncommitted sexual encounter involving kissing to intercourse without an understood promise of a continued relationship.

Pornography: Sexually explicit words, images, or videos that have the intent to arouse the user.

Religiosity: In this study, religiosity was measured by self-reports of religious importance and religious affiliations. "Religious" individuals were those who scored high on religious importance and also identified with an organized religion, while those who were "not religious" either did not identify with a religious affiliation or did belong to a religion but did not consider their religion personally important. Sexual Script Theory: Rooted in the widely used script theory, which teaches that human behavior is dictated by patterns called "scripts" that individuals "act out" due to exposure and conditioning. Sexual scripts are culturally available messages that define what 'counts' as sex, or how to act during a sexual encounter.

Social Learning Theory: States that individuals learn not only by their own experiences, but also through the observation of others' behaviors.

Chapter 9
Loneliness, Disclosure, and Facebook Usage:
Results From a Hong Kong Survey

Fung Yin Lee
Hong Kong Baptist University, China

Lynne M. Webb
Florida International University, USA

ABSTRACT

The authors conducted an online survey of 241 emerging adults in Hong Kong, China to assess potential associations between loneliness, Facebook usage, and self-disclosure on Facebook. Loneliness was not associated with Facebook usage, but rather inversely related with negative disclosure; the lonelier the Facebook user, the less he/she disclosed negative information. The pattern of associations between Facebook usage and self-disclosure indicted that the more time users spent on Facebook, the more they revealed positive disclosures and the less they revealed negative disclosures. The authors argue that these findings may provide evidence of a "remain positive" norm among emerging adult Facebook users in Hong Kong. They note that their findings may be unique to their cultural context.

INTRODUCTION

Emerging Adult Theory argues that a distinct life stage exists between adolescence and adulthood, a time when individuals "have not yet settled into the long-term choices and life-paths that make up adulthood" (Bigham, 2012, p. 533). As originally conceived by Arnett (2015), this life stage extended from late teens through the 20s when individuals address the challenging tasks that typically accompany the transition into adulthood. Munsey (2006) identified five features of emerging adulthood:

DOI: 10.4018/978-1-7998-1063-6.ch009

- Identity exploration concerning lifestyles and believe systems (e.g., religion, politics)
- Instability. Individuals may change residents frequently, moving frequently for education, work, and/or family reasons. They may change intimate partners and friends frequently as well. The challenge for emerging adults is to find stability including negotiating on-going, positive interpersonal relationships and moving along a chosen career path that allows life in primarily one location.
- Self-focus. Given the above described instability and focus on identity exploration, emerging adults remain self-focused until they begin making commitments to specific career paths and to significant others—commitments that lead to adulthood.
- Feeling in between. Individuals know they are not children or teenagers anymore, but often do not see themselves as adults yet.
- Endless possibilities. This time of exploration and confusion leaves emerging adults with a sense of incompleteness but also with a sense of wonder and endless possibilities. The experience of endless possibilities can lead to a sense of empowerment or feeling overwhelming by too many options.

The Theory of Emerging Adulthood is not without its critics (Hendry & Kloep, 2007). Some adherents have argued that tying the definition of emerging adulthood to its challenges rather than specific ages is more sensible, given that individuals complete development tasks at differing paces (Bigham, 2012). Additionally, researchers argue that ethnicity (Munsey, 2006) and culture (e.g., Arseth, Kroger, Martinussen, & Bakken, 2009) may influence how individuals experience this life stage. Despite these concerns, an on-going line of research has emerged that examines the online behavior of emerging adults (e.g., Wu & Webb, 2016).

This chapter reports the findings of an original research study that continues an exploration of emerging adulthood among these newer concerns (i.e., extended age-frame, cultural differences, and online behaviors). We examined Facebook usage and its relationship to emerging adult users' perceived loneliness and self-disclosure on Facebook in a Hong Kong sample. This study fills a gap in the current body of research in two ways: (a) by examining the inter-relationships among this specific combination of three variables (i.e., loneliness, self-disclosure on Facebook, and Facebook usage per se) as well as (b) collecting data from a culturally unique sample, emerging adults in Hong Kong.

BACKGROUND

Motivations for users to join and use social networking websites (SNS) vary (boyd, 2006; Bryant, Marmo, & Ramirez, 2011; Chen, 2015), but the primary motivation is to communicate and maintain relationships with other users (Dwyer, Hiltz & Passerini, 2007). Individuals can form online communities around shared interests with others outside their pre-existing social group or location (Webb & Lee, 2011). However, many participants in large SNSs like Facebook primary search for and communicate with their offline connections rather than looking for new people to meet (Lampe, Ellison, & Steinfield, 2006; Miller & Mundey, 2015). Nonetheless, the more users want to maintain relationships on social media, the more likely they are to spend time in self-disclosing activities, such as updating Facebook profile information, posting status updates, and uploading photos and videos.

One of the largest, well known, and well-studied SNS in the world is Facebook (Rains & Brunner, 2015). On February 4, 2019, Facebook turned 15 years old and reported 1.5 billion daily, active users world-wide in May 2019 (Facebook, 2019). Indeed, Facebook is big business with offices in 20 U. S. cities and 47 overseas cities, including an office in Hong Kong (Facebook, 2019).

Facebook provides multiple opportunities for self-disclosure, here defined as consciously communicating messages about the self to others. For example, users can reveal personal information on their personal profiles including birthdate, education background, hobbies, sexual orientation, and relationship status. Additionally, users can upload photos and videos of their activities as well as reveal their thoughts and feelings via status updates; this information in turn appears on their friends' news feed. Therefore, it is not surprising that self-disclosure on Facebook is a well-researched topic (Caers et al., 2013). A google-scholar search using the two keywords Facebook and self-disclosure yielded over 30,600 results in May 2019.

This extensive line of research examines users' self-disclosure on Facebook in Argentina (Linne, 2014), Australia (Saling, Cohen, & Cooper, 2019), Germany (Utz, 2015), Japan (Omori & Allen, 2014), Korea (e.g., Kwak, Choi, & Lee, 2014), Mainland China (e.g., Liu & Brown, 2014), Poland (e.g., Blachnio, Przepiorka, & Rudnicka, 2016), Slovenia (e.g., Zlatolas, Welzer, Hericko, & Holbl, 2015), the United Kingdom (e.g., Green, Wilhelmsen, Wilmots, Dodd, & Quin, 2016), and the United States (e.g., Crabtree & Pillow, 2018). However, very little of this research was completed Hong Kong (i.e., Cheung, Lee, & Chan, 2015). Given the unique cultural aspects of Hong Kong, with its 99 years history of British occupation mingled with its ethnically Chinese roots, it is reasonable to question whether Hong Kong Facebook users would follow the same norms of self-disclosure documented in other cultures.

Indeed, perhaps in acknowledgement of its uniqueness, a growing body of over 25 published studies examines various Facebook behaviors of Hong Kong residents, including peer network characteristics (Chan, 2018), talk among colleagues (Nam, Chun, & Hin, 2014), and one specific type of self-disclosure, sharing sex stories (Yeo & Chu, 2017). However, only one previous research has examined Hong Kong Facebook users' self-disclosure as a general matter (Chenug et al., 2015). That study assessed perceived costs and benefits of self-disclosure on Facebook but failed to directly assess the relationship between Hong Kong users' self-disclosure on Facebook with their reported loneliness. This is concerning, given that previous studies linked loneliness and self-disclosure on Facebook among users in Australia (Al-Saggaf & Nielsen, 2014) and Korea (Jin, 2013; Lee, Noh, & Koo, 2013). Our study expands this fledgling line of research by testing whether such a relationship can be similarly documented among Facebook users in a Hong Kong sample.

Many studies have examined the relationship between loneliness and Facebook use (see Song et al, 2014 for a meta-analysis of this research). However, we could locate no previous work that examined this association in Hong Kong users. To address this gap in the literature, we elected to focus our study on Facebook use, loneliness, and self-disclosure among a Hong Kong sample of emerging adults.

Facebook

Facebook is the most popular SNS on Earth (Ahmad, 2019). Users can search for other registered users and initiate requests to become friends. Facebook friends range from established intimate relationships to acquaintances. While the research on self-disclosure and Facebook is extensive, as is the research on loneliness and Facebook use, nonetheless, much of the existing academic research on Facebook has focused on interpersonal processes more indirectly related to loneliness and/or self-disclosure. They include boundary tending (Miller & Mundey, 2015), privacy concerns (Tsay-Vogel, Shanahan, & Signorielli, 2018), feeling connected (Utz, 2015), social anxiety (e.g., Burke & Ruppel, 2015), social cohesion (Hollenbaugh, & Ferris, 2014), general interpersonal relations (Kwak et al., 2014), and the overarching concern of acquiring and maintained social capital (Liu & Brown, 2014). Additionally, recent studies report mixed outcomes associated with frequent Facebook usage including (a) lower depressive symptoms in females with high neuroticism (Simoncic, Kuhlman, Vargas, Houchins, & Lopez-Duran, 2014) but (b) higher stress and lower quality of life among college students (Bevan, Gomez, and Sparks, 2014) as well as associations with narcissism (Blachnio et al., 2016) among emerging and middle-aged adults. In sum, loneliness and self-disclosure remain common targets of both direct and indirect investigation by Facebook researchers.

Loneliness and Facebook Use

We view loneliness as an uncomfortable psychological state associated with a desire for increased human interaction. Loneliness has been linked to reduced social support and reduced life satisfaction (Kong & You, 2013). For lonely individuals, online social media, such as Facebook, may offer a less demanding communication medium than face-to-face (FtF) interaction. Facebook makes connecting with others easy by facilitating connections in the following manner: Its customized features allow users with common interests to easily discover each other and converse.

In their meta-analysis of the research on loneliness and Facebook usage, Song et al. (2014) report that, early on, many studies documented an association between loneliness and Facebook use. Following recognition of this documentation, researchers focused on the question of whether Facebook usage decreased or increased loneliness. While the previous evidence was mixed, Song and associates (2014) presented definitive evidence that loneliness, driven by shyness and low self-esteem, leads to increased Facebook usage. Rather than retest the directionality of the association, our study tested whether loneliness and Facebook usage remain correlated with a Hong Kong sample.

Like Song et al. (2014), we located many studies of loneliness and Facebook use. These studies employed samples of emerging adults in diverse locations including Australia (e.g., Al-Saggaf & Nielsen, 2014), Belgium (e.g., Frison & Eggermont, 2015), Germany (Utz, 2015), Korea (Jin, 2013), Poland (Balachnio, Przepiorka, Boruch, & Balakier, 2016), Scotland (Phu & Gow, 2019), Turkey (Satici, 2019), and the United States (e.g., Wohn & LaRose, 2014). However, this association remain undocumented in a Hong Kong sample. Therefore, we posed the following research question:

RQ1: Is there an association between loneliness and Facebook usage?

Self-Disclosure and Facebook Use

In addition to testing whether Facebook usage is related to loneliness in a Hong Kong sample, we questioned whether either users' loneliness or Facebook usage is associated with their self-disclosure on Facebook. Self-disclosure (here defined as revealing information about the self to others) is widely considered an important factor in the development and maintenance of relationships in FtF and well as social media contexts (Bazarova & Choi, 2014). It has positive effects on online dating (Gibbs, Ellison, & Heino, 2006), online support communities (Turner, Grube, & Myers, 2001), virtual work teams (Walther, Slovacek, & Tidwell, 2001), and online interpersonal relationships (Kwak et al., 2014).

Relationship maintenance, often manifest as self-disclosure, is among the most prominent motivation for using Facebook (Dwyer et al., 2007; Ellison, Vitak, Gray, & Lampe, 2014; Lampe et al., 2006; Park & Lee, 2014). Users stay in touch with their offline relational partners via Facebook, (Miller & Mundey, 2015), including both geographically distant and close friends (Waters & Ackerman, 2011) as well as current and previous romantic partners (Medeiros & Webb, 2019). In addition to relationship maintenance, users may employ Facebook to satisfy engagement and affiliation needs—and both are associated with self-disclosure (Chen, 2015). Furthermore, Ledbetter et al. (2011) reported a link between self-disclosure on Facebook and relational closeness.

Many researches argue for a direct relationship between Facebook use and self-disclosure (Webb & Temple, 2015). For example, Linne identified "interchanging personal information between friends" (in other words, self-disclosure) as one of adolescents' the common uses of Facebook (2014, para. 1). Similarly, Park and Lee (2014) report that college students have four motivations for using Facebook, including self-expression and communication (in other words, self-disclosure). Finally, Hollenbaugh and Ferris (2014) documented an association between the breadth of self-disclosure on Facebook and relational maintenance per se as well as one of its specific components, openness.

A wave of recent studies documented a positive relationship between Facebook use and self-disclosure (Chang & Heo, 2014; Chen & Sharma, 2015; Crabtree & Pillow, 2018; Lee et al., 2013; Park & Baek, 2016; Tsay-Vogel et al., 2018). However, our study is the first to test this relationship using a Hong Kong sample. Such a sample-specific test appears relevant in light of increasing evidence that Facebook usage is influenced by cultural values such as individualism (Shneor & Efrat, 2014). Particularly relevant to our research, two studies reported cultural differences in self-disclosure on Facebook: Lee-Won, Shim, Joo, and Park (2014) documented cultural differences in self-presentation on Facebook between South Korean versus U. S. emerging adults; given that self-disclosure is the primary means through which users present their online identity, these cultural differences provide a warrant for our culturally-specific sample. Similarly, Omori and Allen documented differences in the willingness of emerging adult Facebook users in Japan versus the United States to post pictures of themselves "partying" and drinking (in other words, self-disclosing questionable recreational activities).

Valence of Disclosure

Given the extensive documentation of self-disclosure on Facebook, researchers recently turned their attention to examining the influence of the valence of self-disclosures on Facebook usage and other pertinent variables (e.g., Saling et al., 2019). As early as 1973, researchers noted that the valence of a disclosure (disclosing positive versus negative information) in FtF interactions influenced the receiver's perception of the discloser (Pearce & Sharp, 1973). More recent findings indicate that valence of disclosure also can prove salient in online interactions. We could locate seven previously published studies that examined positive versus negative disclosures on Facebook; their results indicate that salience of Facebook disclosures may be a variable worthy of observation.

- Qiu, Lin, Leung, and Tov (2012) documented that, among a sample of Singapore college students, Facebook users were more likely to disclose positive versus negative emotions.
- Lee-Won et al. (2014) documented that U. S. versus Korean college-student Facebook users engaged in more positive self-presentation (in other words, self-disclosure).

- Liu and Brown (2014) examined self-disclosure among first-year college students at three universities in Beijing in mainland China on Renren, the Chinese version of Facebook. Their results revealed that social skills were positively associated with self-disclosure, which in turn was associated with receiving positive feedback from friends.
- Jin (2013) reported that, among a Korean sample of emerging adults, lonely users were more likely to engage in negative self-disclosure and less likely to engage in positive self-disclosure.
- Bevan et al. (2015) reported that, in a sample of emerging adults in the United States, users preferred to disclose negative life events directly (e.g., status updates) whereas they preferred to disclose positive life events indirectly (e.g., posting pictures).
- Utz (2015) reported that positive (not negative) Facebook disclosures were associated with feelings of connection among a sample of German university students.
- Saling et al., (2019) reported that Australian Facebook users of many ages preferred receiving negative disclosures off-line rather than online.

We extended this exploration of positive versus negative valence of disclosures on Facebook to examine their potential relationships between loneliness, Facebook usage, and positive versus negative self-disclosure on Facebook. We believed that emerging adult Facebook users were likely to disclose positive (versus negative) information about the self to shape desirable online images. Therefore, we posed the following research question:

RQ2: Is there an association between positive or negative self-disclosure on Facebook and Facebook usage?

Loneliness and Self-Disclosure on Facebook

The relationship between the use of Facebook and self-disclosure might be more profound for lonely people who desire social relationships but lack opportunities for self-disclosure in FtF interaction. It is possible that, because of the impersonality and participation equality of online communication, lonely people may be more willing to disclose in greater breadth and depth. Also, Facebook may be a more comfortable place for the lonely to disclose than less interactive online venues such as Instagram and Twitter. If Facebook serves as a comfortable place for lonely people to self-disclose, lonely Facebook users and/or high disclosing users may use Facebook more frequently than less lonely users.

We could locate only three previous studies (Al-Saggaf & Nielsen, 2014; Jin, 2013; Lee et al., 2013) that tested for such associations. Among a sample of Australian users, Al-Saggaf and Nielsen (2014) reported that lonely Facebook users disclosed more personal and more relational information but fewer viewpoints. Lee et al. (2013) reported that loneliness increased self-disclosure on Facebook among their sample of Korean college students. Jin (2013) reported that, among a Korean sample of emerging adults, users' amount of time on Facebook was not associated with loneliness; however, lonely users were more likely to engage in negative self-disclosure and less likely to engage in positive self-disclosure. To explore if this set of previously examined relationships existed in a Hong Kong sample, we posted the following research question:

RQ3: Is there an association between loneliness and positive or negative self-disclosure on Facebook?

It is noteworthy that we could locate no previous study that examined possible associations between the particular array of variables examined in this study (i.e., loneliness, self-disclosure by valence, and Facebook use). Thus, in addition to retesting previously documented associations with a Hong Kong sample of emerging adults, our study fills this additional gap in the research on Facebook.

METHOD

Sample

We recruited 251 Facebook users ages 16 or older residing in Hong Kong, China to complete our online survey. For many reasons explained below, a Hong Kong sample presents an almost ideal sample for studying Facebook behavior generally and an appropriate sample to test the queried associations:

- Hong Kong residents engage in the Chinese cultural practice of "guanxi"; they prize networking and place high value on having and maintaining connections. Thus, they may visit Facebook often and work diligently to maintain their Facebook connections.
- The vast majority of Hong Kong residents culturally identify as Chinese and thus feel an affinity with their immediate neighbor to the north, Mainland China. However, the government of Mainland China forbids the use of Facebook and affirmatively takes step to block its citizen's Facebook usage. Because of this policy, Hong Kong residents prize their access to Facebook and find it useful for maintaining ties with intercity friends in Hong Kong as well as ethnically Chinese friends living in countries other than Mainland China such as Malaysia, Singapore, and Taiwan.
- Because Hong Kong serves as an international hub for law, business, fashion and so forth, native Hong Kong residents often become acquainted with people from multiple countries and cultures. Thus, Hong Kong residents, more than residents of most locations, have the opportunity to communicate with intercultural relational partners around the world via Facebook.
- Because Hong Kong serves as an international hub for law, business, fashion and so forth, many Hong Kong residents are citizens of outside countries and territories. Thus, our sample, collected in Hong Kong, accurately represented a wider variety of foreign nationals than typically seen in most locations.
- Hong Kong is a densely populated urban area and thus residents experience frequent close physical proximity to one another; they often fail to engage in eye contact or interaction as a way to maintain personal space in one of the most densely populated cities in the world. Thus, a fair number of residents may experience loneliness.

Furthermore, recent articles reported on Facebook behavior in Japan (e.g., Omori & Allen, 2014), Korea (e.g., Ha, Kim, Labaque-Saena, Chang, & Park, 2015), Malaysia (e.g., Abdulahi, Samadi, & Gharleghi, 2014), and Singapore (e.g., Qiu et al., 2012). Our study adds to this growing body of knowledge concerning Facebook usage in Asia.

Our sample size of 251 was (a) consistent with recently research reports on the same topic such as Satici's 2019 article examining the relationship between loneliness and Facebook use among 280 Turkish university students and (b) almost identical to the sample size of 264 reported in the only previously published study of self-disclosure on a SNS that substitutes for Facebook among emerging adults in Mainland China (Liu & Brown, 2014).

Typical of survey research of emerging adult Facebook users (e.g., Phu & Gow, 2019), we employed convenience sampling. Our sample included 95 (37.8%) males and 156 (62.2%) females. Most of the respondents (*n* = 157; 62.5%) were ages 20-24. However, the sample also contained younger emerging adults ages 16-19 (14.3%) and older emerging adults ages 25-29 (15.1%). Only 4% of our sample were over age 29. Thus, our Hong Kong sample was almost exclusively comprised of emerging adults.

Respondents reported diverse educational experiences ranging from completing secondary level (13.6%) to holding a certificate or associate degree (11.6%) to an earned baccalaureate degree (61.8%) to a graduate degree (12.8%). The majority reported having a monthly income of HK$10,000 or below (69.7%), followed by HK$10,000-$20,000 (23.5%). The respondents hailed from various walks of life, but were mostly students (60.6%). The second largest group provided social services (8.4%), a typical "starter job" for emerging adults in Hong Kong.

One advantage of collecting data in an international city is the sample's diversity. Our convenience sample contained citizens of seven countries including France, Mainland China, Malaysia, Taiwan, United Kingdom, and the United States—but the majority of respondents claimed Hong Kong citizenship (*n* =231, 92.00%). Similarly, the vast majority of our respondents self-identified as Asian (*n* =247, 98.40%), with the remaining identifying as Caucasian.

Instruments

Because we recruited respondents in Hong Kong, a multi-national city, the survey displayed 64 questions in the city's two dominant languages: English and traditional Chinese characters. We discovered existing instruments in English and then translated them into Chinese. Next, the questions were back translated by graduate students in Communication to ensure consistency and accuracy across the two language versions.

- **Loneliness.** The revised UCLA Loneliness Scale developed by (Russell, Peplau, & Cutrona, 1980) contains 20-items rated on 4-point Likert scales that range from 1 (never) to 4 (often). The scale included items such as "I am outgoing and friendly." The scale proved reliable with our sample, yielding a Cronbach alpha of 0.90.
- **Self-disclosure on Facebook.** The Revised Self Disclosure Scale (RSDS) developed by Wheeless and Grotz (1976) is a self-report instrument of 31 items scored on 5-point Likert scales ranging from 5 (strongly agree) to 1 (strongly disagree). We reworded the items to address self-disclosure on Facebook. For example, one item stated, "I usually disclose positive things about myself on Facebook".

A factor analysis of our respondents' scores using principal components analysis with Varimax rotation yielded two self-disclosure factors, namely negative self-disclosure and positive self-disclosure.[1] Negative self-disclosure was comprised of two items with a Cronbach's alpha of 0.80. Positive self-disclosure was comprised of 13 items identified in previous studies across four dimensions of self-disclosure (i.e., accuracy, depth, breath, intention) with a Cronbach's alpha of 0.81.

- **Facebook Usage.** Following Leung (2002), we employed three measures to assess Facebook usage. We asked (a) how many days a week they visited Facebook, (b) how many hours a day they spent on Facebook, and (c) how much time they typically spent per visit.

Procedures

We pretested our survey with 21 users drawn from the research sample. Based on their feedback, we made minor word changes to the questionnaires to increase clarity; for example, we rewrote instructions using more specific terms.

We posted three versions of the revised survey, each at its own URL. Each version contained the same instruments but in differing, counter-balanced orders to ameliorate order effects. Based on their birth months, we directed approximately a third of the respondents to each of the three URLs.

Typical of survey sampling of Facebook users (e.g., Phu & Gow, 2019), we employed multiple methods of recruitment to increase the size and diversity of our convenience sample. Specifically, the authors each posted an invitation to the survey on their Facebook pages and urged their Facebook friends to *not* take the survey but to repost the recruitment invitation. Thus, members of the researchers' social network served as recruiters but not as respondents in the study, minimizing the introduction of researcher bias. Additionally, the survey's URLs were sent via an invitational email to undergraduate students in Communication classes at a large, state-sponsored university in Hong Kong. The URLs remained live for 14 consecutive days and thus allowed for the collection of 251 completed surveys.

RESULTS

Preliminary Analyses

We factor analyzed the scores from the items on the loneliness and self-disclosure instruments using principal components analysis with Varimax rotation.[1] The loneliness scale factored cleanly and, as mentioned above, the self-disclosure scale reduced to two factors: positive disclosure and negative disclosure.

Next, we examined the frequency distributions for the variables. Three indicators of Facebook usage (days per week, hours per day, and time per visit) were not normally distributed. Therefore, we conducted nonparametric tests for the analyses involving these measures. We conducted parametric tests to assess the potential relationships between loneliness and positive versus negative self-disclosure.

Primary Analyses

We computed Spearman's correlation coefficients to assess (a) the potential association between loneliness and Facebook usage and (b) the potential association between self-disclosure and Facebook usage. Facebook usage was not significantly associated with loneliness (see Table 1), suggesting that Facebook users' loneliness was not associated with increased or decreased Facebook usage. Conversely, both positive and negative self-disclosure were associated with Facebook usage (see Table 1). Positive self-disclosure was positively correlated with two measures of Facebook usage, indicating that the more days per week users visited Facebook as well as the more hours per day they spent on Facebook, the more they engaged on positive self-disclosure on Facebook. Conversely, negative self-disclosure was negatively correlated

Table 1. Correlations between loneliness, self-disclosure, and facebook usage

	Facebook Usage Pattern		
	Days per Week	Hours per Day	Time per Visit
Loneliness	-0.01 (n.s.)	0.08 (n.s.)	-0.01 (n.s.)
Self-disclosure on Facebook			
Positive self-disclosure	0.18**	0.18**	-0.01 (n.s.)
Negative self-disclosure (R)	-0.08 (n.s.)	-0.17**	-0.01 (n.s.)

Notes: $^{**}p<0.01$, n=251

with hours per day on Facebook, suggesting that the more hours per day users spent on Facebook, the less they self-disclosed negatively on Facebook. In all three significant results, increased Facebook usage was associated with either more positive or less negative self-disclosure.

Finally, we calculated Pearson's correlation coefficients to assess the potential correlation between loneliness and self-disclosure on Facebook. Loneliness was not correlated with positive self-disclosure (r = -0.05, p = NS). However, loneliness was negatively correlated with negative self-disclosure (r = -0.22, p = 0.01). The lonelier the Facebook user, the less he/she disclosed negative information.

DISCUSSION

Loneliness and Facebook Usage

Our results answer RQ1 in the negative. Loneliness was not significantly associated with Facebook usage. Our results are consistent with a few previous studies (i.e., Baker & Oswasld, 2010; Wohn & LaRose, 2014) conducted with U.S. freshmen, but inconsistent with the conclusion of Song et al.'s (2014) meta-analysis and with the vast majority of previous studies testing for such an association.

We offer three explanations for our findings: (a) We may be observing cultural differences. Given that Facebook is very popular in Hong Kong, it may be too cool to be on Facebook for anyone to ignore its draw; thus, differences across loneliness scores could not be documented. (b) We assessed positive and negative self-disclosure rather than using overall self-disclosure scores as was typical for the earlier researched that documents a positive correlation. Thus, both measurement and sample differences may explain our results. (c) Previous research indicates that factors other than loneliness influence Facebook usage; such factors include shyness (Baker & Oswald, 2010), self-esteem (e.g., Leighton, Legate, LePine, Anderson, & Grahe, 2018; Varnali & Toker, 2015), self-inferiority (Hong, Huang, Lin, & Chiu, 2014), and stress (Bevan et al., 2014). Thus, loneliness was not associated with Facebook usage across samples in two locations: the United States and now Hong Kong.

For at least two reasons, Facebook may offer limited appeal to lonely users looking for new relational partners online: (a) Facebook users primarily search for and communicate with existing, offline connections rather than looking for new people to meet (Lampe et al., 2006; Miller & Mundey, 2015). (b) Facebook users primarily reveal their profile information to existing, offline connections (Lampe et al., 2006). Attempts to befriend users unknown in the FtF world are typically ignored or rejected.

Instead of Facebook, lonely people may turn to SNS that focus on connecting strangers based on shared interests, political views, or activities like dating websites, blogs, forums, and chatrooms where they can present themselves as more extroverted, less shy, more intelligent, more fun loving, and generally more favorable. In such alternative forums, they can enjoy a greater sense of safety and perceived ability to control anonymity as well as communicate with multiple fellow users in real time.

Loneliness and Facebook Usage

Our results revealed associations between self-disclosure and Facebook usage, thus, answering RQ2 in the affirmative. These results are consistent with previously published findings (Chang & Heo, 2014; Chen & Sharma, 2015; Crabtree & Pillow, 2018; Lee et al., 2013; Park & Baek, 2016; Tsay-Vogel et al., 2018). However, our results are the first to document this association in a Hong Kong sample.

An association between self-disclosure and Facebook usage may be the result of the reciprocity norm of self-disclosure (Pearce & Sharp, 1973). Users' Facebook pages, posts, and comments contain self-information that functions as self-disclosure. Therefore, the more time a user spends on Facebook, the more he/she is exposed to the self-disclosures of others and then may disclose reciprocally, perhaps disclosing in greater depth and breadth to further prompt the disclosure of others.

Additionally, social exchange theories argue that people develop and maintain relationships based on reciprocal exchange of rewards (Dunbar, 2015). Applying this principle to self-disclosure, online interactants may reveal themselves to people who self-disclose to them. Facebook seems an ideal medium for such exchanges.

Valence of Disclosure and Facebook Usage

Perhaps the most interesting findings of the study surround the valence of Facebook self-disclosure. We report three significant findings that add to the growing understanding of how the valence of self-disclosure functions on Facebook.

- First, we adapted our self-disclosure instrument by add the words "on Facebook" to each item. Recall that its factor analysis yielded two factors divided by valence (positive versus negative) rather than the expected four factors found in previous studies (i.e., accuracy, depth, breath, intention). This result was our first indication that valence of disclosure may be a salient factor for our respondents.
- Second, our analyses revealed the significant negative correlation between hours per day on Facebook and negative self-disclosure. The more hours spent per day on Facebook, the less the respondents tended to self-disclosure negatively on Facebook.
- Third, two measures of Facebook usage (number of days per week and hours per day) were positively correlated with positive self-disclosure. The more Facebook usage, the more positive self-disclosure.

Our results, consistent with previously reported findings (Qiu et al., 2012; Lee et al., 2014), indicate that disclosure on Facebook tends to be positive. In fact, our results indicate that the more time spent on Facebook, the less negative self-disclosure. We believe our results provide evidence for the existence of a "stay positive" Facebook norm. As users learn the norms of Facebook, including the norm of posting primarily positive status updates, they might desire to obey the "stay positive" norm as well as to interact in a positive manner to maintain their relationships.

We are not the first researchers to discuss Facebook norms. McLaughlin and Vitak (2012) documented ways users enforce Facebook norms. Miller and Munday (2015) identified three Facebook norms. Our data results may identify a fourth norm: Stay positive in posts and status updates. The notion of a "stay positive" Facebook norm is consistent with the findings of two recent studies: Toma and Carlson (2015) report that college students' perception that they portray a positive version of the self in their Facebook profiles as well as Burke and Ruppel's (2015) finding that users report greater interaction success on Facebook on days when they report more positive self-presentation.

Loneliness and Self-Disclosure on Facebook

Our RQ3 analyses yielded mixed results. Negative self-disclosure correlated negatively with loneliness, whereas positive self-disclosure did not correlate with loneliness. The lonelier the user, the less he/she revealed negative information. Conversely, the less lonely the user, the more he/she revealed negative information. This finding was *not* consistent with previous research findings including Lee et al's (2013) report that that loneliness increased self-disclosure on Facebook among their sample of Korean college students. Also, these results are inconsistent with Jin's (2013) report that, among a Korean sample of emerging adults, lonely users were more likely to engage in negative self-disclosure and less likely to engage in positive self-disclosure. Our results are the first to document this exact relationship: Negative self-disclosure correlated negatively with loneliness, whereas positive self-disclosure did not correlate with loneliness.

Our findings are consistent with recent results documenting that Facebook users prefer receiving negative disclosures offline (Saling et al., 2019). Perhaps lonely users are especially sensitive to communication norms and endeavor to follow them conscientiously. Indeed, lonely users might be attempting to maintain and develop Facebook relationships—and might avoid negative disclosure to do so. Less lonely users may feel sufficiently secure in their relationships to be comfortable revealing negative information.

Loneliness and Facebook Usage

In sum, based on data from our sample and a few previously published studies, loneliness appears to be unrelated to Facebook usage, at least among certain populations. Perhaps previously identified user characteristics such as shyness (Baker & Oswald, 2010), self-esteem (e.g., Varnali & Toker, 2015), self-inferiority (Hong et al., 2014), and stress (Bevan et al., 2014) exercise more influence over Facebook usage than loneliness.

However, loneliness may prompt cautiousness, as loneliness appears to be associated with less negative self-disclosure on Facebook. In general, the more time the emerging adults in our sample spent on Facebook, the more likely they were to engage in positive self-disclosure and the less likely they are to reveal negative information. This pattern of self-disclosure seems reasonable, given that the primary way to interact on Facebook is to post a comment or status update, thus revealing information about the self, and given the potential existence of a Facebook norm of "staying positive."

Given the inconsistences between our findings and previous results with alternative populations, our outcomes may indicate that culture may play a role in Facebook users' communication patterns. Such a conclusion would be consistent with previously published results that emerging adult behavior can differ from culture to culture (Arseth et al., 2009). Additionally, examining valence of self-disclosure may allow more nuanced understandings of the norms governing Facebook disclosures.

LIMITATIONS AND FUTURE RESEARCH DIRECTIONS

We acknowledge multiple limitations to our study. Our sample was gathered in one location, Hong Kong. The sample proved fruitful for a study of Facebook usage, given the many significant findings of the study. However, the generalizability of the findings to other locations awaits testing. Furthermore, multiple Chinese cultural norms (i.e., social hierarchy, monitoring displays of strong emotion, face concerns, and emphasis on group harmony) can influence respondents' replies in research (Kwan, Chun, & Chesla, 2011).

Furthermore, because there is no directory of Facebook users, probability sampling was impossible. Thus, the representativeness of our convenience sample remains unknown. Additionally, because this was a one-time survey, causality could not be established. Future research could examine the causal relationships between loneliness, self-disclosure, and Facebook use, perhaps employing experimental interventions and longitudinal methods. Finally, the limitations of self-report data include recall problems and social-desirability biases.

Although beyond the score of our study, future research might examine further the link between self-disclosure and users' motivations for disclosure on Facebook (Bazarova & Choi, 2014). Certain motivations may account for the amount and valence of disclosures. Additionally, future studies of disclosure could move beyond survey data to examine actual Facebook profiles, as such examinations have proved fruitful in previous studies of Facebook behavior of emerging adults (e.g., Boupha, Grisso, Morris, Webb, & Zakeri, 2013; Taraszow, Aristodemou, Shitta, Laouris, & Arsoy, 2010; Webb, Wilson, Hodges, Smith, & Zakeri, 2012).

CONCLUSION

Despite these limitations, our study contributes to scholarly understanding of user-interactions on SNS. We offer the first examination of the relationships between loneliness, self-disclosure on Facebook, and Facebook usage among a Hong Kong sample of emerging adults. We now know that, at least among one sample of Facebook users, the more time spent on Facebook, the more users engage in positive self-disclosure on Facebook. The more hours per day users spent on Facebook, the less negative self-disclosure they reveal on Facebook. However, two measures of Facebook usage (days per week on Facebook and time spent on Facebook per visit) were not significantly correlated with negative self-disclosure. The higher the loneliness score, the less users reveal negative self-information on Facebook. We offered two logical explanations for our results: the reciprocity norm of self-disclosure and the proposed Facebook norm of remaining positive. Finally, our study offers evidence that Facebook norms may be culture specific and measuring self-discourse valence may provide a more nuanced understanding for those norms.

REFERENCES

Abdulahi, A., Samadi, B., & Gharleghi, B. (2014). A Study on the negative effects of social networking sites such as Facebook among Asia Pacific University scholars in Malaysia. *International Journal of Business and Social Science*, *5*(1), 133–145. Retrieved from http://www.ijbssnet.com/journals/Vol_5_No_10_September_2014/18.pdf

Al-Saggaf, Y., & Nielsen, S. (2014). Self-disclosure on Facebook among female users and its relationship to feelings of loneliness. *Computers in Human Behavior*, *36*, 460–468. doi:10.1016/j.chb.2014.04.014

Arnett, J. J. (2015). *Emerging adulthood: The winding road from the late teens through the twenties* (2nd ed.). New York: Oxford University Press. doi:10.1093/oxfordhb/9780199795574.013.9

Arseth, A. K., Kroger, J., Martinussen, M., & Bakken, G. (2009). Intimacy status, attachment, separation-individuation patterns, and identity status in female university students. *Journal of Social and Personal Relationships*, *26*(5), 697–712. doi:10.1177/0265407509347927

Baker, L. R., & Oswald, D. L. (2010). Shyness and online networking services. *Journal of Social and Personal Relationships*, *27*(7), 873–889. doi:10.1177/0265407510375261

Bazarova, N. N., & Choi, Y. H. (2014). Self-disclosure in social media: Extending the functional approach to disclosure motivations and chacteristics on social network sites. *Journal of Communication*, *64*(4), 635–657. doi:10.1111/jcom.12106

Bevan, J. L., Cummings, M. B., Kubiniec, A., Mogannam, M., Price, M., & Todd, R. (2015). How are important life events disclosed on Facebook? Relationships with likelihood of sharing and privacy. *Cyberpsychology, Behavior, and Social Networking*, *18*(1), 8–12. doi:10.1089/cyber.2014.0373 PMID:25584725

Bevan, J. L., Gomez, R., & Sparks, L. (2014). Disclosures about important life events on Facebook: Relationships with stress and quality of life. *Computers in Human Behavior*, *39*, 246–253. doi:10.1016/j.chb.2014.07.021

Bigham, D. S. (2012). Emerging adulthood in sociolinguists. *Language and Linguistics Compass*, *6*(8), 533–544. doi:10.1002/lnc3.350

Blachnio, A., Przepiorka, A., & Rudnicka, P. (2016). Narcissism and self-esteem as predictors of dimensions of Facebook use. *Personality and Individual Differences*, *90*, 296–301. doi:10.1016/j.paid.2015.11.018

Boupha, S., Grisso, A. D., Morris, J., Webb, L. M., & Zakeri, M. (2013). How college students display ethnic identity on Facebook. In R. A. Lind (Ed.), *Race/Gender/Media: Considering diversity across audiences, content, and producers* (3rd ed.; pp. 107-112). Boston, MA: Pearson. Retrieved on June 10, 2019 from https://www.researchgate.net/publication/225271141_How_college_students_display_ethnic_identity_on_Facebook

boyd, d. m. (2006). Friends, Friendsters, and MySpace Top8: Writing community into being on social network sties. *First Monday, 11*(12). Retrieved Jan 23, 2010 from http://www.firstmonday.org/issues/issue11_12/boyd/

Bryant, E. M., Marmo, J., & Ramirez, A. (2011). A functional approach to social networking sites. In K. B. Wright & L. M. Webb (Eds.), *Computer mediated communication in personal relationships* (pp. 3–20). New York: Peter Lang Publishers.

Burke, T. J., & Ruppel, E. K. (2015). Facebook self-presentation motives: Daily effects on social anxiety and interaction success. *Communication Studies*, *66*(2), 204–217. doi:10.1080/10510974.2014.884014

Caers, R., De Feyter, T., De Couck, M., Stough, T., Vigna, C., & Du Bois, C. (2013). Facebook: A literature review. *New Media & Society*, *15*(6), 982–1002. doi:10.1177/1461444813488061

Chan, M. (2018). Reluctance to talk about politics in Face-to-face and Facebook settings: Examining the impact of fear of isolation, willingness to self-censor, and peer network characteristics. *Mass Communication & Society*, *21*(1), 1–23. doi:10.1080/15205436.2017.1358819

Chang, C. W., & Heo, J. (2014). Visiting theories that predict college students' self-disclosure on Facebook. *Computers in Human Behavior*, *36*, 79–86. doi:10.1016/j.chb.2013.07.059

Chen, G. M. (2015). Why do women bloggers use social media? Recreation and information motivations outweigh engagement motivations. *New Media & Society*, *17*(1), 24–40. doi:10.1177/1461444813504269

Chen, R., & Sharma, S. K. (2015). Learning and self-disclosure behavior on social networking sites: The case of Facebook users. *European Journal of Information Systems*, *24*(1), 93–106. doi:10.1057/ejis.2013.31

Cheung, C. M. K., Lee, Z. W. Y., & Chan, T. K. H. (2015). Self-disclosure in social networking sites: The role of perceived cost, perceived benefits and social influence. *Internet Research*, *2*(2), 279–299. doi:10.1108/IntR-09-2013-0192

Crabtree, M. A., & Pillow, D. R. (2018). Extending the dual factor of Facebook use: Social motives and network density predict Facebook use through impression management and open self-disclosure. *Personality and Individual Differences*, *133*, 34–40. doi:10.1016/j.paid.2017.06.017

Dunbar, N. E. (2015). A review of theoretical approaches to interpersonal power. *Review of Communication*, *15*(1), 1–18. doi:10.1080/15358593.2015.1016310

Dwyer, C., Hiltz, S. R., & Passerini, K. (2007). Trust and privacy concern within social networking sites: A comparison of Facebook and MySpace. *Proceedings of Thirteenth Americas Conference on Information Systems.* Retrieved June 10, 2019 from http://csis.pace.edu/dwyer/research/DwyerAMCIS2007.pdf

Ellison, N. B., Vitak, J., Gray, R., & Lampe, C. (2014). Cultivating social resources on social network sites: Facebook relationship maintenance behaviors and their role in social capital processes. *Journal of Computer-Mediated Communication*, *19*(4), 855–870. doi:10.1111/jcc4.12078

Facebook. (2019). *Stats.* Retrieved May 30, 2019 from https://newsroom.fb.com/company-info/

Frison, E., & Eggermont, S. (2015). Toward an integrated and differential approach to the relationships between loneliness, different types of Facebook use, and adolescents' depressed mood. *Communication Research*, *43*, 279–282. doi:10.1177/0093650215617506

Gibbs, J. L., Ellison, N. B., & Heino, R. D. (2006). Self-presentation in online personals: The role of anticipated future interaction, self-disclosure, and perceived success in Internet dating. *Communication Research*, *33*(2), 1–26. doi:10.1177/0093650205285368

Green, T., Wilhelmsen, T., Wilmots, E., Dood, B., & Quinn, S. (2016). Social anxiety, attributes of online communication and self-disclosure across private and public Facebook communication. *Computers in Human Behavior*, *58*, 206–213. doi:10.1016/j.chb.2015.12.066

Ha, Y. W., Kim, J., Libaque-Saenz, C. F., Chang, Y. H., & Park, M. C. (2015). Use and gratifications of mobile SNSs: Facebook and KakaoTalk in Korea. *Telematics and Informatics*, *32*(3), 425–438. doi:10.1016/j.tele.2014.10.006

Hendry, L. B., & Kloep, M. (2007). Conceptualizing emerging adulthood: Inspecting the emperor's new clothes? *Child Development Perspectives*, *1*(2), 74–79. doi:10.1111/j.1750-8606.2007.00017.x

Hollenbaugh, E. E., & Ferris, A. L. (2014). Facebook and self-disclosure: Examining the role of traits, social cohesion, and motives. *Computers in Human Behavior*, *30*, 50–58. doi:10.1016/j.chb.2013.07.055

Hong, F. Y., Huang, D. H., Lin, H. Y., & Chiu, S. L. (2014). Analysis of the psychological traits, Facebook usage, and Facebook addition model of Taiwanese university students. *Telematics and Informatics*, *31*(4), 597–606. doi:10.1016/j.tele.2014.01.001

Jin, B. (2013). How lonely people use and perceive Facebook. *Computers in Human Behavior*, *29*(6), 2463–2470. doi:10.1016/j.chb.2013.05.034

Kong, F., & You, X. Q. (2013). Loneliness and self-esteem as mediators between social support and life satisfaction in late adolescence. *Social Indicators Research*, *110*(1), 271–279. doi:10.100711205-011-9930-6

Kwak, K. T., Choi, S. K., & Lee, B. G. (2014). SNS flow, SNS self-disclosure and post hoc interpersonal relations change: Focused on Korean Facebook user. *Computers in Human Behavior*, *31*, 294–304. doi:10.1016/j.chb.2013.10.046

Kwan, C. M. L., Chun, K. M., & Chesla, C. A. (2011). Cultural norms shaping research group interviews with Chinese American immigrants. *Asian American Journal of Psychology*, *2*(2), 115–127. doi:10.1037/a0024184 PMID:21760974

Lampe, C., Ellison, N., & Steinfield, C. (2006). A Face(book) in the crowd: Social searching vs. social browsing. In *Proceedings of the 2006 20th Anniversary Conference on Computer Supported Cooperative Work* (pp. 167-170). New York: ACM Press. 10.1145/1180875.1180901

Ledbetter, A. M., Mazer, J. P., DeGroot, J. M., Meyer, K. R., Yuping, M., & Swafford, B. (2011). Attitudes toward online social connection and self-disclosure as predictors of Facebook communication and relational closeness. *Communication Research*, *38*(1), 27–53. doi:10.1177/0093650210365537

Lee, K. T., Noh, M. J., & Koo, D. M. (2013). Lonely people are no longer lonely on social networking sites: The mediating role of self-disclosure and social support. *Cyberpsychology, Behavior, and Social Networking*, *16*(6), 413–418. doi:10.1089/cyber.2012.0553 PMID:23621716

Lee-Won, R. J., Shim, M. S., Joo, Y. K., & Park, S. G. (2014). Who puts the best "face" in Facebook?: Positive self-presentation in online social networking and the role of self-consciousness, actual-to-total friends ratio, and culture. *Computers in Human Behavior*, *39*, 413–423. doi:10.1016/j.chb.2014.08.007

Leighton, D. C., Legate, N., LePine, S., Anderson, S. F., & Grahe, J. E. (2018, January 1). *Self-Esteem, self-disclosure, self-expression, and connection on Facebook: A collaborative replication meta-analysis.* doi:10.31234/osf.io/sx742

Leung, L. (2002). Loneliness, self-disclosure, and ICQ use. *Cyberpsychology & Behavior*, *5*(3), 241–251. doi:10.1089/109493102760147240 PMID:12123247

Linne, J. (2014). Common uses of Facebook among adolescents from different social sectors in Buenos Aires City. *Media Education Research Journal, 43,* 189-197. Retrieved June 10, 2019 from dialnet.unirioja.es/descarga/articulo/4738318/2.pdf

Liu, D., & Brown, B. B. (2014). Self-disclosure on social networking sites, positive feedback, and social capital among Chinese college students. *Computers in Human Behavior*, *38*, 213–219. doi:10.1016/j.chb.2014.06.003

McLaughlin, C., & Vitak, J. (2012). Norm evolution and violation on Facebook. *New Media & Society*, *14*(2), 299–315. doi:10.1177/1461444811412712

Medeiros, D. T., & Webb, L. M. (2019). Remaining Facebook versus face-to-face friends after a romantic breakup. *International Journal of Interactive Communication Systems and Technologies*, *9*(1), 1–16. doi:10.4018/IJICST.2019010101

Miller, B., & Mundey, P. (2015). Follow the rules and no one will get hurt: Performing boudary work to avoid negative interactions when using social network sites. *Information Communication and Society*, *18*(2), 187–201. doi:10.1080/1369118X.2014.946433

Munsey, C. (2006). Emerging adults: The in-between age. *Monitor (Charlottetown)*, *37*, 68. Retrieved from http://www.apa.org/monitor/jun06/emerging.aspx

Nam, M., Chun, B., & Hin, L. C. (2014). Impoliteness in Facebook Status updates: Stategic talk among colleagues "outside" the workplace. *Text & Talk*, *34*, 165–188. doi:10.1515/text-2013-0042

Omori, K., & Allen, M. (2014). Cultural differences between American and Japanese self-presentation on SNSs. *International Journal of Interactive Communication Systems and Technologies*, *4*(1), 47–60. doi:10.4018/ijicst.2014010104

Park, N., & Baek, K. (2016). Effects of Facebook users' self-disclosure, Facebook use intensity, privacy concern and trust on continuous use intention of Facebook: Focusing on moderating effect of privacy protection skill. *Journal of Korean Content Association*, *16*(11), 53–62. doi:10.5392/JKCA.2016.16.11.053

Park, N. K., & Lee, S. Y. (2014). College students' motivations for facebook use and psychological outcomes. *Journal of Broadcasting & Electronic Media*, *58*(4), 601–620. doi:10.1080/08838151.2014.966355

Pearce, W. B., & Sharp, S. M. (1973). Self-disclosing communication. *Journal of Communication*, *23*(4), 409–425. doi:10.1111/j.1460-2466.1973.tb00958.x PMID:4589176

Phu, B., & Gow, A. J. (2019). Facebook use and its association with subjective happiness and loneliness. *Computers in Human Behavior*, *92*, 151–159. doi:10.1016/j.chb.2018.11.020

Qiu, L., Lin, H., Leung, A. K., & Tov, W. (2012). Putting their best foot forward: Emotional disclosure on Facebook. *Cyberpsychology, Behavior, and Social Networking*, *15*(10), 569–572. doi:10.1089/cyber.2012.0200 PMID:22924675

Rains, S. A., & Brunner, S. R. (2015). What can we learn about social network sites by studying Facebook? A call and recommendations for research on social network sites. *New Media & Society*, *17*(1), 114–131. doi:10.1177/1461444814546481

Russell, D., Peplau, L. A., & Cutrona, C. E. (1980). The revised UCLA Loneliness Scale: Concurrent and discriminant validity evidence. *Journal of Personality Assessment*, *42*, 290–294. doi:10.120715327752jpa4203_11 PMID:660402

Saling, L. L., Cohen, D. B., & Cooper, D. (2019). Not close enough for comfort: Facebook users eschew high intimacy negative disclosures. *Personality and Individual Differences*, *142*, 103–109. doi:10.1016/j.paid.2019.01.028

Satici, S. A. (2019). Facebook addiction and subjective well-being: A study of the mediating role of shyness and loneliness. *International Journal of Mental Health and Addiction*, *17*(1), 41–55. doi:10.100711469-017-9862-8

Shneor, R., & Efrat, K. (2014). Analyzing the impact of culture on average time spent on special media networking sites. *Journal of Promotion Management*, *20*(4), 413–435. doi:10.1080/10496491.2014.930281

Simoncic, T. E., Kuhlman, K. R., Vargas, I., Houchins, S., & Lopez-Duran, N. L. (2014). Facebook use and depressive symptomatology: Investigating the role of neuroticism and extraversion in youth. *Computers in Human Behavior*, *40*, 1–5. doi:10.1016/j.chb.2014.07.039 PMID:25861155

Song, H., Zmyslinski-Seeling, A., Kim, J. Y., Drent, A., Victor, A., Omori, K., & Allen, M. (2014). Does Facebook make you lonely? A meta-analysis. *Computers in Human Behavior*, *36*, 446–452. doi:10.1016/j.chb.2014.04.011

Taraszow, T., Aristodemou, E., Shitta, G., Laouris, Y., & Arsoy, A. (2010). Disclosure of personal contact information by young people in social networking sites: An analysis using Facebook as an example. *International Journal of Media and Cultural Politics*, *6*(1), 81–102. doi:10.1386/macp.6.1.81/1

Toma, C. L., & Carlson, C. L. (2015). How do Facebook users believe they come across in their profiles?: A meta-perception approach to investigating Facebook self-presentation. *Communication Research Reports*, *32*(1), 93–101. doi:10.1080/08824096.2014.990557

Tsay-Vogel, M., Shanahan, J., & Signorielli, N. (2018). Social media cultivating perceptions of privacy: A 5-year analysis of privacy attitudes and self-disclosure behavior among Facebook users. *New Media & Society*, 1–21. doi:10.1177/1461444816660731

Turner, J. W., Grube, J. A., & Myers, J. (2001). Developing an optimal match within online communities: An exploration of CMC support communities and traditional support. *Journal of Communication*, *51*(2), 231–251. doi:10.1111/j.1460-2466.2001.tb02879.x

Utz, S. (2015). The function of self-disclosure on social networking sites: Not only intimate, but also positive and entertaining self-disclosures increase feelings of connection. *Computers in Human Behavior*, *45*, 1–10. doi:10.1016/j.chb.2014.11.076

Varnali, K., & Toker, A. (2015). Self-disclosure on social networking sites. *Social Behavior and Personality*, *43*(1), 1–13. doi:10.2224bp.2015.43.1.1

Walther, J. B., Slovacek, C. L., & Tidwell, L. C. (2001). Is a picture worth a thousand words? Photographic images in long-term and short-term computer-mediated communication. *Communication Research*, *28*(1), 105–134. doi:10.1177/009365001028001004

Waters, S., & Ackerman, J. (2011). Exploring privacy management on Facebook: Motivations and perceived consequences of voluntary disclosure. *Journal of Computer-Mediated Communication*, *17*(1), 101–115. doi:10.1111/j.1083-6101.2011.01559.x

Webb, L. M., & Lee, B. S. (2011). Mommy blogs: The centrality of community in the performance of online maternity. In M. Moravec (Ed.), *Motherhood online: How online communities shape modern motherhood* (pp. 244-257). Newcastle upon Tyne, UK: Cambridge Scholars Publishing. Retrieved June 10, 2019 from https://www.researchgate.net/profile/Lynne_Webb/publication/225271136_Mommy_blogs_The_centrality_of_community_in_the_performance_of_online_maternity/links/0fcfd4fcffab5514ca000000.pdf

Webb, L. M., & Temple, N. (2015). Social media and gender issues. In B. Guzzetti & M. Lesley (Eds.), *Handbook of research on the societal impact of digital media* (pp. 638–669). Hershey, PA: IGI Global. doi:10.4018/978-1-4666-8310-5.ch025

Webb, L. M., Wilson, M. L., Hodges, M., Smith, P. A., & Zakeri, M. (2012). Facebook: How college students work it. In H. S. Noor Al-Deen & J. A. Hendricks (Eds.), *Social media: Usage and impact* (pp. 3–22). Lanham, MD: Lexington Books.

Wheeless, L. R., & Grotz, J. (1976). Conceptualization and measurement of reported self-disclosure. *Human Communication Research*, *2*(4), 338–346. doi:10.1111/j.1468-2958.1976.tb00494.x

Wohn, D. Y., & LaRose, R. (2014). Effects of loneliness and differential usage of Facebook on college adjustment of first-year students. *Computers & Education*, *76*, 158–167. doi:10.1016/j.compedu.2014.03.018

Wu, C. W., & Webb, L. M. (2016). Chinese international students' messages on the Family Forum: Topics, goals, and types of assistance. In M. F. Wright (Ed.), *Identity, sexuality, and relationships among emerging adults in the digital age* (pp. 128–149). Hershey, PA: IGI Global. doi:10.4018/978-1-5225-1856-3.ch009

Yeo, T. E. D., & Chu, T. H. (2017). Sharing "sex secrets" on Facebook: A content analysis of youth peer communication and advice exchange on social media about sexual health and intimate relations. *Journal of Health Communication*, *22*(9), 753–762. doi:10.1080/10810730.2017.1347217 PMID:28796578

Zlatolas, L. N., Welzer, T., Hericko, M., & Holbl, M. (2015). Privacy antecedents for SNS self-disclosure: The case of Facebook. *Computers in Human Behavior, 45,* 158-167. doi:10.1016/j.chb.2014.12.012

KEY TERMS AND DEFINITIONS

Emerging Adulthood: A distinct life stage exists between adolescence and full adulthood when individuals are exploring long-term choices.

Facebook Use (or Usage): Active engagement on Facebook across time operationalized as the amount of time the individual spends reading or writing in the social medium platform located at Facebook.com.

Hong Kong, China: A semi-autonomous city-state in the south-eastern corner of China, located on the South China sea. It is a densely populated urban center comprised of one main island and a small part of the mainland territory. Its native language is Mandarin, although English is widely spoken.

Loneliness: The individual experiences an uncomfortable psychological state associated with a desire for increased human interaction.

Self-Disclosure: An individual reveals information about the self to others.

Valence of a Disclosure: The perception of revealed information as either positive versus negative by either the sender, the receiver, or an observer.

Chapter 10
Investigation of Smartphone Use Addiction in Generation Y

Zeynep Güvenç Salabğir
Istanbul University, Turkey

Süphan Nasır
Istanbul University, Turkey

ABSTRACT

In recent years, rapidly developing of communication technology, increasing of internet and social networking applications usage have led to an increase in the level of smartphones dependence. Transformation of smartphone use from habit to addiction and spread of this addiction especially among young adults emphasize seriousness of the matter. In this context, the main purpose of this research is the investigation of smartphone use and addiction in Generation Y that are a part of the digital world. An online survey was conducted with 887 respondents who own a smartphone from Turkey. Five dimensions of smartphone addiction were extracted from the factor analysis, namely tolerance, accompany/fellowship, withdrawal, social network dependence, and health problems. In order to classify smartphone addiction groups, K-means cluster analysis was used on the extracted factors. Four groups named "nonaddicts," "heavy addicts," "realistic addicts," and "emotional addicts" were determined.

INTRODUCTION

In the digital age, mobile devices have become essential for people around the world and smartphone owners are becoming increasingly reliant on their devices, especially because of such devices' advanced capabilities. Even though the smartphone revolution is relatively young, every year the smartphone access becomes more penetrating. Smartphones are essential and it accompanies and participates in most people's daily rituals. In this regard, smartphone penetration continues to increase with each passing day (Ericsson, 2015a; Deloitte, 2015).

Research on mobile phone/smartphone usage reveal this distinct penetration all over the world. Ericson Mobility Report (2016) stated that the total number of mobile subscriptions at the end of 2015 was

DOI: 10.4018/978-1-7998-1063-6.ch010

around 7.3 billion; there was an increase of 68 million subscriptions during fourth quarter of 2015. Global mobile penetration reached 100% in the same period. The number of smartphone users is forecasted to grow from 1.5 billion in 2014 to around 2.5 billion in 2019 and over 36% of the world's population is projected to use a smartphone by 2018 with an increase from about 10% in 2011 (Statista, 2015a).

A Consumers and Mobile Financial Services Report (2015) focused on consumers' use of mobile technology to access financial services and make financial decisions; according to the report, 87% of adults in the United States (US) has a mobile phone and 71% of mobile phones are smartphones, a substantial increase of smartphone use over the 61% rate in 2013. In addition, smartphone adoption is higher among 18-29 year olds than 30-44 year olds (Federal Reserve Board, 2015).

According to findings of a Pew Research Center's (2016) survey, gathered from among 45,435 respondents from 40 nations from March 25, 2015 to May 27, 2015, there was a noticeable rise over the past two years in the percentage of people who own a smartphone in the emerging and developing nations. Smartphone ownership rates have rapidly increased in many countries since 2013 from 21% to 37% in 2015. Additionally, within nearly every country, people who are between the ages of 18-34 are more likely to be internet and smartphone users. South Korea is noticiable country with the highest smartphone ownership rate of 88%. The smartphone ownership rate is 58% in China, 39% in Japan, 72% in the US, 67% in Canada, 68% in the United Kingdom, 60% in Germany, 77% in Australia, and 45% in Russia.

Approximately 29.5% of the global population used smartphones in 2014 and there were 196.6 million smartphone users in Europe, 163.9 million smartphone users in the US, and 944 million smartphone users in China (RapidValue, 2014). TNS/Google's (2014) Connected Consumer Study report is a global research which contains 57 country and helps to provide a better understanding of media markets and media related infrastructures. Findings from this report revealed that Singapore has a 85% smartphone penetration rate, the U.K. has a rate of 68%, Germany of 50%, and France of 49%.

It is predicted that around 90% of mobile data traffic will be from smartphones by the end of 2021 (Ericsson, 2015b). Furthermore, the Asia Pacific region will have the largest share of total smartphone traffic and smartphone subscriptions in the Middle East and Africa regions will grow more than 200% in 2021. The number of smartphone users in China which is the most populous country in the world is forecasted to grow from around 480 million in 2013 to almost 690 million in 2019 (Statista, 2015a). Around half of the Chinese population is projected to use a smartphone by 2018. Moreover, the number of smartphone users was around 170 million in US in 2014. By 2019, this number is expected to increase to 236 million.

Smartphones have become indispensable to daily life in Turkey too. Between July 2011 and July 2012 Turkey was one of the top ten fatest growing smartphone markets in the world (The Boston Consulting Group, 2013). The Our Mobile Planet Turkey report involved interviewing 1,000 Turkish adults between 18 and 64 years of age (Google Iposos MediaCT, 2013). Smartphone penetration was 14% in the first quarter of 2011, with this rate increasing to 30% in the first quarter of 2013 (Google Ipsos MediaCT, 2013) and increasing again to 56% in 2015 (Consumer Barometer Report, 2015). According to TNS/ Google's (2014) Connected Consumer Study report, smartphone penetration in Turkey is 39%.

There have been significant increases in the number of people who have access to the internet in Turkey where 72% of people use the internet at least occasionally or own a smartphone, up from 41% in 2013 (Pew Research Center, 2015). Smartphone usage is higher among younger generations than older with a 93% of Turkish millennials (ages 18-34) owning a smartphone compared with 53% of Turkish people who were 35 or older (Pew Research Center, 2016). In 2016, the number of smartphone users in

Turkey is estimated to reach 35.2 million while this number was 16 million in 2013. By 2019 the number of smartphone users in the Turkey is expected to increase to 48 million (Statista, 2015b).

Mobile Addiction

Mobile addiction is a disease of modern age and it has negative physical, psychological, and social impacts on people's lives (Hayatı Kaçırma, 2015). The term "addiction" is mostly explained in relation to specific objects and a narrow pattern of behavior such as alcoholism, heroin dependence, or cocaine dependence (Shaffer, 1996). However, this term is used widely to explain behavioral addictions such as gambling and excessive Internet, gaming, and mobile phone use (Kwon et al., 2013).

Behavioral addiction for mobile phones/smartphones is defined as obsessive use of a mobile phone/smartphone (Davey & Davey, 2014), and it has various names, including mobile phone dependence (Nikhita, Jadhav, & Ajinkya, 2015; Toda, Monden, Kubo, & Morimoto, 2006), mobile phone addiction (Babadi-Akashe, Zamani, & Hedayati, 2014; Chen, Yan, Tang, Yang, Xie, & He, 2016; Chung, 2011; Chóliz, 2012; Hong, Chiu, & Huang, 2012; Leung, 2008), problematic mobile phone use (Augner & Hacker, 2012; Beranuy, Oberst, Carbonell, & Chamarro, 2009; Bianchi & Phillips, 2005; Billieux, Van Der Linden, & Rochat, 2008; Takao, 2014; Hadlington, 2015), and smartphone addiction (Kwon, et al., 2013; Kwon, Kim, Cho, & Yang, 2013; Aljomaa, Al.Qudah, Albursan, Bakhiet, & Abduljabbar, 2016; Bian & Leung, 2015; Darcin, Kose, Noyan, Nurmedov, Yılmaz, & Dilbaz, 2016; Davey & Davey, 2014; Pavia, Cavani, Di Blasi, & Giordano, 2016).

The characteristics of mobile phone/smartphones addiction are excessive use, problems with parents related to excessive use of mobile phones/smartphones, interference with school or personal activities, emotional changes (Chóliz, 2012), physical disorders, withdrawal symptoms, developing tolerance to overuse, and deviant behavior (Chung, 2011).

People who can not stop using their phone even though it is harming their daily life are on the pathway to mobile phone/smartphones addiction (Heid, 2016). A survey based on 15,747 US smartphone owners found that 51% of women and 41% of men admitted they cannot live without their smartphone (Ligato, 2015). Approximately 15% of Americans between the ages of 18 and 29 are heavily dependent on a smartphone for online access and 46% of smartphone owners say that it is something they "couldn't live without" (Pew Research Center, 2015). Furthermore, 72% of people in one survey state that there is a very little chance that they will ever be more than 5 feet away from their phone (Addictiontips, 2015).

Most research suggests that people spend lots of time on their phones and check their device without receiving any notification (Heid, 2016). About 80% of the people in one study have experienced false vibrations and around 30% have heard ringing that simply did not exist. According to a 2013 internet study, the average mobile phone user checks their device 150 times a day while the more addicted check their phones as much as 900 times a day and they swipe the screen to unlock their phone an average of 110 times every day (Ligato, 2015; Addictiontips, 2015). U.K. consumers, especially younger age groups, look at their smartphones 400 billion times a year. In addition, 30% of smartphone owners check their phones unprompted "very often" or "almost always" to see whether any messages or updates have arrived (Deloitte, 2015).

According to one survey conducted between April 13-26, 2015 with 1000 US adults, 44% of respondents say that they could not make it through the day without their mobile device (Bank of America, 2015). People who were between the ages of 25-34 years old and between ages of the 35-49 years old are more dependent on their smartphones. In addition, 36% of repondents say that they check their smartphone constantly each day. Younger millennials (54%) who were between ages of the 18-24 are more likely to constantly check their mobile phones. Findings also revealed that 82% of adults considering returning home for their smartphone if they left it at home.

Most people in one survey believed that phones helps them feel normal and reduce their panic (Addictiontips, 2015). This study found that 58% of men and 47% of women felt fearful without their smartphone.

Problematic use of smartphones also influences the health of users. According to HuffPost/YouGov survey (2014), 38% of US smartphone owners reported that they fall asleep with a smartphone or other digital device in bed with them and that number was approximately 41% among those adults between the ages of 18-29. In another study, 80% of people between 18-24 slept with their phones right next to them (Addictiontips, 2015). Smartphone use late at night is associated with less sleep, less engagement at work, and morning depletion. Furthermore, many car accidents occur as a result of people using their phones while driving (Flynn, 2014; Addictiontips, 2015).

Symptoms of mobile addiction have been reported in Turkey too. According to Google Ipsos MediaCT's (2013) Our Mobile Planet Turkey report, 76% of Turkish people do not leave home without their devices. Deloitte's Global Mobile Consumer Survey 2015 reveals significant data related to mobile addiction among 1000 Turkish people between 18-50 years of age. The report indicates that Turkey has high rates of mobile addiction. More than 80% of participants were addictive above the average level. The highest level of mobile addiction occurred around the age of 30. According to the survey findings, 71.7% of smartphone owners looked at their devices more than 50 times a day and 47% of participants checked their smartphones "very often" about 100 times a day. One in three smartphone owners reaches for their devices after waking whithin 5 minutes and 28% of them do this immediately. Roughly 20% of smartphone owners used their devices while driving and crossing the road. Such use also influences the social life of Turkish people, with 41% of smartphone owners using their devices to talk with their family and friends (Deloitte, 2016).

Literature Review on Mobile Addiction

Increasing attention has been given to mobile addiction including mobile phone and smartphone addiction in literature. Most of these studies suggest the importance of personality, psychological, and physical effects of mobile phone/smartphone addiction. Bianchi and Phillips (2005) predicted problematic mobile phone use from extraversion, self-esteem, and neuroticism. Data were gathered from 195 participants ages at 18 to 85 years. Findings revealed that extraversion and low self-esteem were important factors in predicting problematic mobile phone use, especially for young people. James and Drennan (2005) explored addictive use of mobile phones through ten semi-structured interviews and a focus group with six participants. They found that attitudinal characteristics of addictive mobile phone users include believing in the importance of mobile phone in one's life, a sense of self identity with mobile phone, fear of group exclusion, and the device's entertainment or hedonistic value. Behavioral characteristics related to addictive mobile phone include impulsiveness, mounting tension prior to using the device, failure of control strategies, and withdrawal symptoms.

Toda, Monden, Kubo, and Morimoto (2006) found associations between the intensity of mobile phone use and health-related lifestyle. In addition, Billieux et al. (2007) found that urgency and lack of perseverance were positively correlated with perceived dependence on mobile phones among 108 female undergraduate psychology students. The following year, Billieux, Van Der Linden and Rochat

(2008) developed and validated a new questionnaire of problematic mobile phone use and explored the link between problematic mobile phone use (e.g., prohibited use, dangerous use, dependence, financial problems) and impulsivity containing urgency, lack of premeditation, lack of perseverance, and sensation seeking. They found that high urgency and lack of perseverance were significant predictors of dependence on mobile phones, high urgency and high sensation seeking were predictors of dangerous use of mobile phones, low premeditation was a predictor of prohibited use of mobile phones, high urgency was a predictor of dependence on mobile phones, and high urgency and low perseverance were predictors of financial problems due to mobile phone use. Ha et al. (2008) researched the psychological and behavioral characteristics of excessive cell phone use and related behaviors among 595 high school students in Korea. The participants classified as the excessive user group were strongly addicted to their cellular phone and had more depressive symptoms, higher interpersonal anxiety, and lower self-esteem.

Leung (2008) examined mobile phone addiction symptoms and its relationship with psychological attributes, such as leisure boredom, sensation seeking, and self-esteem, among 402 teenagers and young adults aged 14–20 in Hong Kong. According to the findings, 27.4% of participants were identified as mobile phone addicts and had leisure boredom, sensation seeking issues, and poor self-esteem. In another study, Takao, Takahashi, and Kitamura (2009) investigated the relationship between problematic mobile phone use and personality traits among 444 Japanese university students who owned and used a mobile phone regularly. High self-monitoring and approval motivation predicted problematic mobile phone use, while loneliness did not predict problematic mobile phone. Beranuy, Oberst, Carbonell, and Chamarro (2009) explored maladaptive use of the internet and mobile phones and its relationship with psychological distress and mental disorders among 365 undergraduate students in Spain. Maladaptive use of internet and mobile phones were related to psychological distress.

Chung (2011) investigated the relationship between the use of mobile phones and the maintenance of interpersonal solidarity among 188 female adolescents in Korea. Results revealed that adolescents who have a greater tendency to be addicted used mobile phones excessively and that they did so to maintain interpersonal solidarity. Hong, Chiu, and Huang (2012) explored the relationship between psychological characteristics, mobile phone addiction, and mobile phone usage among 269 female university students in Taiwan. The study's findings revealed that there is a stronger relationship between female students' psychological characteristics and their mobile phone addiction. Moreover, there was a positive correlation between social extroversion and anxiety and mobile phone addiction. Augner and Hacker (2012) examined the associations between excessive use of mobile phones and certain indicators of psychological and physical health among 196 students in Austria. High chronic stress and low emotional stability were the best predictors of high problematic mobile phone use; depression and extraversion were also positively related to problematic mobile phone use. A similar study was conducted by Babadi-Akashe, Zamani and Hedayati (2014) who focused on the mobile phone addictive behavior and mental health among 296 university students in Iran. They found an inverse relationship between mobile phone addiction and behavioral problems, anxiety, depression, and psychosis.

Çağan, Ünsal and Çelik (2014) found that as daily use of mobile phone increases, the level of dependence on mobile phone increases as well and as the level of mobile phone dependency increases, the severity of depression and academic failure increases among Osmangazi University Health high schol students in Turkey. Takao (2014) examined the correlation between problematic mobile phone use and the big-five personality domains of extraversion, neuroticism, openness-to-experience, agreeableness, and conscientiousness. Problematic mobile phone use was linked to extraversion, neurosis, and openness-to-experience. Lee, Chang, Lin, and Cheng (2014) explored the relationships between psychological traits and stress and the compulsive behaviors of smartphone users. Compulsive usage of smartphones was positively correlated with an external locus of control, materialism, social interaction anxiety, and the need for touch. Furthermore, the findings revealed that compulsive usage of smartphone can trigger stress among smartphone users. Hadlington (2015) investigated the link between internet addiction and problematic mobile phone use, as well as the relationship with cognitive failures among 210 participants between the ages of 18 and 65. Internet addiction and problematic mobile phone use were positively related to higher scores on the cognitive failures in daily life; individuals with higher levels of problematic mobile phone use and internet addiction also had a lower working memory capacity and poorer attentional control.

Bian and Leung (2015) investigated roles of psychological attributes, such as shyness and loneliness, in symptoms of smartphone addiction and the effects of smartphone usage and smartphone addiction on social capital among 414 university students in China. Smartphone addiction was associated positively with loneliness and shyness. Darcin et al. (2016) examined Turkish university students' smartphone use and addiction and its relationship with social anxiety and loneliness. Social anxiety and loneliness were related to excessive smartphone use and loneliness was correlated with smartphone addiction. Participants who used their smartphones to access social networking sites have a higher risk for smartphone addiction than participants who used their smartphones mainly for Internet surfing or making phone calls. Chen et al. (2016) focused on the prevalence of mobile phone addiction among young adults, the differences between mobile phone addicts, possible mobile phone addicts, and nonaddicts in terms of their mobile phone use, and the mediating role of interpersonal problems in the relationship between mobile phone addiction and negative emotions among 1089 young adults in China. The findings revealed that 4% of young adults were mobile phone addicts, more than 58% were possible mobile phone addicts, and 37% were nonaddicts. Mobile phone addiction level was a positive indicator of negative emotions, like depression and social anxiety, and interpersonal problems mediated the relationship between mobile phone addiction levels and negative emotions. Aljomaa et al. (2016) focused on the frequency and indices of smartphone addiction among 416 university students in Saudi Arabia. Findings of the study revealed that 48% of students were addicted to their smarthpone and males used smartphones more often than females. Moreover, overuse and technological dimensions were the strongest predictors of smartphone addiction compared to the psychological-social, preoccupation with smartphones, and the health dimensions.

Studies have also been doncuted on the to effects of mobile addiction on academic performance. Chen (2006) examined the relationships between mobile phones use, mobile phone addiction, social capital, and academic performance among 166 college students in Taiwan. Results showed that mobile phone usage adversely affected heavy mobile phone users' academic performance and learning whereas light mobile phone users' academic performance and learning were influenced less. Findings also revealed that participants valued their mobile phones as a means to improve their relationships with their friends and family; therefore their mobile phones were used as communication tools to enhance their social capital. Lepp, Barkley, and Karpinski (2014) researched the link between cell phone use and academic performance, anxiety, and satisfaction with life among 536 undergraduate students in the US Cell phone use was negatively related to academic performance and satisfaction with life and positively related to anxiety. Participants who used cell phones frequently had lower academic performance, lower satisfaction with life, and higher anxiety. Hawi and Samaha (2016) examined the effects of smartphone addiction on academic performance among 293 university students. Approximately 44.6% of students at high risk for smartphone addiction had low academic performance.

Salehan and Negahban (2013) investigated the effect of using social networking mobile applications on mobile phone addiction. The use of mobile social networking applications was a significant predictor of mobile addiction. Furthermore, Roberts, Petnji Yaya, and Manolis (2014) examined the association between cell-phone activities and cell-phone addiction among 184 college students; the number of calls made a positive effect on cell-phone addiction. Findings also revelaed that women spend an average of 600 minutes on their cell-phone every day compared to 459 minutes for males. Women were more addicted to using their cell-phone than men. Nikhita, Jadhav, and Ajinkya (2015) studied the prevalence of mobile phone dependence among 415 secondary school adolescents in India. Findings revealed that mobile phone dependence was associated with gender, family type, type of mobile phone used, average time per day spent using mobile phone, and years of mobile phone usage. Most of these studies suggest that young people, particularly students, tended to become more addictive to their mobile phone/smartphone. In this regard, the main purpose of this study is to investigate smartphone use and addiction among Generation Y in Turkey.

RESEARCH METHODOLOGY

The aim of this study was to investigate smartphone use and the addiction profile of Generation Y (ages 18-34). An online questionnaire was administered and data were gathered from 970 respondents. The first question of the survey was a filter question about smartphone ownership. Approximately 21 respondents indicated that they did not own a smartphone and 62 participants were not from Generation Y, and they were excluded from data analysis. As a result, a total of 887 usable responses were included in data analysis. Among the 887 participants, 666 were 18-24 and 221 were 25-34. Other demographic characteristics of respondents are shown as frequencies and percentages in Table 1.

There were four frequency questions asked concerning smartphone usage, such as duration of daily smartphone use (recorded in hours), frequency of looking at smartphone in one day, unprompted checking of smartphone in one day, and average monthly paid smartphone service charge. These questions were adapted from Deloitte (2015), Pew Research Center (2015), and Salesforce (2014).

There were 34 items on smartphone addiction used to identify the mobile addiction profile of participants which were measured on a seven-point Likert-type scale (1= "strongly disagree" to 7= "strongly agree"). Six of these items were adapted from Kwon et al.'s (2013) study, 18 were adapted from Kwon, Kim, Cho, and Yang's (2013) study, four were adapted from Bianchi and Phillips's (2005) study, four were adapted from Roberts, Petnji Yaya, and Manolis's (2014) study, two were adapted from Chung's (2011) study, and two were adapted from Chóliz's (2012) study. Data were analyzed with The Statistical

Table 1. Demographic profile of respondents

		N	%			N	%
Gender	Male	371	41.8	**Education**	Formal education	661	74.5
	Female	516	58.2		Open education	15	1.7
Age	18-24	666	75.1		Distance education	6	.7
	25-34	221	24.9		Master program	143	16.1
					Doctor of philosophy program	62	7.0

Package for Social Science (SPSS) version 20. The reliability of the scale that measured smartphone addiction was 0.934 (Cronbach's Alpha).

FINDINGS OF THE STUDY

Smartphone Usage Profile of University Students

Findings related to the duration of smartphone usage, frequency of looking at smartphone, and unprompted checking of smartphone in a day were predictors of dependency on smartphone. Furthermore, 28.2% of students used their devices between 4 and 6 hours, and 21.3% used their devices over 6 hours in a day. Approximately 24% of students looked at their smartphones between 50 and 100 times, 11% looked at their devices between 100 and 150 times, and 11.5% looked at their devices over 150 times a day. Of the students, 40.8% "often" checked their smartphones without any notification and 6.7% of students checked their smartphones "very often". More than half of students paid monthly smartphone service charges of over 30TL (~ $10.46). The smartphone usage profile of respondents are presented as frequencies and percentages in Table 2.

Categorization of Smartphone Addiction

In order to analyze the structure of the smartphone addiction questionnaire, factor analysis was used and the 21 items of smarphone addicton were appropriate for the analysis. The Kaiser-Meyer-Olkin measure of sampling adequacy value was 0.908. Five factors were extracted from the factor analysis and all of factors had eigenvalues greater than 1. The extracted five factors explain 64.98 of the total variance and are named: tolerance, accompany/fellowship, withdrawal, social network dependence, and health

Table 2. Smartphone usuge profile of respondents

		N	%			N	%
Duration of daily smartphone use (hours)	<1	29	3.3	**Unprompted checking of smartphone in a day**	Never	21	2.4
	1-2	133	15.0		Sometimes	445	50.2
	2-4	286	32.2		Often	362	40.8
	4-6	250	28.2		Very Often	59	6.7
	>6	189	21.3				
Frequency of looking at smartphone in a day	Never	2	.2	**Average mounthly paid smartphone service charge**	<20TL	45	5.1
	Under 25 times	88	9.9		20-30TL	371	41.8
	25-50 times	222	25.0		30-40TL	187	21.1
	50-100 times	213	24.0		40-50TL	109	12.3
	100-150 times	98	11.0		50-60TL	66	7.4
	150-200 times	44	5.0		60-70TL	39	4.4
	Over 200 times	58	6.5		>70TL	70	7.9
	Don't know	162	18.3				

problems. Results of factor analysis are included in table 3. Tolerance (6 items) explained 18.089% of the variance and has reliability of 0.841 (Cronbach's Alpha). This factor described lack of time management and inability to prevent increasing use of smartphones. Accompany/fellowship (6 items) explained 14.795% of the variance and has reliability of 0.857 (Cronbach's Alpha). This factor refered to the positive feelings about smartphones and frequent use of it, as well as the belief that smartphones are good for owners and provide a good time to them especially when owners feel lonely or bored. Withdrawal (4 items) explained 13.804% of the variance and has reliability of 0.797 (Cronbach's Alpha). This factor described being anxious, uneasy, and uncomfortable without one's smartphone or when the battery is reduced. Social network dependence (3 items) explained 11.365% of the variance and has reliability of 0.785 (Cronbach's Alpha). This factor referred to the importance of making friendships on one's smartphone's social network applications rather than in real life. Health problems (2 items) explained 6.927% of the vaiance and has reliability of 0.684 (Cronbach's Alpha). This factor included health problems due to excessive use of smartphones, such as experiencing lightheadedness, blurred vision, or feeling pain in different areas of the body.

As shown in Table 3, results revealed that accompany/fellowship ($\mu = 4.64$) and withdrawal ($\mu = 4.34$) were the strongest predictors of smartphone addiction and tolerance ($\mu = 3.90$). The main criterions in defining smartphone addiction among university students are that they use their smartphone rather than talk to others when they feel isolated or lonely ($\mu =5.44$), they think that the most fun thing is to use their smartphnes ($\mu = 4.52$), and they look at their smartphone fruquently ($\mu = 4.93$). Other significant indicators of smartphone addiction among university students include withdrawal symptoms containing anxious feelings when the battery is low ($\mu = 5.04$) and getting agitated when their smartphone is not in sight ($\mu = 4.75$). Tolarance was also a predictor of smartphone addiction which refers the lack of time management for reducing smartphone use ($\mu = 4.44$) and that they spent more time on their smartphones than they intended ($\mu = 4.03$).

Clustering of Smartphone Addiction Groups

In order to classify smartphone addiction groups, K-means cluster analysis was used on the extracted factors. Four groups were determined and classified into "nonaddicts", "heavy addicts", "realistic addicts", and "emotional addicts". To determine whether there were group differences between smartphone addiction in terms of tolerance, accompany/fellowship, withdrawal, social network dependence, and health problems, One Way Analysis of Variance (ANOVA) was used. Results revealed that tolerance, accompany/fellowship, withdrawal, social network dependence, and health problems were signicantly different from each other, with the biggest difference found for withdrawal.

The final cluster centers shown in Table 5 represent the mean values of the four groups and allow for the differentiation between the characteristics of clusters in terms of smartphone addiction.

Cluster 1-Nonaddicts: Students in this cluster represent 25.1% of total university students who not dependent on their smartphones. Although they think using their smartphone is fun, they do not experience the lack of time management related to failing to reduce smartphone use, are not anxious, uneasy, or uncomfortable without their smartphone, experience no health problems due to excessive use of smartphones, and do not prefer to make friendships on smartphone's social network applications.

Table 3. Results of factor analysis

Factors and Items	Factor Loading	Mean	Cronbach Alpha α	Eigenvalue
Factor 1: Tolerance		**3.90**	**.841**	**7.44**
Missing planned work due to smartphone use	.737	3.73		
Having a hard time concentrating in class, while doing assignments, or while working due to smartphone use	.759	3.74		
Always thinking that I should shorten my smartphone use time	.755	4.44		
The people around me tell me that I use my smartphone too much	.617	3.02		
I spend more time than I should on my cell phone.	.813	4.03		
Having used my smartphone when I am not supposed to (in class, during a meeting, etc.)	.439	3.78		
Factor 2: Accompany/Fellowship		**4.64**	**.857**	**2.18**
Constantly checking my smartphone so as not to miss conversations between other people on Twitter or Facebook	.565	4.36		
I look at my mobile phone frequently	.621	4.93		
When I have my mobile phone with me, I can't stop using it	.497	4.14		
I have used my mobile phone to talk to others when I was feeling isolated	.651	5.44		
There is nothing more fun to do than using my smartphone	.783	4.52		
Feeling great meeting more people via smartphone use	.775	4.46		
Factor 3: Withdrawal		**4.34**	**.797**	**1.90**
When out of range for some time, I become preoccupied with the thought of missing a call	.766	4.07		
I become irritable if I have to switch off my mobile phone for meetings, dinner engagements, or at the movies	.665	3.52		
I become anxious when the battery is low	.680	5.04		
I get agitated when my cell phone is not in sight	.776	4.75		
Factor 4: Social Network Dependence		**2.12**	**.785**	**1.09**
Feeling that my relationships with my smartphone buddies are more intimate than my relationships with my real-life friends	.819	2.24		
Preferring talking with my smartphone buddies to hanging out with my real-life friends or with the other members of my family	.833	2.09		
I have argued with my parents or family members about the cost of my mobile phone	.751	2.04		
Factor 5: Health Problems		**2.90**	**.684**	**1.01**
Experiencing lightheadedness or blurred vision due to excessive smartphone use	.710	2.41		
Feeling pain in the wrists or at the back of the neck while using a smartphone	.742	3.39		

Table 4. ANOVA Table Based on Cluster Analysis

	Cluster		Error		F	Sig.
	Mean Square	df	Mean Square	df		
Tolerance	423.430	3	1.216	883	348.151	.000
Accompany/Fellowship	292.377	3	.930	883	314.548	.000
Withdrawal	469.496	3	1.032	883	454.800	.000
Social Network Dependence	131.287	3	1.580	883	83.071	.000
Health Problems	435.548	3	1.229	883	354.534	.000

Cluster 2-Heavy Addicts: This cluster involves 22% of university students who are excessively addicted to their smartphones. They feel fun or excitement when they use their devices and they would rather use their devices when they feel lonely than talk to others. They check their smartphones and look at their smartphones frequently. They have an inability to prevent themselves from using smartphone at an increasing frequency. Moreover, they feel anxious without their smartphone and they become agitated when the battery is reduced. They have problems related to controlling smartphone use and they experience some health problems due to excessive use of smartphones. They also believe that friendships made through smartphones are more intimate than real life friends.

Cluster 3-Realistic Addicts: Realistic addicts represent 15.7% of university students and they believe that the smartphone is a good fellow and can help them feel good so they look at and check their devices frequently. They experience lack of time management, inability to prevent increasing use of the smartphone, and also have health problems. They have less withdrawal symptoms. Their social network dependence level is very low and they do not believe that friendship made through smartphones are more intimate than real life friends.

Cluster 4-Emotional Addicts: They represent 37.2% of university students. Their social network dependence level is very low, they do not experience health problems due to excessive use of smartphones, and they experience lack of time management slightly. Conversely, they feel anxious, uneasy, and uncomfortable without their smartphone and they believe that the smartphone is a good fellow and helps them feel good.

Table 5. Final cluster center analysis of smartphone addiction

	Cluster			
	Nonaddicts (N=223)	Heavy Addicts (N=195)	Realistic Addicts (N=139)	Emotional Addicts (N=330)
Tolerance	2.26	5.61	4.67	3.68
Accompany/Fellowship	3.19	5.96	4.25	5.02
Withdrawal	2.57	5.77	3.41	5.11
Social Network Dependence	1.64	3.37	1.72	1.90
Health Problems	1.73	4.43	4.48	2.13

CONCLUSION

Research on mobile addiction revealed that smartphone addiction is becoming more prevalent, especially among adolescent and university students. The present study revealed significant information associated with smartphone use and addiction among Generation Y who were university sudents aged 18-34 in Turkey. The findings revealed that 28.2% of students used their devices between 4-6 hours and 21.3% used their devices over 6 hours a day. Furthermore, 22.5% of students looked at their devices over 100 times a day and 40.8% of students "often" checked their smartphones without receiving any notifications.

In order to analyze the structure of the smartphone addiction questionnaire, factor analysis was performed. Five factors were extracted from the factor analysis, explaining 64.981% of the total variance. The factors included tolerance, accompany/fellowship, withdrawal, social network dependence, and health problems. Accompany/fellowship and withdrawal were the strongest predictors of smartphone addiction. In this context, smartphone is a good fellow for students so they use their smartphone rather than talk to others when they feel isolated or lonely; they think that the most fun thing to do is to use their smartphones. Moreover, they experience withdrawal symptoms, such as anxious feelings, when the battery is low and become agitated when their smartphone is not in their sight.

To classify smartphone addiction groups and reveal the smartphone addiction profile of university students, cluster analysis was used on the extracted factors. The analysis provided significant understandig of smartphone addiction among university students. Four groups were identified, including "nonaddicts", "heavy addicts", "realistic addicts", and "emotional addicts". Nonaddicts comprised 25.1% of the total university students. Roughly 74.9% of university students have indicators of smartphone addiction. This percentage denotes that the smartphones have become indispensable for life among university students. Being isolated from real life, having an inability to prevent themselves from using smartphone, problems with parents, having withdrawal symptoms, having problems related to controlling smartphone, experiencing lack of time management and health problems are the most significant issues related to excessive use of smartphones.

Today not only university students but also adolescents and children experience these problems. It is crucial that there is a strong trend of children owning and using a smartphone and, they grow up dependent on their phones. Future studies should investigate compulsive use of smartphone among children and give advice for parents to reduce smartphone addiction of children.

This study gives explanation about profile of smartphone users and, provides important information related to their addictive use. Future researches should also investigate factors that trigger and increase mobile addiction among children and adolescents.

REFERENCES

Addictiontips. (2015). *25 Surprising Facts About Phone Addiction*. Retrieved May 10, 2016 from http://www.addictiontips.net/phone-addiction/phone-addiction-facts/

Aljomaa, S. S., Al.Qudah, M. F., Albursan, I. S., Bakhiet, S. F., & Abduljabbar, A. S. (2016). Smartphone addiction among university students in the light of some variables. *Computers in Human Behavior, 61*, 155–164. doi:10.1016/j.chb.2016.03.041

Augner, C., & Hacker, G. W. (2012). Associations between problematic mobile phone use and psychological parameters in young adults. *International Journal of Public Health, 57*(2), 437–441. doi:10.100700038-011-0234-z PMID:21290162

Babadi-Akashe, Z., Zamani, B. E., & Hedayati, N. (2014). The Relationship between Mental Health and Addiction to Mobile Phones among University Students of Shahrekord, Iran. *Addiction & Health, 6*(3-4), 93–99. PMID:25984275

Bank of America. (2015). *Trends in Consumer Mobility Report.* Retrieved May 20, 2016 from http://newsroom.bankofamerica.com/files/doc_library/additional/2015_BAC_Trends_in_Consumer_Mobility_Report.pdf

Beranuy, M., Oberst, U., Carbonell, X., & Chamarro, A. (2009). Problematic Internet and Mobile Phone Use and Clinical Symptoms in College Students: The Role of Emotional Intelligence. *Computers in Human Behavior, 25*(5), 1182–1187. doi:10.1016/j.chb.2009.03.001

Bian, M., & Leung, L. (2015). Linking Loneliness, Shyness, Smartphone Addiction Symptoms, and Patterns of Smartphone Use to Social Capital. *Social Science Computer Review, 31*(1), 61–79. doi:10.1177/0894439314528779

Bianchi, A., & Phillips, J. G. (2005). Psychological Predictors of Problem Mobile Phone Use. *Cyberpsychology & Behavior, 8*(1), 39–51. doi:10.1089/cpb.2005.8.39 PMID:15738692

Billieux, J., Van der Linden, M., d'Acremont, M., Ceschi, G., & Zermatten, A. (2007). Does Impulsivity Relate to Perceived Dependence on and Actual Use of the Mobile Phone? *Applied Cognitive Psychology, 21*(4), 527–537. doi:10.1002/acp.1289

Billieux, J., Van Der Linden, M., & Rochat, L. (2008). The Role of Impulsivity in Actual and Problematic Use of the Mobile Phone. *Applied Cognitive Psychology, 22*(9), 1195–1210. doi:10.1002/acp.1429

Çağan, Ö., Ünsal, A., & Çelik, N. (2014). Evaluation of College Students'the Level of Addiction to Cellular Phone and Investigation on the Relationsship Between the Addiction and the Level of Depression. *Procedia: Social and Behavioral Sciences, 114*, 831–839. doi:10.1016/j.sbspro.2013.12.793

Chen, L., Yan, Z., Tang, W., Yang, F., Xie, X., & He, J. (2016). Mobile Phone Addiction Levels and Negative Emotions Among Chinese Young Adults: The Mediating Role of Interpersonal Problems. *Computers in Human Behavior, 55*, 856–866. doi:10.1016/j.chb.2015.10.030

Chen, Y.-F. (2006). Social phenomena of mobile phone use: An exploratory study in Taiwanese. *Information for Social Research, 11*, 219–244.

Chóliz, M. (2012). Mobile-phone addiction in adolescence: The Test of Mobile Phone Dependence (TMD). *Progress in Health Sciences*, *2*(1), 33–44.

Chung, N. (2011). Korean Adolescent Girls' Addictıve Use Of Mobile Phones To Maintain Interpersonal Solidarity. *Social Behavior and Personality*, *39*(10), 1349–1358. doi:10.2224bp.2011.39.10.1349

Darcin, A. E., Kose, S., Noyan, C. O., Nurmedov, S., Yılmaz, O., & Dilbaz, N. (2016). Smatphone Addiction and Its Relationship with Social Anxiety and Loneliness. *Behaviour & Information Technology*, 1–6.

Davey, S., & Davey, A. (2014). Assessment of Smartphone Addiction in Indian Adolescents: A Mixed Method Study by Systematic-review and Meta-analysis Approach. *International Journal of Preventive Medicine*, *5*(12), 1500–1511. PMID:25709785

Deloitte. (2015). *Deloitte Mobile Consumer 2015: The UK Cut Game Of Phones.* Retrieved April 16, 2016 from https://www.deloitte.co.uk/mobileuk/assets/pdf/Deloitte-Mobile-Consumer-2015.pdf

Deloitte. (2016). *Deloitte Global Mobil Kullanıcı Anketi 2015 Türkiye.* Retrieved May 28, 2016 from https://www2.deloitte.com/content/dam/Deloitte/tr/Documents/technology-media-telecommunications/deloitte-global-mobil-kullanici-anketi-2015-f.pdf

Ericsson. (2015a, June). *Ericsson Mobility Report.* Retrieved May 2, 2016 from https://www.ericsson.com/res/docs/2015/ericsson-mobility-report-june-2015.pdf

Ericsson. (2015b, November). *Ericsson Mobility Report.* Retrieved April 16, 2016 from //www.ericsson.com/res/docs/2015/mobility-report/ericsson-mobility-report-nov-2015.pdf

Ericsson. (2016). *Ericsson Mobility Report.* Retrieved May 27, 2016 from http://www.ericsson.com/res/docs/2016/mobility-report/ericsson-mobility-report-feb-2016-interim.pdf

Federal Reserve Board. (2015). *Consumers and Mobile Financial Services 2015.* Retrieved April 16, 2016 from http://www.federalreserve.gov/econresdata/consumers-and-mobile-financial-services-report-201503.pdf

Google Ipsos Media, C. T. (2011, April). *The Mobile Movement Understanding Smartphone Users.* Retrieved April 16, 2016 from http://www.gstatic.com/ads/research/en/2011_TheMobileMovement.pdf

Google Ipsos Media, C. T. (2013). *Our Mobile Planet:Understanding the Mobile Consumer.* Retrieved April 16, 2016 from http://services.google.com/fh/files/misc/omp-2013-tr-en.pdf

Ha, J. H., Chin, B., Park, D.-H., Ryu, S.-H., & Yu, J. (2008). Characteristics of Excessive Cellular Phone Use in Korean Adolescents. *Cyberpsychology & Behavior*, *11*(6), 783–784. doi:10.1089/cpb.2008.0096 PMID:18991536

Hadlington, L. (2015). Cognitive failures in daily life: Exploring the link with Internet addiction and problematic mobile phone use. *Computers in Human Behavior*, *51*, 75–81. doi:10.1016/j.chb.2015.04.036

Hawi, N. S., & Samaha, M. (2016). To Excel or Not to Excel: Strong Evidence on The Adverse Effect of smartphone Addiction on Academic Performance. *Computers & Education*, *98*, 81–89. doi:10.1016/j.compedu.2016.03.007

Hayatı Kaçırma. (2015). Retrieved March 23, 2016 from Mobil Bağımlılık: http://hayatikacirma.org/telefonu-birak-muhabbete-bak/

Heid, M. (Dü.). (2016). *You Asked: Am I Addicted to My Phone?* Retrieved May 10, 2016 from http://time.com/4234366/phone-smartphone-addiction/

Hong, F.-Y., Chiu, S.-I., & Huang, D.-H. (2012). A model of the Relationship Between Psychological Characteristics, Mobile Phone Addiction and Use of Mobile Phones by Taiwanese University Female Students. *Computers in Human Behavior*, 1–8.

James, D., & Drennan, J. (2005). Exploring Addictive Consumption of Mobile Phone Technology. *ANZMAC 2005: Broadening the Boundaries: Conference Proceedings.*

Kwon, M., Kim, D.-J., Cho, H., & Yang, S. (2013). The Smartphone Addiction Scale: Development and Validation of a Short Version for Adolescents. *PLoS One*, *8*(2), 1–7. doi:10.1371/journal.pone.0056936 PMID:24391787

Kwon, M., Lee, J.-Y., Won, W.-Y., Park, J.-W., Min, J.-A., Hahn, C., ... Kim, D.-J. (2013). Development and Validation of a Smartphone Addiction Scale (SAS). *PLoS One*, *8*(2), 1–7. doi:10.1371/journal.pone.0056936 PMID:23468893

Lee, Y.-K., Chang, C.-T., Lin, Y., & Cheng, Z.-H. (2014). The Dark Side of Smartphone Usage: Psychological Traits, Compulsive Behavior and Technostress. *Computers in Human Behavior*, *31*, 373–383. doi:10.1016/j.chb.2013.10.047

Lepp, A., Barkley, J. E., & Karpinski, A. C. (2014). The Relationship Between Cell Phone Use, Academic Performance, Anxiety, and Satisfaction with Life in College Students. *Computers in Human Behavior*, *31*, 343–350. doi:10.1016/j.chb.2013.10.049

Leung, L. (2008). Linking Psychological Attributes to Addictıon and Improper Use of The Mobile Phone Among Adolescents in Hong Kong. *Journal of Children and Media*, *2*(2), 93–113. doi:10.1080/17482790802078565

Ligato, L. (2015). *An Embarrassing Number Of People Say They Couldn't Live Without Their Smartphone*. Retrieved May 10, 2016 from http://www.huffingtonpost.com/2015/07/13/smartphone-dependence-addiction_n_7785782.html

Nikhita, C. S., Jadhav, P. R., & Ajinkya, S. A. (2015, November). Prevalence of Mobile Phone Dependence in Secondary School Adolescents. *Journal of Clinical and Diagnostic Research: JCDR*, *9*(11), 6–9. PMID:26672469

Pavia, L., Cavani, P., Di Blasi, M., & Giordano, C. (2016). Smartphone Addiction Inventory (SPAI): Psychometric properties and confirmatory factor analysis. *Computers in Human Behavior*, *63*, 170–178. doi:10.1016/j.chb.2016.05.039

Pew Research Center. (2015, April). *U.S. Smartphone Use in 2015.* Retrieved April 16, 2016 from http://www.pewinternet.org/files/2015/03/PI_Smartphones_0401151.pdf

Pew Research Center. (2016). *Smartphone Ownership and Internet Usage Continues to Climb in Emerging Economies.* Retrieved May 20, 2016 from http://www.pewglobal.org/files/2016/02/pew_research_center_global_technology_report_final_february_22__2016.pdf

RapidValue. (2014). *Internet, Smartphone & Social Media Usage Statistics.* Retrieved May 20, 2016 from http://www.rapidvaluesolutions.com/wp-content/uploads/2014/11/Internet-Smartphone-and-Social-Media-Usage-Statistics-by-RapidValue-Solutions.pdf

Report, C. B. (2015). *Trended Data from Google for Turkey.* Retrieved May 20, 2016 from https://www.consumerbarometer.com/en/trending/?countryCode=TR&category=TRN-NOFILTER-ALL

Roberts, J. A., Petnji Yaya, L. H., & Manolis, C. (2014). The Invisible Addiction: Cell-Phone Activities and Addiction Among Male and Female College Students. *Journal of Behavioral Addictions*, *3*(4), 254–265. doi:10.1556/JBA.3.2014.015 PMID:25595966

Salehan, M., & Negahban, A. (2013). Social Networking on Smartphones: When Mobile Phones Become. *Computers in Human Behavior*, *29*(6), 2632–2639. doi:10.1016/j.chb.2013.07.003

Salesforce. (2014). *2014 Mobile Behavior Report.* Retrieved April 16, 2016 from https://brandcdn.exacttarget.com/sites/exacttarget/files/deliverables/etmc-2014mobilebehaviorreport.pdf

Shaffer, H. J. (1996). Understanding the Means and Objects of Addiction:Technology, the Internet, and Gambling. *Journal of Gambling Studies*, *12*(4), 461–469. doi:10.1007/BF01539189 PMID:24234163

Statista. (2015a). *Smartphone users worldwide 2014-2019.* Retrieved 20 May, 2016 from http://www.statista.com/statistics/330695/number-of-smartphone-users-worldwide/

Statista. (2015b). *Turkey smartphone users 2013-2019.* Retrieved May 20, 2016 from http://www.statista.com/statistics/467181/forecast-of-smartphone-users-in-turkey

Takao, M. (2014). Problematic Mobile Phone Use and Big-Five Personality Domains. *Indian Journal of Community Medicine*, *39*(2), 111–113. doi:10.4103/0970-0218.132736 PMID:24963228

Takao, M., Takahashi, S., & Kitamura, M. (2009). Addictive Personality and Problematic Mobile Phone Use. *Cyberpsychology & Behavior*, *12*(5), 501–507. doi:10.1089/cpb.2009.0022 PMID:19817562

The Boston Consulting Group. (2013). *Turkey Online How The Internet is Trensforming the Turkish Ekonomi.* Retrieved April 16, 2016 from http://www.bcg.com.tr/documents/file129539.pdf

TNS/Google. (2014). *Connected Consumer Study 2014 Global Results.* Retrieved May 20, 2016 from storage.googleapis.com/think-v2 emea/docs/research_study/Connected_Consumer_Study_2014.pdf

Toda, M., Monden, K., Kubo, K., & Morimoto, K. (2006). Mobile Phone Dependence And Health-Related Lifestyle Of University Students. *Social Behavior and Personality*, *34*(10), 1277–1284. doi:10.2224bp.2006.34.10.1277

Chapter 11
Benefits and Risks Associated With Use of Social Media by People With Health Issues:
Focusing on Mental Illness, HIV/AIDS, Cancer, Intellectual Disability, and Diabetes

Tatsuya Imai
Nanzan University, Japan

ABSTRACT

Previous studies have found that individuals with various health issues use social media for various purposes. Social media help them obtain support from other users and manage identity. However, past research also pointed out risks and challenges associated with the use of social media by those with health issues. One of the risks is stigmatization they could experience when using social media. Even though previous studies revealed serious issues related to stigma in face-to-face settings, the negative effects of stigmatization on social media are left unexplored. To facilitate research on the issues, first, this chapter reviews past works focusing on the use of social media by those with various health issues. Next, previous studies on stigma associated with these illnesses and disabilities are reviewed. Finally, this chapter proposes future directions of research on the issues.

INTRODUCTION

In 2019, the number of social media users worldwide was 3.534 billion, up 11% from the prior year; 46% of people actively use social media around the world (We Are Social, 2019). The number of users is expected to continue to increase in the future (Statista, 2019a). Compared to other regions, the United States (U.S.) has the top social media penetration rate, roughly 70% (Statista, 2019b) and most emerging adults in the U.S. use social media (Bjornsen, 2018). Also, 90% of American young adults (18

DOI: 10.4018/978-1-7998-1063-6.ch011

to 29 years) used at least one SNS (social network site), which is one form of social media, compared with 12% in 2005 (Perrin, 2015). The time spent on SNSs among emerging adults is high, around 52 minutes every day (Coyne, Padilla-Walker, & Howard, 2013; Jacobsen & Forste, 2011). Emerging adults use social media for various purposes, such as maintaining friendships (Barker, 2009) and developing romantic relationships (Fox, Warber, & Makstaller, 2013). Previous studies showed that the use of social media is associated with various positive outcomes for the users; in particular, the number of Facebook friends is related to perceived social support, reduced stress, and less physical illness (Nabi, Prestin, & So, 2013) and the use of Facebook is also related to psychological well-being, especially for those with low self-esteem and low life satisfaction (Ellison, Steinfield, & Lampe, 2007).

Consequently, it is not surprising that people with health issues use social media with the intent to improve their quality of life (e.g., Househ, Borycki, & Kushniruk, 2014; Moorhead et al., 2013; Shpigelman & Gill, 2014a). Househ et al. (2014) reviewed 12 studies on the use of social media by patients with various health issues and found that social media empowered the patients in various ways. For example, people with health issues used YouTube to share their experiences regarding their illness and coping methods, and other people with the same illness can gain useful knowledge and information by viewing the video. Similarly, Moorhead et al., (2013) reviewed 98 studies on social media use for health communication among patients, general public, and health professionals. The findings indicate that social media could provide patents with opportunities to interact with others such as other patients and health professionals and could help them gain emotional support from other patients. Further, Shpigelman and Gill (2014a) surveyed individuals suffering from disabilities, such as physical disability, Autism, hearing disability, and mental illness, to examine these individuals' use of Facebook. Results showed that 69% of the participants visited Facebook at least once a day and 48% of them reported having up to 200 Facebook friends. In addition, 10.1% of them reported that they did not have Facebook friends with disabilities, while 89.9% of them indicated that they had Facebook friends with disabilities. Qualitative analyses of responses to the open-ended questions suggested that people with disabilities use Facebook to seek support and advice from other users. These findings revealed that social media play significant roles for those with health issues in maintaining and developing interpersonal relationships as well as obtaining support.

However, when using social media, those with health issues experience stigma associated with their health issues (Imai & Dailey, 2015; Newman et al., 2011), similar to the stigma they might experience offline (e.g., Goffman, 1963; Schneider, 2005). The stigma those with health issues experience may threaten their identity (Newman, Lauterbach, Munson, Resnick, & Morris, 2011; Schabert, Browne, Mosely, & Speight, 2013). For example, some individuals struggling with diabetes may want to share their health condition on social media to seek emotional support (Newman et al., 2011). However, they are concerned about the possibility that disclosing their health issue threatens their socially desired identity. In fact, most teenage hospital patients in a study (van der Velden & El Emam, 2013) answered that they tried not to show their health information on Facebook such as their diagnosis and treatment because SNSs are places they want to act as "regular" individuals. The issues related to the identity of patients might be particularly concerning for emerging adults, whose main task is to establish a sense of identity (Schwartz, Donnellan, Ravert, Luyckx, & Zamboanga, 2013).

Despite the significant effect of stigma associated with health issues on social media, little research has been conducted on this topic. To address the issue, this chapter describes the current state of the literature on social media use by those with health issues and the stigma associated with various health issues. This chapter first introduces past studies investigating how those individuals with various health issues use social media for different purposes. Next, previous research on stereotypes and stigmatization associated with health issues is reviewed. Finally, this chapter describes future research directions on stigmatizing effects of social media on emerging adults with health issues.

USE OF SOCIAL MEDIA BY THOSE WITH HEALTH ISSUES

Before starting to discuss the use of social media by people with health issues, it is important to clarify the difference between social media and SNSs, which are often used interchangeably. Social media are defined as a group of internet-based applications that build on the ideological and technological foundations of Web 2.0 on which people can create and exchange various contents (Kaplan & Haenlein, 2010). SNSs can be defined as web-based services that allow people to build a public profile, articulate a list of other users with whom they develop a connection, and view and traverse the connection (boyd & Ellison, 2008). Therefore, social media include SNSs, blogs, collaborative projects (e.g., Wikipedia), content communities (e.g., YouTube), and virtual game/social worlds (Kaplan & Haenlein, 2010). This chapter discusses the use of social media by those with health issues rather than focusing only on the use of SNSs because those with health issues use various types of social media such as online support communities (e.g., Mo & Coulson, 2008) and YouTube (Naslund, Grande, Aschbrenner, & Elwyn, 2014). The following sections discuss the use of social media by those with various health issues such as a mental illness, HIV/AIDS, cancer, an intellectual disability, and diabetes.

Mental Illness

Five features of mental illnesses are described by Stein et al. (2010). First, a mentally ill individual demonstrates a clinically significant behavioral or psychological syndrome or pattern. Second, the syndrome or pattern is related to present distress or disability or to a considerably increased risk of suffering death, pain, disability, or an important loss of freedom. Third, the syndrome or pattern is not an expectable and culturally sanctioned response to a specific event (e.g., the death of a loved one). Fourth, the individual shows a behavioral, psychological, or biological dysfunction. Finally, neither deviant behaviors nor conflicts between the individual and society can be classified as mental illness, unless the deviance or conflict is a symptom of dysfunction in the individual. Fitting these criteria, there are a variety of types of mental illnesses, such as schizophrenia, substance-related disorders, mood disorders, anxiety disorders, and eating disorders as described in the *Diagnostic and Statistical Manual of Mental Disorders* (DSM-V; American Psychiatric Association, 2013). Based on the results of a meta-analysis of mental health surveys conducted worldwide from 1980 through 2013, one in five adults (17.6%) has suffered from mental disorders within the past 12 months and 29.2% across their lifetime (Steel et al., 2014). In 2017, the prevalence of people with a major depressive episode was highest among emerging adults (18 to 25 years; 13.1%; National Institute of Mental Health, 2019).

Past studies delineate various aspects of the use of social media by mentally ill individuals. Gowen et al. (2012) surveyed 207 emerging adults (18 to 24 years) comprised of 128 individuals with a mental illness and 79 individuals without a mental illness to explore their use of SNSs. Results showed that 94% of those with mental illness used SNSs for a variety of purposes. Compared with those without a mental illness, mentally ill people tended to use SNSs more often to make new friends, share interests, and blog. The main communication methods they use on SNSs were sending private messages, posting public messages, sharing information and links, and commenting on blogs. Through the use of SNSs, those with mental illness desire to find information on independent living skills, strategies to overcome social isolation, and ways to develop interpersonal relationships. This research illustrates mentally ill emerging adults' active use of SNSs to gain various support that would not be available in face-to-face (FtF) interactions.

However, the active use of SNSs may not always bring positive outcomes. Rice et al. (2014) reviewed past studies on effectiveness of social media interventions for the treatment of depression. They found a mixed picture of the effectiveness; that is, some studies found benefits of SNS use and others found harms of SNS use. Direct one-to-one communication on SNSs engaged by depressed individuals was associated with improved well-being and symptoms. SNS use was also associated with various positive outcomes that hypothetically lead to mental health benefits such as supportive relationships, belongingness, and self-esteem. They also pointed out a potential function of SNSs as a screening tool for at-risk individuals through status update posts. The findings are consistent with the results of another study showing that a quarter of Facebook users who are juniors and seniors in a college posted comments that meet the criteria as symptoms of depression received social support from Facebook friends (Moreno et al., 2011). On the other hand, Rice et al. (2014) also revealed that some studies indicated potential risks of SNS use by mentally ill individuals such as cyberbullying, harassment, sexting, and privacy concerns. Further, negative interactions with SNS were linked with greater depressive symptoms and negative affect. The systematic review identified a mixed picture of the effectiveness of social media use especially for depressed individuals.

Naslund, Grande, Aschbrenner, and Elwyn (2014) investigated YouTube as a potential tool to develop peer support for individuals with severe mental illness. They qualitatively analyzed about 3,000 comments posted on YouTube videos uploaded by those with a mental illness such as bipolar disorder and schizophrenia to explore how the videos function to facilitate peer support for other mentally ill individuals. Topics of the videos include managing symptoms, challenges, coping strategies, and efforts to help others who have a similar illness. Four main themes of the comments emerged: minimizing a sense of isolation and providing hope, finding peer support through peer exchange and reciprocity, coping with day-to-day challenges, and learning from shared experiences of medication use and seeking mental health care. Regardless of the types of functions, YouTube seemed to provide mentally ill individuals with peer support that improved their quality of life. However, authors pointed out potential risks of the use of YouTube such as privacy concerns of those who upload videos and the reliability of the contents of the video. Taken together, many mentally ill individuals actively use SNSs for various purposes, but risks associated with the use should not be overlooked.

HIV/AIDS

There were approximately 34 million people living with HIV/AIDS in 2014 (WHO, 2015). The WHO (2015) reports that in 2014 about 1.2 million people died from HIV-related causes and approximately 2 million people became newly infected with HIV globally. There is no cure for the HIV infection, but effective treatments with antiretroviral drugs are available to control the virus, leading to healthy and productive lives of those with HIV. Specifically, about 57,200 emerging adults (18 to 24 years) were living with HIV in the United States at the end of 2012 (Centers for Disease Control & Prevention, 2016). Among them, 25,300 were living with undiagnosed HIV, that was the highest rate of undiagnosed HIV in any age group. Also, 21% of them were prescribed HIV medicines and 16% had a suppressed viral load, that is the lowest rates of any age group.

Some research illustrates the use of social media by those individuals living with HIV/AIDS. Horvath et al. (2012) surveyed individuals living with HIV regarding their use of SNSs and found that 76% of these individuals used SNSs at least once a week. The most widely used SNS was Facebook, which was used by 62% of individuals living with HIV in this study. In addition, 22% of the participants reported that they participated in at least one of two online groups focusing on HIV. Several themes emerged from responses to the open-ended questions assessing their ideal SNS. Forty-five percent of the participants reported that their ideal SNS would be one in which they could connect with other people, whether the people live with HIV or not. On the other hand, another 14% of them reported that they would not like to participate in a SNS focusing on HIV. An additional 26% of them were concerned about the privacy issues related to their participating in HIV-focused SNSs. For example, some users living with HIV were worried that others would find out they were HIV positive by participating in online groups focusing on HIV. Overall, people living with HIV use SNSs to develop interpersonal relationships and participate in online communities focusing on HIV, although privacy is a barrier to using SNSs.

In order to closely investigate online interactions of individuals living with HIV/AIDS, Mo and Coulson (2008) analyzed the contents of 1,138 messages exchanged in an online HIV/AIDS support group. Of these messages, there were 171 unique message sender names identified in the selected threads and the HIV status of 145 members could be identified as HIV-positive on their profiles. Among all the messages, 986 messages contained at least one type of social support and the supportive messages were categorized into five social support message types: information support (44.5%), emotional support (35.2%), esteem support (12.4%), network support (6.9%), and tangible assistance (1.0%). Information support is advice messages providing suggestions or guidance for coping with HIV/AIDS symptoms. Emotional support is offered by messages to express care and concern to other members. Esteem support is provided through compliment messages, which convey positive assessments of the recipient and his or her abilities. Network support involves messages that broaden the recipients' social network by developing access to new members. Tangible support involves messages in which senders are offering to perform a direct task related to a request.

Although these studies emphasized benefits of social media use for those living with HIV/AIDS, Mo and Coulson (2013) explored disadvantages associated with online support groups for those living with HIV/AIDS. Responses to open-ended questions from patients living with HIV/AIDS were analyzed and categorized into four groups. First, some patients expressed dissatisfying interaction with other members because of the limited FtF and physical contact with them. Second, they were worried about their experience of inappropriate behaviors by other members such as being attacked and ridiculed. Third, some participants expressed concerns that their participation in online social groups might decrease real life relationships. Fourth, information overloaded and misinformation on online social support groups sometimes confused and depressed them. Taggart, Grewe, Conserve, Gliwa, and Isler (2015) added another possible risk which is stigma associated with HIV/AIDS. When using social media, anonymity should be guaranteed especially for those living with HIV/AIDS to prevent HIV/AIDS-related stigma from negatively affecting them.

In short, social media such as SNSs and online support communities for those living with HIV/AIDS could help them seek various types of information and support while some studies show possible risks of social media use. Even though these studies did not focus on emerging adults, the information of

HIV/AIDS provided in online communities are helpful for emerging adults living with HIV who tend to lack enough accurate information of the disease (Centers for Disease Control & Prevention, 2016).

Cancer

Cancer represents around 12% of all-cause mortality worldwide (International Agency for Research on Cancer, 2008). In 2012, there were 14.1 million new cancer cases, 8.2 million cancer deaths, and 32.6 million people living with cancer (WHO, 2012). In the world, the most common causes of cancer death are cancers of the lungs (1.59 million deaths), liver (745,000 deaths), stomach (723,000 deaths), colorectal (694,000 deaths), breast (521,000 deaths), and oesophageal cancer (400,000 deaths).

Social media play a critical role in providing a variety of support for people having cancer. Bender, Jimenez-Marroquin, and Jadad (2011) examined 620 breast cancer groups on Facebook to identify the purposes, use, and creators of the groups. They analyzed the contents of the groups and found four main types of breast cancer groups: fundraising groups, awareness-raising groups, support groups, and "promote-a-site" groups. The fundraising groups are created to attract financial resources for breast cancer through events, products, or services. The awareness-raising groups aim to bring attention to the significance of breast cancer in general. Support groups attempt to meet the information and emotional needs of breast cancer survivors as well as affected family members and friends. The "promote-a-site" groups are formed to increase the prominence of external websites raising funds.

To examine actual interaction on such support groups, Abramson, Keefe, and Chou (2015) investigated the contents of wall posts posted on a cancer awareness page on Facebook. Five main themes emerged in their analyses. First, some posts indicate that the breast cancer organization functions as an open gathering place for users to share information and ideas. Second, some wall posts encourage users to participate in campaigns to promote awareness with scarce cancer-related health information. Third, the breast cancer organization has posts that emphasize on online purchasing as a means to support breast cancer research. Fourth, some contents of conversations are not directly related to the contents of the original posts. Fifth, users use feminine imagery and language to engage other users and the types of products being sold are likely to be stereotypically feminine items.

Participating in support groups regarding cancer was associated with increased social support, leading to reduced stress and depression (Beaudoin & Tao, 2007). Erfani, Blount, and Abedin (2016) also found that ovarian cancer patients who participated in a Facebook page to support cancer patients reported that their participation allowed them to experience social connectedness, receive social support, and engage in effective communication, that lead to the increases in their happiness and satisfaction.

The population of these studies was not emerging adults. However, one study interviewing emerging adults (20 to 25 years) with cancer revealed that their needs such as necessary information and interpersonal support were not met (Patterson, Millar, Desille, & McDonald, 2012). Thus, if emerging adults with cancer participate in the support groups on social media, their needs could be met through interaction with other social media users.

Intellectual Disability

According to the American Association of Intellectual and Developmental Disabilities (AAIDD; 2013), an intellectual disability (ID) is defined as significant limitations on both intellectual functions and in adaptive behavior, which includes everyday conceptual, social, and practical skills, and this disability originates before the age of 18. The adaptive behavior specifically includes language, literacy, interpersonal skills, self-esteem, occupational skills, and transportation. Approximately 200 million people in the world have an intellectual disability (Special Olympics, 2015).

Shpigelman and Gill (2014b) examined various aspects regarding the use of Facebook by 58 people with a learning disability and/or ADD/ADHD. The participants visited Facebook at least once a week (67.2%) and they used it mainly for connecting with people they meet in FtF settings, such as friends, family members, and caregivers. The results also revealed that 68% of the participants reported that making new friends is easier on Facebook than in person. Also, 82% of them said that they felt more comfortable talking with people on Facebook than FtF. Some responses to open-ended questions referred to the emotional effect of communication on Facebook. For instance, Facebook helped the participants feel connected with others when they felt lonely. The findings indicate that those with ID make use of social media to gain benefits that are not easy to achieve in FtF interaction.

Shpigelman (2016) also conducted qualitative interviews with 20 individuals with ID to explore their experience of Facebook use and found five major themes from the contents of the interviews. First, the use of Facebook allowed them to feel like non-disabled others. The users found the participation in Facebook to be a positive status they wanted to adopt. Second, by using Facebook, they could stay connected to their real-world friends and family members. Third, the participation in Facebook helped them be visible to others through using a Like function and sharing information. Fourth, the visibility they achieved on Facebook made them feel popular that is hard to achieve in a real life. Five, the activities above made them experience both positive and negative feelings. For example, the visibility and popularity due to their participation in Facebook contributed to their psychological well-being. On the other hand, some technical difficulties they faced when using Facebook made them feel stressed and frustrated. Some social media users with ID are well aware of the risks of social media use such as being hurt or ending up in undesirable situations (Molin, Sorbring, & Lofgren-Martenson, 2017). Therefore, they might be more careful when they use social media than those without ID.

Research found that young adults with ID reported that their interpersonal networks were composed of only a few people who tended to be support professionals, leading to feelings of being isolated from others (Starke, 2013). To help emerging adults with ID develop relationships with other youth, SNS may be useful as shown in the results above.

Diabetes

Diabetes is the eighth leading cause of death in the world (WHO, 2014a). In 2014, the global prevalence of diabetes was estimated to be 9% among adults (WHO, 2014b). Common symptoms of diabetes are urinating often, feeling very thirsty, extreme fatigue, and blurry vision (American Diabetes Association, 2015).

Greene, Choudhry, Kilabuk, and Shrank (2010) qualitatively examined the 15 most recent wall posts and the 15 most recent discussion topics from the 10 largest Facebook groups focusing on diabetes management. The study sample included 690 individual posts on wall pages and discussion board posts written by 480 users. The main themes identified included posts about information-sharing, patient-centered management, and community-building. As for the main function of the Facebook groups, 62% of the posts involved sharing of personal experiences with diabetes management. Furthermore, 24% of posts contained sensitive aspects of patient-centered diabetes management. For instance, posts described how to count carbohydrates to enable extended alcoholic drinking sessions among individuals with Type

I Diabetes. Some posts also functioned to form a supportive community to seek interpersonal support from group members. These findings imply that Facebook groups specifically focusing on diabetes allow diabetes patients to share and seek information related to their illness.

To understand further why and how people with diabetes share their health information on SNSs and online support communities, Newman et al. (2011) interviewed 14 individuals struggling with diabetes and weight loss management. By analyzing the contents of transcripts of the interviews, Newman and colleagues found that the main goal of the individuals using SNSs and online support communities was to receive emotional support. Through online support communities, it was easier to find people who had similar struggles, so the participants could obtain positive and encouraging messages from other users. The researchers also revealed that SNS users with diabetes had concerns regarding their identity management on SNSs. Although they would emphasize their identity as healthy people, they wanted to obtain support by being open about their struggles. One study focusing on young adults with diabetes found that they believed that talking about their diabetes-related distress with others and joining peer support groups moderate their distress caused by diabetes (Balfe, Doyle, Smith, Sreenan, Brugha, Hevey, & Conroy, 2013). Thus, social media might help emerging adults with diabetes talk about their distress with other users to moderate the distress.

In summary, the studies introduced in this section suggest that social media could help users with health issues improve their quality of life by sharing and seeking important information on their conditions through social media and developing online interpersonal relationships. However, some studies above suggest that the use of social media by those with health issues could be associated with risks of stigmatization. People with a mental illness should be careful about using YouTube as a place where they talk about their illness because mentally ill individuals tend to be targets of stigmatization (Naslund et al., 2014). Taggart et al. (2015) also pointed out that privacy settings should be appropriately done to prevent HIV/AIDS-related stigma from affecting the users living with HIV/AIDS. Newman et al. (2011) revealed that people with diabetes tried to show their identity as healthy people because of their concern about being seen as an unhealthy patient. Even though the researchers pointed out the potential risks of stigma effects on social media, the effects have not been fully examined. To consider the issues, the next section introduces the definition and characteristics of stigma followed by previous studies focusing on various influences of illness or disability stigma on communication.

STIGMA

Stigma is defined as an attribute or characteristic that conveys a social identity that is discredited and devalued in a particular context (Goffman, 1963; Schneider, 2005). Link and Phelan (2001) argue that a set of events need to take place in order for stigma to manifest. First, people distinguish and label targets based on the differences they have from others. Second, the differences are associated with negative stereotypes. Third, the labels are given for specific categories that separate "us" from "them." Fourth, people who receive stigmatizing labels experience status loss and discrimination, leading to unequal outcomes. Finally, the stigmatization the targets experience is related to social, economic, and political power that may identify their differences, construct stereotypes, and separate them into distinct categories.

Additionally, stigma has six dimensions (Jones et al., 1984). The essential dimension is concealability. For example, facial disfigurement and physical disabilities are harder to conceal than a history of mental illness, a prison record, or homosexuality. The second dimension is called time course. Some conditions, such as AIDS, may worsen over time whereas other conditions, such as diabetes, may improve. On the other hand, some types of physical disabilities, such as blindness and paralysis, may not change. The third dimension is aesthetic value. For instance, obesity, facial scars, and body disfigurement are related to physical attractiveness whereas AIDS may not be associated with attractiveness. How stigmatized conditions are generated is another crucial dimension called stigma origins. This dimension is related to whether a stigmatized individual is seen as responsible for the stigma. For example, some conditions, including obesity, a criminal record, and homosexuality, may be seen as matters of choice. However, other conditions, such as cancer and physical disability, are perceived to be outside of the control of the stigmatized individuals. People often blame or devalue individuals with conditions that are seen to be caused by their choice or to be in their control. The fifth dimension is whether the stigmatizing condition is perceived to put other people in danger. For example, people might see those with criminal records to be dangerous. People with HIV may make others more afraid of contamination than those diagnosed with cancer. The final dimension is disruptiveness—the degree to which the stigma interrupts social interactions. For example, interactions with schizophrenic individuals might be disruptive because they often have symptoms of speech dysfunctions.

STIGMA ASSOCIATED WITH SPECIFIC HEALTH ISSUES

Previous studies suggest that different illnesses and disabilities carry different stigmas and the different types of stigma influence communication involving those with health issues.

Mental Illness

Stigma associated with a general label of "mental illness" (i.e., not a specific mental illness) impacts interpersonal communication in various ways. First, Modified Labeling Theory explains how a mental illness label influences those labeled in various situations, such as interpersonal interactions, job opportunities, and quality of life (Link, 1982). According to this theory, if people believe a mentally ill individual is devalued and rejected, they worry that they would also be rejected if they have a mental illness. When they realize that they have a mental illness, the belief (e.g., people with mental illness are rejected) will bring them negative consequences, such as demoralization, income loss, and unemployment. Furthermore, Link, Cullen, Struening, Shrout, and Dohrenwend (1989) found several possible consequences associated with the fear of being labeled with a mental illness, including secrecy, withdrawal, and education. Secrecy involves concealing a history of treatment, such as being hospitalized and being prescribed medications. Labeled individuals may also withdraw from potentially threatening situations, such as a party with people who stigmatize mentally ill individuals. Education includes the active attempt at educating others in hopes of enlightening them to ward off negative attitudes. Among these strategies, the withdrawing behaviors may lead to poorer social support from others.

Second, mental illness stigma also affects others' interpersonal behaviors toward those with mental illness. Sibicky and Dovidio (1986) found that people who believed that an individual is mentally ill leads to negative perceptions and behaviors toward that individual. In their study, participants were told that their interactant was a regular undergraduate student or a student seeking psychotherapy. After they interacted, the audio of the interaction was coded. Results revealed that the participants in the experimental condition had a more negative impression of their interactant and the coded speech of the participants toward their interactant was less open and secure compared with the control condition. In short, when individuals believe that someone is mentally ill, their perceptions and behaviors toward the person tend to be negative. Mental illness stigma may impact mentally ill individuals as well as others around them.

Depression

Depressed individuals are perceived as more violent than those without any mental illness (Link, Phelan, Bresnahan, Stueve, & Pescosolido, 1999). People also believe that depressed individuals tend to be angry, afraid, alone, tired, sad, unhappy (Horowitz, French, Lapid, & Wecker, 1982), and dependent (Rippere, 1977). These negative ideas of depression make people reject those with depression (Link et al., 1999).

Several theoretical accounts explain how the stigma of depression impacts others' perceptions toward depressed individuals. Cane and Gotlib (1985) argued that stereotypes of depression function as a cognitive framework influencing people's interpretations of depressed individuals' characteristics and behaviors. Thus, people are likely to perceive behaviors engaged in by depressed individuals consistent with depression stereotypes, such as being alone and sad. In addition, Sacco and Vaughan (2006) developed the Social-Cognitive Interpersonal Process Model with an emphasis on interpersonal factors influencing depression. Similar to the ideas of Cane and Gotlib (1985), this model argues that people explain behaviors of depressed individuals in negative ways because of a negative schema associated with depressed individuals.

These theoretical frameworks are consistent with findings of empirical studies on the stigma of depression. Individuals who interacted with a confederate who they believed to be depressed evaluated the confederate more negatively on both depression-related traits and depression-unrelated traits as compared to a control condition (Nicholson & Sacco, 1999). In another study conducted by Yarkin, Harvey, and Bloxom (1981), participants were told before interacting with a confederate that the confederate was distressed or not distressed (the distressing behaviors were similar to symptoms of depression), but the confederate behaved neutrally in both conditions. The confederate in the distressed condition was evaluated more negatively than that in the control condition.

These negative evaluations of depressed individuals might lead people to reject those with depression. In the study by Yarkin et al. (1981), participants who believed that a confederate was distressed maintained a larger distance from the confederate, displayed shorter durations of eye contact, engaged in a more negatively-valenced conversation, and spoke for shorter periods of time than those who were not told that the confederate was distressed. In addition, Nicholson and Sacco (1999) revealed that participants who interacted with a confederate who they believed to be depressed showed that they were less willing to interact with the confederate again than a nondepressed confederate. Furthermore, participants who only imagined interactions with depressed individuals indicated more rejecting attitudes than did participants in a control group (Gotlib & Beatty, 1985). Taken together, depression stereotypes negatively affect others' perceptions of depressed individuals' behaviors, leading to rejection of these individuals.

Schizophrenia

Individuals suffering from schizophrenia are more seriously stigmatized than those with depression. Compared with depressed individuals, schizophrenic individuals tend to be seen as more dangerous and unpredictable and consequently, they are more often rejected (Angermeyer & Matschinger, 1997, 2003; Link et al., 1999). A depressed individual could elicit more positive emotions in others, such as a desire to help and empathy, whereas a schizophrenic individual elicits more fear, uneasiness, and insecurity in others (Angermeyer & Matschinger, 2003). People may have such negative feelings toward a schizophrenic individual because they believe schizophrenia is difficult to cure. For example, people believe schizophrenia is caused by biological factors, such as a chemical imbalance in the brain, more than depression and alcohol dependence (Link et al., 1999). Angermeyer and Matschinger (2003) also found that depression is believed to be caused by social factors, such as stress at work, and life events, whereas schizophrenia is perceived to be caused by more biological and genetic factors, such as brain disease and heredity; consequently, schizophrenia is believed to be more likely to deteriorate and be harder to cure than depression.

Previous studies further reveal a strong negative effect of the stigma attached to schizophrenia on interpersonal communication. Jenkins and Carpenter-Song (2009) interviewed those diagnosed with schizophrenia and 96% of them reported experiencing stigmatization across a variety of social settings, including interactions with strangers, in work places, and within close relationships. Schizophrenic individuals reported that verbal and nonverbal communication by strangers was expressed in a way to signal that a schizophrenic individual is strange, frightening, and has less intellectual/social capacity (Jenkins & Carpenter-Song, 2009). The experience of being stigmatized was associated with low quality interpersonal relationships and with low frequency of contact with friends and acquaintances (Lysaker, Roe, & Yanos, 2007). Norman et al. (2010) assessed others' perception of schizophrenic individuals in an experiment and found people possessing stigmatizing attitudes toward schizophrenic individuals did not desire to be physically close to them. In sum, research has revealed that schizophrenic individuals are more seriously stigmatized than those with depression, and consequently these individuals often treated more negatively.

HIV/AIDS

Although the perception of HIV/AIDS has improved over the past 20 years (Herek, 2014), among those without correct knowledge about HIV transmission, 34% of them reported that they would be uncomfortable working with people with HIV and 65% of them reported that they would be uncomfortable about having food prepared by people with HIV (Washington Post & Kaiser Family Foundation, 2012). Because individuals with HIV are aware of the stigma associated with HIV, they may hesitate to disclose their diagnosis even to people they feel close to (Greene, 2009). In fact, after disclosing their HIV-positive status, they receive negative emotional reactions and perceive being treated differently (Greene & Faulkner, 2002). Consequently, those with HIV perceive that they receive social rejection and social isolation (File & Wright, 2000). Furthermore, people often associate HIV/AIDS with homosexuality and IV drug use, and they believe that the patient is responsible for having HIV/AIDS because they engaged in such deviant behaviors.

Cancer

The stigma attached to cancer is caused primarily by fear of the illness itself (File & Wright, 2000). For instance, people tend to associate cancer with death (Chapple, Ziebland, & McPherson, 2004). Results of a survey conducted in India, Italy, Japan, Mexico, and South Africa to examine people's perceptions of cancer showed that 30% of these individuals believed that people with cancer cannot survive (Neal et al., 2010). Sixteen percent of them believed that cancer is contagious and 25% of them believed that people with cancer bring it on themselves. These negative images associated with cancer make people reject those with cancer (File & Wright, 2000). People with cancer have difficulties obtaining social resources and their social activities are restricted (Bloom & Kessler, 1994).

Intellectual Disability

Past research suggests that there are negative stereotypes attached to people with ID. Some people believe that those with ID are aggressive (Slevin & Sines, 1996) and threatening (van Alphen, Dijker, Bos, van Den Borne, & Curfs, 2012), so people are sometimes fearful of those with ID (Jahoda, Wilson, Stalker, & Cairney, 2010). These stereotypes make those with ID experience stigmatization in various social contexts. In school, some individuals with ID are ridiculed and called names by other students and teachers sometimes refuse to help them (Cooney, Jahoda, Gumley, & Knott, 2006). Parents are willing to include children with mild and moderate ID in school, but they oppose the inclusion of children with severe ID (Rafferty, Boettcher, & Griffin, 2001). The teacher-student relationship of children with ID are of poorer quality than that of typically developing students (McIntyre, Blacher, & Baker, 2006). Stigma associated with ID also plays a role in employment. Only 21% of working-age people with ID are employed, according to U.S. Bureau of Labor Statistics (2010). Even when they get a job, they tend to be bullied and ignored in the workplace (Johoda et al., 2010). In fact, some individuals would like to avoid working with those with ID (Bickley, 1990).

Diabetes

Studies have shown that people who do not have diabetes are likely to perceive diabetes as a non-stigmatized condition (e.g., Schabert, Brown, Mosely, & Speight, 2013), but those with diabetes experience being stigmatized (e.g., Brod, Kongso, Lessard, & Christensen, 2009). To treat diabetes, patients may have to use syringes, but using them in public may make them feel embarrassed and afraid of being rejected (Brod et al., 2009). Those with diabetes might have to be careful about what they eat, so they sometimes need to refuse unhealthy food at social events, leading to embarrassment (Wellard, Rennie, & King, 2008). Patients also feel that few people around them understand diabetes correctly, so they are afraid of disclosing their health status even to their fiancés and parents (Sato et al., 2003). Some patients reported that they were afraid to lose their job if they disclosed their health status to people they work with (Shiu, Kwan, & Wong, 2003). Patients who worry about stigmatization described above are likely to suffer from depression and psychological distress (Schabert, Brown, Mosely, & Speight, 2013).

Taken together, past studies indicate that different illnesses and disabilities are associated with various stigmas. As mentioned in the previous section, the stigma associated with health issues on social media has not been fully researched. However, some research implies that people with health issues experience stigma while using social media. For example, some Facebook users with diabetes avoid showing their concerns and distress about their health issue because of the stigma associated with diabetes even though they desire support from others on social media by disclosing their inner state (Newman et al., 2011). Bender et al. (2011) also suggest that features of social media such as the visibility of user profiles and personal networks reduce the anonymity, so users who are concerned about stigma associated with their health issue might hesitate sharing their experience on social media. Thus, stigma of health issues may prevent social media users with health issues from seeking information and support on social media. Especially for emerging adults, most of whom are struggling to manage their identity (Schwartz et al.,

2013), the negative effect of stigma on social media might be significant. In fact, on Facebook, emerging adults try to engage in identity management by presenting multiple facets of the self such as the real self, the ideal self, and the false self (Michikyan, Dennis, & Subrahmanyam, 2015).

FUTURE DIRECTIONS: STIGMA OF HEALTH ISSUES ON SNS

The previous sections introduce research on the use of social media by individuals with health issues and the stigma associated with specific health issues. Considering the frequency of social media use by individual with health issues and their negative experiences related to the stigma, it is necessary to investigate how stigma would impact their social media use. In fact, social identification model of deindividuation effects (Postmes, Spears, & Lea, 2000) suggests that people evaluate others based on the social categories that they belong to (e.g., a group of mentally ill patients, Asians, females) especially in the online interaction. Therefore, on social media, people might have negative perceptions of an individual with health issues due to the stigma associated with the health issues.

On social media, health issues can be revealed in various ways. For example, social media users with a health issue may disclose their health issues on a wall that other users can see. People could also disclose their health issue by sending a message only to someone they want to disclose their illness to. People may realize others' illness by seeing interactions on social media that are open to other users or by seeing that others belong to an organization to which only people with a specific health issue are allowed to belong.

Consequently, it is important to consider various situations in which people with a health issue communicate with others on social media, but little research has examined stigma effects of a specific health issue on online communication. Thus, the following sections discuss how stigma of a specific health issue influences communication on social media with Facebook as a particular focus, since this SNS has the highest number of users (Pew Research Center, 2014) and 82% of emerging adults who use the Internet use Facebook; the percentage is the highest of any age group (Pew Research Center, 2015). Also, Facebook has been used as the main social media by people with a health issue (e.g., Bender et al., 2011; Shpigelman & Gill, 2014a). Possible research questions are also proposed to drive research in these areas.

Sending and Receiving Messages

On most social media, users can send and receive private online messages to each other. Gowen et al. (2012) found that one of the main ways to use social media for mentally ill people is sending messages. Such direct one-to-one communication on social media was positively associated with enhanced well-being for depressed individuals (Rice et al., 2014). However, if people realize that their interactant has a health issue, they may negatively change their message to the interactant. For instance, people may see someone's wall in which the person's friends discuss a health issue the person has. After realizing the person has the issue, messages sent to the person may be negatively altered. To address the possibility that mental illness stigma influences online messages to a mentally ill individual, Imai and Dailey (2015) examined mental illness stigma effects on a request for a favor from a mentally ill individual on Facebook. Participants (97% of them were emerging adults: 18 to 29 years) interacted with a hypothetical target on Facebook, who was believed to have schizophrenia, depression, or a cavity (i.e., the control group). Participants were asked to rate the favor request in terms of face threat in addition to writing a response which was then coded by researchers. Results indicated that a request by a schizophrenic target threatened participants' positive face more significantly than that of a target with depression or without any mental illness. Also, participants' responses to the schizophrenic target were more likely to be polite, but less warm, whereas responses to the depressed target were more likely to be accepting messages. The results indicate that emerging adults who realize that their interactant on SNSs has a health issue, their message to the interactant may be negatively altered.

Stigma may also influence messages those with health issues send to others. Disclosing health issues to someone may be effective in obtaining social support from others (e.g., Chesney & Smith, 1999). Thus, it is possible for those with health issues to disclose their illness or disability by using online messages because these exchanged messages are not seen by others except for the specific recipient. However, people may decide not to disclose their illness because of the stigma associated with the illness (Greene, 2009). Research shows that people living with HIV hesitate to disclose their HIV positive status because of expected negative reactions caused by the stigma of HIV (Miller & Rubin, 2007). Consistent with these theoretical accounts, Newman et al. (2011) found that some social media users with diabetes emphasize their identity as healthy people to avoid being seen as patients struggling with their health issue. Taggart et al. (2015) also argue that using social media, anonymity should be guaranteed especially for those living with HIV/AIDS because of the possible negative effects caused by stigma associated with HIV/AIDS. Further, by reviewing studies on social media use by depressed patients, Rice et al. (2014) suggested that users should be aware of potential risks of social media use such as cyberbullying, harassment, and sexting that could occur while communicating through private messages. Those concerns associated with stigma attached to some health issues might prevent users with the health issues from sending private messages to others because of concerns about negative consequences. In fact, some social media users with ID are aware of these risks such as being hurt, so they are very careful about interacting with others on social media (Molin et al., 2017).

Especially for emerging adults, it is difficult to talk about their health issues through online messages. Research interviewing youth living with HIV (17 to 21 years) revealed that most participants had great difficulty disclosing their diagnosis (Hosek, Harper, & Domanico, 2000). One participant told that he or she could not disclose the diagnosis even to his or her parents because of the stigma attached to HIV. Another study specifically examining diagnosis disclosure of adolescents living with HIV found that one third of the participants disclosed their diagnosis only to immediate family members and a few close friends (Wiener & Battles, 2006). Taken together, as the previous studies show possible stigma effects of messages exchanged on SNSs, future research should examine the effects by exploring the following research questions:

RQ1: If people know their Facebook friend has a health issue, will their online message to the friend be negatively influenced?

RQ2: If people with a health issue expect to be stigmatized after disclosing their issue, will they be unwilling to disclose their issue through the use of online messages?

Communication on Walls

A main usage of social media is interaction on walls where users can exchange opinions that are seen by other users. For example, on Facebook, they can post an update status on their wall that allows them to show other Facebook friends what they are doing and how they are feeling. In turn, their Facebook friends can write comments on the updated status. Also, Facebook users can use a Like button to let other users know they like other's postings such as a status updates, pictures, and shared websites. Similarly, each YouTube video has a wall below the video where users discuss regarding the contents of the video. These functions play important roles in communication on social media. For instance, messages on a wall of YouTube function as a naturally occurring peer support where mentally ill individuals provide and receive support and information (Naslund et al., 2014). Shpigelman (2016) also found that the participation in Facebook by people with ID allowed them to be visible to others through interaction on Facebook walls. The visibility made them feel popular that is not easy to achieve in FtF settings for them.

However, if people know their Facebook friend has health issues, it is possible that their communication on walls involving the friend is negatively affected. For example, some individuals struggling with weight loss management reported that when they mentioned they worried about their weight on a Facebook wall, they received sarcastic and negative comments from others (Newman et al., 2011). Also, Naslund et al. (2014) suggested risks associated with interaction below videos uploaded on YouTube by those with severe mental illness such as schizophrenia. Since some users with a mental illness upload videos and post comments below them without hiding their identity, they could be targets of stigmatization because some mental illnesses such as schizophrenia carry severe stigma (Angermeyer & Matschinger, 1997, 2003; Link et al., 1999). These ideas indicate a possibility that stigma attached to illnesses and disabilities could negatively influence behaviors of others toward targets with health issues on social media.

To research the stigma effect on how those health issues interact with others on a wall, Modified Labeling Theory (Link, 1982) is useful. This theory specifically focuses on mental illness stigma, but some concepts in this theory are applicable to other health issues. A core theoretical idea of the theory is that individuals with health issues would avoid interacting with others because they are afraid of being rejected or ignored by others due to possible stigma effects. In that vein, individuals living with HIV/AIDS who participated in online support groups for HIV/AIDS showed concerns about being attacked or ridiculed because of HIV/AIDS stigma (Mo & Coulson, 2013; Taggart et al., 2015). Shpigelman (2016) also suggest that social media users with ID were worried about being hurt or ending up in undesirable situations through interaction on social media (Molin et al., 2017). These concerns might prevent those with health issues from engaging in interaction on walls, that potentially reduces chances to obtain support from others.

Modified Labeling Theory also predicts that those with health issues would try to educate other Facebook friends to obviate the negative effects of stigma. They may share websites that show the facts of the illness or disability to combat the myths of the illness or disability. They may also write comments on friends' walls if the friends write incorrect information about mental illnesses. Exchanging useful information about illnesses and disabilities among social media users with health issues has been observed in various studies (e.g., Househ et al., 2014). Future studies should explore if and how individuals with health issues provide those *without* health issues with correct health information to ward off the negative influences of stigma.

The stigma impact on interaction using the wall may be significant particularly for emerging adults. Schwartz et al. (2013) suggest that emerging adults undertake experimentation to explore who they are through interpersonal interaction. For example, to establish their identity, emerging adults may show their different facets of the self to others to see if they get feedback that is consistent with who they think they are. In fact, emerging adults present the real self, the ideal self, and even the false self on Facebook to explore their identity (Michikyan et al., 2015). Thus, if the emerging adults are aware that their health issues are stigmatized, they would not reveal the information about the issues on walls of SNSs. In fact, some hospital patients tried not to show their health information such as their diagnosis and treatment on a Facebook wall because SNSs are places they want to act as "regular" individuals without being labeled as patients struggling with illnesses. Based on these theoretical ideas, future research should examine the following research questions:

RQ3: If people know their Facebook friend has a health issue, will their comments on the friend's wall be negatively influenced?
RQ4: If an individual with a health issue believes their health status is known by Facebook friends, will the individual decline to participate in conversations taking place on walls?
RQ5: If an individual with a health issue believes their health status is known by Facebook friends, will the individual try to educate the friends by providing information related to the health issue?

Mixed-Mode Relationships

Past research argues that some online relationships migrate to FtF settings (Anthenunis, Valkenburg, & Peter, 2012). Such relationships are called mixed-mode relationships (MMRs), in which people meet online and migrate offline (Walther & Parks, 2002). Those with health issues actively seek new relationships on social media (e.g., Gowen et al., 2012), so it is possible for them to try to meet people they met on social media in a FtF setting. In a study by Molin et al. (2017), some adolescents with ID reported experiences of developing a romantic relationship with others through social media and some of the relationship lasted for a long time. Although it is not clear from the study whether or not they met their partner offline, it is natural that they might have been motivated to meet their partner FtF.

However, stigma associated with health issues might influence the decision for social media users with or without health issues to meet offline. For instance, people tried to avoid physically meeting a schizophrenic individual they know only on Facebook because of the stigma associated with the illness (Imai, 2016). Stigma may also impact people with health issues' decision to meet others offline. Modified Labeling Theory (Link 1982) suggests that people with health issues try to avoid potentially threatening situations, such as social gatherings where they may be rejected and isolated. Thus, people may avoid physically meeting someone they know only on social media because they are afraid to lose the social ties they developed online.

Research showed that the main motive to use SNSs for emerging adults is to stay in touch with friends they know offline, but one third of them use SNSs to meet and make friends with new people (Subrahmanyam, Reich, Waechter, & Espinoza 2008). The stigma associated with their health issues may prevent emerging adults with health issues from developing new relationships online that could develop social support offline. According to these accounts, the following research questions are posed:

RQ6: If people know their Facebook friend has a health issue, will they avoid meeting the friend in FtF settings?
RQ7: If individuals with health issues believe their health status is known by their Facebook friends, will the friend decline to meet in FtF settings?

CONCLUSION

Previous research revealed that some emerging adults with health issues have a hard time developing close relationships with others and obtaining interpersonal support (Patterson et al., 2012; Starke, 2013). Social media could provide valuable opportunities for them to achieve such relationships and support (e.g., Barker, 2009; Nabi, Prestin, & So, 2013). However, those with health issues are at risk of experiencing stigma while using social media (Imai & Dailey, 2015; Newman et al., 2011) and this experience may have a negative impact on emerging adults' identity management (Schwartz et al., 2013). Despite the predicted risks, there has been little research investigating the stigma effect on social media users with health issues. To facilitate research on this issue, this chapter described the current literature on the use of social media by individuals with health issues. Previous research has revealed that people with health issues actively use social media for various reasons such as obtaining support (Mo & Coulson, 2008; Moorhead et al., 2013) and managing their identity (Newman et al., 2011; Shpigelman, 2016). However, some studies indicate potential negative consequences related to the use of social media by those with health issues such as stigmatization (Taggart et al., 2015), cyberbullying, harassment, sexting, Rice et al. (2014), and being hurt, attacked, and ridiculed (Mo & Coulson, 2013; Mollin et al., 2017). To help researchers address these issues further, this chapter poses research questions that future studies should explore. Addressing these questions will make social media better places for emerging adults with health issues to develop interpersonal relationships and improve their quality of life.

REFERENCES

Abramson, K., Keefe, B., & Chou, W. S. (2015). Communicating about cancer through Facebook: A qualitative analysis of a breast cancer awareness page. *Journal of Health Communication*, *20*(2), 237–243. doi:10.1080/10810730.2014.927034 PMID:25495200

American Association of Intellectual and Developmental Disabilities. (2013). *Definition of intellectual disability*. Retrieved from http://aaidd.org/intellectual-disability/definition#.Vd0xTKaZ5EI

American Diabetes Association. (2015). *Diabetes symptoms*. Retrieved from http://www.diabetes.org/diabetes-basics/symptoms/

American Psychiatric Association. (2013). *Diagnostic and statistical manual of mental disorders* (5th ed.). Arlington, VA: American Psychiatric Publishing.

Angermeyer, M. C., & Matschinger, H. (1997). Social distance towards the mentally ill: Results of representative surveys in the Federal Republic of Germany. *Psychological Medicine*, *27*(1), 131–141. doi:10.1017/S0033291796004205 PMID:9122293

Angermeyer, M. C., & Matschinger, H. (2003). Public beliefs about schizophrenia and depression: Similarities and differences. *Social Psychiatry and Psychiatric Epidemiology*, *38*(9), 526–534. doi:10.100700127-003-0676-6 PMID:14504738

Anthenunis, M. L., Valkenburg, P. M., & Peter, J. (2012). The quality of online, offline, and mixed-mode friendships among users of a social net- working site. *Cyberpsychology (Brno)*, *6*, 6. Retrieved from http://www.cyberpsychology.eu/view.php? cisloclanku=2012120304&article=6

Balfe, M., Doyle, F., Smith, D., Sreenan, S., Brugha, R., Hevey, D., & Conroy, R. (2013). What's distressing about having type 1 diabetes? A qualitative study of young adults' perspectives. *BMC Endocrine Disorders*, *13*(1), 1–14. doi:10.1186/1472-6823-13-25 PMID:23885644

Barker, V. (2009). Older adolescents' motivations for social network site use: The influence of gender, group identity, and collective self-esteem. *Cyberpsychology & Behavior*, *12*(2), 209–213. doi:10.1089/cpb.2008.0228 PMID:19250021

Beaudoin, C. E., & Tao, C. C. (2007). Benefiting from social capital in online support groups: An empirical study of cancer patients. *Cyberpsychology & Behavior*, *10*(4), 587–590. doi:10.1089/cpb.2007.9986 PMID:17711369

Bender, J. L., Jimenez-Marroquin, M. C., & Jadad, A. R. (2011). Seeking support on facebook: A content analysis of breast cancer groups. *Journal of Medical Internet Research*, *13*(1), e16. doi:10.2196/jmir.1560 PMID:21371990

Bickley, S. R. (1990). Dental hygienists' attitudes towards dental care for people with a mental handicap and the perceptions of adequacy of their training. *Dental Education*, *168*, 361–364. PMID:2140515

Bjornsen, C. (2018). Social media use and emerging adulthood. In M. Zupančič & M. Puklek Levpušček (Eds.), Prehod v odraslost: Sodobni trendi in raziskave [Emerging adulthood: Current trends and research] (pp. 193–223). Ljubljana, Slovenia: Znanstvena založba Filozofske fakultete.

Bloom, J. R., & Kessler, L. (1994). Emotional support following cancer: A test of the stigma and social activity hypotheses. *Journal of Health and Social Behavior*, *35*(2), 118–133. doi:10.2307/2137360 PMID:8064120

boyd, D., & Ellison, N. (2008). Social network sites: Definition, history and scholarship. *Journal of Computer-Mediated Communication, 13,* 212-216.

Brod, M., Kongso, J. H., Lessard, S., & Christensen, T. L. (2009). Psychological insulin resistance: Patient beliefs and implications for diabetes management. *Quality of Life Research: An International Journal of Quality of Life Aspects of Treatment, Care and Rehabilitation*, *18*(1), 23–32. doi:10.100711136-008-9419-1 PMID:19039679

Cane, D. B., & Gotlib, I. H. (1985). Implicit conceptualizations of depression: Implications for an interpersonal perspective. *Social Cognition*, *3*(4), 341–368. doi:10.1521oco.1985.3.4.341

Centers for Disease Control & Prevention. (2016). *HIV Among Youth.* Retrieved from http://www.cdc.gov/hiv/group/age/youth/

Chapple, A., Ziebland, S., & McPherson, A. (2004). Stigma, shame, and blame experienced by patients with lung cancer: Qualitative study. *British Medical Journal*, *328*(7454), 1470–1473. doi:10.1136/bmj.38111.639734.7C PMID:15194599

Chesney, M. A., & Smith, A. W. (1999). Critical delays in HIV testing and care: The potential role of stigma. *The American Behavioral Scientist*, *42*(7), 1162–1174. doi:10.1177/00027649921954822

Cooney, G., Jahoda, A., Gumley, A., & Knott, F. (2006). Young people with learning disabilities attending mainstream and segregated schooling: Perceived stigma, social comparisons and future aspirations. *Journal of Intellectual Disability Research, 50*(6), 432–445. doi:10.1111/j.1365-2788.2006.00789.x PMID:16672037

Coyne, S. M., Padilla-Walker, L. M., & Howard, E. (2013). Emerging in a digital world: A decade review of media use, effects, and gratifications in emerging adulthood. *Emerging Adulthood, 1*(2), 125–137. doi:10.1177/2167696813479782

Ellison, N. B., Steinfield, C., & Lampe, C. (2007). The benefits of Facebook "friends:" Social capital and college students use of online social network sites. *Journal of Computer-Mediated Communication, 12*(4), 1143–1168. doi:10.1111/j.1083-6101.2007.00367.x

Erfani, S. S., Blount, Y., & Abedin, B. (2016). The influence of health-specific social network site use on the psychological well-being of cancer-affected people. *Journal of the American Medical Informatics Association, 23*(3), 467–476. doi:10.1093/jamia/ocv170 PMID:26911816

File, B. L., & Wright, E. R. (2000). The dimensionality of stigma: A comparison of its impact on the self of persons with HIV/AIDS and cancer. *Journal of Health and Social Behavior, 41*(1), 50–67. doi:10.2307/2676360 PMID:10750322

Fox, J., Warber, K. M., & Makstaller, D. (2013). The role of Facebook in romantic relationship development: An exploration of Knapp's relational stage model. *Journal of Social and Personal Relationships, 30*(6), 771–794. doi:10.1177/0265407512468370

Goffman, E. (1963). *Stigma: Notes on the management of spoiled identity*. Englewood Cliffs, NJ: Prentice Hall.

Gotlib, I. H., & Beatty, M. E. (1985). Negative responses to depression: The role of attribution style. *Cognitive Therapy and Research, 9*(1), 91–103. doi:10.1007/BF01178753

Gowen, L. K., Deschaine, M., Gruttadaro, D., & Markey, D. C. (2012). Young adults with mental health conditions and social networking websites: Decreasing social isolation. *Psychiatric Rehabilitation Journal, 35*, 245–250. doi:10.2975/35.3.2012.245.250 PMID:22246123

Greene, J. A., Choudhry, N. K., Kilabuk, E., & Shrank, W. H. (2010). Online social networking by patients with diabetes: A qualitative evaluation of communication with facebook. *Journal of General Internal Medicine, 26*(3), 287–292. doi:10.100711606-010-1526-3 PMID:20945113

Greene, K. (2009). An integrated model of health disclosure decision-making. In T. D. Afifi & W. A. Afifi (Eds.), *Uncertainty, information management, and disclosure decisions: Theories and applications* (pp. 226–253). New York: Routledge.

Greene, K., & Faulkner, S. L. (2002). Self-disclosure in relationships of HIV-positive African American adolescent females. *Communication Studies, 53*, 297–317. doi:10.1080/10510970209388595

Herek, G. M. (2014). HIV-related stigma. In P. W. Corrigan (Ed.), *The stigma of disease and disability: Empirical models and implications for change* (pp. 121–138). Washington, DC: American Psychological Association.

Horowitz, L. M., French, R. de S., Lapid, J. S., & Weckler, D. A. (1982). Symptoms and interpersonal problems: The prototypes as an integrating concept. In J. C. Anchin & D. J. Kiesler (Eds.), Handbook of interpersonal psychotherapy (pp. 168-189). New York: Pergamon.

Horvath, K. J., Danilenko, G. P., Williams, M. L., Simoni, J., Amico, K. R., Oakes, J. M., & Rosser, B. R. S. (2012). Technology use and reasons to participate in social networking health websites among people living with HIV in the US. *AIDS and Behavior*, *16*(4), 900–910. doi:10.100710461-012-0164-7 PMID:22350832

Hosek, S. G., Harper, G. W., & Domanico, R. (2000). Psychological and social difficulties of adolescents living with HIV: A qualitative analysis. *Journal of Sex Education and Therapy*, *25*(4), 269–276. doi:1 0.1080/01614576.2000.11074360

Househ, M., Borycki, E., & Kushniruk, A. (2014). Empowering patients through social media: The benefits and challenges. *Health Informatics Journal*, *20*(1), 50–58. doi:10.1177/1460458213476969 PMID:24550564

Imai, T. (2016). Influences of mental illness stigma in a computer-mediated communication context: Investigating mediating roles of predicted outcome value and negative affect. *Japanese Journal of Communication Studies*, *44*, 135–150.

Imai, T., & Dailey, R. M. (2015). Influences of mental illness stigma on perceptions of and responses to requests for favors. *Health Communication*, *31*(7), 863–872. doi:10.1080/10410236.2015.1012630 PMID:26642875

International Agency for Research on Cancer. (2008). *World Cancer Report 2008* (P. Boyle & B. Levin, Eds.). Lyon, France: Author.

Jacobsen, W. C., & Forste, R. (2011). The wired generation: Academic and social outcomes of electronic media use among university students. *Cyberpsychology, Behavior, and Social Networking*, *14*(5), 275–280. doi:10.1089/cyber.2010.0135 PMID:20961220

Jahoda, A., Wilson, A., Stalker, K., & Cairney, A. (2010). Living with stigma and the self perceptions of people with mild learning disabilities. *The Journal of Social Issues*, *66*(3), 521–534. doi:10.1111/j.1540-4560.2010.01660.x

Jenkins, J. H., & Carpenter-Song, E. A. (2009). Awareness of stigma among persons with schizophrenia: Marking the contexts of lived experience. *The Journal of Nervous and Mental Disease*, *197*(7), 520–529. doi:10.1097/NMD.0b013e3181aad5e9 PMID:19597360

Jones, E. E., Farina, A., Hastorf, A. H., Markus, H., Miller, D. T., & Scott, R. A. (1984). *Social stigma: The psychology of marked relationships*. New York: Freeman.

Kaplan, A., & Haenlein, M. (2010). Users of the world, unite! The challenges and opportunities of social media. *Business Horizons*, *53*(1), 59–68. doi:10.1016/j.bushor.2009.09.003

Link, B. G. (1982). Mental patient status, work, and income: An examination of the effects of a psychiatric label. *American Sociological Review*, *47*(2), 202–215. doi:10.2307/2094963 PMID:7091929

Link, B. G., Cullen, F. T., Struening, E., Shrout, P. E., & Dohrenwend, B. P. (1989). A modified labeling theory approach to mental disorders: An empirical assessment. *American Sociological Review*, *54*(3), 400–423. doi:10.2307/2095613

Link, B. G., & Phelan, J. C. (2001). Conceptualizing stigma. *Annual Review of Sociology*, *27*(1), 363–385. doi:10.1146/annurev.soc.27.1.363

Link, B. G., Phelan, J. C., Bresnahan, M., Stueve, A., & Pescosolido, B. A. (1999). Public conceptions of mental illness: Labels, causes, dangerousness and social distance. *American Journal of Public Health*, *89*(9), 1328–1333. doi:10.2105/AJPH.89.9.1328 PMID:10474548

Lysaker, P. H., Roe, D., & Yanos, P. T. (2007). Toward understanding the insight paradox: Internalized stigma moderates the association between insight and social functioning, hope, and self-esteem among people with schizophrenia spectrum disorders. *Schizophrenia Bulletin*, *33*(1), 192–199. doi:10.1093chbulbl016 PMID:16894025

McIntyre, L. L., Blacher, J., & Baker, B. L. (2006). Transition to school: Adaptation in young children with and without developmental delays. *Journal of Intellectual Disability Research*, *50*, 349–361. doi:10.1111/j.1365-2788.2006.00783.x PMID:16629928

Michikyan, M., Dennis, J., & Subrahmanyam, K. (2015). Can you guess who I am? Real, ideal, and false self-presentation on Facebook among emerging adults. *Emerging Adulthood*, *3*(1), 55–64. doi:10.1177/2167696814532442

Miller, A. N., & Rubin, D. L. (2007). Factors leading to self-disclosure of a positive HIV diagnosis in Nairobi, Kenya. *Qualitative Health Research*, *17*(5), 586–598. doi:10.1177/1049732307301498 PMID:17478642

Mo, P. K. H., & Coulson, N. S. (2008). Exploring the communication of social support within virtual communities: A content analysis of messages posted to an online HIV/AIDS support group. *Cyberpsychology & Behavior*, *11*(3), 371–374. doi:10.1089/cpb.2007.0118 PMID:18537512

Mo, P. K. H., & Coulson, N. S. (2013). Online support group use and psychological health for individuals living with HIV/AIDS. *Patient Education and Counseling*, *93*(3), 426–432. doi:10.1016/j.pec.2013.04.004 PMID:23669152

Molin, M., Sorbring, E., & Löfgren-Mårtenson, L. (2017). New Em@ncipatory landscapes? Young people with intellectual disabilities, Internet use and identification processes. *Advances in Social Work*, *18*(2), 645–662. doi:10.18060/21428

Moorhead, S. A., Hazlett, D. E., Harrison, L., Carroll, J. K., Irwin, A., & Hoving, C. (2013). A new dimension of Health Care: Systematic Review of the Uses, Benefits and Limitations of Social Media for Health Communication. *Journal of Medical Internet Research*, *15*(4), e85. doi:10.2196/jmir.1933 PMID:23615206

Moreno, M. A., Jelenchick, L. A., Egan, K. G., Cox, E., Young, H., Gannon, K. E., & Becker, T. (2011). Feeling bad on Facebook: Depression disclosures by college students on a social networking site. *Depression and Anxiety*, *28*(6), 447–455. doi:10.1002/da.20805 PMID:21400639

Nabi, R. L., Prestin, A., & So, J. (2013). Facebook Friends with (Health) Benefits?: Exploring the Palliative Effects of Social Network Sites Compared to Interpersonal Networks. *Cyberpsychology, Behavior, and Social Networking*, *16*, 721–727. doi:10.1089/cyber.2012.0521

Naslund, J. A., Grande, S. W., Aschbrenner, K. A., & Elwyn, G. (2014). Naturally occurring peer support through social media: The experiences of individuals with severe mental illness using YouTube. *PLoS One*, *9*(10), e110171. doi:10.1371/journal.pone.0110171 PMID:25333470

National Institute of Mental Health. (2019). *Major Depression.* Retrieved from https://www.nimh.nih.gov/health/statistics/major-depression.shtml

Neal, C., Beckjord, E., Rechis, R., Schaeffer, J., Berno, D., & Duchover, Y. (2010). *Cancer stigma and silence around the world: A LIVESTRONG report.* Retrieved from http://images.livestrong.org/downloads/flatfiles/what-we-do/our-approach/reports/cancer-stigma/LSGlobalResearchReport.pdf

Newman, M. W., Lauterbach, D., Munson, S. A., Resnick, P., & Morris, M. E. (2011). It's not that I don't have problems, I'm just not putting them on Facebook: Challenges and opportunities in using online social networks for health. In *Proceedings of the ACM 2011 Conference on Computer Supported Cooperative Work* (pp. 341- 350). Hangzhou, China: ACM. 10.1145/1958824.1958876

Nicholson, K. J., & Sacco, W. P. (1999, August). *Interpersonal responses to depression: Negative social-cognition, affect, and non-genuine support.* Poster session presented at the annual meeting of the American Psychological Association, Boston, MA.

Norman, R. M. G., Gawronski, G., Hampson, E., Sorrentno, R. M., Szeto, A., & Ye, Y. (2010). Physical proximity in anticipation of meeting someone with schizophrenia: The role of explicit evaluations, implicit evaluations and cortisol levels. *Schizophrenia Research*, *124*(1-3), 74–80. doi:10.1016/j.schres.2010.07.021 PMID:20713306

Patterson, P., Millar, B., Desille, N., & McDonald, F. (2012). The unmet needs of emerging adults with a cancer diagnosis: A qualitative study. *Cancer Nursing*, *35*(3), 32–40. doi:10.1097/NCC.0b013e31822d9105 PMID:22538263

Perrin, A. (2015). *Social media usage 2005-2015.* Retrieved from http://www.pewinternet.org/2015/10/08/social-networking-usage-2005-2015/

Pew Research Center. (2014). *Social networking fact sheet.* Retrieved from http://www.pewinternet.org/fact-sheets/social-networking-fact-sheet/

Pew Research Center. (2015). *The demographics of social media users.* Retrieved from http://www.pewinternet.org/2015/08/19/the-demographics-of-social-media-users/

Postmes, T., Spears, R., & Lea, M. (2000). The formation of group norms in computermediated communication. *Human Communication Research*, *26*(3), 341–371. doi:10.1111/j.1468-2958.2000.tb00761.x

Rafferty, J., Boettcher, C., & Griffin, K. W. (2001). Benefits and risks of reverse inclusion for preschoolers with and without disabilities: Parents' perspectives. *Journal of Early Intervention*, *24*(4), 266–286. doi:10.1177/105381510102400403

Rice, S. M., Goodall, J., Hetrick, S. E., Parker, A. G., Gilbertson, T., Amminger, G. P., ... Alvarez-Jimenez, M. (2014). Online and social networking interventions for the treatment of depression in young people: A systematic review. *Journal of Medical Internet Research, 16*(9), e206. doi:10.2196/jmir.3304 PMID:25226790

Rippere, V. (1977). Commonsense beliefs about depression and antidepressive behaviour: A study of social consensus. *Behaviour Research and Therapy, 15*(6), 465–473. doi:10.1016/0005-7967(77)90002-X PMID:603479

Sacco, W. P., & Vaughan, C. A. (2006). Depression and the response of others: A social-cognitive interpersonal process model. In T. E. Joiner, J. S. Brown, & J. Kistner (Eds.), *The interpersonal, social and cognitive nature of depression*. Mahwah, NJ: Lawrence Erlbaum Associates.

Sato, E., Ohsawa, I., Kataoka, J., Miwa, M., Tsukagoshi, F., Sato, J., ... Sato, Y. (2003). Socio-psychological problems of patients with late adolescent onset type 1 diabetes – analysis by qualitative research. *Nagoya Journal of Medical Science, 66*, 21–29. PMID:12848418

Schabert, J., Browne, J. L., Mosely, K., & Speight, J. (2005). Social stigma in diabetes: A framework to understand a growing problem for an increasing epidemic. *Patient, 6*(1), 1–10. doi:10.100740271-012-0001-0 PMID:23322536

Schneider, D. J. (2005). *The psychology of stereotyping*. New York: Guilford Press.

Schwartz, S. J., Donnellan, M. B., Ravert, R. D., Luyckx, K., & Zamboanga, B. L. (2013). Identity development, personality, and well-being in adolescence and emerging adulthood: Theory, research, and recent advances. In Handbook of psychology, vol. 6: Developmental psychology (pp. 339-364). New York: John Wiley and Sons.

Shiu, A. T., Kwan, J. J. Y., & Wong, R. Y. (2003). Social stigma as a battier to diabetes self-management: Implications for multi-level interventions. *Journal of Clinical Nursing, 12*(1), 149–150. doi:10.1046/j.1365-2702.2003.00735.x PMID:12519263

Shpigelman, C.-N. (2016, July). *Sense of belonging of Facebook users with intellectual disabilities.* Paper presented at the Fifth Conference of Alter, European Society for Research on Disability, Stockholm, Sweden.

Shpigelman, C.-N., & Gill, C. J. (2014a). Facebook use by persons with disabilities. *Journal of Computer-Mediated Communication, 19*(3), 610–624. doi:10.1111/jcc4.12059

Shpigelman, C.-N., & Gill, C. J. (2014b). How do adults with intellectual disabilities use Facebook? *Disability & Society, 29*(10), 1601–1616. doi:10.1080/09687599.2014.966186

Sibicky, M., & Dividio, J. F. (1986). Stigma of psychological therapy: Stereotypes, interpersonal reactions, and the self-fulfilling prophecy. *Journal of Counseling Psychology, 33*(2), 148–154. doi:10.1037/0022-0167.33.2.148

Slevin, E., & Sines, D. (1996). Attitudes of nurses in general hospital towards people with learning disabilities: Influences of contact, and graduate – non-graduate status, a comparative study. *Journal of Advanced Nursing, 24*(6), 1116–1126. doi:10.1111/j.1365-2648.1996.tb01016.x PMID:8953346

Special Olympics. (2015). *What is intellectual disability?* Retrieved from http://www.specialolympics.org/Sections/Who_We_Are/What_Is_Intellectual_Disability.aspx

Starke, M. (2013). Everyday life of young adults with intellectual disabilities: Inclusionary and exclusionary processes among young adults of parents with intellectual disability. *Intellectual and Developmental Disabilities*, *51*(3), 164–175. doi:10.1352/1934-9556-51.3.164 PMID:23834213

Statista. (2019a). *Number of global social media users 2010-2021*. Retrieved from https://www.statista.com/statistics/278414/number-of-worldwide-social-network-users/

Statista. (2019b). *Social media usage in the United States*. Retrieved from https://www.statista.com/topics/3196/social-media-usage-in-the-united-states/

Steel, Z., Marnane, C., Iranpour, C., Chey, T., Jackson, J. W., Patel, V., & Silove, D. (2014). The global prevalence of common mental disorders: A systematic review and meta-analysis 1980-2013. *International Journal of Epidemiology*, *43*(2), 476–493. doi:10.1093/ije/dyu038 PMID:24648481

Stein, D. J., Phillips, K. A., Bolton, D., Fulford, K. W. M., Sadler, J. Z., & Kendler, K. S. (2010). What is a mental/psychiatric disorder? From DSM-IV to DSM-V. *Psychological Medicine*, *40*(11), 1759–1765. doi:10.1017/S0033291709992261 PMID:20624327

Subrahmanyam, K., Reich, S. M., Waechter, N., & Espinoza, G. (2008). Online and offline social networks: Use of social networking sites by emerging adults. *Journal of Applied Developmental Psychology*, *29*(6), 420–433. doi:10.1016/j.appdev.2008.07.003

Taggart, T., Grewe, M. E., Conserve, D. F., Gliwa, C., & Isler, M. R. (2015). Social media and HIV: A systematic review of uses of social media in HIV communication. *Journal of Medical Internet Research*, *17*(11), e248. doi:10.2196/jmir.4387 PMID:26525289

U.S. Bureau of Labor Statistics. (2010). Employment status of the civilian population by sex, age, and disability status, not seasonally adjusted [Data file]. Retrieved from http://www.bls.gov

van Alphen, L. M., Dijker, A. J. M., Bos, A. E. R., Van den Borne, B., & Curfs, L. M. G. (2012). The influence of group size and stigma severity on social acceptance: The case of people with intellectual disability moving into neighborhoods. *Journal of Community & Applied Social Psychology*, *22*(1), 38–50. doi:10.1002/casp.1094

van der Velden, M., & El Emam, K. (2013). "Not all my friends need to know:" a qualitative study of teenage patients, privacy, and social media. *Journal of the American Medical Informatics Association*, *20*(1), 16–24. doi:10.1136/amiajnl-2012-000949 PMID:22771531

Walther, J. B., & Parks, M. R. (2002). Cues filtered out, cues filtered in: Computer-mediated communication and relationships. In M. L. Knapp & J. A. Daly (Eds.), *Handbook of interpersonal communication* (3rd ed.; pp. 529–563). Thousand Oaks, CA: Sage.

Washington Post-Kaiser Family Foundation. (2012). *2012 survey of Americans of HIV/AIDS.* Retrieved from https://kaiserfamilyfoundation.files.wordpress.com/2013/01/8334-f.pdf

We Are Social. (2019). *Digital 2019.* Retrieved from https://wearesocial.com/blog/2019/07/global-social-media-users-pass-3-5-billion

Wellard, S. J., Rennie, S., & King, R. (2008). Perceptions of people with type 2 diabetes about self-management and the efficiency of community based services. *Contemporary Nurse, 29*(2), 218–226. doi:10.5172/conu.673.29.2.218 PMID:18844535

Wiener, L. S., & Battles, H. B. (2006). Untangling the web: A close look at diagnosis disclosure among HIV-infected adolescents. *The Journal of Adolescent Health, 38*(3), 307–309. doi:10.1016/j.jadohealth.2005.03.024 PMID:16488835

World Health Organization. (2012). *Cancer fact sheet.* Retrieved from http://globocan.iarc.fr/Pages/fact_sheets_cancer.aspx

World Health Organization. (2014a). *The top 10 causes of death.* Retrieved from http://www.who.int/mediacentre/factsheets/fs310/en/

World Health Organization. (2014b). *Diabetes.* Retrieved from http://www.who.int/mediacentre/factsheets/fs312/en/

World Health Organization. (2015). *HIV/AIDS.* Retrieved from http://www.who.int/mediacentre/factsheets/fs360/en/

Yarkin, K. L., Harvey, J. H., & Bloxom, B. M. (1981). Cognitive sets, attribution, and social interaction. *Journal of Personality and Social Psychology, 41*(2), 243–252. doi:10.1037/0022-3514.41.2.243

KEY TERMS AND DEFINITIONS

AIDS: The final stage of HIV infection in which the body is vulnerable to diseases and those with AIDS may develop various serious health conditions.

Cancer: A group of different and distinctive diseases caused by an uncontrolled abnormal cell growth.

Diabetes: A group of metabolic diseases in which the body cannot control the amount of sugar in blood.

HIV: HIV interferes with the function of the immune system that fights off diseases.

Intellectual Disability: A disability characterized by impaired intellectual abilities and a lack of skills necessary for day-to-day life.

Mental Illness: A mental health condition that interferes with an individual's cognitive, emotional, or behavioral functioning.

Social Networking Sites: A web-based services that enable users to create a public profile and develop relationships with other users online.

Stigma: A negative stereotype associated with a specific group of people, leading to the unequal treatment for them.

Chapter 12
Self-Comparison in the Digital World:
The Impact to Self-Esteem

Clara Moningka
Universitas Pembangunan Jaya, Indonesia

ABSTRACT

In this chapter, the author is interested in studying self-comparison in social media and its effect to the self-esteem in emerging adults. In Indonesia, social media are widely used by various groups. Jakarta is even referred as the capital of a text-based social media. Data in 2016 indicated that social media users in Indonesia have reached high ranking. Indonesia ranked fourth in the world for social media users and ranked first with Facebook with 111 million users, followed by Twitter. Indonesian Internet Service Provider Association explained that the biggest users were dominated by adolescents, amounting to 75.50% of the total users. The use of social media can be influenced by collective culture. This culture can influence how individuals evaluate themselves, including their self-esteem. The topic of the psychological effects of social media has been much discussed. A lot of research conducted on the effect of social on development of self-esteem. Social media becoming a place for comparing oneself to others and it turn out it has a great effect.

INTRODUCTION

Mashall, McLuhan, communication theorist, coined the phrase, "the medium is the message" (Steers, Wickham, & Acitelli, 2014). McLuhan did not mean to imply that individuals should ignore communication through a certain medium, but that people should not only be aware of a medium's properties but also be aware of how it subtly influences culture and how it may redefine human interactions.

The use of social media is growing rapidly worldwide. Kaplan and Haenlein (2010) explain that social media is a group of internet-based applications that are designed for social relationships and allow for the creation and exchange of user-generated content. Leonsis (cited by Hardy, 2016) explained that social media is a place where users can be entertained, communicate with each other, and participate

DOI: 10.4018/978-1-7998-1063-6.ch012

in the social environment. Brenner and Smith (2014) found that Facebook and Twitter were the most popular social media websites among Indonesian emerging adults. Kimbrough, Guadagno, Muscannel, and Dill (2013) explained that social media users usually are young people, especially women. Research conducted by "We are Social" in 2018 stated that on average Indonesians spend at least three hours or more a day accessing various types of social media, such as Facebook, Twitter, Instagram, and Google Plus. The other popular forms of social media are YouTube as a media sharing network and WordPress or Tumblr to share articles with fellow users.

Ayun (2015) explains that adolescents in Indonesia use social media as a means of presenting themselves or forming identities. They often carry out activities such as sharing personal messages with other users and sharing status about their condition at that time. They also share their current locations and photos or videos related to the places or events that they have visited. This behavior indicates that social media can show self-existence. For adolescents and young adults, self-existence and self-esteem are very important. They can display a positive self-image through social media. They can show the enjoyable parts of their life and hope to receive positive responses from other social media users (Foo in Moningka, 2017). This behavior is a strategy to boost their self-esteem.

Statistics showed that the highest users groups of Facebook are teens and emerging adults; young emerging adults over the age of 18 years occupy 42% of total users, followed by older emerging adults aged 25-34 years at 21% (Sandra 2012). According to the data collected in 2014, 87% American adults were connected to internet and more than 50% owned internet connected devices. These numbers increased to 97% and 83% of users between ages of 18 and 29 (Davis, 2016). Davis (2016) explained that social media permeate all aspects of our life, such as work, education, politics, and even social life, including the developments of self and identity.

Indonesian internet users are considered some of the most social people on Earth. Indonesian youth see social media as an everyday necessity (Kemp, 2011). These youths will sacrifice other 'luxuries' to ensure their phones have sufficient credit to access mobile data. Indonesians between the ages of 13 and 24 years old have the highest level of interactions through the internet when compared to other cohorts. Arnett (2006) mentioned that emerging adults around age 18 to 25 are the highest users of social media. This period is characterized by instability and the search for stability and transition. The transition from adolescence to emerging adulthood is a crucial period in the formation of self-esteem as a part of self-concept.

The self is an important part of humans. The self relates to how we see ourselves and it also helps us to adapt to the environment. It is formed from the interaction between the potential that exists within us and within the environment. The environment might include parenting style, schools, neighborhoods, and the peer group. Nowadays, the digital world is becoming part of our environment. The aim of this chapter is to examine the effects of social media on self-esteem. The use of social media is massively increasing. This phenomenon can affect the formation of self. Social media allows people to easily observe other people, accessing any information, and knowing about other people's lives. It can also lead to upward or downward self-comparison that leads to how they respect themselves. The concept of how individuals value themselves is known as self-esteem.

BACKGROUND

Mazzoni and Zanazzi (2014) described changes in the global market that have affected social structure. This social change allowed people to find new channels of communication and to maintain their social networks through social media. Arakali (2015) reported that approximately 63 million people in Indonesia access social media such as Facebook at least once a month in 2015. This year also marked the culmination of mobile phone use. Indonesia has the 3rd largest country population accessing Facebook, after the United States and India; the percentage of Facebook users from Indonesia who access the platform via mobile phones is higher than in any other country. By the end of 2015, it is estimated that users of social media will reach 100 million, and will continue to increase in 2016. Furthermore, Indonesia will reach the top five of internet users in 2017, overtaking Japan. Indonesian Internet Service Provider Association (2018) explained that the biggest social media users were dominated by adolescents with an age range of 13 to 18 years, amounting to 75.50% of the total users.

Social media can basically be something beneficial, but the use of social media needs a lot of attention. Social media can help us build social networks and expand social interactions, but on the other hand, social media also includes some risks that could affect aspects of human life, whether cognitive, affective, or behavioral. Davis (2016) explained that digital social technologies have an effect on identity. Excessive use of social media can create a difficulty for individuals to adapt to the real environment. Basically, the social media environment limits individuals from learning to interrelate in the real world. Another thing that can happen is that individuals do not present “the real” self through social media because they are trying to create a good self-image and are trying to boost their self-esteem. The other negative effect of social media is the emergence of aggressive behavior, such as cyberbullying (Andriani, 2016). Even nowadays the use of social is common to spread hoaxes and hate speech.

Many efforts have been made to overcome the negative impacts of social media. In 2013, Japan’s government was very concern about internet addiction and they believed that this addiction would disrupt children’s development. Children and adolescents who use the internet intensely are more likely to experience depression, obesity, and developmental disorders. One way to deal with addiction is to send children to Internet fasting camps, where there is no internet connection. This type of camp tries to encourage children to communicate directly with others. In Indonesia In 2017, the societies of 7 cities in Indonesia, including Jakarta, Bandung, Semarang, Solo, Wonosobo, Jogjakarta and Surabaya, declared an “Anti-hoax Declaration”. Anyone can participate and sign up to participate declaring themselves to be part of the anti-hoax community. This activity was initiated by the Indonesian Anti Hoax Society, led by Septiaji Eko Nugroho. The Ministry of Communication and Information strongly supports these activities and movements. This event was supported by journalists and media associates, social media activists, celebrities, and public figures (Press Conference No. 2/HM/KOMINFO/01/2017). These movements show that the use of social media has a great effect on individuals. How can social media influence the way we see ourselves?

At birth, we were given a name that became part of our identity. Along with our physical and mental development, we also develop other types of identity, such as gender identity, ethnic identity, and a concept of who we are. The knowledge about ourselves is known as self-concept. Self-concept is defined as a person’s sense of self, shaped through interaction with the environment, other people, and the group in which we belong to. Sandra (2014) and Sanderson (2010) elaborate further that self-concept is a picture of how people describe themselves, which covers their point of view and how they think and judge themselves. Self-concept also includes how we value ourselves. This concept is known as self-esteem.

A positive self-concept including self-esteem is very important for improving mental health and various behaviors, such as academic achievement and the resiliency to cope with negative interactions (Chapman, Tunmer, & Prochnov, 2000).

The formation of self-concept is not limited to the interaction with the family, school, and the peer group, which can occur offline or through cyberspace. Myers (2013) explained that the self-esteem especially in collective culture correlates closely with what others think of oneself and the group they're belong to. The great advances of technology make it possible for us to be close to each other, even when we are far from each other. Social networking websites allow us to easily observe the activities of other individuals.

Vogel et al. (2014) explained that social media, such as Facebook, provides abundant social comparison opportunities. The concern is that individuals tend to upload photos, activities, or statuses that they find pleasant that reflect the most exciting part of their lives (Uhlir, 2016). These posts were intended to create a flattering depiction of themselves in order to boost their self-esteem. Kim and Lee (2011) argued that this activity is a way to present themselves to others, which is known as self-presentation; in this case, the individual is trying to present the good side of their self. This activity involves presenting themselves in a selective manner, emphasizing favorable and appropriate images. This behavior can boost self-esteem and also lead to social comparisons. It is human nature that people tend to see others as luckier and better than themselves. Myers and Twenge (2013) explained that most people are actually motivated to maintain their self-esteem. A study found that college students preferred a boost to their self-esteem to eating, seeing their friend, or having sexual activity (Bushman, Moeller, & Crocker, 2011). The self-esteem can be threatened by failure of an unflattering comparison. Self-esteem threats can occur among friends, whose success can be more threatening than strangers.

In connection with this matter, Uhlir (2016) also explained that there is the phenomenon called "the Facebook depression", which is caused by social comparison on social media. This phenomenon occurs because the individual can simply observe other people's lives through social media. Such comparison may relate to the formation of the self and may influence psychological well-being. People can choose to present their ideal self or false self on social media. They might do so for deception, exploration, or impressing others. Discrepancies between the ideal self and real self can lead to devaluation of the self and presentation of the false self. It is also linked to low self-esteem and depression.

Interaction Between Self-Esteem and Self-Comparison

Around the world, children are growing up in high-technology environments. Children are masters of technology, including the Internet and how to interact in social media. Foo (2003) suggests that the interaction with the Internet leads to the development of unlimited self-identity. Development of information technology can encourage the growth of creativity and knowledge, but also increases interactions on social networking websites, where people can explore the life of others and also expect positive feedback from such interaction. Good interaction through social networking websites also lead to life satisfaction and better relationships in the real world. Research conducted by Jackson, Zhao, Witt, Fitzgerald, Von Eye, and Harold (2009) revealed that interactions in the virtual world can build positive self-concepts. Individuals can acquire social support and a sense of comfort through their interaction in social media. Other studies have found the opposite result. Other research conducted by Sandra (2012) in four large cities in Indonesia, Jakarta (Capital City), Yogyakarta (Central Java), and Denpasar (Bali) revealed that Internet use also has negative impacts. For instance, people tend to pretend and present an unreal self-identity. This is very possible in social media because social media allows people to be anyone they want to be. Jang, Park, and Song (2016) examined social comparison on Facebook, and they did not find a significant relationship between social comparison and self-esteem, although research conducted by Vogel, Rose, Roberts, and Eckles (2014) found a significant relationship between social comparison and self-esteem; by making social comparisons, individuals can find new standards for their self-esteem.

Self-comparison theory was purposed by Leon Festinger. This theory explains that individuals tend to compare themselves to others, when they need guidance or a standard to compare their ability to. Individuals process information from their social environment by comparing themselves to established similarities and differences. This information might be sought for a reason or purpose (Krayer, Ingledew, & Iphofen, 2008). Sanderson (2010) stated that self-comparison explains what we think about ourselves and can be different for each person, depending on the nature of comparison we are making. People make social comparisons to reduce uncertainty about their performance or abilities. Therefore, they need an external standard to compare with. White, Langer, Yariv, and Welch (2006) explained that social-comparison can be used as a coping mechanism. For instance, when we compare ourselves with others who are less fortunate than us, we sometimes feel relieved.

Self-comparison plays an important role in evaluating our abilities. Sanderson's research on college students (2010) explained that first year college students suddenly felt not so smart, even though they used to be a star in their previous schools. In a new environment, they can be surrounded by smarter students, which can lower their self-esteem. A contemporary psychoanalyst, Bolt (2010) explained that some people were raised in a society that taught them to compare themselves with others. Children might learn this during their early years and it is common that some parents compare their children with other children in order to control their children's undesirable behavior. Such comparisons might reduce or boost one's ego. Bolt explained that the effects of social comparison has two distinct outcomes, depending on the meaning we assigned to the comparison. A person who does not measure up to the comparison might feel exhausted and depressed, withdrawing from others. On the other hand, when an individual feels that he or she is superior to other individuals, feelings of superiority increase. White, Langer, Yariv, and Welch (2006) explained that frequent social comparison are associated with destructive emotions and behaviors, such as envy and depression.

Dark Side of Social Comparison and the Impact to Self-Esteem

Lyubomirsky and Ross (1997) found that unhappy people tend to compare themselves to others. The comparison occurs spontaneously and frequently. These findings are also similar to research from Giordano, Wood, and Michela (2000) and Swallow and Kuiper (1992), that unhappy people make numerous comparisons. They also found that people with depression also made frequent social comparison. Furthermore, Stapel and Blanton (2004) explained that social comparison occurs automatically and we often are not aware of it. With social media, people can easily compare themselves with others, either automatically or purposefully.

White, Langer, Yarif, and Welch (2006) suggests that individuals who often make social comparison with others are people who are dissatisfied with themselves. Frequent social comparison positively correlated with destructive emotions and behaviors, such as envy, guilt, regret, and lying. Many studies have revealed that envy affects behaviors. Smith and Kim (2007) explained that Facebook is an easier place to engage in comparisons. Furthermore, Krasnova, Wenninger, Widjaja, and Buxmann (2013) also stated that the more people use Facebook, the more envious these individuals feel and the more dissatisfied they are with their lives.

Moningka (2015) conducted research in Jakarta, Indonesia regarding social comparison. The research was conducted in Jakarta, because it is the metropolis city and also the capital city of the Indonesia in which the population of social media users is quite high. This study's aim was to understand the purpose of using social media and what participants felt when they're using it. From the 90 respondents (ages ranged from 17 to 45), more than 80% (72 respondents) used social media as a tool to entertain themselves. They also accessed social media daily and used it on average more than 1 hour a day. More than 40% of respondents felt anxious or irritated if they were not able to access social media. Other respondents stated that they felt bored if they could not access social media. But there were around 20% of respondents who felt relief if they could not access social media. Feeling relief indicated that they would feel a sense of freedom from social media. They felt free from social media, because for them social media could cause them to feel anxious and discomfort.

Moningka (2015) also explained that activities on social media consisted of updating statuses or seeing other people's statuses and photos and the participants felt excited to read others status or knowing their friend's activities. This preliminary research also found that most of the respondents felt envious about what was happening on social media and sometimes they lied to boost their self-esteem. These activities are unhealthy and can lead to stress, even depression. After interviewing eight people, Moningka concluded that these individuals were quite happy with their self; however, when they accessed social media frequently, they felt that others were happier and luckier. They pretended like things were going well in their lives to boost their self-esteem. They mentioned that they felt happy for their friends and colleagues' accomplishments but because they did not experience the success themselves, they sometimes felt negative emotions. Subsequent research was conducted in 2018 by Moningka and Permatasari to determine the relationship between self-comparison and self-esteem. The study was conducted in Jakarta with 200 adolescents as respondent. The research found that there was a significant negative correlation between self-comparison and self-esteem. The more people do self-comparison, the more likely they are to have low self-esteem. In this case, the individuals will feel pressured if they continue to compare themselves with other individuals they consider better.These findings are consistent with a study carried out by Lyuborsky and Ross (1997). In their study, they found that unhappy people felt worse when paired with better performers. These unhappy people compared themselves with worse performers. Social media gives us a lot of chances to compare ourselves to others. We might do so unconsciously at first.

From this research, we can conclude that social media was important to their lives but could affect their emotions. These findings were similar to the results from a study conducted in Semarang, Central Java by Soliha (2015). In her research on 100 undergraduate students, Soliha (2015) found a positive correlation between social anxiety and dependence on social media. Vogel et al. (2014) also found that the individuals with more exposure to social media tended to evaluate themselves more poorly while average users reported more upward comparisons than downward social comparison. Comparisons on Facebook allow individuals to compare themselves on a variety of topics, including their looks or physical performance. From the research conducted by Moningka (2015), it was found that women tend to compare their activities and their performance to their Facebook friends' more than men. Furthermore, women were generally more curious about what their social media friends did in comparison to men. Sagioglou and Greitemeyer (2014) also found similar patterns, even though both genders experience negative moods resulting from their social comparisons. Fardouly, Diedrichs, Vartanian, and Halliwell (2015) found that women reported negative mood after brief exposure in Facebook than after exposure to an appearance-neutral website. In this case, it is very obvious that social media can influence the development of the self (Krayer, Ingledew, & Iphofen, 2008). This research also revealed that body dissatisfaction increases when individuals viewed or read appearance-focused material or were exposed to peer messages about thinness.

Sandra (2012) also explained that people try to get noticed or gain attention in cyberspace. Furthermore, people desire to be accepted through cyberspace as well by altering their names or profile updates to fit in with others. In another study, Vaswani (2012) explained that young people in Indonesia, especially in the big city or urban areas, use social media because it is one way for young Indonesians to feel connected to some of the more famous and powerful people. To be connected with someone famous might boost their self-esteem. These individuals identify themselves with the social figure they followed and sometimes they compared themselves with the social figure and adopted his or her way of thinking. It is similar to the concept of BIRGing (Basking in reflected glory). It refers to the tendency of individuals to associate themselves with the successful or famous person even though they are not related in the real world.

Teenagers and emerging adults are the highest social media users in Indonesia, and they are in a transition phase from children to adults that is characterized by changes in cognition, physical, and socio-emotional development (Santrock, 2011). Research conducted by Penter & Mehdizadeh on adolescents aged 13 to 19 years (cited by Charoensukmongkol, 2017) states that adolescents are the largest age group that uses social media to publish a positive self-image, to make a good impression, and to maintain their self-esteem. This makes it easier for adolescents to be vulnerable to conducting social comparisons (Tandoc in Charoensukmongkol, 2017) because teenage behavior is easily formed based on its social context, such as peers and parents who have a strong influence on their lives (Charoensukmongkol, 2017). Other studies conducted by Eisert & Kahle (2015) found that late adolescents (with an average age of 16 years) were more prone to social comparison because they compared their status to peers.

Self-esteem as the most vulnerable part of this social comparison can predict positive emotion, leading to happiness; however, when we frequently compare ourselves to others, we might feel dissatisfied with ourselves, leading to negative emotions and behaviors. In support of this conclusion, Vogel and colleagues (2014) found that frequent Facebook users believed that other users were happier and more successful than themselves. It appears that the people compared their realistic self with their idealized online selves. Kim and Lee (2011) explained that self-presentation on Facebook is reinforced by improvements in mood and self-esteem; social media in some ways can increase happiness, although social comparison is a mediator in the association between the use of Facebook and depressive symptoms.

The impact of exposure to activities shared on social media for other users is that it can be used as inspiration (for positive content; Triastuti, Prabowo, & Nurul, 2017); it can also can trigger jealousy, low life satisfaction (Krasnova in Sagioglou & Greitemeyer, 2014), and reduced positive mood (Greitemeyer, Mugge, & Bollermann in Sagioglou & Greitemeyer, 2014).

SOLUTIONS AND RECOMMENDATIONS

Indonesia has entered the era of industrial revolution. In this era, social media is very common and is needed in many ways. On the other hand, this borderless world causes individuals to easily access many things. Without realizing it, they can compare themselves with others. These activities can influence how individuals see and value themselves. Once self-comparison leads to negative outcomes, individuals can experience stress and poorer psychological well-being. In this case, there is a need to control the use of internet and social media. There has to be awareness that technology is needed for human welfare and not to harm other. Social media is not to blame, but rather how individuals can control themselves and use social media more wisely. So let's go digital and stay human!

REFERENCES

Andriani, I. (2016). *Model of cyberbullying behavior influenced by external and internal factors* (Doctoral Dissertation). University of Gunadarma, Jakarta, Indonesia.

Arakali, H. (2015). *Emerging Markets Like Indonesia, India Top US In Facebook Mobile Access.* Retrieved January 30, 2016 from http://www.ibtimes.com/emerging-markets-indonesia-india-top-us-facebook-mobile-access-1792686Bolt

Bolt, J. (2010, August 9). How to Wreck Your Self Esteem: Compare Yourself with Others. *Psychology Today*. Retrieved from http://www.psychologytoday.com/blog/your-zesty- self/201008/how-wreck-your-self-esteem-compare-youself-others

Bushman, B. J., Moeller, S. J., & Crocker, J. (2011). Sweets, sex or self-esteem? Comparing the calue of self-esteem boosts with other pleasant rewards. *Journal of Personality*, *79*(5), 993–1012. doi:10.1111/j.1467-6494.2011.00712.x PMID:21950264

Chapman, J., Turner, W., & Prochnow, J. (2000). Early reading related to performance, reading self-concept and the development of academic self-concept. *Journal of Educational Psychology*, *92*(4), 703–708. doi:10.1037/0022-0663.92.4.703

Davis, J. L. (2016). Identity theory in a digital age. In J. E. Stets & R. T. Serpe (Eds.), *New directions in identity theory and research*. Oxford University Press. doi:10.1093/acprof:oso/9780190457532.003.0006

Fardouly, J., Diedrichs, P. C., Vartanian, L. R., & Halliwell, E. (2015). Social comparison on social media: The impact of Facebook on young womans body image concern and mood. *Body Image*, *13*, 38–45. doi:10.1016/j.bodyim.2014.12.002 PMID:25615425

Foo, C. T. (2003). Child of the internet. *Cyberpsychology & Behavior*, *6*(2), 195–199. doi:10.1089/109493103321640392 PMID:12804032

Giordano, C., Wood, J. V., & Michela, J. L. (2000). Depressive personality style, dysphoria, and social comparison in everyday life. *Journal of Personality and Social Psychology*, *79*(3), 438–451. doi:10.1037/0022-3514.79.3.438 PMID:10981845

Hardy. (2016). *8 jenis sosial media dan perkembangannya*. Retrieved from: https://www.progresstech.co.id/blog/jenis-sosial-media/

Jackson, L. A., Zhao, Y., Witt, E. A., Fitzgerald, H. E., Von Eye, A., & Harold, R. (2009). Self-concept, self-esteem, gender, race, and information technology use. *Cyberpsychology & Behavior*, *12*(4), 437–440. doi:10.1089/cpb.2008.0286 PMID:19514819

Kaplan, A. M., & Haenlein, M. (2010). Users of the world, unite! The challenges and opportunities of Social Media. *Business Horizons*, *53*(1), 59–68. doi:10.1016/j.bushor.2009.09.003

Kemp, S. (2011). *Social, digital, and mobile in Indonesia*. Retrieved January 5, 2016 from http://weare-social.sg/blog/2011/12/social-digital-mobile-indonesia/

Kim, J., & Lee, J. R. (2011). The Facebook paths to happiness: Effects of the number Facebook friends and self-presentation on subjective well-being. *Cyberpsychology, Behavior, and Social Networking*, *14*(6), 359–364. doi:10.1089/cyber.2010.0374 PMID:21117983

Kimbrough, A. M., Guadagno, R. E., Muscanell, N. L., & Dill, J. (2013). Gender differences in mediated communication: Women connect more than do men. *Computers in Human Behavior*, *29*(3), 896–900. doi:10.1016/j.chb.2012.12.005

Krasnova, H., Wenninger, H., Widjaja, T., & Buxmann, P. (2013). Envy on Facebook: A Hidden Threat to Users' Life Satisfaction? *Wirtschaftsinformatik Proceedings 2013*. Retrieved from http:// www.ara.cat/tecnologia/facebook_ARAFIL20130128_0001.pdf

Krayer, A., Ingledew, D. K., & Iphofen, R. (2008). Social comparison and body image in adolescence: A grounded theory approach. *Health Education Research*, *23*(5), 892–903. doi:10.1093/her/cym076 PMID:18156148

Lyubormirsky, S., & Ross, L. (1997). Hedonic consequences of social comparison: A contrast of happy and unhappy people. *Journal of Personality and Social Psychology*, *73*(6), 1141–1157. doi:10.1037/0022-3514.73.6.1141 PMID:9418274

Mazzoni, E., & Zanazzi, L. (2014). Comparing the use of SNSs among adults and emerging adults. Journal of e-Learning and knowledge. *Society*, *10*(3), 25–36.

Moningka, C. (2015). *The use of social media in Jakarta. Unpublished research.* Jakarta: Gunadarma University.

Moningka, C., & Permatasari, R. E. (2018). *The effect of social comparison on self-esteem*. Unpublished manuscript. Tangerang Selatan: Universitas Pembangunan Jaya.

Myers, D. G., & Twenge, J. M. (2013). Social psychology (11th ed.). New York: McGraw-Hill.

Sagioglou, C., & Greitemeyer, T. (2014). Facebooks emotional consequences: Why Facebook causes a decrease in mood and why people still use it. *Computers in Human Behavior, 35*, 359–363. doi:. chb.2014.03.003 doi:10.1016/j

Samakow, J. (2013). *Japan Internet 'Fasting Camps' Aim to Treat Screen-Addicted Kids*. Retrieved January, 8, 2016 from http://www.huffingtonpost.com/2013/08/28/japan-internet-fasting-camp_n_3824697.html

Sanderson, C. A. (2010). *Social psychology*. New York: John Wiley & Sons, Inc.

Sandra, L. (2012). *The dynamics interaction of psychological self-concept and on-line identity* (Unpublished Doctoral Dissertation). University of Gajah Mada, Yogyakarta.

Setyawan, D. (2014). *KPAI ingatkan orang tua: waspadai kejahatan seksual pada anak melalui media sosial.* Retrieved, January, 8, 2016 from http://www.kpai.go.id/berita/kpai-ingatkan-orang-tua-waspadai-kejahatan-seksual-pada-anak-melalui-media-sosial/

Smith, R. H., & Kim, S. H. (2007). Comprehending envy. *Psychological Bulletin, 133*(1), 46–64. doi:10.1037/0033-2909.133.1.46 PMID:17201570

Soliha, S. F. (2015). Tingkat ketergantungan pengguna media sosial dan kecemasan sosial. *Jurnal Interaksi, 4*(1), 1–10.

Srivastava, R., & Joshi, S. (2014). Relationship between self-concept and self-esteem in adolescent. *Journal of Advanced Research, 2*(2), 36–43.

Stapel, D. A., & Blanton, H. (2004). From seeing to being: Subliminal social comparison affect implicit and explicit self-evaluation. *Journal of Personality and Social Psychology, 87*(4), 468–481. doi:10.1037/0022-3514.87.4.468 PMID:15491272

Steers, M. N., Wickham, R. E., & Acitelli, L. K. (2014). Seeing everyone elses highlight reels: How Facebook usage is linked to depressive symptoms. *Journal of Social and Clinical Psychology, 33*(8), 701–731. doi:10.1521/jscp.2014.33.8.701

Swallow, S. R., & Kuiper, N. A. (1992). Mild depression and frequency of social comparison behavior. *Journal of Social and Clinical Psychology, 11*(2), 167–180. doi:10.1521/jscp.1992.11.2.167

Uhlir, J. L. (2016). Social comparison and self-presentation on social media of depressive symptoms. *Scripps Senior Theses Paper 756*. Retrieved, August 18, 2016 from http://scolarship.claremont.edu/scripps_theses/756

Vaswani, K. (2012). *Indonesia's love affair with social media*. Retrieved, January 8, 2016 from http://www.bbc.com/news/world-asia-17054056

Vogel, E. A., Rose, J. P., Roberts, L. R., & Eckles, K. (2014). Social comparison, social media, and self-esteem. *Psychology of Popular Media Culture, 3*(4), 206–222. doi:10.1037/ppm0000047

White, J. B., Langer, E. J., Yariv, L., & Welch, J. C. IV. (2006). Frequent social comparison and destructive emotions and behaviors: The dark side of social comparison. *Journal of Adult Development, 13*(1), 36–44. doi:10.100710804-006-9005-0

Chapter 13
The Onlife in Emerging Adulthood:
Experimentation, Exploration, and Change in the Digital Era

Martina Benvenuti
Istituto per le Tecnologie Didattiche (ITD), Italian National Research Council (CNR), Italy

Sara Giovagnoli
Department of Psychology, University of Bologna, Italy

Melanie Keep
https://orcid.org/0000-0001-9516-0303
Faculty of Health Sciences, The University of Sydney, Australia

Elvis Mazzoni
https://orcid.org/0000-0002-7258-5381
Department of Psychology, University of Bologna, Italy

Patrizia Selleri
Department of Psychology, University of Bologna, Italy

ABSTRACT

Internet revolutionized our lifestyle. New generation devices like smartphones and tablets allow us to be always connected: the web represents a significant part of our days. These epochal changes bring with them questions about the potentialities and the risks of web. This chapter introduces a research whose purpose is to investigate the Onlife during emerging adulthood divided into two groups—youngerEA (18-24) and olderEA (25-29)—considering both the problematic and the functional side of the use of the internet. Self-esteem, self-control, online and offline social support were considered as factor that influenced the internet use habits. Typology of social networks, time spent online, device used, and number of online contacts are considered. Results show significant differences between youngerEA and olderEA in the use of the web both in problematic and functional way.

DOI: 10.4018/978-1-7998-1063-6.ch013

INTRODUCTION

The Internet is an important part of our daily lives, and represents a basic tool for finding information, social interactions, and the consequent construction of knowledge (Frozzi & Mazzoni, 2011; Mazzoni & Zanazzi, 2014). The evolution of the Internet has been accompanied by, and it could be argued facilitated by, changes in the types of devices used to access the online world: tablets, laptops, and smartphones. These have transformed the ways in which people use the internet, where they do so from, and the people with whom they interact. Millions of people have chosen to engage with each other using virtual platforms, such as blogs, social networks, chat, and e-mail, sometimes in preference to interacting face to face, which generally requires more time and the geographical negotiation of the people involved (Lee & Cheung, 2014).

The integration between being online and offline is an important part of the psychology of human beings in current Western society (Turkle, 2012). In some cases, it is possible to find a balance between offline and online engagement that is functional for working, studying, and carry out daily activities. In other cases, though, people run the risk of pursuing behaviors that lead to problematic outcomes (Davis, 2001). These discussions about the outcomes of the online life are particularly relevant to emerging adults, as they navigate changing social networks, and explore and develop their own identity. The internet provides new and unique opportunities for identity creation and peer interactions that require further exploration. Particularly, in this chapter starting from the concepts described in the Onlife Manifesto (2015) we explored the factors involved in the use of the internet and web technologies during the emerging adulthood. To this end, we outline the current research into the impact of social media use on emerging adults, explore the ideas around functional and problematic Internet use, and discuss our own findings from a large online survey of internet use among emerging adults.

INTERNET USE DURING EMERGING ADULTHOOD: PROCESSES OF EXPERIMENTATION, EXPLORATION, AND CHANGE

Arnett (2000) defined emerging adulthood as being between 18-29 years with a particular focus on 18-25. He argues that this is a distinct life stage where (commonly) individuals are afforded greater freedom than adolescents (for example, with fewer parental constraints) without the same level of responsibilities as adulthood (for example, parenthood or a mortgage). Arnett describes emerging adulthood as being characterized by identity exploration, instability, self-focus, feeling in-between, and possibilities.

Identity exploration extends the process started in adolescence where young people experiment with love, work, and their worldviews. During emerging adulthood, individuals work towards achieving greater confidence in, and stability of, their romantic relationships (e.g. cohabitation, marriage), employment and study (focus on careers in contrast to casual or part time work for supplementary income), and worldviews (examining or re-examining beliefs learnt from families or exposed to through university/travel to form independent thoughts).

Emerging adulthood is also considered the age of instability by Arnett (2000). He writes that as part of their process of exploration, emerging adults are often changing residences, workplaces or roles and potentially romantic relationships. This leads to great instability in their daily lives. As a result of this process of exploration and instability, emerging adulthood is also described as the age of feeling in-between. People aged in their twenties perceive the process of becoming an adult as being gradual and so feel that their transition is gradual as well. As such, they report feeling neither adolescent nor adult.

Given the decisions that they are required to make independently, Arnett (2000) also conceptualizes emerging adulthood as being an age of self-focus, more so than other life stages. He explains that without parents, siblings, teachers to be accountable to in adolescence, or partners or mortgage lenders in adulthood, emerging adults have greater self-focus in daily lives. They are responsible for a range of decisions (without necessarily consulting family or friends) from what to eat for dinner or when to do laundry, to switching degrees/majors or ending a relationship. As these decisions about relationships, work, and worldviews have yet to be finalized, emerging adulthood is also seen as an age of possibilities. Emerging adults perceive the future as being open and hopeful with a range of different paths that they can take.

It is important to note that emerging adulthood sits between, and is distinct from both, adolescence and adulthood. Adolescence is catalyzed and (to an extent) characterized by physical changes such as the onset of puberty. Socially, adolescents are commencing their transition from relationships bounded to family and parents to those forged with peers. This period, however, is conceptualized as being more tumultuous than emerging adulthood where individuals are closer to decisions and focused more on stable conceptions of love and relationships, work, and worldviews. Adolescents are also likely to be experiencing greater parental influence/control than emerging adults.

Emerging adulthood is also neither adulthood nor young adulthood. The latter implies that adulthood has been reached, and this is not the case when considering societal markers of adulthood (for example, parenthood, established careers or home life) or the perceptions of people aged between 18-29 years. These individuals, however, are making more serious attempts and greater strides at adulthood than those during adolescence.

Why Is It Important to Study This Group?

Emerging adults are the largest users of social media, including social networking sites (SNSs) in America (Smith & Anderson, 2018), Australia (Sensis, 2018) the UK (Office for National Statistics, 2018) and Italy (Pew Research Center, 2018), where our data was collected. Social media is an umbrella term that consists of platforms that enable users to share content such as text, images, or videos. These include WhatsApp, Second Life, and Facebook. SNSs, in contrast, are a specific type of social media. SNSs allow users to create a profile with personalized content, share content with others and interact with their content, and build networks by connecting with others (Boyd & Ellison, 2007). Examples include Facebook, Instagram, and Snapchat.

Given their functionality, social media provides unique opportunities for developing and maintaining relationships (both existing offline ones and new online ones) and self-expression (Nadkarni & Hofmann, 2012). As emerging adulthood is characterized by exploring relationships and identity, and the greatest users of these tools, it is important to consider how social media is being used, and the outcomes of this use, among emerging adults.

Why Is It Important to Distinguish Between Younger and Older Emerging Adults?

As a transitional period (Arnett, 2000), emerging adulthood is characterized by a gradual change in the individual. Given this, the experiences of an individual at the start of this life stage is likely to be different to the individual who is towards the end of this life stage. For example, a 28-year-old person may have made more decisions about their relationships, work life, and worldviews than someone who is 18 years old. As such, research is needed to understand this process of transition and how digital technologies and online interactions affects emerging adults at the start and towards the end of this life stage.

Additionally, research suggests age differences in social media consumption even within the emerging adulthood life stage. For example, the Pew Research Centre found that Snapchat, Instagram and Twitter were more commonly used by Americans aged 18-24 years old than those in their late twenties (Smith & Anderson, 2018). This suggests a need to take a nuanced approach to understanding social media use in emerging adults by considering those at the start and towards the end of this life stage separately.

It is important to note, though, that despite evidence of adolescents and emerging adults being the highest users of digital technologies, that the assumptions around digital natives are incorrect. Young people, having grown up with technology, were assumed highly proficient users (certainly with superior technology skills to previous generations) who were disengaged with education systems that were "old-fashioned" and not technologically as exciting as what the young people were capable of (Bennett, Maton, & Kervin, 2008). This, however, has been found to be untrue (for a summary, see Corrin, Apps, Beckman, & Bennett, 2019). Technology use among adolescents and emerging adults is complex and contextual. Recent research, for example, has shown that while university students report confidence and competence in using common technologies (such as word-processing or video editing); they were not confidence in using those technologies in professional contexts (Lam et al., 2016). Therefore, in research and discourse about emerging adults, the incorrect assumptions about digital natives should be taken into account, and conclusions drawn with this understanding in mind.

OUTCOMES OF INTERNET USE

Recent media attention has sparked interest in the outcome of internet use for emerging adults. Discussions have used terms such as "addiction" and focused on negative experiences such as cyberbullying ("How children interact with digital media", 2019). The Internet, and social media, is framed as something for parents to protect their children from a potential source of predators and depressive symptoms. Although there is, some research to support this (Chang, et al., 2015), the findings regarding the impact of social media on the well-being of emerging adults is not consistent.

Take the research on depression and loneliness, for example. Studies into image sharing have found that greater Instagram use, especially when coupled with interactions with strangers, is linked with greater negative social comparison and depressive symptoms (Lup, Trub, & Rosenthal, 2015). Moreover, these negative effects of social media on mood seem to last for months after initial Instagram use. Frison and Eggermont (2017), for instance, found that frequency of browsing Instagram (but not frequency of posting images or liking others' posts) significantly and positively predicted severity of depressive mood seven months later. Other research has similarly shown that SNS use predicted loneliness among emerging adults (Lou, Yan, Nickerson, & McMorris, 2012).

In contrast, other research has shown no relationship between the time spent on Facebook and depressive symptoms (Jelenchick, Eickhoff, & Moreno, 2013), and others still found that Facebook use can decrease loneliness. Using an experimental design, Deters and Mehl (2013) randomly allocated either university students to an experimental condition (where they were asked to increase the number of status updates they made every day over seven days) or a control condition (no change to their current frequency of status updates). The researchers found that participants in the experimental condition reported less loneliness as a result of feeling more connected with their friends due to their increased posting. This benefit was not affected by the amount of feedback they received (i.e., number of comments on their status update). A recent meta-analysis examining literature on Facebook use and loneliness found that the most adequate explanation of the data was that people who are lonely use Facebook rather than the SNS making its users lonely (Song et al., 2014). This highlights the need to consider a more nuanced approach to understanding the outcomes of SNS use that considers motivations and user characteristics as potential factors for explaining why emerging adults feel the way they do after they use social media.

In addition, research is needed to consider both the positive and negative outcomes of using SNSs. Social media, at its core, is a tool aimed at building connections between individuals. Studies have shown that social media use has been linked to greater sense of connection among users (Grieve, Indian, Witteveen, Tolan, & Marrington, 2013), increased social support (Gaysynsky, Romansky-Poulin, & Arpadi, 2015), and reduced loneliness (Deters & Mehl, 2013). Therefore, it seems that social media use can lead to a range of well-being outcomes, but more research is needed to understand why. Additionally, research should include measures of positive and negative outcomes together. The studies cited above focused only on either positive or negative outcomes. By investigating the two together, researchers can begin to draw a more complete picture of the factors that affect what outcomes SNS users' experience. Some of this research has been done with adolescents (Anderson & Jiang, 2018), but more is needed to consider the emerging adulthood life stage, and to compare between people at the early and later parts of this developmental stage.

THEORETICAL BACKGROUND AND POTENTIAL EXPLANATIONS

In working towards a more holistic and nuanced understanding of the factors influencing social media use, and the outcomes of SNS interactions, researchers have explored the role of user motivation, particularly their need to belong, their self-esteem, and self-control.

The Uses and Gratifications (U&G) framework (Katz, 1973; Katz, Blumler, & Gurevitch, 1974) has been used to explore why people use social media. According to this model, users make active decisions about media use (from radio to television to the Internet) based on their individual needs, or gratifications. For example, some people use SNSs to build and maintain relationships, others use it to manage others' impressions of them, and others still use social media to document life events (Keep, Janssen, & Amon, 2019). Consequently, the ways in which individuals use social media will differ according to their motivations, and so the outcomes of their use will differ. For example, people who are motivated by a fear of missing out might share fewer posts than users using SNSs as an online archive of significant life events. In their original framing of the U&G model, Katz et al. (1974) also suggest that motivations could positively impact well-being if individuals feel their needs are met by the ways in which they are interacting with various media.

Relationships and Social Support

One recurring motivator for SNS use is the desire to belong, and to build and maintain relationships (Orchard, 2019). According to the belonging hypothesis (Baumeister & Leary, 1995), humans have an innate desire for interpersonal relationships, so they create and foster positive social interactions to achieve this goal. These ideas are also consistent with Maslow's hierarchy of needs (Maslow, 1954) where the need to belong and have fulfilling relationships are core to being human. Research has also shown that individuals who report feeling a stronger sense of belonging also report greater relationship and life satisfaction (Mellor, Stokes, Firth, Hayashi, & Cummins, 2008), higher self-esteem (Gailliot & Baumeister, 2007), and reduced loneliness (Masi, Chen, Hawkley, & Cacioppo, 2011).

Given this, people who perceive their offline interactions to be insufficient for fulfilling this need for belonging and positive relationships may go online to address this need. A recent study by Sheldon, Abad, and Hinsch (2011) suggests that this may be the case. The study found that first year university students who reported higher levels of perceived disconnectedness used Facebook more frequently, and in turn, this increased Facebook use increased students' sense of connection with peers. Similarly, offline loneliness has also been suggested as a cause for going online (Song et al., 2014). So, people who do not feel supported offline may turn to the Internet to fulfil their needs.

The role of offline support as a motivator for online interactions is particularly clear when observing online support communities for people with health concerns. They report accessing online support groups when their offline support is insufficient. This can include inadequate support from family/friends or existing networks, inappropriate services for their condition, or having a rare or stigmatised condition (Coulson, 2019). Research into offline support as a motivator for online behaviours, however, should also be explored in non-health related SNS interactions. For emerging adults, during this time of changing relationships and locations, exploration and transition, offline support may be inadequate. Also, there is limited understanding about the role of online support and how this may further entice emerging adults to use social media for support.

Self-Esteem

In the previous section, we describe the Internet as a space that can compensate for limitations in people's offline experiences. This is a variation of the Social Compensation hypothesis (Zywica & Danowski, 2008). Conceived to explore social interactions and popularity in SNSs, this hypothesis states that individuals who are limited offline will engage with others online to offset these limitations. So, according to this perspective, people with lower self-esteem offline will engage with social media to increase their self-esteem (Zywica & Danowski, 2008). An alternative view is the Social Enhancement, or rich-get-richer, hypothesis. According to this view, those who benefit socially offline will have their benefits increased online. For example, an individual who has more self-esteem offline than their friends will continue to have more self-esteem online.

Self-esteem refers to an individual's perceived self-worth and value (Rosenberg, 1985), and individuals with high self-esteem report greater confidence, independence, autonomy, and positivity compared to individuals with low self-esteem (Zywica & Danowski, 2008). Research has suggested that people with higher self-esteem seek to enhance it, and people with lower self-esteem seek to compensate for it (Tice, 1993). Regarding social media usage, studies exploring self-esteem have yielded mixed results. Some suggested that high self-esteem predicted less time on Facebook (Kalpidou, Costin, & Morris,

2011), while others found that high self-esteem predicted more Facebook use, even to the extent of addictive tendencies (Wilson, Fornasier, & White, 2010). Other studies still found no relationship between self-esteem and Facebook usage (Hong, Huang, Lin, & Chiu, 2014; Krämer & Winter, 2008). Further research is required to understand how self-esteem interacts with other motivators to predict social media use more generally, as well as the outcomes of this use. Though research into self-esteem as a predictor of social media use is mixed, as a construct, self-esteem may allow researchers to develop a more nuanced understanding of why some users experience positive outcomes and why others do not.

Self-Control

Self-control, sometimes referred to in the computer-mediated communication literature as self-regulation, is conceptualized as the conscious effort to monitor and react to stimuli (Bandura, 1991). To date, it has been studied primarily in the context of negative internet use. For example, Khang, Kim, and Kim (2013) surveyed university students on their self-control, immersion while using the Internet, and videogame, Internet, and mobile "addiction". The researchers found that self-control significantly and negatively predicted higher scores on each of the three addiction scales. This suggested that as users lose control over their use of digital technologies, they may more likely engage in extreme usage with potentially adverse outcomes.

It is possible, though, that self-control may influence positive outcomes for social media use. For example, if emerging adults use the internet to build and maintain fulfilling relationships, they may engage in deliberately engage in positive interactions with others. So, having high self-control may lead to the benefits that come with positive relationships with others. This, however, requires further investigation. Research is needed to explore the potential impact of self-control on positive outcomes of social media use.

THE CURRENT STUDY

Emerging adults are at a critical life stage where they explore and experiment with changing relationships, world views, and work arrangements. People currently in this age group (18-29 year olds) are also high users of digital technologies. With social media being designed to foster and maintain relationships, these tools provide a unique opportunity for understanding the intersection between personal characteristics and motivation (specifically, social support, self-esteem, and self-control) and SNS use among younger (18-24) and older emerging adults (25-29). This study addresses these research gaps by exploring the following questions:

1. How do emerging adults use social media and the Internet?
2. How do factors such as self-esteem, online and offline social support, self-control, influence the use of the Internet in positive and negative ways?
3. Does the relationship between self-esteem, social support and self-control, and internet use differ between younger and older emerging adults?

Method

An online questionnaire, hosted on Qualtrics, was designed to answer the previous research questions. The questionnaire was promoted on the main social networking websites such as Facebook, Youtube, and LinkedIn.

The regional ethics committee of the University of Bologna approved the research protocol and all participants provided their informed consent. The research was carried out in accordance with The Code of Ethics of the World Medical Association (Declaration of Helsinki).

Materials and Procedure

Sample Description

A total sample of 817 Italian subjects (mean age=21.56; SD=3.15), 506 females and 31 males completed the survey. Of this, 657 subjects were classified as Younger Emerging Adults (407 females and 250 males, aged between 18 and 24 years; mean age=20.32; SD=2.01) and 160 classified as Late Emerging Adults (99 females and 61 males, aged between 25 and 29 years old; mean age=26.64; SD=1.34).

Measures

The questionnaire included the following subsections: (1) demographic measures, (2) device used, (3) time spent online, (4) number of online contacts, (5) Onlife measures.

Demographic Measures

Participants responded to questions regarding their gender, age, nationality, country of residence, profession, educational qualification and relationship status. In this chapter we report the demographics measures for describing the internet use habits.

Device Used

The respondents indicated which devices they used to access the internet. Options included smartphone, tablet and computer.

Time Spent Online

The respondents are asked to indicate how many hours per day they spent online.

Number of Online Contacts

Three questions in the questionnaire concern the number of online contacts that refers to acquaintances (i.e. those with whom you do not interact regularly, online or in everyday life) and refers to friends (i.e. those with whom you usually interact, beyond simply knowing them, online and in everyday life) are included.

Onlife Measures

General Self-Esteem was measured using the Rosenberg Self-Esteem Scale (Rosenberg, 1965). The scale has been translated and validated in different languages; including Italian, which is utilized in the current research. The scale is composed of 10-points Likert-scale items with 5 points each.

The Social Support was measured using the Offline Social Support Scale created by Wang and Wang (2013) and adapted by Leung and Lee (2005). Participants rate items on a 5-point Likert scale. Additionally, the Offline Social Support Scale was adapted to measure the Online Social Support.

Self-control was measured using the Brief Self-control Scale by Tangey, Baumeister, and Boone (2004), and re-validated by Maloney, Grawitch, and Barber (2012). Participants respond to items about their self-control on a 5-point Likert scale. The two authors through exploratory and confirmatory factor analysis individuated two different dimensions of the self-control: restraint and impulsivity. According to the scholars these two dimensions have different impact on the outcomes of self-control.

Problematic Internet use (PIU) was measured using the Generalized Problematic Internet Use Scale 2 (Caplan, 2010), consisting of 15 7-point Likert items. The definition of problematic use was preferred over concepts related to pathological addiction since it included a wider range of experiences and it is closer to the experience of the users. The theoretical background on which the PIU scale is based is the cognitive-behavioral theory of Davis (2001). The scale was validated in Italian by Fioravanti, Primi, and Casale (2013).

Finally, a brief functional internet use (FIU) scale was specifically created for this study. The scale was named Web Useful and is composed of 4 items: (1) "being connected increases my ability to reach certain goals", (2) "being connected improves my productivity", (3) "being connected is useful for carrying out my activities", (4) "being connected improves my performances". It is measured on a 7-point Likert scale from 1= strongly disagree to 7= strongly agree.

Results

Emerging Adults' Use of Social Media: Differences Between OlderEA and YoungerEA

The first research question sought to understand how emerging adults are using technology and the Internet, and whether there are differences between the use of these tools among OlderEA and YoungerEA. Results showed that 91.2% (n=745) of the subjects declare to own a smartphone (92.1% of YoungerEA and 87.5% of OlderEA), 24.4% (n=199) have a tablet (23.6% of YoungerEA and 27.5% of OlderEA) and 95.1% (n=777) have a personal computer (95% of YoungerEA and 95.6% of OlderEA).

All participants who reported owning a specific device were asked to indicate on average how many hours a day they spend connected with each device. Figure 1 summarises the differences between YoungerEA and OlderEA on the time spent on devices. On average, OlderEA (M=8.9h, SD=7.5h) spend more time connected with the smartphone compared to YoungerEA (M=8.3h, SD=6.7h). OlderEA (M=5.6h, SD=4.2h) also spend more time on computers than YoungerEA (M=3.8, SD=3.6). In contrast, OlderEA spend less time on tablets (2.0h, SD=2.0h) compared with YoungerEA (M=2.8, SD=3.8h). This could be due to the fact that most OlderEA are already involved in working contexts, in which computers are the most important devices to connect, while many YoungerEA are in majority connected to the university in which smartphone and tablet are the most used.

Figure 1. Connection time (hours) declared by the YoungerEA group and OlderEA group by means the use of Smartphone, Tablet and PC. Histograms represent means, Error bars represent standard deviation

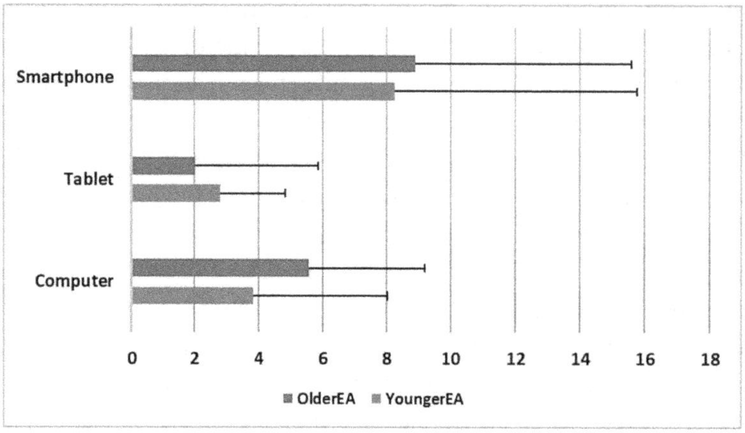

Figure 2 summarises the number of the Online friends and the Online Acquaintances that OlderEA and YoungerEA have. YoungerEA report both more Online friends (n=87,4, SD=153,1) and more Online Acquaintances (n=656,9, SD=1015,4) than OlderEA (Friends=56,8; SD=72,1; Acquaintances =542,6; SD=773,7). This seems to reflect the transitions that emerging adults are experiencing, and the changes that occur even within this life stage. YoungerEA are starting to construct their future and are living in a period characterized by many changes in their life, particularly residential changes that come from going to university or being independent from family. Thus, online friends and acquaintances, i.e., their social capital, is particularly important to face up to these changes. For OlderEA, who are living a phase of construction of their professional identity and probably have already face up with many changes, it is more important selecting acquaintances and friends to have a stronger professional impact and more stable friendship groups.

Figure 3 shows the most commonly used application during the day (directly from the web or in mobile App version) Emerging Adults mostly use Facebook (90,8%) and WhatsApp (82,3%) followed by

Figure 2. Number of Online Friends and Online Acquaintances declared by the YoungerEA group and OlderEA group. Histograms represent means, Error bars represent standard deviation.

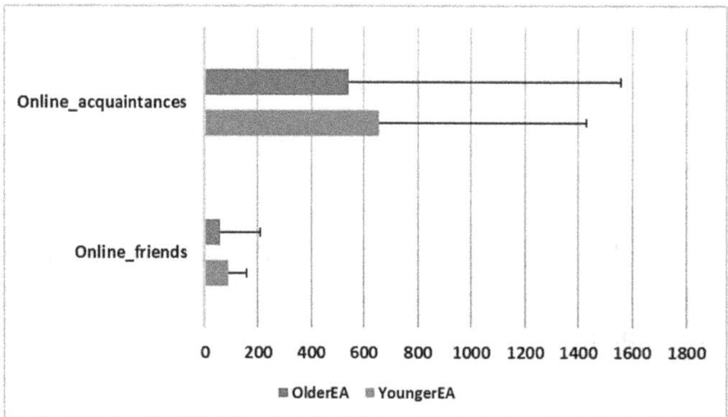

Figure 3. Web tools used during the day by the YoungerEA group and OlderEA group. Histograms represent percentage of subjects that declare to use the different tools

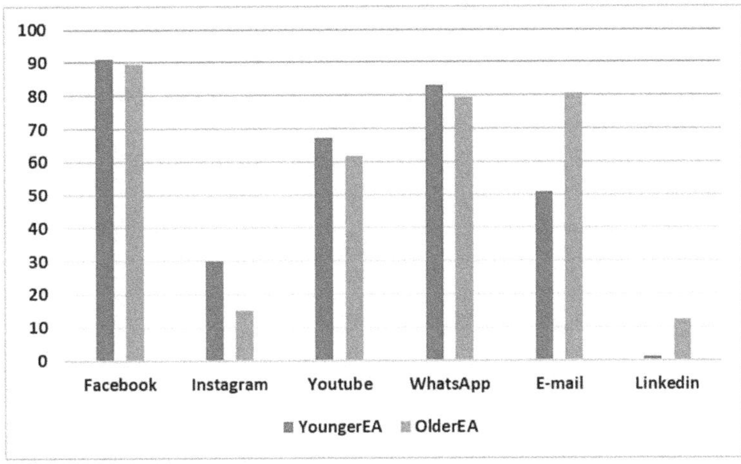

the use of YouTube (66,2%) and E-mail (56,7%). Instagram (27,1%) and LinkedIn (3,4%) are used less commonly. As can be seen from figure 3, the YoungerEA report a greater use of social media compared to OlderEA, except for E-mail and LinkedIn, which is mostly used by the OlderEA.

The greater use of the latter two applications by OlderEA could be linked to the fact that they are mainly used in the working world, for professional tools to look for work or for communications/exchanges of work materials. The different phase of life of YoungerEA and OlderEA are well described by their used of applications. While Facebook and WhatsApp are similarly used by the two groups, as described before, OlderEA are the ones who mostly use applications connected to working contexts, such as e-mail and LinkedIn, while YoungerEA are more connected to those applications related to leisure time, such as Instagram and YouTube.

Figures 4 and 5 show the differences in time spent using different social media for recreational and work/study purposes, respectively, among older and younger emerging adults. No significant difference can be observed in time spent using the web tools between YoungerEA and OlderEA. However, it is interesting to note that the application that is mostly used is WhatsApp for both YoungerEA and OlderEA, showing a percentage of subjects who use the application more than 10 hours per day equal to 11% for the YoungerEA and equal to 8% for the OlderEA. Perhaps unsurprisingly, LinkedIn is the least used application in leisure time for both YoungerEA and OlderEA.

Figure 5 presents the distribution of the time spent using the different web tools during work or study time. Again, no significant differences can be observed in time spent using the web tools between YoungerEA and OlderEA. However, as for the time-distribution concerning work or study time, LinkedIn remains the least used application for both YoungerEA and OlderEA. WhatsApp is the most used application for both YoungerEA and OlderEA, showing a percentage of subjects who use the application more than 10 hours per day equal to 11% for the YoungerEA, and equal to 7% for the OlderEA (very similar to the percentages identified in leisure time). Instagram is used less during work/study time compared to recreational time: 88% of OlderEA use Instagram less than 1 hour a day and only the 12% use it for a time between 1 and 3 hours while the 83% of YoungerEA use Instagram for less than 1 hour, 14% between 1 and 3 hours and only the 3% use it a time between 3 and 7 hours.

Figure 4. Time distribution spent Online with the different web tools during free time declared by OlderEA and Younger EA. Different colors represent different time-range chosen by the subjects in percentage

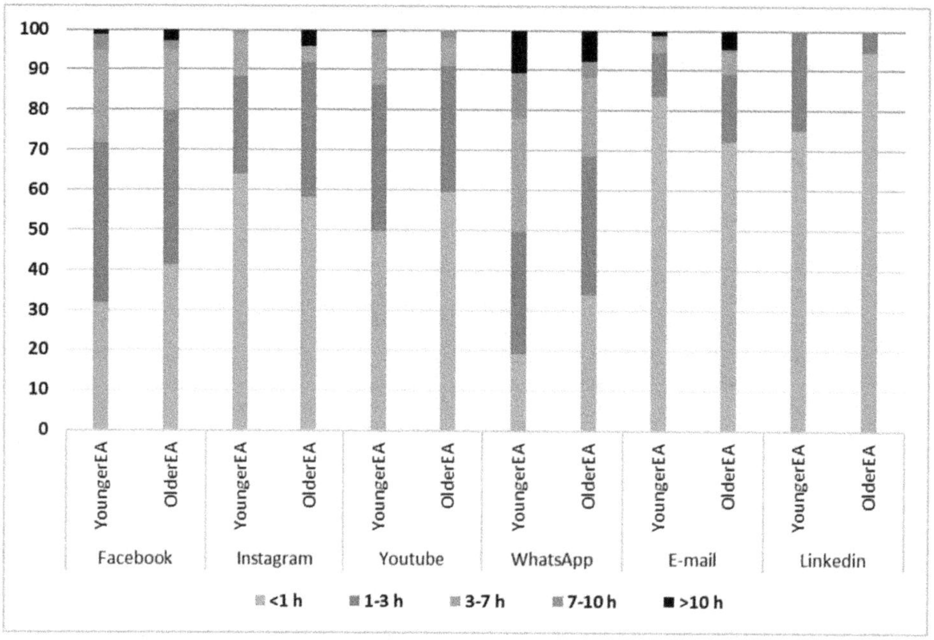

Factors Influencing Functional and Problematic Internet Use

The next component of the study explored the role of subjective factors, such as social support perceived both in the online life and in the offline life, self-esteem and self-control, in influencing the functional and problematic Internet use. To analyze if and in which way the four factors listed above predict the FIU (Functional Internet Use) and PIU (Problematic Internet Use) a Multiple Regression Analysis was applied. Results show a general significant influence of the Online SS ($F_{(2,807)}$=44.528; *p<.01*), Offline SS ($F_{(2,807)}$=31.40; *p<.01)*, Self-control ($F_{(2,807)}$=53.63; *p<.01)* and Self-esteem ($F_{(2,807)}$=17.16; *p<.01)* on the Internet use (both Problematic and Functional).

By analysing the relation between the different factors and the FIU, we found that Online SS and self-esteem significantly predicts FIU in a positive way (see table 1). Therefore, it appears that a perception of high Online Social Support, as well as high levels of self-esteem predict higher levels of functional use of the Internet. In contrast, perceived offline social support significantly and negatively predicted FIU (see table 1). This result indicates that the greater the Offline social support perceived and the less functional the use of the internet will be, so the lower the Offline SS the more the use of internet will be functional (Lower Offline SS predict higher FIU levels). Self-control does not appear to be a significant predictor of the FIU.

Results of the multiple regression analysis showed that Offline social support, Self-esteem and Self-control significantly and negatively predict PIU. Participants who report higher Self-esteem reported lower scores on problematic Internet use, as well as high Self-control and high level of Offline SS predict low PIU. Conversely, the higher the perception of the subject is Online Social Support, the higher the level of Problematic Internet Use.

Figure 5. Time distribution spent Online with the different web tools during work or study time declared by OlderEA and Younger EA. Different colors represent different time-range chosen by the subjects in percentage

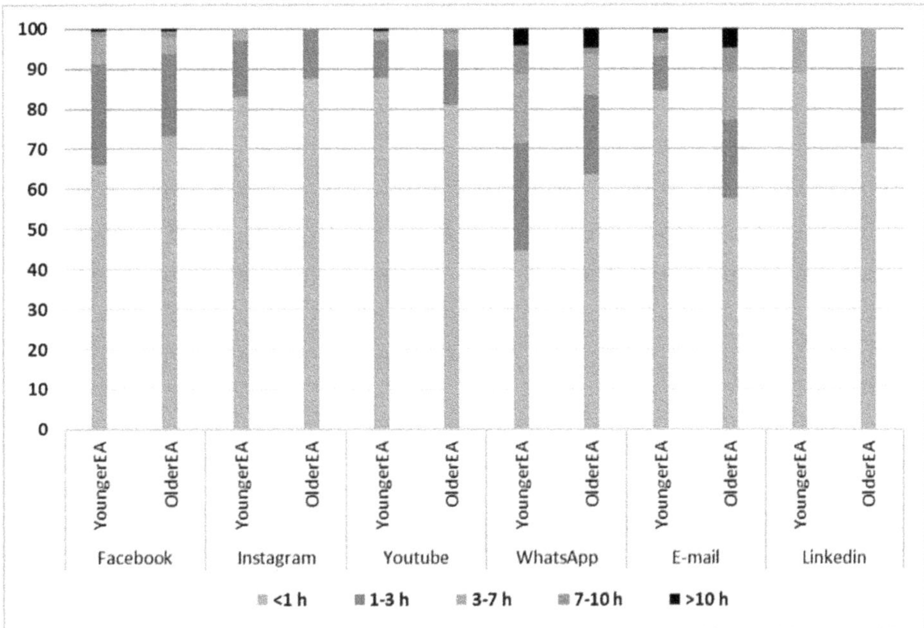

Finally, a Multivariate Analysis of Variance was used to analyze the differences between males and females, and between YoungerEA and OlderEA on the Problematic Internet use, The Functional Internet use and on the factors related to the use of Internet (Online and Offline Social Support, Self-control and Self-esteem). In addition, the interaction effect gender by age has been analyzed on the same dependent variables.

Table 1. Multiple Regression Analysis conducted by means of GLM procedure, dependent variable: Functional Internet Use (FIU) and Problematic Internet Use (PIU). Due to some missing data, 813 subjects compose the total sample included in this analysis (n=813)

		B	*SE*	*t*
FIU	Online SS	.87	.21	4.12**
	Offline SS	-1.42	.29	-4.84**
	Self-control	.02	.03	.77
	Self-esteem	.25	.07	3.65**
PIU	Online SS	5.40	.59	9.10**
	Offline SS	-5.81	.83	-7.05**
	Self-control	-.85	.09	-10.04**
	Self-esteem	-.73	.19	-3.86**

Note *p < .05 **p < .01

As shown in table 2, a significant gender main effect and a significant age main effect was found. There was no significant interaction effect of gender by age.

Regarding gender, males showed significantly higher PIU and of FIU compared to the females, while the females show a significantly greater Offline Social Support than the males. No significant gender differences has been found regarding Online Social Support, Self-control and Self-esteem (see figure 6).

Table 2. Multivariate Analysis of Variance conducted by means of GLM procedure, dependent variables: PIU, FIU, OnlineSS, OfflineSS, Self-control and self-esteem; factors: gender and age (n=813)

Gender	$F_{(6,804)}$=***11.68*****		Females (*mean±SE)*	Males (*mean±SE)*
PIU	$F_{(1,809)}$=7.00**		38,87±1.07	43,45±1.36
FIU	$F_{(1,809)}$=24.35**		13,58±.32	16,15±.41
Online SS	$F_{(1,809)}$=2.67		3,12±.06	2,96±.07
Offline SS	$F_{(1,809)}$=40.64**		4,08±.04	3,64±.05
Self-control	$F_{(1,809)}$=2.12		43,36±.41	42,40±.52
Self-esteem	$F_{(1,809)}$=.15		21,85±.19	21,97±.24
Age	$F_{(6,804)}$=***9.45*****		*YoungerAE (mean±SE)*	OlderAE *(mean±SE)*
PIU	$F_{(1,809)}$=9.40**		43,82±.77	38,50±1.55
FIU	$F_{(1,809)}$=24.15**		13,59±.23	16,14±.47
Online SS	$F_{(1,809)}$=6.51*		3,16±.04	2,92±.08
Offline SS	$F_{(1,809)}$=1.20		3,90±.03	3,82±.06
Self-control	$F_{(1,809)}$=15.87**		41,57±.29	44,20±.59
Self-esteem	$F_{(1,809)}$=10.91**		21,41±.14	22,42±.27
Gender*Age	$F_{(6,804)}$=***.47***		Females *(mean±SE)*	Males *(mean±SE)*
PIU	$F_{(1,809)}$=.38	YoungerAE	40,99±.95	46,65±1.21
		OlderAE	36,75±1.92	40,26±2.44
FIU	$F_{(1,809)}$=.03	YoungerAE	12,26±.28	14,92±.36
		OlderAE	14,91±.58	17,38±.73
OnlineSS	$F_{(1,809)}$=.24	YoungerAE	3,26±.05	3,06±.07
		OlderAE	2,97±.10	2,87±.13
OfflineSS	$F_{(1,809)}$=.32	YoungerAE	4,10±.04	3,70±.05
		OlderAE	4,06±.08	3,58±.10
Self-control	$F_{(1,809)}$=.58	YoungerAE	42,30±.36	40,84±.46
		OlderAE	44,42±.73	43,97±.93
Self-esteem	$F_{(1,809)}$=.31	YoungerAE	21,26±.17	21,55±.21
		OlderAE	22,44±.34	22,39±.43

Note *p < .05 **p < .01

Figure 6. Difference between Females and Males on PIU, FIU, Self-control, Self-esteem, OnlineSS and OfflineSS

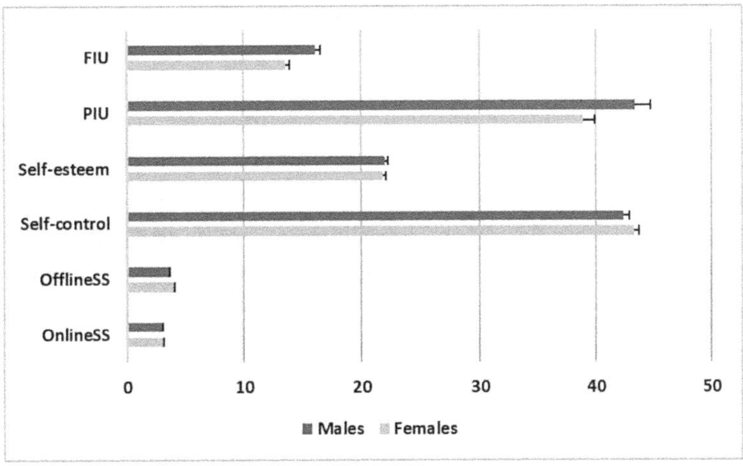

YoungerEA reported higher scores in PIU and in Online Social Support and lower FIU, Self-control and Self-esteem levels compared to OlderEA. No significant difference were found for the offline social support (see figure 7).

No interaction effect of age by gender was found for the different aspects related to the internet use. This result shows that males and females do not change their behavior in the functional or problematic use of Internet or in the factors associated with it as a function of their age change, or considering the transition between one age group and another (see table 2).

Figure 7. Difference between YoungerEA and OlderEA on PIU, FIU, Self-control, Self-esteem, OnlineSS and OfflineSS

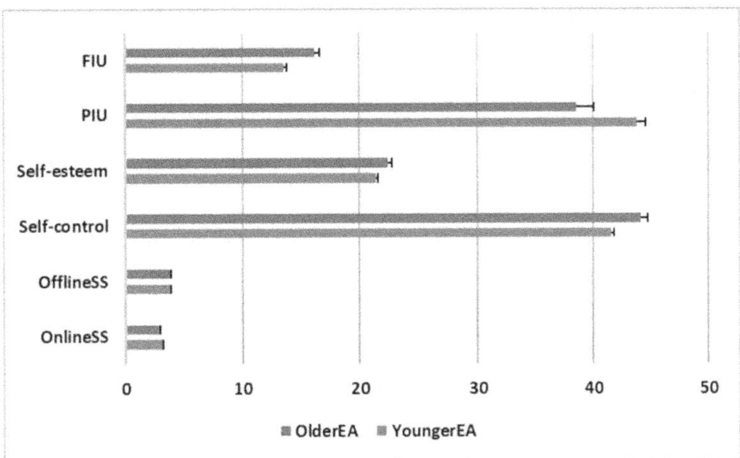

Results Interpretation

This study confirmed previous findings that showed emerging adults to be frequent users of social media (Smith & Anderson, 2018). It was also found that OlderEA and YoungerEA differed in their use of different social media platforms. For example, a greater number of OlderEA participants used e-mail and LinkedIn compared to YoungerEA participants. This is likely to reflect the fact that OlderEA are moving towards more stable careers (in contrast to frequent changes in jobs in YoungerEA), and these are tools more commonly associated with work and professional networks. The Uses and Gratifications framework can also be applied here. As OlderEA participants are more established in professions, they may be more likely to use email in the workplace and engage with LinkedIn as they build their professional profiles. YoungerEA participants, on the other hand, may not be motivated by careers in the same way, or have jobs that require the use of email and so will use these tools less frequently.

The second part of this study focused on factors that predicted PIU and FIU among participants. It was found that Online social support, Offline social support, Self-control and Self-esteem are factors that can significantly predict PIU and FIU levels. Specifically, participants with higher Self-esteem were more likely to engage in functional internet use, and less likely to engage in problematic use.

With regard to Social Support, it is important to note that a high Online Social Support predicted both high PIU and FIU. In other words, participants who report feeling supported online both engaged in functional Internet use (i.e. feeling productive and purposeful online) and problematic Internet use (i.e. excessive Internet use that interferes with offline relationships). This may be because positive online social support is self-reinforcing, and dependent on the nature of the online support. For example, participants may feel supported by a productive and positive group that encourages prosocial behaviour. The positive interactions with others in this group would lead to more functional Internet use. On the other hand, if the online social support focuses too much on the online community or encourages the individual to ignore their offline commitments, then the person might still perceive high online social support but engage in problematic Internet use.

A similar phenomenon is observed for the Offline Social Support. Offline social support is negatively linked both to FIU and PIU. High perceived offline social support predicted reduced functional Internet use and reduced problematic Internet use. This finding partially supports the rich-get-richer or Social Enhancement perspective where users who perceive a lack of support offline may choose to engage more in online communities and pay less attention to their offline commitments. Individuals may search Online for what is missing in his real life. The increase in Internet use, and the increasing needs of Internet, could lead to a dysfunctional Internet use but, paradoxically, could contribute to improve the correct and functional use of the social media as a place where the subject finds rewarding answers to social needs. On the other hand, the finding can also be explained by the Social Compensation hypothesis. Here, users who perceive their offline support to be insufficient or unsatisfactory so turn to the online world for support and more positive engagement.

One potential explanation for these findings is self-control. In this study, it was found that participants with high self-control are less at risk to develop problematic internet use. In combination with the above findings about online and offline social support, this suggests that self-control is the factor that determines whether perceived social support will lead to problematic or functional Internet use. Perhaps users with higher self-control remember their offline responsibilities and can better manage their online experiences, even when these experiences are very positive. This may also be related to the Uses and Gratifications explanation. Users with higher self-control may have more needs for positive and functional Internet use, whereas users with lower self-control may be focussing on their need for enjoyment. In this way, users focussed on enjoyment may more likely continue engaging with the Internet even when it is interfering with their offline life. Further research on the exact needs or gratifications of emerging adults, and how these relate to perceptions of online and offline social support, is needed.

Of note, it is also important to state that these findings suggest that PIU and FIU are not the two poles of a same scale, but two separated aspects of the use of the Web. Both seem to be affected by perceived online and offline social support in the same way which suggests that they may be distinct constructs. It is important then, for research to consider these two variables distinctly and not just test one and make assumptions about the other.

SOLUTIONS AND RECOMMENDATIONS

Although much research has highlighted the negative impact of online life on human development (i.e. Caplan, 2005; Davis, 2001), studies have also found that online life has a positive effect on the offline one (Ellison, Steinfield & Lampe, 2007; Benvenuti, Mazzoni, & Piobbico, 2016; Mazzoni & Iannone, 2014; Mazzoni, Baiocco, Cannata & Dimas, 2016). The results described in this chapter show which factors and relationships can be influenced in order to prevent PIU on the one hand, and to promote FIU on the other. Concerning its theoretical implications, this research has partly filled a gap in literature which has thus far been excessively unbalanced towards PIU. Indeed, the results regarding FIU show how the Internet (and its applications) could represent a tool to support activities for both youngerEA and olderEA. In this regard, social support online and offline and the number of online contacts plays an important role for younger emerging adults in facing life's challenges and changes, such as moving to another city to study or for work. Moreover, concerning the practical implications for emerging adults, these results could help universities, companies and traditional job search channels (e.g. employment agencies), to further promote informal information dissemination tools (e.g. pages on SNSs), compared to traditional institutional/professional media (e.g. company website, university website). This should have the aim of raising awareness about a more informed use and warning people against the possible risks deriving from a dysfunctional use of the Internet.

FUTURE RESEARCH DIRECTIONS

Future research must clarify a number of concepts which have only been touched upon in this study and which could further explore certain issues suggested by the theoretical framework and empirical results. For a better understanding of Internet use, studies should be conducted in different cultural, social, and economic contexts to investigate the connections between the factors involved: self-control, online social-support, offline social-support and self-esteem. Moreover, the findings from this study revealed differences between youngerEA and olderEA in Italy. It would be very interesting to compare the differences between age groups in different cultures. In addition, future researchers should better analyze the relationships which are strictly related to the concept of FIU in greater depth as it is still limited in literature, and try to develop a suitable tool for identifying the dynamics and behaviors that lead emerging adults, both Younger and Older, to a functional use of the Internet and Web applications/tools.

CONCLUSION

The chapter aimed to fill a gap in the studies dealing with the understanding of the relationship in the emerging adult's onlife. In this regard, the main goal is to focus the attention not only on understanding factors that determine a problematic use of the Internet, but also on those factors that allow emerging adults to achieve the developmental and career goals that characterize their daily activities. This perspective, that was born into the wider field of positive psychology (Riva et al., 2012), could have important implications to improve the effectiveness of certain human functions in everyday contexts, thanks to the attention placed on the awareness of the negative and positive aspects of the Internet.

Nonetheless, this study presents three limitations: sample limitations, structural limitations and theoretical limitations. The sample limitations are a direct consequence of the data collection method. Although the number of participants is high for statistical purposes it is not representative of the large and diverse population to which it refers. The channels used (principally social networking sites) allowed to reach mainly the researchers' contacts and the contacts of researchers' contacts, limiting the study to those people belonging to middle/high social class, highly educated, and with good ability in the use of technology. The presence of students is much higher than it would have been for a random sample.

Structural limitations are due to the very nature of the phenomenon studied. Internet is a huge thing; it has entered in the life of most people pervasively, and in many different aspects. Moreover, internet changes at an extremely high rate, and online there is already who is talking about a web 3.0 - still more personalized and based on semantic - that will replace in few years web 2.0. Faced this incredible speed of changes, the research in general, and the psychology in particular, have to run very fast and, until now, they have always been some steps behind. Anyway, the psychological research of the last 15 years converges on the importance of some variables like self-control and self-esteem to predict the dysfunctional use of the web. We can ask, in the future, for a better collaboration between software engineers, web sociologists and cyber-psychologists to study the new changes that will occur in the web before they become obsolete.

REFERENCES

Arnett, J. J. (2000). Emerging adulthood: A theory of development from the late teens through the twenties. *The American Psychologist, 55*(5), 469–480. doi:10.1037/0003-066X.55.5.469 PMID:10842426

Bandura, A. (1991). Social cognitive theory of self-regulation. *Organizational Behavior and Human Decision Processes, 50*(2), 248–287. doi:10.1016/0749-5978(91)90022-L

Baumeister, R. F., & Leary, M. R. (1995). The need to belong: Desire for interpersonal attachments as a fundamental human motivation. *Psychological Bulletin, 117*(3), 497–529. doi:10.1037/0033-2909.117.3.497 PMID:7777651

Bennett, S., Maton, K., & Kervin, L. (2008). The 'digital natives' debate: A critical review of the evidence. *British Journal of Educational Technology, 39*(5), 775–786. doi:10.1111/j.1467-8535.2007.00793.x

Benvenuti, M., Mazzoni, E., & Piobbico, G. (2016). Being Online in Emerging Adulthood: Between Problematic or Functional. In *Identity, Sexuality, and Relationships among Emerging Adults in the Digital Age*. Hershey, PA: IGI Global.

Boyd, D. M., & Ellison, N. B. (2007). Social network sites: Definition, history, and scholarship. *Journal of Computer-Mediated Communication, 13*(1), 210–230. doi:10.1111/j.1083-6101.2007.00393.x

Caplan, S.E. (2005). A social skill account of problematic Internet use. *Journal of Communication, 55*, 721-736.

Caplan, S. E. (2010). Theory and measurement of generalized problematic Internet use: A two-step approach. *Computers in Human Behavior, 26*(5), 1089–1097. doi:10.1016/j.chb.2010.03.012

Chang, F.-C., Chiu, C.-H., Miao, N.-F., Chen, P.-H., Lee, C.-M., Chiang, J.-T., & Pan, Y.-C. (2015). The relationship between parental mediation and Internet addiction among adolescents, and the association with cyberbullying and depression. *Comprehensive Psychiatry, 57*, 21–28. doi:10.1016/j.comppsych.2014.11.013 PMID:25487108

Corrin, L., Apps, T., Beckman, K., & Bennett, S. (2019). The Myth of the Digital Native and What It Means for Higher Education. In A. Attrill-Smith, C. Fullwood, M. Keep, & D. J. Kuss (Eds.), *The Oxford Handbook of Cyberpsychology*. Oxford, UK: Oxford University Press.

Coulson, N. S. (2019). Online Support Communities. In A. Attrill-Smith, C. Fullwood, M. Keep, & D. J. Kuss (Eds.), *The Oxford Handbook of Cyberpsychology*. Oxford, UK: Oxford University Press.

Davis, R. A. (2001). A cognitive-behavioral model of pathological Internet use. *Computers in Human Behavior, 17*(2), 187–195. doi:10.1016/S0747-5632(00)00041-8

Deters, F., & Mehl, M. R. (2013). Does Posting Facebook Status Updates Increase or Decrease Loneliness? An Online Social Networking Experiment. *Social Psychological & Personality Science, 4*(5), 579–586. doi:10.1177/1948550612469233 PMID:24224070

Ellison, N., Steinfield, C., & Lampe, C. (2007). The benefits of Facebook "friends": Social capital and college students' use of online social network sites. *Journal of Computer-Mediated Communication, 12*(4), 1143–1168. doi:10.1111/j.1083-6101.2007.00367.x

Fioravanti, G., Primi, C., & Casale, S. (2013). Psychometric evaluation of the generalized problematic internet use scale 2 in an Italian sample. *Cyberpsychology, Behavior, and Social Networking, 16*(10), 761–766. doi:10.1089/cyber.2012.0429 PMID:23742149

Floridi, L. (2015). *The Online Manifesto: Being Human in a Hyperconnected Era*. Springer.

Frison, E., & Eggermont, S. (2017). Browsing, Posting, and Liking on Instagram: The Reciprocal Relationships Between Different Types of Instagram Use and Adolescents' Depressed Mood. *Cyberpsychology, Behavior, and Social Networking, 20*(10), 603–609. doi:10.1089/cyber.2017.0156 PMID:29039700

Frozzi, G., & Mazzoni, E. (2011). On the importance of social network sites in the transitions which characterize "emerging adulthood.". *ICST Transactions on E-Education and E-Learning, 11*(7-9), 1–11.

Gailliot, M. T., & Baumeister, R. F. (2007). Self-esteem, belongingness, and worldview validation: Does belongingness exert a unique influence upon self-esteem? *Journal of Research in Personality, 41*(2), 327–345. doi:10.1016/j.jrp.2006.04.004

Gaysynsky, A., Romansky-Poulin, K., & Arpadi, S. (2015). “My YAP Family”: Analysis of a Facebook Group for Young Adults Living with HIV. *AIDS and Behavior*, *19*(6), 947–962. doi:10.100710461-014-0887-8 PMID:25186783

Grieve, R., Indian, M., Witteveen, K., Tolan, G. A., & Marrington, J. (2013). Face-to-face or Facebook: Can social connectedness be derived online? *Computers in Human Behavior*, *29*(3), 604–609. doi:10.1016/j.chb.2012.11.017

Hong, F.-Y., Huang, D.-H., Lin, H.-Y., & Chiu, S.-L. (2014). Analysis of the psychological traits, Facebook usage, and Facebook addiction model of Taiwanese university students. *Telematics and Informatics*, *31*(4), 597–606. doi:10.1016/j.tele.2014.01.001

How children interact with digital media. (2019, Jan. 3). *The Economist*. Retrieved from https://www.economist.com/special-report/2019/01/03/how-children-interact-with-digital-media

Jelenchick, L. A., Eickhoff, J. C., & Moreno, M. A. (2013). “Facebook Depression?” Social Networking Site Use and Depression in Older Adolescents. *The Journal of Adolescent Health*, *52*(1), 128–130. doi:10.1016/j.jadohealth.2012.05.008 PMID:23260846

Kalpidou, M., Costin, D., & Morris, J. (2011). The relationship between Facebook and the well-being of undergraduate college students. *Cyberpsychology, Behavior, and Social Networking*, *14*(4), 183–189. doi:10.1089/cyber.2010.0061 PMID:21192765

Katz, E., Blumler, J. G., & Gurevitch, M. (1973). Uses and Gratifications Research. *Public Opinion Quarterly*, *37*(4), 509–523. doi:10.1086/268109

Katz, E., Blumler, J. G., & Gurevitch, M. (1974). Utilization of mass communication by the individual. In J. G. Blumer & E. Katz (Eds.), *The uses of mass communications: Current perspectives on gratifications research* (pp. 19–32). Beverly Hills, CA: Sage.

Keep, M., Janssen, A., & Amon, K. (2019). Image Sharing on Social Networking Sites: Who, What, Why, and So What? In A. Attrill-Smith, C. Fullwood, M. Keep, & D. J. Kuss (Eds.), *The Oxford Handbook of Cyberpsychology*. Oxford, UK: Oxford University Press.

Khang, H., Kim, J. K., & Kim, Y. (2013). Self-traits and motivations as antecedents of digital media flow and addiction: The Internet, mobile phones, and video games. *Computers in Human Behavior*, *29*(6), 2416–2424. doi:10.1016/j.chb.2013.05.027

Krämer, N. C., & Winter, S. (2008). Impression Management 2.0. *Journal of Media Psychology*, *20*(3), 106–116. doi:10.1027/1864-1105.20.3.106

Lam, M. K., Hines, M., Lowe, R., Nagarajan, S., Keep, M., Penman, M., & Power, E. (2016). Preparedness for eHealth: Health Sciences Students’ Knowledge, Skills, and Confidence. *Journal of Information Technology Education: Research*, *15*, 305–334. doi:10.28945/3523

Lee, Z. W. Y., & Cheung, C. M. K. (2014). Problematic use of social networking sites: The role of self-esteem. *International Journal of Business and Information*, *9*(2), 143.

Leung, L., & Lee, P. S. (2005). Multiple determinants of life quality: The roles of Internet activities, use of new media, social support, and leisure activities. *Telematics and Informatics*, *22*(3), 161–180. doi:10.1016/j.tele.2004.04.003

Lou, L. L., Yan, Z., Nickerson, A., & McMorris, R. (2012). An examination of the reciprocal relationship of loneliness and Facebook use among first-year college students. *Journal of Educational Computing Research*, *46*(1), 105–117. doi:10.2190/EC.46.1.e

Lup, K., Trub, L., & Rosenthal, L. (2015). Instagram #Instasad?: Exploring associations among Instagram use, depressive symptoms, negative social comparison, and strangers followed. *Cyberpsychology, Behavior, and Social Networking*, *15*(5), 247–252. doi:10.1089/cyber.2014.0560 PMID:25965859

Maloney, P. W., Grawitch, M. J., & Barber, L. K. (2012). The multi-factor structure of the Brief Self-Control Scale: Discriminant validity of restraint and impulsivity. *Journal of Research in Personality*, *46*(1), 111–115. doi:10.1016/j.jrp.2011.10.001

Masi, C. M., Chen, H.-Y., Hawkley, L. C., & Cacioppo, J. T. (2011). A meta-analysis of interventions to reduce loneliness. *Personality and Social Psychology Review*, *15*(3), 219–266. doi:10.1177/1088868310377394

Maslow, A. (1954). *Motivation and personality*. New York, NY: Harper.

Mazzoni, E., Baiocco, L., Cannata, D., & Dimas, I. (2016). Is Internet the cherry on top or a crutch? Offline social support as moderator of the outcomes of online social support on Problematic Internet Use. *Computers in Human Behavior*, *56*, 369–374. doi:10.1016/j.chb.2015.11.032

Mazzoni, E., & Iannone, M. (2014). From high school to university: Impact of social networking sites on social capital in the transitions of emerging adults. *British Journal of Educational Technology*, *45*(2), 303–315. doi:10.1111/bjet.12026

Mazzoni, E., & Zanazzi, L. (2014). Comparing the Use of SNSs Among Adults and Emerging Asults. *Journal of e-Learning and Knowledge Society, 10*, 25-36.

Mellor, D., Stokes, M., Firth, L., Hayashi, Y., & Cummins, R. (2008). Need for belonging, relationship satisfaction, loneliness, and life satisfaction. *Personality and Individual Differences*, *45*(3), 213–218. doi:10.1016/j.paid.2008.03.020

Nadkarni, A., & Hofmann, S. G. (2012). Why do people use Facebook? *Personality and Individual Differences*, *52*(3), 243–249. doi:10.1016/j.paid.2011.11.007 PMID:22544987

Office for National Statistics. (2018). *Internet access - households and individuals*. Retrieved from https://www.ons.gov.uk/peoplepopulationandcommunity/householdcharacteristics/homeinternetandsocialmediausage/datasets/internetaccesshouseholdsandindividualsreferencetables

Orchard, L. J. (2019). Uses and Gratifications of Social Media: Who Uses It and Why? In A. Attrill-Smith, C. Fullwood, M. Keep, & D. J. Kuss (Eds.), *The Oxford Handbook of Cyberpsychology*. Oxford, UK: Oxford University Press.

Poushter, J., Bishop, C., & Chwe, H. (2018). *Social Media Use Continues to Rise in Developing Countries but Plateaus Across Developed Ones*. Retrieved from: http://assets.pewresearch.org/wp-content/uploads/sites/2/2018/06/15135408/Pew-Research-Center_Global-Tech-Social-Media-Use_2018.06.19.pdf

Riva, G. (2012). *Psicologia dei nuovi media. Azione, presenza, identità e relazioni*. Il mulino.

Rosenberg, M. (1965). Rosenberg self-esteem scale (RSE). Acceptance and Commitment Therapy. Measures Package, 61. *Society and the Adolescent Self-Image*.

Rosenberg, M. (1985). Self-Concept and Psychological Well-Being in Adolescence. In R. L. Leahy (Ed.), *The Development of the Self*. Orlando, FL: Academic Press.

Sensis. (2018). *Yellow Social Media Report 2018 Part 1 - Consumers*. Retrieved from Melbourne: https://www.yellow.com.au/wp-content/uploads/2018/06/Yellow-Social-Media-Report-2018-Consumer.pdf

Sheldon, K. M., Abad, N., & Hinsch, C. (2011). A two-process view of Facebook use and relatedness need-satisfaction: Disconnection drives use, and connection rewards it. *Psychology of Popular Media Culture, 1*(S), 2-15. doi:10.1037/2160-4134.1.S.2

Smith, A., & Anderson, M. (2018). *Social Media Use in 2018*. Retrieved from http://www.pewinternet.org/2018/03/01/social-media-use-in-2018/

Song, H., Zmyslinski-Seelig, A., Kim, J., Drent, A., Victor, A., Omori, K., & Allen, M. (2014). Does Facebook make you lonely?: A meta analysis. *Computers in Human Behavior, 36*, 446–452. doi:10.1016/j.chb.2014.04.011

Tangney, J. P., Baumeister, R. F., & Boone, A. L. (2004). High self-control predicts good adjustment, less pathology, better grades, and interpersonal success. *Journal of Personality, 72*(2), 271–324. doi:10.1111/j.0022-3506.2004.00263.x PMID:15016066

Tice, D. M. (1993). The social motivations of people with low self-esteem. In R. F. Baumeister (Ed.), *Self-Esteem: The Puzzle of Low Self-Regard* (pp. 37–54). New York, NY: Plenum Press. doi:10.1007/978-1-4684-8956-9_3

Wang, E. S. T., & Wang, M. C. H. (2013). Social Support and Social Interaction Ties on Internet Addiction: Integrating Online and Offline Contexts. *Cyberpsychology, Behavior, and Social Networking, 16*(11), 843–849. doi:10.1089/cyber.2012.0557 PMID:23848959

Wilson, K., Fornasier, S., & White, K. M. (2010). Psychological Predictors of Young Adults' Use of Social Networking Sites. *Cyberpsychology, Behavior, and Social Networking, 13*(2), 173–177. doi:10.1089/cyber.2009.0094 PMID:20528274

Zywica, J., & Danowski, J. (2008). The Faces of Facebookers: Investigating Social Enhancement and Social Compensation Hypotheses; Predicting Facebook™ and Offline Popularity from Sociability and Self-Esteem, and Mapping the Meanings of Popularity with Semantic Networks. *Journal of Computer-Mediated Communication, 14*(1), 1–34. doi:10.1111/j.1083-6101.2008.01429.x

ADDITIONAL READING

Arnett, J. J. (2015). *Emerging adulthood: The winding road from late teens through the twenties*. Oxford: Oxford university Press. doi:10.1093/oxfordhb/9780199795574.013.9

Attrill-Smith, A., Fullwood, C., Keep, M., & Kuss, D. J. (Eds.). (2019). *The Oxford Handbook of Cyberpsychology*. Oxford: Oxford University Press. doi:10.1093/oxfordhb/9780198812746.001.0001

Benvenuti, M., & Mazzoni, E. (2016). Online and Offline life: Key factors for a functional use of the Internet. *Annual Review of Cybertherapy and Telemedicine*, *2016*, 177.

Błachnio, A., Przepiorka, A., Benvenuti, M., Mazzoni, E., & Seidman, G. (2018). Relations Between Facebook Intrusion, Internet Addiction, Life Satisfaction, and Self-Esteem: A Study in Italy and the USA. *International Journal of Mental Health and Addiction*, 1–13.

Błachnio, A., Przepiórka, A., Gorbaniuk, A., Benvenuti, M., Ciobanu, A. M., Senol-Durak, M., ... Ben-Ezra, M. (2019). Culural Correlates of Internet Addiction. *Cyberpsychology, Behavior, and Social Networking*, *22*(4), 258–263. doi:10.1089/cyber.2018.0667

Boyd, D. (2015). *It's complicated: The social lives of networked teens*. Connecticut: Yale University Press.

Coyne, S., Padilla-Walker, S., & Howard, E. (2013). Emerging in a digital world: A decade review of media use, effects, and gratifications in emerging adulthood. *Emerging Adulthood*, *1*(2), 125–137. doi:10.1177/2167696813479782

Mazzoni, E., Baiocco, L., Benvenuti, M., Cannata, D., Fossi, E., & Zanazzi, L. (2014). Beyond Internet Addiction A New Framework To Understand Risks And Benefits Of Being Online. *Ict, Society and Human Beings 2014 Web Based Communities and Social Media 2014 E-Commerce 2014*, 405.

Mazzoni, E., Baiocco, L., Cannata, D., & Dimas, I. (2016). Is Internet the cherry on top or a crutch? Offline social support as moderator of the outcomes of online social support on Problematic Internet Use. *Computers in Human Behavior*, *56*, 369–374. doi:10.1016/j.chb.2015.11.032

KEY TERMS AND DEFINITIONS

Emerging Adulthood: The life stage between adolescence and adulthood. Usually between 18 years and 30 years old, where individuals are transitioning to more stable relationships, and work and home life.

Functional Internet Use: A set of actions that lead people to use the Internet for purposes that can improve their activities, facilitate goal achievement, and empower their life.

Onlife: It is the set of actions and relationships that a person performs and has when he/she has when he/she is both connected and disconnected.

Problematic Internet Use: A set of actions that lead a person to use the Internet in a way which leads to problems during its excessive use.

Self-Control: It is a measure of how much people control themselves and their actions.

Self-Esteem: It is a measure of how much people perceive to be popular and successful in their social interactions.

Social Support: It is the set of information that come to a person thanks to social interactions and that transmit the individual the feeling of being loved, valued and able, as well as being part of a network from which derive mutual obligations.

Compilation of References

Abdulahi, A., Samadi, B., & Gharleghi, B. (2014). A Study on the negative effects of social networking sites such as Facebook among Asia Pacific University scholars in Malaysia. *International Journal of Business and Social Science*, *5*(1), 133–145. Retrieved from http://www.ijbssnet.com/journals/Vol_5_No_10_September_2014/18.pdf

Abramson, K., Keefe, B., & Chou, W. S. (2015). Communicating about cancer through Facebook: A qualitative analysis of a breast cancer awareness page. *Journal of Health Communication*, *20*(2), 237–243. doi:10.1080/10810730.2014.927034 PMID:25495200

Access Hollywood. (2010). *Access extended: Rihanna: 'I couldn't say no to Eminem' for 'Love the Way You Lie'*. Accessed January 22, 2018: http://www.accesshollywood.com/rihanna-icouldnt-say-no-to-eminem-to-record-love-the-way-you-lie_video_1240713

Addictiontips. (2015). *25 Surprising Facts About Phone Addiction*. Retrieved May 10, 2016 from http://www.addictiontips.net/phone-addiction/phone-addiction-facts/

Albury, K., & Byron, P. (2016). Safe on my phone? Same-sex attracted young people's negotiations of intimacy, visibility, and risk on digital hook-up apps. *Social Media+Society, 2*(4).

Albury, K., & Byron, P. (2014). Queering sexting and sexualization. *Media International Australia*, *153*(1), 138–147. doi:10.1177/1329878X1415300116

Alderson, K., & Samimi, P. (2014). Sexting among undergraduate students. *Computers in Human Behavior*, *31*, 230–241. doi:10.1016/j.chb.2013.10.027

Alexy, E. M., Burgess, A. W., Baker, T., & Smoyak, S. A. (2005). Perceptions of cyberstalking among college students. *Brief Treatment and Crisis Intervention*, *5*(3), 279–289. doi:10.1093/brief-treatment/mhi020

Aljomaa, S. S., Al.Qudah, M. F., Albursan, I. S., Bakhiet, S. F., & Abduljabbar, A. S. (2016). Smartphone addiction among university students in the light of some variables. *Computers in Human Behavior*, *61*, 155–164. doi:10.1016/j.chb.2016.03.041

Allard, E. R., & Williams, D. F. (2008). Listeners' perceptions of speech and language disorders. *Journal of Communication Disorders*, *41*(2), 108–123. doi:10.1016/j.jcomdis.2007.05.002 PMID:17586521

Almog, R., & Kaplan, D. (2017). The nerd and his discontent: The seduction community and the logic of the game as a geeky solution to the challenges of young masculinity. *Men and Masculinities*, *20*(1), 27–48. doi:10.1177/1097184X15613831

Alper, S., & Raharinirina, S. (2006). Assistive technology for individuals with disabilities: A review and synthesis of the literature. *Journal of Special Education Technology*, *21*(2), 47–64. doi:10.1177/016264340602100204

Al-Saggaf, Y., & Nielsen, S. (2014). Self-disclosure on Facebook among female users and its relationship to feelings of loneliness. *Computers in Human Behavior*, *36*, 460–468. doi:10.1016/j.chb.2014.04.014

Alvarez-Garcia, D., Nunez Perez, J. C., Gonzalez, A. D., & Perez, C. R. (2015). Risk factors associated with cyber victimization in adolescence. *International Journal of Clinical and Health Psychology*, *15*(3), 226–235. doi:10.1016/j.ijchp.2015.03.002 PMID:30487840

American Association of Intellectual and Developmental Disabilities. (2013). *Definition of intellectual disability*. Retrieved from http://aaidd.org/intellectual-disability/definition#.Vd0xTKaZ5EI

American Diabetes Association. (2015). *Diabetes symptoms*. Retrieved from http://www.diabetes.org/diabetes-basics/symptoms/

American Psychiatric Association. (2013). *Diagnostic and statistical manual of mental disorders* (5th ed.). Arlington, VA: American Psychiatric Publishing.

Anderson, M., Perrin, A., & Jiang, J. (2018). 11% of Americans don't use the internet. Who are they? *Pew Research Center.* Retrieved from http://www.pewresearch.org/fact-tank/2018/03/05/some-americans-dont-use-the-internet-who-are-they/

Anderson, C. A., Carnagey, N. L., & Eubanks, J. (2003). Exposure to violent media: The effects of songs with violent lyrics on aggressive thoughts and feelings. *Journal of Personality and Social Psychology*, *84*(5), 960–971. doi:10.1037/0022-3514.84.5.960 PMID:12757141

Andriani, I. (2016). *Model of cyberbullying behavior influenced by external and internal factors* (Doctoral Dissertation). University of Gunadarma, Jakarta, Indonesia.

Angermeyer, M. C., & Matschinger, H. (1997). Social distance towards the mentally ill: Results of representative surveys in the Federal Republic of Germany. *Psychological Medicine*, *27*(1), 131–141. doi:10.1017/S0033291796004205 PMID:9122293

Angermeyer, M. C., & Matschinger, H. (2003). Public beliefs about schizophrenia and depression: Similarities and differences. *Social Psychiatry and Psychiatric Epidemiology*, *38*(9), 526–534. doi:10.100700127-003-0676-6 PMID:14504738

Anthenunis, M. L., Valkenburg, P. M., & Peter, J. (2012). The quality of online, offline, and mixed-mode friendships among users of a social net- working site. *Cyberpsychology (Brno)*, *6*, 6. Retrieved from http://www.cyberpsychology.eu/view.php? cisloclanku=2012120304&article=6

Apter, A., Kotler, M., Sevy, S., Plutchik, R., Brown, S. L., Foster, H., ... van Praag, H. M. (1991). Correlates of risk of suicide in violent and nonviolent psychiatric patients. *The American Journal of Psychiatry*, *148*(7), 883–837. doi:10.1176/ajp.148.7.883 PMID:2053628

Arakali, H. (2015). *Emerging Markets Like Indonesia, India Top US In Facebook Mobile Access*. Retrieved January 30, 2016 from http://www.ibtimes.com/emerging-markets-indonesia-india-top-us-facebook-mobile-access-1792686Bolt

Archer, M. S. (2000). *Being human: The problem of agency*. Cambridge University Press. doi:10.1017/CBO9780511488733

Archer, M. S. (2007). *Making our way through the world: Human reflexivity and social mobility*. Cambridge University Press. doi:10.1017/CBO9780511618932

Archer, M. S. (2012). *The reflexive imperative in late modernity*. Cambridge University Press. doi:10.1017/CBO9781139108058

Ardila-Rey, A., Killen, M., & Brenick, A. (2009). Moral reasoning in violent contexts: Displaced and non-displaced Colombian children's evaluations of moral transgressions, retaliation, and reconciliation. *Social Development*, *18*(1), 181–209. doi:10.1111/j.1467-9507.2008.00483.x PMID:25722543

Armstrong, E. A., Hamilton, L., & England, P. (2010). Is Hooking Up Bad for Young Women? *Contexts*, *9*(3), 22–27. doi:10.1525/ctx.2010.9.3.22

Arnett, J. J., & Schwab, J. (2012). *The Clark University Poll of Emerging Adults: Thriving, Sturgglin, & Hopeful*. Retrieved from: https://www.clarku.edu/clarkpoll-emerging-adults/pdfs/clark-university-poll-emerging-adults-findings.pdf

Arnett, J. (2000). Emerging adulthood: A theory of development from late teens through the twenties. *The American Psychologist*, *55*(5), 469–480. doi:10.1037/0003-066X.55.5.469 PMID:10842426

Arnett, J. J. (2002). The psychology of globalization. *The American Psychologist*, *57*(10), 774–783. doi:10.1037/0003-066X.57.10.774 PMID:12369500

Arnett, J. J. (2007). Socialization in emerging adulthood: From the family to the wider world, from socialization to self-socialization. In J. E. Grusec & P. D. Hastings (Eds.), *Handbook of Socialization: Theory and Research* (pp. 208–231). New York: Guilford Press.

Arnett, J. J. (2015). *Emerging adulthood: The winding road from the late teens through the twenties* (2nd ed.). New York: Oxford University Press. doi:10.1093/oxfordhb/9780199795574.013.9

Arnett, J., & Jensen, L. (2002). A congregation of one: Individualized religious beliefs among emerging adults. *Journal of Adolescent Research*, *17*(5), 451–467. doi:10.1177/0743558402175002

Arseth, A. K., Kroger, J., Martinussen, M., & Bakken, G. (2009). Intimacy status, attachment, separation-individuation patterns, and identity status in female university students. *Journal of Social and Personal Relationships*, *26*(5), 697–712. doi:10.1177/0265407509347927

Ashcroft, J. (2001). *Stalking and domestic violence: A report to Congress (No. NCJ 186157)*. Washington, DC: U.S. Department of Justice.

Asongu, S. A. (2013). How has mobile phone penetration stimulated financial development in Africa? *Journal of African Business*, *14*(1), 7–18. doi:10.1080/15228916.2013.765309

Attwood, F. (2005). What do people do with porn? Qualitative research into the consumption, use, and experience of pornography and other sexually explicit media. *Sexuality & Culture*, *9*(2), 65–86. doi:10.100712119-005-1008-7

Augner, C., & Hacker, G. W. (2012). Associations between problematic mobile phone use and psychological parameters in young adults. *International Journal of Public Health*, *57*(2), 437–441. doi:10.100700038-011-0234-z PMID:21290162

Avagianou, P. A., & Zafiropoulou, M. (2008). Parental bonding and depression: Personality as a mediating factor. *International Journal of Adolescent Medicine and Health*, *20*(3), 261–270. doi:10.1515/IJAMH.2008.20.3.261 PMID:19097563

Babadi-Akashe, Z., Zamani, B. E., & Hedayati, N. (2014). The Relationship between Mental Health and Addiction to Mobile Phones among University Students of Shahrekord, Iran. *Addiction & Health*, *6*(3-4), 93–99. PMID:25984275

Backe, E. L., Lilleston, P., & McCleary-Sills, J. (2018). Networked individuals, gendered violence: A literature review of cyberviolence. *Violence and Gender*, *5*(3), 135–146. doi:10.1089/vio.2017.0056

Badger, S., Nelson, L., & Barry, C. M. N. (2006). Perceptions of the transition to adulthood among Chinese and American emerging adults. *International Journal of Behavioral Development*, *30*(1), 84–93. doi:10.1177/0165025406062128

Baker, L. R., & Oswald, D. L. (2010). Shyness and online networking services. *Journal of Social and Personal Relationships*, *27*(7), 873–889. doi:10.1177/0265407510375261

Balfe, M., Doyle, F., Smith, D., Sreenan, S., Brugha, R., Hevey, D., & Conroy, R. (2013). What's distressing about having type 1 diabetes? A qualitative study of young adults' perspectives. *BMC Endocrine Disorders*, *13*(1), 1–14. doi:10.1186/1472-6823-13-25 PMID:23885644

Bandura, A. (1977). *Social Learning Theory*. Englewood Cliffs, NJ: Prentice-Hall.

Bandura, A. (1991). Social cognitive theory of self-regulation. *Organizational Behavior and Human Decision Processes*, *50*(2), 248–287. doi:10.1016/0749-5978(91)90022-L

Bank of America. (2015). *Trends in Consumer Mobility Report.* Retrieved May 20, 2016 from http://newsroom.bankofamerica.com/files/doc_library/additional/2015_BAC_Trends_in_Consumer_Mobility_Report.pdf

Bannink, R., Broeren, S., van de Looij-Jansen, P. M., de Waart, F. G., & Raat, H. (2014). Cyber and traditional bullying victimization as a risk factor for mental health problems in adolescents. *PLoS One*, *9*, e94026. doi:10.1371/journal.pone.0094026 PMID:24718563

Barak, A., Fisher, W. A., Belfry, S., & Lashambe, D. R. (1999). Sex, guys, and cyberspace: Effects of internet pornography and individual differences on men's attitudes toward women. *Journal of Psychology & Human Sexuality*, *11*(1), 63–91. doi:10.1300/J056v11n01_04

Bargh, J. A., McKenna, K. Y. A., & Fitzsimons, G. M. (2002). Can you see the real me? Activation and expression of the "true self" on the Internet. *The Journal of Social Issues*, *58*(1), 33–48. doi:10.1111/1540-4560.00247

Barker, E. D., Arseneault, L., Brendgen, M., Fontaine, N., & Maughan, B. (2008). Joint development of bullying and victimization in adolescence: Relations to delinquency and self-harm. *Journal of the American Academy of Child and Adolescent Psychiatry*, *47*(9), 1030–1038. PMID:18665001

Barker, V. (2009). Older adolescents' motivations for social network site use: The influence of gender, group identity, and collective self-esteem. *Cyberpsychology & Behavior*, *12*(2), 209–213. doi:10.1089/cpb.2008.0228 PMID:19250021

Barrow, K. (2010, December 27). Difference is the norm on these dating sites. *The New York Times*. Retrieved from http://www.nytimes.com

Barry, C. M., Madsen, S. D., Nelson, L. J., Carroll, J. S., & Badger, S. (2009). Friendship and romantic relationship qualities in emerging adulthood: Differential associations with identity development and achieved adulthood criteria. *Journal of Adult Development*, *16*(4), 209–222. doi:10.100710804-009-9067-x

Bartholomew, K., & Horowitz, L. M. (1991). Attachment styles among young adults: A test of a four- category model. *Journal of Personality and Social Psychology*, *61*(2), 226–244. doi:10.1037/0022-3514.61.2.226 PMID:1920064

Bauman, Z. (2003). *Liquid Love: On the frailty of human bonds*. John Wiley & Sons.

Baumeister, R. F., & Leary, M. R. (1995). The need to belong: Desire for interpersonal attachments as a fundamental human motivation. *Psychological Bulletin*, *117*(3), 497–529. doi:10.1037/0033-2909.117.3.497 PMID:7777651

Baum, K., Catalano, S., Rand, M., & Rose, K. (2009). *Stalking victimization in the United States*. Washington, DC: Department of Justice Bureau of Justice Statistics. Available from https://www.justice.gov/sites/default/files/ovw/legacy/2012/08/15/bjs-stalking-rpt.pdf

Baym, N. (2010). *Personal connections in the digital age*. Cambridge, UK: Polity Press.

Bazarova, N. N., & Choi, Y. H. (2014). Self-disclosure in social media: Extending the functional approach to disclosure motivations and chacteristics on social network sites. *Journal of Communication, 64*(4), 635–657. doi:10.1111/jcom.12106

Beaudoin, C. E., & Tao, C. C. (2007). Benefiting from social capital in online support groups: An empirical study of cancer patients. *Cyberpsychology & Behavior, 10*(4), 587–590. doi:10.1089/cpb.2007.9986 PMID:17711369

Beck, A. T., & Steer, R. A. (1993). *Beck anxiety inventory manual.* San Antonio, TX: Harcourt Brace.

Beck, A. T., Steer, R. A., & Brown, G. K. (1996). *Manual for the beck inventory-II.* San Antonio, TX: Psychological Corporation.

Bender, J. L., Jimenez-Marroquin, M. C., & Jadad, A. R. (2011). Seeking support on facebook: A content analysis of breast cancer groups. *Journal of Medical Internet Research, 13*(1), e16. doi:10.2196/jmir.1560 PMID:21371990

Bennett, C. L. (2017). Disability-disclosure preferences and practices in online dating communities. *XRDS, 24*(2), 30–33. doi:10.1145/3155120

Bennett, D. C., Guran, E. L., Ramos, M. C., & Margolin, G. (2011). College students' electronic victimization in friendships and dating relationships: Anticipated distress and associations with risky behaviors. *Violence and Victims, 26*(4), 410–429. doi:10.1891/0886-6708.26.4.410 PMID:21882666

Bennett, S., Maton, K., & Kervin, L. (2008). The 'digital natives' debate: A critical review of the evidence. *British Journal of Educational Technology, 39*(5), 775–786. doi:10.1111/j.1467-8535.2007.00793.x

Benvenuti, M., Mazzoni, E., & Piobbico, G. (2016). Being Online in Emerging Adulthood: Between Problematic or Functional. In *Identity, Sexuality, and Relationships among Emerging Adults in the Digital Age.* Hershey, PA: IGI Global.

Beranuy, M., Oberst, U., Carbonell, X., & Chamarro, A. (2009). Problematic Internet and Mobile Phone Use and Clinical Symptoms in College Students: The Role of Emotional Intelligence. *Computers in Human Behavior, 25*(5), 1182–1187. doi:10.1016/j.chb.2009.03.001

Bergdall, A. R., Kraft, J. M., Andes, K., Carter, M., Hatfield-Timajchy, K., & Hock-Long, L. (2012). Love and hooking up in the new millennium: Communication technology and relationships among urban African American and Puerto Rican young adults. *Journal of Sex Research, 49*(6), 570–582. doi:10.1080/00224499.2011.604748 PMID:21854226

Berg, J., Dickhaut, J., & McCabe, K. (1995). Trust, reciprocity, and social history. *Games and Economic Behavior, 10*(1), 122–142. doi:10.1006/game.1995.1027

Berns, N. (2001). Degendering the problem and degendering the blame: Political discourse on violence and women. *Gender & Society, 15*(2), 262–281. doi:10.1177/089124301015002006

Berns, N. (2004). *Framing the victim: Domestic violence, media, and social problems.* New York: Taylor & Francis.

Bersamin, M. M., Zamboanga, B. L., Schwartz, S. J., Donnellan, M. B., Hudson, M., Weisskirch, R. S., & Caraway, S. J. (2014). Risky business: Is there an association between casual sex and mental health among emerging adults? *Journal of Sex Research, 51*(1), 43–51. doi:10.1080/00224499.2013.772088 PMID:23742031

Bessi, A., Coletto, M., Davidescu, G. A., Scala, A., Caldarelli, G., & Quattrociocchi, W. (2015). Science vs conspiracy: Collective narratives in the age of misinformation. *PLoS One, 10*(2), e0118093. doi:10.1371/journal.pone.0118093 PMID:25706981

Bevan, J. L., Cummings, M. B., Kubiniec, A., Mogannam, M., Price, M., & Todd, R. (2015). How are important life events disclosed on Facebook? Relationships with likelihood of sharing and privacy. *Cyberpsychology, Behavior, and Social Networking, 18*(1), 8–12. doi:10.1089/cyber.2014.0373 PMID:25584725

Bevan, J. L., Gomez, R., & Sparks, L. (2014). Disclosures about important life events on Facebook: Relationships with stress and quality of life. *Computers in Human Behavior*, *39*, 246–253. doi:10.1016/j.chb.2014.07.021

Beymer, M. R., Weiss, R. E., Bolan, R. K., Rudy, E. T., Bourque, L. B., Rodriguez, J. P., & Morisky, D. E. (2014). Sex on demand: Geosocial networking phone apps and risk of sexually transmitted infections among a cross-sectional sample of men who have sex with men in Los Angeles county. *Sexually Transmitted Infections*, *90*(7), 567–572. doi:10.1136extrans-2013-051494 PMID:24926041

Bhattacharya, S. (2015). Swipe and burn. *New Scientist*, *225*(3002), 30–33. doi:10.1016/S0262-4079(15)60032-X

Bianchi, A., & Phillips, J. G. (2005). Psychological Predictors of Problem Mobile Phone Use. *Cyberpsychology & Behavior*, *8*(1), 39–51. doi:10.1089/cpb.2005.8.39 PMID:15738692

Bian, M., & Leung, L. (2015). Linking Loneliness, Shyness, Smartphone Addiction Symptoms, and Patterns of Smartphone Use to Social Capital. *Social Science Computer Review*, *31*(1), 61–79. doi:10.1177/0894439314528779

Bickley, S. R. (1990). Dental hygienists' attitudes towards dental care for people with a mental handicap and the perceptions of adequacy of their training. *Dental Education*, *168*, 361–364. PMID:2140515

Bigham, D. S. (2012). Emerging adulthood in sociolinguists. *Language and Linguistics Compass*, *6*(8), 533–544. doi:10.1002/lnc3.350

Billieux, J., Van der Linden, M., d'Acremont, M., Ceschi, G., & Zermatten, A. (2007). Does Impulsivity Relate to Perceived Dependence on and Actual Use of the Mobile Phone? *Applied Cognitive Psychology*, *21*(4), 527–537. doi:10.1002/acp.1289

Billieux, J., Van Der Linden, M., & Rochat, L. (2008). The Role of Impulsivity in Actual and Problematic Use of the Mobile Phone. *Applied Cognitive Psychology*, *22*(9), 1195–1210. doi:10.1002/acp.1429

Birtchnell, J. (1996). *How Humans Relate: A New Interpersonal Theory*. Hove, UK: Psychology Press.

Birtchnell, J., Hammond, S., Horn, E., De Jong, C., & Kalaitzaki, A. (2013). A cross-national comparison of a shorter version of the Person's Relating to Others Questionnaire. *Clinical Psychology & Psychotherapy*, *20*(1), 36–48. doi:10.1002/cpp.789 PMID:21960317

Bisson, M. A., & Levine, T. R. (2009). Negotiating a friends with benefits relationship. *Archives of Sexual Behavior*, *38*(1), 66–73. doi:10.100710508-007-9211-2 PMID:17851750

Bjornsen, C. (2018). Social media use and emerging adulthood. In M. Zupančič & M. Puklek Levpušček (Eds.), Prehod v odraslost: Sodobni trendi in raziskave [Emerging adulthood: Current trends and research] (pp. 193–223). Ljubljana, Slovenia: Znanstvena založba Filozofske fakultete.

Blachnio, A., Przepiorka, A., & Rudnicka, P. (2016). Narcissism and self-esteem as predictors of dimensions of Facebook use. *Personality and Individual Differences*, *90*, 296–301. doi:10.1016/j.paid.2015.11.018

Black, M. C., Basile, K. C., Breiding, M. J., Smith, S. G., Walters, M. L., Merrick, M. T., & Stevens, M. R. (2011). National intimate partner and sexual violence survey. Atlanta, GA: Centers for Disease Control and Prevention.

Black, B. M., Weisz, A. N., & Bennett, L. W. (2010). Graduating social work students' perspectives on domestic violence. *Affilia*, *25*(2), 173–184. doi:10.1177/0886109910364824

Blackhart, G. C., Fitzpatrick, J., & Williamson, J. (2014). Dispositional factors predicting use of online dating sites and behaviors related to online dating. *Computers in Human Behavior*, *33*, 113–118. doi:10.1016/j.chb.2014.01.022

Blackwell, C., Birnholtz, J., & Abbott, C. (2015). Seeing and being seen: Co-situation and impression formation using Grindr, a location-aware gay dating app. *New Media & Society*, *17*(7), 1117–1136. doi:10.1177/1461444814521595

Blair, K. L., & Pukall, C. F. (2014). Can less be more? Comparing duration vs. frequency of sexual encounters in same-sex and mixed-sex relationships. *The Canadian Journal of Human Sexuality*, *23*(2), 123–136. doi:10.3138/cjhs.2393

Blood, I. M. (1997). The hearing aid effect: Challenges for counseling. *Journal of Rehabilitation*, *63*, 59–62.

Bloom, J. R., & Kessler, L. (1994). Emotional support following cancer: A test of the stigma and social activity hypotheses. *Journal of Health and Social Behavior*, *35*(2), 118–133. doi:10.2307/2137360 PMID:8064120

Bogart, K. R., Rottenstein, A., Lund, E. M., & Bouchard, L. (2017). Who self-identifies as disabled? An examination of impairment and contextual predictors. *Rehabilitation Psychology*, *62*(4), 553–562. doi:10.1037/rep0000132 PMID:28581320

Bogle, K. A. (2008). *Hooking up: sex, dating, and relationships on campus*. New York: New York University Press.

Bollen, K. A., & Curran, P. J. (2006). *Latent curve models: A structural equation perspective*. New York, NY: Wiley.

Bolt, J. (2010, August 9). How to Wreck Your Self Esteem: Compare Yourself with Others. *Psychology Today*. Retrieved from http://www.psychologytoday.com/blog/your-zesty- self/201008/how-wreck-your-self-esteem-compare-youself-others

Borrajo, E., Gámez-Guadix, M., & Calvete, E. (2015). Cyber dating abuse: Prevalence, context, and relationship with offline dating aggression. *Psychological Reports*, *116*(2), 565–585. doi:10.2466/21.16.PR0.116k22w4 PMID:25799120

Boupha, S., Grisso, A. D., Morris, J., Webb, L. M., & Zakeri, M. (2013). How college students display ethnic identity on Facebook. In R. A. Lind (Ed.), *Race/Gender/Media: Considering diversity across audiences, content, and producers* (3rd ed.; pp. 107-112). Boston, MA: Pearson. Retrieved on June 10, 2019 from https://www.researchgate.net/publication/225271141_How_college_students_display_ethnic_identity_on_Facebook

Boutyline, A., & Willer, R. (2017). The social structure of political echo chambers: Variation in ideological homophily in online networks. *Political Psychology*, *38*(3), 551–569. doi:10.1111/pops.12337

Bowker, N. I. (2010). Understanding barriers to online experience for people with physical and sensory disabilities using discursive social psychology. *Universal Access in the Information Society*, *9*(2), 121–136. doi:10.100710209-009-0162-3

boyd, d. m. (2006). Friends, Friendsters, and MySpace Top8: Writing community into being on social network sties. *First Monday, 11*(12). Retrieved Jan 23, 2010 from http://www.firstmonday.org/issues/issue11_12/boyd/

boyd, D., & Ellison, N. (2008). Social network sites: Definition, history and scholarship. *Journal of Computer-Mediated Communication, 13,* 212-216.

Boyd, D. M., & Ellison, N. B. (2007). Social network sites: Definition, history, and scholarship. *Journal of Computer-Mediated Communication*, *13*(1), 210–230. doi:10.1111/j.1083-6101.2007.00393.x

Boyle, A. M., & O'Sullivan, L. F. (2016). Staying connected: Computer-mediated and face-to-face communication in college students' dating relationships. *Cyberpsychology, Behavior, and Social Networking*, *19*(5), 299–307. doi:10.1089/cyber.2015.0293 PMID:27148761

Bradshaw, C., Kahn, A. S., & Saville, B. K. (2010). To hook up or date: Which gender benefits? *Sex Roles*, *62*(9-10), 661–669. doi:10.100711199-010-9765-7

Braithwaite, S. R., Coulson, G., Keddington, K., & Fincham, F. D. (2015). The influence of pornography on sexual scripts and hooking up among emerging adults in college. *Archives of Sexual Behavior*, *44*(1), 111–123. doi:10.100710508-014-0351-x

Braithwaite, S. R., Delevi, R., & Fincham, F. D. (2010). Romantic relationships and the physical and mental health of college students. *Personal Relationships*, *17*(1), 1–12. doi:10.1111/j.1475-6811.2010.01248.x

Braun-Courville, D. K., & Rojas, M. (2009). Exposure to sexually explicit websites and adolescent sexual attitudes and behaviors. *The Journal of Adolescent Health*, *45*(2), 156–162. doi:10.1016/j.jadohealth.2008.12.004 PMID:19628142

Brenick, A., Flannery, K., & Rankin, E. (2017). Victimization or entertainment? How attachment and rejection sensitivity relate to sexting experiences, evaluations, and victimization. In M. F. Wright (Ed.), *Identity, Sexuality, and Relationships among Emerging Adults in the Digital Age* (pp. 201–223). Hershey, PA: IGI Global. doi:10.4018/978-1-5225-1856-3.ch013

Brenick, A., & Killen, M. (2014). Moral judgments about Jewish–Arab intergroup exclusion: The role of cultural identity and contact. *Developmental Psychology*, *50*(1), 86–99. doi:10.1037/a0034702 PMID:24188040

Brenick, A., & Romano, K. (2016). Perceived peer and parent outgroup norms, cultural identity, and adolescents' reasoning about peer intergroup exclusion. *Child Development*, *87*(5), 1392–1408. doi:10.1111/cdev.12594 PMID:27684394

Bridges, A. J., Sun, C. F., Ezzell, M. B., & Johnson, J. (2016). Sexual scripts and the sexual behavior of men and women who use pornography. *Sexualization, Media, & Society*, *2*(4).

Bridges, A. J., Wosnitzer, R., Scharrer, E., Sun, C., & Liberman, R. (2010). Aggression and sexual behavior in best-selling pornography videos: A content analysis update. *Violence Against Women*, *16*(10), 1065–1085. doi:10.1177/1077801210382866 PMID:20980228

Brighi, A., Melotti, G., Guarini, A., Genta, M. L., Ortega, R., Mora-Merchan, J., … Thompson, F. (2012). Self-esteem and loneliness in relation to cyberbullying in three European countries. In Q. Ling, D. Cross, & P. K. Smith (Eds.), Cyberbullying in the global playground (pp. 52-56). West Sussex, UK: Blackwell Publishing.

Brod, M., Kongso, J. H., Lessard, S., & Christensen, T. L. (2009). Psychological insulin resistance: Patient beliefs and implications for diabetes management. *Quality of Life Research: An International Journal of Quality of Life Aspects of Treatment, Care and Rehabilitation*, *18*(1), 23–32. doi:10.100711136-008-9419-1 PMID:19039679

Bromwich, J. E. (2017, December 18). Tinder and Bumble are hungry for your love. *The New York Times.* Retrieved from https://www.nytimes.com/2018/12/18/style/dating-apps-tinder-bumble-content.html

Bromwich, J. E. (2018, December 20). Tinder and Bumble Are Hungry for Your Love. *The New York Times.* Retrieved from https://www.nytimes.com/2018/12/18/style/dating-apps-tinder-bumble-content.html

Brown, J. D., & L'Engle, K. L. (2009). X-rated sexual attitudes and behaviors associated with US early adolescents exposure to sexually explicit media. *Communication Research*, *36*(1), 129–151. doi:10.1177/0093650208326465

Brown, J., & Trevethan, R. (2010). Shame, internalized homophobia, identity formation, attachment style, and the connection to relationship status in gay men. *American Journal of Men's Health*, *4*(3), 267–276. doi:10.1177/1557988309342002 PMID:20413384

Brownstein, A. (2000). In the campus shadows, women are stalkers as well as the stalked. *The Chronicle of Higher Education*, *47*(15), 40–42.

Bryant, E. M., Marmo, J., & Ramirez, A. (2011). A functional approach to social networking sites. In K. B. Wright & L. M. Webb (Eds.), *Computer mediated communication in personal relationships* (pp. 3–20). New York: Peter Lang Publishers.

Burgess, K. (2016). *Consumer survey: The best way to "swipe" a mate*. Retrieved from http://consumersresearch.org/consumer-survey-the-best-way-to-swipe-amate/

Burke, S. C., Wallen, M., Vail-Smith, K., & Knox, D. (2011). Using technology to control intimate partners: An exploratory study of college undergraduates. *Computers in Human Behavior*, *27*(3), 1162–1167. doi:10.1016/j.chb.2010.12.010

Burke, T. J., & Ruppel, E. K. (2015). Facebook self-presentation motives: Daily effects on social anxiety and interaction success. *Communication Studies*, *66*(2), 204–217. doi:10.1080/10510974.2014.884014

Burkett, M. (2015). Sex(t) talk: A qualitative analysis of young adults' negotiations of the pleasures and perils of sexting. *Sexuality & Culture: An Interdisciplinary Quarterly*, *19*(4), 835–863. doi:10.100712119-015-9295-0

Bushman, B. J., Moeller, S. J., & Crocker, J. (2011). Sweets, sex or self-esteem? Comparing the calue of self-esteem boosts with other pleasant rewards. *Journal of Personality*, *79*(5), 993–1012. doi:10.1111/j.1467-6494.2011.00712.x PMID:21950264

Buzawa, E. S., Buzawa, C. G., & Stark, E. D. (2017). *Responding to domestic violence: The integration of criminal justice and human services* (5th ed.). New York, NY: Sage. doi:10.1007/978-3-319-56721-1

Byers, E. S., & Demmons, S. (1999). Sexual satisfaction and sexual self-disclosure within dating relationships. *Journal of Sex Research*, *36*(2), 180–189. doi:10.1080/00224499909551983

Byrne, P. (2009). Why psychiatrists should watch films (or What has cinema ever done for psychiatry?). *Advances in Psychiatric Treatment*, *15*(4), 286–296. doi:10.1192/apt.bp.107.005306

Caers, R., De Feyter, T., De Couck, M., Stough, T., Vigna, C., & Du Bois, C. (2013). Facebook: A literature review. *New Media & Society*, *15*(6), 982–1002. doi:10.1177/1461444813488061

Çağan, Ö., Ünsal, A., & Çelik, N. (2014). Evaluation of College Students'the Level of Addiction to Cellular Phone and Investigation on the Relationsship Between the Addiction and the Level of Depression. *Procedia: Social and Behavioral Sciences*, *114*, 831–839. doi:10.1016/j.sbspro.2013.12.793

Campbell, J. C., Webster, D., Koziol-McLain, J., Block, C., Campbell, D., Curry, M. A., ... Sharps, P. (2003). Risk factors for femicide in abusive relationships: Results from a multisite case control study. *American Journal of Public Health*, *93*(7), 1089–1097. doi:10.2105/AJPH.93.7.1089 PMID:12835191

Campbell, M., Kleinplatz, P. J., Mehak, L., Menard, A. D., Paquet, M. P., Paradis, N., & Zuccarino, D. (2009). The components of optimal sexuality: A portrait of" great sex. *The Canadian Journal of Human Sexuality*, *18*(1-2), 1–14.

Cane, D. B., & Gotlib, I. H. (1985). Implicit conceptualizations of depression: Implications for an interpersonal perspective. *Social Cognition*, *3*(4), 341–368. doi:10.1521oco.1985.3.4.341

Caplan, S.E. (2005). A social skill account of problematic Internet use. *Journal of Communication*, *55*, 721-736.

Caplan, S. E. (2010). Theory and measurement of generalized problematic Internet use: A two-step approach. *Computers in Human Behavior*, *26*(5), 1089–1097. doi:10.1016/j.chb.2010.03.012

Cappadocia, M. C., Craig, W. M., & Pepler, D. (2013). Cyberbullying: Prevalence, stability and risk factors during adolescence. *Canadian Journal of School Psychology*, *28*(2), 171–192. doi:10.1177/0829573513491212

Carroll, J. S., Busby, D. M., Willoughby, B. J., & Brown, C. C. (2017). The porn gap: Differences in men's and women's pornography patterns in couple relationships. *Journal of Couple & Relationship Therapy*, *16*(2), 146–163. doi:10.1080/15332691.2016.1238796

Carroll, J. S., Padilla-Walker, L. M., Nelson, L. J., Olson, C. D., Barry, C. M., & Madsen, S. D. (2008). Generation XXX: Pornography acceptance and use among emerging adults. *Journal of Adolescent Research*, *23*(1), 6–30. doi:10.1177/0743558407306348

Carroll, J. S., Willoughby, B., Badger, S., Nelson, L. J., Barry, C. M., & Madsen, S. D. (2007). So close, yet so far away: The impact of varying marital horizons on emerging adulthood. *Journal of Adolescent Research*, *22*(3), 219–247. doi:10.1177/0743558407299697

Carson, R. (2014). *Adolescent cyberbullying in New Zealnd and the implications of parenting styles* (Unpublished doctoral thesis). University of Canterbury.

Cassidy, J. (2001). Truth, lies, and intimacy: An attachment perspective. *Attachment & Human Development*, *3*(2), 121–155. doi:10.1080/14616730110058999 PMID:11708734

Castells, M. (1997). *The power of identity: The information age. Economy, Society and Culture* (Vol. 2). West Sussex, UK: John Wiley & Sons.

Celizic, M. (2009). *Her Teen Committed Suicide Over Sexting*. Retrieved from http://www.today.com/parents/her-teen-committed-suicide-over-sexting-2D80555048#.VRwMLvnF-So

Center for Disease Control and Prevention (CDC). (2011). *Self-directed violence surveillance: Uniform definitions and recommended data elements*. Retrieved from: http://www.cdc.gov/violenceprevention/pdf/SelfDirected-Violence-a.pdf

Centers for Disease Control & Prevention. (2016). *HIV Among Youth*. Retrieved from http://www.cdc.gov/hiv/group/age/youth/

Chang, C. W., & Heo, J. (2014). Visiting theories that predict college students' self-disclosure on Facebook. *Computers in Human Behavior*, *36*, 79–86. doi:10.1016/j.chb.2013.07.059

Chang, F.-C., Chiu, C.-H., Miao, N.-F., Chen, P.-H., Lee, C.-M., Chiang, J.-T., & Pan, Y.-C. (2015). The relationship between parental mediation and Internet addiction among adolescents, and the association with cyberbullying and depression. *Comprehensive Psychiatry*, *57*, 21–28. doi:10.1016/j.comppsych.2014.11.013 PMID:25487108

Chan, L. S. (2018). Ambivalence in networked intimacy: Observations from gay men using mobile dating apps. *New Media & Society*, *20*(7), 2566–2581. doi:10.1177/1461444817727156

Chan, M. (2018). Reluctance to talk about politics in Face-to-face and Facebook settings: Examining the impact of fear of isolation, willingness to self-censor, and peer network characteristics. *Mass Communication & Society*, *21*(1), 1–23. doi:10.1080/15205436.2017.1358819

Chapman, J., Turner, W., & Prochnow, J. (2000). Early reading related to performance, reading self-concept and the development of academic self-concept. *Journal of Educational Psychology*, *92*(4), 703–708. doi:10.1037/0022-0663.92.4.703

Chapple, A., Ziebland, S., & McPherson, A. (2004). Stigma, shame, and blame experienced by patients with lung cancer: Qualitative study. *British Medical Journal*, *328*(7454), 1470–1473. doi:10.1136/bmj.38111.639734.7C PMID:15194599

Check, J. V., & Malamuth, N. M. (1986). Pornography and sexual aggression: A social learning theory analysis. *Annals of the International Communication Association*, *9*(1), 181–213. doi:85.1986.11678607 doi:10.1080/238089

Chen, G. M. (2015). Why do women bloggers use social media? Recreation and information motivations outweigh engagement motivations. *New Media & Society*, *17*(1), 24–40. doi:10.1177/1461444813504269

Chen, L., Yan, Z., Tang, W., Yang, F., Xie, X., & He, J. (2016). Mobile Phone Addiction Levels and Negative Emotions Among Chinese Young Adults: The Mediating Role of Interpersonal Problems. *Computers in Human Behavior*, *55*, 856–866. doi:10.1016/j.chb.2015.10.030

Chen, R. K., Brodwin, M. G., Cardoso, E., & Chan, F. (2002). Attitudes toward people with disabilities in the social context of dating and marriage: A comparison of American, Taiwanese, and Singaporean college students. *Journal of Rehabilitation*, *68*, 5–11.

Chen, R., & Sharma, S. K. (2015). Learning and self-disclosure behavior on social networking sites: The case of Facebook users. *European Journal of Information Systems*, *24*(1), 93–106. doi:10.1057/ejis.2013.31

Chen, Y.-F. (2006). Social phenomena of mobile phone use: An exploratory study in Taiwanese. *Information for Social Research*, *11*, 219–244.

Chesney, M. A., & Smith, A. W. (1999). Critical delays in HIV testing and care: The potential role of stigma. *The American Behavioral Scientist*, *42*(7), 1162–1174. doi:10.1177/00027649921954822

Cheung, C. M. K., Lee, Z. W. Y., & Chan, T. K. H. (2015). Self-disclosure in social networking sites: The role of perceived cost, perceived benefits and social influence. *Internet Research*, *2*(2), 279–299. doi:10.1108/IntR-09-2013-0192

Choi, E. P. H., Wong, J. Y. H., & Fong, D. Y. T. (2018). An emerging risk factor of sexual abuse: The use of smartphone dating applications. *Sexual Abuse*, *30*(4), 343–366. PMID:27698090

Choi, H., Ouytsel, J. V., & Temple, J. R. (2016). Association between sexting and sexual coercion among female adolescents. *Journal of Adolescence*, *53*, 164–168. doi:10.1016/j.adolescence.2016.10.005 PMID:27814493

Choi, K. (2008). Computer crime victimization and integrated theory: An empirical assessment. *International Journal of Cyber Criminology*, *2*, 308–333.

Chóliz, M. (2012). Mobile-phone addiction in adolescence: The Test of Mobile Phone Dependence (TMD). *Progress in Health Sciences*, *2*(1), 33–44.

Chung, N. (2011). Korean Adolescent Girls' Addictive Use Of Mobile Phones To Maintain Interpersonal Solidarity. *Social Behavior and Personality*, *39*(10), 1349–1358. doi:10.2224bp.2011.39.10.1349

Clayton, R. B., Nagurney, A., & Smith, J. R. (2013). Cheating, breakup, and divorce: Is Facebook use to blame? *Cyberpsychology, Behavior, and Social Networking*, *16*(10), 717–720. doi:10.1089/cyber.2012.0424 PMID:23745615

Clevenger, S. L., Navarro, J. N., & Gilliam, M. (2018). Technology and the endless "cat and mouse" game: A review of the interpersonal cybervictimization literature. *Sociology Compass*, *12*(12), e12639. doi:10.1111oc4.12639

Cohen, L. E., & Felson, M. (1979). Social change and crime rate trends: A routine activity approach. *American Sociological Review*, *44*(4), 588–608. doi:10.2307/2094589

Coleman, E. (2011). Impulsive/compulsive sexual behavior: Assessment and treatment. The Oxford Handbook of Impulse Control Disorders, 375.

Coleman, J. M., Brunell, A. B., & Haugen, I. M. (2015). Multiple forms of prejudice: How gender and disability stereotypes influence judgments of disabled men and women. *Current Psychology (New Brunswick, N.J.)*, *34*(1), 177–189. doi:10.100712144-014-9250-5

Collins, N. (1996). *Revised Adult Attachment Scale* [Measurement Instrument]. Retrieved from https://labs.psych.ucsb.edu/collins/nancy/UCSB_Close_Relationships_Lab/Resources_files/Adult%20Attachment%20Scale.doc

Collins, V. E., & Carmody, D. C. (2011). Deadly love images of dating violence in the "Twilight Saga.". *Affilia*, *26*(4), 382–394. doi:10.1177/0886109911428425

Collins, W. A. (2003). More than myth: The developmental significance of romantic relationships during adolescence. *Journal of Research on Adolescence*, *13*(1), 1–24. doi:10.1111/1532-7795.1301001

Cooney, G., Jahoda, A., Gumley, A., & Knott, F. (2006). Young people with learning disabilities attending mainstream and segregated schooling: Perceived stigma, social comparisons and future aspirations. *Journal of Intellectual Disability Research, 50*(6), 432–445. doi:10.1111/j.1365-2788.2006.00789.x PMID:16672037

Copes, H., Kerley, K., Huff, R., & Kane, J. (2010). Differentiating identity theft: An exploratory study of victims using a national victimization survey. *Journal of Criminal Justice, 38*(5), 1045–1052. doi:10.1016/j.jcrimjus.2010.07.007

Copsey, R. (2010). Eminem and Rihanna break YouTube record. *Digital Spy*. Accessed January 22, 2018. http://www.digitalspy.com/music/news/a258634/eminem-andrihanna-break-youtube-record.html

Corrin, L., Apps, T., Beckman, K., & Bennett, S. (2019). The Myth of the Digital Native and What It Means for Higher Education. In A. Attrill-Smith, C. Fullwood, M. Keep, & D. J. Kuss (Eds.), *The Oxford Handbook of Cyberpsychology*. Oxford, UK: Oxford University Press.

Coulson, N. S. (2019). Online Support Communities. In A. Attrill-Smith, C. Fullwood, M. Keep, & D. J. Kuss (Eds.), *The Oxford Handbook of Cyberpsychology*. Oxford, UK: Oxford University Press.

Cowie, H. (2013). Cyberbullying and its impact on young people's emotional health and well-being. *The Psychiatrist, 37*(5), 167–170. doi:10.1192/pb.bp.112.040840

Coyne, S. M., & Padilla-Walker, L. M. (2015). Sex, violence, & rock n'roll: Longitudinal effects of music on aggression, sex, and prosocial behavior during adolescence. *Journal of Adolescence, 41*, 96–104. doi:10.1016/j.adolescence.2015.03.002 PMID:25828552

Coyne, S. M., Padilla-Walker, L. M., & Howard, E. (2013). Emerging in a digital world: A decade review of media use, effects, and gratifications in emerging adulthood. *Emerging Adulthood, 1*(2), 125–137. doi:10.1177/2167696813479782

Coyne, S. M., Stockdale, L., Busby, D., Iverson, B., & Grant, D. M. (2011). "I luv u:)!": A descriptive study of the media use of individuals in romantic relationships. *Family Relations, 60*(2), 150–162. doi:10.1111/j.1741-3729.2010.00639.x

Crabtree, M. A., & Pillow, D. R. (2018). Extending the dual factor of Facebook use: Social motives and network density predict Facebook use through impression management and open self-disclosure. *Personality and Individual Differences, 133*, 34–40. doi:10.1016/j.paid.2017.06.017

Crawford, M., & Popp, D. (2003). Sexual double standards: A review and methodological critique of two decades of research. *Journal of Sex Research, 40*(1), 13–26. doi:10.1080/00224490309552163 PMID:12806528

Crosslin, K. L., & Crosslin, M. B. (2014). Cyberbullying at a Texas university—A mixed-methods approach to examining online aggression. *Texas Public Health Journal, 66*, 26–31.

Crystal, D. S., Killen, M., & Ruck, M. (2008). It is who you know that counts: Intergroup contact and judgments about race-based exclusion. *British Journal of Developmental Psychology, 26*(1), 51–70. doi:10.1348/026151007X198910 PMID:25505355

Dailey, R. M., Rossetto, K. R., Pfiester, A., & Surra, C. A. (2009). A qualitative analysis of on-again/off-again romantic relationships: "It's up and down, all around". *Journal of Social and Personal Relationships, 26*(4), 443-466. doi:10.1177/0265407509351035

Dailey, R. M., Jin, B., Pfiester, A., & Beck, G. (2011). On-again/Off-again dating relationships: What keeps partners coming back? *The Journal of Social Psychology, 151*(4), 417–440. doi:10.1080/00224545.2010.503249 PMID:21755653

Dake, J., Price, J., Maziarz, L., & Ward, B. (2012). Prevalence and correlates of sexting behavior in adolescents. *American Journal of Sexuality Education, 7*(1), 1–15. doi:10.1080/15546128.2012.650959

Darbyshire, D., & Baker, P. (2012). A systematic review and thematic analysis of cinema in medical education. *Medical Humanities*, *38*(1), 28–33. doi:10.1136/medhum-2011-010026 PMID:22282424

Darcin, A. E., Kose, S., Noyan, C. O., Nurmedov, S., Yılmaz, O., & Dilbaz, N. (2016). Smatphone Addiction and Its Relationship with Social Anxiety and Loneliness. *Behaviour & Information Technology*, 1–6.

Davey, S., & Davey, A. (2014). Assessment of Smartphone Addiction in Indian Adolescents: A Mixed Method Study by Systematic-review and Meta-analysis Approach. *International Journal of Preventive Medicine*, *5*(12), 1500–1511. PMID:25709785

Davis, J. L. (2016). Identity theory in a digital age. In J. E. Stets & R. T. Serpe (Eds.), *New directions in identity theory and research*. Oxford University Press. doi:10.1093/acprof:oso/9780190457532.003.0006

Davis, R. A. (2001). A cognitive-behavioral model of pathological Internet use. *Computers in Human Behavior*, *17*(2), 187–195. doi:10.1016/S0747-5632(00)00041-8

Del Vicario, M., Vivaldo, G., Bessi, A., Zollo, F., Scala, A., Caldarelli, G., & Quattrociocchi, W. (2016). Echo chambers: Emotional contagion and group polarization on facebook. *Scientific Reports*, *6*(1), 37825. doi:10.1038rep37825 PMID:27905402

Delevi, R., & Weisskirch, R. (2012). Its ovr b/n u n me: Technology use, attachment styles, and gender roles in relationship dissolution. *Cyberpsychology, Behavior, and Social Networking*, *15*(9), 486–490. doi:10.1089/cyber.2012.0169 PMID:22823329

Delevi, R., & Weisskirch, R. (2013). Attachment style and conflict resolution skills predicting technology use in relationship dissolution. *Computers in Human Behavior*, *29*(6), 2530–2534. doi:10.1016/j.chb.2013.06.027

Deloitte. (2015). *Deloitte Mobile Consumer 2015: The UK Cut Game Of Phones*. Retrieved April 16, 2016 from https://www.deloitte.co.uk/mobileuk/assets/pdf/Deloitte-Mobile-Consumer-2015.pdf

Deloitte. (2016). *Deloitte Global Mobil Kullanıcı Anketi 2015 Türkiye*. Retrieved May 28, 2016 from https://www2.deloitte.com/content/dam/Deloitte/tr/Documents/technology-media-telecommunications/deloitte-global-mobil-kullanici-anketi-2015-f.pdf

Derogatis, L. R. (1993). *BSI, Brief Symptom Inventory: Administration, scoring & procedures manual*. Minneapolis, MN: National Computer Systems.

Derogatis, L. R. (2001). *Brief Symptom Inventory (BSI)-18. Administration, scoring and procedures manual*. Minneapolis, MN: NCS Pearson, Inc.

Deters, F., & Mehl, M. R. (2013). Does Posting Facebook Status Updates Increase or Decrease Loneliness? An Online Social Networking Experiment. *Social Psychological & Personality Science*, *4*(5), 579–586. doi:10.1177/1948550612469233 PMID:24224070

Dewing, M. (2010). *Social media: Who uses them?* Library of Parliament Background Paper. Retrieved from publications.gc.ca/site/eng/370191/publication.html

Dill, K. E. (2009). *How fantasy becomes reality: Seeing through media influence*. Oxford University Press.

Dilmac, N. (2009). Psychological needs as a predict of cyber bullying: A preliminary report on college students. *Educational Sciences: Theory and Practice*, *9*(3), 1307–1325.

Dir, A. L., & Cyders, M. A. (2015). Risks, risk factors, and outcomes associated with phone and Internet sexting among university students in the United States. *Archives of Sexual Behavior*, *44*(6), 1675–1684. doi:10.100710508-014-0370-7 PMID:25358950

Donath, J., & Boyd, D. (2004). Public displays of connection. *BT Technology Journal*, *22*(4), 71–82. doi:10.1023/B:BTTJ.0000047585.06264.cc

Doucette, H., Collibee, C., Hood, E., Gittins Stone, D. I., DeJesus, B., & Rizzo, C. J. (2018). Perpetration of electronic intrusiveness among adolescent females: Associations with in-person dating violence. *Journal of Interpersonal Violence*. PMID:30516429

Downey, G., & Feldman, S. (1996). Implications of rejection sensitivity for intimate relationships. *Journal of Personality and Social Psychology*, *70*(6), 1327–1343. doi:10.1037/0022-3514.70.6.1327 PMID:8667172

Downey, G., Freitas, A., Michaelis, B., & Khouri, H. (1998). The self-fulfilling prophecy in close relationships: Rejection sensitivity and rejection by romantic partners. *Journal of Personality and Social Psychology*, *75*(2), 545–560. doi:10.1037/0022-3514.75.2.545 PMID:9731324

Downey, G., Nesdale, D., Trevaskis, S., & Zimmer-Gembeck, M. (2014). Relational victimization, loneliness and depressive symptoms: Indirect associations via self and peer reports of rejection sensitivity. *Journal of Youth and Adolescence*, *43*(4), 568–582. doi:10.100710964-013-9993-6 PMID:23955324

Downing-Matibag, T. M., & Geisinger, B. (2009). Hooking up and sexual risk taking among college students: A health belief model perspective. *Qualitative Health Research*, *19*(9), 1196–1209. doi:10.1177/1049732309344206 PMID:19690202

Draucker, C. B., & Marstolf, D. S. (2010). The role of electronic communication technology in adolescent dating violence. *Journal of Child and Adolescent Psychiatric Nursing*, *23*(3), 133–142. doi:10.1111/j.1744-6171.2010.00235.x PMID:20796096

Dreßing, H., Bailer, J., Anders, A., Wagner, H., & Gallas, C. (2014). Cyberstalking in a large sample of social network users: Prevalence, characteristics, and impact upon victims. *Cyberpsychology, Behavior, and Social Networking*, *17*(2), 61–67. doi:10.1089/cyber.2012.0231 PMID:24106979

Drouin, M., & Landgraff, C. (2012). Texting, sexting, and attachment in college students' romantic relationships. *Computers in Human Behavior*, *28*(2), 444–449. doi:10.1016/j.chb.2011.10.015

Drouin, M., Ross, J., & Tobin, E. (2015). Sexting: A new, digital vehicle for intimate partner aggression? *Computers in Human Behavior*, *50*, 197–204. doi:10.1016/j.chb.2015.04.001

Drouin, M., & Tobin, E. (2014). Unwanted but consensual sexting among young adults: Relations with attachment and sexual motivations. *Computers in Human Behavior*, *31*, 412–418. doi:10.1016/j.chb.2013.11.001

Drouin, M., Vogel, K. N., Surbey, A., & Stills, J. R. (2013). Let's talk about sexting, baby: Computer-mediated sexual behaviors among young adults. *Computers in Human Behavior*, *29*(5), A25–A30. doi:10.1016/j.chb.2012.12.030

Duggan, M. (2014). *Pew Research Center. Photo and Video Sharing Grow Online*. Available at: http://pewInternet.org/Reports/2013/Photos-and-videos.aspx

Duggan, M. (2014). *Online harassment*. Washington, DC: Pew Research Center. Retrieved from http://www.pewinternet.org/2014/10/22/onlineharassment/#

Duguay, S. (2017). Dressing up Tinderella: Interrogating authenticity claims on the mobile dating app Tinder. *Information Communication and Society*, *20*(3), 351–367. doi:10.1080/1369118X.2016.1168471

Dunbar, N. E. (2015). A review of theoretical approaches to interpersonal power. *Review of Communication*, *15*(1), 1–18. doi:10.1080/15358593.2015.1016310

Duncan, Z., & March, E. (2019). Using Tinder® to start a fire: Predicting antisocial use of Tinder® with gender and the Dark Tetrad. *Personality and Individual Differences*, *145*, 9–14. doi:10.1016/j.paid.2019.03.014

Dunn, D. (2015). *The social psychology of disability*. New York: Oxford University Press.

Dwyer, C., Hiltz, S. R., & Passerini, K. (2007). Trust and privacy concern within social networking sites: A comparison of Facebook and MySpace. *Proceedings of Thirteenth Americas Conference on Information Systems*. Retrieved June 10, 2019 from http://csis.pace.edu/dwyer/research/DwyerAMCIS2007.pdf

Edwards, G., & Barber, B. (2010). The relationship between rejection sensitivity and compliant condom use. *Archives of Sexual Behavior*, *39*(6), 1381–1388. doi:10.100710508-009-9520-8 PMID:19760145

Ellison, N. B., Steinfield, C., & Lampe, C. (2007). The benefits of Facebook "friends:" Social capital and college students use of online social network sites. *Journal of Computer-Mediated Communication*, *12*(4), 1143–1168. doi:10.1111/j.1083-6101.2007.00367.x

Ellison, N. B., Vitak, J., Gray, R., & Lampe, C. (2014). Cultivating social resources on social network sites: Facebook relationship maintenance behaviors and their role in social capital processes. *Journal of Computer-Mediated Communication*, *19*(4), 855–870. doi:10.1111/jcc4.12078

Elphinston, R. A., & Noller, P. (2011). Time to face it! Facebook intrusion and the implications for romantic jealousy and relationship satisfaction. *Cyberpsychology, Behavior, and Social Networking*, *14*(11), 631–635. doi:10.1089/cyber.2010.0318 PMID:21548798

Emerson, R. M. (1976). Social exchange theory. *Annual Review of Sociology*, *2*(1), 335–362. doi:10.1146/annurev.so.02.080176.002003

England, P. (n.d.). *Online College Social Life Survey, 2005-2011*. New York University [data file and codebook]. Retrieved from: http://www.nyu.edu/projects/england/ocsls/

Erfani, S. S., Blount, Y., & Abedin, B. (2016). The influence of health-specific social network site use on the psychological well-being of cancer-affected people. *Journal of the American Medical Informatics Association*, *23*(3), 467–476. doi:10.1093/jamia/ocv170 PMID:26911816

Ericsson. (2015a, June). *Ericsson Mobility Report*. Retrieved May 2, 2016 from https://www.ericsson.com/res/docs/2015/ericsson-mobility-report-june-2015.pdf

Ericsson. (2015b, November). *Ericsson Mobility Report*. Retrieved April 16, 2016 from //www.ericsson.com/res/docs/2015/mobility-report/ericsson-mobility-report-nov-2015.pdf

Ericsson. (2016). *Ericsson Mobility Report*. Retrieved May 27, 2016 from http://www.ericsson.com/res/docs/2016/mobility-report/ericsson-mobility-report-feb-2016-interim.pdf

Erikson, E. H. (1964). Inner and outer space: Reflections on womanhood. *Daedalus*, *93*(2), 582–606. Retrieved from http://www.jstor.org/stable/20026847

Erikson, E. H. (1968). *Identity: Youth and crisis*. New York, NY: Norton.

Erozkan, A. (2009). Rejection sensitivity levels with respect to attachment styles, gender, and parenting styles: A study with Turkish students. *Social Behavior and Personality*, *37*(1), 1–14. doi:10.2224bp.2009.37.1.1

Eyal, K., & Kunkel, D. (2008). The effects of sex in television drama shows on emerging adults sexual attitudes and moral judgments. *Journal of Broadcasting & Electronic Media*, *52*(2), 161–181. doi:10.1080/08838150801991757

Facebook. (2019). *Stats.* Retrieved May 30, 2019 from https://newsroom.fb.com/company-info/

Fagundes, C. P. (2012). Getting over you: Contributions of attachment theory for postbreakup emotional adjustment. *Personal Relationships*, *19*(1), 37–50. doi:10.1111/j.1475-6811.2010.01336.x

Fardouly, J., Diedrichs, P. C., Vartanian, L. R., & Halliwell, E. (2015). Social comparison on social media: The impact of Facebook on young womans body image concern and mood. *Body Image*, *13*, 38–45. doi:10.1016/j.bodyim.2014.12.002 PMID:25615425

Federal Reserve Board. (2015). *Consumers and Mobile Financial Services 2015.* Retrieved April 16, 2016 from http://www.federalreserve.gov/econresdata/consumers-and-mobile-financial-services-report-201503.pdf

Feeney, J. A., & Noller, P. (1990). Attachment style as a predictor of adult romantic relationships. *Journal of Personality and Social Psychology*, *58*(2), 281–291. doi:10.1037/0022-3514.58.2.281

Feinstein, B. A., Bhatia, V., & Davila, J. (2014). Rumination mediates the association between cybervictimization and depressive symptoms. *Journal of Interpersonal Violence*, *29*(9), 1732–1746. doi:10.1177/0886260513511534 PMID:24346650

Feldman, R. S., Forrest, J. A., & Happ, B. R. (2002). Self-presentation and verbal deception: Do self-presenters lie more? *Basic and Applied Social Psychology*, *24*(2), 163–170. doi:10.1207/S15324834BASP2402_8

Felson, M., & Cohen, L. E. (1980). Human ecology and crime: A routine activity approach. *Human Ecology*, *8*(4), 389–406. doi:10.1007/BF01561001

Felson, M., & Eckert, M. (2016). *Crime and everyday life.* Sage publications.

Feragen, K. B., Stock, N. M., Sharratt, N. D., & Kvalem, I. L. (2016). Self-perceptions of romantic appeal in adolescents with a cleft lip and/or palate. *Body Image*, *18*, 143–152. doi:10.1016/j.bodyim.2016.06.009 PMID:27459395

Ferdon, C. D., & Hertz, M. F. (2007). Electronic media, violence, and adolescents. An emerging public health problem. *The Journal of Adolescent Health*, *41*(6), 1–5. doi:10.1016/j.jadohealth.2007.08.020 PMID:17577527

Festl, R., & Quandt, T. (2013). Social relations and cyberbullying: The influence of individual and structural attributes on victimization and perpetration via the internet. *Human Communication Research*, *39*(1), 101–126. doi:10.1111/j.1468-2958.2012.01442.x

Fielder, R. L., & Carey, M. P. (2010). Predictors and consequences of sexual "hookups" among college students: A short-term prospective study. *Archives of Sexual Behavior*, *39*(5), 1105–1119. doi:10.100710508-008-9448-4 PMID:19130207

File, B. L., & Wright, E. R. (2000). The dimensionality of stigma: A comparison of its impact on the self of persons with HIV/AIDS and cancer. *Journal of Health and Social Behavior*, *41*(1), 50–67. doi:10.2307/2676360 PMID:10750322

Fincham, F. D., & Cui, M. (Eds.). (2010). *Romantic relationships in emerging adulthood.* Cambridge University Press; doi:10.1017/CBO9780511761935

Finkel, E. J., Eastwick, P. W., Karney, B. R., Reis, H. T., & Sprecher, S. (2012). Online dating: A critical analysis from the perspective of psychological science. *Psychological Science in the Public Interest*, *13*(1), 3–66. doi:10.1177/1529100612436522 PMID:26173279

Finn, J. (2004). A survey of online harassment at a university campus. *Journal of Interpersonal Violence*, *19*(4), 468–483. doi:10.1177/0886260503262083 PMID:15038885

Fioravanti, G., Primi, C., & Casale, S. (2013). Psychometric evaluation of the generalized problematic internet use scale 2 in an Italian sample. *Cyberpsychology, Behavior, and Social Networking*, *16*(10), 761–766. doi:10.1089/cyber.2012.0429 PMID:23742149

Fischer, E. H., Dornelas, E. A., & Goethe, J. W. (2001). Characteristics of people lost to attrition in psychiatric follow-up studies. *The Journal of Nervous and Mental Disease*, *189*(1), 49–55. doi:10.1097/00005053-200101000-00009 PMID:11206665

Fletcher, A., Fitzgerald-Yau, N., Jones, R., Allen, E., Viner, R. M., & Bonell, C. (2014). Brief report: Cyberbullying perpetration and its associations with socio-demographics, aggressive behaviour at school, and mental health outcomes. *Journal of Adolescence*, *37*(8), 1393–1398. doi:10.1016/j.adolescence.2014.10.005 PMID:25448835

Floridi, L. (2015). *The Online Manifesto: Being Human in a Hyperconnected Era*. Springer.

Foo, C. T. (2003). Child of the internet. *Cyberpsychology & Behavior*, *6*(2), 195–199. doi:10.1089/109493103321640392 PMID:12804032

Fox, J., Osborn, J. L., & Warber, K. M. (2014). Relational dialectics and social networking sites: The role of Facebook in romantic relationship escalation, maintenance, conflict, and dissolution. *Computers in Human Behavior*, *35*, 527–534. doi:10.1016/j.chb.2014.02.031

Fox, J., & Tokunaga, R. S. (2015). Romantic Partner Monitoring After Breakups: Attachment, Dependence, Distress, and Post-Dissolution Online Surveillance via Social Networking Sites. *Cyberpsychology, Behavior, and Social Networking*, *18*(9), 491–498. doi:10.1089/cyber.2015.0123 PMID:26348808

Fox, J., & Warber, K. M. (2014). Social networking sites in romantic relationships: Attachment, uncertainty, and partner surveillance on facebook. *Cyberpsychology, Behavior, and Social Networking*, *17*(1), 3–7. doi:10.1089/cyber.2012.0667 PMID:23952623

Fox, J., Warber, K. M., & Makstaller, D. C. (2013). The role of Facebook in romantic relationship development: An exploration of Knapp's relational stage 216 model. *Journal of Social and Personal Relationships*, *30*(6), 771–794. doi:10.1177/0265407512468370

Fox, K. A., & Cook, C. L. (2011). Is knowledge power? The effects of a victimology course on victim blaming. *Journal of Interpersonal Violence*, *26*(17), 3407–3427. doi:10.1177/0886260511403752 PMID:21602202

Fox, K. A., Gover, A. R., & Kaukinen, C. (2009). The rffects of low self control and childhood maltreatment on stalking victimization among men and women. *American Journal of Criminal Justice*, *34*(3-4), 181–197. doi:10.100712103-009-9064-4

Franiuk, R., Coleman, J., & Apa, B. (2017). The influence of non-misogynous and mixed portrayals of intimate partner violence in music on beliefs about intimate partner violence. *Violence Against Women*, *23*(2), 243–257. doi:10.1177/1077801216637473 PMID:26985047

Friedman, E. J., & Resnick, P. (2001). The social cost of cheap pseudonyms. *Journal of Economics & Management Strategy, 10*(2), 173-199.

Frison, E., & Eggermont, S. (2015). Toward an integrated and differential approach to the relationships between loneliness, different types of Facebook use, and adolescents' depressed mood. *Communication Research*, *43*, 279–282. doi:10.1177/0093650215617506

Frison, E., & Eggermont, S. (2017). Browsing, Posting, and Liking on Instagram: The Reciprocal Relationships Between Different Types of Instagram Use and Adolescents' Depressed Mood. *Cyberpsychology, Behavior, and Social Networking*, *20*(10), 603–609. doi:10.1089/cyber.2017.0156 PMID:29039700

Frith, H., & Kitzinger, C. (2001). Reformulating sexual script theory: Developing a discursive psychology of sexual negotiation. *Theory & Psychology*, *11*(2), 210. doi:10.1177/0959354301112004

Frozzi, G., & Mazzoni, E. (2011). On the importance of social network sites in the transitions which characterize "emerging adulthood.". *ICST Transactions on E-Education and E-Learning*, *11*(7-9), 1–11.

Gailliot, M. T., & Baumeister, R. F. (2007). Self-esteem, belongingness, and worldview validation: Does belongingness exert a unique influence upon self-esteem? *Journal of Research in Personality*, *41*(2), 327–345. doi:10.1016/j.jrp.2006.04.004

Garcia, F. D., & Thibaut, F. (2010). Sexual addictions. *The American Journal of Drug and Alcohol Abuse*, *36*(5), 254–260. doi:10.3109/00952990.2010.503823 PMID:20666699

Garcia, J. R., Reiber, C., Massey, S. G., & Merriwether, A. M. (2012). Sexual Hookup Culture: A Review. *Review of General Psychology*, *16*(2), 161–176. doi:10.1037/a0027911 PMID:23559846

Gaysynsky, A., Romansky-Poulin, K., & Arpadi, S. (2015). "My YAP Family": Analysis of a Facebook Group for Young Adults Living with HIV. *AIDS and Behavior*, *19*(6), 947–962. doi:10.100710461-014-0887-8 PMID:25186783

Geiger, A., & Livingston, G. (2019, February 13). *8 facts about love and marriage in America*. Retrieved April 29, 2019, from https://www.pewresearch.org/fact-tank/2019/02/13/8-facts-about-love-and-marriage/

Gibbs, J. L., Ellison, N. B., & Heino, R. D. (2006). Self-presentation in online personals: The role of anticipated future interaction, self-disclosure, and perceived success in internet dating. *Communication Research*, *33*(2), 152–177. doi:10.1177/0093650205285368

Gill, C. J. (1996). Dating and relationship issues. *Sexuality and Disability*, *14*(3), 183–190. doi:10.1007/BF02590076

Gilovich, T., Griffin, D., & Kahneman, D. (Eds.). (2002). *Heuristics and biases: The psychology of intuitive judgment*. Cambridge university press. doi:10.1017/CBO9780511808098

Giordano, P. C., Flannigan, C. M., Manning, W. D., & Longmore, M. A. (2009). *Developmental shifts in the character of romantic relationships from adolescence to early adulthood*. National Center for Family & Marriage Research Working Paper Series.

Giordano, C., Wood, J. V., & Michela, J. L. (2000). Depressive personality style, dysphoria, and social comparison in everyday life. *Journal of Personality and Social Psychology*, *79*(3), 438–451. doi:10.1037/0022-3514.79.3.438 PMID:10981845

Giordano, P. C., Longmore, M. A., Schroeder, R. D., & Seffrin, P. M. (2008). A life-course perspective on spirituality and desistance from crime. *Criminology*, *46*(1), 99–132. doi:10.1111/j.1745-9125.2008.00104.x

Giugliano, J. R. (2013). Sex addiction as a mental health diagnosis: Coming together or coming apart? *Sexologies*, *22*(3), e77–e80. doi:10.1016/j.sexol.2012.08.018

Goffman, E. (1963). *Stigma: Notes on the management of spoiled identity*. Englewood Cliffs, NJ: Prentice Hall.

Goodman, S. (2012, March 22). Online dating with a disability. *The Guardian*. Retrieved from http://www.theguardian.com/lifeandstyle/2012/mar/22/online-dating-with-disability

Google Ipsos Media, C. T. (2011, April). *The Mobile Movement Understanding Smartphone Users*. Retrieved April 16, 2016 from http://www.gstatic.com/ads/research/en/2011_TheMobileMovement.pdf

Google Ipsos Media, C. T. (2013). *Our Mobile Planet:Understanding the Mobile Consumer*. Retrieved April 16, 2016 from http://services.google.com/fh/files/misc/omp-2013-tr-en.pdf

Gordon-Messer, D., Bauermeister, J. A., Grodzinski, A., & Zimmerman, M. (2013). Sexting among young adults. *The Journal of Adolescent Health*, *52*(3), 301–306. doi:10.1016/j.jadohealth.2012.05.013 PMID:23299018

Gotlib, I. H., & Beatty, M. E. (1985). Negative responses to depression: The role of attribution style. *Cognitive Therapy and Research*, *9*(1), 91–103. doi:10.1007/BF01178753

Gowen, L. K., Deschaine, M., Gruttadaro, D., & Markey, D. C. (2012). Young adults with mental health conditions and social networking websites: Decreasing social isolation. *Psychiatric Rehabilitation Journal*, *35*, 245–250. doi:10.2975/35.3.2012.245.250 PMID:22246123

Gozza-Cohen, M., & May, D. (2012). Individuals with disabilities and internet use. In Z. Yan (Ed.), *Encyclopedia of Cyber Behavior* (pp. 242–258). Hershey, PA: IGI Global. doi:10.4018/978-1-4666-0315-8.ch021

Gradinger, P., Strohmeier, D., & Spiel, C. (2015). Traditional bullying and cyberbullying: Identification of risk groups for adjustment problems. *The Journal of Psychology*, *217*, 205–213.

Green, S. M., Turner, D., & Logan, R. G. (2018). *Exploring the effect of sharing common Facebook friends on the sexual risk behaviors of tinder users*. Academic Press.

Greene, J. A., Choudhry, N. K., Kilabuk, E., & Shrank, W. H. (2010). Online social networking by patients with diabetes: A qualitative evaluation of communication with facebook. *Journal of General Internal Medicine*, *26*(3), 287–292. doi:10.100711606-010-1526-3 PMID:20945113

Greene, K. (2009). An integrated model of health disclosure decision-making. In T. D. Afifi & W. A. Afifi (Eds.), *Uncertainty, information management, and disclosure decisions: Theories and applications* (pp. 226–253). New York: Routledge.

Greene, K., & Faulkner, S. L. (2002). Self-disclosure in relationships of HIV-positive African American adolescent females. *Communication Studies*, *53*, 297–317. doi:10.1080/10510970209388595

Greenfield, R. (2013). Tinder: A hook-up app women actually use. *Atlantic (Boston, Mass.)*.

Green, S. M., Turner, D. A., & Logan, R. G. (2018, July). Exploring the Effect of Sharing Common Facebook Friends on the Sexual Risk Behaviors of Tinder Users. *Cyberpsychology, Behavior, and Social Networking*, *21*(7), 457–462. doi:10.1089/cyber.2017.0581

Green, T., Wilhelmsen, T., Wilmots, E., Dood, B., & Quinn, S. (2016). Social anxiety, attributes of online communication and self-disclosure across private and public Facebook communication. *Computers in Human Behavior*, *58*, 206–213. doi:10.1016/j.chb.2015.12.066

Grieve, R., Indian, M., Witteveen, K., Tolan, G. A., & Marrington, J. (2013). Face-to-face or Facebook: Can social connectedness be derived online? *Computers in Human Behavior*, *29*(3), 604–609. doi:10.1016/j.chb.2012.11.017

Grigg, D. W. (2010). Cyber-aggression: Definition and concept of cyberbullying. *Australian Journal of Guidance & Counselling*, *20*(2), 143–156. doi:10.1375/ajgc.20.2.143

Groban, M. S. (2016). Intimate partner cyberstalking - Terrorizing intimate partners with 21st Century technology. United States Attorneys'. *Bulletin*, *64*(3), 12–16.

Grubbs, J. B., Wright, P. J., Braden, A. L., Wilt, J. A., & Kraus, S. W. (2019). Internet pornography use and sexual motivation: a systematic review and integration. *Annals of the International Communication Association*, 1-39.

Grubbs, J. B., & Perry, S. L. (2019). Moral incongruence and pornography use: A critical review and integration. *Journal of Sex Research*, *56*(1), 29–37. doi:10.1080/00224499.2018.1427204 PMID:29412013

Guadagno, R. E., Okdie, B. M., & Kruse, S. A. (2012). Dating deception: Gender, online dating, and exaggerated self-presentation. *Computers in Human Behavior*, *28*(2), 642–647. doi:10.1016/j.chb.2011.11.010

Gunter, B. (2007). Internet dating: A British survey. *Aslib Proceedings*, *60*(2), 88–98. doi:10.1108/00012530810862437

Hadlington, L. (2015). Cognitive failures in daily life: Exploring the link with Internet addiction and problematic mobile phone use. *Computers in Human Behavior*, *51*, 75–81. doi:10.1016/j.chb.2015.04.036

Hafen, C., Spilker, A., Chango, J., Marston, E., & Allen, J. (2014). To accept or reject? The impact of adolescent rejection sensitivity on early adult romantic relationships. *Journal of Research on Adolescence*, *24*(1), 55–64. doi:10.1111/jora.12081 PMID:24729668

Hahn, H. A., You, D. S., Sferra, M., Hubbard, M., Thamotharan, S., & Fields, S. A. (2018). Is it too soon to meet? Examining differences in geosocial networking app use and sexual risk behavior of emerging adults. *Sexuality & Culture*, *22*(1), 1–21. doi:10.100712119-017-9449-3

Ha, J. H., Chin, B., Park, D.-H., Ryu, S.-H., & Yu, J. (2008). Characteristics of Excessive Cellular Phone Use in Korean Adolescents. *Cyberpsychology & Behavior*, *11*(6), 783–784. doi:10.1089/cpb.2008.0096 PMID:18991536

Hald, G. M., Seaman, C., & Linz, D. (2014). Sexuality and pornography. In D. Tolman, L. Diamond, J. Bauermeister, W. George, J. Pfaus, & L. Ward, (Eds.), APA Handbook of Sexuality and Psychology, Vol. 1: Person-based approaches. American Psychological Association. doi:10.1037/14194-001

Hald, G. M. (2006). Gender differences in pornography consumption among young heterosexual Danish adults. *Archives of Sexual Behavior*, *35*(5), 577–585. doi:10.100710508-006-9064-0 PMID:17039402

Hald, G. M., Kuyper, L., Adam, P. C., & Wit, J. B. (2013). Does viewing explain doing? Assessing the association between sexually explicit materials use and sexual behaviors in a large sample of Dutch adolescents and young adults. *Journal of Sexual Medicine*, *10*(12), 2986–2995. doi:10.1111/jsm.12157 PMID:23621804

Hald, G. M., & Malamuth, N. M. (2008). Self-perceived effects of pornography consumption. *Archives of Sexual Behavior*, *37*(4), 614–625. doi:10.100710508-007-9212-1 PMID:17851749

Hald, G. M., Malamuth, N. M., & Yuen, C. (2010). Pornography and attitudes supporting violence against women: Revisiting the relationship in non-experimental studies. *Aggressive Behavior*, *36*(1), 14–20. doi:10.1002/ab.20328 PMID:19862768

Hall, P. (2014). Sex addiction–An extraordinarily contentious problem. *Sexual and Relationship Therapy*, *29*(1), 68–75. doi:10.1080/14681994.2013.861898

Halpern-Meekin, S., Manning, W. D., Giordano, P. C., & Longmore, M. A. (2013). Relationship churning in emerging adulthood on/off relationships and sex with an ex. *Journal of Adolescent Research*, *28*(2), 166–188. doi:10.1177/0743558412464524 PMID:24535913

Halpern-Meekin, S., Manning, W. D., Giordano, P. C., & Longmore, M. A. (2013). Relationship churning, physical violence, and verbal abuse in young adult relationships. *Journal of Marriage and the Family*, *75*(1), 2–12. doi:10.1111/j.1741-3737.2012.01029.x PMID:24000263

Hardey, M. (2004). Mediated relationships. *Information Communication and Society*, *7*(2), 207–222. doi:10.1080/1369118042000232657

Hardin, R. (2002). *Trust and trustworthiness*. Russell Sage Foundation.

Hardy. (2016). *8 jenis sosial media dan perkembangannya*. Retrieved from: https://www.progresstech.co.id/blog/jenis-sosial-media/

Hawi, N. S., & Samaha, M. (2016). To Excel or Not to Excel: Strong Evidence on The Adverse Effect of smartphone Addiction on Academic Performance. *Computers & Education, 98*, 81–89. doi:10.1016/j.compedu.2016.03.007

Ha, Y. W., Kim, J., Libaque-Saenz, C. F., Chang, Y. H., & Park, M. C. (2015). Use and gratifications of mobile SNSs: Facebook and KakaoTalk in Korea. *Telematics and Informatics, 32*(3), 425–438. doi:10.1016/j.tele.2014.10.006

Hayatı Kaçırma. (2015). Retrieved March 23, 2016 from Mobil Bağımlılık: http://hayatikacirma.org/telefonu-birak-muhabbete-bak/

Hay, C., & Meldrum, R. (2010). Bullying victimization and adolescent self-harm: Testing hypotheses from General Strain Theory. *Journal of Youth and Adolescence, 39*(5), 446–459. doi:10.100710964-009-9502-0 PMID:20072852

Heasley, S. (2019, January 30). Graduation rate for students with disabilities shows improvement. *Disability Scoop.* Retrieved from https://www.disabilityscoop.com/2019/01/30/graduation-rate-shows-improvement/25962/

Hechter, M. (1988). *Principles of group solidarity*. Univ of California Press.

Heid, M. (Dü.). (2016). *You Asked: Am I Addicted to My Phone?* Retrieved May 10, 2016 from http://time.com/4234366/phone-smartphone-addiction/

Heideman, E. (2014, August 1). Disabled woman tackles the dating site trolls. *The Daily Beast.* Retrieved from http://www.thedailybeast.com/articles/2014/08/01/dropping-the-d-bomb- online-dating-with-a-disability.html

Heinze, J., & Horn, S. (2014). Do adolescents' evaluations of exclusion differ based on gender expression and sexual orientation? *The Journal of Social Issues, 70*(1), 63–80. doi:10.1111/josi.12047

Helweg-Larsen, M., Harding, H. G., & Kleinman, K. E. (2008). Risk perceptions of dating violence among college women: The role of experience and depressive symptoms. *Journal of Social and Clinical Psychology, 27*(6), 600–617. doi:10.1521/jscp.2008.27.6.600

Hendry, L. B., & Kloep, M. (2007). Conceptualizing emerging adulthood: Inspecting the emperor's new clothes? *Child Development Perspectives, 1*(2), 74–79. doi:10.1111/j.1750-8606.2007.00017.x

Henning, K. R., & Klesges, L. M. (2002). Utilization of counseling and supportive services by female victims of domestic abuse. *Violence and Victims, 17*(5), 623–636. doi:10.1891/vivi.17.5.623.33714 PMID:12477102

Herek, G. M. (2014). HIV-related stigma. In P. W. Corrigan (Ed.), *The stigma of disease and disability: Empirical models and implications for change* (pp. 121–138). Washington, DC: American Psychological Association.

Hinduja, S., & Patchin, J. W. (2010). Bullying, cyberbullying, and suicide. *Archives of Suicide Research, 14*(3), 206–221. doi:10.1080/13811118.2010.494133 PMID:20658375

Hitsch, G. J., Hortacsu, A., & Ariely, D. (2010). What makes you click? – Mate preferences in online dating. *Quantitative Marketing and Economics, 8*(4), 393–427. doi:10.100711129-010-9088-6

Hobbs, M., Owen, S., & Gerber, L. (2017). Liquid love? Dating apps, sex, relationships and the digital transformation of intimacy. *Journal of Sociology (Melbourne, Vic.), 53*(2), 271–284. doi:10.1177/1440783316662718

Hoeve, M., Dubas, J. S., Eichelsheim, V. I., van der Laan, P. H., Smeenk, W., & Gerris, J. R. M. (2009). The relationship between parenting and delinquency: A meta-analysis. *Journal of Abnormal Child Psychology, 37*(6), 749–775. doi:10.100710802-009-9310-8 PMID:19263213

Hollenbaugh, E. E., & Ferris, A. L. (2014). Facebook and self-disclosure: Examining the role of traits, social cohesion, and motives. *Computers in Human Behavior, 30*, 50–58. doi:10.1016/j.chb.2013.07.055

Holmes, E. K., Brown, G., Shafer, K., & Stoddard, N. (2017). Healthy transitions to family formation. In L. M. Padilla-Walker & L. J. Nelson (Eds.), *Flourishing in emerging adulthood: Positive development during the third decade of life* (pp. 70–97). New York, NY: Oxford University Press.

Holmes, K. M., & O'Loughlin, N. (2014). The experience of people with learning disabilities on social networking sites. *British Journal of Learning Disabilities, 42*(1), 1–5. doi:10.1111/bld.12001

Holt-Lunstad, J., Robles, T. F., & Sbarra, D. A. (2017). Advancing social connection as a public health priority in the United States. *The American Psychologist, 72*(6), 517–530. doi:10.1037/amp0000103 PMID:28880099

Holt, T. J., & Bossler, A. M. (2009). Examining the applicability of lifestyle-routine activities theory for cybercrime victimization. *Deviant Behavior, 30*(1), 1–25. doi:10.1080/01639620701876577

Holt, T. J., & Bossler, A. M. (2014). An assessment of the current state of cybercrime scholarship. *Deviant Behavior, 35*(1), 20–40. doi:10.1080/01639625.2013.822209

Holt, T. J., Fitzgerald, S., Bossler, A. M., Chee, G., & Nq, E. (2016). Assessing the risk factors of cyber and mobile phone bullying victimization in a nationally representative sample of Singapore youth. *International Journal of Offender Therapy and Comparative Criminology, 60*(5), 598–615. doi:10.1177/0306624X14554852 PMID:25326463

Hong, F. Y., Huang, D. H., Lin, H. Y., & Chiu, S. L. (2014). Analysis of the psychological traits, Facebook usage, and Facebook addition model of Taiwanese university students. *Telematics and Informatics, 31*(4), 597–606. doi:10.1016/j.tele.2014.01.001

Hong, F.-Y., Chiu, S.-I., & Huang, D.-H. (2012). A model of the Relationship Between Psychological Characteristics, Mobile Phone Addiction and Use of Mobile Phones by Taiwanese University Female Students. *Computers in Human Behavior*, 1–8.

Horn, S. S., & Nucci, L. (2006). Harassment of gay and lesbian youth and school violence in America: An analysis and directions for intervention. In C. Daiute, Z. F. Beykont, C. Higson-Smith, & L. Nucci (Eds.), *International perspectives on youth conflict and development* (pp. 139–155). New York, NY: Oxford University Press. doi:10.1093/acprof:oso/9780195178425.003.0009

Horowitz, L. M., French, R. de S., Lapid, J. S., & Weckler, D. A. (1982). Symptoms and interpersonal problems: The prototypes as an integrating concept. In J. C. Anchin & D. J. Kiesler (Eds.), Handbook of interpersonal psychotherapy (pp. 168-189). New York: Pergamon.

Horvath, K. J., Danilenko, G. P., Williams, M. L., Simoni, J., Amico, K. R., Oakes, J. M., & Rosser, B. R. S. (2012). Technology use and reasons to participate in social networking health websites among people living with HIV in the US. *AIDS and Behavior, 16*(4), 900–910. doi:10.100710461-012-0164-7 PMID:22350832

Hosek, S. G., Harper, G. W., & Domanico, R. (2000). Psychological and social difficulties of adolescents living with HIV: A qualitative analysis. *Journal of Sex Education and Therapy, 25*(4), 269–276. doi:10.1080/01614576.2000.11074360

Househ, M., Borycki, E., & Kushniruk, A. (2014). Empowering patients through social media: The benefits and challenges. *Health Informatics Journal, 20*(1), 50–58. doi:10.1177/1460458213476969 PMID:24550564

How children interact with digital media. (2019, Jan. 3). *The Economist*. Retrieved from https://www.economist.com/special-report/2019/01/03/how-children-interact-with-digital-media

Howland, C. A., & Rintala, D. H. (2001). Dating behaviors of women with physical disabilities. *Sexuality and Disability, 19*(1), 41–70. doi:10.1023/A:1010768804747

Hudson, H. K., & Fetro, J. V. (2015). Sextual activity: Predictors of sexting behaviors and intentions to sext among selected undergraduate students. *Computers in Human Behavior, 49*, 615–622. doi:10.1016/j.chb.2015.03.048

Hume, D. (2003). *A treatise of human nature*. Courier Corporation.

Hwang, W. (2013). Who are people willing to date? Ethnic and gender patterns in online dating. *Race and Social Problems, 5*(1), 28–40. doi:10.100712552-012-9082-6

Hyatt, C. S., Berke, D. S., Miller, J. D., & Zeichner, A. (2017). Do beliefs about gender roles moderate the relationship between exposure to misogynistic song lyrics and men's female-directed aggression? *Aggressive Behavior, 43*(2), 123–132. doi:10.1002/ab.21668 PMID:27527124

Imai, T. (2016). Influences of mental illness stigma in a computer-mediated communication context: Investigating mediating roles of predicted outcome value and negative affect. *Japanese Journal of Communication Studies, 44*, 135–150.

Imai, T., & Dailey, R. M. (2015). Influences of mental illness stigma on perceptions of and responses to requests for favors. *Health Communication, 31*(7), 863–872. doi:10.1080/10410236.2015.1012630 PMID:26642875

International Agency for Research on Cancer. (2008). *World Cancer Report 2008* (P. Boyle & B. Levin, Eds.). Lyon, France: Author.

Jackson, L. A., Zhao, Y., Witt, E. A., Fitzgerald, H. E., Von Eye, A., & Harold, R. (2009). Self-concept, self-esteem, gender, race, and information technology use. *Cyberpsychology & Behavior, 12*(4), 437–440. doi:10.1089/cpb.2008.0286 PMID:19514819

Jacobsen, W. C., & Forste, R. (2011). The wired generation: Academic and social outcomes of electronic media use among university students. *Cyberpsychology, Behavior, and Social Networking, 14*(5), 275–280. doi:10.1089/cyber.2010.0135 PMID:20961220

Jaeger, P. T. (2012). *Disability and the internet: Confronting a digital divide*. Boulder, CO: Lynne Rienner Publishers.

Jahoda, A., Wilson, A., Stalker, K., & Cairney, A. (2010). Living with stigma and the self perceptions of people with mild learning disabilities. *The Journal of Social Issues, 66*(3), 521–534. doi:10.1111/j.1540-4560.2010.01660.x

James, D., & Drennan, J. (2005). Exploring Addictive Consumption of Mobile Phone Technology. *ANZMAC 2005: Broadening the Boundaries: Conference Proceedings*.

Jelenchick, L. A., Eickhoff, J. C., & Moreno, M. A. (2013). "Facebook Depression?" Social Networking Site Use and Depression in Older Adolescents. *The Journal of Adolescent Health, 52*(1), 128–130. doi:10.1016/j.jadohealth.2012.05.008 PMID:23260846

Jenkins, J. H., & Carpenter-Song, E. A. (2009). Awareness of stigma among persons with schizophrenia: Marking the contexts of lived experience. *The Journal of Nervous and Mental Disease, 197*(7), 520–529. doi:10.1097/NMD.0b013e3181aad5e9 PMID:19597360

Jensen, L. A., & Arnett, J. J. (2012). Going global: New pathways for adolescents and emerging adults in a changing world. *The Journal of Social Issues, 68*(3), 473–492. doi:10.1111/j.1540-4560.2012.01759.x

Jin, B. (2013). How lonely people use and perceive Facebook. *Computers in Human Behavior, 29*(6), 2463–2470. doi:10.1016/j.chb.2013.05.034

John, O. P., Donahue, E. M., & Kentle, R. L. (1991). *The Big Five Inventory--Versions 4a and 54*. Berkeley, CA: Institute of Personality and Social Research.

John, O. P., & Srivastava, S. (1999). The Big Five trait taxonomy: History, measurement, and theoretical perspectives. In L. A. Pervin & O. P. John (Eds.), *Handbook of personality: Theory and research* (pp. 102–138). New York: Guilford Press.

Johnson, J. A., Ezzell, M. B., Bridges, A. J., & Sun, C. F. (2019). Pornography and heterosexual women's intimate experiences with a partner. *Journal of Women's Health, 28*(9), 1254–1265. doi:10.1089/jwh.2018.7006 PMID:30998084

Joinson, A. N. (2001). Self-disclosure in computer-mediated communication: The role of self-awareness and visual anonymity. *European Journal of Social Psychology, 31*(2), 170–192. doi:10.1002/ejsp.36

Jones, E. E., Farina, A., Hastorf, A. H., Markus, H., Miller, D. T., & Scott, R. A. (1984). *Social stigma: The psychology of marked relationships*. New York: Freeman.

Judge, A. (2012). Sexting among U.S. adolescents: Psychological and legal perspectives. *Harvard Review of Psychology, 20*(2), 86–96. doi:10.3109/10673229.2012.677360 PMID:22512742

Kalaitzaki, A. E. (2017). Cyberstalking victimization and perpetration among Greek college students. In M. F. Wright (Ed.), *Identity, Sexuality, and Relationships among Emerging Adults in the Digital Age*. IGI Global. doi:10.4018/978-1-5225-1856-3.ch015

Kalaitzaki, A. E., & Birtchnell, J. (2016). The Person's Relating to Others Questionnaire (PROQ). In J. Birtchnell, M. Newberry, & A. E. Kalaitzaki (Eds.), *Relating Theory: Clinical, Forensic and other Applications*. London: Palgrave Macmillan. doi:10.1057/978-1-137-50459-3_3

Kalichman, S. C., & Rompa, D. (1995). Sexual sensation seeking and sexual compulsivity scales: Validity, and predicting HIV risk behavior. *Journal of Personality Assessment, 65*(3), 586–601. doi:10.120715327752jpa6503_16 PMID:8609589

Kalof, L. (1999). The effects of gender and music video imagery on sexual attitudes. *The Journal of Social Psychology, 139*(3), 378–385. doi:10.1080/00224549909598393 PMID:10410622

Kalpidou, M., Costin, D., & Morris, J. (2011). The relationship between Facebook and the well-being of undergraduate college students. *Cyberpsychology, Behavior, and Social Networking, 14*(4), 183–189. doi:10.1089/cyber.2010.0061 PMID:21192765

Kaplan, A., & Haenlein, M. (2010). Users of the world, unite! The challenges and opportunities of social media. *Business Horizons, 53*(1), 59–68. doi:10.1016/j.bushor.2009.09.003

Karavasilis, L., Doyle, A. B., & Markiewicz, D. (2003). Associations between parenting style and attachment to mother in middle childhood and adolescence. *International Journal of Behavioral Development, 27*(2), 153–164. doi:10.1080/0165025024400015

Kashy, D. A., & DePaulo, B. M. (1996). Who lies? *Journal of Personality and Social Psychology, 70*(5), 1037–1051. doi:10.1037/0022-3514.70.5.1037 PMID:8656334

Katz, E., Blumler, J. G., & Gurevitch, M. (1973). Uses and Gratifications Research. *Public Opinion Quarterly, 37*(4), 509–523. doi:10.1086/268109

Katz, E., Blumler, J. G., & Gurevitch, M. (1974). Utilization of mass communication by the individual. In J. G. Blumer & E. Katz (Eds.), *The uses of mass communications: Current perspectives on gratifications research* (pp. 19–32). Beverly Hills, CA: Sage.

Keep, M., Janssen, A., & Amon, K. (2019). Image Sharing on Social Networking Sites: Who, What, Why, and So What? In A. Attrill-Smith, C. Fullwood, M. Keep, & D. J. Kuss (Eds.), *The Oxford Handbook of Cyberpsychology*. Oxford, UK: Oxford University Press.

Kelley, H. H., & Thibaut, J. W. (1978). *Interpersonal relations: A theory of interdependence*. New York: Wiley-Interscience.

Kemp, S. (2011). *Social, digital, and mobile in Indonesia*. Retrieved January 5, 2016 from http://weare-social.sg/blog/2011/12/social-digital-mobile-indonesia/

Kernsmith, P. D., Victor, B. G., & Smith-Darden, J. P. (2018). Online, offline, and over the line: Coercive sexting among adolescent dating partners. *Youth & Society*, *50*(7), 891–904. doi:10.1177/0044118X18764040

Khang, H., Kim, J. K., & Kim, Y. (2013). Self-traits and motivations as antecedents of digital media flow and addiction: The Internet, mobile phones, and video games. *Computers in Human Behavior*, *29*(6), 2416–2424. doi:10.1016/j.chb.2013.05.027

Killen, M., Lee-Kim, J., McGlothlin, H., Stangor, C., & Helwig, C. C. (2002). How children and adolescents evaluate gender and racial exclusion. *Monographs of the Society for Research in Child Development*, *67*, i-129. PMID:12557595

Killen, M., & Rutland, A. (2011). *Children and Social Exclusion: Morality, Prejudice, and Group Identity*. Hoboken, NJ: Wiley. doi:10.1002/9781444396317

Kimbrough, A. M., Guadagno, R. E., Muscanell, N. L., & Dill, J. (2013). Gender differences in mediated communication: Women connect more than do men. *Computers in Human Behavior*, *29*(3), 896–900. doi:10.1016/j.chb.2012.12.005

Kim, J., & Lee, J. R. (2011). The Facebook paths to happiness: Effects of the number Facebook friends and self-presentation on subjective well-being. *Cyberpsychology, Behavior, and Social Networking*, *14*(6), 359–364. doi:10.1089/cyber.2010.0374 PMID:21117983

Kimmel, M. (2008). *Guyland: The perilous world where boys become men*. New York: Harper Perennial.

Kim, Y. S., Leventhal, B. L., Koh, Y. J., & Boyce, W. T. (2009). Bullying increased suicide risk: Prospective study of Korean adolescents. *Archives of Suicide Research*, *13*(1), 15–30. doi:10.1080/13811110802572098 PMID:19123106

Kingston, D. A., & Malamuth, N. M. (2011). Problems with aggregate data and the importance of individual differences in the study of pornography and sexual aggression: Comment on Diamond, Jozifkova, and Weiss (2010). *Archives of Sexual Behavior*, *40*(5), 1045–1048. doi:10.100710508-011-9743-3

Klaassen, M. J., & Peter, J. (2015). Gender (in) equality in Internet pornography: A content analysis of popular pornographic Internet videos. *Journal of Sex Research*, *52*(7), 721–735. doi:10.1080/00224499.2014.976781 PMID:25420868

Klettke, B., Hallford, D., & Mellor, D. (2014). Sexting prevalence and correlates: A systematic literature review. *Clinical Psychology Review*, *34*(1), 44–53. doi:10.1016/j.cpr.2013.10.007 PMID:24370714

Klinger, L. (2016). Hookup Culture on College Campuses: Centering College Women, Communication Barriers, and Negative Outcomes. *College Student Affairs Leadership*, *3*(2), 5.

Kokkinos, C. M., Antoniadou, N., & Markos, A. (2014). Cyber-bullying: An investigation of the psychological profile of university student participants. *Journal of Applied Developmental Psychology*, *35*(3), 204–214. doi:10.1016/j.appdev.2014.04.001

Kong, F., & You, X. Q. (2013). Loneliness and self-esteem as mediators between social support and life satisfaction in late adolescence. *Social Indicators Research*, *110*(1), 271–279. doi:10.100711205-011-9930-6

Kopecký, K. (2014). Cyberbullying and sexting between children and adolescents –Comparative study. *Procedia: Social and Behavioral Sciences*, *149*, 467–471. doi:10.1016/j.sbspro.2014.08.292

Korte, R. F. (2009). How newcomers learn the social norms of an organization: A case study of the socialization of newly hired engineers. *Human Resource Development Quarterly*, *20*(3), 285–306. doi:10.1002/hrdq.20016

Kowalski, R. M., & Limber, S. P. (2007). Electronic bullying among middle school students. *The Journal of Adolescent Health*, *41*(6), 22–30. doi:10.1016/j.jadohealth.2007.08.017 PMID:18047942

Kowalski, R. M., & Limber, S. P. (2012). Psychological, physical, and academic correlates of cyberbullying and traditional bullying. *The Journal of Adolescent Health*, *53*, 513–520. PMID:23790195

Krämer, N. C., & Winter, S. (2008). Impression Management 2.0. *Journal of Media Psychology*, *20*(3), 106–116. doi:10.1027/1864-1105.20.3.106

Krasnova, H., Wenninger, H., Widjaja, T., & Buxmann, P. (2013). Envy on Facebook: A Hidden Threat to Users' Life Satisfaction? *Wirtschaftsinformatik Proceedings 2013*. Retrieved from http:// www.ara.cat/tecnologia/facebook_ARAFIL20130128_0001.pdf

Krayer, A., Ingledew, D. K., & Iphofen, R. (2008). Social comparison and body image in adolescence: A grounded theory approach. *Health Education Research*, *23*(5), 892–903. doi:10.1093/her/cym076 PMID:18156148

Kreager, D. A., Cavanagh, S. E., Yen, J., & Yu, M. (2014). "Where have all the good men gone?" Gendered interactions in online dating. *Journal of Marriage and the Family*, *76*(2), 387–410. doi:10.1111/jomf.12072 PMID:24910472

Kuzma, J. M., & Black, D. W. (2008). Epidemiology, prevalence, and natural history of compulsive sexual behavior. *The Psychiatric Clinics of North America*, *31*(4), 603–611. doi:10.1016/j.psc.2008.06.005 PMID:18996301

Kwak, K. T., Choi, S. K., & Lee, B. G. (2014). SNS flow, SNS self-disclosure and post hoc interpersonal relations change: Focused on Korean Facebook user. *Computers in Human Behavior*, *31*, 294–304. doi:10.1016/j.chb.2013.10.046

Kwan, C. M. L., Chun, K. M., & Chesla, C. A. (2011). Cultural norms shaping research group interviews with Chinese American immigrants. *Asian American Journal of Psychology*, *2*(2), 115–127. doi:10.1037/a0024184 PMID:21760974

Kwon, M., Kim, D.-J., Cho, H., & Yang, S. (2013). The Smartphone Addiction Scale: Development and Validation of a Short Version for Adolescents. *PLoS One*, *8*(2), 1–7. doi:10.1371/journal.pone.0056936 PMID:24391787

LaBelle, S., Booth-Butterfield, M., & Rittenour, C. E. (2013). Attitudes toward profoundly hearing impaired and deaf individuals: Links with intergroup anxiety, social dominance orientation, and contact. *Western Journal of Communication*, *77*(4), 489–506. doi:10.1080/10570314.2013.779017

Ladau, E. (2017, Sept. 27). Playing the online dating game, in a wheelchair. *The New York Times*. Retrieved from https:// www.nytimes.com/2017/09/27/opinion/online-dating-disability.html

LaMendola, W. (2010). Social work and social presence in an online world. *Journal of Technology in Human Services*, *28*(1-2), 108–119. doi:10.1080/15228831003759562

Lam, M. K., Hines, M., Lowe, R., Nagarajan, S., Keep, M., Penman, M., & Power, E. (2016). Preparedness for eHealth: Health Sciences Students' Knowledge, Skills, and Confidence. *Journal of Information Technology Education: Research*, *15*, 305–334. doi:10.28945/3523

Lampe, C., Ellison, N., & Steinfield, C. (2006). A Face(book) in the crowd: Social searching vs. social browsing. In *Proceedings of the 2006 20th Anniversary Conference on Computer Supported Cooperative Work* (pp. 167-170). New York: ACM Press. 10.1145/1180875.1180901

Landoll, R. R., La Greca, A. M., & Lai, B. S. (2013). Aversive peer experiences on social networking sites: Development of the Social Networking-Peer Experiences Questionnaires (SN-PEQ). *Journal of Research on Adolescence*, *23*(4), 695–705. doi:10.1111/jora.12022 PMID:24288449

Landovitz, R. J., Tseng, C. H., Weissman, M., Haymer, M., Mendenhall, B., Rogers, K., ... Shoptaw, S. (2013). Epidemiology, sexual risk behavior, and HIV prevention practices of men who have sex with men using GRINDR in Los Angeles, California. *Journal of Urban Health*, *90*(4), 729–739. doi:10.100711524-012-9766-7 PMID:22983721

Lanz, M., & Tagliabue, S. (2007). Do I really need someone in order to become an adult? Romantic relationships during emerging adulthood in Italy. *Journal of Adolescent Research*, *22*(5), 531–549. doi:10.1177/0743558407306713

Lathouwers, K., de Moor, J., & Didden, R. (2009). Access to and use of Internet by adolescents who have a physical disability: A comparative study. *Research in Developmental Disabilities*, *30*(4), 702–711. doi:10.1016/j.ridd.2008.09.003 PMID:19022618

Lauckner, C., Truszczynski, N., Lambert, D., Kottamasu, V., Meherally, S., Schipani-McLaughlin, A. M., ... Hansen, N. (2019). "Catfishing," cyberbullying, and coercion: An exploration of the risks associated with dating app use among rural sexual minority males. *Journal of Gay & Lesbian Mental Health*, 1–18.

Ledbetter, A. M., Mazer, J. P., DeGroot, J. M., Meyer, K. R., Yuping, M., & Swafford, B. (2011). Attitudes toward online social connection and self-disclosure as predictors of Facebook communication and relational closeness. *Communication Research*, *38*(1), 27–53. doi:10.1177/0093650210365537

Lee, B. H., & O'Sullivan, L. F. (2014). The ex-factor: Characteristics of online and offline post-relationship contact and tracking among canadian emerging adults. *The Canadian Journal of Human Sexuality*, *23*(2), 96–105. doi:10.3138/cjhs.2415

Lee, E., Choi, T. R., Lee, T. D., & Sung, Y. (2019). Using Instagram While "In a Relationship". *Journal of Individual Differences*, *40*(2), 111–117. doi:10.1027/1614-0001/a000282

Lee, K. T., Noh, M. J., & Koo, D. M. (2013). Lonely people are no longer lonely on social networking sites: The mediating role of self-disclosure and social support. *Cyberpsychology, Behavior, and Social Networking*, *16*(6), 413–418. doi:10.1089/cyber.2012.0553 PMID:23621716

Lee, M., & Crofts, T. (2015). Gender, pressure, coercion and pleasure: Untangling motivations for sexting between young people. *British Journal of Criminology*, *55*(3), 454–473. doi:10.1093/bjc/azu075

Lee-Won, R. J., Shim, M. S., Joo, Y. K., & Park, S. G. (2014). Who puts the best "face" in Facebook?: Positive self-presentation in online social networking and the role of self-consciousness, actual-to-total friends ratio, and culture. *Computers in Human Behavior*, *39*, 413–423. doi:10.1016/j.chb.2014.08.007

Lee, Y.-K., Chang, C.-T., Lin, Y., & Cheng, Z.-H. (2014). The Dark Side of Smartphone Usage: Psychological Traits, Compulsive Behavior and Technostress. *Computers in Human Behavior*, *31*, 373–383. doi:10.1016/j.chb.2013.10.047

Lee, Z. W. Y., & Cheung, C. M. K. (2014). Problematic use of social networking sites: The role of self-esteem. *International Journal of Business and Information*, *9*(2), 143.

LeFebvre, L. E. (2018). Swiping me off my feet: Explicating relationship initiation on Tinder. *Journal of Social and Personal Relationships*, *35*(9), 1205–1229. doi:10.1177/0265407517706419

Lefkowitz, E. S., & Gillen, M. M. (2006). *"Sex is just a normal part of life": Sexuality in emerging adulthood*. Academic Press.

Leighton, D. C., Legate, N., LePine, S., Anderson, S. F., & Grahe, J. E. (2018, January 1). *Self-Esteem, self-disclosure, self-expression, and connection on Facebook: A collaborative replication meta-analysis.* doi:10.31234/osf.io/sx742

Lenahan, P., & Shapiro, J. (2005). Facilitating the emotional education of medical students: Using literature and film in training about intimate partner violence. *Family Medicine*, *37*(8). PMID:16145628

Lenhart, A. Ybaraa, M., & Price-Feeney, M. (2016). *Nonconsensual Image Sharing: One in 25 Americans has been a Victim of "Revenge Porn."* Academic Press.

Lenhart, A., Ybarra, M., Zickuhr, K., & Price-Feeney, M. (2016). *Online Harassment, Digital Abuse, and Cyberstalking in America.* Data & Society Research Institute. Retrieved from https://www.datasociety.net/pubs/oh/Online_Harassment_2016.pdf

Leonhardt, N. D., Spencer, T. J., Butler, M. H., & Theobald, A. C. (2018). An organizational framework for sexual media's influence on short-term versus long-term sexual quality. *Archives of Sexual Behavior*, 1–17. PMID:30014336

Leonhardt, N. D., & Willoughby, B. J. (2018). Longitudinal links between pornography use, marital importance, and permissive sexuality during emerging adulthood. *Marriage & Family Review*, *54*(1), 64–84. doi:10.1080/01494929.2017.1359811

Leonhardt, N. D., Willoughby, B. J., & Young-Petersen, B. (2018). Damaged goods: Perception of pornography addiction as a mediator between religiosity and relationship anxiety surrounding pornography use. *Journal of Sex Research*, *55*(3), 357–368. doi:10.1080/00224499.2017.1295013 PMID:28287845

Lepp, A., Barkley, J. E., & Karpinski, A. C. (2014). The Relationship Between Cell Phone Use, Academic Performance, Anxiety, and Satisfaction with Life in College Students. *Computers in Human Behavior*, *31*, 343–350. doi:10.1016/j.chb.2013.10.049

Leung, L. (2002). Loneliness, self-disclosure, and ICQ use. *Cyberpsychology & Behavior*, *5*(3), 241–251. doi:10.1089/109493102760147240 PMID:12123247

Leung, L. (2008). Linking Psychological Attributes to Addictıon and Improper Use of The Mobile Phone Among Adolescents in Hong Kong. *Journal of Children and Media*, *2*(2), 93–113. doi:10.1080/17482790802078565

Leung, L., & Lee, P. S. (2005). Multiple determinants of life quality: The roles of Internet activities, use of new media, social support, and leisure activities. *Telematics and Informatics*, *22*(3), 161–180. doi:10.1016/j.tele.2004.04.003

Levine, T. R. (2014). Truth-Default Theory (TDT): A theory of human deception and deception detection. *Journal of Language and Social Psychology*, *33*(4), 378–392. doi:10.1177/0261927X14535916

Levine, T. R., Kima, R. K., & Hamela, L. M. (2010). People Lie for a Reason: Three Experiments Documenting the Principle of Veracity. *Communication Research Reports*, *4*(4), 271–285. doi:10.1080/08824096.2010.496334

Levinson, D. J. (1978). *The seasons of a man's life*. Random House LLC.

Levitin, D. J. (2014). *The Organized Mind.* New York: Penguin Random House.

Liddiard, K., & Slater, J. (2018). "Like, pissing yourself is not a particularly attractive quality, let's be honest": Learning to contain through youth, adulthood, disability and sexuality. *Sexualities*, *21*(3), 319–333. doi:10.1177/1363460716688674

Lietz, C., Langer, C., & Furman, R. (2006). Establishing trustworthiness in social work research: Implications from a study regarding spirituality. *Qualitative Social Work: Research and Practice*, *5*(4), 441–458. doi:10.1177/1473325006070288

Ligato, L. (2015). *An Embarrassing Number Of People Say They Couldn't Live Without Their Smartphone*. Retrieved May 10, 2016 from http://www.huffingtonpost.com/2015/07/13/smartphone-dependence-addiction_n_7785782.html

Liles, R. E. (2007). The use of feature films as teaching tools in social work education. *Journal of Teaching in Social Work, 27*(3-4), 45–60. doi:10.1300/J067v27n03_04

Limoncin, E., Carta, R., Gravina, G. L., Carosa, E., Ciocca, G., Di Sante, S., ... Jannini, E. A. (2014). The sex.ual attraction toward disabilities: A preliminary internet- based study. *International Journal of Impotence Research, 26*(2), 51–54. doi:10.1038/ijir.2013.34 PMID:24048013

Link, B. G. (1982). Mental patient status, work, and income: An examination of the effects of a psychiatric label. *American Sociological Review, 47*(2), 202–215. doi:10.2307/2094963 PMID:7091929

Link, B. G., Cullen, F. T., Struening, E., Shrout, P. E., & Dohrenwend, B. P. (1989). A modified labeling theory approach to mental disorders: An empirical assessment. *American Sociological Review, 54*(3), 400–423. doi:10.2307/2095613

Link, B. G., & Phelan, J. C. (2001). Conceptualizing stigma. *Annual Review of Sociology, 27*(1), 363–385. doi:10.1146/annurev.soc.27.1.363

Link, B. G., Phelan, J. C., Bresnahan, M., Stueve, A., & Pescosolido, B. A. (1999). Public conceptions of mental illness: Labels, causes, dangerousness and social distance. *American Journal of Public Health, 89*(9), 1328–1333. doi:10.2105/AJPH.89.9.1328 PMID:10474548

Linne, J. (2014). Common uses of Facebook among adolescents from different social sectors in Buenos Aires City. *Media Education Research Journal, 43,* 189-197. Retrieved June 10, 2019 from dialnet.unirioja.es/descarga/articulo/4738318/2.pdf

Lippman, J. R., & Campbell, S. W. (2014). Damned if you do, damned if you don't… if you're a girl: Relational and normative contexts of adolescent sexting in the United States. *Journal of Children and Media, 8*(4), 371–386. doi:10.1080/17482798.2014.923009

Lipton, J. D. (2011). Combating cyber-victimization. *Berkeley Technology Law Journal, 26,* 1104–1126.

Little, R. J. A., & Rubin, D. B. (1989). The analysis of social science data with missing values. *Sociological Methods & Research, 18*(2-3), 292–326. doi:10.1177/0049124189018002004

Liu, D., & Brown, B. B. (2014). Self-disclosure on social networking sites, positive feedback, and social capital among Chinese college students. *Computers in Human Behavior, 38,* 213–219. doi:10.1016/j.chb.2014.06.003

Loeber, R., & Farrington, D. P. (2014). Age-Crime Curve. In G. Bruinsma & D. Weisburd (Eds.), *Encyclopedia of Criminology and Criminal Justice.* New York, NY: Springer. doi:10.1007/978-1-4614-5690-2_474

Lofgren-Martenson, L. (2008). Love in cyberspace: Swedish young people with intellectual disabilities and the internet. *Scandinavian Journal of Disability Research, 10*(2), 125–138. doi:10.1080/15017410701758005

Löfgren-Mårtenson, L., & Månsson, S. A. (2010). Lust, love, and life: A qualitative study of Swedish adolescents perceptions and experiences with pornography. *Journal of Sex Research, 47*(6), 568–579. doi:10.1080/00224490903151374

Lopes, M. R., & Vogel, C. (2017, August). Women's perspective on using Tinder: a user study of gender dynamics in a mobile device application. In *Proceedings of the 35th ACM International Conference on the Design of Communication* (p. 12). ACM. 10.1145/3121113.3121220

Loseke, D. R. (2001). Lived realities and formula stories of "battered women." In J. F. Gubrium & J. A. Holstein (Eds.), *Institutional selves: Troubled identities in a postmodern world* (pp. 107–126). New York: Oxford University Press.

Lou, L. L., Yan, Z., Nickerson, A., & McMorris, R. (2012). An examination of the reciprocal relationship of loneliness and Facebook use among first-year college students. *Journal of Educational Computing Research, 46*(1), 105–117. doi:10.2190/EC.46.1.e

Lo, V. H., & Wei, R. (2002). Third-person effect, gender, and pornography on the internet. *Journal of Broadcasting & Electronic Media*, *46*(1), 13–33. doi:10.120715506878jobem4601_2

Lucero, J. L., Weisz, A. N., Smith-Darden, J., & Lucero, S. M. (2014). Exploring gender differences: Socially interactive technology use/abuse among dating teens. *Affilia*, *29*(4), 478–491. doi:10.1177/0886109914522627

Lup, K., Trub, L., & Rosenthal, L. (2015). Instagram #Instasad?: Exploring associations among Instagram use, depressive symptoms, negative social comparison, and strangers followed. *Cyberpsychology, Behavior, and Social Networking*, *15*(5), 247–252. doi:10.1089/cyber.2014.0560 PMID:25965859

Lutz, C., & Ranzini, G. (2017). Where dating meets data: Investigating social and institutional privacy concerns on tinder. *Social Media+ Society*, *3*(1).

Lysaker, P. H., Roe, D., & Yanos, P. T. (2007). Toward understanding the insight paradox: Internalized stigma moderates the association between insight and social functioning, hope, and self-esteem among people with schizophrenia spectrum disorders. *Schizophrenia Bulletin*, *33*(1), 192–199. doi:10.1093chbulbl016 PMID:16894025

Lyubormirsky, S., & Ross, L. (1997). Hedonic consequences of social comparison: A contrast of happy and unhappy people. *Journal of Personality and Social Psychology*, *73*(6), 1141–1157. doi:10.1037/0022-3514.73.6.1141 PMID:9418274

MacInnes, M. (2011). Altar-bound? The effect of disability on the hazard of entry into a first marriage. *International Journal of Sociology*, *41*(1), 87–103. doi:10.2753/IJS0020-7659410105 PMID:23946548

MacKenzie, R. D., Mullen, P. E., Ogloff, J. R. P., McEwan, T. E., & James, D. V. (2008). Parental bonding and adult attachment styles in different types of stalker. *Journal of Forensic Sciences*, *53*(6), 1443–1449. doi:10.1111/j.1556-4029.2008.00869.x PMID:18798773

Mackinnon, S. P., Nosko, A., Pratt, M. W., & Norris, J. E. (2011). Intimacy in young adults' narratives of romance and friendship predICT's Eriksonian generativity: A mixed method analysis. *Journal of Personality*, *79*(3), 587–617. doi:10.1111/j.1467-6494.2011.00692.x PMID:21534965

Malamuth, N. M. (1996). Sexually explicit media, gender differences, and evolutionary theory. *Journal of Communication*, *46*(3), 8–31. doi:10.1111/j.1460-2466.1996.tb01486.x

Malamuth, N. M., & Check, J. V. (1985). The effects of aggressive pornography on beliefs in rape myths: Individual differences. *Journal of Research in Personality*, *19*(3), 299–320. doi:10.1016/0092-6566(85)90021-2

Malamuth, N. M., Hald, G. M., & Koss, M. (2012). Pornography, individual differences in risk and mens' acceptance of violence against women in a representative sample. *Sex Roles*, *66*(7-8), 427–439. doi:10.100711199-011-0082-6

Maloney, P. W., Grawitch, M. J., & Barber, L. K. (2012). The multi-factor structure of the Brief Self-Control Scale: Discriminant validity of restraint and impulsivity. *Journal of Research in Personality*, *46*(1), 111–115. doi:10.1016/j.jrp.2011.10.001

Manning, W. D., Giordano, P. C., Longmore, M. A., & Hocevar, A. (2009). *Romantic relationships and academic/career trajectories in early adulthood.* Retrieved from The Center for Family and Demographic Research website: http://www.bgsu.edu/organizations/cfdr

Manning, W. D., Brown, S. L., & Payne, K. K. (2014). Two decades of stability and change in age at first union formation. *Journal of Marriage and the Family*, *76*(2), 247–260. doi:10.1111/jomf.12090 PMID:25147410

Mansson, D. H., & Myers, S. A. (2011). An initial examination of college students' expressions of affection through Facebook. *The Southern Communication Journal*, *76*(2), 155–168. doi:10.1080/10417940903317710

March, E., Grieve, R., Marrington, J., & Jonason, P. K. (2017). Trolling on Tinder® (and other dating apps): Examining the role of the Dark Tetrad and impulsivity. *Personality and Individual Differences*, *110*, 139–143. doi:10.1016/j.paid.2017.01.025

Marcum, C. D., Higgins, G. E., & Ricketts, M. L. (2014). Juveniles and cyber stalking in the United States: An analysis of theoretical predictors of patterns of online perpetration. *International Journal of Cyber Criminology*, *8*, 47–56.

Markham, A. (2013). Remix Cultures, Remix Methods. Global Dimensions of Qualitative Inquiry, 63-81.

Markowitz, D. M., & Hancock, J. T. (2018). Deception in mobile dating conversations. *Journal of Communication*, *68*(3), 547–569. doi:10.1093/joc/jqy019

Marshall, T. C., Bejanyan, K., Di Castro, G., & Lee, R. A. (2013). Attachment styles as predictors of Facebook-related jealousy and surveillance in romantic relationships. *Personal Relationships*, *20*(1), 1–22. doi:10.1111/j.1475-6811.2011.01393.x

Martino, S. C., Collins, R. L., Elliott, M. N., Strachman, A., Kanouse, D. E., & Berry, S. H. (2007). Exposure to degrading versus nondegrading music lyrics and sexual behavior among youth. *Pediatrics*, *118*(2), e430–e441. doi:10.1542/peds.2006-0131 PMID:16882784

Marwick, A. E. (2015). Instafame: Luxury Selfies in the Attention Economy. *Public Culture, 27*(175), 137-160.

Marwick, A. E., & boyd. (2011). I tweet honestly, I tweet passionately: Twitter users, context collapse, and the imagined audience. *New Media & Society*, *13*(1), 114–133. doi:10.1177/1461444810365313

Masi, C. M., Chen, H.-Y., Hawkley, L. C., & Cacioppo, J. T. (2011). A meta-analysis of interventions to reduce loneliness. *Personality and Social Psychology Review*, *15*(3), 219–266. doi:10.1177/1088868310377394

Maslow, A. (1954). *Motivation and personality*. New York, NY: Harper.

Mathias, Z., & Harcourt, D. (2014). Dating and intimate relationships of women with below-knee amputation: An exploratory study. *Disability and Rehabilitation*, *36*(5), 395–402. doi:10.3109/09638288.2013.797509 PMID:23721496

May, K. T. (2013, February 14). 7 things we learned about online dating from the co-founder of OKCupid [blog post]. Retrieved from http://blog.ted.com/7- things-we-learned-about-online-dating-from-the-co-founder-of-okcupid/

Mayo, R., & Mayo, C. M. (2013). College students' perspectives on dating a person who stutters. *College Student Journal*, *47*, 169–177.

Mazur, E., & Kozarian, L. (2010). Self-presentation and interaction in blogs of adolescents and young emerging adults. *Journal of Adolescent Research*, *25*(1), 124–144. doi:10.1177/0743558409350498

Mazzoni, E., & Zanazzi, L. (2014). Comparing the Use of SNSs Among Adults and Emerging Asults. *Journal of e-Learning and Knowledge Society, 10*, 25-36.

Mazzoni, E., Baiocco, L., Cannata, D., & Dimas, I. (2016). Is Internet the cherry on top or a crutch? Offline social support as moderator of the outcomes of online social support on Problematic Internet Use. *Computers in Human Behavior*, *56*, 369–374. doi:10.1016/j.chb.2015.11.032

Mazzoni, E., & Iannone, M. (2014). From high school to university: Impact of social networking sites on social capital in the transitions of emerging adults. *British Journal of Educational Technology*, *45*(2), 303–315. doi:10.1111/bjet.12026

Mazzoni, E., & Zanazzi, L. (2014). Comparing the use of SNSs among adults and emerging adults.Journal of e-Learning and knowledge. *Society*, *10*(3), 25–36.

McCartney, J. (2010). Eminem and Rihanna's brutality chic is a bit beyond me. *The Telegraph*. Retrieved from http://www.telegraph.co.uk/comment/columnists/ jennymccartney/7957505/Emimen-and-Rihannas-brutality-chic-is-a-bit-beyond-me.html

McDonald, S. M. (2010, July 26). As ADA turns 20, Harris interactive survey finds lifestyle and economic gaps still remain between Americans with and without disabilities. *The Kessler Foundation*. Retrieved from http://www.2010disabilitysurveys.org/

McIntosh, A. (1999). When the deaf and the hearing interact: Communication features, relationship, and disability issues. In D. O. Braithwaite & T. L. Thompson (Eds.), *Handbook of Communication and People with Disabilities: Research and Application* (pp. 353–368). Mahwah, NJ: Routledge.

McIntyre, L. L., Blacher, J., & Baker, B. L. (2006). Transition to school: Adaptation in young children with and without developmental delays. *Journal of Intellectual Disability Research*, *50*, 349–361. doi:10.1111/j.1365-2788.2006.00783.x PMID:16629928

McKee, A. (2007). The relationship between attitudes towards women, consumption of pornography, and other demographic variables in a survey of 1,023 consumers of pornography. *International Journal of Sexual Health*, *19*(1), 31–45. doi:10.1300/J514v19n01_05

McKenna, K. Y., Green, A. S., & Gleason, M. E. J. (2002). Relationship formation on the Internet: What's the big attraction? *The Journal of Social Issues*, *58*(1), 9–31. doi:10.1111/1540-4560.00246

McLaughlin, C., & Vitak, J. (2012). Norm evolution and violation on Facebook. *New Media & Society*, *14*(2), 299–315. doi:10.1177/1461444811412712

McMahon, S., Postmus, J. L., Warrener, C., Plummer, S., & Schwartz, R. (2013). Evaluating the effect of a specialized MSW course on violence against women. *Journal of Social Work Education*, *49*(2), 307–320. doi:10.1080/10437797.2013.768484

Medeiros, D. T., & Webb, L. M. (2019). Remaining Facebook versus face-to-face friends after a romantic breakup. *International Journal of Interactive Communication Systems and Technologies*, *9*(1), 1–16. doi:10.4018/IJICST.2019010101

Meijer, R. R., de Vries, R. M., & van Bruggen, V. (2011). An evaluation of the Brief Symptom Inventory-18 using item response theory: Which items are most strongly related to psychological distress? *Psychological Assessment*, *23*(1), 193–202. doi:10.1037/a0021292 PMID:21280957

Mellor, D., Stokes, M., Firth, L., Hayashi, Y., & Cummins, R. (2008). Need for belonging, relationship satisfaction, loneliness, and life satisfaction. *Personality and Individual Differences*, *45*(3), 213–218. doi:10.1016/j.paid.2008.03.020

Membrives, M. D., Isern, M. T. I., & Matheu, M. C. L. (2016). Literature review: Use of commercial films as a teaching resource for health sciences students. *Nurse Education Today*, *36*, 264–267. doi:10.1016/j.nedt.2015.10.002 PMID:26490325

Ménard, K. S., & Pincus, A. L. (2012). Predicting overt and cyber stalking perpetration by male and female college students. *Journal of Interpersonal Violence*, *27*(11), 2183–2207. doi:10.1177/0886260511432144 PMID:22203630

Meyers, M. (1994). News of battering. *Journal of Communication*, *44*(2), 47–63. doi:10.1111/j.1460-2466.1994.tb00676.x

Michikyan, M., Dennis, J., & Subrahmanyam, K. (2015). Can you guess who I am? Real, ideal, and false self-presentation on Facebook among emerging adults. *Emerging Adulthood*, *3*(1), 55–64. doi:10.1177/2167696814532442

Mikulincer, M. (2006). Attachment, caregiving, and sex within romantic relationships. *Dynamics of Romantic Love: Attachment, Caregiving, and Sex*, 23-42.

Mikulincer, M., & Shaver, P. R. (2016). *Attachment in adulthood: Structure, dynamics, and change* (2nd ed.). New York: Guilford Press.

Milbrodt, T. (2019). Dating websites and disability identity: Presentations of the disabled self in online dating profiles. *Western Folklore, 78*, 66–100.

Miller, A. N., & Rubin, D. L. (2007). Factors leading to self-disclosure of a positive HIV diagnosis in Nairobi, Kenya. *Qualitative Health Research, 17*(5), 586–598. doi:10.1177/1049732307301498 PMID:17478642

Miller, B., & Mundey, P. (2015). Follow the rules and no one will get hurt: Performing boudary work to avoid negative interactions when using social network sites. *Information Communication and Society, 18*(2), 187–201. doi:10.1080/1369118X.2014.946433

Miller, E., Chen, R., Glover-Graf, N. M., & Kranz, P. (2009). Willingness to engage in personal relationships with persons with disabilities. *Rehabilitation Counseling Bulletin, 52*(4), 211–224. doi:10.1177/0034355209332719

Miller, S. A., & Byers, E. S. (2004). Actual and desired duration of foreplay and intercourse: Discordance and misperceptions within heterosexual couples. *Journal of Sex Research, 41*(3), 301–309. doi:10.1080/00224490409552237 PMID:15497058

Mishna, F., Khoury-Kassabri, M., Gadalla, T., & Daciuk, J. (2012). Risk factors for involvement in cyber bullying: Victims, bullies and bully-victims. *Children and Youth Services Review, 34*(1), 63–70. doi:10.1016/j.childyouth.2011.08.032

Mishna, F., McLuckie, A., & Saini, M. (2009). Real-world dangers in an online reality: A qualitative study examining online relationships and cyber abuse. *Social Work Research, 33*(2), 107–118. doi:10.1093wr/33.2.107

Molin, M., Sorbring, E., & Löfgren-Mårtenson, L. (2017). New Em@ncipatory landscapes? Young people with intellectual disabilities, Internet use and identification processes. *Advances in Social Work, 18*(2), 645–662. doi:10.18060/21428

Moningka, C., & Permatasari, R. E. (2018). *The effect of social comparison on self-esteem.* Unpublished manuscript. Tangerang Selatan: Universitas Pembangunan Jaya.

Moningka, C. (2015). *The use of social media in Jakarta. Unpublished research.* Jakarta: Gunadarma University.

Montgomery-Graham, S., & Kohut, T. (2019). Pornography problems due to moral incongruence. *Archives of Sexual Behavior, 48*(2), 425–429.

Monto, M. A., & Carey, A. G. (2014). A new standard of sexual behavior? Are claims associated with the "hookup culture" supported by general social survey data? *Journal of Sex Research, 51*(6), 605–615. doi:10.1080/00224499.2014.906031 PMID:24750070

Moorhead, S. A., Hazlett, D. E., Harrison, L., Carroll, J. K., Irwin, A., & Hoving, C. (2013). A new dimension of Health Care: Systematic Review of the Uses, Benefits and Limitations of Social Media for Health Communication. *Journal of Medical Internet Research, 15*(4), e85. doi:10.2196/jmir.1933 PMID:23615206

Mo, P. K. H., & Coulson, N. S. (2008). Exploring the communication of social support within virtual communities: A content analysis of messages posted to an online HIV/AIDS support group. *Cyberpsychology & Behavior, 11*(3), 371–374. doi:10.1089/cpb.2007.0118 PMID:18537512

Mo, P. K. H., & Coulson, N. S. (2013). Online support group use and psychological health for individuals living with HIV/AIDS. *Patient Education and Counseling, 93*(3), 426–432. doi:10.1016/j.pec.2013.04.004 PMID:23669152

Moreno, M. A., Jelenchick, L. A., Egan, K. G., Cox, E., Young, H., Gannon, K. E., & Becker, T. (2011). Feeling bad on Facebook: Depression disclosures by college students on a social networking site. *Depression and Anxiety*, *28*(6), 447–455. doi:10.1002/da.20805 PMID:21400639

Morgan, E. M. (2011). Associations between young adults use of sexually explicit materials and their sexual preferences, behaviors, and satisfaction. *Journal of Sex Research*, *48*(6), 520–530. doi:10.1080/00224499.2010.543960 PMID:21259151

Morgan, E. M., & Korobov, N. (2012). Interpersonal identity formation in conversations with close friends about dating relationships. *Journal of Adolescence*, *35*(6), 1471–1483. doi:10.1016/j.adolescence.2011.09.005 PMID:21986354

Mosher, D. L., & MacIan, P. (1994). College men and women respond to X-rated videos intended for male or female audiences: Gender and sexual scripts. *Journal of Sex Research*, *31*(2), 99–113. doi:10.1080/00224499409551736

Muise, A., Christofides, E., & Desmarais, S. (2009). More information than you ever wanted: Does Facebook bring out the green-eyed monster of jealousy? *Cyberpsychology & Behavior*, *12*(4), 441–444. Retrieved from http://sexresearchandthecity.com/content/uploads/2011/04/Facebook-Jealousy.pdf doi:10.1089/cpb.2008.0263 PMID:19366318

Munsey, C. (2006). Emerging adults: The in-between age. *Monitor (Charlottetown)*, *37*, 68. Retrieved from http://www.apa.org/monitor/jun06/emerging.aspx

Murphy, A. (2018). Dating Dangerously: Risks Lurking within Mobile Dating Apps. *Catholic University Journal of Law and Technology*, *26*(1), 7.

Murray, C. E., & Campbell, E. C. (2015). The pleasures and perils of technology in intimate relationships. *Journal of Couple & Relationship Therapy*, *14*(2), 116–140. doi:10.1080/15332691.2014.953651

Murray, C., & Kardatzke, K. (2007). Dating violence among college students: Key issues for college counselors. *Journal of College Counseling*, *10*(1), 79–89. doi:10.1002/j.2161-1882.2007.tb00008.x

Myers, D. G., & Twenge, J. M. (2013). Social psychology (11th ed.). New York: McGraw-Hill.

Nabi, R. L., Prestin, A., & So, J. (2013). Facebook Friends with (Health) Benefits?: Exploring the Palliative Effects of Social Network Sites Compared to Interpersonal Networks. *Cyberpsychology, Behavior, and Social Networking*, *16*, 721–727. doi:10.1089/cyber.2012.0521

Nabors, E. L., Dietz, T. L., & Jasinski, J. L. (2006). Domestic violence beliefs and perceptions among college students. *Violence and Victims*, *21*(6), 779–795. doi:10.1891/0886-6708.21.6.779 PMID:17220019

Nadkarni, A., & Hofmann, S. G. (2012). Why do people use Facebook? *Personality and Individual Differences*, *52*(3), 243–249. doi:10.1016/j.paid.2011.11.007 PMID:22544987

Nam, M., Chun, B., & Hin, L. C. (2014). Impoliteness in Facebook Status updates: Stategic talk among colleagues "outside" the workplace. *Text & Talk*, *34*, 165–188. doi:10.1515/text-2013-0042

Naslund, J. A., Grande, S. W., Aschbrenner, K. A., & Elwyn, G. (2014). Naturally occurring peer support through social media: The experiences of individuals with severe mental illness using YouTube. *PLoS One*, *9*(10), e110171. doi:10.1371/journal.pone.0110171 PMID:25333470

Natarajan, G., Somasundaram, C. P., & Sundaram, K. R. (2011). Relationship between attachment security and rejection sensitivity in early adolescence. *Psychological Studies*, *56*(4), 378–386. doi:10.100712646-011-0108-8

National Institute of Mental Health. (2019). *Major Depression.* Retrieved from https://www.nimh.nih.gov/health/statistics/major-depression.shtml

Neal, C., Beckjord, E., Rechis, R., Schaeffer, J., Berno, D., & Duchover, Y. (2010). *Cancer stigma and silence around the world: A LIVESTRONG report.* Retrieved from http://images.livestrong.org/downloads/flatfiles/what-we-do/our-approach/reports/cancer-stigma/LSGlobalResearchReport.pdf

Nelson, L. J., Padilla-Walker, L. M., & Carroll, J. S. (2010). I believe it is wrong but I still do it: A comparison of religious young men who do versus do not use pornography. *Psychology of Religion and Spirituality*, *2*(3), 136–147. doi:10.1037/a0019127

Nelson, L., & Barry, C. (2005). Distinguishing features of emerging adulthood: The role of self-classification as an adult. *Journal of Adolescent Research*, *20*(2), 242–262. doi:10.1177/0743558404273074

Nemeth, S. A. (2000). Society, sexuality, and disabled/ablebodied romantic relationships. In D. O. Braithwaite & T. L. Thompson (Eds.), *Handbook of communication and people with disabilities* ((pp. 37–48). Mahwah, NJ: Lawrence Erlbaum.

Newberry, M. (2016). Negative Relating and Psychopathy. In J. Birtchnell, M. Newberry, & A. E. Kalaitzaki (Eds.), *Relating Theory: Clinical, Forensic and other Applications*. London: Palgrave Macmillan. doi:10.1057/978-1-137-50459-3_20

Newberry, M., & Birtchnell, J. (2011). Negative relating and offense type. *Journal of Criminal Psychology*, *1*(1), 24–35. doi:10.1108/20093829201100003

Newman, L., Wagner, M., Knokey, A. M., Marder, C., Nagle, K., Shaver, D., ... Schwarting, M. (2011). *The post-high school outcomes of young adults with disabilities up to 8 years after high school. A report from the National Longitudinal Transition Study-2 (NLTS2)* (NCSER 2011-3005). Menlo Park, CA: SRI International.

Newman, M. W., Lauterbach, D., Munson, S. A., Resnick, P., & Morris, M. E. (2011). It's not that I don't have problems, I'm just not putting them on Facebook: Challenges and opportunities in using online social networks for health. In *Proceedings of the ACM 2011 Conference on Computer Supported Cooperative Work* (pp. 341- 350). Hangzhou, China: ACM. 10.1145/1958824.1958876

Nicholson, K. J., & Sacco, W. P. (1999, August). *Interpersonal responses to depression: Negative social-cognition, affect, and non-genuine support.* Poster session presented at the annual meeting of the American Psychological Association, Boston, MA.

Nikhita, C. S., Jadhav, P. R., & Ajinkya, S. A. (2015, November). Prevalence of Mobile Phone Dependence in Secondary School Adolescents. *Journal of Clinical and Diagnostic Research: JCDR*, *9*(11), 6–9. PMID:26672469

Nobles, M. R., Reyns, B. W., Fox, K. A., & Fisher, B. S. (2014). Protection against pursuit: A conceptual and empirical comparison of cyberstalking and stalking victimization among a national sample. *Justice Quarterly*, *31*(6), 986–1014. doi:10.1080/07418825.2012.723030

Norman, R. M. G., Gawronski, G., Hampson, E., Sorrentno, R. M., Szeto, A., & Ye, Y. (2010). Physical proximity in anticipation of meeting someone with schizophrenia: The role of explicit evaluations, implicit evaluations and cortisol levels. *Schizophrenia Research*, *124*(1-3), 74–80. doi:10.1016/j.schres.2010.07.021 PMID:20713306

Norona, J. C., Roberson, P. N. E., & Welsh, D. P. (2016). Rejection sensitivity and depressive symptoms: Longitudinal actor-partner effects in adolescent romantic relationships. *Journal of Adolescence*, *51*, 6–18. doi:10.1016/j.adolescence.2016.05.007 PMID:27254083

Norona, J. C., Salvatore, J. F., Welsh, D. P., & Darling, N. (2014). Rejection sensitivity and adolescents' perceptions of romantic interactions. *Journal of Adolescence*, *37*(8), 1257–1267. doi:10.1016/j.adolescence.2014.09.003 PMID:25282535

Nosek, M. A., Howland, B. A., Rintala, D. H., Young, M. E., & Chanpong, G. (2001). National study of women with physical disabilities: Final report. *Sexuality and Disability, 19*, 5-39.

Novak, S. P., & Clayton, R. R. (2001). The influence of school environment and self-regulation on transitions between stages of cigarette smoking: A multilevel analysis. *Health Psychology, 20*(3), 196–207. doi:10.1037/0278-6133.20.3.196 PMID:11403217

O'Riordan, C., & O'Connell, M. (2014). Predicting adult involvement in crime: Personality measures are significant, socio-economic measures are not. *Personality and Individual Differences, 68*, 98–101. doi:10.1016/j.paid.2014.04.010

Odaci, H., & Kalkan, M. (2010). Problematic Internet use, loneliness and dating anxiety among young adult college students. *Computers & Education, 55*(3), 1091–1097. doi:10.1016/j.compedu.2010.05.006

Office for National Statistics. (2018). *Internet access - households and individuals.* Retrieved from https://www.ons.gov.uk/peoplepopulationandcommunity/householdcharacteristics/homeinternetandsocialmediausage/datasets/internetaccesshouseholdsandindividualsreferencetables

Olkin, R. (1999). *What psychotherapists should know about disability.* New York: Guilford Press.

Olmstead, S. B., Negash, S., Pasley, K., & Fincham, F. D. (2013). Emerging adults expectations for pornography use in the context of future committed romantic relationships: A qualitative study. *Archives of Sexual Behavior, 42*(4), 625–635. doi:10.100710508-012-9986-7 PMID:22886349

Omori, K., & Allen, M. (2014). Cultural differences between American and Japanese self-presentation on SNSs. *International Journal of Interactive Communication Systems and Technologies, 4*(1), 47–60. doi:10.4018/ijicst.2014010104

Orchard, L. J. (2019). Uses and Gratifications of Social Media: Who Uses It and Why? In A. Attrill-Smith, C. Fullwood, M. Keep, & D. J. Kuss (Eds.), *The Oxford Handbook of Cyberpsychology.* Oxford, UK: Oxford University Press.

Owen, J., Fincham, F. D., & Moore, J. (2011). Short-term prospective study of hooking up among college students. *Archives of Sexual Behavior, 40*(2), 331–341. doi:10.100710508-010-9697-x

Ozen, A., Sumer, N., & Demir, M. (2010). Predicting friendship quality with rejection sensitivity and attachment security. *Journal of Social and Personal Relationships*, 163–181. doi:10.1177/0265407510380607

Paasonen, S., Light, B., & Jarrett, K. (2019). The dick pic: harassment, curation, and desire. *Social Media+ Society, 5*(2).

Padgett, V. R., Brislin-Slütz, J. A., & Neal, J. A. (1989). Pornography, erotica, and attitudes toward women: The effects of repeated exposure. *Journal of Sex Research, 26*(4), 479–491. doi:10.1080/00224498909551529

Paolacci, G., Chandler, J., & Ipeirotis, P. G. (2010). Running experiments on amazon mechanical turk. *Judgment and Decision Making, 5*(5), 411–419.

Papp, L., Danielewicz, J., & Cayemberg, C. (2012). "Are we Facebook official?" Implications of dating partners' Facebook use and profiles for intimate relationship. *Cyberpsychology & Behavior, 15*(2), 85–99. doi:10.1089/cyber.2011.0291 PMID:21988733

Parant, A., Schiano-Lomoriello, S., & Marchan, F. (2017). How would I live with a disability? Expectations of bio-psychological consequences and assistive technology use. *Disability and Rehabilitation. Assistive Technology, 12*(7), 681–685. doi:10.1080/17483107.2016.1218555 PMID:27677931

Park, M. (2018, March 26). *Dating app dangers: is swiping safe?* Retrieved May 12, 2019, from The Daily Universe website: https://universe.byu.edu/2018/03/26/dating-apps-can-present-predatory-dangers-to-users1/

Parker, K., & Livingston, G. (2018, June 13). *7 facts about American fathers.* Retrieved April 29, 2019, from https://www.pewresearch.org/fact-tank/2018/06/13/fathers-day-facts/

Parker, G., Tupling, H., & Brown, L. B. (1979). A Parental Bonding Instrument. *The British Journal of Medical Psychology, 52*(1), 1–10. doi:10.1111/j.2044-8341.1979.tb02487.x

Parker, T. S., Blackburn, K. M., Perry, M. S., & Hawks, J. M. (2013). Sexting as an intervention: Relationship satisfaction and motivation considerations. *The American Journal of Family Therapy, 41*(1), 1–12. doi:10.1080/01926187.2011.635134

Park, N. K., & Lee, S. Y. (2014). College students' motivations for facebook use and psychological outcomes. *Journal of Broadcasting & Electronic Media, 58*(4), 601–620. doi:10.1080/08838151.2014.966355

Park, N., & Baek, K. (2016). Effects of Facebook users' self-disclosure, Facebook use intensity, privacy concern and trust on continuous use intention of Facebook: Focusing on moderating effect of privacy protection skill. *Journal of Korean Content Association, 16*(11), 53–62. doi:10.5392/JKCA.2016.16.11.053

Park, Y., & Killen, M. (2010). When is peer rejection justifiable? Children's understanding across two cultures. *Cognitive Development, 25*(3), 290–301. doi:10.1016/j.cogdev.2009.10.004 PMID:21076660

Patterson, P., Millar, B., Desille, N., & McDonald, F. (2012). The unmet needs of emerging adults with a cancer diagnosis: A qualitative study. *Cancer Nursing, 35*(3), 32–40. doi:10.1097/NCC.0b013e31822d9105 PMID:22538263

Patterson, R., & Price, J. (2012). Pornography, religion, and the happiness gap: Does pornography impact the actively religious differently? *Journal for the Scientific Study of Religion, 51*(1), 79–89. doi:10.1111/j.1468-5906.2011.01630.x PMID:22616090

Patton, C. L., Nobles, M. R., & Fox, K. A. (2010). Look who's stalking: Obsessive pursuit and attachment theory. *Journal of Criminal Justice, 38*(3), 282–290. doi:10.1016/j.jcrimjus.2010.02.013

Paul, E. L., McManus, B., & Hayes, A. (2000). Hookups: Characteristics and correlates of college students spontaneous and anonymous sexual experiences. *Journal of Sex Research, 37*(1), 76–88. doi:10.1080/00224490009552023

Pausch, N. C., Winter, K., Halama, D., Wirtz, C., Yildirim, V., & Nattapong, S. (2016). Psychosocial acceptance of cleft patients: Has something changed? *Oral and Maxillofacial Surgery, 20*(1), 19–26. doi:10.100710006-015-0518-1 PMID:26212596

Pavia, L., Cavani, P., Di Blasi, M., & Giordano, C. (2016). Smartphone Addiction Inventory (SPAI): Psychometric properties and confirmatory factor analysis. *Computers in Human Behavior, 63*, 170–178. doi:10.1016/j.chb.2016.05.039

Pearce, W. B., & Sharp, S. M. (1973). Self-disclosing communication. *Journal of Communication, 23*(4), 409–425. doi:10.1111/j.1460-2466.1973.tb00958.x PMID:4589176

Peluchette, J. V., Karl, K., Wood, C., & Williams, J. (2015). Cyberbullying victimization: Do victims' personality and risky social network behaviors contribute to the problem? *Computers in Human Behavior, 52*, 424–435. doi:10.1016/j.chb.2015.06.028

Perkins, S. A., & Turiel, E. (2007). To lie or not to lie: To whom and under what circumstances. *Child Development, 78*(2), 609–621. doi:10.1111/j.1467-8624.2007.01017.x PMID:17381793

Perrin, A. (2015). *Social media usage 2005-2015*. Retrieved from http://www.pewinternet.org/2015/10/08/social-networking-usage-2005-2015/

Perrin, A., & Duggan, M. (2015). *Americans' internet access: 2000-2015*. Retrieved from: http://www.pewin ternet.org/2015/06/26/americans-internet-access-2000-2015/

Perry, S. L., & Schleifer, C. (2019). Race and trends in pornography viewership, 1973–2016: Examining the moderating roles of gender and religion. *Journal of Sex Research, 56*(1), 62–73. doi:10.1080/00224499.2017.1404959 PMID:29244541

Peter, J., & Valkenburg, P. M. (2007). Adolescents' exposure to a sexualized media environment and their notions of women as sex objects. *Sex Roles*, *56*(5-6), 381–395. doi:10.100711199-006-9176-y

Petersen, J. L., & Hyde, J. S. (2011). Gender Differences in Sexual Attitudes and Behaviors: A Review of Meta-Analytic Results and Large Datasets. *Journal of Sex Research*, *48*(2–3), 149–165. doi:10.1080/00224499.2011.551851 PMID:21409712

Peters, J. (2008). Measuring myths about domestic violence: Development and initial validation of the domestic violence myth acceptance scale. *Journal of Aggression, Maltreatment & Trauma*, *16*(1), 1–21. doi:10.1080/10926770801917780

Peterson, A. (2014). *How I rebuilt Tinder and discovered the shameful secret of attraction*. Academic Press.

Pew Research Center. (2014). *Social networking fact sheet*. Retrieved from http://www.pewinternet.org/fact-sheets/social-networking-fact-sheet/

Pew Research Center. (2015). *The demographics of social media users*. Retrieved from http://www.pewinternet.org/2015/08/19/the-demographics-of-social-media-users/

Pew Research Center. (2015, April). *U.S. Smartphone Use in 2015*. Retrieved April 16, 2016 from http://www.pewinternet.org/files/2015/03/PI_Smartphones_0401151.pdf

Pew Research Center. (2016). *Smartphone Ownership and Internet Usage Continues to Climb in Emerging Economies*. Retrieved May 20, 2016 from http://www.pewglobal.org/files/2016/02/pew_research_center_global_technology_report_final_february_22__2016.pdf

Pfeiffer, J. P., & Pinquart, M. (2011). Attainment of developmental tasks by adolescent with visual impairments and sighted adolescents. *Journal of Visual Impairment & Blindness*, *105*(1), 33–44. doi:10.1177/0145482X1110500104

Phillips, B., Hajela, R., & Hilton, D. L. Jr. (2015). Sex addiction as a disease: Evidence for assessment, diagnosis, and response to critics. *Sexual Addiction & Compulsivity*, *22*(2), 167–192. doi:20162.2015.1036184 doi:10.1080/107

Phu, B., & Gow, A. J. (2019). Facebook use and its association with subjective happiness and loneliness. *Computers in Human Behavior*, *92*, 151–159. doi:10.1016/j.chb.2018.11.020

Pietromonaco, P. R., & Collins, N. L. (2017). Interpersonal mechanisms linking close relationships to health. *The American Psychologist*, *72*(6), 531–542. doi:10.1037/amp0000129 PMID:28880100

Pinquart, M., & Pfeiffer, J. P. (2012). What is essential is invisible to the eye: Intimate relationships of adolescents with visual impairment. *Sexuality and Disability*, *30*(2), 139–147. doi:10.100711195-011-9248-y

Plentyoffishmedia. (2015, October 23). Retrieved from http://www.pof.com/

Policastro, C., & Payne, B. K. (2013). The blameworthy victim: Domestic violence myths and the criminalization of victimhood. *Journal of Aggression, Maltreatment & Trauma*, *22*(4), 329–347. doi:10.1080/10926771.2013.775985

Postmes, T., Spears, R., & Lea, M. (2000). The formation of group norms in computermediated communication. *Human Communication Research*, *26*(3), 341–371. doi:10.1111/j.1468-2958.2000.tb00761.x

Postmus, J. L., McMahon, S., Warrener, C., & Macri, L. (2011). Factors that influence attitudes, beliefs, and behaviors of students toward survivors of violence. *Journal of Social Work Education*, *47*(2), 303–319. doi:10.5175/JSWE.2011.200900122

Poulsen, F. O., Busby, D. M., & Galovan, A. M. (2013). Pornography use: Who uses it and how it is associated with couple outcomes. *Journal of Sex Research*, *50*(1), 72–83. doi:10.1080/00224499.2011.648027 PMID:22449010

Poushter, J., Bishop, C., & Chwe, H. (2018). *Social Media Use Continues to Rise in Developing Countries but Plateaus Across Developed Ones*. Retrieved from: http://assets.pewresearch.org/wp-content/uploads/sites/2/2018/06/15135408/Pew-Research-Center_Global-Tech-Social-Media-Use_2018.06.19.pdf

Purcell, R., Pathé, M., & Mullen, P. E. (2004). Stalking: Defining and prosecuting a new category. *International Journal of Law and Psychiatry*, *27*(2), 157–169. doi:10.1016/j.ijlp.2004.01.006 PMID:15063640

Purdie, V., & Downey, G. (2000). Rejection sensitivity and adolescent girls' vulnerability to relationship-centred difficulties. *Child Maltreatment*, *5*(4), 338–349. doi:10.1177/1077559500005004005 PMID:11232261

Qiu, L., Lin, H., Leung, A. K., & Tov, W. (2012). Putting their best foot forward: Emotional disclosure on Facebook. *Cyberpsychology, Behavior, and Social Networking*, *15*(10), 569–572. doi:10.1089/cyber.2012.0200 PMID:22924675

Rafferty, J., Boettcher, C., & Griffin, K. W. (2001). Benefits and risks of reverse inclusion for preschoolers with and without disabilities: Parents' perspectives. *Journal of Early Intervention*, *24*(4), 266–286. doi:10.1177/105381510102400403

Rafferty, R., & Vander Ven, T. (2014). "I hate everything about you": A qualitative examination of cyberbullying and on-line aggression in a college sample. *Deviant Behavior*, *35*(5), 364–377. doi:10.1080/01639625.2013.849171

Rains, S. A., & Brunner, S. R. (2015). What can we learn about social network sites by studying Facebook? A call and recommendations for research on social network sites. *New Media & Society*, *17*(1), 114–131. doi:10.1177/1461444814546481

Ranzini, G., & Lutz, C. (2017). Love at first swipe? Explaining Tinder self-presentation and motives. *Mobile Media & Communication*, *5*(1), 80–101. doi:10.1177/2050157916664559

RapidValue. (2014). *Internet, Smartphone & Social Media Usage Statistics*. Retrieved May 20, 2016 from http://www.rapidvaluesolutions.com/wp-content/uploads/2014/11/Internet-Smartphone-and-Social-Media-Usage-Statistics-by-RapidValue-Solutions.pdf

Ravneberg, B. (2012). Usability and abandonment of assistive technology. *Journal of Assistive Technologies*, *6*(4), 259–269. doi:10.1108/17549451211285753

Rayner, G. (2016, March 3). *Match.com rapist jailed for life as judge raises concerns about safety of dating websites*. Retrieved from https://www.telegraph.co.uk/news/uknews/crime/12181869/Match.com-rapist-Jason-Lawrance-jailed-for-attacking-women-met-on-dating-site.html

Reed, L. A., Tolman, R. M., & Ward, L. M. (2016). Snooping and sexting: Digital media as a context for dating aggression and abuse among college students. *Violence Against Women*, *22*(13), 1556–1576. doi:10.1177/1077801216630143 PMID:26912297

Reed, L. A., Tolman, R. M., & Ward, L. M. (2017). Gender matters: Experiences and consequences of digital dating abuse victimization in adolescent dating relationships. *Journal of Adolescence*, *59*, 79–89. doi:10.1016/j.adolescence.2017.05.015 PMID:28582653

Reed, L. A., Tolman, R. M., Ward, L. M., & Safyer, P. (2016). Keeping tabs: Attachment anxiety and electronic intrusion in high school dating relationships. *Computers in Human Behavior*, *58*, 259–268. doi:10.1016/j.chb.2015.12.019

Reed, L. A., Ward, L. M., Tolman, R. M., Lippman, J. R., & Seabrook, R. C. (2018). The association between stereotypical gender and dating beliefs and digital dating abuse perpetration in adolescent dating relationships. *Journal of Interpersonal Violence*. PMID:30261802

Regnerus, M., & Uecker, J. (2010). *Premarital sex in America: How young americans meet, mate, and think about marrying*. Oxford University Press. doi:10.1093/acprof:oso/9780199743285.001.0001

Reich, R. R., Cummings, J. R., Greenbaum, P. E., Moltisanti, A. J., & Goldman, M. S. (2015). *The temporal "pulse" of drinking: Tracking 5 years of binge drinking in emerging adults*. Academic Press.

Reimer-Reiss, M. L., & Wacher, R. R. (2000). Factors associated with assistive technology discontinuance among individuals with disabilities. *Journal of Rehabilitation*, *66*, 44–50.

Renfrow, D. G., & Rollo, E. A. (2014). Sexting on campus: Minimizing perceived risks and neutralizing behaviors. *Deviant Behavior*, *35*(11), 903–920. doi:10.1080/01639625.2014.897122

Report, C. B. (2015). *Trended Data from Google for Turkey*. Retrieved May 20, 2016 from https://www.consumerbarometer.com/en/trending/?countryCode=TR&category=TRN-NOFILTER-ALL

Resch, M. N., & Alderson, K. G. (2014). Female partners of men who use pornography: Are honesty and mutual use associated with relationship satisfaction? *Journal of Sex & Marital Therapy*, *40*(5), 410–424. doi:10.1080/0092623X.2012.751077 PMID:23898992

Reyns, B. W. (2010). A situational crime prevention approach to cyberstalking victimization: Preventive tactics for Internet users and online place managers. *Crime Prevention and Community Safety*, *12*(2), 99–118. doi:10.1057/cpcs.2009.22

Reyns, B. W. (2018). Online pursuit in the twilight zone: Cyberstalking perpetration by college students. *Victims & Offenders*. doi:10.1080/15564886.2018.1557092

Reyns, B. W., & Fisher, B. S. (2018). The relationship between offline and online stalking victimization: A gender-specific analysis. *Violence and Victims*, *33*(4), 769–786. doi:10.1891/0886-6708.VV-D-17-00121 PMID:30567773

Reyns, B. W., Fisher, B. S., & Randa, R. (2018). Explaining cyberstalking victimization against college women using a multitheoretical approach: Self-control, opportunity, and control balance. *Crime and Delinquency*, *64*(13), 1742–1764. doi:10.1177/0011128717753116

Reyns, B. W., Henson, B., & Fisher, B. S. (2012). Stalking in the twilight zone: Extent of cyberstalking victimization and offending among college students. *Deviant Behavior*, *33*(1), 1–25. doi:10.1080/01639625.2010.538364

Reyns, B. W., Henson, B., & Fisher, B. S. (2016). Guardians of the cyber galaxy: An empirical and theoretical analysis of the guardianship concept from routine activity theory as it applies to online forms of victimization. *Journal of Contemporary Criminal Justice*, *32*(2), 148–168. doi:10.1177/1043986215621378

Rheingold, H. (2012). *Net smart: How to thrive online*. Mit Press.

Rhodes, N., Potocki, B., & Masterson, D. S. (2018). Portrayals of intimate partner violence in music videos: Effects on perceptions of IPV warning signs. *Media Psychology*, *21*(1), 137–156. doi:10.1080/15213269.2016.1267648

Rice, E., Holloway, I., Winetrobe, H., Rhoades, H., Barman-Adhikari, A., Gibbs, J., ... & Dunlap, S. (2012). Sex risk among young men who have sex with men who use Grindr, a smartphone geosocial networking application. *Journal of AIDS and Clinical Research*, (Suppl. 4).

Rice, S. M., Goodall, J., Hetrick, S. E., Parker, A. G., Gilbertson, T., Amminger, G. P., ... Alvarez-Jimenez, M. (2014). Online and social networking interventions for the treatment of depression in young people: A systematic review. *Journal of Medical Internet Research*, *16*(9), e206. doi:10.2196/jmir.3304 PMID:25226790

Rideout, V. J., Roberts, D. F., & Foehr, U. G. (2005). *Generation M: Media in the lives of 8-18-year-olds: Executive summary*. Menlo Park, CA: Henry J. Kaiser Family Foundation.

Riessman, C. K., & Quinney, L. (2005). Narrative in social work: A critical review. *Qualitative Social Work: Research and Practice*, *4*(4), 391–412. doi:10.1177/1473325005058643

Ringrose, J., Harvey, L., Gill, R., & Livingstone, S. (2013). Teen girls, sexual double standards and 'sexting': Gendered value in digital image exchange. *Feminist Theory, 14*(3), 305–323. doi:10.1177/1464700113499853

Rintala, D. H., Howland, C. A., Nosek, M. A., Bennett, J. L., Young, M. E., Foley, C. C., ... Chanpong, G. (1997). Dating issues for women with physical disabilities. *Sexuality and Disability, 15*(4), 219–242. doi:10.1023/A:1024717313923

Rippere, V. (1977). Commonsense beliefs about depression and antidepressive behaviour: A study of social consensus. *Behaviour Research and Therapy, 15*(6), 465–473. doi:10.1016/0005-7967(77)90002-X PMID:603479

Riva, G. (2012). *Psicologia dei nuovi media. Azione, presenza, identità e relazioni.* Il mulino.

Roberts, J. A., Petnji Yaya, L. H., & Manolis, C. (2014). The Invisible Addiction: Cell-Phone Activities and Addiction Among Male and Female College Students. *Journal of Behavioral Addictions, 3*(4), 254–265. doi:10.1556/JBA.3.2014.015 PMID:25595966

Roberts, L. (2008). Jurisdictional and definitional concerns with computer related interpersonal crimes: An analysis on cyber stalking. *International Journal of Cyber Criminology, 2*, 271–285.

Rocque, M., Posick, C., & Hoyle, J. (2016). Age and crime. In W. G. Jennings, G. E. Higgins, D. N. Khey, & M. M. Maldonado-Molina (Eds.), *Encyclopedia of Crime and Punishment.* Hoboken, NJ: Wiley.

Romito, P., & Beltramini, L. (2011). Watching pornography: Gender differences, violence and victimization. An exploratory study in Italy. *Violence Against Women, 17*(10), 1313–1326. doi:10.1177/1077801211424555 PMID:21997464

Rosenberg, M. (1965). Rosenberg self-esteem scale (RSE). Acceptance and Commitment Therapy. Measures Package, 61. *Society and the Adolescent Self-Image.*

Rosenberg, M. (1985). Self-Concept and Psychological Well-Being in Adolescence. In R. L. Leahy (Ed.), *The Development of the Self.* Orlando, FL: Academic Press.

Roth, M. E., & Gillis, J. M. (2015). "Convenience with the click of a mouse": A survey of adults with autism spectrum disorder on online dating. *Sexuality and Disability, 33*(1), 133–150. doi:10.100711195-014-9392-2

Rozler, J., & Lavinthal, A. (2010). *The hookup handbook: A single girl's guide to living it up.* Simon and Schuster.

Rubin, K. H., & Coplan, R. (2010). *The development of shyness and social withdrawal.* New York, NY: Guilford Press.

Russell, D. (1996). UCLA Loneliness Scale (Version 3): Reliability, validity, and factor structure. *Journal of Personality Assessment, 66*(1), 20–40. doi:10.120715327752jpa6601_2 PMID:8576833

Russell, D., Peplau, L. A., & Cutrona, C. E. (1980). The revised UCLA Loneliness Scale: Concurrent and discriminant validity evidence. *Journal of Personality Assessment, 42*, 290–294. doi:10.120715327752jpa4203_11 PMID:660402

Rutland, A., Killen, M., & Abrams, D. (2010). A new social-cognitive developmental perspective on prejudice: The interplay between morality and group identity. *Perspectives on Psychological Science, 5*(3), 279–291. doi:10.1177/1745691610369468 PMID:26162160

Sacco, W. P., & Vaughan, C. A. (2006). Depression and the response of others: A social-cognitive interpersonal process model. In T. E. Joiner, J. S. Brown, & J. Kistner (Eds.), *The interpersonal, social and cognitive nature of depression.* Mahwah, NJ: Lawrence Erlbaum Associates.

Sagioglou, C., & Greitemeyer, T. (2014). Facebooks emotional consequences: Why Facebook causes a decrease in mood and why people still use it. *Computers in Human Behavior, 35*, 359–363. doi:.chb.2014.03.003 doi:10.1016/j

Salas-Wright, C. P., Vaughn, M. G., & Maynard, B. R. (2014). Profiles of religiosity and their association with risk behavior among emerging adults in the United States. *Emerging Adulthood.*

Salehan, M., & Negahban, A. (2013). Social Networking on Smartphones: When Mobile Phones Become. *Computers in Human Behavior, 29*(6), 2632–2639. doi:10.1016/j.chb.2013.07.003

Salesforce. (2014). *2014 Mobile Behavior Report.* Retrieved April 16, 2016 from https://brandcdn.exacttarget.com/sites/exacttarget/files/deliverables/etmc-2014mobilebehaviorreport.pdf

Saling, L. L., Cohen, D. B., & Cooper, D. (2019). Not close enough for comfort: Facebook users eschew high intimacy negative disclosures. *Personality and Individual Differences, 142*, 103–109. doi:10.1016/j.paid.2019.01.028

Saltes, N. (2013). Disability, identity, and disclosure in the online dating environment. *Disability & Society, 28*(1), 96–109. doi:10.1080/09687599.2012.695577

Samakow, J. (2013). *Japan Internet 'Fasting Camps' Aim to Treat Screen-Addicted Kids.* Retrieved January, 8, 2016 from http://www.huffingtonpost.com/2013/08/28/japan-internet-fasting-camp_n_3824697.html

Sandelowski, M. (1995). Sample size in qualitative research. *Research in Nursing & Health, 18*(2), 179–183. doi:10.1002/nur.4770180211 PMID:7899572

Sanderson, C. A. (2010). *Social psychology.* New York: John Wiley & Sons, Inc.

Sandra, L. (2012). *The dynamics interaction of psychological self-concept and on-line identity* (Unpublished Doctoral Dissertation). University of Gajah Mada, Yogyakarta.

Sansone, R. A., Wiederman, M. W., & Sansone, L. A. (1998). The Self-Harm Inventory (SHI): Development of a scale of identifying self-destructive behaviors and borderline personality disorder. *Journal of Clinical Psychology, 54*(7), 973–983. doi:10.1002/(SICI)1097-4679(199811)54:7<973::AID-JCLP11>3.0.CO;2-H PMID:9811134

Santuzzi, A. M., & Waltz, P. R. (2016). Disability in the workplace: A unique and variable identity. *Journal of Management, 42*(5), 1111–1135. doi:10.1177/0149206315626269

Satici, S. A. (2019). Facebook addiction and subjective well-being: A study of the mediating role of shyness and loneliness. *International Journal of Mental Health and Addiction, 17*(1), 41–55. doi:10.100711469-017-9862-8

Sato, E., Ohsawa, I., Kataoka, J., Miwa, M., Tsukagoshi, F., Sato, J., ... Sato, Y. (2003). Socio-psychological problems of patients with late adolescent onset type 1 diabetes – analysis by qualitative research. *Nagoya Journal of Medical Science, 66*, 21–29. PMID:12848418

Schabert, J., Browne, J. L., Mosely, K., & Speight, J. (2005). Social stigma in diabetes: A framework to understand a growing problem for an increasing epidemic. *Patient, 6*(1), 1–10. doi:10.100740271-012-0001-0 PMID:23322536

Schenk, A. M., & Fremouw, W. J. (2012). Prevalence, psychological impact, and coping of cyberbully victims among college students. *Journal of School Violence, 11*(1), 21–37. doi:10.1080/15388220.2011.630310

Schmitt, D. P., Allik, J., McCrae, R. R., & Benet-Martinez, V. (2007). The geographic distribution of Big Five personality traits: Patterns and profiles of human self-description across 56 nations. *Journal of Cross-Cultural Psychology, 38*(2), 173–212. doi:10.1177/0022022106297299

Schneider, D. J. (2005). *The psychology of stereotyping.* New York: Guilford Press.

Schur, L., Kruse, D., & Blanck, P. (2013). *People with Disabilities: Sidelined or Mainstreamed?* New York: Cambridge University Press. doi:10.1017/CBO9780511843693

Schwartz, S. J., Donnellan, M. B., Ravert, R. D., Luyckx, K., & Zamboanga, B. L. (2013). Identity development, personality, and well-being in adolescence and emerging adulthood: Theory, research, and recent advances. In Handbook of psychology, vol. 6: Developmental psychology (pp. 339-364). New York: John Wiley and Sons.

Schwartz, S. J., Côté, J. E., & Arnett, J. J. (2005). Identity and Agency in Emerging Adulthood Two Developmental Routes in the Individualization Process. *Youth & Society*, *37*(2), 201–229. doi:10.1177/0044118X05275965

Selkie, E. M., Kota, R., Chan, Y., & Moreno, M. (2015). Cyberbullying, depression, and problem alcohol use in female college students: A multisite study. *Cyberpsychology, Behavior, and Social Networking*, *18*(2), 79–86. doi:10.1089/cyber.2014.0371 PMID:25684608

Senft, T. (2008). *CamGirls: Celebrity and Community in the Age of Social Networks*. New York: Peter Lang Publishing.

Sensis. (2018). *Yellow Social Media Report 2018 Part 1 - Consumers*. Retrieved from Melbourne: https://www.yellow.com.au/wp-content/uploads/2018/06/Yellow-Social-Media-Report-2018-Consumer.pdf

Sessoms, J. (2011). *The cyber pornography use inventory: Comparing a religious and secular sample*. Academic Press.

Seto, M. C., Maric, A., & Barbaree, H. E. (2001). The role of pornography in the etiology of sexual aggression. *Aggression and Violent Behavior*, *6*(1), 35–53. doi:10.1016/S1359-1789(99)00007-5

Setyawan, D. (2014). *KPAI ingatkan orang tua: waspadai kejahatan seksual pada anak melalui media sosial*. Retrieved, January, 8, 2016 from http://www.kpai.go.id/berita/kpai-ingatkan-orang-tua-waspadai-kejahatan-seksual-pada-anak-melalui-media-sosial/

Sevi, B. (2019). Brief Report: Tinder Users Are Risk Takers and Have Low Sexual Disgust Sensitivity. *Evolutionary Psychological Science*, *5*(1), 104–108. doi:10.100740806-018-0170-8

Seymour, W., & Lupton, D. (2004). Holding the line online: Exploring wired relationships for people with disabilities. *Disability & Society*, *19*(4), 291–305. doi:10.1080/09687590410001689421

Shaffer, H. J. (1996). Understanding the Means and Objects of Addiction:Technology, the Internet, and Gambling. *Journal of Gambling Studies*, *12*(4), 461–469. doi:10.1007/BF01539189 PMID:24234163

Shapiro, G. K., Tatar, O., Sutton, A., Fisher, W., Naz, A., Perez, S., & Rosberger, Z. (2017). Correlates of Tinder use and risky sexual behaviors in young adults. *Cyberpsychology, Behavior, and Social Networking*, *20*(12), 727–734. doi:10.1089/cyber.2017.0279 PMID:29211500

Sharratt, N. D., Jenkinson, E., Moss, T., Clarke, A., & Rumsey, N. (2018). Understanding and experiences of visible difference and romantic relationships: A qualitative exploration. *Body Image*, *27*, 32–42. doi:10.1016/j.bodyim.2018.08.002 PMID:30125758

Shaver, P., & Hazan, C. (1987). Being lonely, falling in love: Perspectives from attachment theory. *Journal of Social Behavior and Personality*.

Sheldon, K. M., Abad, N., & Hinsch, C. (2011). A two-process view of Facebook use and relatedness need-satisfaction: Disconnection drives use, and connection rewards it. *Psychology of Popular Media Culture*, *1*(S), 2-15. doi:10.1037/2160-4134.1.S.2

Sherman, A. J., & Tocantins, N. (2004). *The happy hook up: A single girl's guide to casual sex*. Springer Science & Business.

Shirky, C. (2008). *Here comes everybody: The power of organizing without organizations*. Penguin.

Shiu, A. T., Kwan, J. J. Y., & Wong, R. Y. (2003). Social stigma as a battier to diabetes self-management: Implications for multi-level interventions. *Journal of Clinical Nursing, 12*(1), 149–150. doi:10.1046/j.1365-2702.2003.00735.x PMID:12519263

Shneor, R., & Efrat, K. (2014). Analyzing the impact of culture on average time spent on special media networking sites. *Journal of Promotion Management, 20*(4), 413–435. doi:10.1080/10496491.2014.930281

Short, E., Linford, S., Wheatcroft, J. M., & Maple, C. (2014). The impact of cyberstalking: The lived experience-a thematic analysis. *Studies in Health Technology and Informatics, 199*, 133–137. doi:10.3233/978-1-61499-401-5-133 PMID:24875706

Shpiegel, Y., Klomek, A. B., & Apter, A. (2015). Bullying, cyberbullying, depression and suicide ideation among youth. Comparing online to paper-and-pencil questionnaires. *International Journal of Child and Adolescent Health, 8*, 161–167.

Shpigelman, C.-N. (2016, July). *Sense of belonging of Facebook users with intellectual disabilities.* Paper presented at the Fifth Conference of Alter, European Society for Research on Disability, Stockholm, Sweden.

Shpigelman, C.-N., & Gill, C. J. (2014a). Facebook use by persons with disabilities. *Journal of Computer-Mediated Communication, 19*(3), 610–624. doi:10.1111/jcc4.12059

Shpigelman, C.-N., & Gill, C. J. (2014b). How do adults with intellectual disabilities use Facebook? *Disability & Society, 29*(10), 1601–1616. doi:10.1080/09687599.2014.966186

Shulman, S., & Connolly, J. (2013). The challenge of romantic relationships in emerging adulthood: Reconceptualization of the field. *Emerging Adulthood, 1*(1), 27–39. doi:10.1177/2167696812467330

Shuttleworth, R. P. (2000). The search for sexual intimacy for men with cerebral palsy. *Sexuality and Disability, 18*(4), 263–282. doi:10.1023/A:1005646327321

Sibicky, M., & Dividio, J. F. (1986). Stigma of psychological therapy: Stereotypes, interpersonal reactions, and the self-fulfilling prophecy. *Journal of Counseling Psychology, 33*(2), 148–154. doi:10.1037/0022-0167.33.2.148

Silverman, A. M., Molton, I. R., Smith, A. E., Jensen, M. P., & Cohen, G. L. (2017). Solace in solidarity: Disability friendship networks buffer well-being. *Rehabilitation Psychology, 62*(4), 525–533. doi:10.1037/rep0000128 PMID:28394146

Simoncic, T. E., Kuhlman, K. R., Vargas, I., Houchins, S., & Lopez-Duran, N. L. (2014). Facebook use and depressive symptomatology: Investigating the role of neuroticism and extraversion in youth. *Computers in Human Behavior, 40*, 1–5. doi:10.1016/j.chb.2014.07.039 PMID:25861155

Singh-Kurtz, S. (2018). *Dating apps are trying to spin your terrible dates as exciting misadventures.* Retrieved May 9, 2019, from Quartzy website: https://qz.com/quartzy/1500645/dating-apps-are-trying-to-spin-your-terrible-dates-as-exciting-misadventures/

Slevin, E., & Sines, D. (1996). Attitudes of nurses in general hospital towards people with learning disabilities: Influences of contact, and graduate – non-graduate status, a comparative study. *Journal of Advanced Nursing, 24*(6), 1116–1126. doi:10.1111/j.1365-2648.1996.tb01016.x PMID:8953346

Smart, J. (2011). *Disability across the developmental lifespan.* New York: Springer.

Smetana, J. G., Jambon, M., & Ball, C. (2014). The social domain approach to children's moral and social judgments. In M. Killen & J. G. Smetana (Eds.), *Handbook of moral development* (2nd ed.; pp. 23–45). New York, NY: Psychology Press. doi:10.4324/9780203581957.ch2

Smith, A. (2016). *15% of American adults use online dating sites or mobile apps.* Retrieved from PEW Research Center website: http://www.pewinternet.org/2016/02/11/15-percent-of-american-adults-have-used-online-dating-sites-or-mobile-dating-apps/

Smith, A. (2016, February 11). 15% of American adults have used online dating sites or mobile dating apps. *Pew Research Center*. Retrieved from http://www.pewinternet.org/2016/02/11/15-percent-of-american-adults- have-used-online-dating-sites-or-mobile-dating-apps/

Smith, A., & Anderson, M. (2016, February 29). 5 facts about online dating. *Pew Research Center.* Retrieved from http://www.pewresearch.org/fact-tank/2016/02/29/5-facts-about-online- dating/

Smith, A., & Anderson, M. (2018). *Social Media Use in 2018.* Retrieved from http://www.pewinternet.org/2018/03/01/social-media-use-in-2018/

Smith, A., & Anderson, M. (2018, March 1). Social media use in 2018. *Pew Research Center.* Retrieved from http://www.pewinternet.org/2018/03/01/social-media-use-in-2018/

Smith, A., & Anderson, M. (2019, April 17). *Social Media Use 2018: Demographics and Statistics.* Retrieved April 29, 2019, from https://www.pewinternet.org/2018/03/01/social-media-use-in-2018/

Smith, A., & Duggan, M. (2013). *Online Dating & Relationships.* Pew Internet & American Life Project. Retrieved from http://www.pewInternet.org/Reports/2013/Online-Dating.aspx

Smith, A., Rainie, L., & Zickuhr, K. (2011). *College students and technology.* Retrieved from http://www.pe winternet.org/2011/07/19/college-students-and-technology/

Smith, M. A. (2009, February 18). Electrification of the interaction order, or, eGoffman. *Connected Action.*

Smith, J. W., & Kandath, K. (1999). Communication and the blind or visually impaired. In D. O. Braithwaite & T. L. Thompson (Eds.), *Handbook of Communication and People with Disabilities: Research and Application* (pp. 389–404). Mahwah, NJ: Routledge.

Smith, M. A. (2000). Some social implications of ubiquitous wireless networks. *Mobile Computing and Communications Review*, *4*(2), 25–36. doi:10.1145/367045.367049

Smith, P. K., Mahdavi, J., Carvalho, M., Fisher, S., Russell, S., & Tippett, N. (2008). Cyberbullying: Its nature and impact in secondary school pupils. *Journal of Child Psychology and Psychiatry, and Allied Disciplines*, *49*(4), 376–385. doi:10.1111/j.1469-7610.2007.01846.x PMID:18363945

Smith, R. H., & Kim, S. H. (2007). Comprehending envy. *Psychological Bulletin*, *133*(1), 46–64. doi:10.1037/0033-2909.133.1.46 PMID:17201570

Smoker, M., & March, E. (2017). Predicting perpetration of intimate partner cyberstalking: Gender and the dark tetrad. *Computers in Human Behavior*, *72*, 390–396. doi:10.1016/j.chb.2017.03.012

Soderstrom, S. (2013). Digital differentiation in young people's internet use – eliminating or reproducing disability stereotypes. *Future Internet*, *5*(2), 190–204. doi:10.3390/fi5020190

Soliha, S. F. (2015). Tingkat ketergantungan pengguna media sosial dan kecemasan sosial. *Jurnal Interaksi*, *4*(1), 1–10.

Solvang, P. (2007). The amputee body desired: Beauty destabilized? Disability re-valued? *Sexuality and Disability*, *25*(2), 51–64. doi:10.100711195-007-9036-x

Song, H., Zmyslinski-Seeling, A., Kim, J. Y., Drent, A., Victor, A., Omori, K., & Allen, M. (2014). Does Facebook make you lonely? A meta-analysis. *Computers in Human Behavior*, *36*, 446–452. doi:10.1016/j.chb.2014.04.011

Sontag, L. M., Clemans, K. H., Graber, J. A., & Lyndon, S. T. (2011). Traditional and cyber aggressors and victims: A comparison of psychosocial characteristics. *Journal of Youth and Adolescence*, *40*(4), 392–404. doi:10.100710964-010-9575-9 PMID:20680425

Special Olympics. (2015). *What is intellectual disability?* Retrieved from http://www.specialolympics.org/Sections/Who_We_Are/What_Is_Intellectual_Disability.aspx

Spitzberg, B. H. (2014). Toward a model of meme diffusion (M3D). *Communication Theory*, *24*(3), 311–339. doi:10.1111/comt.12042

Spitzberg, B. H., & Cupach, W. R. (2001). Paradoxes of pursuit: Toward a relational model of stalking-related phenomena. In J. A. Davis (Ed.), *Stalking crimes and victim protection: Prevention, intervention, threat assessment, and case management* (pp. 97–136). Boca Raton, FL: CRC Press. doi:10.1201/9781420041743.ch6

Spitzberg, B. H., & Cupach, W. R. (2007). The state of the art of stalking: Taking stock of the emerging literature. *Aggression and Violent Behavior*, *12*(1), 64–86. doi:10.1016/j.avb.2006.05.001

Spitzberg, B. H., & Hoobler, G. (2002). Cyberstalking and the technologies of interpersonal terrorism. *New Media & Society*, *4*(1), 71–92. doi:10.1177/14614440222226271

Sprankles, J. (2015, October 26). *The Most Common Abuse On Tinder Faced by Women Is Truly Revolting — INFOGRAPHIC*. Retrieved May 12, 2019, from https://www.bustle.com/articles/119408-the-most-common-abuse-on-tinder-faced-by-women-is-truly-revolting-infographic

Srivastava, R., & Joshi, S. (2014). Relationship between self-concept and self-esteem in adolescent. *Journal of Advanced Research*, *2*(2), 36–43.

Stack, S., Wasserman, I., & Kern, R. (2004). Adult social bonds and use of Internet pornography. *Social Science Quarterly*, *85*(1), 75–88. doi:10.1111/j.0038-4941.2004.08501006.x

Stanley, S. M., Rhoades, G. K., & Fincham, F. D. (2011). *Understanding romantic relationships among emerging adults: The significant roles of cohabitation and ambiguity*. Cambridge University Press.

Stapel, D. A., & Blanton, H. (2004). From seeing to being: Subliminal social comparison affect implicit and explicit self-evaluation. *Journal of Personality and Social Psychology*, *87*(4), 468–481. doi:10.1037/0022-3514.87.4.468 PMID:15491272

Starke, M. (2013). Everyday life of young adults with intellectual disabilities: Inclusionary and exclusionary processes among young adults of parents with intellectual disability. *Intellectual and Developmental Disabilities*, *51*(3), 164–175. doi:10.1352/1934-9556-51.3.164 PMID:23834213

Statista. (2015a). *Smartphone users worldwide 2014-2019*. Retrieved 20 May, 2016 from http://www.statista.com/statistics/330695/number-of-smartphone-users-worldwide/

Statista. (2015b). *Turkey smartphone users 2013-2019*. Retrieved May 20, 2016 from http://www.statista.com/statistics/467181/forecast-of-smartphone-users-in-turkey

Statista. (2019a). *Number of global social media users 2010-2021*. Retrieved from https://www.statista.com/statistics/278414/number-of-worldwide-social-network-users/

Statista. (2019b). *Social media usage in the United States*. Retrieved from https://www.statista.com/topics/3196/social-media-usage-in-the-united-states/

Steel, Z., Marnane, C., Iranpour, C., Chey, T., Jackson, J. W., Patel, V., & Silove, D. (2014). The global prevalence of common mental disorders: A systematic review and meta-analysis 1980-2013. *International Journal of Epidemiology*, *43*(2), 476–493. doi:10.1093/ije/dyu038 PMID:24648481

Steers, M. N., Wickham, R. E., & Acitelli, L. K. (2014). Seeing everyone elses highlight reels: How Facebook usage is linked to depressive symptoms. *Journal of Social and Clinical Psychology*, *33*(8), 701–731. doi:10.1521/jscp.2014.33.8.701

Stein, D. J., Phillips, K. A., Bolton, D., Fulford, K. W. M., Sadler, J. Z., & Kendler, K. S. (2010). What is a mental/psychiatric disorder? From DSM-IV to DSM-V. *Psychological Medicine*, *40*(11), 1759–1765. doi:10.1017/S0033291709992261 PMID:20624327

Steinfield, C., Ellison, N. B., & Lampe, C. (2008). Social capital, self-esteem, and use of online social network sites: A longitudinal analysis. *Journal of Applied Developmental Psychology*, *29*(6), 434–445. doi:10.1016/j.appdev.2008.07.002

Stevens, S. B., & Morris, T. L. (2007). College dating and social anxiety: Using the Internet as a means of connecting to others. *Cyberpsychology & Behavior*, *10*(5), 680–688. doi:10.1089/cpb.2007.9970 PMID:17927536

Stewart, D. N., & Szymanski, D. M. (2012). Young adult women's reports of their male romantic partners pornography use as a correlate of their self-esteem, relationship quality, and sexual satisfaction. *Sex Roles*, *67*(5-6), 257–271. doi:10.100711199-012-0164-0

Stonard, K. E. (2018). The prevalence and overlap of technology-assisted and offline adolescent dating violence. *Current Psychology (New Brunswick, N.J.)*, 1–15.

Strawhun, J., Adams, N., & Huss, M. T. (2013). The assessment of cyberstalking: An expanded examination including social networking, attachment, jealousy, and anger in relation to violence and abuse. *Violence and Victims*, *28*(4), 715–730. doi:10.1891/0886-6708.11-00145 PMID:24047049

Štulhofer, A., Buško, V., & Landripet, I. (2010). Pornography, sexual socialization, and satisfaction among young men. *Archives of Sexual Behavior*, *39*(1), 168–178. doi:10.100710508-008-9387-0 PMID:18561012

Subrahmanyam, K., Reich, S. M., Waechter, N., & Espinoza, G. (2008). Online and offline social networks: Use of social networking sites by emerging adults. *Journal of Applied Developmental Psychology*, *29*(6), 420–433. doi:10.1016/j.appdev.2008.07.003

Sumter, S. R., Vandenbosch, L., & Ligtenberg, L. (2017). Love me Tinder: Untangling emerging adults' motivations for using the dating application Tinder. *Telematics and Informatics*, *34*(1), 67–78. doi:10.1016/j.tele.2016.04.009

Suri, S., & Watts, D. J. (2011). Cooperation and contagion in web-based, networked public goods experiments. *PLoS One*, *6*(3), e16836. doi:10.1371/journal.pone.0016836 PMID:21412431

Swallow, S. R., & Kuiper, N. A. (1992). Mild depression and frequency of social comparison behavior. *Journal of Social and Clinical Psychology*, *11*(2), 167–180. doi:10.1521/jscp.1992.11.2.167

Swanson, J. A., & Walker, E. (2015) Academic versus non-academic emerging adult college student technology use. *Technology, Knowledge and Learning*, 1-12.

Sykes, T. (2014, January 18). Online dating is hard enough. Try doing it with a disability. *The Guardian*. Retrieved from http://www.theguardian.com/commentisfree/2014/jan/18/online-dating-with-disability-match

Taggart, T., Grewe, M. E., Conserve, D. F., Gliwa, C., & Isler, M. R. (2015). Social media and HIV: A systematic review of uses of social media in HIV communication. *Journal of Medical Internet Research*, *17*(11), e248. doi:10.2196/jmir.4387 PMID:26525289

Takao, M. (2014). Problematic Mobile Phone Use and Big-Five Personality Domains. *Indian Journal of Community Medicine*, *39*(2), 111–113. doi:10.4103/0970-0218.132736 PMID:24963228

Takao, M., Takahashi, S., & Kitamura, M. (2009). Addictive Personality and Problematic Mobile Phone Use. *Cyberpsychology & Behavior*, *12*(5), 501–507. doi:10.1089/cpb.2009.0022 PMID:19817562

Tang, D. T. S. (2017). All I get is an emoji: Dating on lesbian mobile phone app Butterfly. *Media Culture & Society*, *39*(6), 816–832. doi:10.1177/0163443717693680

Tang, J., Ma, Y., Guo, T., Ahmed, N. I., Yu, Y., & Wang, J. (2013). Association of aggression and non-suicidal self-injury: A school-based sample of adolescents. *PLoS One*, *8*(1), e78149. doi:10.1371/journal.pone.0078149 PMID:24205132

Tangney, J. P., Baumeister, R. F., & Boone, A. L. (2004). High self-control predicts good adjustment, less pathology, better grades, and interpersonal success. *Journal of Personality*, *72*(2), 271–324. doi:10.1111/j.0022-3506.2004.00263.x PMID:15016066

Taraszow, T., Aristodemou, E., Shitta, G., Laouris, Y., & Arsoy, A. (2010). Disclosure of personal contact information by young people in social networking sites: An analysis using Facebook as an example. *International Journal of Media and Cultural Politics*, *6*(1), 81–102. doi:10.1386/macp.6.1.81/1

Taylor, D. M. (2018, November). *Americans with Disabilities: 2014.* Current Population Reports, P70-152, U.S. Census Bureau, Washington, DC. Retrieved from https://www.census.gov/content/dam/Census/library/publications/2018/demo/p70-152.pdf

Taylor, S., & Xia, Y. (2018). Cyber partner abuse: A systematic review. *Violence and Victims*, *33*(6), 983–1011. doi:10.1891/0886-6708.33.6.983 PMID:30573547

Tennant, J. E., Demaray, M. K., Coyle, S., & Malecki, C. K. (2015). The dangers of the webs: Cybervictimization, depression, and social support in college students. *Computers in Human Behavior*, *50*, 348–357. doi:10.1016/j.chb.2015.04.014

Thaller, J., & Messing, J. T. (2014). (Mis) Perceptions around intimate partner violence in the music video and lyrics for "Love the Way You Lie.". *Feminist Media Studies*, *14*(4), 623–639. doi:10.1080/14680777.2013.826267

The Boston Consulting Group. (2013). *Turkey Online How The Internet is Trensforming the Turkish Ekonomi.* Retrieved April 16, 2016 from http://www.bcg.com.tr/documents/file129539.pdf

Thompson, L. (2018). "I can be your Tinder nightmare": Harassment and misogyny in the online sexual marketplace. *Feminism & Psychology*, *28*(1), 69–89. doi:10.1177/0959353517720226

Tice, D. M. (1993). The social motivations of people with low self-esteem. In R. F. Baumeister (Ed.), *Self-Esteem: The Puzzle of Low Self-Regard* (pp. 37–54). New York, NY: Plenum Press. doi:10.1007/978-1-4684-8956-9_3

Timmermans, E., & Courtois, C. (2018). From swiping to casual sex and/or committed relationships: Exploring the experiences of Tinder users. *The Information Society*, *34*(2), 59–70. doi:10.1080/01972243.2017.1414093

Timmermans, E., & De Caluwé, E. (2017). To Tinder or not to Tinder, that's the question: An individual differences perspective to Tinder use and motives. *Personality and Individual Differences*, *110*, 74–79. doi:10.1016/j.paid.2017.01.026

Tjaden, P., & Thoennes, N. (1998). *Stalking in America: Findings from the National Violence Against Women Survey (Research in Brief NCJ 169592).* Washington, DC: National Institute of Justice and Centers for Disease Control and Prevention.

Tjaden, P., & Thoennes, N. (2000). *Full report of the prevalence, incidence, and consequences of violence against women series: Research report.* Atlanta, GA: Centers for Disease Control and Prevention.

TNS/Google. (2014). *Connected Consumer Study 2014 Global Results*. Retrieved May 20, 2016 from storage.googleapis.com/think-v2 emea/docs/research_study/Connected_Consumer_Study_2014.pdf

Toda, M., Monden, K., Kubo, K., & Morimoto, K. (2006). Mobile Phone Dependence And Health-Related Lifestyle Of University Students. *Social Behavior and Personality*, *34*(10), 1277–1284. doi:10.2224bp.2006.34.10.1277

Tokunaga, R. S. (2011). Social networking site or social surveillance site? Understanding the use of interpersonal electronic surveillance in romantic relationships. *Computers in Human Behavior*, *27*(2), 705–713. doi:10.1016/j.chb.2010.08.014

Tokunaga, R. S., & Aune, K. S. (2017). Cyber-defense: A taxonomy of tactics for managing cyberstalking. *Journal of Interpersonal Violence*, *32*(10), 1451–1475. doi:10.1177/0886260515589564 PMID:26082443

Tolman, D. L., Diamond, L. M., Bauermeister, J. A., George, W. H., Pfaus, J. G., & Ward, L. (2014). APA Handbook of Sexuality and Psychology, Vol. 2: Contextual approaches. APA.

Toma, C. L. (2015). Online dating. In C. Berger & M. Roloff (Eds.), *The international encyclopedia of interpersonal communication* (pp. 1–5). Hoboken, NJ: John Wiley & Sons, Inc. doi:10.1002/9781118540190.wbeic118

Toma, C. L., & Carlson, C. L. (2015). How do Facebook users believe they come across in their profiles?: A meta-perception approach to investigating Facebook self-presentation. *Communication Research Reports*, *32*(1), 93–101. doi:10.1080/08824096.2014.990557

Toma, C. L., Hancock, J. T., & Ellison, N. B. (2008). Separating fact from fiction: An examination of deceptive self-presentation in online dating profiles. *Personality and Social Psychology Bulletin*, *34*(8), 1023–1036. doi:10.1177/0146167208318067 PMID:18593866

Tonin, E. (2004). The attachment styles of stalkers. *Journal of Forensic Psychiatry & Psychology*, *15*(4), 584–590. doi:10.1080/14789940410001729644

Topcu, C., Erdur-Baker, O., & Capa, A. Y. (2008). Examination of cyber-bullying experiences among Turkish students from different school types. *Cyberpsychology & Behavior*, *11*(6), 644–648. doi:10.1089/cpb.2007.0161 PMID:18783345

Traen, B., Nilsen, T. S., & Stigum, H. (2006). Use of pornography in traditional media and on the internet in Norway. *Journal of Sex Research*, *43*(3), 245–254. doi:10.1080/00224490609552323 PMID:17599247

Tsay-Vogel, M., Shanahan, J., & Signorielli, N. (2018). Social media cultivating perceptions of privacy: A 5-year analysis of privacy attitudes and self-disclosure behavior among Facebook users. *New Media & Society*, 1–21. doi:10.1177/1461444816660731

Tumin, D. (2016). Marriage trends among Americans with childhood-onset disabilities, 1997-2013. *Disability and Health Journal*, *9*(4), 713–718. doi:10.1016/j.dhjo.2016.05.004 PMID:27265773

Turiel, E. (1983). *The Development of Social Knowledge: Morality and Convention Cambridge*. Cambridge University Press.

Turiel, E. (2014). Morality: Epistemology, development, and social opposition. In M. Killen & J. G. Smetana (Eds.), *Handbook of moral development* (2nd ed.; pp. 3–22). New York, NY: Psychology Press. doi:10.4324/9780203581957.ch1

Turkle, S. (2011). *Alone together: Why we expect more from technology and less from each other*. New York: Basic Books.

Turner, J. W., Grube, J. A., & Myers, J. (2001). Developing an optimal match within online communities: An exploration of CMC support communities and traditional support. *Journal of Communication*, *51*(2), 231–251. doi:10.1111/j.1460-2466.2001.tb02879.x

Tversky, A., & Kahneman, D. (1973). Availability: A heuristic for judging frequency and probability. *Cognitive Psychology, 5*(2), 207–232. doi:10.1016/0010-0285(73)90033-9

Twenge, J. M., Sherman, R. A., & Wells, B. E. (2017). Sexual inactivity during young adulthood is more common among us millennials and igen: Age, period, and cohort effects on having no sexual partners after age 18. *Archives of Sexual Behavior, 46*(2), 433–440. doi:10.100710508-016-0798-z PMID:27480753

U.S. Bureau of Labor Statistics. (2010). Employment status of the civilian population by sex, age, and disability status, not seasonally adjusted [Data file]. Retrieved from http://www.bls.gov

U.S. Dating Website or App Usage by Age Group. (2019). Retrieved from Statista: www.statista.com/statistics/310344/us-online-dating-app-site-usage-age/

Uhlir, J. L. (2016). Social comparison and self-presentation on social media of depressive symptoms. *Scripps Senior Theses Paper 756*. Retrieved, August 18, 2016 from http://scolarship.claremont.edu/ scripps_theses/756

Umemura, T., Lacinová, L., & Macek, P. (2014). Is emerging adults' attachment preference for the romantic partner transferred from their attachment preferences for their mother, father, and friends? *Emerging Adulthood.*

Urquhart, C., & Fraser-Thoms, E. (2012, December 30). Online dating surges as lonely hearts look to kickstart some post-Christmas romance. *The Observer.* Retrieved from http://www.theguardian.com/lifeandstyle/2012/dec/29/online-dating-christmas-romance

Uteda, A. (2017). *Young Gay Adults' Personal Engagement with Contemporary Hookup Culture Through the Use of Mobile Apps*. Unpublished M.A. thesis.

Utz, S. (2015). The function of self-disclosure on social networking sites: Not only intimate, but also positive and entertaining self-disclosures increase feelings of connection. *Computers in Human Behavior, 45*, 1–10. doi:10.1016/j.chb.2014.11.076

van Alphen, L. M., Dijker, A. J. M., Bos, A. E. R., Van den Borne, B., & Curfs, L. M. G. (2012). The influence of group size and stigma severity on social acceptance: The case of people with intellectual disability moving into neighborhoods. *Journal of Community & Applied Social Psychology, 22*(1), 38–50. doi:10.1002/casp.1094

van Baak, C., & Hayes, B. E. (2018). Correlates of cyberstalking victimization and perpetration among college students. *Violence and Victims, 33*(6), 1036–1054. doi:10.1891/0886-6708.33.6.1036 PMID:30573549

van der Velden, M., & El Emam, K. (2013). "Not all my friends need to know:" a qualitative study of teenage patients, privacy, and social media. *Journal of the American Medical Informatics Association, 20*(1), 16–24. doi:10.1136/amiajnl-2012-000949 PMID:22771531

Vanden Abeele, V., Campbell, M., Eggermont, S., & Roe, K. (2014). Sexting, mobile porn use, and peer group dynamics: Boys' and girls' self-perceived popularity, need for popularity, and perceived peer pressure. *Media Psychology, 17*(1), 6–33. doi:10.1080/15213269.2013.801725

Vander Ven, T. (2011). *Getting wasted: why college students drink too much and party so hard.* New York: New York University Press.

Varnali, K., & Toker, A. (2015). Self-disclosure on social networking sites. *Social Behavior and Personality, 43*(1), 1–13. doi:10.2224bp.2015.43.1.1

Vaswani, K. (2012). *Indonesia's love affair with social media.* Retrieved, January 8, 2016 from http:// www.bbc.com/news/world-asia-17054056

Vaterlaus, J. M., Tulane, S., Porter, B. D., & Beckert, T. E. (2018). The Perceived Influence of Media and Technology on Adolescent Romantic Relationships. *Journal of Adolescent Research*, *33*(6), 651–671. doi:10.1177/0743558417712611

Velotti, P., Balzarotti, S., Tagliabue, S., English, T., Zavattini, G. C., & Gross, J. J. (2015). Emotional suppression in early marriage: Actor, partner, and similarity effects on marital quality. *Journal of Social and Personal Relationships*.

Vitis, L., & Gilmour, F. (2017). Dick pics on blast: A woman's resistance to online sexual harassment using humour, art and Instagram. *Crime, Media, Culture*, *13*(3), 335–355. doi:10.1177/1741659016652445

Vogel, E. A., Rose, J. P., Roberts, L. R., & Eckles, K. (2014). Social comparison, social media, and self-esteem. *Psychology of Popular Media Culture*, *3*(4), 206–222. doi:10.1037/ppm0000047

Wade, L. (2017). *American Hookup: The New Culture of Sex on Campus*. W.W. Norton & Company, Inc.

Walker, C., Sockman, B., & Koehn, S. (2011). An exploratory study of cyberbullying with undergraduate university students. *TechTrends*, *55*(2), 31–38. doi:10.100711528-011-0481-0

Walker, S., Sanci, L., & Temple-Smith, M. (2013). Sexting: Young women's and men's views on its nature and origins. *The Journal of Adolescent Health*, *52*(6), 697–701. doi:10.1016/j.jadohealth.2013.01.026 PMID:23587784

Wall, D. (2007). *Cybercrime: The Transformation of Crime in the Information Age*. Polity.

Waltermaurer, E. (2012). Public justification of intimate partner violence: A review of the literature. *Trauma, Violence & Abuse*, *13*(3), 167–175. doi:10.1177/1524838012447699 PMID:22643069

Walther, J. B., & Parks, M. R. (2002). Cues filtered out, cues filtered in: Computer-mediated communication and relationships. In M. L. Knapp & J. A. Daly (Eds.), *Handbook of interpersonal communication* (3rd ed.; pp. 529–563). Thousand Oaks, CA: Sage.

Walther, J. B., Slovacek, C. L., & Tidwell, L. C. (2001). Is a picture worth a thousand words? Photographic images in long-term and short-term computer-mediated communication. *Communication Research*, *28*(1), 105–134. doi:10.1177/009365001028001004

Wang, E. S. T., & Wang, M. C. H. (2013). Social Support and Social Interaction Ties on Internet Addiction: Integrating Online and Offline Contexts. *Cyberpsychology, Behavior, and Social Networking*, *16*(11), 843–849. doi:10.1089/cyber.2012.0557 PMID:23848959

Washington Post-Kaiser Family Foundation. (2012). *2012 survey of Americans of HIV/AIDS*. Retrieved from https://kaiserfamilyfoundation.files.wordpress.com/2013/01/8334-f.pdf

Waters, S., & Ackerman, J. (2011). Exploring privacy management on Facebook: Motivations and perceived consequences of voluntary disclosure. *Journal of Computer-Mediated Communication*, *17*(1), 101–115. doi:10.1111/j.1083-6101.2011.01559.x

We Are Social. (2019). *Digital 2019*. Retrieved from https://wearesocial.com/blog/2019/07/global-social-media-users-pass-3-5-billion

Webb, L. M., & Lee, B. S. (2011). Mommy blogs: The centrality of community in the performance of online maternity. In M. Moravec (Ed.), *Motherhood online: How online communities shape modern motherhood* (pp. 244-257). Newcastle upon Tyne, UK: Cambridge Scholars Publishing. Retrieved June 10, 2019 from https://www.researchgate.net/profile/Lynne_Webb/publication/225271136_Mommy_blogs_The_centrality_of_community_in_the_performance_of_online_maternity/links/0fcfd4fcffab5514ca000000.pdf

Webb, L. M., & Temple, N. (2015). Social media and gender issues. In B. Guzzetti & M. Lesley (Eds.), *Handbook of research on the societal impact of digital media* (pp. 638–669). Hershey, PA: IGI Global. doi:10.4018/978-1-4666-8310-5.ch025

Webb, L. M., Wilson, M. L., Hodges, M., Smith, P. A., & Zakeri, M. (2012). Facebook: How college students work it. In H. S. Noor Al-Deen & J. A. Hendricks (Eds.), *Social media: Usage and impact* (pp. 3–22). Lanham, MD: Lexington Books.

Weigman, O., & Schie, E. (1998). Video game playing and its relations with aggressive and prosocial behaviors. *British Journal of Social Psychology, 37*(3), 367–378. doi:10.1111/j.2044-8309.1998.tb01177.x PMID:9738313

Weinberg, M. S., Williams, C. J., Kleiner, S., & Irizarry, Y. (2010). Pornography, normalization, and empowerment. *Archives of Sexual Behavior, 39*(6), 1389–1401. doi:10.100710508-009-9592-5 PMID:20127507

Weiss, D. S., & Marmar, C. R. (1996). The Impact of Event Scale - Revised. In J. Wilson & T. M. Keane (Eds.), *Assessing psychological trauma and PTSD* (pp. 399–411). New York: Guilford.

Weisskirch, R., & Delevi, R. (2011). "Sexting" and adult romantic attachment. *Computers in Human Behavior, 27*(5), 1697–1701. doi:10.1016/j.chb.2011.02.008

Wellard, S. J., Rennie, S., & King, R. (2008). Perceptions of people with type 2 diabetes about self-management and the efficiency of community based services. *Contemporary Nurse, 29*(2), 218–226. doi:10.5172/conu.673.29.2.218 PMID:18844535

Wheeless, L. R., & Grotz, J. (1976). Conceptualization and measurement of reported self-disclosure. *Human Communication Research, 2*(4), 338–346. doi:10.1111/j.1468-2958.1976.tb00494.x

White, J. B., Langer, E. J., Yariv, L., & Welch, J. C. IV. (2006). Frequent social comparison and destructive emotions and behaviors: The dark side of social comparison. *Journal of Adult Development, 13*(1), 36–44. doi:10.100710804-006-9005-0

Whitton, S. W., Dyar, D., Newcomb, M. E., & Mustanski, B. (2018). Romantic involvement: A protective factor for psychological health in racially-diverse young sexual minorities. *Journal of Abnormal Psychology, 127*(3), 265–275. doi:10.1037/abn0000332 PMID:29389141

Whitty, M. T. (2008). Revealing the "real" me, searching for the "actual" you: Presentations of self on an internet dating site. *Computers in Human Behavior, 24*(4), 1707–1723. doi:10.1016/j.chb.2007.07.002

Widman, L., Welsh, D. P., McNulty, J. K., & Little, K. C. (2006). Sexual Communication and Contraceptive Use in Adolescent Dating Couples. *The Journal of Adolescent Health, 39*(6), 893–899. doi:10.1016/j.jadohealth.2006.06.003 PMID:17116521

Wiegerink, D., Roebroeck, M. E., Donkervoort, M., Stam, H. J., & Cohen-Kettenis, P. T. (2006). Social and sexual relationships of adolescents and young adults with cerebral palsy: A review. *Clinical Rehabilitation, 20*(12), 1023–1031. doi:10.1177/0269215506071275 PMID:17148513

Wiegerink, D., Roebroeck, M. E., Van Der Slot, W. M., Stam, H. J., & Cohen-Kettenis, P. T. (2010). Importance of peers and dating in the development of romantic relationships and sexual activity of young adults with cerebral palsy. *Developmental Medicine and Child Neurology, 52*(6), 576–582. doi:10.1111/j.1469-8749.2010.03620.x PMID:20187888

Wiener, L. S., & Battles, H. B. (2006). Untangling the web: A close look at diagnosis disclosure among HIV-infected adolescents. *The Journal of Adolescent Health, 38*(3), 307–309. doi:10.1016/j.jadohealth.2005.03.024 PMID:16488835

Wilkinson, S. (1998). Focus groups in feminist research: Power, Interaction, and the Co-construction of meaning. *Women's Studies International Forum, 21*(1), 111–125. doi:10.1016/S0277-5395(97)00080-0

Willoughby, B. J., & Busby, D. M. (2015). In the eye of the beholder: Exploring variations in the perceptions of pornography. *Journal of Sex Research*, 1–11. PMID:26643148

Willoughby, B. J., Carroll, J. S., Busby, D. M., & Brown, C. C. (2015). Differences in pornography use among couples: Associations with satisfaction, stability, and relationship processes. *Archives of Sexual Behavior*, ▪▪▪, 1–14.

Willoughby, B. J., Carroll, J. S., Nelson, L. J., & Padilla-Walker, L. M. (2014). Associations between relational sexual behaviour, pornography use, and pornography acceptance among US college students. *Culture, Health & Sexuality*, *16*(9), 1052–1069. doi:10.1080/13691058.2014.927075 PMID:25023726

Willoughby, B. J., & Hall, S. S. (2015). Enthusiasts, delayers, and the ambiguous middle: Marital paradigms among emerging adults. *Emerging Adulthood*, *3*(2), 123–135. doi:10.1177/2167696814548478

Willoughby, B. J., Hall, S. S., & Luczak, H. P. (2013). Marital paradigms: A conceptual framework for marital attitudes, values, and beliefs. *Journal of Family Issues*.

Willoughby, B. J., Young-Petersen, B., & Leonhardt, N. D. (2018). Exploring trajectories of pornography use through adolescence and emerging adulthood. *Journal of Sex Research*, *55*(3), 297–309. doi:10.1080/00224499.2017.1368977 PMID:28972398

Wilson, K., Fornasier, S., & White, K. M. (2010). Psychological Predictors of Young Adults' Use of Social Networking Sites. *Cyberpsychology, Behavior, and Social Networking*, *13*(2), 173–177. doi:10.1089/cyber.2009.0094 PMID:20528274

Wohn, D. Y., & LaRose, R. (2014). Effects of loneliness and differential usage of Facebook on college adjustment of first-year students. *Computers & Education*, *76*, 158–167. doi:10.1016/j.compedu.2014.03.018

Wolak, J., Mitchell, K., & Finkelhor, D. (2007). Does online harassment constitute bullying? An exploration of online harassment by known peers and online-only contacts. *The Journal of Adolescent Health*, *41*(6), 51–58. doi:10.1016/j.jadohealth.2007.08.019 PMID:18047945

Wood, M. (2015, February 4). Led by Tinder, the mobile dating game surges. *The New York Times*, p. B8.

Worden, A. P., & Carlson, B. E. (2005). Attitudes and beliefs about domestic violence: Results of a public opinion survey II. Beliefs about causes. *Journal of Interpersonal Violence*, *20*(10), 1219–1243. doi:10.1177/0886260505278531 PMID:16162487

Working to Halt Online Abuse (WHOA). (2011). *Cyberstalking statistics*. Retrieved on 8th January 2015, from http://www.haltabuse.org/resources/stats/2011Statistics.pdf

Working to Halt Online Abuse. (2013). *Online Harassment / Cyberstalking statistics*. Retrieved on 25th March, 2019, from http://www.haltabuse.org/resources/stats/2013Statistics.pdf

World Health Organization. (2012). *Cancer fact sheet*. Retrieved from http://globocan.iarc.fr/Pages/fact_sheets_cancer.aspx

World Health Organization. (2014a). *The top 10 causes of death*. Retrieved from http://www.who.int/mediacentre/factsheets/fs310/en/

World Health Organization. (2014b). *Diabetes*. Retrieved from http://www.who.int/mediacentre/factsheets/fs312/en/

World Health Organization. (2015). *HIV/AIDS*. Retrieved from http://www.who.int/mediacentre/factsheets/fs360/en/

Wright, B. (1983). *Physical disability: A psychosocial approach*. New York: Harper & Row. doi:10.1037/10589-000

Wright, M. F. (2015). Cyber victimization and perceived stress: Linkages to late adolescents' cyber aggression and psychological functioning. *Youth & Society*, *47*(6), 789–810. doi:10.1177/0044118X14537088

Wright, M. F., & Li, Y. (2012). Kicking the digital dog: A longitudinal investigation of young adults' victimization and cyber-displaced aggression. *Cyberpsychology, Behavior, and Social Networking, 15*(9), 44–454. doi:10.1089/cyber.2012.0061 PMID:22974350

Wright, M. F., & Li, Y. (2013). Normative beliefs about aggression and cyber aggression among young adults: A longitudinal investigation. *Aggressive Behavior, 39*(3), 161–170. doi:10.1002/ab.21470 PMID:23440595

Wright, M. F., Li, Y., & Shi, J. (2014). Chinese adolescents' social status goals: Associations with behaviors and attributions for relational aggression. *Youth & Society, 46*(4), 566–588. doi:10.1177/0044118X12448800

Wright, P. J., Tokunaga, R. S., & Kraus, A. (2015). A meta-analysis of pornography consumption and actual acts of sexual aggression in general population studies. *Journal of Communication.*

Wu, C. W., & Webb, L. M. (2016). Chinese international students' messages on the Family Forum: Topics, goals, and types of assistance. In M. F. Wright (Ed.), *Identity, sexuality, and relationships among emerging adults in the digital age* (pp. 128–149). Hershey, PA: IGI Global. doi:10.4018/978-1-5225-1856-3.ch009

Yang, C., Brown, B. B., & Braun, M. F. (2013). From Facebook to cell calls: Layers of electronic intimacy in college students' interpersonal relationships. *New Media & Society, 0*(0), 1–19. doi:10.1177/1461444812472486

Yarkin, K. L., Harvey, J. H., & Bloxom, B. M. (1981). Cognitive sets, attribution, and social interaction. *Journal of Personality and Social Psychology, 41*(2), 243–252. doi:10.1037/0022-3514.41.2.243

Ybarra, M. L., Alexander, C., & Mitchell, K. J. (2005). Depressive symptomology, youth internet use, and online interactions: A national survey. *The Journal of Adolescent Health, 36*(1), 9–18. doi:10.1016/j.jadohealth.2003.10.012 PMID:15661591

Ybarra, M. L., Diener-West, M., & Leaf, P. J. (2007). Examining the overlap in internet harassment and school bullying: Implications for school intervention. *The Journal of Adolescent Health, 41*(6), S42–S50. doi:10.1016/j.jadohealth.2007.09.004 PMID:18047944

Ybarra, M. L., & Mitchell, K. J. (2004). Online aggressor/targets, aggressors, and targets: A comparison of associated youth characteristics. *Journal of Child Psychology and Psychiatry, and Allied Disciplines, 45*(7), 1308–1316. doi:10.1111/j.1469-7610.2004.00328.x PMID:15335350

Yeo, T. E. D., & Chu, T. H. (2017). Sharing "sex secrets" on Facebook: A content analysis of youth peer communication and advice exchange on social media about sexual health and intimate relations. *Journal of Health Communication, 22*(9), 753–762. doi:10.1080/10810730.2017.1347217 PMID:28796578

Yeo, T. E. D., & Fung, T. H. (2016, July). Relationships form so quickly that you won't cherish them: mobile dating apps and the culture of instantaneous relationships. In *Proceedings of the 7th 2016 International Conference on Social Media & Society* (p. 2). ACM. 10.1145/2930971.2930973

Young, B. J., & Furman, W. (2007). Interpersonal factors in the risk for sexual victimization and its recurrence during adolescence. *Journal of Youth and Adolescence, 37*(3), 297–309. doi:10.100710964-007-9240-0

Young, K. S. (2008). Internet sex addiction risk factors, stages of development, and treatment. *The American Behavioral Scientist, 52*(1), 21–37. doi:10.1177/0002764208321339

Zeinali, A., Sharifi, H., Enayati, M., Asgari, P., & Pasha, G. (2011). The mediational pathway among parenting styles, attachment styles and self-regulation with addiction susceptibility of adolescents. *Journal of Research in Medical Sciences, 16*(9), 1105–1121. PMID:22973379

Zhao, X., Schwanda Sosik, V., & Cosley, D. (2012). It's complicated: how romantic partners use Facebook. In *Proceedings of the SIGCHI Conference on Human Factors in Computing Systems* (pp. 771-780). ACM. 10.1145/2207676.2207788

Zimmer-Gembeck, M., & Duffy, A. (2014). Heightened emotional sensitivity intensifies associations between relational aggression and victimization among girls but not boys: A longitudinal study. *Development and Psychopathology*, *26*(3), 661–673. doi:10.1017/S0954579414000303 PMID:25047290

Zlatolas, L. N., Welzer, T., Hericko, M., & Holbl, M. (2015). Privacy antecedents for SNS self-disclosure: The case of Facebook. *Computers in Human Behavior, 45,* 158-167. doi:10.1016/j.chb.2014.12.012

Zweig, J. M., Dank, M., Yahner, J., & Lachman, P. (2013). The rate of cyber dating abuse among teens and how it relates to other forms of teen dating violence. *Journal of Youth and Adolescence*, *42*(7), 1063–1077. doi:10.100710964-013-9922-8 PMID:23412689

Zywica, J., & Danowski, J. (2008). The Faces of Facebookers: Investigating Social Enhancement and Social Compensation Hypotheses; Predicting Facebook™ and Offline Popularity from Sociability and Self-Esteem, and Mapping the Meanings of Popularity with Semantic Networks. *Journal of Computer-Mediated Communication*, *14*(1), 1–34. doi:10.1111/j.1083-6101.2008.01429.x

Related References

To continue our tradition of advancing academic research, we have compiled a list of recommended IGI Global readings. These references will provide additional information and guidance to further enrich your knowledge and assist you with your own research and future publications.

Ababio, G. K. (2018). Nutraceuticals: The Dose Makes the Difference – It's All in the Dose. In A. Verma, K. Srivastava, S. Singh, & H. Singh (Eds.), *Nutraceuticals and Innovative Food Products for Healthy Living and Preventive Care* (pp. 24–47). Hershey, PA: IGI Global. doi:10.4018/978-1-5225-2970-5.ch002

Adams, M. G. (2018). Systematically Investigating Instructor Impact on Student Satisfaction in Graduate Programs. In D. Polly, M. Putman, T. Petty, & A. Good (Eds.), *Innovative Practices in Teacher Preparation and Graduate-Level Teacher Education Programs* (pp. 200–214). Hershey, PA: IGI Global. doi:10.4018/978-1-5225-3068-8.ch012

Akgül, Y., & Tunca, M. Z. (2018). Proliferating View of Knowledge Management and Balanced Scorecard Outcome Linkage. In N. Baporikar (Ed.), *Global Practices in Knowledge Management for Societal and Organizational Development* (pp. 168–193). Hershey, PA: IGI Global. doi:10.4018/978-1-5225-3009-1.ch008

Alcaraz-Valencia, P. A., Gaytán-Lugo, L. S., & Gallardo, S. C. (2018). An Exploratory Study on the Interaction Beyond Virtual Environments to Improve Listening Ability When Learning English as a Second Language. In F. Cipolla-Ficarra (Ed.), *Optimizing Human-Computer Interaction With Emerging Technologies* (pp. 306–331). Hershey, PA: IGI Global. doi:10.4018/978-1-5225-2616-2.ch013

Altıntaş, F. Ç., & Kavurmacı, C. (2018). Value Statements in Web Pages of Turkish State Universities: A Basic Classification. In U. Thomas (Ed.), *Advocacy in Academia and the Role of Teacher Preparation Programs* (pp. 302–316). Hershey, PA: IGI Global. doi:10.4018/978-1-5225-2906-4.ch017

Amoroso, D. L. (2018). The Importance of Advocacy on Reputation and Loyalty: Comparison of Japanese, Chinese, and the Filipino Consumers. In P. Ordóñez de Pablos (Ed.), *Management Strategies and Technology Fluidity in the Asian Business Sector* (pp. 114–125). Hershey, PA: IGI Global. doi:10.4018/978-1-5225-4056-4.ch007

Atiku, S. O., & Fields, Z. (2018). Organisational Learning Dimensions and Talent Retention Strategies for the Service Industries. In N. Baporikar (Ed.), *Global Practices in Knowledge Management for Societal and Organizational Development* (pp. 358–381). Hershey, PA: IGI Global. doi:10.4018/978-1-5225-3009-1.ch017

Ayoola-Amale, A. (2018). Women in Leadership: Why We Need More Women Leaders. In B. Cook (Ed.), *Handbook of Research on Examining Global Peacemaking in the Digital Age* (pp. 211–222). Hershey, PA: IGI Global. doi:10.4018/978-1-5225-3032-9.ch015

Baran, A. G. (2018). Through the Syrians Refuge in Turkey Towards the Creation of the War Migration Theory. In Ş. Erçetin (Ed.), *Social Considerations of Migration Movements and Immigration Policies* (pp. 178–196). Hershey, PA: IGI Global. doi:10.4018/978-1-5225-3322-1.ch011

Beckett-Camarata, J. (2018). Public Choice and Financing Local Government Fiscal Reform in Albania. In H. Levine & K. Moreno (Eds.), *Positioning Markets and Governments in Public Management* (pp. 197–208). Hershey, PA: IGI Global. doi:10.4018/978-1-5225-4177-6.ch015

Bedford, D. A. (2018). Sustainable Knowledge Management Strategies: Aligning Business Capabilities and Knowledge Management Goals. In N. Baporikar (Ed.), *Global Practices in Knowledge Management for Societal and Organizational Development* (pp. 46–73). Hershey, PA: IGI Global. doi:10.4018/978-1-5225-3009-1.ch003

Benaouda, A., & García-Peñalvo, F. J. (2018). Towards an Intelligent System for the Territorial Planning: Agricultural Case. In F. García-Peñalvo (Ed.), *Global Implications of Emerging Technology Trends* (pp. 158–178). Hershey, PA: IGI Global. doi:10.4018/978-1-5225-4944-4.ch010

Beneventi, P. (2018). When Technology Becomes Popular: A Multimedia, Shared Production for the Information Age. In *Technology and the New Generation of Active Citizens: Emerging Research and Opportunities* (pp. 23–44). Hershey, PA: IGI Global. doi:10.4018/978-1-5225-3770-0.ch002

Bernal, L. D., & Cusi, M. L. (2018). Corporate Entrepreneurship in Colombia: Contrast Cases of Two Colombian Manufacturing SMEs. In R. Perez-Uribe, C. Salcedo-Perez, & D. Ocampo-Guzman (Eds.), *Handbook of Research on Intrapreneurship and Organizational Sustainability in SMEs* (pp. 368–390). Hershey, PA: IGI Global. doi:10.4018/978-1-5225-3543-0.ch017

Berning, S. C., & Ambrosius, J. (2018). How the Human Resource Practices of Chinese MNEs in Africa Create Economic Growth and Livelihood Options. In S. Hipsher (Ed.), *Examining the Private Sector's Role in Wealth Creation and Poverty Reduction* (pp. 85–109). Hershey, PA: IGI Global. doi:10.4018/978-1-5225-3117-3.ch005

Bharti, A., & Mittal, A. (2018). Perishable Goods Supply Cold Chain Management in India. In A. Kumar & S. Saurav (Eds.), *Supply Chain Management Strategies and Risk Assessment in Retail Environments* (pp. 232–246). Hershey, PA: IGI Global. doi:10.4018/978-1-5225-3056-5.ch013

Bhattacharya, S., Kumar, R. V., & Dutta, A. (2018). Exploring Kapferer's Brand Identity Prism Applicability in Indian Political Marketing Aspect With Special Focus to Youth Voters. In Rajagopal, & R. Behl (Eds.), Start-Up Enterprises and Contemporary Innovation Strategies in the Global Marketplace (pp. 136-152). Hershey, PA: IGI Global. doi:10.4018/978-1-5225-4831-7.ch010

Bhattarai, R. K. (2018). Enterprise Immune System. In *Enterprise Resiliency in the Continuum of Change: Emerging Research and Opportunities* (pp. 88–111). Hershey, PA: IGI Global. doi:10.4018/978-1-5225-2627-8.ch003

Bhattarai, R. K. (2018). Enterprise Philosophy. In *Enterprise Resiliency in the Continuum of Change: Emerging Research and Opportunities* (pp. 1–43). Hershey, PA: IGI Global. doi:10.4018/978-1-5225-2627-8.ch001

Bhattarai, R. K. (2018). Enterprise Resiliency. In *Enterprise Resiliency in the Continuum of Change: Emerging Research and Opportunities* (pp. 112–137). Hershey, PA: IGI Global. doi:10.4018/978-1-5225-2627-8.ch004

Bisen, S. S., & Deshpande, Y. (2018). The Impact of the Internet in Twenty-First Century Addictions: An Overview. In B. Bozoglan (Ed.), *Psychological, Social, and Cultural Aspects of Internet Addiction* (pp. 1–19). Hershey, PA: IGI Global. doi:10.4018/978-1-5225-3477-8.ch001

Biswal, S. K. (2018). Branding Culture: A Study of Telugu Film Industry. In S. Dasgupta, S. Biswal, & M. Ramesh (Eds.), *Holistic Approaches to Brand Culture and Communication Across Industries* (pp. 1–23). Hershey, PA: IGI Global. doi:10.4018/978-1-5225-3150-0.ch001

Blake, S., & Burkett, C. M. (2018). Individual Creativity: Predictors and Characteristics. In *Creativity in Workforce Development and Innovation: Emerging Research and Opportunities* (pp. 88–104). Hershey, PA: IGI Global. doi:10.4018/978-1-5225-4952-9.ch005

Blomeley, S., & Hamilton, A. H. (2018). Writing Partners: Bridging the Personal and Social in the Service-Learning Classroom. In O. Delano-Oriaran, M. Penick-Parks, & S. Fondrie (Eds.), *Culturally Engaging Service-Learning With Diverse Communities* (pp. 202–222). Hershey, PA: IGI Global. doi:10.4018/978-1-5225-2900-2.ch012

Bohra, M., & Visen, A. (2018). Nutraceutical Properties in Flowers. In A. Verma, K. Srivastava, S. Singh, & H. Singh (Eds.), *Nutraceuticals and Innovative Food Products for Healthy Living and Preventive Care* (pp. 217–235). Hershey, PA: IGI Global. doi:10.4018/978-1-5225-2970-5.ch010

Boyd, L. N. (2018). Fortifying Parent Partnerships Through the Black Church Space. In K. Norris & S. Collier (Eds.), *Social Justice and Parent Partnerships in Multicultural Education Contexts* (pp. 118–137). Hershey, PA: IGI Global. doi:10.4018/978-1-5225-3943-8.ch007

Bozoglan, B. (2018). The Role of Family Factors in Internet Addiction Among Children and Adolescents: An Overview. In B. Bozoglan (Ed.), *Psychological, Social, and Cultural Aspects of Internet Addiction* (pp. 146–168). Hershey, PA: IGI Global. doi:10.4018/978-1-5225-3477-8.ch008

Briz-Ponce, L., Juanes-Méndez, J. A., & García-Peñalvo, F. J. (2018). Current Situation and Appraisal Tendencies of M-Learning. In F. García-Peñalvo (Ed.), *Global Implications of Emerging Technology Trends* (pp. 115–129). Hershey, PA: IGI Global. doi:10.4018/978-1-5225-4944-4.ch007

Brkljačić, T., Majetić, F., & Wertag, A. (2018). I'm Always Online: Well-Being and Main Sources of Life Dis/Satisfaction of Heavy Internet Users. In B. Bozoglan (Ed.), *Psychological, Social, and Cultural Aspects of Internet Addiction* (pp. 72–89). Hershey, PA: IGI Global. doi:10.4018/978-1-5225-3477-8.ch004

Brown, M. A. Sr. (2018). Defining Your Team. In *Motivationally Intelligent Leadership: Emerging Research and Opportunities* (pp. 1–22). Hershey, PA: IGI Global. doi:10.4018/978-1-5225-3746-5.ch001

Brown, M. A. Sr. (2018). Empowering Leaders With Tools. In *Motivationally Intelligent Leadership: Emerging Research and Opportunities* (pp. 72–96). Hershey, PA: IGI Global. doi:10.4018/978-1-5225-3746-5.ch006

Brown, M. A. Sr. (2018). Sensemaking Theory. In *Motivationally Intelligent Leadership: Emerging Research and Opportunities* (pp. 46–55). Hershey, PA: IGI Global. doi:10.4018/978-1-5225-3746-5.ch004

Brown, S., & Bousalis, R. (2018). Best Practices in K-12 Arts Integration: Curricular Connections. In *Curriculum Integration in Contemporary Teaching Practice: Emerging Research and Opportunities* (pp. 95–124). Hershey, PA: IGI Global. doi:10.4018/978-1-5225-4065-6.ch004

Brown, S., & Bousalis, R. (2018). Interdisciplinary Curriculum in K-12 Schools: Current Practices in the Field. In *Curriculum Integration in Contemporary Teaching Practice: Emerging Research and Opportunities* (pp. 125–143). Hershey, PA: IGI Global. doi:10.4018/978-1-5225-4065-6.ch005

Bullock, C. A. (2018). Collaboration: Academes, Government, and Community to Drive Economic Uplift and Empowerment. In S. Burton (Ed.), *Engaged Scholarship and Civic Responsibility in Higher Education* (pp. 1–24). Hershey, PA: IGI Global. doi:10.4018/978-1-5225-3649-9.ch001

Burdenko, E. V., & Mudrova, S. V. (2018). Indicators System as a Measure of Development Level of Knowledge Economy: Application of World Bank Methodology. In N. Baporikar (Ed.), *Global Practices in Knowledge Management for Societal and Organizational Development* (pp. 74–105). Hershey, PA: IGI Global. doi:10.4018/978-1-5225-3009-1.ch004

Burston, B., & Collier-Stewart, S. (2018). STEM for All: The Importance of Parent/School/Community Partnerships Across the K-12 Pipeline and Beyond. In K. Norris & S. Collier (Eds.), *Social Justice and Parent Partnerships in Multicultural Education Contexts* (pp. 274–288). Hershey, PA: IGI Global. doi:10.4018/978-1-5225-3943-8.ch015

Carboni, M., & Perelli, C. (2018). "Beyond" Religious Tourism: The Case of Fez. In H. El-Gohary, D. Edwards, & R. Eid (Eds.), *Global Perspectives on Religious Tourism and Pilgrimage* (pp. 71–83). Hershey, PA: IGI Global. doi:10.4018/978-1-5225-2796-1.ch005

Cascella, M., Muzio, M. R., Bimonte, S., & Cuomo, A. (2018). Nutraceuticals for Prevention of Chemotherapy-Induced Peripheral Neuropathy. In A. Verma, K. Srivastava, S. Singh, & H. Singh (Eds.), *Nutraceuticals and Innovative Food Products for Healthy Living and Preventive Care* (pp. 236–259). Hershey, PA: IGI Global. doi:10.4018/978-1-5225-2970-5.ch011

Cena, F., Rapp, A., Likavec, S., & Marcengo, A. (2018). Envisioning the Future of Personalization Through Personal Informatics: A User Study. *International Journal of Mobile Human Computer Interaction, 10*(1), 52–66. doi:10.4018/IJMHCI.2018010104

Chandiramani, J., & Airy, A. (2018). Urbanization and Socio-Economic Growth in South Asia Region. In U. Benna & I. Benna (Eds.), *Urbanization and Its Impact on Socio-Economic Growth in Developing Regions* (pp. 130–154). Hershey, PA: IGI Global. doi:10.4018/978-1-5225-2659-9.ch007

Chang, Y., Choi, S. B., Lee, J., & Jin, W. C. (2018). Population Size vs. Number of Crimes: Is the Relationship Superlinear? *International Journal of Information Systems and Social Change*, *9*(1), 26–39. doi:10.4018/IJISSC.2018010102

Chaudhary, N. S., & Yadav, R. (2018). Cross-Cultural Conflicts: Concept, Causes, and Elucidations. In N. Sharma, V. Singh, & S. Pathak (Eds.), *Management Techniques for a Diverse and Cross-Cultural Workforce* (pp. 79–96). Hershey, PA: IGI Global. doi:10.4018/978-1-5225-4933-8.ch005

Chirisa, I., Mukarwi, L., & Matamanda, A. R. (2018). Social Costs and Benefits of the Transformation of the Traditional Families in an African Urban Society. In U. Benna & I. Benna (Eds.), *Urbanization and Its Impact on Socio-Economic Growth in Developing Regions* (pp. 179–197). Hershey, PA: IGI Global. doi:10.4018/978-1-5225-2659-9.ch009

Chitima, S. S., & Ndlovu, I. (2018). Incorporating Indigenous Knowledge in the Preservation of Collections at the Batonga Community Museum in Zimbabwe. In P. Ngulube (Ed.), *Handbook of Research on Heritage Management and Preservation* (pp. 396–407). Hershey, PA: IGI Global. doi:10.4018/978-1-5225-3137-1.ch019

Choudhury, D. K., & Rao, P. (2018). Determinants of FDI Inflows in Developing Countries: A Dynamic Panel Approach. In V. Malepati & C. Gowri (Eds.), *Foreign Direct Investments (FDIs) and Opportunities for Developing Economies in the World Market* (pp. 25–45). Hershey, PA: IGI Global. doi:10.4018/978-1-5225-3026-8.ch002

Cipolla-Ficarra, F. V., Carré, J., Quiroga, A., & Ficarra, V. M. (2018). Anti-Models for Architectural Graphic Expression and UX Education. In F. Cipolla-Ficarra, M. Ficarra, M. Cipolla-Ficarra, A. Quiroga, J. Alma, & J. Carré (Eds.), *Technology-Enhanced Human Interaction in Modern Society* (pp. 218–233). Hershey, PA: IGI Global. doi:10.4018/978-1-5225-3437-2.ch011

Cipolla-Ficarra, F. V., Ficarra, V. M., & Cipolla-Ficarra, M. (2018). Inverted Semanteme Into Financial Information Online. In F. Cipolla-Ficarra, M. Ficarra, M. Cipolla-Ficarra, A. Quiroga, J. Alma, & J. Carré (Eds.), *Technology-Enhanced Human Interaction in Modern Society* (pp. 263–283). Hershey, PA: IGI Global. doi:10.4018/978-1-5225-3437-2.ch013

Cipolla-Ficarra, F. V., Quiroga, A., & Ficarra, V. M. (2018). Kernel of the Labyrinths Hypertextuals. In F. Cipolla-Ficarra, M. Ficarra, M. Cipolla-Ficarra, A. Quiroga, J. Alma, & J. Carré (Eds.), *Technology-Enhanced Human Interaction in Modern Society* (pp. 122–142). Hershey, PA: IGI Global. doi:10.4018/978-1-5225-3437-2.ch006

Coffey, S. M. (2018). Unveilings Through Transformative Pedagogy: Striving for Realization of Du Bois' Educational Paradigm. In U. Thomas (Ed.), *Advocacy in Academia and the Role of Teacher Preparation Programs* (pp. 206–224). Hershey, PA: IGI Global. doi:10.4018/978-1-5225-2906-4.ch012

da Rocha, J. P. (2018). Process Outcomes. In *Political Mediation in Modern Conflict Resolution: Emerging Research and Opportunities* (pp. 155–164). Hershey, PA: IGI Global. doi:10.4018/978-1-5225-5118-8.ch004

Dahiya, K., & Dhankhar, R. (2018). Role of Nutraceuticals in Cancer. In A. Verma, K. Srivastava, S. Singh, & H. Singh (Eds.), *Nutraceuticals and Innovative Food Products for Healthy Living and Preventive Care* (pp. 176–194). Hershey, PA: IGI Global. doi:10.4018/978-1-5225-2970-5.ch008

Dasgupta, S., & Kothari, R. (2018). The Impact of Digital Word-of-Mouth Communication on Consumer Decision-Making Processes: With Special Reference to Fashion Apparel Industry. In S. Dasgupta, S. Biswal, & M. Ramesh (Eds.), *Holistic Approaches to Brand Culture and Communication Across Industries* (pp. 176–198). Hershey, PA: IGI Global. doi:10.4018/978-1-5225-3150-0.ch010

Dávila, F. A. (2018). Relationship Lending and Entrepreneurial Behavior: A Game-Theoretic-Based Modeling. In Rajagopal, & R. Behl (Eds.), Start-Up Enterprises and Contemporary Innovation Strategies in the Global Marketplace (pp. 65-86). Hershey, PA: IGI Global. doi:10.4018/978-1-5225-4831-7.ch006

de Sousa, J. C. (2018). Memory. In *Neuromarketing and Big Data Analytics for Strategic Consumer Engagement: Emerging Research and Opportunities* (pp. 92–100). Hershey, PA: IGI Global. doi:10.4018/978-1-5225-4834-8.ch006

de Sousa, J. C. (2018). Sensory and Motor System. In *Neuromarketing and Big Data Analytics for Strategic Consumer Engagement: Emerging Research and Opportunities* (pp. 68–91). Hershey, PA: IGI Global. doi:10.4018/978-1-5225-4834-8.ch005

Deka, D. B., & Jadeja, M. (2018). Childhood Sexual Abuse: Prevention and Intervention. In R. Gopalan (Ed.), *Social, Psychological, and Forensic Perspectives on Sexual Abuse* (pp. 127–146). Hershey, PA: IGI Global. doi:10.4018/978-1-5225-3958-2.ch010

Dobell, E., Herold, S., & Buckley, J. (2018). Spreadsheet Error Types and Their Prevalence in a Healthcare Context. *Journal of Organizational and End User Computing*, *30*(2), 20–42. doi:10.4018/JOEUC.2018040102

Donert, K., & Papoutsis, P. (2018). School on the Cloud: Connecting Education to the Cloud for Digital Citizenship. In K. Koutsopoulos, K. Doukas, & Y. Kotsanis (Eds.), *Handbook of Research on Educational Design and Cloud Computing in Modern Classroom Settings* (pp. 157–182). Hershey, PA: IGI Global. doi:10.4018/978-1-5225-3053-4.ch008

Downton, M. P. (2018). Preparation for Future Teaching: Authentic Activities in a Teacher Education Classroom. In D. Polly, M. Putman, T. Petty, & A. Good (Eds.), *Innovative Practices in Teacher Preparation and Graduate-Level Teacher Education Programs* (pp. 293–305). Hershey, PA: IGI Global. doi:10.4018/978-1-5225-3068-8.ch016

Drivas, G., Sotiriou, C., Bonanou, H., Saliari, S., Balafouti, M., & Tsevi, H. (2018). The Sky Is the Limit! In K. Koutsopoulos, K. Doukas, & Y. Kotsanis (Eds.), *Handbook of Research on Educational Design and Cloud Computing in Modern Classroom Settings* (pp. 101–121). Hershey, PA: IGI Global. doi:10.4018/978-1-5225-3053-4.ch006

Erçetin, Ş. Ş., & Bisaso, S. M. (2018). Migration and Refugee Crisis: Structural and Managerial Implications for Education. In Ş. Erçetin (Ed.), *Educational Development and Infrastructure for Immigrants and Refugees* (pp. 47–71). Hershey, PA: IGI Global. doi:10.4018/978-1-5225-3325-2.ch003

Erçetin, Ş. Ş., & Kubilay, S. (2018). Educational Expectations of Refugee Mothers for Their Children. In Ş. Erçetin (Ed.), *Educational Development and Infrastructure for Immigrants and Refugees* (pp. 171–195). Hershey, PA: IGI Global. doi:10.4018/978-1-5225-3325-2.ch009

Erçetin, Ş. Ş., Potas, N., Açıkalın, Ş. N., Özdemir, N., & Doğan, A. M. (2018). Municipalities and Refugee Crisis: Ansar Policies and Numbers. In Ş. Erçetin (Ed.), *Social Considerations of Migration Movements and Immigration Policies* (pp. 46–57). Hershey, PA: IGI Global. doi:10.4018/978-1-5225-3322-1.ch003

Erkekoğlu, L. C., & Madi, İ. (2018). The Hashemite Kingdom of Jordan. In S. Ozdemir, S. Erdogan, & A. Gedikli (Eds.), *Handbook of Research on Sociopolitical Factors Impacting Economic Growth in Islamic Nations* (pp. 95–121). Hershey, PA: IGI Global. doi:10.4018/978-1-5225-2939-2.ch006

Essien, E. D. (2018). Strengthening Performance of Civil Society Through Dialogue and Critical Thinking in Nigeria: Its Ethical Implications. In S. Chhabra (Ed.), *Handbook of Research on Civic Engagement and Social Change in Contemporary Society* (pp. 82–102). Hershey, PA: IGI Global. doi:10.4018/978-1-5225-4197-4.ch005

Feza, N. N. (2018). The Socioeconomic Status Label Associated With Mathematics. In I. Tshabangu (Ed.), *Global Ideologies Surrounding Children's Rights and Social Justice* (pp. 186–203). Hershey, PA: IGI Global. doi:10.4018/978-1-5225-2578-3.ch012

Fleener, J., Lu, L., Dun, J., & Mingquan, Y. (2018). Sustaining a Teacher Professional Learning Community in China Through Technology. In H. Spires (Ed.), *Digital Transformation and Innovation in Chinese Education* (pp. 80–99). Hershey, PA: IGI Global. doi:10.4018/978-1-5225-2924-8.ch005

Forge, J. (2018). Defence. In *The Morality of Weapons Design and Development: Emerging Research and Opportunities* (pp. 52–77). Hershey, PA: IGI Global. doi:10.4018/978-1-5225-3984-1.ch004

Forge, J. (2018). Justification. In *The Morality of Weapons Design and Development: Emerging Research and Opportunities* (pp. 78–93). Hershey, PA: IGI Global. doi:10.4018/978-1-5225-3984-1.ch005

Forge, J. (2018). Projectile Weapons. In *The Morality of Weapons Design and Development: Emerging Research and Opportunities* (pp. 94–117). Hershey, PA: IGI Global. doi:10.4018/978-1-5225-3984-1.ch006

Forge, J. (2018). Proportionality, Just War Theory, and Weapons Design. In *The Morality of Weapons Design and Development: Emerging Research and Opportunities* (pp. 139–154). Hershey, PA: IGI Global. doi:10.4018/978-1-5225-3984-1.ch008

Forge, J. (2018). Purposes and Means. In *The Morality of Weapons Design and Development: Emerging Research and Opportunities* (pp. 34–51). Hershey, PA: IGI Global. doi:10.4018/978-1-5225-3984-1.ch003

Fudge, M. (2018). The Inequity of User Fees and the Overreliance by Communities to Generate Revenue. In H. Levine & K. Moreno (Eds.), *Positioning Markets and Governments in Public Management* (pp. 147–158). Hershey, PA: IGI Global. doi:10.4018/978-1-5225-4177-6.ch011

Furumoto, R. R. (2018). Mexican-American Parents Using Critical Literacy to Address Climate Change. In K. Norris & S. Collier (Eds.), *Social Justice and Parent Partnerships in Multicultural Education Contexts* (pp. 187–208). Hershey, PA: IGI Global. doi:10.4018/978-1-5225-3943-8.ch010

Gabay, D. (2018). Who's Represented in Canadian Teaching and Learning Centres? In B. Blummer, J. Kenton, & M. Wiatrowski (Eds.), *Promoting Ethnic Diversity and Multiculturalism in Higher Education* (pp. 172–198). Hershey, PA: IGI Global. doi:10.4018/978-1-5225-4097-7.ch010

Garner, G. (2018). Foundations for Yoga Practice in Rehabilitation. In S. Telles & N. Singh (Eds.), *Research-Based Perspectives on the Psychophysiology of Yoga* (pp. 263–307). Hershey, PA: IGI Global. doi:10.4018/978-1-5225-2788-6.ch015

Geethanjali, P. (2018). Bio-Inspired Techniques in Human-Computer Interface for Control of Assistive Devices: Bio-Inspired Techniques in Assistive Devices. In D. Lopez & M. Durai (Eds.), *HCI Challenges and Privacy Preservation in Big Data Security* (pp. 23–46). Hershey, PA: IGI Global. doi:10.4018/978-1-5225-2863-0.ch002

Gharote, M. (2018). Common Features Between Findings in Traditional Texts and Contemporary Science: Yoga Texts and Contemporary Science. In S. Telles & N. Singh (Eds.), *Research-Based Perspectives on the Psychophysiology of Yoga* (pp. 309–315). Hershey, PA: IGI Global. doi:10.4018/978-1-5225-2788-6.ch016

Giosi, A., Zaccaro, E., & Testarmata, S. (2018). Social Responsibility, Shared Value, and Business Modelling: An Integrated Approach. In M. Risso & S. Testarmata (Eds.), *Value Sharing for Sustainable and Inclusive Development* (pp. 100–121). Hershey, PA: IGI Global. doi:10.4018/978-1-5225-3147-0.ch005

Grădinaru, C., Toma, S. I., & Marinescu, P. I. (2018). Entrepreneurial Thinking in the Educational System. In M. Risso & S. Testarmata (Eds.), *Value Sharing for Sustainable and Inclusive Development* (pp. 29–48). Hershey, PA: IGI Global. doi:10.4018/978-1-5225-3147-0.ch002

Güler, A. (2018). PKK-Related Asylum Applications from Turkey: Counter-Terrorism Measures vs. Refugee Status. In Ş. Erçetin (Ed.), *Social Considerations of Migration Movements and Immigration Policies* (pp. 117–142). Hershey, PA: IGI Global. doi:10.4018/978-1-5225-3322-1.ch008

Gupta, S. K. (2018). Sexual Abuse of Children and Adults With Intellectual Disabilities: Preventive, Supportive, and Intervention Strategies for Clinical Practice. In R. Gopalan (Ed.), *Social, Psychological, and Forensic Perspectives on Sexual Abuse* (pp. 197–206). Hershey, PA: IGI Global. doi:10.4018/978-1-5225-3958-2.ch014

Gürcan, Ö. F., & Gümüşsoy, Ç. A. (2018). Factors Influencing Effective Knowledge Transfer in Organizations. In N. Baporikar (Ed.), *Global Practices in Knowledge Management for Societal and Organizational Development* (pp. 271–292). Hershey, PA: IGI Global. doi:10.4018/978-1-5225-3009-1.ch013

Hagen, I., Kofoed, S., & Nayar, U. (2018). Yoga for Psychological Wellbeing in Modern Life and Contexts. In S. Telles & N. Singh (Eds.), *Research-Based Perspectives on the Psychophysiology of Yoga* (pp. 316–334). Hershey, PA: IGI Global. doi:10.4018/978-1-5225-2788-6.ch017

Handayani, B. (2018). The Paradox of Authenticity and Its Implications for Contemporary and "Bizarre" Tourism Campaigns. In S. Sarma (Ed.), *Global Observations of the Influence of Culture on Consumer Buying Behavior* (pp. 48–65). Hershey, PA: IGI Global. doi:10.4018/978-1-5225-2727-5.ch003

Huamaní, G. A., Fernández-López, S., Gómez, I. N., Rey-Ares, L., Rodríguez-Gulías, M. J., & Rodeiro-Pazos, D. (2018). The Role Models as Determinants of New Technology-Based Firms: An Exploratory Study. In A. Carrizo Moreira, J. Guilherme Leitão Dantas, & F. Manuel Valente (Eds.), *Nascent Entrepreneurship and Successful New Venture Creation* (pp. 272–288). Hershey, PA: IGI Global. doi:10.4018/978-1-5225-2936-1.ch013

Hucks, D., Sturtz, T., & Tirabassi, K. (2018). Building, Shaping, and Modeling Tools for Literacy Development and Civic Engagement. In *Fostering Positive Civic Engagement Among Millennials: Emerging Research and Opportunities* (pp. 22–35). Hershey, PA: IGI Global. doi:10.4018/978-1-5225-2452-6.ch002

Hucks, D., Sturtz, T., & Tirabassi, K. (2018). Insights, Next Steps, and Future Research. In *Fostering Positive Civic Engagement Among Millennials: Emerging Research and Opportunities* (pp. 65–72). Hershey, PA: IGI Global. doi:10.4018/978-1-5225-2452-6.ch005

Iguisi, O. V. (2018). Comparative Analysis of Hofstede's Culture Dimensions for West African Regions (WAF) and Nigeria. In S. Sarma (Ed.), *Global Observations of the Influence of Culture on Consumer Buying Behavior* (pp. 190–205). Hershey, PA: IGI Global. doi:10.4018/978-1-5225-2727-5.ch012

Islam, M. R. (2018). Abuse Among Child Domestic Workers in Bangladesh. In I. Tshabangu (Ed.), *Global Ideologies Surrounding Children's Rights and Social Justice* (pp. 1–21). Hershey, PA: IGI Global. doi:10.4018/978-1-5225-2578-3.ch001

Ito, K., & Hilliker, S. M. (2018). Supporting University International Students Through Supportive ESL Instruction and Corrective Feedback. In B. Blummer, J. Kenton, & M. Wiatrowski (Eds.), *Promoting Ethnic Diversity and Multiculturalism in Higher Education* (pp. 40–58). Hershey, PA: IGI Global. doi:10.4018/978-1-5225-4097-7.ch003

Iurato, G. (2018). A Brief Account of Ignacio Matte Blanco Theory and Other Related Psychoanalytic Themes. In *Computational Psychoanalysis and Formal Bi-Logic Frameworks* (pp. 114–135). Hershey, PA: IGI Global. doi:10.4018/978-1-5225-4128-8.ch003

Iurato, G. (2018). First Attempts to Formalize Some Main Aspects of Psychoanalysis: Towards a Computational Psychoanalysis. In *Computational Psychoanalysis and Formal Bi-Logic Frameworks* (pp. 136–205). Hershey, PA: IGI Global. doi:10.4018/978-1-5225-4128-8.ch004

Jacobsen, M., Friesen, S., & Brown, B. (2018). Teachers' Professional Learning Focused on Designs for Early Learners and Technology. In D. Polly, M. Putman, T. Petty, & A. Good (Eds.), *Innovative Practices in Teacher Preparation and Graduate-Level Teacher Education Programs* (pp. 417–438). Hershey, PA: IGI Global. doi:10.4018/978-1-5225-3068-8.ch022

Jensen, A. A., & Thomassen, A. O. (2018). Teachers' Reflective Practice in Lifelong Learning Programs. In Z. Djoub (Ed.), *Fostering Reflective Teaching Practice in Pre-Service Education* (pp. 25–45). Hershey, PA: IGI Global. doi:10.4018/978-1-5225-2963-7.ch002

Jiang, K., Barnett, G. A., Taylor, L. D., & Feng, B. (2018). Dynamic Co-Evolutions of Peace Frames in the United States, Mainland China, and Hong Kong: A Semantic Network Analysis. In B. Cook (Ed.), *Handbook of Research on Examining Global Peacemaking in the Digital Age* (pp. 145–168). Hershey, PA: IGI Global. doi:10.4018/978-1-5225-3032-9.ch010

Jiménez-González, S. G., Mendoza-González, R., & Luna-García, H. (2018). Guidelines Based on Need-Findings Study and Communication Types to Design Interactions for MOOCs. In F. Cipolla-Ficarra (Ed.), *Optimizing Human-Computer Interaction With Emerging Technologies* (pp. 210–231). Hershey, PA: IGI Global. doi:10.4018/978-1-5225-2616-2.ch008

Johnson, N. N. (2018). Effectively Managing Bias in Teacher Preparation. In U. Thomas (Ed.), *Advocacy in Academia and the Role of Teacher Preparation Programs* (pp. 146–160). Hershey, PA: IGI Global. doi:10.4018/978-1-5225-2906-4.ch008

Joseph, C. (2018). The Role of Government in a Liberal Market Economy: A Double-Edge Sword. In H. Levine & K. Moreno (Eds.), *Positioning Markets and Governments in Public Management* (pp. 53–61). Hershey, PA: IGI Global. doi:10.4018/978-1-5225-4177-6.ch005

Kade, D., Lindell, R., Ürey, H., & Özcan, O. (2018). Supporting Motion Capture Acting Through a Mixed Reality Application. In F. Cipolla-Ficarra (Ed.), *Optimizing Human-Computer Interaction With Emerging Technologies* (pp. 248–273). Hershey, PA: IGI Global. doi:10.4018/978-1-5225-2616-2.ch010

Karataş, S., Kukul, V., & Özcan, S. (2018). How Powerful Is Digital Storytelling for Teaching?: Perspective of Pre-Service Teachers. In D. Polly, M. Putman, T. Petty, & A. Good (Eds.), *Innovative Practices in Teacher Preparation and Graduate-Level Teacher Education Programs* (pp. 511–529). Hershey, PA: IGI Global. doi:10.4018/978-1-5225-3068-8.ch027

Kavaklı, N. (2018). Hate Speech Towards Syrian Refugees in Turkish Online Reader Comments. In C. Akrivopoulou (Ed.), *Global Perspectives on Human Migration, Asylum, and Security* (pp. 127–142). Hershey, PA: IGI Global. doi:10.4018/978-1-5225-2817-3.ch007

Kaynak, S. (2018). Pakistan. In S. Ozdemir, S. Erdogan, & A. Gedikli (Eds.), *Handbook of Research on Sociopolitical Factors Impacting Economic Growth in Islamic Nations* (pp. 293–313). Hershey, PA: IGI Global. doi:10.4018/978-1-5225-2939-2.ch015

Korstanje, M. E. (2018). Thana-Capitalism and the Sense of Reality: Lessons Unlearned. In C. Akrivopoulou (Ed.), *Global Perspectives on Human Migration, Asylum, and Security* (pp. 1–20). Hershey, PA: IGI Global. doi:10.4018/978-1-5225-2817-3.ch001

Korstanje, M. E. (2018). The Lost Paradise: The Religious Nature of Tourism. In H. El-Gohary, D. Edwards, & R. Eid (Eds.), *Global Perspectives on Religious Tourism and Pilgrimage* (pp. 129–141). Hershey, PA: IGI Global. doi:10.4018/978-1-5225-2796-1.ch008

Korstanje, M. E., & George, B. P. (2018). Emotionality, Reason, and Dark Tourism: Discussions Around the Sense of Death. In M. Korstanje & B. George (Eds.), *Virtual Traumascapes and Exploring the Roots of Dark Tourism* (pp. 1–25). Hershey, PA: IGI Global. doi:10.4018/978-1-5225-2750-3.ch001

Kougioumtzis, G. A., & Louka, D. (2018). Advocacy and Teacher Mentoring. In U. Thomas (Ed.), *Advocacy in Academia and the Role of Teacher Preparation Programs* (pp. 65–87). Hershey, PA: IGI Global. doi:10.4018/978-1-5225-2906-4.ch004

Kousar, H. (2018). Gender Violence in Academia. In N. Mahtab, T. Haque, I. Khan, M. Islam, & I. Wahid (Eds.), *Handbook of Research on Women's Issues and Rights in the Developing World* (pp. 144–155). Hershey, PA: IGI Global. doi:10.4018/978-1-5225-3018-3.ch009

Koutsafti, M., & Politi, N. (2018). Career Counseling: The "Model of Personal Career Management". In K. Koutsopoulos, K. Doukas, & Y. Kotsanis (Eds.), *Handbook of Research on Educational Design and Cloud Computing in Modern Classroom Settings* (pp. 410–429). Hershey, PA: IGI Global. doi:10.4018/978-1-5225-3053-4.ch020

Koutsopoulos, K. (2018). From Ground to Cloud: The School on the Cloud. In K. Koutsopoulos, K. Doukas, & Y. Kotsanis (Eds.), *Handbook of Research on Educational Design and Cloud Computing in Modern Classroom Settings* (pp. 1–21). Hershey, PA: IGI Global. doi:10.4018/978-1-5225-3053-4.ch001

Kovacevic, Z., Klimek, B., & Drower, I. S. (2018). Refugee Children and Parental Involvement in School Education: A Field Model. In K. Norris & S. Collier (Eds.), *Social Justice and Parent Partnerships in Multicultural Education Contexts* (pp. 139–161). Hershey, PA: IGI Global. doi:10.4018/978-1-5225-3943-8.ch008

Kratky, A. (2018). Personal Touch: A Viewing-Angle-Compensated Multi-Layer Touch Display. In F. Cipolla-Ficarra (Ed.), *Optimizing Human-Computer Interaction With Emerging Technologies* (pp. 232–247). Hershey, PA: IGI Global. doi:10.4018/978-1-5225-2616-2.ch009

Kuang, Y. (2018). Application of the "Teaching Innovation Practice Platform" in English Reading Instruction: A Case Study of a Public Middle School in Shanghai. In H. Spires (Ed.), *Digital Transformation and Innovation in Chinese Education* (pp. 249–271). Hershey, PA: IGI Global. doi:10.4018/978-1-5225-2924-8.ch014

Kubilay, S., & Yardibi, N. (2018). Refugee Parents' Preferential Values in Education. In Ş. Erçetin (Ed.), *Educational Development and Infrastructure for Immigrants and Refugees* (pp. 72–84). Hershey, PA: IGI Global. doi:10.4018/978-1-5225-3325-2.ch004

Kumar, T. P. (2018). Impact of Corporate Social Responsibility on Service Performance in Mediating Effect of Brand Equity With Reference To Banks in India. In Rajagopal, & R. Behl (Eds.), Start-Up Enterprises and Contemporary Innovation Strategies in the Global Marketplace (pp. 88-99). Hershey, PA: IGI Global. doi:10.4018/978-1-5225-4831-7.ch007

LaPlante, J. M. (2018). Unequal Opportunities and Inequitable Outcomes: Rethinking Education Finance Policy Design for a Global Society. In H. Levine & K. Moreno (Eds.), *Positioning Markets and Governments in Public Management* (pp. 209–239). Hershey, PA: IGI Global. doi:10.4018/978-1-5225-4177-6.ch016

Lau, B. T., & Win, K. M. (2018). Differentiated Animated Social Stories to Enhance Social Skills Acquisition of Children With Autism Spectrum Disorder. In V. Bryan, A. Musgrove, & J. Powers (Eds.), *Handbook of Research on Human Development in the Digital Age* (pp. 300–329). Hershey, PA: IGI Global. doi:10.4018/978-1-5225-2838-8.ch014

Lee, J. K., & Chirino-Klevans, I. (2018). Cosmopolitanism in a World of Teachers: American Student Teachers in a Chinese School. In H. Spires (Ed.), *Digital Transformation and Innovation in Chinese Education* (pp. 232–248). Hershey, PA: IGI Global. doi:10.4018/978-1-5225-2924-8.ch013

Lee, S. (2018). Expatriate Cantonese Learners in Hong Kong: Adult L2 Learning, Identity Negotiation, and Social Pressure. In D. Velliaris (Ed.), *Study Abroad Contexts for Enhanced Foreign Language Learning* (pp. 151–168). Hershey, PA: IGI Global. doi:10.4018/978-1-5225-3814-1.ch007

Lee, S. C. (2018). Mother America: Cold War Maternalism and the Origins of Korean Adoption. In F. Topor (Ed.), *Ethical Standards and Practice in International Relations* (pp. 157–186). Hershey, PA: IGI Global. doi:10.4018/978-1-5225-2650-6.ch007

Li, Y., & Wang, X. (2018). Seeking Health Information on Social Media: A Perspective of Trust, Self-Determination, and Social Support. *Journal of Organizational and End User Computing*, *30*(1), 1–22. doi:10.4018/JOEUC.2018010101

Livers, S. D., & Lin, L. (2018). Elementary Teacher Candidates' Perspectives on the Teaching and Learning of English Learners. In U. Thomas (Ed.), *Advocacy in Academia and the Role of Teacher Preparation Programs* (pp. 23–41). Hershey, PA: IGI Global. doi:10.4018/978-1-5225-2906-4.ch002

López-Cózar-Navarro, C., & Priede-Bergamini, T. (2018). Nascent Social Entrepreneurship: Economic, Legal, and Financial Framework. In A. Carrizo Moreira, J. Guilherme Leitão Dantas, & F. Manuel Valente (Eds.), *Nascent Entrepreneurship and Successful New Venture Creation* (pp. 132–152). Hershey, PA: IGI Global. doi:10.4018/978-1-5225-2936-1.ch006

Lu, S. (2018). Financial Literacy Education Program Post Financial Housing Crisis: Community Based Financial Literacy Education Program. In S. Burton (Ed.), *Engaged Scholarship and Civic Responsibility in Higher Education* (pp. 49–66). Hershey, PA: IGI Global. doi:10.4018/978-1-5225-3649-9.ch003

Luyombya, D. (2018). Management of Records and Archives in Uganda's Public Sector. In P. Ngulube (Ed.), *Handbook of Research on Heritage Management and Preservation* (pp. 275–297). Hershey, PA: IGI Global. doi:10.4018/978-1-5225-3137-1.ch014

Luyombya, D., Kiyingi, G. W., & Naluwooza, M. (2018). The Nature and Utilisation of Archival Records Deposited in Makerere University Library, Uganda. In P. Ngulube (Ed.), *Handbook of Research on Heritage Management and Preservation* (pp. 96–113). Hershey, PA: IGI Global. doi:10.4018/978-1-5225-3137-1.ch005

Lytras, M. D., Papadopoulou, P., Marouli, C., & Misseyanni, A. (2018). Higher Education Out-of-the-Box: Technology-Driven Learning Innovation in Higher Education. In S. Burton (Ed.), *Engaged Scholarship and Civic Responsibility in Higher Education* (pp. 67–100). Hershey, PA: IGI Global. doi:10.4018/978-1-5225-3649-9.ch004

Mafumbate, R. (2018). Child Resilience, Survival, and Development: Voices of Orphans in Zimbabwe. In I. Tshabangu (Ed.), *Global Ideologies Surrounding Children's Rights and Social Justice* (pp. 239–252). Hershey, PA: IGI Global. doi:10.4018/978-1-5225-2578-3.ch015

Malmierca, M. J. (2018). Cloud Computing for Rural and Isolated Schools. In K. Koutsopoulos, K. Doukas, & Y. Kotsanis (Eds.), *Handbook of Research on Educational Design and Cloud Computing in Modern Classroom Settings* (pp. 376–394). Hershey, PA: IGI Global. doi:10.4018/978-1-5225-3053-4.ch018

Maroofi, F. (2018). Knowledge Management and Organizational Performance in Service Industry: Transformational Leadership Versus Transactional Leadership. In N. Baporikar (Ed.), *Global Practices in Knowledge Management for Societal and Organizational Development* (pp. 194–212). Hershey, PA: IGI Global. doi:10.4018/978-1-5225-3009-1.ch009

Mattson, T., & Aurigemma, S. (2018). Running with the Pack: The Impact of Middle-Status Conformity on the Post-Adoption Organizational Use of Twitter. *Journal of Organizational and End User Computing*, *30*(1), 23–43. doi:10.4018/JOEUC.2018010102

Medhekar, A., & Haq, F. (2018). Urbanization and New Jobs Creation in Healthcare Services in India: Challenges and Opportunities. In U. Benna & I. Benna (Eds.), *Urbanization and Its Impact on Socio-Economic Growth in Developing Regions* (pp. 198–218). Hershey, PA: IGI Global. doi:10.4018/978-1-5225-2659-9.ch010

Meletiou-Mavrotheris, M., & Koutsopoulos, K. (2018). Projecting the Future of Cloud Computing in Education: A Foresight Study Using the Delphi Method. In K. Koutsopoulos, K. Doukas, & Y. Kotsanis (Eds.), *Handbook of Research on Educational Design and Cloud Computing in Modern Classroom Settings* (pp. 262–290). Hershey, PA: IGI Global. doi:10.4018/978-1-5225-3053-4.ch012

Miller, J. (2018). Causes and Ramifications of Public Pension Fund Underfunding: A Case Study of the New Jersey Pension Funds. In H. Levine & K. Moreno (Eds.), *Positioning Markets and Governments in Public Management* (pp. 114–146). Hershey, PA: IGI Global. doi:10.4018/978-1-5225-4177-6.ch010

Milović, B. (2018). Developing Marketing Strategy on Social Networks. In S. Sarma (Ed.), *Global Observations of the Influence of Culture on Consumer Buying Behavior* (pp. 66–82). Hershey, PA: IGI Global. doi:10.4018/978-1-5225-2727-5.ch004

Mosweu, O., & Kenosi, L. S. (2018). Theories of Appraisal in Archives: From Hillary Jenkinson to Terry Cook's Times. In P. Ngulube (Ed.), *Handbook of Research on Heritage Management and Preservation* (pp. 24–46). Hershey, PA: IGI Global. doi:10.4018/978-1-5225-3137-1.ch002

Mukherjee, S., & Pradeep, K. (2018). Does Internationalization of Business-Group-Affiliated Firms Depend on Their Performance? In Rajagopal, & R. Behl (Eds.), Start-Up Enterprises and Contemporary Innovation Strategies in the Global Marketplace (pp. 153-165). Hershey, PA: IGI Global. doi:10.4018/978-1-5225-4831-7.ch011

Mutisya, P. M., & Conway, C. S. (2018). Quality Mentoring: A Prerequisite for Faculty at HBCUs. In C. Conway (Ed.), *Faculty Mentorship at Historically Black Colleges and Universities* (pp. 15–34). Hershey, PA: IGI Global. doi:10.4018/978-1-5225-4071-7.ch002

Nagabhushan, P. (2018). Mean Level Changes in College Students' Academic Motivation and Engagement. In *Engaging Adolescent Students in Contemporary Classrooms: Emerging Research and Opportunities* (pp. 142–174). Hershey, PA: IGI Global. doi:10.4018/978-1-5225-5155-3.ch006

Naranjo, J. (2018). Meeting the Need for Inclusive Educators Online: Teacher Education in Inclusive Special Education and Dual-Certification. In D. Polly, M. Putman, T. Petty, & A. Good (Eds.), *Innovative Practices in Teacher Preparation and Graduate-Level Teacher Education Programs* (pp. 106–122). Hershey, PA: IGI Global. doi:10.4018/978-1-5225-3068-8.ch007

Nirmala, T., & Aram, I. A. (2018). Newspaper Framing of Climate Change and Sustainability Issues in India. *International Journal of E-Politics*, *9*(1), 15–28. doi:10.4018/IJEP.2018010102

Novak, J. I., & Loy, J. (2018). Digital Technologies and 4D Customized Design: Challenging Conventions With Responsive Design. In V. Bryan, A. Musgrove, & J. Powers (Eds.), *Handbook of Research on Human Development in the Digital Age* (pp. 403–426). Hershey, PA: IGI Global. doi:10.4018/978-1-5225-2838-8.ch018

Ögeyik, M. C. (2018). Measuring Phonological and Orthographic Similarity: The Case of Loanwords in Turkish and English. In D. Buğa & M. Coşgun Ögeyik (Eds.), *Psycholinguistics and Cognition in Language Processing* (pp. 49–67). Hershey, PA: IGI Global. doi:10.4018/978-1-5225-4009-0.ch003

Oling-Sisay, M. (2018). Don't Touch My Hair: Culturally Responsive Engagement in Service-Learning. In O. Delano-Oriaran, M. Penick-Parks, & S. Fondrie (Eds.), *Culturally Engaging Service-Learning With Diverse Communities* (pp. 43–55). Hershey, PA: IGI Global. doi:10.4018/978-1-5225-2900-2.ch003

Ololube, N. P., Ingiabuna, E. T., & Dudafa, U. J. (2018). Effective Decision Making for Knowledge Development in Higher Education: A Case Study of Nigeria. In N. Baporikar (Ed.), *Global Practices in Knowledge Management for Societal and Organizational Development* (pp. 382–399). Hershey, PA: IGI Global. doi:10.4018/978-1-5225-3009-1.ch018

Oritsejafor, E. O. (2018). Enhancing Competitiveness of Public Utilities in Nigeria: The Case of the Power Holding Company of Nigeria (PHCN). In H. Levine & K. Moreno (Eds.), *Positioning Markets and Governments in Public Management* (pp. 240–252). Hershey, PA: IGI Global. doi:10.4018/978-1-5225-4177-6.ch017

Otunla, A. O., & Olatunji, O. T. (2018). Clients' Perception, Extent of Adoption, and Level of Satisfaction With Multi-Platform Advertising Media Strategies (MuPAMS): Among Business Organisations in Ibadan, South-Western Nigeria. In K. Yang (Ed.), *Multi-Platform Advertising Strategies in the Global Marketplace* (pp. 54–80). Hershey, PA: IGI Global. doi:10.4018/978-1-5225-3114-2.ch003

Owuor, N. A. (2018). Oil and Gas Discoveries in Kenya: Important Global Exploration and Production Value Chain Lessons for the Society. In M. Risso & S. Testarmata (Eds.), *Value Sharing for Sustainable and Inclusive Development* (pp. 322–337). Hershey, PA: IGI Global. doi:10.4018/978-1-5225-3147-0.ch015

Özdemir, E., & Yılmaz, M. (2018). Omni-Channel Retailing: The Risks, Challenges, and Opportunities. In A. Kumar & S. Saurav (Eds.), *Supply Chain Management Strategies and Risk Assessment in Retail Environments* (pp. 97–118). Hershey, PA: IGI Global. doi:10.4018/978-1-5225-3056-5.ch006

Panko, T. R., & George, B. P. (2018). Animal Sexual Abuse and the Darkness of Touristic Immorality. In M. Korstanje & B. George (Eds.), *Virtual Traumascapes and Exploring the Roots of Dark Tourism* (pp. 175–189). Hershey, PA: IGI Global. doi:10.4018/978-1-5225-2750-3.ch009

Paraschiv, M. M. (2018). Elif Shafak's Works: A Means of Preventing Honor Based Violence. In M. Badea & M. Suditu (Eds.), *Violence Prevention and Safety Promotion in Higher Education Settings* (pp. 36–49). Hershey, PA: IGI Global. doi:10.4018/978-1-5225-2960-6.ch003

Paravastu, N., Simmers, C. A., & Anandarajan, M. (2018). Non-Compliant Mobile Device Usage and Information Systems Security: A Bystander Theory Perspective. *International Journal of Information Systems and Social Change, 9*(1), 1–25. doi:10.4018/IJISSC.2018010101

Pathak, B. (2018). Process Documentation of Interfaith Peacebuilding Cycle: A Case Study From Nepal. In B. Cook (Ed.), *Handbook of Research on Examining Global Peacemaking in the Digital Age* (pp. 70–93). Hershey, PA: IGI Global. doi:10.4018/978-1-5225-3032-9.ch006

Pathak, S. J. (2018). Women Painters of Mithila: A Quest for Identity. In N. Mahtab, T. Haque, I. Khan, M. Islam, & I. Wahid (Eds.), *Handbook of Research on Women's Issues and Rights in the Developing World* (pp. 370–381). Hershey, PA: IGI Global. doi:10.4018/978-1-5225-3018-3.ch023

Patro, C. S., & Raghunath, K. M. (2018). Corporate Social Responsibility: A Conscientious Take. In M. Risso & S. Testarmata (Eds.), *Value Sharing for Sustainable and Inclusive Development* (pp. 75–99). Hershey, PA: IGI Global. doi:10.4018/978-1-5225-3147-0.ch004

Pérez-Uribe, R. I., Torres, D. A., Jurado, S. P., & Prada, D. M. (2018). Cloud Tools for the Development of Project Management in SMEs. In R. Perez-Uribe, C. Salcedo-Perez, & D. Ocampo-Guzman (Eds.), *Handbook of Research on Intrapreneurship and Organizational Sustainability in SMEs* (pp. 95–120). Hershey, PA: IGI Global. doi:10.4018/978-1-5225-3543-0.ch005

Perrotta, K. A., & Mattson, M. F. (2018). Using Counterstories and Reflective Writing Assignments to Promote Critical Race Consciousness in an Undergraduate Teacher Preparation Course. In U. Thomas (Ed.), *Advocacy in Academia and the Role of Teacher Preparation Programs* (pp. 42–64). Hershey, PA: IGI Global. doi:10.4018/978-1-5225-2906-4.ch003

Poli, A., Gambini, A., Pezzotti, A., Broglia, A., Mazzola, A., Muschiato, S., ... Costa, F. (2018). Digital Diorama: An Interactive Multimedia Resource for Learning the Life Sciences. In F. Cipolla-Ficarra (Ed.), *Optimizing Human-Computer Interaction With Emerging Technologies* (pp. 52–82). Hershey, PA: IGI Global. doi:10.4018/978-1-5225-2616-2.ch003

Presadă, D. (2018). Literature and Aesthetic Reading as Means of Promoting Nonviolence. In M. Badea & M. Suditu (Eds.), *Violence Prevention and Safety Promotion in Higher Education Settings* (pp. 94–109). Hershey, PA: IGI Global. doi:10.4018/978-1-5225-2960-6.ch006

Punetha, H., Kumar, S., Mudila, H., & Prakash, O. (2018). Brassica Meal as Source of Health Protecting Neuraceutical and Its Antioxidative Properties. In A. Verma, K. Srivastava, S. Singh, & H. Singh (Eds.), *Nutraceuticals and Innovative Food Products for Healthy Living and Preventive Care* (pp. 108–131). Hershey, PA: IGI Global. doi:10.4018/978-1-5225-2970-5.ch005

Puri, R., & Sengupta, P. (2018). Application of Statistics in Human Resource Management. In D. Bhattacharyya (Ed.), *Statistical Tools and Analysis in Human Resources Management* (pp. 15–37). Hershey, PA: IGI Global. doi:10.4018/978-1-5225-4947-5.ch002

Putnik, N., & Milošević, M. (2018). Trends in Peace Research: Can Cyber Détente Lead to Lasting Peace? In B. Cook (Ed.), *Handbook of Research on Examining Global Peacemaking in the Digital Age* (pp. 1–18). Hershey, PA: IGI Global. doi:10.4018/978-1-5225-3032-9.ch001

Rana, S., & Sharma, R. (2018). An Overview of Employer Branding With Special Reference to Indian Organizations. In N. Sharma, V. Singh, & S. Pathak (Eds.), *Management Techniques for a Diverse and Cross-Cultural Workforce* (pp. 116–131). Hershey, PA: IGI Global. doi:10.4018/978-1-5225-4933-8.ch007

Randa, I. O. (2018). Leveraging Knowledge Management for Value Creation in Service-Oriented Organisations of Namibia. In N. Baporikar (Ed.), *Global Practices in Knowledge Management for Societal and Organizational Development* (pp. 145–167). Hershey, PA: IGI Global. doi:10.4018/978-1-5225-3009-1.ch007

Rekun, M. S. (2018). A Swift Kick: Russian Diplomatic Practice in Bulgaria, 1879-1883. In F. Topor (Ed.), *Ethical Standards and Practice in International Relations* (pp. 49–72). Hershey, PA: IGI Global. doi:10.4018/978-1-5225-2650-6.ch003

Rodil, K., Nielsen, E. B., & Nielsen, J. B. (2018). Sharing Memories: Co-Designing Assistive Technology with Aphasic Adults and Support Staff. *International Journal of Sociotechnology and Knowledge Development, 10*(1), 21–36. doi:10.4018/IJSKD.2018010102

Samli, R. (2018). A Review of Internet Addiction on the Basis of Different Countries (2007–2017). In B. Bozoglan (Ed.), *Psychological, Social, and Cultural Aspects of Internet Addiction* (pp. 200–220). Hershey, PA: IGI Global. doi:10.4018/978-1-5225-3477-8.ch011

Sánchez-García, J. C., & Hernández-Sánchez, B. R. (2018). Nascent Entrepreneurs, Psychological Characteristics, and Sociocultural Background: Psycho-Sociocultural Background of Nascent Entrepreneurs. In A. Carrizo Moreira, J. Guilherme Leitão Dantas, & F. Manuel Valente (Eds.), *Nascent Entrepreneurship and Successful New Venture Creation* (pp. 111–131). Hershey, PA: IGI Global. doi:10.4018/978-1-5225-2936-1.ch005

Santana-Mansilla, P., Costaguta, R., & Schiaffino, S. (2018). A Multi-Agent Model for Personalizing Learning Material for Collaborative Groups. In F. Cipolla-Ficarra (Ed.), *Optimizing Human-Computer Interaction With Emerging Technologies* (pp. 343–375). Hershey, PA: IGI Global. doi:10.4018/978-1-5225-2616-2.ch015

Santos, C. E., Lima de Oliveira, D., & Freitas, M. D. (2018). The Role of Pibid in Graduation Courses: Discussing Teachers' Education. In Z. Djoub (Ed.), *Fostering Reflective Teaching Practice in Pre-Service Education* (pp. 218–234). Hershey, PA: IGI Global. doi:10.4018/978-1-5225-2963-7.ch012

Sarkar, J. (2018). Methodological Considerations for Research in Compensation Management. In D. Bhattacharyya (Ed.), *Statistical Tools and Analysis in Human Resources Management* (pp. 142–168). Hershey, PA: IGI Global. doi:10.4018/978-1-5225-4947-5.ch007

Sarofim, S., & Tolba, A. (2018). When Age, Religion, and Culture Matter: The Impact of Aging, Religiosity, and Cultural Differences on Consumers' Emotions and Behavior. In S. Sarma (Ed.), *Global Observations of the Influence of Culture on Consumer Buying Behavior* (pp. 261–278). Hershey, PA: IGI Global. doi:10.4018/978-1-5225-2727-5.ch015

Schroth, S. T., & Helfer, J. A. (2018). Differentiated Fieldwork and Practicum Experiences: Matching Teacher Candidate Assignments to Their Skills and Needs. In D. Polly, M. Putman, T. Petty, & A. Good (Eds.), *Innovative Practices in Teacher Preparation and Graduate-Level Teacher Education Programs* (pp. 306–326). Hershey, PA: IGI Global. doi:10.4018/978-1-5225-3068-8.ch017

Schwartz, H. M. (2018). States via Markets and Markets via States: Symbiosis and Change, Not Conflict. In H. Levine & K. Moreno (Eds.), *Positioning Markets and Governments in Public Management* (pp. 1–10). Hershey, PA: IGI Global. doi:10.4018/978-1-5225-4177-6.ch001

Semali, L. M. (2018). Indigenous Knowledge as Resource to Sustain Self-Employment in Rural Development. In S. Chhabra (Ed.), *Handbook of Research on Civic Engagement and Social Change in Contemporary Society* (pp. 142–158). Hershey, PA: IGI Global. doi:10.4018/978-1-5225-4197-4.ch008

Seraphin, H., & Gowreesunkar, V. (2018). On the Use of Qualitative Comparative Analysis to Identify the Bright Spots in Dark Tourism. In M. Korstanje & B. George (Eds.), *Virtual Traumascapes and Exploring the Roots of Dark Tourism* (pp. 67–83). Hershey, PA: IGI Global. doi:10.4018/978-1-5225-2750-3.ch004

Shahidi, N., Tossan, V., & Cacho-Elizondo, S. (2018). Assessment of A Mobile Educational Coaching App: Exploring Adoption Patterns and Barriers in France. *International Journal of Technology and Human Interaction, 14*(1), 22–43. doi:10.4018/IJTHI.2018010102

Sikira, A. N., Matekere, T., & Urassa, J. K. (2018). Engaging Men in Women's Economic Empowerment in Butiama District, Mara Region, Tanzania. In N. Mahtab, T. Haque, I. Khan, M. Islam, & I. Wahid (Eds.), *Handbook of Research on Women's Issues and Rights in the Developing World* (pp. 252–268). Hershey, PA: IGI Global. doi:10.4018/978-1-5225-3018-3.ch015

Silveira, D. G. (2018). Diffusion of Innovation and Role of Opinion Leaders. In S. Sarma (Ed.), *Global Observations of the Influence of Culture on Consumer Buying Behavior* (pp. 83–93). Hershey, PA: IGI Global. doi:10.4018/978-1-5225-2727-5.ch005

Simard, D. A., Martin, M., Mockry, J., Puliatte, A., & Squires, M. E. (2018). Introduction: Mental Health and Well-Being of College Students. In M. Martin, J. Mockry, A. Puliatte, D. Simard, & M. Squires (Eds.), *Raising Mental Health Awareness in Higher Education: Emerging Research and Opportunities* (pp. 1–20). Hershey, PA: IGI Global. doi:10.4018/978-1-5225-3793-9.ch001

Sosnin, P. (2018). Experimental Actions With Conceptual Objects. In *Experience-Based Human-Computer Interactions: Emerging Research and Opportunities* (pp. 47–97). Hershey, PA: IGI Global. doi:10.4018/978-1-5225-2987-3.ch003

Sosnin, P. (2018). Lack of Naturalness in Human-Computer Interactions. In *Experience-Based Human-Computer Interactions: Emerging Research and Opportunities* (pp. 9–46). Hershey, PA: IGI Global. doi:10.4018/978-1-5225-2987-3.ch002

Spaseski, N. (2018). Fractal and Wavelet Market Analysis in Pattern Recognition. In *Alternative Decision-Making Models for Financial Portfolio Management: Emerging Research and Opportunities* (pp. 254–309). Hershey, PA: IGI Global. doi:10.4018/978-1-5225-3259-0.ch007

Spaseski, N. (2018). Theory and Modelling. In *Alternative Decision-Making Models for Financial Portfolio Management: Emerging Research and Opportunities* (pp. 1–19). Hershey, PA: IGI Global. doi:10.4018/978-1-5225-3259-0.ch001

Spires, H. A., Green, K. E., & Liang, P. (2018). Chinese Parents' Perspectives on International Higher Education and Innovation. In H. Spires (Ed.), *Digital Transformation and Innovation in Chinese Education* (pp. 272–287). Hershey, PA: IGI Global. doi:10.4018/978-1-5225-2924-8.ch015

Spires, H. A., Himes, M., & Wang, L. (2018). Designing a State-of-the-Art High School in Suzhou, China: Connecting to the Future. In H. Spires (Ed.), *Digital Transformation and Innovation in Chinese Education* (pp. 191–210). Hershey, PA: IGI Global. doi:10.4018/978-1-5225-2924-8.ch011

Squires, M. E., Martin, M., Mockry, J., Puliatte, A., & Simard, D. A. (2018). Campus-Wide Initiatives. In M. Martin, J. Mockry, A. Puliatte, D. Simard, & M. Squires (Eds.), *Raising Mental Health Awareness in Higher Education: Emerging Research and Opportunities* (pp. 77–104). Hershey, PA: IGI Global. doi:10.4018/978-1-5225-3793-9.ch005

Standing, K., & Parker, S. L. (2018). Girls' and Women's Rights to Menstrual Health in Nepal. In N. Mahtab, T. Haque, I. Khan, M. Islam, & I. Wahid (Eds.), *Handbook of Research on Women's Issues and Rights in the Developing World* (pp. 156–168). Hershey, PA: IGI Global. doi:10.4018/978-1-5225-3018-3.ch010

Stępień, B., & Hinner, M. (2018). From Love to Rebuff: How Culture Shapes the Perception of Luxury Goods Among Consumers. In S. Sarma (Ed.), *Global Observations of the Influence of Culture on Consumer Buying Behavior* (pp. 24–47). Hershey, PA: IGI Global. doi:10.4018/978-1-5225-2727-5.ch002

Tantau, A. D., & Frăţilă, L. C. (2018). Trends and Conclusions for Business Development in the Renewable Energy Industry. In *Entrepreneurship and Business Development in the Renewable Energy Sector* (pp. 351–376). Hershey, PA: IGI Global. doi:10.4018/978-1-5225-3625-3.ch010

Terry, D. L., & Amudalat, E. A. (2018). Data Documentation and Informed Consent in Research. In C. Sibinga (Ed.), *Ensuring Research Integrity and the Ethical Management of Data* (pp. 127–154). Hershey, PA: IGI Global. doi:10.4018/978-1-5225-2730-5.ch008

Toma, S. I., Marinescu, P., & Grădinaru, C. (2018). Creating Shared Value in the 21st Century: The Case of Toyota Motor Company. In M. Risso & S. Testarmata (Eds.), *Value Sharing for Sustainable and Inclusive Development* (pp. 155–184). Hershey, PA: IGI Global. doi:10.4018/978-1-5225-3147-0.ch007

Travis, F. T. (2018). Long-Term Changes in Experienced Yoga Practitioners: Growth of Higher States of Consciousness. In S. Telles & N. Singh (Eds.), *Research-Based Perspectives on the Psychophysiology of Yoga* (pp. 35–51). Hershey, PA: IGI Global. doi:10.4018/978-1-5225-2788-6.ch003

Tripp, L. O., Love, A., Thomas, C. M., & Russell, J. (2018). Teacher Education Advocacy for Multiple Perspectives and Culturally Sensitive Teaching. In U. Thomas (Ed.), *Advocacy in Academia and the Role of Teacher Preparation Programs* (pp. 161–181). Hershey, PA: IGI Global. doi:10.4018/978-1-5225-2906-4.ch009

Tshabangu, I. (2018). Child Poverty and Social Inequalities in Africa: A Social Justice Perspective. In I. Tshabangu (Ed.), *Global Ideologies Surrounding Children's Rights and Social Justice* (pp. 74–87). Hershey, PA: IGI Global. doi:10.4018/978-1-5225-2578-3.ch005

Tugjamba, N., Yembuu, B., Gantumur, A., & Gezel, U. (2018). Research Study on Climate Change Education for Sustainable Development in Mongolia. In P. Ordóñez de Pablos (Ed.), *Management Strategies and Technology Fluidity in the Asian Business Sector* (pp. 192–214). Hershey, PA: IGI Global. doi:10.4018/978-1-5225-4056-4.ch012

Upadhye, B. D., & Bandopadhyay, N. (2018). The Taxonomy of Methodological Approaches in Marketing Research: Retrospect and Prospect. In Rajagopal, & R. Behl (Eds.), Start-Up Enterprises and Contemporary Innovation Strategies in the Global Marketplace (pp. 276-293). Hershey, PA: IGI Global. doi:10.4018/978-1-5225-4831-7.ch021

Uvanesh, K., Nayak, S. K., Sagiri, S. S., Banerjee, I., Ray, S. S., & Pal, K. (2018). Effect of Non-Ionic Hydrophilic and Hydrophobic Surfactants on the Properties on the Stearate Oleogels: A Comparative Study. In A. Verma, K. Srivastava, S. Singh, & H. Singh (Eds.), *Nutraceuticals and Innovative Food Products for Healthy Living and Preventive Care* (pp. 260–279). Hershey, PA: IGI Global. doi:10.4018/978-1-5225-2970-5.ch012

Vallverdú, J., Nishida, T., Ohmoto, Y., Moran, S., & Lázare, S. (2018). Fake Empathy and Human-Robot Interaction (HRI): A Preliminary Study. *International Journal of Technology and Human Interaction, 14*(1), 44–59. doi:10.4018/IJTHI.2018010103

Van Deur, P. (2018). Assessing Self-Directed Learning at School Level. In *Managing Self-Directed Learning in Primary School Education: Emerging Research and Opportunities* (pp. 61–77). Hershey, PA: IGI Global. doi:10.4018/978-1-5225-2613-1.ch003

Van Deur, P. (2018). Case Study: The Relationship Between Curriculum Focus on Inquiry and Self-Directed Learning. In *Managing Self-Directed Learning in Primary School Education: Emerging Research and Opportunities* (pp. 95–111). Hershey, PA: IGI Global. doi:10.4018/978-1-5225-2613-1.ch005

Van Deur, P. (2018). Describing Self-Directed Learning in Primary Students. In *Managing Self-Directed Learning in Primary School Education: Emerging Research and Opportunities* (pp. 33–59). Hershey, PA: IGI Global. doi:10.4018/978-1-5225-2613-1.ch002

Vargas-Hernández, J. G., Almanza-Jiménez, R., Calderón, P. C., & Casas-Cardenaz, R. (2018). Organizational Learning and Performance Under the Approach of Organizational Theories. In N. Baporikar (Ed.), *Global Practices in Knowledge Management for Societal and Organizational Development* (pp. 106–125). Hershey, PA: IGI Global. doi:10.4018/978-1-5225-3009-1.ch005

Vega, J. A., Arquette, C. M., Lee, H., Crowe, H. A., Hunzicker, J. L., & Cushing, J. (2018). Ensuring Social Justice for English Language Learners: An Innovative English as a Second Language (ESL) Endorsement Program. In D. Polly, M. Putman, T. Petty, & A. Good (Eds.), *Innovative Practices in Teacher Preparation and Graduate-Level Teacher Education Programs* (pp. 48–66). Hershey, PA: IGI Global. doi:10.4018/978-1-5225-3068-8.ch004

Verma, A. K., Singh, A., & Negi, M. S. (2018). Nutriproteomics: An Advance Methodology of Nutrichemical Analysis. In A. Verma, K. Srivastava, S. Singh, & H. Singh (Eds.), *Nutraceuticals and Innovative Food Products for Healthy Living and Preventive Care* (pp. 1–23). Hershey, PA: IGI Global. doi:10.4018/978-1-5225-2970-5.ch001

Verma, J., & Verma, R. (2018). Innovation in the Provision of Medical Services in India. In Rajagopal, & R. Behl (Eds.), Start-Up Enterprises and Contemporary Innovation Strategies in the Global Marketplace (pp. 16-27). Hershey, PA: IGI Global. doi:10.4018/978-1-5225-4831-7.ch002

Verrini, A. (2018). Strategists From the Past, as Encrypted Cognitive Maps, Whose Access Code Is the Will of Learning Solutions. In L. dall'Acqua, & D. Lukose (Eds.), Improving Business Performance Through Effective Managerial Training Initiatives (pp. 196-209). Hershey, PA: IGI Global. doi:10.4018/978-1-5225-3906-3.ch009

Veselinova, E., & Samonikov, M. G. (2018). Driving Brand Equity With Radical Transparency. In *Building Brand Equity and Consumer Trust Through Radical Transparency Practices* (pp. 18–62). Hershey, PA: IGI Global. doi:10.4018/978-1-5225-2417-5.ch002

Veselinova, E., & Samonikov, M. G. (2018). Henkel: Radical Transparency and Sustainability. In *Building Brand Equity and Consumer Trust Through Radical Transparency Practices* (pp. 337–389). Hershey, PA: IGI Global. doi:10.4018/978-1-5225-2417-5.ch009

Veselinova, E., & Samonikov, M. G. (2018). The 3M Company: How to Use Radical Transparency to Generate Value for the Company. In *Building Brand Equity and Consumer Trust Through Radical Transparency Practices* (pp. 185–318). Hershey, PA: IGI Global. doi:10.4018/978-1-5225-2417-5.ch007

Vila, A. R. (2018). Latin American and Caribbean Literature Transposed Into Digital: Corpus, Ecosystem, Canon, and Cartonera Publishing. In F. García-Peñalvo (Ed.), *Global Implications of Emerging Technology Trends* (pp. 34–58). Hershey, PA: IGI Global. doi:10.4018/978-1-5225-4944-4.ch003

Vorkapic, C. F. (2018). Yoga for Children. In S. Telles & N. Singh (Eds.), *Research-Based Perspectives on the Psychophysiology of Yoga* (pp. 104–120). Hershey, PA: IGI Global. doi:10.4018/978-1-5225-2788-6.ch007

Vu, N. T. (2018). Pros and Cons of Integrating Non-Financial Services in Microfinance. In S. Hipsher (Ed.), *Examining the Private Sector's Role in Wealth Creation and Poverty Reduction* (pp. 171–199). Hershey, PA: IGI Global. doi:10.4018/978-1-5225-3117-3.ch008

Wani, K. A., Manzoor, J., Anjum, J., Bashir, M., & Mamta. (2018). Pesticides in Vegetables: Their Impact on Nutritional Quality and Human Health. In A. Verma, K. Srivastava, S. Singh, & H. Singh (Eds.), *Nutraceuticals and Innovative Food Products for Healthy Living and Preventive Care* (pp. 132-157). Hershey, PA: IGI Global. doi:10.4018/978-1-5225-2970-5.ch006

Weiss-Randall, D. (2018). DOI Theoretical Framework: Adopting Innovative Technologies. In *Utilizing Innovative Technologies to Address the Public Health Impact of Climate Change: Emerging Research and Opportunities* (pp. 144–166). Hershey, PA: IGI Global. doi:10.4018/978-1-5225-3414-3.ch005

Weiss-Randall, D. (2018). Sustainable Development. In *Utilizing Innovative Technologies to Address the Public Health Impact of Climate Change: Emerging Research and Opportunities* (pp. 167–203). Hershey, PA: IGI Global. doi:10.4018/978-1-5225-3414-3.ch006

Whitelaw, L., & Taddei, L. M. (2018). Using Reflection to Explore Cultural Responsiveness of Preservice Teachers. In Z. Djoub (Ed.), *Fostering Reflective Teaching Practice in Pre-Service Education* (pp. 166–188). Hershey, PA: IGI Global. doi:10.4018/978-1-5225-2963-7.ch009

Wongsurawat, W., & Shrestha, V. (2018). Information Technology, Globalization, and Local Conditions: Implications for Entrepreneurs in Southeast Asia. In P. Ordóñez de Pablos (Ed.), *Management Strategies and Technology Fluidity in the Asian Business Sector* (pp. 163–176). Hershey, PA: IGI Global. doi:10.4018/978-1-5225-4056-4.ch010

Woodman, K., & Kourtis-Kazoullis, V. (2018). Facebook, Tele-Collaboration, and International Access to Technology in the Classroom. In F. Cipolla-Ficarra (Ed.), *Optimizing Human-Computer Interaction With Emerging Technologies* (pp. 274–286). Hershey, PA: IGI Global. doi:10.4018/978-1-5225-2616-2.ch011

Woods, R. J., Johnson, S., & Pope, M. L. (2018). Teaching in an Anti-Deficit Pedagogical Mindset. In U. Thomas (Ed.), *Advocacy in Academia and the Role of Teacher Preparation Programs* (pp. 190–205). Hershey, PA: IGI Global. doi:10.4018/978-1-5225-2906-4.ch011

Wright, M. (2018). Cyberbullying: Description, Definition, Characteristics, and Outcomes. In F. Cipolla-Ficarra (Ed.), *Optimizing Human-Computer Interaction With Emerging Technologies* (pp. 161–182). Hershey, PA: IGI Global. doi:10.4018/978-1-5225-2616-2.ch006

Xu, D. (2018). Multimodal Semiotics in China. In H. Spires (Ed.), *Digital Transformation and Innovation in Chinese Education* (pp. 60–79). Hershey, PA: IGI Global. doi:10.4018/978-1-5225-2924-8.ch004

Yaokumah, W., & Kumah, P. (2018). Exploring the Impact of Security Policy on Compliance. In F. García-Peñalvo (Ed.), *Global Implications of Emerging Technology Trends* (pp. 256–274). Hershey, PA: IGI Global. doi:10.4018/978-1-5225-4944-4.ch014

Yaokumah, W., & Okai, E. S. (2018). Inter-Organizational Study of Access Control Security Measures. *International Journal of Technology and Human Interaction, 14*(1), 60–79. doi:10.4018/IJTHI.2018010104

Zheng, X., Liu, H., Lin, D., & Li, J. (2018). Achieving Rural Teachers' Development Through a WeChat Professional Learning Community: Two Cases From Guangdong Province. In H. Spires (Ed.), *Digital Transformation and Innovation in Chinese Education* (pp. 307–318). Hershey, PA: IGI Global. doi:10.4018/978-1-5225-2924-8.ch017

About the Contributors

Michelle F. Wright, Ph.D., is a Research Associate at The Pennsylvania State University and a research fellow at Masaryk University in Brno, the Czech Republic. Her research focus is on the contextual factors which influence children's, adolescents', and young adults' involvement in aggressive behaviors, with a special interest in social goals, peer status, and cultural values. She has published on these topics, with her most recent work focused on culture and anonymity, and their role in cyberbullying among adolescents.

* * *

Martina Benvenuti is a Postdoctoral Research Fellow at the Istituto per le Tecnologie Didattiche (ITD) that is one of the research institutes of the Italian National Research Council (CNR). She is particularly interested on the dynamics of the integration of ICT in different educational settings (e.g. school, university, business).

Alaina Brenick, Ph.D., Associate Professor of Human Development and Family Sciences at the University of Connecticut, received a pre-doctoral traineeship from the National Institute of Child Health and Human Development to obtain her Ph.D. at the University of Maryland prior to her postdoctoral fellowship at the Friedrich Schiller University, Germany. She analyzes how diverse groups of youth in the U.S. and other regions of the world—sometimes with vastly different societal structures, norms, and expectations—experience, reason about, and respond to intergroup peer relations and group-based victimization. This work is translated into contextually and developmentally appropriate intervention programs, designed to promote social equity and positive intergroup relations.

Daniell Carvalheiro is a doctoral student in Human Development and Family Sciences at the University of Connecticut. His research interests focus on children's peer relations, temperament, parent-child relationships, diversity, and quantitative methodology. He serves as a research assistant for the Center for the Study of Culture, Health, and Human Development (CHHD) and the Developmental Approaches to Identities, Inequalities, and Intergroup Relations Lab (DAIIIR). Several of the research projects he has worked on include a cross-cultural comparison of parents' and teachers' ideas about school involvement, a study assessing how parents' and peers' influence on adolescents' evaluations of intergroup relations varies by age and gender, and an evaluation of interventions for reducing prejudice among youth in Israel. He was awarded the Scholarship for Developmental, Child, & Family Psychology to attend the ICPSR Summer Program in Quantitative Methods of Social Research in 2019.

Kaitlin Flannery earned her Ph.D. in Developmental Psychology at the University of Connecticut. She is currently an assistant professor in the Department of Psychology at SUNY Cortland. Her research is focused on social and emotional development among adolescents and emerging adults. Specifically, she is interested in friendships, friendship dissolution, and romantic relationships. Her research also examines social media use and its associations with adjustment.

Sara Giovagnoli, Psychologist, PhD, Assistant professor in psychometrics at the Department of Psychology, University of Bologna. She deals with research in psychometric statistics and psychological research methodology. Furthermore, she is co-head of the SPEV (Service for neuropsychological assessment and intervention for children and adolescent) of the same Department and carry out research in the field of Specific Learning Disorders and of visual perception.

Zeynep Güvenç Salabğir graduated from Istanbul University, departments of Public Administration and International Relations. She got master's degree in International Business. She is now a PhD student in department of Business Administration at İstanbul University.

Brenna Helm (BA, Sociology at Otterbein University) is a graduate student in sociology at Ohio University. Her research interests are found in the intersection of criminology, deviance, gender, sexuality, and sexual deviance. Helm's MA thesis investigates the ways in which college students navigate hookup culture through the use of dating or "hookup apps". Her research explores the ways in which user experiences and match outcomes are influenced by communication and expectations.

Tatsuya Imai is an assistant professor in the Department of British and American Studies at Nanzan University. His research interests include interpersonal communication and prejudice.

Argyroula Kalaitzaki (BA, MSc, PhD, CPsychol), female, is an Assistant Professor of Clinical Psychology at the Department of Social Work and Head of the Laboratory of Interdisciplinary Approaches for the Enhancement of Quality of Life (Quality of Life Lab; QoL), affiliated at the School of Health at the Hellenic Mediterranean University (ex Technological Educational Institute of Crete). She has a number of peer-reviewed papers, chapters in books, presentations in national and international conferences and she has also co-authored a book. She has educational experience over 18 years during which she has taught various courses related to Clinical Psychology. Her research interests include, among others, interpersonal relating within families of persons with various psychiatric disorders, social networks and problems of misuse (e.g., internet addiction, cyberstalking), Positive Psychology, PP technologies and mental health apps, Aging, Dementia and Alzheimer's disease.

Emily Karr is pursuing her J.D. at the University of Connecticut School of Law. She graduated magna cum laude from The University of Connecticut as an honors scholar with a Bachelor of Arts degree in Human Development and Family Studies and a minor in Political Science. She has developed an interest in research to understand the issues being faced by children, emerging adults, and families in America today to better prepare her for a future career as a guardian ad litem. In addition to this chapter, she has also coauthored a book chapter on prejudice in schools.

Melanie Keep (née Nguyen) is currently a Senior Lecturer in the Faculty of Health Sciences at The University of Sydney. Her cyberpsychology and eHealth research examines computer-mediated communication in social and therapeutic contexts. This includes social media, online support groups and telehealth. Additionally, she is interested in using technology (specifically learning analytics, online discussion forums and interactive video resources) to enhance the student learning experience. She regularly presents on and writes about computer-mediated communication and higher education.

Judy Krysik, MSW, PhD, is an Associate Professor in the ASU School of Social Work and Director of the ASU Center for Child Well-Being. Her overarching goal is to better serve children and families who have experienced trauma. She has extensive research experience with Healthy Families Arizona, a child abuse and neglect prevention program aimed at high risk families from birth through age five and delivered in the home, and Safe Babies Court Teams in Arizona, a program for infants and toddlers removed from their parents' care due to maltreatment. The Center for Child Well-Being is host to the National Children of Incarcerated Parents conference.

Walter LaMendola is Professor Emeritus, Graduate School of Social Work (GSSW), University of Denver. A pioneer in the integration of technology, human services and education, Dr. LaMendola developed a small computer system for human service agencies in 1978 that won national recognition and awards. He opened an Information Technology Center at GSSW in 1983. He is a founding father of HUSITA. In addition to consulting in various countries, he co-founded a number of early computer networks, and has written about communication and information technology interactions with culture, social justice, inequity, human presence, sustainability, and every day life. Dr. LaMendola is co-author of five books and over a hundred articles and technical reports. He received his BA from St. Vincent College, MSW in Community Organization from the University of Pittsburgh, diploma in Sociology and Social Welfare from the University of Stockholm, and PhD in Social Work from the University of Minnesota.

Fung Yin Lee (BA with Honours, 2010, Hong Kong Baptist University) works as an Immigration Officer in Hong Kong, China. This research report is based on her senior honours thesis, directed by the second author while she served as a visiting professor.

Megan Lindsay Brown, MSW, PhD, is currently a Research Assistant Professor at Arizona State University in the Schoo of Social Work. During her doctoral studies, Brown's research focused on the use of information communication technologies (ICT) and the impact of mediated spaces on human development, specifically young adult women. Her work has examined young adult dating relationships, online harassment, interventions using ICT, and the ways ICT interaction impacts individual perceptions during development. Currently, her research is focused on the ways digital culture fosters violence against women and finding ways to safely deliver online interventions for women experience sexual and domestic violence.

Elizabeth Mazur is Professor of Psychology at Penn State University, Greater Allegheny campus. She received her M.A. and Ph.D. in Developmental Psychology from University of Michigan, completed a postdoc at Arizona State University's Center for Prevention Research, and previously taught at Eastern Kentucky University and University of Michigan, Flint. She has served on the Committee for Disability

Issues in Psychology of the American Psychological Association and currently co-chairs the Special Committee on Women and Disability for the Society for the Psychology of Women (Div. 35 of APA).

Elvis Mazzoni, Ph.D., Associate Professor of Developmental and Educational Psychology at the University of Bologna. His research focus is on the effects of digital technologies use on human behaviours, and robotics in human development. He is members of many scientific and technical committee of international conferences in these fields and he is Managing Editor of the European Journal of Psychology of Education.

Clara Moningka graduated from Doctoral Program of Psychology, Gunadarma University in Jakarta and worked as a lecturer in 2002. Clara has taught at various universities, such as Gunadarma University, UKRIDA. Esa Unggul University, Universitas Bunda Mulia and Bina Nusantara. Since 2017, he has been a permanent lecturer at Pembangunan Jaya University. He served as head of the Psychological services in Ukrida, Head of the Psychology Department and Manager of the Student Advisory Center at Bunda Mulia University. Clara was also a resource person for several media, having served as a PIC for the Nusantara Scientific Psychology Consortium. Clara also took part in the Asian Association of Social Psychology summer school program (Yogyakarta) and 2015 (Philippines). Actively involved as an organizing committee for the 2015 Social Psychological Scientific Meeting and the 2017 Asian Psychological Association.

Süphan Nasir is Professor at Department of Business Administration, İstanbul University. She is chairman of marketing subdicipline and coordinator of business administration e-learning program. She worked as chief editor at International Journal of E-Entrepreneurship and Innovation 2010-2014, and she is also editor of Yükseköğretim Dergisi/ Journal of Higher Education (Turkey) since 2010. She also undertaken important roles such as organization committee member and advisory board member of international conferences. Her articles were published in reputable academic journals and she has written chapters for well-known books. Her latest books entitled Modern Entrepreneurship and E-Business Innovations and CRM Strategies in the Digital Era were published in USA in 2013 and 2015, respectively. She has also presented her papers at major international conferences and attended some international conference as keynote speaker. CRM as well as mobile marketing, consumer behavior, innovation management and entrepreneurship are the scope of her interest area.

Jonel Thaller, PhD, MSW, is an Associate Professor of Social Work at Ball State University whose primary research focus has been the prevention of violence against women and children, specifically the sociocultural and developmental factors that contribute to violence against women and children as well as the effectiveness of individual interventions for the prevention of such violence.

Thomas Vander Ven (Ph.D., University of Cincinnati, 1998) is Professor of Sociology and Director of Graduate Studies in Sociology at Ohio University. He has authored and co-authored research publications in the areas of college drinking culture and harm reduction, criminological theory, juvenile delinquency, and serial violence. Vander Ven's study on college drinking culture, Getting Wasted: Why College Students Drink Too Much and Party So Hard, was published by NYU Press in 2011.

Lynne M. Webb (PhD, University of Oregon, 1980) serves as Professor Emeritus in Communication, Florida International University, Miami, Florida. Her research examines three objects of study: social media, family communication, and romantic communication. She has published three scholarly readers and over 100 essays, including multiple theories, research reports, pedagogical essays, and methods pieces. Her work has appeared in numerous national and international journals including the Journal of Family Communication, Journal of Applied Communication, Health Communication, Computers in Human Behavior, and the International Journal of Social Research and Methodology as well as in prestigious edited volumes including the Handbook of Family Communication (Sage, 2014) and numerous IGI Global collections. She has presented over 100 papers at conferences in the U.S. and abroad. Dr. Webb has received numerous research, teaching, and service awards during her 40 years as a university professor; she is the 2015 recipient of the Southern States Communication Association's highest award, the Osborn Teacher/Scholar Award for excellence in teaching, research, and service. In 2018, she received the National Communication Association's highest honor for scholarship in family communication, the Brommel Award.

Howard T. Welser (PhD, University of Washington) is an associate professor of sociology at Ohio University. His published research investigates how micro-level processes generate collective outcomes across diverse social settings: diffusion of innovation among Wikipedia editors, emergence of social roles in online discussion, how cooperation emerges among competing teams, and how forms of influence and organization emerge online and spread into real world groups. Dr. Welser uses quantitative methods and social network analysis to study the intersections of social media, inequality and social change in contemporary social settings. He is increasingly interested in studying how social media involvement alters the nature of social groups, organizations, sub-cultures and institutions. His work appears in a wide variety of journals: Social Science Research, Information Communication and Society, Small Group Research, Rationality and Society, Rural Sociology, Journal of Social Structure, Journal of Computer Mediated Communication; as well as edited volumes and conference proceedings: iConference, HICSS, WWW, and ICWSM.

Brian Willoughby is an associate professor in the School of Family Life at Brigham Young University. Dr. Willoughby is also the Director of the RELATE Institute, a non-profit organization dedicated to studying and improving romantic relationships. Dr. Willoughby's research focuses on young adult dating and relationship patterns. Dr. Willoughby's specific expertise areas include dating, sexuality, cohabitation, marriage formation, and marital attitudes/beliefs.

Bonnie Young-Petersen is a recent graduate of BYU's Marriage and Family Therapy program and currently lives and works in Barcelona, Spain.

Index

A

C

D

E

F

G

H

I

www.ingramcontent.com/pod-product-compliance
Lightning Source LLC
LaVergne TN
LVHW062135300926
849161LV00010B/2543